FORM AND SUBSTANCE IN THE LAW OF OBLIGATIONS

The chapters in this book were originally presented at the *Ninth Biennial Conference on the Law of Obligations*, which was co-hosted by Melbourne Law School and the Faculty of Law at the University of Oxford and held in Melbourne in July 2018. They explore the relationship between form and substance in the law of obligations. The volume builds on the rich tradition of legal thought that deploys these concepts to inform our understanding of the common law. The essays offer multiple conceptions of form and substance and cover an array of private law subjects, scholarly approaches and jurisdictions. The collection makes it clear that the interplay between form and substance is a key element of the dynamism that characterises this area of the law.

Form and Substance in the Law of Obligations

Edited by
Andrew Robertson
and
James Goudkamp

•HART•
OXFORD • LONDON • NEW YORK • NEW DELHI • SYDNEY

HART PUBLISHING

Bloomsbury Publishing Plc

Kemp House, Chawley Park, Cumnor Hill, Oxford, OX2 9PH, UK

HART PUBLISHING, the Hart/Stag logo, BLOOMSBURY and the Diana logo are trademarks of Bloomsbury Publishing Plc

First published in Great Britain 2019

A catalogue record for this book is available from the British Library.

Library of Congress Cataloging-in-Publication data

Names: Robertson, Andrew, 1966- editor. | Goudkamp, James, 1980- editor.

Title: Form and substance in the law of obligations / edited by Andrew Robertson and James Goudkamp.

Description: Oxford, UK ; Chicago, Illinois : Hart Publishing, 2019. | Includes bibliographical references and index.

Identifiers: LCCN 2019021112 (print) | LCCN 2019021912 (ebook) | ISBN 9781509929467 (EPub) | ISBN 9781509929450 (hardback : alk. paper)

Subjects: LCSH: Obligations (Law)

Classification: LCC K830 (ebook) | LCC K830 .F67 2019 (print) | DDC 346.02—dc23

LC record available at https://lccn.loc.gov/2019021112

ISBN: HB: 978-1-50992-945-0
ePDF: 978-1-50992-947-4
ePub: 978-1-50992-946-7

Typeset by Compuscript Ltd, Shannon
Printed and bound in Great Britain by CPI Group (UK) Ltd, Croydon CR0 4YY

FSC www.fsc.org MIX Paper from responsible sources FSC® C013604

ACKNOWLEDGEMENTS

This volume contains a selection of essays originally presented at the *Ninth Biennial Conference on the Law of Obligations*, which was co-hosted by Melbourne Law School and the Faculty of Law at the University of Oxford and held in Melbourne in July 2018. We thank Professor Pip Nicholson, the Dean of Melbourne Law School, and Professor Anne Davies, the Dean of the Faculty of Law at the University of Oxford, for supporting the venture.

We are very grateful to Hart Publishing for sponsoring the conference and for their ongoing support for the Obligations conference series. Particular thanks are also due to Allan J Myers AC QC, Chancellor of the University of Melbourne, who provided generous financial support for the Obligations IX conference.

Georgia Davis performed an indispensable role as assistant convener of the conference, and as editorial assistant for this collection. Her outstanding work contributed greatly to both the conference and this book. We also thank Tom Carroll, Yujie Du, Peggy Gusah, Isobel Orford, Matas Ruseckas, Esther Taylor and Eliza Wallace for their assistance during the conference. We gratefully acknowledge the contributions of all of the presenters, chairs and participants in the conference to the discussion of the theme of this collection and the individual chapters.

Andrew Robertson and James Goudkamp
1 March 2019

CONTENTS

CONTRIBUTORS

Kit Barker is a Professor of Law at the University of Queensland.

Elise Bant is a Professor of Law at the University of Melbourne.

Andrew Burrows is Professor of the Law of England at the University of Oxford and Senior Research Fellow of All Souls College, Oxford.

Ben Chen is a Lecturer in Law at the University of Sydney.

Jeff Gordon is a Lecturer in Law at the University of Sydney.

James Goudkamp is Professor of the Law of Obligations at the University of Oxford and Fellow of Keble College, Oxford.

Birke Häcker is Professor of Comparative Law and Director of the Institute for European and Comparative Law at the University of Oxford and Professorial Fellow of Brasenose College, Oxford.

Eleni Katsampouka is a Lecturer in Law at Keble College, Oxford.

James Lee is Reader in English Law at The Dickson Poon School of Law, King's College London.

Pey-Woan Lee is an Associate Professor of Law at Singapore Management University.

Mark Leeming is a Judge of Appeal of the Supreme Court of New South Wales and Challis Lecturer in Equity, University of Sydney.

Ben McFarlane is a Professor of Law at University College London.

Liam Murphy is Herbert Peterfreund Professor of Law and Professor of Philosophy at New York University.

Jason W Neyers is a Professor of Law at Western University Canada.

Jeannie Marie Paterson is a Professor of Law at the University of Melbourne.

Dan Priel is an Associate Professor at Osgoode Hall Law School, York University.

Andrew Robertson is a Professor of Law at the University of Melbourne.

Robert Stevens is the Herbert Smith Freehills Professor of Private Law at the University of Oxford.

William Swadling is Reader in the Law of Property at the University of Oxford and the Senior Law Fellow at Brasenose College, Oxford.

Man Yip is an Associate Professor of Law at Singapore Management University.

TABLE OF CASES

All decisions of the Privy Council are cited in the Table as UK cases.

Australia

Bermuda

Canada

Hong Kong

Ireland

Jersey

New Zealand

Singapore

United Kingdom

United States of America

TABLE OF LEGISLATION

Australia

France

Germany

Hong Kong

New Zealand

Singapore

United Kingdom

Statutory Instruments

United States of America

1

Between Form and Substance

ANDREW ROBERTSON AND JAMES GOUDKAMP

This collection of essays is drawn from the *Ninth Biennial Conference on the Law of Obligations*, which was focused on the theme of this book. The theme was inspired by PS Atiyah and Robert Summers' influential comparative study *Form and Substance in Anglo-American Law*, which was published a little over 30 years ago.[1] Atiyah and Summers explored the relationship between *formal reasoning* (the application of rules without reference either to the justifications that underlie the rules being applied, or to other potentially relevant considerations of justice or welfare) and *substantive reasoning* (direct reference to considerations of justice, purpose, welfare or convenience). Duncan Kennedy was also concerned with form and substance in this sense in his landmark article 'Form and Substance in Private Law Adjudication', which preceded Atiyah and Summers' study.[2] Kennedy argued that a lawmaker's choice of form correlates with a substantive preference, with individualism corresponding with a preference for rules and altruism with a preference for standards. Form and substance are also distinguished in various other ways in the law of obligations. A form and substance dichotomy that is more familiar to private lawyers in the common law world is the distinction between what might broadly be described as appearance on the one hand and underlying truth on the other. In this vein, distinctions are commonly drawn between the form of a legal instrument, transaction or relationship, and its intended or actual legal effect. A related distinction is sometimes drawn between the form of a legal or equitable doctrine and its substantive effect. This book explores the insights provided by various manifestations of the form and substance dichotomy.[3]

The primary purpose of Atiyah and Summers' analysis of form and substance was comparative. They claimed that a profound difference – perhaps the most

[1] PS Atiyah and RS Summers, *Form and Substance in Anglo-American Law: A Comparative Study of Legal Reasoning, Legal Theory, and Legal Institutions* (Oxford, Clarendon Press, 1987).

[2] D Kennedy, 'Form and Substance in Private Law Adjudication' (1976) 89 *Harvard Law Review* 1685.

[3] K Barker, 'Form and Substance: Three Observations on the State of Debate', this volume, ch 18, text accompanying nn 5–9, identifies no fewer than 13 different kinds of distinction between form and substance.

profound difference – between the English legal system and those of the US was that the English approach to law was highly formal, while the American was more focused on and driven by matters of substance, in each case excessively so. Atiyah and Summers helpfully captured their thesis in the idea of contrasting 'visions' of law, with the English vision of law being essentially that of 'a system of rules', while the American vision of law was of 'an outward expression of the community's sense of right or justice.'[4]

The differences between English and American approaches to law, Atiyah and Summers showed, have deep roots. The English understanding of law has long been dominated by Austinian positivism, while the American long influenced by notions of natural law and of law as an instrument of social and economic policy.[5] Atiyah and Summers suggested that those different conceptions of law and the respective levels of formality in legal reasoning both influenced, and were influenced by, wide ranging differences in legal education, legal scholarship, the conception of legal rules, the doctrine of precedent, the capacity of the courts to develop and reform the common law, the legislative process, law reform processes, the drafting of statutes, statutory interpretation, various aspects of civil and criminal procedure including the role of juries, access to justice, the court structure, the appointment of judges and composition of the judiciary, and the structure of the legal profession.[6] Atiyah and Summers compared each of those aspects of the English and American legal systems and others in detail.

The focus of this collection is on the interplay between form and substance in the law of obligations, including legal and equitable doctrines, judicial reasoning, the drafting of statutes, statutory interpretation, and private law theory.

I. False Appearance and Inner Truth

The form and substance dichotomy that is most familiar to private lawyers is the distinction between what Andrew Burrows describes in Chapter 2 as 'false appearance and inner truth'.[7] In this context, the form and substance dichotomy

[4] Atiyah and Summers, above n 1, 19–21 (on the impossibility or impracticability of a legal system that eschews either form or substance entirely) and 5 (on the contrasting visions of law). Atiyah and Summers (ibid 411–15) provide a more detailed account of differences between the formal and substantive visions of law in their concluding chapter.

[5] ibid, chs 8 and 9 (on contrasting theories of law).

[6] Atiyah and Summers, ibid 411, suggested that these factors 'mutually reinforce each other', but were careful not to make any claims about the existence of any identifiable causal connections (ibid 410–11). It has been suggested that the relationship between the institutional features of the two legal systems and their respective levels of formality might be better described as symbiotic, rather than causal: C Osakew, 'Rethinking the Communion Between the Common Laws of England and the United States' (1988) 82 *Northwestern University Law Review* 855. Cf MT Sigillito, 'Book Review' (1990) 34 *St Louis University Law Journal* 389.

[7] A Burrows, 'Form and Substance: Fictions and Judicial Power', this volume, ch 2, text following n 8.

is invoked to justify looking beyond a chosen legal form to the true nature of a transaction or relationship in order to ensure that it has the consequences, either as between the parties or in the public interest, that it ought to have. Pey-Woan Lee notes in Chapter 4 that transactions may be 'recharacterised' in order to prevent the avoidance of the legal incidents of a particular category of transaction or relationship at common law, or to prevent the avoidance of the consequences of a statutory regime.[8] In this context substance is preferred to form where the form of a transaction or relationship is seen as artificial and the substance is considered to reflect the underlying reality of the situation. Whether transactions and relationships should be recharacterised is a familiar question in relation to employment, leases, trusts, mortgages and charges.

Looking more broadly at the category of false appearance and inner truth, substance is preferred to form in a number of different situations, and those situations can be classified in different ways. In Chapter 3, Birke Häcker distinguishes between the category of cases in which *content prevails over name* (such as employee/independent contractor and lease/licence), the broader category of cases in which *legal substance prevails over factual appearance* (including sham transactions and cases in which the equitable remedy of rectification is granted), and cases in which *economic substance prevails over legal form*.[9] Häcker's economic substance/legal form category is exemplified by the understanding of contractual penalties adopted by the High Court of Australia in *Andrews v Australia and New Zealand Banking Group Limited*,[10] in which a contractual provision can constitute a penalty – even if it is not triggered by a breach of contract – if 'as a matter of substance' it is collateral to a primary stipulation, on the failure of which it imposes an additional detriment to the benefit of the other party.[11]

Within the broad category of form and substance in the sense of appearance and underlying truth, a more basic distinction can be drawn between the form and substance of *legal transactions and legal relationships* on the one hand and the form and substance of *legal doctrines and judicial reasoning* on the other. As we see in this volume, the notion of form and substance as *appearance and underlying truth* is not distinct from the notion of form and substance in the sense of *rules and reasons*. On the contrary, the two conceptions are heavily intertwined. The essential reason for this is that whether a transaction, relationship or legal doctrine should be understood or treated differently from its surface appearance is not

[8] PW Lee, 'Form, Substance and Recharacterisation', this volume, ch 4.

[9] B Häcker, '"Substance Over Form": Has the Pendulum Swung Too Far?', this volume, ch 3.

[10] *Andrews v Australia and New Zealand Banking Group Ltd* [2012] HCA 30, (2012) 247 CLR 205 [10], contra *Cavendish Square Holding BV v Makdessi; ParkingEye Limited v Beavis* [2015] UKSC 67, [2016] AC 1172 [42]; see further Häcker, above n 9, text accompanying nn 93–97.

[11] See, however, B McFarlane, 'Form and Substance in Equity', this volume, ch 9, text accompanying nn 27–28 on the limits of the notion that the court can look beyond the form adopted by the parties in this context.

simply a factual question of its inner truth or reality, but is an issue that requires consideration of normative questions of justice between the parties and the social and economic consequences of different characterisations.

A. Recharacterising and Adjusting Transactions and Relationships

The legal and equitable processes of looking beyond the name, form or appearance of a legal transaction or relationship encompass wholesale recharacterisations as well as more limited adjustments such as those made through the doctrine of rectification. A foundational question in this context is what constitutes the 'substance' that is to be preferred to the legal form. As Ben McFarlane notes in Chapter 9, the relevant equitable maxim is sometimes expressed as 'equity looks to the *substance* rather than the form' and sometimes as 'equity looks to the *intent* rather than the form'.[12] Clearly party intent is the determining criterion in many instances. In such instances the courts are generally not concerned with the transactional form or form of words intended by the parties but with the rights and obligations they intended to create. In this respect, as Pey-Woan Lee observes in Chapter 4, the courts tend to apply formal criteria in order to determine the substance of a transaction. Whether and when a transaction should be recharacterised, however, raises questions of substance in the sense of considerations of justice and community welfare.[13] That is because recharacterisation raises normative questions about matters such as the implications of the avoidance – or inappropriate invocation – of the common law incidents of particular categories of relationship, and the appropriateness of constraining party autonomy.[14] Lee argues in Chapter 4 that in some instances these questions of substance need to be more openly acknowledged and explicitly addressed in recharacterisation cases. In her analysis of this topic Lee illustrates the deep and important connection between the two conceptions of form and substance.

Another strong example of the connection and interplay between the two kinds of form and substance (appearance/reality and rules/reasons) is provided by the decision of the English Court of Appeal in *Shell UK Ltd v Total UK Ltd*, which is subjected to sustained critical analysis in three chapters in this volume.[15] The court in that case held that the beneficial owner of property could recover damages for economic loss that is consequent upon physical damage to that

[12] B McFarlane, 'Form and Substance in Equity', this volume, ch 9, fn 2, citing J Heydon, M Leeming and P Turner (eds), *Meagher, Gummow and Lehane's Equity: Doctrines and Remedies*, 5th edn (Sydney, LexisNexis, 2015) para 3.145.

[13] ibid.

[14] ibid.

[15] [2010] EWCA Civ 180, [2011] QB 86 ('*Shell v Total*'), discussed by B Häcker, above n 9; McFarlane, above n 12 and W Swadling, 'In Defence of Formalism', this volume, ch 5.

property caused by the defendant's negligence, provided the trustee is joined in the proceedings. In doing so, the court departed from the general rule that only the legal owner or a person with a possessory interest in property can recover damages for loss caused by the destruction of or damage to that property. The court further eroded the general rule against liability for pure economic loss in negligence. It also departed from the foundational notion that a beneficiary under a trust does not have a right to the trust asset itself, but only rights against the trustee (which may affect third parties who deal with the trustee).[16] The court was influenced by a concern that legal rules must not stand in the way of 'practical justice', noting that it would be 'legalistic' to deny a right to recovery to the 'real owner' of the property, and that it '*should not* be legally relevant' that the '"real" owner' had chosen to vest legal title in another company. The court concluded that it 'it would be a triumph of form over substance to deny a remedy to the beneficial owner of property when the legal owner is a bare trustee for that beneficial owner'.[17]

The court's concern to do 'practical justice' in *Shell v Total* led to a development which was incompatible with the concept of the trust as conventionally understood. Substance in the shape of 'real ownership' (underlying truth) and 'practical justice' (reasons) prevailed over recognised legal forms (rules and concepts), and what was taken to be a 'legalistic' (formalistic) understanding of the law. If one accepts the force of the widespread criticism of the decision in *Shell v Total*,[18] then it provides a good example of what Atiyah and Summers called 'substantivistic' reasoning: a favouring of substance (in the sense of both underlying reality and a loose sense of justice) over form (in the sense of both appearance and rules) which may be considered excessive when judged by the standards of the jurisdiction in which it was made.[19] The analysis of *Shell v Total* by Häcker, McFarlane and Swadling in this volume suggests that the decision illustrates the dangers of too great a willingness to dismiss a concern with form and the application of settled principles as 'legalistic' and 'formalistic'. Doing so in this case, that analysis suggests, not only resulted in the distortion of legal forms, but also in inadequate consideration of the significant issues of substance raised by the case. That an English appellate court could be accused of such insufficient attention to form in an important case is clearly noteworthy in view of Atiyah and Summers' thesis, although this must be seen in the light of the criticism that the decision

[16] J Edelman, 'Two Fundamental Questions for the Law of Trusts' (2013) 129 *LQR* 66, 85; Swadling, above n 15, text accompanying nn 47–60; McFarlane, above n 12, Pt III.

[17] [2010] EWCA Civ 180, [2011] QB 86 [143]. See also at [132].

[18] See, eg, PG Turner, 'Consequential Economic Loss and the Trust Beneficiary' (2010) 69 *CLJ* 445, 446 ('This holding does a disservice to tort and trust law'), K Low, 'Economic Title and Economic Loss' (2010) 126 *LQR* 507 and the works cited by Häcker, above n 9, fn 139.

[19] Atiyah and Summers, above n 1, 30–31.

has attracted in this volume and elsewhere. That critical response points to the strength of the continuing commitment to form in English legal culture.

B. Recharacterising Legal Doctrines and Judicial Reasoning

Points of contrast between the false appearance and inner truth of legal reasoning provide the primary focus of Andrew Burrows' Chapter 2.[20] Burrows' concern is with legal fictions: artificial concepts or lines of reasoning used by judges which obscure their true motivations or reasons. Burrows suggests that fictions in judicial reasoning conceal or underplay the power that judges exercise, but argues that judges ought to embrace rather than fear acknowledgment of that power. Open recognition of the fact that judges make law, for example, provides an opportunity for that power to be explained, rationalised and used carefully in light of the relationship between the judiciary and the legislature. The eradication of fictions forces judges to confront difficult questions, but those questions must, Burrows argues, be addressed in order to promote rationality and transparency in the law. It is on this basis that Burrows celebrates the recent decision of the Supreme Court of the UK in *Patel v Mirza*.[21] In that case, the Court held by a narrow majority that, in asking whether the defence of illegality applies to a claim in unjust enrichment, it is necessary openly to discuss and balance the competing policy considerations that weigh in favour of, and against, the application of the defence.

Another overlap is encountered between the two notions of form and substance (appearance/reality and rules/reasons) in relation to questions of taxonomy. As Andrew Robertson argues in Chapter 11, notions of form and substance underlie the standard 'lumping' and 'splitting' taxonomical analyses and disputes.[22] A conventional taxonomic argument is that the form of the law does not reflect some underlying truth, either because what is understood as a single doctrine is in fact more complex and deals with a number of different types of case which would better be understood separately or, conversely, two or more separate doctrines operate in circumstances that are so closely analogous that they are in substance doing the same work or producing inconsistent results in analogous cases. This may be seen as an issue concerning form and substance in the sense of appearance and underlying reality. But it is also fundamentally a question about rules and reasons, as Chapter 11 shows, because taxonomic issues ultimately turn on the purposes served by the doctrines in question, and on the unity or disunity of the issues of justice and policy in the different categories of case.

[20] Burrows, above n 7.
[21] [2016] UKSC 42, [2017] AC 467.
[22] A Robertson, 'The Form and Substance of Equitable Estoppel', this volume, ch 11.

II. Rules and Reasons

A. The Relationship between Rules and Rationales

One of the dominant scholarly methodologies in the law of obligations in the common law world is interpretive: its aim is to understand the law at a deep level, to reveal the rationales and purposes underlying the law and to explain why the law is as it is. An interpretive theory of the common law is generally tested through some combination of the following criteria: *fit* (consistency between the theory and established legal rules and the outcomes of the cases), *coherence* (the extent to the theory presents the law as coherent or reveals an 'intelligible order' in the law), *justification* (the extent to which the theory presents the law in its best normative light, and shows it to be consistent with whatever normative influences there are or should be on the law, such as notions of right and wrong or economic efficiency), and *fidelity* (consistency with the reasons given by the judges in the cases).[23] That broad interpretive methodology covers a wide range of different scholarly approaches because the elements can be combined in different ways, with differing levels of weight accorded to the different criteria, and in some instances particular criteria given no weight at all.[24]

An interesting question raised by the contributions to this volume by Liam Murphy and Robert Stevens is the relationship between form and substance, in the sense of rules and reasons broadly understood, in an interpretive theory of law. For Robert Stevens, form controls substance.[25] Following Weinrib,[26] Stevens argues that the bilateral form of private law imposes strict limits on the kinds of reasons that can justify it and to which, consequently, judges should be permitted to have recourse. The distinguishing feature of private law duties, Stevens contends, is that they are owed to other people who have control over them. While the power to sue is usually an aspect of that control, Stevens argues that is not the defining feature of a private law right because it is neither unique to private law nor a necessary feature of a private law right/duty relationship. Rather, the distinguishing feature of a private law duty is the control enjoyed by the right-holder in the form of a power to consent to non-performance or release the obligor from the duty. Since the private law right/duty relationship is in this way bilateral at is core, the reasons that justify those legal relations must also be bilateral, in the sense that they must apply equally to both parties. For Stevens, therefore, one-sided arguments (such as the need to deter the defendant or the desire to see that the claimant is compensated for his or her loss) cannot be understood to

[23] SA Smith, *Contract Theory* (Oxford, Oxford University Press, 1993) 7–13; Murphy, 'The Formality of Contractual Obligation', this volume, ch 7.

[24] A Robertson, 'Rights, Pluralism and the Duty of Care' in D Nolan and A Robertson (eds), *Rights and Private Law* (Oxford, Hart Publishing, 2012) 437–9.

[25] R Stevens, 'Private Law and the Form of Reasons', this volume, ch 6.

[26] EJ Weinrib, *The Idea of Private Law* (Cambridge, MA, Harvard University Press, 1995).

underlie private law rights and duties: if they do not apply equally to both parties then they are not 'right-shaped reasons'. The form of private law, on this view, dictates the kinds of reasons of substance that can be understood to justify it.

A fundamentally different understanding of the relationship between form and substance or rules and reasons in interpretive legal theory is adopted by Liam Murphy in Chapter 7. Murphy's focus is *content formality*, which is the extent to which a rule or reason is – or can be seen to be – shaped by underlying concerns of substance, such as justice or policy. If a legal rule has low content formality, then its form clearly does not control the reasons of substance that can be understood to underlie it. Atiyah and Summers suggest that a rule has high content formality if its content is shaped by fiat – ie, somewhat arbitrary – or is 'under-inclusive or over-inclusive in relation to its objectives'.[27] The rule that one must drive on the left or right-hand side of a road has high content formality because its content is chosen arbitrarily: what matters is that there must be a rule, rather than which side is chosen.[28] Atiyah and Summers also cite the requirement that a will must be attested by two witnesses as an example of a highly formal rule, not because of its arbitrariness, but because it is over-inclusive. The purpose of the rule is to ensure that a will was signed by the testator, but a will may be struck down by the rule even though there is other reliable evidence that it was signed by the testator.[29] The Australian statutory prohibition on misleading or deceptive conduct in trade or commerce, by way of contrast, has very low content formality because its content is shaped more or less entirely by reasons of substance.[30] The rule prohibits the very kind of conduct that is its purpose to prevent.

Murphy suggests that a rule can be understood to have high content formality if it does not state its rationale, and can be understood as more substantive the more it makes clear its purpose. On that basis, Murphy argues that contract law as a whole has high content formality because it is instrumental, and the purposes it pursues are not evident in the rules and principles of contract law. On its face, contract law seems to be based on the idea that the law of contract enforces promises and agreements because people ought, as a matter of right and wrong, to keep their promises and agreements. But Murphy's analysis proceeds on the premise that there are no natural promissory rights and duties. Rather, Murphy suggests that promissory morality is dependent on the existence of a conventional social practice requiring the keeping of promises. If that premise is accepted, then the best understanding of the purpose of contract law is that it is to promote the beneficial social practices of keeping promises and agreements. Since that purpose is

[27] Atiyah and Summers, above n 1, 13.

[28] ibid.

[29] As Kennedy, above n 2, 1695 notes, some over-inclusion and under-inclusion inevitably result from the use of a rule rather than a standard, and 'are the price of avoiding the potential arbitrariness and uncertainty of a standard'.

[30] Australian Consumer Law, s 18; see J Paterson and E Bant, 'Misrepresentation, Misleading Conduct and Statute through the Lens of Form and Substance', this volume, ch 17.

not evident in even the most fundamental principles of contract law, contract law as a whole must be understood to have a high level of content formality.

The flexibility of interpretive legal methodology is exemplified by the fact that it is followed by two groups of scholars who hold fundamentally different, perhaps even ultimately irreconcilable, understandings of law and approaches to legal scholarship. In Chapter 8, Dan Priel distinguishes two different kinds of 'formalism' in obligations scholarship: conceptualism and doctrinalism.[31] Doctrinalism is an approach which begins with the cases and seeks to identify structure, coherence and general principles by way of induction. Priel suggests that this approach is 'formalist' in the sense that it places faith in the development of dispositive legal categories.[32] Conceptualism, in contrast, begins with relations between individuals and develops universal ideas about law on the basis of reason. Conceptualism is ultimately grounded in notions of natural law and takes relations between individuals as its governing forms. While doctrinal scholarship rarely drills down to deep jurisprudential levels, most doctrinal scholarship is consistent with a positivist understanding of law. Priel's analysis of the tenets, techniques, strengths, weaknesses, points of connection and divergences between these two kinds of 'formalism' offers a deep and potentially very productive understanding of the dominant forms of contemporary obligations scholarship.

B. The Form and Substance of Equity

The maxim that 'equity looks to the substance rather than the form' is potentially misleading to the extent that it suggests that the common law is unconcerned with substance and that equity is unconcerned with form. As Ben McFarlane observes in Chapter 9, courts look to the substance of transactions for the purpose of determining the parties' common law rights as well as the application of equitable principles. Moreover, McFarlane argues, form is vitally important in equity, and in understanding equity. Equity may look beyond the form of a trustee's ownership to recognise the beneficiary as the 'true owner', but, McFarlane's analysis suggests, the notion that the beneficiary's 'ownership' can be equated with legal ownership is dangerously misleading, as exemplified by *Shell v Total*. McFarlane argues that it helps us to understand equity to see that it commonly operates by controlling the enforcement or acquisition of legal rights. Thus, a beneficiary's right under a trust is not best understood as a form of ownership, but as a right against the trustee's right.[33] McFarlane does not argue that this is all equity does, nor that the common law does not control the acquisition and enforcement of rights, but that many equitable rules operate in this way, that it is consistent with the notion of

[31] D Priel, 'Two Forms of Formalism', this volume, ch 8.
[32] ibid, text preceding fn 26.
[33] B McFarlane and R Stevens, 'The nature of equitable property' (2010) 4 *Journal of Equity* 1.

equity as a supplement to the common law, and that paying attention to this form helps us to understand equity as a second order system.

Of course, as Man Yip reminds us in Chapter 10, it is in the very nature of equity to favour reasons over rules in particular instances.[34] Equity developed as a substance-driven response to the restrictive rules of the common law, and even in its contemporary, more rule-based form routinely calls for direct consideration of underlying issues of justice and questions of right and wrong. The primary vehicle for consideration of issues of substance in equity is, of course, the notion of conscience. Man Yip argues that English equity has, in recent years, taken a turn away from formality and towards substance. She identifies symptoms of that trend (the treatment of precedent, the rise of discretion and increased sensitivity to context) and suggests some causes (increasing diversity of fact situations, rising complexity and a turn to pragmatism). She identifies two different models by which considerations of substance are given priority in recent equity jurisprudence: the first is the 'open discretion model' which involves a 'range of factors' or 'in the round' analysis in the first instance, the second involves the softening of a primary rule by way of a 'residual discretion' which allows the court to do justice on the facts of the particular case.

One of the symptoms of the turn to substance in English equity identified by Man Yip is the role played by precedent in judicial reasoning: the approach taken to conflicting authorities, the extent of deference to precedent and the interaction between precedent on the one hand and justice and policy on the other. For Atiyah and Summers, a significant dimension of form and substance in legal reasoning was the treatment of precedent, a topic to which they devoted considerable attention.[35] They observed that through a variety of accepted practices and techniques, American judges enjoyed much greater powers – and had much greater willingness – to disregard, overrule and evade precedent than English judges. English judges generally took pains to reconcile, explain and distinguish conflicting authorities[36] and, of course, the House of Lords considered that it was bound by its own decisions until 1966. Perhaps most tellingly, Atiyah and Summers noted that English judges were more inclined on a day-to-day basis to be more deferential to colleagues whose judgments were not binding on them even if they disagreed with them.[37] It is noteworthy, then, that Man Yip identifies a greater willingness in the Supreme Court of the UK to resolve difficult questions by direct reference to the underlying issues of substance without feeling compelled to reconcile and rationalise conflicting lines of authority.[38]

[34] Man Yip, 'Modern Equity – At the Edge of Formal Reasoning?', this volume, ch 10.

[35] Atiyah and Summers, above n 1, ch 5.

[36] ibid 129.

[37] ibid 127.

[38] Cf the analysis offered by James Lee in his chapter in this volume of several decisions of the Supreme Court of the UK in the law of torts. We discuss Lee's chapter in the section below.

C. Form and Substance in the Law of Torts

Atiyah and Summers touched on certain decisions in the law of torts but, by and large, did not engage with that branch of the law of obligations at any length. Several chapters in this volume, therefore, seek to apply the Atiyah and Summers' framework with a view to illuminating this area of private law. Jason Neyers in his chapter focuses on the tort of deceit and, in particular, the requirement that the plaintiff suffer actionable damage. He lays siege to a loss-based understanding of that tort, that is, one that comprehends the idea of damage as meaning that the plaintiff has been made factually worse off, and contends that that account of the damage element is animated by a highly formal assessment of the relevant cases. His overarching thesis is that '[t]his formalistic view has prevented English scholars from providing compelling justifications for the results of leading deceit cases on damages and thereby from unearthing the core principle animating the tort.'[39] Superior to the traditional loss-based account of deceit in terms of its power to explain leading cases in the field, Neyers contends, is the notion that the damage element of the tort requires 'the non-consensual dispossession of a right previously held by the claimant'.[40] Although Neyers grapples only with the tort of deceit, it is doubtful that his understanding of the concept of damage is meant to be confined to that tort. It may well be that his analysis sheds light on how the concept of damage is to be understood in relation to all torts of which damage is an ingredient.

James Goudkamp and Eleni Katsampouka in Chapter 14 engage with the jurisdiction to award punitive damages, which jurisdiction is either available only in the context of tort law or is predominantly enlivened in connection with claims in tort, depending on the legal system with which one is concerned. Atiyah and Summers singled out the decision of the House of Lords in *Rookes v Barnard*[41] as powerful evidence in support of their claim that English law is excessively formal. In that case, Lord Devlin controversially held that precedent required that the award of punitive damages be limited to just three categories of case (ie, cases where the defendant was a government servant and, acting in that capacity, engaged in oppressive, arbitrary or unconstitutional conduct, instances where the defendant had a profit motive, and situations where statute mandated the availability of punitive damages). *Rookes* certainly exemplifies formalistic reasoning. It does so partly because of Lord Devlin's extensive reliance on, and fine-grained analysis of, precedent but more fundamentally because it denies the availability of punitive damages in all cases that do not fall within one of the identified categories, irrespective of whether the reasons for awarding punitive damages (which the courts identify as being punishment and deterrence) suggest that an award should

[39] J Neyers, 'Form and Substance in the Tort of Deceit', this volume, ch 13.
[40] ibid, text following n 7.
[41] [1964] AC 1129.

be made. Goudkamp and Katsampouka build on Atiyah and Summers' analysis of this topic with reference to the contemporary law. Their essential concern is not to make any particular claims regarding how the law of punitive damages should be structured but to facilitate understanding of the existing law in this regard by scrutinising it through the prism of Atiyah and Summers' work. In the spirit of Atiyah and Summers' project, they examine the position in England and the US, but also in Australia and Canada. Their conclusion is that, in so far as the award of punitive damages is concerned, Atiyah and Summers' thesis that English law is dominated by formal reasoning while in the US substantive reasoning prevails holds good, although the gulf is not as great as it was at the time that Atiyah and Summers were writing. This is partly because judges at the ultimate appellate level in England have, since the turn of the twenty-first century, shown increased willingness to shape the law of punitive damages by reference to the rationales for the award.[42]

James Lee's chapter[43] analyses the balance between form and substance in a series of decisions of the Supreme Court of the UK in several topics in the law of torts. His primary focus is on two fields in which the Court has been particularly active in recent years: the duty of care element of the tort of negligence and vicarious liability. Interestingly, Lee's analysis reveals the employment of different types of reasoning across these areas. In relation to duty of care, Lee points out that recent decisions have (at least) marginalised or retreated from the *Caparo* test,[44] the third stage of which explicitly calls for consideration of substantive reasons.[45] Instead, the Supreme Court has emphasised in several recent decisions[46] the overriding importance of allegiance to precedent. The basic idea underpinning the cases concerned is that it is illegitimate to ask *de novo* in each and every situation whether policy favours or militates against the recognition of a duty of care and to recognise or deny the existence of a duty accordingly. Instead, the starting point is whether an existing case settles the position. It is only in truly novel matters that it is permissible, on this approach, to enquire as to what policy demands. Lee emphasises that the Supreme Court's recent jurisprudence on duty of care plainly contrasts radically with that in relation to vicarious liability. As to the latter doctrine, the Supreme Court[47] has extended relentlessly the circumstances

[42] See, in particular, *Kuddus v Chief Constable of Leicestershire* [2001] UKHL 29, [2002] 2 AC 122.

[43] J Lee, 'Trends in Tort Law: Bad Form and Addictive Substance?', this volume, ch 12.

[44] *Caparo Industries Plc v Dickman* [1990] 2 AC 605.

[45] See further A Robertson, 'Justice, Community Welfare and the Duty of Care' (2011) 127 *LQR* 370, 'On the Function of the Law of Negligence' (2013) 33 *OJLS* 31 and 'Policy-Based Reasoning in Duty of Care Cases' (2013) 33 *Legal Studies* 119.

[46] *Michael v Chief Constable of South Wales Police* [2015] UKSC 2, [2015] AC 1732; *Robinson v Chief Constable of West Yorkshire* [2018] UKSC 4, [2018] AC 736; *Darnley v Croydon Health Services NHS Trust* [2018] UKSC 50; [2018] 3 WLR 1153.

[47] *Various Claimants v Catholic Child Welfare Society* [2012] UKSC 56, [2013] 2 AC 1; *Cox v Ministry of Justice* [2016] UKSC 10, [2016] AC 660; *Armes v Nottinghamshire County Council* [2017] UKSC 60, [2018] AC 355; *Mohamud v Wm Morrison Supermarkets Plc* [2016] UKSC 11, [2016] AC 677.

in which vicarious liability arises by reference to the perceived reasons for that principle of liability and, further, has placed policy considerations front and centre in the determination of whether vicarious liability should be imposed. The reason why the Supreme Court has employed fundamentally different modes of reasoning in these two important (and closely related) parts of tort law more or less simultaneously is unclear, although it is doubtful that the difference is due to differently constituted benches.

D. Form and Substance in Legislation

Atiyah and Summers regarded statutes as inherently formal.[48] Whereas judges must give reasons for their decisions from which the rationale for the rule in issue may be discerned, a statute is simply a series of commands. Those commands must be faithfully applied and take precedence automatically (subject to constitutional principles) over other sources of law and other reasons that legal actors may have for action. Historically, statute has played a relatively unimportant role in the law of obligations, with the great bulk of the rules that constitute this part of the law having been created by judges. This pattern, however, is changing, with legislation having an increasingly significant impact on private law rights and duties. As such, one may expect that, generally speaking, the rise of statute would be gradually rendering the law of obligations increasingly formal.

Although there is an inherent formality to statutes, the degree of formality in statute law is neither uniform nor straightforward, for a number of reasons. In the first place, the level of content formality varies greatly. While some statutes exhibit high content formality, others, as noted earlier, are manifestly substantive in content. This is a recurring theme of Jeannie Paterson and Elise Bant's chapter.[49] Paterson and Bant compare the English Misrepresentation Act 1967 (UK) with the statutory prohibition of misleading conduct in Australia. They emphasise that the English statute is far more narrow and prescriptive than the Australian legislation, and this has significant consequences for its interpretation and therefore, arguably, its effectiveness. They write that '[t]he prescriptive expression of the Misrepresentation Act has encouraged the English judicial proclivity for formal reasoning'.[50] By contrast, they contend that legislation such as the Australian prohibition on misleading conduct, which draws on 'open-textured standards', prompts a more substantive approach to interpretation in which the courts construe the legislation with direct reference to its purposes. Paterson and Bant examine the judicial responses to contracting parties' attempts to contract around the English and Australian legislation, and this provides an illuminating contrast between the two different styles of legislative drafting and interpretation.

[48] Atiyah and Summers, above n 1, 96–98.
[49] Paterson and Bant, above n 30.
[50] ibid, text following n 142.

Secondly, the formality of statutes is in some instances diminished by provisions that expressly allow or even require substantive considerations to be taken into account in their interpretation. Such provisions sometimes govern the interpretation of particular statutes,[51] and are sometimes promulgated as general principles of statutory interpretation. An example of the latter is the provision enacted by the Australian Commonwealth Parliament that requires 'the interpretation that would best achieve the purpose or object' of an act 'to be preferred to each other interpretation.'[52] It sits alongside a provision allowing courts to have recourse to extrinsic material for certain specified purposes.[53] Ben Chen and Jeff Gordon explain in Chapter 16 how the enactment of those provisions ushered in a markedly less formal, more contextualist approach to statutory interpretation in Australia.

Thirdly, statutes and the common law are fundamentally interlinked at a number of levels.[54] For example, a significant proportion of the common law comprises judge-created rules that gloss statutes and tell us how they are to be understood (so called 'statutory common law'). Some statutes 'preserve' the common law, which presents issues of formidable complexity,[55] such as whether the relevant common law is thereby ossified as at the date of the statute and rendered incapable of further development. Further, many statutes would simply be unintelligible if considered in isolation but anticipate, like equity, the existence of a substantial body of common law principles. Such statutes are inextricably linked with the common law. Even so called 'codes' are, as Ben Chen and Jeff Gordon observe,[56] not written on a *tabula rasa*. Chen and Gordon argue that the displacement of the common law by legislation is not binary but continuous, and may best be understood by reference to the idea of a 'displacement continuum', with complete codes at one end, modification or supplementation in the middle, and minimal displacement at the other end.[57] On the relationship between statutes and the common law, it should finally be noted that there is, of course, a profound and difficult question of the extent to which the common law should be adapted in view of a relevant statute.[58] On one view, the superiority of statute as a source of law, both authoritatively but also increasingly in terms of its importance and ubiquity, requires that the judge-made law evolve in a manner that is coherent with statute.

[51] See, eg, Murphy, above n 23, text accompanying n 9.

[52] Acts Interpretation Act 1901 (Cth), s 15AA ('In interpreting a provision of an Act, the interpretation that would best achieve the purpose or object of the Act (whether or not that purpose or object is expressly stated in the Act) is to be preferred to each other interpretation').

[53] ibid, s 15AB.

[54] For valuable analysis, see A Burrows, 'The relationship between common law and statute in the law of obligations' (2012) 128 *LQR* 232.

[55] For illuminating discussion, see R Munday 'Legislation that would "preserve" the common law: the case of the (hearsay) declaration of intention' (2008) 124 *LQR* 46.

[56] B Chen and J Gordon, 'Interpretive Formalism in the Law of Obligations: Thirty Years after *Form and Substance*', this volume, ch 16, text accompanying n 79.

[57] ibid, text accompanying nn 62–89.

[58] The classic analysis of this issue is PS Atiyah, 'Common Law and Statute Law' (1985) 48 *MLR* 1.

A fourth complicating factor is that judges are the ultimate arbiters of what statutes mean, with the result that different approaches to statutory interpretation can render statutes either more or less formal. For example, a highly formal approach to construction concentrates simply on the text, whereas a more substantive approach takes account of the purposes and policies underlying the statute, which may even be given primacy over the words used.[59] As Atiyah and Summers note, those purposes can be gleaned or inferred from the text itself, or identified through other sources such as legislative history.[60] This fourth consideration is the primary focus of Ben Chen and Jeff Gordon's chapter in this volume, which compares approaches to statutory interpretation in Australia and US.[61]

At the risk of oversimplifying Chen and Gordon's nuanced analysis, their overarching thesis is that while the Australian approach to statutory interpretation has become significantly most substantive, the approach followed in the US has become markedly more formal. Chen and Gordon note the observation made by Lord Scarman in a lecture in Melbourne in 1980 that the High Court of Australia was 'more English than the English' in its approach to statutory interpretation.[62] Legislative reform followed almost immediately and the courts subsequently developed a more contextual approach.[63] Patrick Atiyah speculated in 1992 that Australia might occupy 'a position somewhere between England and America' in the level of formality of its legal system.[64] Chen and Gordon argue that, in the realm of contract interpretation, Australian law now oscillates between textualism and contextualism, in contrast with a strong trend in favour of textualism in the US. In the field of statutory interpretation, Chen and Gordon argue, Australian law has become firmly contextualist, while Justice Scalia has led the US courts in a strongly textualist direction.

The complexity of the interaction between the common law and statute, and the importance of being attentive to that interaction, is emphasised by Mark Leeming's chapter in this volume.[65] Leeming focuses on three occasions where legislation and the common law coalesce (or contrast) with each other. These are the availability or otherwise of apportionment for contributory negligence in claims for breach of contract, the law of punitive damages and the different approaches to the interpretation of judgments and statutory text, and the statutory modification in Australia of the concept of unconscionable conduct. The first of these issues has particular

[59] Atiyah and Summers, above n 1, 100.

[60] ibid 15.

[61] Chen and Gordon, above n 56.

[62] ibid, text accompanying n 35, quoting L Scarman, 'Ninth Wilfred Fullagar Memorial Lecture: The Common Law Judge and the Twentieth Century – Happy Marriage or Irretrievable Breakdown?' (1980) 7 *Monash Law Review* 1.

[63] Chen and Gordon, above n 56, text following n 35.

[64] PS Atiyah, 'Justice and Predictability in the Common Law' (1992) 15 *University of New South Wales Law Journal* 448, 454 (noting that he was 'not sufficiently familiar with trends in Australian law today' to do more than speculate on the question).

[65] M Leeming, 'Statute Law in the Law of Obligations: Dimensions of Form and Substance', this volume, ch 15. See, further M Leeming, *The Statutory Foundations of Negligence* (Sydney, Federation Press, 2019).

relevance in the present context. In England, it has long been the law that damages in a claim for breach of contract cannot be reduced for contributory negligence unless the contractual duty concerned is one that requires the taking of reasonable care and a parallel obligation arises in the tort of negligence.[66] The Court of Appeal arrived at this conclusion without reference to the statutory language of the Law Reform (Contributory Negligence) Act 1945 (UK), but in view of what it ultimately thought was a just and fair rule to adopt.[67] By contrast, the High Court of Australia held in dramatic fashion[68] that materially identical legislation in South Australia had no application to contractual claims with the result that, where a plaintiff had concurrent claims in tort and contract, the award in the contractual claim would be unaffected by any contributory negligence of which the plaintiff may be guilty. The High Court arrived at that conclusion following close attention to the legislative text. The difference between the judicial methodologies in England (more substantive) and Australia (more formal) is stark. One of Leeming's concerns is to rebut certain criticisms that have been made of the High Court's decision, which was promptly overturned by statutes enacted across Australia. He emphasises that the High Court's decision was an exercise in legislative interpretation and that the words of the statute were quite clearly directed at the position in tort and to tort alone.

III. Conclusion

The essays in this volume show that the form and substance dichotomy provides a productive frame of reference for studying the law of obligations. It allows illuminating comparisons to be drawn across time, between jurisdictions, between different subject areas and between different approaches to myriad factual, doctrinal and theoretical problems. Above all, this volume shows that form and substance are inextricably intertwined in the common law of obligations. Both form and substance are essential elements of legal reasoning in this area of the law, and dangers lie in the neglect of either. Strong arguments are made in this book for favouring form over substance in some situations, and for choosing substance over form in others. This collection suggests that not only is it 'possible to be formalist in one way and substantivist in another', as Kit Barker observes in his concluding chapter,[69] but it is also necessary. Just as common law method requires frequent movement back and forth between fact and value, it also requires frequent movement back and forth between form and substance. That movement between form and substance is a vital element of the dynamism of the common law of obligations.

[66] For discussion, see J Goudkamp, 'The Contributory Negligence Doctrine: Four Commercial Law Problems' [2017] *Lloyd's Maritime and Commercial Law Quarterly* 213, 219–228.

[67] *Forsikringsaktieselskapet Vesta v Butcher* [1989] AC 852.

[68] *Astley v Austrust Ltd* [1999] HCA 6, (1999) 197 CLR 1.

[69] Barker, above n 3.

2

Form and Substance: Fictions and Judicial Power

ANDREW BURROWS*

I. Introduction

Although all lawyers are familiar with the terminology of form and substance, there are several very different meanings that one might attach to that distinction. Moreover, it is not clear that those different meanings cohere with each other so that, in truth, it is probably a distinction that is best avoided. In other words, it can be powerfully argued that, to avoid confusion, it is better always to use other labels to describe precisely what one has in mind. It is this very uncertainty as to what is meant by form and substance that renders the distinction so eminently suitable for discussion and debate.

The central focus of this chapter is on fictions but, in order to explain the move from the theme of form and substance to the specific topic of fictions, the chapter starts by looking generally at form and substance. One might regard this as an unusually large hors d'ouevre before the main dish of the day.

II. Different Meanings of Form and Substance

If it is correct that the distinction between form and substance has different and apparently unrelated meanings, what are some of these different meanings? I will briefly mention two of these – although there are shades of meaning within each of those two – before I come to what is probably the primary meaning of form and substance, at least in English law, which is the distinction between false appearance and inner reality.

*I would like to thank Andrew Robertson and James Goudkamp for inviting me to the Obligations IX conference in Melbourne in July 2018 at which this chapter was presented as a plenary paper. I would also like to thank participants in the conference for their comments.

A. Rules/Doctrine and Balancing of Factors/Policies Behind the Rules

The first of these different meanings is that the distinction captures the contrast between a rule-based approach to judicial decision-making and an approach concerned with a flexible balancing of particular factors. Hence one might describe the move made by the UK Supreme Court in relation to the illegality defence in *Patel v Mirza*[1] as a move from a formalistic rules approach to a substantive balancing approach.[2] Somewhat similarly, if one thinks of the great judges of the latter part of the last century, one might say that Lord Diplock was a formalist in the sense that he strongly believed in the application of fixed and clear rules; whereas Lord Denning preferred substance over form because he believed in reaching decisions flexibly by looking at the overall merits or fairness of the case. Indeed, form and substance here replicate the tension between certainty and justice.

One might also say that that same basic idea underpins the contrast between legal reasoning in English and American law drawn by Professors Atiyah and Summers in their book written over 30 years ago *Form and Substance in Anglo-American Law* which, as I understand it, was one of the inspirations for this book.[3] They described English law as more formalistic than American law in the sense that the latter is more concerned with the substance of the matter. Although it is not easy to pinpoint exactly what they meant by this contrast, they appeared to have in mind that the predominant judicial approach in English law is to formulate and apply rules, justified internally by legal logic, whereas in American law there is a greater focus on articulating and applying the reasons behind the rules, so that a judge looks more at the policies and moral considerations behind the legal rules in order to reach a decision.[4] I am insufficiently knowledgeable about the practical

[1] *Patel v Mirza* [2016] UKSC 42, [2017] AC 467.

[2] The same might be said of the modern move in the English law on vicarious liability in tort (see especially *Armes v Nottinghamshire County Council* [2017] UKSC 60, [2018] AC 355: vicarious liability extended so that local authority held liable for sexual abuse by foster parents) to considering a range of factors. Indeed, as R Bagshaw, 'The Rise of "Evaluative Judgment" in the Law of Torts' (Society of Legal Scholars Conference, Oxford, September 2016), has explained, across many areas of tort law there has been what he succinctly describes as the 'rise of evaluative judgment'.

[3] PS Atiyah and RS Summers, *Form and Substance in Anglo-American Law: A Comparative Study of Legal Reasoning, Legal Theory, and Legal Institutions* (Oxford, Clarendon Press, 1987).

[4] In their words, ibid 1–3, 'A substantive reason is a moral, economic, political, institutional, or other social consideration … A formal reason is a different kind of reason from a substantive reason … [It] is a legally authoritative reason on which judges … are empowered or required to base a decision … [that] … excludes from consideration, overrides, or at least diminishes the weight of any countervailing substantive reason arising at the point of decision … [O]ur primary thesis [is] that the English legal system inclines to the greater use of formal reasons, while the American legal system inclines to the greater use of reasons of substance'. To put it another way, Atiyah and Summers appear to be arguing that English judicial reasoning is more formalistic in the sense that the judges have a greater concern with black letter law and doctrine and see law as an autonomous institution; whereas American judicial reasoning, under the influence of the realist movement, is more substantive in the sense that it has a greater focus on the underlying policies behind the law and sees law as part of the multi-disciplinary social sciences.

workings of the US law courts to know whether that was, and remains, an accurate contrast in relation to judicial reasoning generally across the US.[5]

B. Trivial Rules and Rules of Central Importance

A second and very different understanding of the distinction between form and substance is that it contrasts legal rules that are relatively trivial, so that a court might ignore non-compliance with them or might allow them to be 'cured', and rules that are of such central importance that they cannot be ignored or evaded.[6] This is the distinction in mind when it is said that particular rules are matters of *mere* form as opposed to substance. To give a practical example from the criminal courts, although this could equally apply to a civil case: what are the consequences if a purported expert's report does not comply with the procedural rules for such a report?[7] Say, for example, contrary to the rules, the expert does not confirm that he or she understands the expert's duty to the court or does not add a declaration of truth. It has been stressed that those procedural rules are not merely matters of form but of substance so that non-compliance with those rules may have the consequence that an expert's report is held to be inadmissible in evidence, even if relevant. Sharp LJ giving the judgment of the Court of Appeal in *R v Berberi* said: 'Those are not matters of form but of substance. [They lay down the] matters with which an expert's report must deal so the court can assess the admissibility and weight of such evidence'.[8]

C. False Appearance and Inner Reality

However, neither of those two usages of form and substance so far looked at correlates to, or, indeed, appears to have anything to do with, what is probably the primary meaning given to form and substance in English law. This is the distinction, applied to a legal rule, concept or line of reasoning, between the outward false appearance and the inner real truth. In other words, one is here distinguishing between, on the one hand, the legal form, which is false or misleading, and, on the other hand, the legal substance, which is the truth or reality.

[5] Looking at US legal academia and law schools compared to UK legal academic and law schools one can detect the sort of contrast that Atiyah and Summers are drawing, albeit that the contrast is less pronounced today than it was 30 years ago.

[6] Very similar is where a particular legal practice is regarded as essentially the same as another, albeit that it is presented differently. One might then say that the difference in presentation is a matter of form not substance, ie it is an unimportant (trivial) difference. This was the meaning of the distinction used by the EAT in *Commissioner of Police of the Metropolis v Shaw* [2012] ICR 464 [25], [28] (Underhill J) when he said that the difference between the Scottish practice of there being one award of damages for 'injured feelings' which might be increased because of aggravating features and the English practice of there being two heads of damages – damages for injured feelings and aggravated damages – was a difference of form not substance.

[7] Now contained in the Criminal Procedure Rules 2015, Pt 19, (SI 2015/1490).

[8] *R v Berberi* [2014] EWCA Crim 2961, [2015] 2 Cr App R 11 [17].

Four illustrations from the law of obligations of this primary usage of form and substance will now be explored before turning, within this general idea, to the wide-ranging example – the judicial use of fictions – that is the focus of this chapter.

A first and wide-ranging illustration is in relation to the classification of contracts. The courts may be required to decide, because different consequential rules may flow from this, whether a particular arrangement, while formally presented as being one type of contract, is in substance another type of contract. For example, in *Welsh Development Agency v Export Finance Co Ltd* the question was whether an agreement was a contract for the sale of goods (by Parrot to Exfinco) or a contract of loan (by Exfinco to Parrot) secured by a charge (in favour of Exfinco over Parrot's goods).[9] The practical importance of that classification was that, if the latter, the charge was likely to be void for non-registration. As it was, the Court of Appeal decided that there was no registration issue because the former classification was correct, ie this was a contract for the sale of goods. But the important point is that in deciding that, the Court made clear that it was looking at the substance not the form of the agreement. In the words of Dillon LJ, a court 'looks at the substance of the transaction and not at the labels which the parties have chosen to put on it'.[10] Staughton LJ said that, in deciding this type of question, the courts have used a variety of terms to stress that they are concerned with substance not form. He said the following: 'substance, truth, reality, genuine are good words; disguise, cloak, mask, colourable device, label, form, artificial, sham, stratagem and pretence are "bad names"'.[11]

A second illustration concerns the distinction between an injunction and specific performance. In the well-known line of cases running from *Lumley v Wagner*[12] through to *LauritzenCool AB v Lady Navigation Inc*[13] the courts have been concerned

[9] *Welsh Development Agency v Export Finance Co Ltd* [1992] BCC 270 ('*Welsh Development*').

[10] *Welsh Development* [1992] BCC 270, 278.

[11] *Welsh Development* [1992] BCC 270, 300. The phrase 'bad names' was from Dixon J in *Palette Shoes Proprietary Ltd v Krohn* (1937) 58 CLR 1, 28. Staughton LJ went on to draw an influential distinction between an external and an internal route to classification. A similar issue of classification has arisen in the very different context of deciding whether a person is an employee or worker, so as to have the benefit of employment protection legislation, or is, in contrast, an independent contractor. For example, in *Autoclenz Ltd v Belcher* [2011] UKSC 41, [2011] 4 All ER 745 ('*Autoclenz*'), the Supreme Court decided that car valet cleaners were employees or workers and not independent contractors even though the contract stated expressly that the valeters were independent contractors and not employees. What mattered was the substance – the parties' true common intentions – and not the form of the transaction; and one could treat a transaction as a sham even if there was no intention to deceive. Lord Clarke, giving the leading judgment, approved, at [25], the reasoning to this effect of Elias J in the Employment Appeal Tribunal in *Consistent Group Ltd v Kalwak* [2007] IRLR 560, including the following sentence: 'Tribunals should take a sensible and robust view of these matters in order to prevent form undermining substance'. The overruling of Elias J by the Court of Appeal (*Consistent Group Ltd v Kalwak* [2008] EWCA Civ 430, [2008] IRLR 505) in that case was disapproved by Lord Clarke. See, somewhat similarly, *Pimlico Plumbers Ltd v Smith* [2018] UKSC 29, [2018] ICR 1511. Although *Autoclenz* was not referred to in the Supreme Court, it was referred to in the Court of Appeal in that case, *Pimlico Plumbers Ltd v Smith* [2017] EWCA Civ 51, [2017] ICR 657, and at [144] Underhill LJ said, 'The tribunals will look narrowly at lawyer-drafted documentation which does not appear to correspond to the reality of the relationship'.

[12] *Lumley v Wagner* (1852) 1 De G M & G 604, 42 ER 687.

[13] *LauritzenCool AB v Lady Navigation Inc* [2005] EWCA Civ 579, [2005] 1 WLR 3686.

to decide whether what is in form a prohibitory injunction restraining breach of a negative contractual obligation is in substance an order of specific performance ordering performance of a positive contractual obligation. This matters because if one is in substance dealing with specific performance, the more restrictive rules applicable to specific performance should be applied, in particular the rule that there cannot be specific performance of a contract for personal service.

A third example of the distinction between form and substance, as meaning outward appearance and inner reality, falls within the law of unjust enrichment. It concerns the decision whether an enrichment of the defendant was 'at the expense of' the claimant. In *Investment Trust Companies v HMRC* the Supreme Court narrowed the scope of unjust enrichment by clarifying that, to satisfy the 'at the expense of' requirement, one normally needs a direct transfer of value from the claimant to the defendant.[14] But Lord Reed, giving the judgment with which all their Lordships agreed, pointed out that past cases, such as *Banque Financiere de la Cite v Parc (Battersea) Ltd* and *Bank of Cyprus UK Ltd v Menelaou*,[15] could only be explained by accepting that sometimes co-ordinated transactions should be treated as forming a single scheme or transaction with the consequence that the need for a direct transfer from claimant to defendant was satisfied even though there was an intervening transaction involving a third party. In Lord Reed's words: 'the court has treated a set of related transactions, operating in a co-ordinated way, as forming a single scheme or transaction, on the basis that to answer the question by considering each of the individual transactions separately would be unrealistic'.[16] And in line with this, Lord Neuberger in *Meneloau* said that to deny the bank's claim would represent 'a triumph of form over substance'.[17]

[14] *Investment Trust Companies v HMRC* [2017] UKSC 29, [2017] 2 WLR 1200 ('*Investment Trust*').

[15] *Banque Financiere de la Cite v Parc (Battersea) Ltd* [1999] 1 AC 221 ('*BFC v Parc*'); *Bank of Cyprus UK Ltd v Menelaou* [2015] UKSC 66, [2016] AC 176 ('*Menelaou*').

[16] *Investment Trust* [2017] UKSC 29, [2017] 2 WLR 1200 [61]. This picks up the theme of Lord Steyn's judgment in *BFC v Parc* that the interposition between the claimant, BFC, and the defendants, Parc/OOL, of a transaction between BFC and a third party (Mr Herzig), did not alter the substance of the matter. In Lord Steyn's words: 'To allow the interposition of Mr Herzig to alter the substance of the transaction would be pure formalism' (*BFC v Parc* [1999] 1 AC 221, 227). Again, in the *Menelaou* case, a bank had allowed the Menelaou parents to extend a loan so as to enable them to sell one house (Rush Green Hall) to buy a property (Great Oak Court) for their daughter, Melissa. The bank did so on the basis that there would be a charge over Great Oak Court securing repayment by the parents, but no valid charge was created. However, it was held that, in order to reverse Melissa's unjust enrichment at the expense of the bank, the bank should be subrogated to the unpaid vendor's lien over her property. The two transactions (between the bank and the parents, and the parents and Melissa) were treated as, in reality, one single scheme so that Melissa's enrichment could be said to have been not only at the expense of her parents but also at the expense of the bank. In Lord Clarke's words: 'It is not … in dispute that, if the bank had received all the proceeds of sale of Rush Green Hall and had then re-advanced the moneys required for the purchase of Great Oak Court, it would be entitled to succeed whether or not the re-advance was to the Menelaou parents or to Melissa … [I]f that is so, it would be pure formalism for subrogation to be precluded simply because the moneys remained in [the parents' solicitor's] client account … between the sale of Rush Green Hall and the purchase of Great Oak Court' *Menelaou* [2015] UKSC 66, [2016] AC 176 [26].

[17] *Menelaou* [2015] UKSC 66, [2016] AC 176 [99].

A final illustration of substance and form, as referring to an outward appearance and an inner reality, concerns the defence of estoppel in the law of unjust enrichment. As a matter of form, estoppel acts as an 'all or nothing' defence to a claim for restitution of a mistaken payment.[18] However, in substance the courts have applied it in a proportionate way by making it a condition of the estoppel that the defendant pays back any balance of the enrichment where it is unconscionable for the defendant to retain that balance. For example, in *Scottish Equitable plc v Derby* the claimant had mistakenly overpaid the defendant's retirement pension by £172,450.[19] The defendant had changed his position as to £9,600 in reliance on the claimant's representation that that pension payment was correct. It was held that, while estoppel was an all or nothing defence, it would be unconscionable for the defendant to have that defence unless it paid back £162,650. In substance and reality, therefore, despite the formal outward appearance, estoppel was being applied proportionately and not in an all or nothing way.

III. Fictions

With all that by way of lengthy introduction, we now turn to the central focus of this chapter which is an examination of one major and wide-ranging aspect of form and substance as meaning false appearance and inner reality. This is the use made in judicial reasoning of fictions.[20]

Although there is difficulty in providing a watertight definition of a fiction, it is sufficient for our purposes – putting to one side the now obsolete fictions involved in pleading the old forms of action – to define a legal fiction as a rule or concept or line of reasoning that is used by judges but obscures their true reasoning.

Jeremy Bentham famously despised fictions. In his words: '[I]n English law, fiction is a syphilis, which runs in every vein, and carries into every part of the system, the principle of rottenness'.[21] More recently, Peter Birks saw it as important in enhancing the rational transparency of the law to excise fictions.[22] Lord Nicholls, in his dissenting speech in the economic tort case of *OBG v Allen*, said: '[F]ictions, of their nature, conceal what is going on. They are a pretence … I would like to think that, as a mature legal system, English law had outgrown

[18] *Avon CC v Howlett* [1983] 1 WLR 605.

[19] *Scottish Equitable plc v Derby* [2001] EWCA Civ 369, [2001] 3 All ER 818. See also *National Westminster Bank plc v Somer International (UK) Ltd* [2001] EWCA Civ 970, [2002] QB 1286.

[20] See generally on fictions M Del Mar and W Twining (eds), *Legal Fictions in Theory and Practice* (Cham, Springer, 2015). For a helpful review of this book, see L Shmilovits, 'Legal Fictions in Theory and Practice' (2017) 76 *CLJ* 683.

[21] J Bowring (ed), *The Works of Jeremy Bentham* (Edinburgh, William Tait, vol 5, 1962) p 92.

[22] 'In the Birksian world there was no place for labels and fictions that were misleading or obscure': 'Peter Birks Obituary', *The Times* (London, 9 July, 2004).

the need for legal fictions'.[23] And in *Forsyth-Grant v Allen* in looking at 'waiver of tort' in the context of damages for the tort of nuisance, Toulson LJ, as he then was, remarked that the 'modern tendency has been to eschew resort to legal fictions'.[24]

In contrast, Lon Fuller in his difficult but seminal analysis of fictions in a trio of articles in the Illinois Law Review in 1930 regarded some fictions as having a legitimate role.[25] Indeed, his very definition of a fiction, which has been cited in many articles since, incorporated the idea that some fictions are useful even though known to be false. Hence, according to Fuller, 'A fiction is either, (1) a statement propounded with a complete or partial consciousness of its falsity, or (2) a false statement recognized as having utility'.[26] Fuller's view was that it was impossible and, in any event, inadvisable to rid the law of all fictions, whether by rejection or by redefinition, because, for example, they express useful concepts or are useful shorthand. More generally, they have utility because they meet the 'desire to keep the form of the law persuasive'.[27] In Fuller's words, 'Metaphor is the traditional device of persuasion. Eliminate metaphor from the law and you have reduced its power to convince and convert'.[28] Equally important for my theme is that Fuller went on to explore the motive for adopting fictions and argued that 'conservatism' of various types lay behind the use of fictions. He wrote, 'Speaking in general terms, one may say … that the impulse is one of conservatism'.[29] He labelled one type of conservatism as 'the conservatism of policy',[30] which he illustrated by it being convenient for judges, in deciding cases, to declare the law so as to 'obscure the process of legislating'.[31] And earlier

[23] *OBG v Allen* [2007] UKHL 21, [2008] 1 AC 1 [228]–[229]. In the context of the tort of conversion, and his view (dissenting) that that tort should extend generally to interference with intangible rights, Lord Nicholls was specifically focussing at the fiction of equating the value of a document as a chattel or piece of paper with the value of the rights embodied or recorded on it.

[24] *Forsyth-Grant v Allen* [2008] EWCA Civ 505, [2008] 2 EGLR 16 [45]. In the context of restitution for torts, Toulson LJ was specifically referring to 'waiver of tort' which, as he explained, is a fiction because the wronged party was not in truth waiving the wrong but was electing between alternative remedies.

[25] L Fuller, 'Legal Fictions' (1930–31) 25 *Illinois Law Review* 363–99, 513–46, 877–910. These were subsequently reprinted in a monograph, *Legal Fictions* (Stanford, Stanford University Press, 1967). For modern defences of fictions see, eg, F Schauer, 'Legal Fictions Revisited' and M Del Mar, 'Legal Fictions and Legal Change' in M Del Mar and W Twining (eds), *Legal Fictions in Theory and Practice* (Cham, Springer, 2015) 113–29, 225–53. As Schauer recognises at 113, 'defences of legal fictions are increasingly rare … and the accusation of using a "legal fiction" may have overtaken "formalist" as the most ubiquitous and ill-defined of jurisprudential condemnations'.

[26] Fuller, *Illinois Law Review*, above n 25, 369.

[27] ibid 380.

[28] ibid.

[29] ibid 519.

[30] ibid. Fuller also talked of 'emotional conservatism', 'the conservatism of convenience' and 'intellectual conservatism' (ibid 519).

[31] ibid. See similarly the reference by Milsom in *A Natural History of the Common Law* to Bentham's view that fictions were used by judges for surreptitiously 'stealing legislative power' (SFC Milsom, *A Natural History of the Common Law* (New York, Columbia University Press, 2003)).

he spoke of fictions concerned with 'the concealment by the court of the exercise of legislative power'.[32]

Also of great interest is Fuller's clarification of what is *not* a fiction. This he did by contrasting a fiction with lots of similar ideas in legal reasoning. For example, he made clear that a fiction is not the same as a lie, because there is no intent to deceive, and is also not the same as flawed or mistaken reasoning, so that we would not say that just because a judge takes a false step in legal reasoning he or she is employing a fiction. Again, Fuller helpfully argued that we must distinguish a fiction from a presumption (which is a rule of evidence), from the non-problematic general metaphorical use of language (such as the 'breaking' of a contract or the 'meeting of minds'), and from legal maxims such as 'equity treats as done that which ought to be done' (which are legal rules).[33]

Fuller's analysis is plainly of great importance and contains many fascinating and subtle insights. But Fuller does not really meet the major criticism of those who oppose fictions, which is that, even if they have proved useful to the judiciary, that is not a good reason for their retention given that, as Fuller accepted, they obscure true judicial reasoning. I therefore prefer the views of Bentham, Birks, Nicholls and others that, in a modern legal system, fictions should be excised, or at least we should attempt to excise them, simply because they are an obstacle to clarity in the law and irrespective of the fact that the judiciary has found them useful.

My concern in this chapter is not to agonise about the correct definition of a fiction, although I accept the point made by, for example, Liron Shmilovits in his review of the excellent 2015 collection of essays on legal fictions edited by Del Mar and Twining, that one's very definition of a fiction can influence one's approach to them.[34] Instead, using the rough working definition set out above – a fiction is a rule or concept or line of reasoning that is used by judges but obscures their true reasoning – my central thesis, developing Fuller's idea of the motivation of conservatism, is that one major reason *why* judges resort to fictions is to underplay their power.

In developing that argument for the rest of this chapter, we shall look first at fictions as to the role of the courts both in relation to the common law and statutes before turning, secondly, to fictions in the law of unjust enrichment and contract.

Before doing so, it should be clarified that I am not suggesting that there is some sort of conspiracy of dishonesty by the judges to conceal the truth.

[32] ibid 367. See also 390: 'The peculiar force which the fiction has [is] in rendering easier alterations in the law by appeasing the longing for an appearance of conservatism'.

[33] More difficult is the distinction between a fiction and a legal construct, such as a trust or a company/corporation. Some have treated the legal personality of a company as a fiction, but Schauer, above n 25, 123, n 17, is surely correct that, because a company has no pre-legal or extra-legal meaning, 'there is nothing fictional about treating a corporation as if it were a natural person'.

[34] As Shmilovits writes in the book review (above n 20, 684) 'The definition of legal fiction is hotly debated. It is hard to find two people who have the same understanding of the term – and those understandings pre-determine the results of inquiries into legal fictions'.

Nevertheless, in line with Fuller, it is accurate to say that there has been institutional judicial conservatism so that, whether consciously or sub-consciously, the judges have found it natural and useful to rely on fictions in order to avoid exposing a particular power being exercised and thereby avoiding opening up the judiciary to criticism. My argument is that the judges ought not to fear the open recognition of their power and that, instead of hiding behind fictions, the correct strategy across the board should be to explain rationally and transparently the judicial power, and its limits, that is being exercised.

IV. Fictions as to the Role of the Courts in Relation to Common Law and Statutes

A. Development of the Common Law

If one were ranking legal fictions in order of importance, top of the list would be the fiction that the courts do not make the common law but rather discover or find it. Often referred to as the declaratory theory, the underlying fairy tale in mind is that judges are given the secret password to a cave wherein lies the common law written on tablets of stone.

Laugh as we might, it is astonishing that that fairy tale was only denounced judicially in the UK as late as 1971. In perhaps the greatest law paper ever written by a UK judge – fittingly delivered to the annual conference of the Society of Public Teachers of Law (now the Society of Legal Scholars) – Lord Reid explained that, because we do not believe in fairy tales any more, it should be openly recognised that the judges in developing the common law make new law.[35] In Lord Reid's classic words:

> There was a time when it was thought almost indecent to suggest that the judges make law – they only declare it. Those with a taste for fairy tales seem to have thought that in some Aladdin's cave there is hidden the Common Law in all its splendour and that on a judge's appointment there descends on him knowledge of the magic words Open Sesame. Bad decisions are given when the judge has muddled the password and the wrong door opens. But we do not believe in fairy tales any more. So we must accept the fact that for better or for worse judges do make law, and tackle the question how do they approach their task and how should they approach it.[36]

Once one accepts that appellate judges can and do make law by developing the common law, a number of difficult questions arise concerning the limits, if any, of that creative power which, it is important to stress, allows retrospective law-making by an unelected judiciary. In his wonderful speech in *Woolwich Equitable*

[35] J Reid, 'The Judge as Law-Maker' (1972) 12 *Journal of the Society of Public Teachers of Law* 22.
[36] ibid 22.

Building Society v Inland Revenue Commissioners,[37] in which the common law of unjust enrichment was developed to allow the restitution as of right of payments obtained by a public authority ultra vires, Lord Goff said that, while he was aware of the boundary line between developing the common law and holding back for the legislature, he was never very sure where to find it. Lord Goff pointed out that if judges had held back we would not have had the modern tort of negligence, freezing injunctions or the modern law of judicial review. One can add that we would also not have had other famous examples of common law development such as the removal of the rule that a husband cannot rape his wife,[38] or the award of mental distress damages in contract,[39] or the removal of the mistake of law bar to restitution in the law of unjust enrichment.[40]

In deciding where the boundary line lies between legitimate judicial law-making and leaving matters to the legislature, it is very important to recognise just how different judge-made law is from legislation. As Lord Goff made clear in *Kleinwort Benson Ltd v Lincoln City Council*,[41] the traditional common law technique, centred on precedent, is characterised by incremental steps that, in most cases, have been anticipated in previous case law. Provided a judge respects these constraints of the common law technique – and, if applicable, the rules of precedent including the 1966 Practice Statement – there is little to fear from judicial law reform because these constraints prevent a judge starting afresh by imposing his or her own preferred political views. In other words, while the judges may be regarded in some cases as making law, provided they act within the traditional historical institutional constraints they are not acting as mini-legislators.[42] In any event, in the UK system of parliamentary sovereignty, there is an ultimate check on judicial power because Parliament is always free to pass legislation overriding what the courts have decided.

It follows from this that it should in practice be rare for the UK Supreme Court to decline to develop the common law in a way that it otherwise believes to be appropriate on the ground that the development is better left to Parliament.[43]

[37] *Woolwich Equitable Building Society v Inland Revenue Commissioners* [1993] AC 70.

[38] *R v R* [1992] 1 AC 599; upheld *R v R* [1992] 1 AC 599. This was not a pure common law development because rape was defined by statute in the Sexual Offences (Amendment) Act 1976 (UK), s 1(1). See generally A Burrows, 'Common Law Retrospectivity' in A Burrows, D Johnston and R Zimmermann (eds), *Judge and Jurist: Essays in Memory of Lord Rodger of Earlsferry* (Oxford, Oxford University Press, 2013) 543, 551–56.

[39] *Jarvis v Swan's Tours Ltd* [1973] QB 233.

[40] *Kleinwort Benson Ltd v Lincoln City Council* [1999] 2 AC 349 ('*Kleinwort*').

[41] *Kleinwort* [1999] 2 AC 349.

[42] This is emphasised by J Gardner, *Law as a Leap of Faith: Essays on Law in General* (Oxford, Oxford University Press, 2012) 19–53, especially 37–42.

[43] This is not to say that, in practice, there is no boundary. It is clear, for example, that, not least because of the intense objection to retrospective punishment (an additional factor is that new crimes need to be supported by a regime of rules concerning the type of offence and possible sentences that the courts are not in a position to lay down) – and common law reform is almost inevitably retrospective (on the possibility of prospective overruling, see *Re Spectrum Plus Ltd* [2005] UKHL 41, [2005] 2 AC 680; *cf Royal Bank of Scotland plc v Etridge (No 2)* [2001] UKHL 44, [2002] 2 AC 773;

But the really important point for the theme of this chapter is that one can readily see that difficult questions about the scope of judicial power, the relationship between the courts and the legislature, and the role of the judiciary in a modern democracy, are brought to the fore once one departs from the fiction that the judges do not make the common law but merely declare what it has always been. Recognition of those difficult questions immediately reveals why that fiction might have been thought useful while it lasted. In a nutshell, the fiction kept the courts out of political controversy.

The removal of the fictional fairy tale need not alarm the judiciary. This is because, once judicial reasoning is properly opened up and scrutinised for what it really is, it can be seen that the judges are making law in a distinctive non-political way; and that the form of law-making in question is one for which, as top-rate lawyers, they are supremely well-qualified despite not having a direct democratic mandate.

B. Statutory Interpretation

Few, if any, would now seek to deny that judges are law-makers when they develop the common law. Yet it is sometimes overlooked that there is a parallel set of issues that arise in relation to statutory interpretation. The fiction here is that all the courts are doing when they interpret a statute is putting into effect the intention of Parliament. The judges, so it is said, are not here exercising any law-making power but are simply the mouthpieces for the Legislature and are applying what the legislator intended even if that was not fully expressed in the statute.

The cases are full of references to this being the ultimate aim of statutory interpretation. How many times do we see judges writing that the statute means this because this is what Parliament must have intended; or that the statute cannot mean that because that cannot be what Parliament intended.

M Arden, 'Prospective Overruling' (2004) 120 *LQR* 7) – the courts should not develop the common law to add new crimes (see *Knuller (Publishing, Printing and Promotions) Ltd v DPP* [1973] AC 435; *cf Shaw v DPP* [1962] AC 220). There may also be occasional cases in which the courts are asked to develop the common law where the issue involves such a controversial issue of social policy that the courts should be inclined not to change the law. A good example is *R (Nicklinson) v Ministry of Justice* [2014] UKSC 38, [2015] AC 65, in which the courts decided, correctly in my view, that there should be no development of the common law of necessity as a defence to murder so as to accommodate certain cases of euthanasia because that was a matter for Parliament. The common law arguments were dealt with in the Divisional Court (led by Toulson LJ), [2012] EWHC 2381 (Admin), [2015] AC 657, and the Court of Appeal, [2013] EWCA Civ 961, [2015] AC 657, but were not taken up to the Supreme Court, which focussed purely on the Human Rights Act 1998 (UK). Toulson LJ said that the matter was for Parliament not the courts. '[I]t is for Parliament to decide whether to change the law on euthanasia … The reasons have to do with competence, constitutionality and control of the consequences' ([75]). '[I]t is one thing for the courts to adapt and develop the principles of the common law incrementally in order to keep up with the requirements of justice in a changing society, but major changes involving matters of controversial social policy are for Parliament.' ([79]). He also rejected the Human Rights Act 1998 (UK) argument as 'these are matters for Parliament to decide.' ([150]).

Recognising that this is a mask or fiction is less straightforward than exposing the fiction that the judges find, and do not make, the common law. But the best way of seeing the truth here is to ask, what exactly does the reference to Parliamentary intention mean?

Plainly it cannot mean that one should be looking at the actual subjective intentions of all those involved – the Minister, the government, the MPs, the Lords, the drafters, the bill team – because those intentions cannot be practically ascertained and, in any event, they are most unlikely to coincide other than at a very general and unhelpful level.

While accepting that, Dr Richard Ekins in his thought-provoking 2012 book *The Nature of Legislative Intent*, nevertheless argues that 'group theory' explains what is meant by parliamentary intention.[44] The legislature is a complex group and what is meant by legislative intention is that Parliament as a group acts with a rational plan, with linked procedures, to change the law in some way. So, in Dr Ekins' view, it is a mistake to argue that any fiction is involved in perpetuating the long-standing tradition of referring to the intention of the legislature.

However, even if one were to accept that Dr Ekins is providing a valid explanation for the traditional reference to parliamentary intention, it is clear that the explanation provides no assistance at a practical level in answering the questions on statutory interpretation that the courts face. In other words, to say that Parliamentary intention means that Parliament as a 'group' intends to change the law in some way by following the rules and procedures required in passing a statute is to say nothing more than that Parliament has validly passed a particular statute so that that statute is law; and plainly that banal observation does not help the courts in deciding a dispute on statutory interpretation. Rather, in deciding on the best interpretation of a statute, the courts need to rely on more concretised ideas that revolve around the judicial analysis of the best meaning today, with the benefit of hindsight, of the words laid down in the light of the statute's context and purpose.[45]

Again, as with the common law fairy tale, one can readily understand why it is that the courts have relied on the pretence that they are merely giving effect to parliamentary intention. Dressing a decision up as effecting parliamentary intention helps to divert attention away from scrutinising the role of the unelected judges. However, in an age of rational transparency the correct strategy should not be to shy away from the truth but to make clear that, while in interpreting legislation, the judges exercise the power to decide what the law is, that power is very different from that exercised by the legislature. Whether their role is interpreting statutes or developing the common law, the judges are clearly not free,

[44] R Ekins, *The Nature of Legislative Intent* (Oxford, Oxford University Press, 2012).

[45] See A Burrows, *Thinking about Statutes: Interpretation, Improvement, Interaction* (Hamlyn Lectures, 2017) (Cambridge, Cambridge University Press, 2018) 13–34. I there clarify that it is hard to reconcile parliamentary intention with the 'always speaking' doctrine.

as a legislator would be, simply to impose anew their own preferred policies. On the contrary, the statutory interpretative exercise is precisely constrained by the words, context and purpose of the statute. Moreover, as has already been mentioned, in the UK's system of parliamentary sovereignty there is an ultimate check on judicial power because Parliament can always pass new or amending legislation overriding what the courts have decided.

V. Fictions in the Law of Unjust Enrichment

No subject has been more bedevilled by fiction than the law of unjust enrichment. Until relatively recently the cause of action of unjust enrichment was not recognised and, in particular, most of the common law part of the subject[46] was hidden behind the fiction that restitution was granted because there was an implied contract between the parties to make restitution. Hence the traditional label for this part of the law was the mysterious 'quasi-contract'.

In English law the authoritative recognition of unjust enrichment did not occur until *Lipkin Gorman v Karpnale Ltd*[47] in 1991 and it was not until the House of Lords' decision in *Westdeutsche Landesbank Girozentrale v Islington London BC*[48]

[46] More specifically, that part of common law unjust enrichment concerned with the actions for money had and received to the claimant's use, money paid to the defendant's use, quantum meruit, and quantum valebat. William Swadling in a fascinating article (W Swadling, 'The Fiction of the Constructive Trust' (2011) 64 *Current Legal Problems* 399) has argued, in a similar way to Donovan Waters (D Waters, *The Constructive Trust: The Case for a New Approach in English Law* (London, The Athlone Press, 1964)) that, in relation to much of the equitable law of unjust enrichment, the use and language of a constructive trust is a fiction. But it is important to note that, for Swadling, the substance is that there is no trust and that that language merely serves to obscure that either a personal monetary remedy is being awarded (this is 'accounting as a constructive trustee') or that there is a mandatory injunction ordering the defendant to reconvey title to the claimant where a monetary award would be inadequate. In contrast to US writers such as Austin Scott (A Scott, 'Constructive Trusts' (1955) *LQR* 39, see also W Seavey and A Scott, 'Restitution' (1938) 54 *LQR* 29), Swadling is not focusing his main attention on what triggers those 'constructive trust' remedies. Scott's main argument was that a constructive trust is a fiction, directly parallel to the implied contract fiction, because it rests on the court imposing a remedy for unjust enrichment rather than upholding the parties' intentions through an express ('intention-based') trust. If the latter is the fiction in mind, it directly falls within the thesis of this chapter because that fiction might again be seen as obscuring the judicial power in reversing an unjust enrichment rather than effecting the parties' intentions.

[47] *Lipkin Gorman v Karpnale Ltd* [1991] 2 AC 548.

[48] *Westdeutsche Landesbank Girozentrale v Islington London Borough Council* [1996] AC 669 ('*Westdeutsche*'). In *Westdeutsche*, it was common ground by the time the case reached the House of Lords that the claimants were entitled to restitution in a personal common law action for money paid under an open void interest-rate swap. Lord Browne-Wilkinson, with whom Lords Slynn and Lloyd agreed, took the opportunity to overrule *Sinclair v Brougham* [1914] AC 398 (which had denied a common law claim for money had and received under a contract that was void because ultra vires) and in so doing his Lordship said the following: 'The common law restitutionary claim is based not on implied contract but on unjust enrichment: in the circumstances the law imposes an obligation to repay rather than implying an entirely fictitious agreement to repay … In my judgment, your Lordships should now unequivocally and finally reject the concept that the claim for moneys had and received is based on an implied contract' (*Westdeutsche* [1996] AC 669, 710 (footnotes omitted)).

(confirmed again by the Court of Appeal in *Haugesund Kommune v Depfa Bank*)[49] that the implied contract fiction was explicitly buried in favour of unjust enrichment.

The question here being asked is, why did the obvious fiction of an implied contract survive for as long as it did? While no doubt it had historical roots in the pleading rules for the common law money counts, it is very hard to see that history could have explained its continuation after the forms of action were abolished in the late nineteenth century. Rather, it is submitted that a plausible reason for the fiction is that it served to obscure the power of the judiciary. Seeing restitution as based on the parties' agreement, which the courts were simply upholding, was far less controversial – and appeared to respect freedom of contract – than accepting that the courts were themselves imposing a solution on the parties where there was no agreement. Once one recognises that this area of law does not rest on the parties' intentions but, like tort, is imposed on the parties subject to any agreement to the contrary, questions inevitably arise as to why the courts are imposing restitution in some situations and not others; and, linking in with the general scrutiny of the law-making power of the judiciary, it may be asked whether the solution is one that is appropriately formulated by unelected judges.

All of this may explain but does not, of course, justify the implied contract fiction. It is essential that we scrutinise the judges' real reasoning and, as the decisions turn on questions of legal principle and policy that do not involve political choices, there is no need for judges to fear the open recognition of their law-making role.

It is helpful to consider very briefly two other fictions in areas of the law that arguably fall within the law of unjust enrichment:[50] first, the law on tracing and, secondly, the law on subrogation.

The law on tracing, as traditionally understood, rests on the idea that a proprietary right over an original asset persists and extends into a different substitute asset so that the justification for a proprietary right over the traced asset is the same as that which justified a proprietary right over the original asset. In other words, proprietary rights in respect of traced assets have nothing to do with the creation of new rights to reverse unjust enrichment. All that is happening is that an existing proprietary right continues in relation to, and sweeps up, different assets. Birks was in no doubt that this involved a fiction and labelled it 'the fiction of persistence'.[51] In *Foskett v McKeown*[52] the House of Lords appeared to embrace that fiction by rejecting unjust enrichment reasoning yet providing no satisfactory explanation as to why what starts off as a proprietary right to one asset ends up as a proprietary right to an entirely different asset. If one is entitled to trace from a

[49] *Haugesund Kommune v Depfa Bank* [2010] EWCA Civ 579, [2012] QB 549.

[50] There is ongoing controversy as to whether or not these areas are best explained as reversing unjust enrichment.

[51] P Birks, *Unjust Enrichment*, 2nd edn (Oxford, Oxford University Press, 2005) 35.

[52] *Foskett v McKeown* [2001] 1 AC 102.

pig to a horse to a car, one surely cannot say, without invoking fiction (the fiction of persistence), that one has proprietary rights in the car merely because one had proprietary rights in the pig that has now been substituted by the car.

If that is a fiction, one might again say that it serves to disguise judicial power. To regard proprietary rights to traced assets as involving nothing more than the natural application of pre-existing proprietary rights is far less controversial than overtly accepting that the judges are here creating new proprietary rights.

Non-contractual subrogation allows one party, without a contract, to 'step into the shoes' of another party as regards some or all of that party's extinguished or subsisting rights. Non-contractual subrogation rests on a fiction because, in itself, it does not explain how or why one person's rights are transferred to another. The fiction is particularly clear where the rights in question have been extinguished so that the claimant is treated as if 'taking over' rights that no longer exist. It is strongly arguable that the underlying truth, as regards both extinguished and subsisting rights, is that the claimant is being given new rights to reverse an unjust enrichment. The significance of that for my theme here is that, to view the claimant as taking over another's previous rights, as if by assignment, again serves to divert attention away from the power the courts are here controversially exercising of creating new rights in favour of the claimant, including new proprietary rights, where, as in *Menelaou*,[53] there is subrogation to secured rights. By not overtly recognising that there are new rights created by the courts, the courts avoid the need to justify how or why those rights are being transferred. Indeed, on its proprietary side, the fiction involved in subrogation may be seen as analogous to the fiction involved in tracing. More generally, there was the added fiction that some of the law on subrogation was falsely seen as based on a contract: this was analogous to the implied contract theory of unjust enrichment and again obscured a judicially imposed and hence more controversial justification based on unjust enrichment by the pretence of there being an agreement between the parties explaining this. The House of Lords in *BFC v Parc*[54] rid the law of that particular fiction and recognised that, alongside contractual subrogation, there is non-contractual subrogation which is best explained as reversing the defendant's unjust enrichment at the claimant's expense.

VI. Fictions in the Law of Contract

The central fiction that will here be looked at is the expansive role, in explaining the rules of contract, of the intentions of the parties. While, not surprisingly, many areas of contract law can properly be said to rest on the intention of the parties, albeit objectively ascertained – for example, the formation of contract, and the

[53] *Menelaou* [2015] UKSC 66, [2016] AC 176.
[54] *BFC v Parc* [1999] 1 AC 221.

incorporation, interpretation and implication of contract terms – there are other areas where the courts often rely on the parties' intentions even though, in reality, they are imposing a fair solution on the parties.[55]

Take, for example, common mistake and frustration. Traditionally English law sought to manage without a doctrine of common mistake and instead explained the cases as resting on an implied term in the contract.[56] Similarly, the juristic basis of frustration has traditionally been said to rest on an implied term in the contract[57] and/or its construction. But, as has more recently been generally recognised, these are situations where in truth, the contract has 'run out' and a fair solution is being imposed on the parties by the courts.

Why have the courts been reluctant openly to recognise this? Again, the answer is that it is far less controversial if the courts are seen to be merely putting into effect what the contracting parties have already themselves agreed rather than accepting that the judges are interfering with freedom of contract by imposing a fair solution on the parties.

The same applies to the law on damages not least remoteness in contract. I have written at length elsewhere in the festschrift for Lord Hoffmann,[58] and will not repeat that analysis again now, as to why it was misleading of Lord Hoffmann in *The Achilleas*[59] to see his concept of an 'assumption of responsibility' as agreement-centred rather than imposing a fair solution – a fair allocation of risk – on the parties based on a range of external factors.[60]

[55] In contrast, civilian systems have been far readier to recognise that they are applying rules imposed for policy reasons. In his seminal article on this topic, Professor Barry Nicholas wrote: 'In the field of contract, a fundamental difference between French law and the traditional Common law is that the Common law habitually attempts to derive all the consequences of a contract from the will of those who made it … whereas the French law (and the Civil law generally) will often have recourse to rules' (B Nicholas, 'Rules and Terms – Civil Law and Common Law' (1974) 48 *Tulane Law Review* 946, 948–49).

[56] An implied condition precedent.

[57] An implied condition subsequent.

[58] A Burrows, 'Lord Hoffmann and Remoteness in Contract' in P Davies and J Pila (eds), *The Jurisprudence of Lord Hoffmann* (Oxford, Hart Publishing, 2015) 251.

[59] *Transfield Shipping Inc v Mercator Shipping Inc* (*The Achilleas*) [2008] UKHL 48, [2009] 1 AC 61.

[60] Applying that approach, it is in general fair and reasonable to allocate the risk of loss to the contract-breaker if the defendant, at the time of the contract, could contemplate that type of loss as a serious possibility of the breach. But 'assumption of responsibility' has an inclusionary effect where the whole purpose of the duty broken is to guard against the risk of the type of loss that has occurred. And it also has an exclusionary effect where the type of loss is exceptional in relation to the standard purpose of the duty. In that situation, it is not fair and reasonable for the risk of that type of loss to be allocated to the defendant unless the defendant at the very least has the requisite knowledge of the particular risk (and hence the opportunity to limit the liability). However, knowledge may be insufficient. Although not articulated in past cases, it can be suggested that further relevant factors may include how disproportionate the loss is compared to the price, whether there has been any adjustment to the price to take account of the risk, the extent to which the parties are insured against, or could be expected to insure against, that loss and, perhaps, how exceptional the type of loss is in relation to the standard purpose of the duty. It follows from this that I agree with the approach of Professor Andrew Robertson: '[T]he remoteness rule is not an agreement-based rule, which is concerned with identifying an implicit allocation of risk made by the contracting parties, but a gap-filling device, which is concerned with ensuring that a contract breaker is not subjected to an unreasonable burden' (A Robertson, 'The Basis

The important point for the thesis in this chapter is that to see remoteness as agreement-based is a fiction which serves to divert attention away from the judicial exercise of power. To view remoteness as resting on the parties' agreement, which the courts are simply upholding, is far less controversial – and appears more respectful of freedom of contract – than accepting that the courts are themselves imposing a solution on the parties. But it is the real reasoning of the courts that we need to be assessing and scrutinising and the courts should have no fears about such open debate not least because deciding the best solution on remoteness does not involve a political choice but is a question of legal principle and policy which the judges are eminently well-qualified to decide.

VII. Conclusion

To conclude, all fictions in judicial reasoning should be exposed for what they are and, in the search for rational transparency, they should be eradicated. However, it is important to understand why fictions have been used; and the thesis of this chapter is that fictions have very often been used in judicial reasoning to underplay the power exercised by the judges.

That thesis most obviously applies, at a general level, to the fictions that apply in respect of the courts' role in developing the common law and in interpreting statutes. But the same can also be said in relation to fictions in unjust enrichment and contract. In particular, fictions have served to present what is in reality the judicial imposition of a fair solution as if it were effecting the parties' intentions, whether by implying a contract where none existed or by artificially extending an existing contract.

Whether one agrees with this thesis or not, it is hoped that, at the very least, it may provide an interesting lens through which to view one aspect of the distinction between form and substance.

of the Remoteness Rule in Contract' (2008) 28 *Legal Studies* 172, 172. Note also that in *Siemens Building Technologies FE Ltd v Supershield Ltd* [2010] EWCA Civ 7, [2010] 1 Lloyd's Rep 349 [40], Toulson LJ referred to the law on remoteness in contract as grounded on policy.

3

'Substance Over Form': Has the Pendulum Swung Too Far?

BIRKE HÄCKER*

I. Introduction

In *R v Hammersmith and Fulham London Borough Council, ex parte Burkett*, Lord Steyn said that '[i]n public law the emphasis should be on substance rather than form'.[1] This chapter is about the extent to which modern *private* law does and should accord 'substance' priority over 'form'. Given that the relationship between form and substance is a topic to which whole monographs have been devoted,[2] the present contribution can do no more than scratch the surface, and it attempts to do so only in respect of the (English) common law. Its aim is twofold. Firstly, to identify different possible senses and fields of application of the 'substance over form' doctrine, and secondly, to drive home the point that occasionally the idea is taken a step too far. Whatever the legitimate ambit of 'substance over form', it is good to remember that – as a starting point – the established 'form' of some legal act or transaction is not to be disregarded lightly and, indeed, is often at least as important as its 'substance'.

The idea of privileging 'substance over form' has a long historical pedigree. Broadly speaking, there has been an apparently universal long-term evolution of the law, away from strict formalities and legal formalism, and towards according greater weight to what the relevant actors really wanted and emphasising the 'substantive merits' of a given case.[3] There are countless examples illustrating

* I am very grateful to Christine Osterloh-Konrad, Luke Rostill, and William Swadling for discussing various aspects of the paper with me, and to Matt Dyson and James Goudkamp for their perceptive comments and suggestions.

[1] *R v Hammersmith and Fulham London Borough Council, ex p Burkett* [2002] UKHL 23, [2002] 1 WLR 1593 [31].

[2] See especially PS Atiyah and RS Summers, *Form and Substance in Anglo-American Law: A Comparative Study of Legal Reasoning, Legal Theory, and Legal Institutions* (Oxford, Clarendon Press, 1987).

[3] The terminology of 'substance' and 'form' is somewhat elusive, with various associations and meanings. The present understanding in its various facets differs somewhat from that used by Atiyah and Summers (ibid) who distinguish between the law's 'formal features' and its 'substantive content' and focus primarily on legal reasoning and judicial techniques (but *cf* section V. below).

this trend over the past two and a half millennia. In Roman times, for instance, the early formality of verbal contracts[4] was relaxed and gradually gave way to so-called 'consensual' and 'innominate' contracts.[5] Formal conveyancing rituals fell into disuse and were superseded and eventually replaced by relatively informal modes of transfer.[6] The rigid *ius civile* became supplemented by a more flexible, merit-based body of Praetorian law (*ius honorarium*). This could happen once the old *legis actio* system of civil procedure had merged into the malleable formulary system which was, in turn, to be supplanted by the informal *cognitio* process. Similar developments took place over the course of English legal history. As the corset of the traditional common law writs became too tight, equity sprang up to counterbalance their rigidity with a conscience-orientated judicial corrective. The forms of actions themselves have since been abolished in favour of substantive causes of action.[7] In the realm of statutory interpretation, we can make out a gradual shift from a grammatical to a more purposive approach,[8] and a parallel shift is evident in respect of the construction[9] of private instruments such as contracts or wills.[10]

[4] The traditional form of the *sponsio* ('spondesne?' – 'spondeo') was widened during the classical period so as to admit other words as well (eg, 'promittis?' – 'promitto'; 'fideiubes?' – 'fideiubeo').

[5] The four 'consensual' contracts of classical Roman law, binding by mere informal agreement, were sale, hire, mandate and partnership. So-called 'innominate contracts' were agreements which did not fall into any of the recognised other categories (verbal, literal, real or consensual contracts) and were therefore in principle unenforceable. However, in due course, a special enforcement action (*actio praescriptis verbis*) was granted to parties who had already fulfilled their side of the bargain. The generalised notion of contract as a multi-purpose vehicle for making agreements binding was only fully developed by seventeenth-century Dutch scholars.

[6] *Mancipatio* and *in iure cessio*, in the old days the proper modes of conveying *res mancipi*, had probably been largely ousted in favour of the ordinary *traditio* (informal delivery) by the end of the classical period. They lost even the last vestiges of theoretical importance when the Emperor Justinian abolished the distinction between *res mancipi* and *res nec mancipi*.

[7] Common Law Procedure Act 1852 (15 and 16 Vict c 76). As a result, it can now be said that where there is a right, there is also a remedy (*ubi ius, ibi remedium*), rather than the other way around.

[8] See, eg, *Carter v Bradbeer* [1975] 1 WLR 1204, 1206–07 (Lord Diplock); *Pepper (Inspector of Taxes) v Hart* [1993] AC 593, especially 617 (Lord Griffiths); SC Styles, 'The Rule of Parliament: Statutory Interpretation after *Pepper* v *Hart*' (1994) 14 *OJLS* 151, 152: 'The rejection of the exclusionary rule is a direct consequence of the move towards a purposive approach to statutory interpretation which has taken place in the UK since the war'; J Burrows, 'The Changing Approach to the Interpretation of Statutes' (2002) 33 *Victoria University of Wellington Law Review* 981. For a critical assessment of this trend, specifically in the tax context, see T Lonnquist, 'The Trend Towards Purposive Statutory Interpretation' (2003) 13 *Revenue Law Journal* 18.

[9] There is a question (not addressed here) over whether 'interpretation' is synonymous with 'construction' or whether the two are in fact separate exercises, with the former identifying the meaning of a word or term and the latter its legal effect: see, eg, *Life Insurance Company of Australia Limited v Phillips* (1925) 36 CLR 60, 78; LB Solum, 'The Interpretation-Construction Distinction' (2010) 27 *Constitutional Commentary* 95. For present purposes, both terms are used synonymously.

[10] See especially *Investors Compensation Scheme Ltd v West Bromwich Building Society* [1998] 1 WLR 896, 912–13 ('*Investors Compensation Scheme*'), where Lord Hoffmann spoke of a 'fundamental change which has overtaken this branch of the law'. According to a famous statement by Wigmore, '[t]he history of the law of interpretation is the history of a progress from a stiff and superstitious formalism to a flexible rationalism': JH Wigmore, *A Treatise on the Anglo-American System of Evidence in Trials at Common Law*, vol 9, 3rd edn (Boston, Little Brown and Co, 1940) 187 (para 2461).

Yet a general trend is not a one-way street. What starts out as an ad hoc response to a particular problem often solidifies into a relatively inflexible rule coming to be applied in a formalistic manner. Equity itself has to some extent become ossified over time and regularly needs to undergo a process of rejuvenation.[11] With regard to the principles of interpretation, it has been convincingly demonstrated that the narrative according to which this followed a straight path from literalism to the teleological approach is misleading.[12] The grammatical dogma of the nineteenth-century approach to statutory interpretation was in fact preceded by a more liberal era, and so periods of literalism have always been interspersed with periods where the rival intention-based stance gained ground.[13] The same could be shown for the principles governing the construction of contracts, wills and (probably) other instruments.[14]

'Substance over form' is thus a paradigm which waxes and wanes. Moreover, it is a paradigm which has many different facets and meanings. The title of this chapter likens it to a pendulum that occasionally swings too far in one direction. What the chapter aims to do is identify and explore four different respects in which the modern (English) common law applies the 'substance over form' idea to private relationships, though admittedly three of these shade into one another. For each category, I will briefly explain what I regard as the proper field of application for the maxim and then discuss particular instances where I think it has either been misapplied, overstretched or is in danger of being taken too far.

The four levels of 'substance over form' we will be looking at are: firstly, 'content over name'; secondly and relatedly, the category here called 'legal substance over

[11] That equity constantly walks a tightrope between remaining flexible and being predictable was openly acknowledged in the recent case of *Gavin Edmondson Solicitors Ltd v Haven Insurance Co Ltd* [2018] UKSC 21, [2018] 1 WLR 2052 [57].

[12] For statutes: S Vogenauer, *Die Auslegung von Gesetzen in England und auf dem Kontinent* (Tübingen, Mohr Siebeck, 2001). For contracts and other private instruments: J McCunn, 'Revolutions in Contractual Interpretation: A Historical Perspective' in S Worthington, A Robertson and G Virgo (eds), *Revolution and Evolution in Private Law* (Oxford, Hart Publishing, 2018) 141, especially 142: 'The history of the law of interpretation is not the history of a straightforward progress, but of cyclical trends.'

[13] Vogenauer, above n 12, especially vol 2, chs 5–7 and 1297–1300. Making the point specifically with respect to late medieval English law: TFT Plucknett, *Statutes & their Interpretation in the First Half of the Fourteenth Century* (Cambridge, Cambridge University Press, 1922). Putting it very strongly: I McLeod, 'Literal and Purposive Techniques of Statutory Interpretation: Some European Community and English Common Law Perspectives' (2004) 29 *Brooklyn Journal of International Law* 1109, 1111: '[W]hen viewed in its proper historical perspective, the nineteenth century flourishing of literalism may be seen as a temporary aberration.'

[14] As far as contracts are concerned, where the 'contextual' approach prominently advocated by Lord Hoffmann in *Investors Compensation Scheme* [1998] 1 WLR 896 held sway for a few decades, we now appear to be witnessing a (still modest) resurgence of literalism: *Arnold v Britton* [2015] UKSC 36, [2015] AC 1619. In *Wood v Capita Insurance Services Ltd* [2017] UKSC 24, [2017] AC 1173, the Supreme Court tried to reconcile both approaches. Looking further back in time: McCunn, above n 12. As far as the construction of wills is concerned, it is worth noting that before courts espoused the strict literalism epitomised in the 'Wigram rules', a number of prominent judges had expressly advocated the intention-based approach: see *Cowper v Cowper* (1734) 2 P Wms 720, 741, 24 ER 930, 937 (Sir Joseph Jekyll MR).

factual appearance'; thirdly, moving slightly further out still, instances of 'economic substance over legal form'; and fourthly, the rise and popularity of the 'substantivist' approach to legal discourse over what is pejoratively labelled doctrinal 'formalism'. The chapter concludes with a remark on comparative law, where the 'function over form' mantra has long been a methodological mainstay.

II. Content Over Name

The 'content over name' category of case concerns the scenario where private parties enter into a particular transaction and call it one thing, but the law looks at the actual nature of the transaction and decides that it is properly speaking another. The name the parties have given to their agreement or instrument is deemed irrelevant to its legal characterisation.

In the old days, if one made what most people nowadays would describe as a 'will' of one's personal estate,[15] but did so without appointing an executor, the document could at most be a so-called 'codicil'. It would not be recognised as a proper 'testament' because (in the words of the 16th century ecclesiastical lawyer Henry Swinburne):[16]

> The generall, substantiall, or essentiall forme common to everie testament, is the naming or appointing of an executor, the which alone dooth make a testament, and without the which no will neither is, neither can be rightly tearmed a testament.

A generalised modern version of the 'content over name' idea may be found in Dillon LJ's judgment in *Welsh Development Agency v Export Finance Co Ltd*, where his Lordship described as 'trite law' the proposition that 'in determining the legal categorisation of an agreement and its legal consequences the court looks at the substance of the transaction and not at the labels which the parties have chosen to put on it'.[17]

If, therefore, Sally and Ben agree that Sally will transfer to Ben title to a rare edition of Blackstone's Commentaries in consideration of Ben paying Sally £10,000, then the parties have a contract for the sale of goods, even if they were to call their arrangement a 'barter'. This is because the Sale of Goods Act 1979 (UK) – or indeed any other applicable statute derived from the Sale of Goods Act 1893 (56 and 57 Vict c 71) – defines such a contract as one 'by which the seller transfers

[15] This is technically imprecise. The word 'will' was originally reserved for dispositions over a testator's real estate (for which the common law courts were responsible). Dispositions concerning a testator's personal estate were properly called 'testaments' (and were until 1858 dealt with by the ecclesiastical courts).

[16] H Swinburne, *A Briefe Treatise of Testaments and Last Willes* (London, John Windet, 1590) Pt IV, § 2 (fol 112r). Swinburne continues (fol 112v): '[S]uch disposition maie be called a codicill, or a will, or otherwise tearmed, but certainlie *a testament*, it is not, neither can be properlie so named'.

[17] *Welsh Development Agency v Export Finance Co Ltd* [1992] BCLC 148, 160 ('*Welsh Development Agency*').

or agrees to transfer the property in goods to the buyer for a money consideration, called the price'.[18] In a contract of barter, by contrast, the parties agree that the consideration will consist not of money used as currency, but in other goods or services.[19] Why is this relevant? It is relevant, for instance, because it is not entirely clear whether title to bartered goods can pass by consent alone as it can in sale.[20] Moreover, to the extent that a statute such as the Sale of Goods Act 1979 (UK), which implies terms into the contract, contains mandatory, non-dispositive provisions, one needs to know whether or not these apply to the transaction at hand.[21]

The problem is more evident in other contexts such as employment law. If a provider of cleaning and maintenance services engages 20 people to act as cleaners in the buildings it services, calling them 'self-employed independent sub-contractors', but supervising them closely and requiring them to be at work between 9am and 5pm every day, taking no more than 30 days off in every calendar year and only after seeking permission in advance, then these people are in reality employees (or at least workers) with the relevant employment rights – working time, minimum wage, protection against unfair dismissal, etc.[22] The relationship is re-classified specifically 'in order to prevent form undermining substance'.[23]

When first starting to ponder the 'content over name' category as an English lawyer, one immediately thinks of *Street v Mountford*,[24] a decision widely hailed as a perfect example of courts stopping form from undermining substance within core private law.[25] In that case, a solicitor by the name of Mr Street had granted Mrs Mountford the right to occupy certain residential premises he owned at a fee of £37 per week, terminable by 14 days' written notice. The agreement was described as a 'licence agreement' and the consideration payable by Mrs Mountford as a 'licence fee' rather than a 'rent', but it was conceded that the agreement granted her exclusive occupation or possession of the premises. The question arose whether Mrs Mountford could rely on the protection afforded to tenants (in those days)

[18] Sale of Goods Act 1979 (UK), s 2. See already s 1 of the Sale of Goods Act 1893 (56 and 57 Vict c 71), upon which much of the modern sale of goods legislation in the common law world is modelled. Until title passes, the contract is called an 'agreement to sell', thereafter it becomes a 'sale'.

[19] This is not to say that there cannot be difficult borderline cases, eg, where the buyer is allowed to substitute part of the contract price for goods or services.

[20] See Sale of Goods Act 1979 (UK), ss 17–18. As regards barter, contrast the Irish case of *Flynn v Mackin* [1974] IR 101, 111–12, holding that a delivery is indispensable, with an obiter dictum in *Cochrane v Moore* (1890) 25 QBD 57, 75, suggesting that the *solo consensu* rule applies wherever a contract envisages the transfer of title to goods for valuable consideration.

[21] Of course, a court may plausibly find that the parties to a contract of barter intended parallel provisions to be contained in their contract as well.

[22] Example (loosely) inspired by *Autoclenz Ltd v Belcher* [2011] UKSC 41, [2011] 4 All ER 745 ('*Autoclenz*'), as well as *Pimlico Plumbers Ltd v Smith* [2018] UKSC 29, [2018] 4 All ER 641.

[23] *Consistent Group Ltd v Kalwak* [2007] UKEAT 0535_06_1805, [2007] IRLR 560 [59] (Elias J), approved by *Autoclenz* [2011] UKSC 41, [2011] 4 All ER 745 [25].

[24] *Street v Mountford* [1985] AC 809 ('*Street*').

[25] In *Welsh Development Agency* [1992] BCLC 148, Dillon LJ specifically referred to *Street* [1985] AC 809 alongside *AG Securities v Vaughan* [1990] 1 AC 417 and the cases cited therein for determining the lease/licence distinction.

by the Rent Acts,[26] despite having expressly acknowledged by her signature that her 'licence' did not amount to a protected tenancy. The House of Lords unanimously held that she did come under the legislation.

The decision is generally taken to stand for the proposition that where someone is granted (i) exclusive possession of land (ii) for a term (iii) at a rent,[27] he or she has, in all bar very exceptional circumstances,[28] a 'tenancy' in the form of a leasehold estate at common law as opposed to a mere contractual 'licence'.[29] As Lord Templeman put it:[30]

> If the agreement satisfied all the requirements of a tenancy, then the agreement produced a tenancy and the parties cannot alter the effect of the agreement by insisting that they only created a licence. The manufacture of a five-pronged implement for manual digging results in a fork even if the manufacturer, unfamiliar with the English language, insists that he intended to make and has made a spade.

The element of 'exclusive possession', when coupled with a fixed period and the payment of consideration,[31] thus apparently turns what would otherwise be a 'licence' – a personal right to occupy the premises (or, put differently, a personal immunity against being regarded a trespasser) – into a property right at common law. This is indeed the traditional view, which the House of Lords in *Street* merely reiterated and reaffirmed.[32] Citing advice given by the Privy Council back in 1904, Lord Templeman said:[33]

> It is not ... a question of words but of substance. If the effect of the instrument is to give the holder an exclusive right of occupation of the land, ... it is in law a demise of the land itself.

In Australia, the High Court decision in *Radaich v Smith* is in the same vein:[34]

> What then is the fundamental right which a tenant has that distinguishes his position from that of a licensee? It is an interest in land as distinct from a personal permission

[26] Rent Act 1968 (UK), consolidated by Rent Act 1977 (UK); largely dismantled by the Thatcher government in the Housing Act 1988 (UK), thereby contributing in no small part to today's housing crisis in the UK.

[27] This is how it was put in *Street* [1985] AC 809, but the consideration may also consist in a one-off lump sum payment. Moreover, in line with general principles, any consideration must be dispensable where the grant is made by deed.

[28] Such as so-called 'service occupancies' by employees, which is actually explicable by the fact that the 'servant's' supposed possession of the premises is legally the 'master's' own.

[29] See, as just one example amongst many, B McFarlane, *The Structure of Property Law* (Oxford, Hart Publishing, 2008) 662: 'The decision [in *Street*] is perfectly correct as a matter of doctrine: it is conceptually impossible for A to give B a right to exclusive control for a limited period and then claim that B has only a licence'.

[30] *Street* [1985] AC 809, 819.

[31] On the need for consideration, see above n 27.

[32] There had been a spate of cases before *Street* [1985] AC 809, beginning with *Errington v Errington* [1952] 1 KB 290 and culminating in *Somma v Hazelhurst* [1978] 1 WLR 1014, which had placed greater store on what sort of right the parties *intended* to create in favour of the occupier.

[33] *Street* [1985] AC 809, 817, citing *Glenwood Lumber Co Ltd v Phillips* [1904] AC 405, 408.

[34] *Radaich v Smith* (1959) 101 CLR 209, 222 (Windeyer J).

> to enter the land and use it for some stipulated purpose or purposes. And how is it to be ascertained whether such an interest in land has been given? By seeing whether the grantee was given a legal right of exclusive possession of the land for a term or from year to year or for a life or lives. If he was, he is a tenant. And he cannot be other than a tenant, because a legal right of exclusive possession is a tenancy and the creation of such a right is a demise. To say that a man who has, by agreement with a landlord, a right of exclusive possession of land for a term is not a tenant is simply to contradict the first proposition by the second.

But if one stops to think about this for a moment, it is actually hard to see why it should be conceptually impossible to grant someone a merely personal right to occupy premises for a certain duration at a stipulated rent. Private law is usually much more restrictive about recognising property rights than it is about allowing people to create personal rights. There is a *numerus clausus* of the former, but not of the latter. In fact, the law normally allows people to replicate or at least emulate any type of property right at the purely personal level.[35] A right which *could* exist as an easement, such as a right of way, can just as easily (indeed, sometimes more readily) be created in the form of a mere licence to cross a neighbour's land. If this is how the parties choose to structure their relationship, successors in title to the owner of the 'servient' tenement such as purchasers will – of course – not be bound by the agreement. But as between the parties themselves, the grantor is contractually bound.

In *IDC Group Ltd v Clark*,[36] one neighbour on St James's Square had granted to another by deed a 'licence' to pass through a door in the communal wall in the case of fire and then to use the neighbouring property as an escape route. When the neighbouring property was sold, the question arose whether the deed was enforceable against the grantor's successors in title. The Court of Appeal held that it was not. Nourse LJ explained:[37]

> I think that one has to take this as being a professionally drawn deed in which the draftsman has deliberately chosen to use the word 'licence' and not the ordinary words associated with the grant of an easement. Therefore, since there is nothing sufficiently clearly pointing in any other direction, I reach the conclusion that the deed did only create a personal licence.

Street, on which counsel for the claimants had relied, was distinguished on the basis that the decision there 'depend[ed] mainly on the exclusive possession given to the licensee, a state of affairs which cannot arise where all that is given is a right to pass and repass over another's land'.[38]

[35] This point is also made by J Hill, 'Intention and the Creation of Proprietary Rights: Are Leases Different?' (1996) 16 *Legal Studies* 200, especially 201, 203–06.

[36] *IDC Group Ltd v Clark* (1993) 65 P & CR 179 ('*IDC*').

[37] *IDC* 184–85, citing what Sir Nicholas Browne-Wilkinson VC had said at first instance ([1992] 1 EGLR 187).

[38] *IDC* 183.

Yet why should the fact of exclusive possession make any difference to the analysis? If a person is granted exclusive possession 'until further notice' or 'until the premises are needed otherwise', without a time period being fixed in advance,[39] the agreement cannot take effect as a regular lease and will only generate personal rights.[40] But if the same person is given exclusive possession for a *certain* term, then not only *may* this arrangement create a proprietary estate in land in the form of a regular leasehold, but apparently is *has* to do so(!). Yet again, if the 'tenant' were to occupy the premises gratuitously otherwise than pursuant to a grant by deed,[41] this could only be under a licence,[42] though a penny's worth of consideration would inescapably turn the relationship into a lease. Apparently the contractual option does not exist here.

One might be tempted to rationalise this result by saying that it is simply a consequence of the doctrine of estates and English law's commitment to relativity of title. If a person has the legal ability to exclude all others from the premises (third parties as well as the grantor himself), then – so one might think – that necessarily amounts to an estate in the land in the form of a lease. However, such

[39] This was arguably the case in *Street*, where the agreement was framed in the following terms: 'I Mrs. Wendy Mountford agree to take from the owner Roger Street the single furnished room number 5 and 6 at 5 St. Clements Gardens, Boscombe, Bournemouth, commencing 7 March 1983 at a licence fee of £37 per week'. It is just about possible, but rather artificial, to treat this as creating a succession of 'implied' one-week leases, automatically renewable, solely on the strength of the fact that the consideration was expressed to be payable on a weekly basis. Yet it is hard to understand how this fits with the letting arrangement being 'terminable' upon giving 14 days' written notice (something which Lord Templeman suggests in his speech, even though the agreement he purports to set out 'in full' makes no mention of it). Surely if, when a given week ran out, Mr Street had told Mrs Mountford that he would not renew, this should have prevented the follow-on tenancy being created at common law, even if it may have amounted to a breach of the contract obliging him to grant the new lease? By contrast, assuming there was a 14-day notice period, the lease in *Street* could be treated as an 'implied' fortnightly tenancy. It should then not have been possible for the parties to 'terminate' it at the end of *any* given week with 14 days' notice, but merely *every other* week.

[40] *Prudential Assurance Co Ltd v London Residuary Body* [1992] 2 AC 386 ('*Prudential*'). To the extent that a so-called 'implied periodic tenancy' arises on the facts, it fulfils the certainty requirement. In the *Prudential* case, Lord Templeman observed (ibid 394) that '[a] tenancy from year to year is saved from being uncertain because each party has power by notice to determine at the end of any year'. The certainty of term requirement recently came under intense scrutiny in *Mexfield Housing Co-operative Ltd v Berrisford* [2011] UKSC 52, [2012] 1 AC 955. The Supreme Court there (just about) declined to overrule the *Prudential* case. It instead ruled that although the parties' agreement lacked sufficient certainty of term to take effect as the intended tenancy, it would prior to 1926 have been treated as a defeasible lease for life at common law and was as such converted by s 146(9) of the Law of Property Act 1925 (UK) into a 90-year lease determinable either on the tenant's death or in accordance with the expressly agreed termination provisions.

[41] Assuming that some form of consideration is indeed integral to a lease created informally: see above n 27 and the accompanying text.

[42] Such situations are often analysed as giving rise to a 'tenancy at will' or a 'tenancy by sufferance', yet in reality there can be nothing more than a personal licence. Any third-party effects such a 'tenancy' creates (such as allowing the 'tenant' to sue trespassers) are based on the *fact* of the claimant' possession rather than any *right* to exclusive possession via-à-vis the 'landlord': see the immediately following text. To the extent that past decisions accorded 'tenants at will' a measure of protection under the Rent Acts, this can best be explained by an expansive, purposive interpretation of the relevant statute – as also argued for below, in the text accompanying nn 53–56.

an argument proves only what it already presupposes. It simply *assumes* that the right to exclude all others goes hand-in-hand with a 'right to exclusive possession' granted by the 'landlord'. But a licensee may well[43] have the same ability to exclude others as a lessee, despite having no more than a personal right as against the grantor. This is because the mere fact of possession can generate a (new) right to possession, a fee simple, which will be good against the whole world save against anyone holding a superior fee simple.[44] What really matters is the tenant's position vis-à-vis the landlord, namely whether it is personal or proprietary. Here everything turns on whether the right to occupy the premises is carved out of the landlord's fee simple and is therefore truly *in rem* as regards the grantor, or whether it is a purely personal right subject to the ordinary rules of privity of contract and therefore not normally[45] binding on the grantor's successors in title such as third-party purchasers.

Looked at this way, there is a glaring gap in the traditional lease/licence dichotomy.[46] We have to recognise the possibility of premises being occupied, with exclusive possession, for a fixed or renewable period and at a periodic rent, pursuant to a contract between 'landlord' and 'tenant' that does *not* amount to the grant of a full-blown lease.

Precisely such a scenario was envisaged by the House of Lords in *Bruton v London & Quadrant Housing Trust*.[47] In that case, the landlord was a charitable housing trust using a council-owned block of flats to provide short-term accommodation to the homeless under a licence agreement with the council. The trust granted Mr Bruton a temporary 'licence' to reside in one of the flats for £18 a week and effectively accorded him exclusive possession of the premises (in the sense

[43] It is impossible within the confines of this chapter to make a fully fledged case for this proposition, so the argument here is very brief and partly relegated to the footnotes (see especially nn 42, 44, 49).

[44] We know that, registration questions apart, even a squatter acquires a fee simple over the land he unlawfully squats on, which is why 'adverse possession' can become an issue. This is so regardless of whether the squatter actually ousted the holder of the superior fee and whether he positively intended to acquire any title: *JA Pye (Oxford) Ltd v Graham* [2002] UKHL 30, [2003] 1 AC 419 ('*Pye*'). The big question is whether or not the same can be said of a contractual licensee. The *Pye* case suggests that everything turns on the presence or absence of the 'paper title owner's' consent to the occupier's presence on the land, but this cannot be correct since possession is established from the occupier perspective – by a sufficient degree of physical control coupled with the 'intention, in one's own name and on one's own behalf, to exclude the world at large': *Powell v McFarlane* (1977) 38 P & CR 452, 471–72 (Slade LJ), approved in *Pye* [2002] UKHL 30, [2003] 1 AC 419 [43], [77]. Many licensees would no doubt regard themselves entitled to bring an action against third-party trespassers and would thus, on the above logic, appear to have a fee simple provided that they also have a sufficient degree of physical control over the land.

[45] Some jurisdictions specifically provide – in deviation from the basic Roman rule that 'sale breaks hire' – for sale not 'breaking' hire, so that (certain) tenancy contracts will bind third-party purchasers from the landlord, despite their *in personam* nature: see, eg, art 1743 of the French *Code civil*; § 566 of the German *BGB*.

[46] As Jonathan Hill, above n 35, 216, has aptly put it: 'It is a mistake to think that the decision in *Taylor v Caldwell* [(1863) 3 B & S 826, 122 ER 309] – that an occupier who does not enjoy exclusive possession cannot be a tenant – logically entails the consequence that where all the conditions for the existence of a lease are satisfied the occupier must be a tenant'.

[47] *Bruton v London & Quadrant Housing Trust* [2000] 1 AC 406 ('*Bruton*').

that he did not have to share with anyone and that the trust did not retain more than a minimum of control over them). The question arose whether Mr Bruton could require the trust to do repair and maintenance work to the premises on the basis of a statutory implied covenant of repair applicable to 'tenancies'.[48] The trust argued that it *could not* have granted a lease to Mr Bruton because it had no estate in the relevant land out of which such a lease could be carved.[49] Although their Lordships apparently accepted that the trust did indeed not have any such estate,[50] they nevertheless found for Mr Bruton. Lord Hoffmann explained:[51]

> [T]he term 'lease' or 'tenancy' describes a relationship between two parties who are designated landlord and tenant. It is not concerned with the question of whether the agreement creates an estate or other proprietary interest which may be binding upon third parties. A lease may, and usually does, create a proprietary interest called a leasehold estate or, technically, a 'term of years absolute.' This will depend upon whether the landlord had an interest out of which he could grant it. Nemo dat quod non habet. But it is the fact that the agreement is a lease which creates the proprietary interest. It is putting the cart before the horse to say that whether the agreement is a lease depends upon whether it creates a proprietary interest.

Lord Hoffmann (with whom the other members of the committee agreed) acknowledged the possible existence of a 'non-proprietary' or purely contractual lease.[52] One could alternatively also describe it as a licence attracting tenancy protection vis-à-vis the grantor.

Although this aspect of the decision is extremely controversial and has been much criticised,[53] Lord Hoffmann actually hit the nail on the head. What mattered in the dispute was not whether or not Mr Bruton had any proprietary entitlement, but simply whether or not his relationship with the housing trust was such that section 11 of the Landlord and Tenant Act 1985 (UK) could be said to apply to it. On a purposive reading of the statute, that possibility could certainly not

[48] Under s 11 of the Landlord and Tenant Act 1985 (UK).

[49] See *Bruton* [2000] 1 AC 406, 409. This was questioned by counsel for Mr Bruton, observing (at 408) that '[t]itle is not absolute. It is relative only. Even a trespasser has a legal estate which is good against the whole world except a person who can show a better title.' It is thus wholly conceivable that the trust *did* have *a* fee simple: see discussion above, n 44, as well as the forceful arguments advanced by J Hill, 'The Proprietary Character of Possession' in E Cooke (ed), *Modern Studies in Property Law*, vol 1 (Oxford, Hart Publishing, 2001) 30; McFarlane, above n 29, 667–68; N Roberts, 'The Bruton Tenancy: A Matter of Relativity' [2012] *Conveyancer and Property Lawyer* 87; A Goymour, '*Bruton v London & Quadrant Housing Trust* [2000]: Relativity of Title, and the Regulation of the "Proprietary Underworld"' in S Douglas, R Hickey and E Waring (eds), *Landmark Cases in Property Law* (Oxford, Hart Publishing, 2015) 151, 160–73.

[50] An assumption which is open to serious doubt: see the references in n 49 immediately above.

[51] *Bruton* [2000] 1 AC 406, 415.

[52] The terms 'non-proprietary lease' and 'contractual lease' are not used by Lord Hoffmann, but were coined by, respectively, M Dixon, 'The Non-Proprietary Lease: The Rise of the Feudal Phoenix' (2000) 59 *CLJ* 25 and S Bright, 'Leases, Exclusive Possession and Estates' (2000) 116 *LQR* 7. Note that Lord Hoffmann in *Bruton* [2000] 1 AC 406, 416 expressly rejected any suggestion that the case turned on there being a so-called 'tenancy by estoppel'.

[53] See, eg, Dixon, above n 52, 27–28; Bright, above n 52, 8–9; K Gray and SF Gray, *Elements of Land Law*, 5th edn (Oxford, Oxford University Press, 2008) 314–15.

be dismissed out of hand. A person who grants another exclusive possession of residential premises and charges rent for them must expect the law to imply into the contract such terms as are normally (and here: compulsorily) part and parcel of these types of agreements.[54]

By the same token, all that mattered in *Street* was whether Mrs Mountford could bring herself under the Rent Acts so as to be protected against Mr Street evicting her or raising the rent willy-nilly. No more needed to be determined by the House of Lords. It would or might at any rate well have been possible to get there by a purposive construction of the word 'tenancy' in its specific statutory context,[55] holding that the purported express disclaimer of a 'protected tenancy' was of no effect.[56] Alternatively, drawing upon consumer protection ideals, Mr Street could simply have been denied the option of granting a mere personal right to someone in Mrs Mountford's comparatively weak position.[57] This would have been a bold, but overt restriction of his freedom to contract in particular circumstances. That their Lordships went further by suggesting that Mr Street *could not*, in law, have granted Mrs Mountford or any other occupier (!) *anything but* a full-blown leasehold estate is a case of proprietary overkill. In the name of prioritising 'substance over form', the House of Lords failed to engage with the nuanced distinctions appropriate to capturing the nature of the parties' relationship and at the same time doing justice to the broader legal framework.

Had their Lordships adopted a less schematic (and in that sense less 'formalistic') approach to the lease/licence dichotomy, they could have done a better job at fine-tuning the law. Occupiers with an indefinite licence, or ones whose 'lease' is of insufficiently certain duration,[58] would in principle be able to benefit from the statutory tenant protection regime, and businesses (at least)[59] would have the option of agreeing to a purely personal right to exclusive possession of commercial premises if, for whatever reason, they preferred a licence arrangement to a leasehold. The fact that there is today a glaring lacuna where a personal right to exclusive possession for a term and at a rent should sit on the map of English private law unhelpfully obscures the real substance of the parties' dispute in *Street* type cases. This is not to say that 'shams' should not be exposed for what they are, but a misapplication of the 'content over name' idea has generated a dogma which, though generally accepted and oft repeated, cannot stand up to scrutiny.

[54] In this vein also McFarlane, above n 29, 668–69.

[55] The Rent Act 1977 (UK), while defining when a tenancy is 'protected' or 'statutory' (ss 1–2), does not provide a definition of the term 'tenancy' as such, but simply presupposes the concept.

[56] See above, text following n 26.

[57] As suggested by Hill, above n 35, 217: 'The drafting of a residential agreement as a licence rather than as a lease is analogous to the inclusion of an unfair contractual term in a consumer sale … Accordingly, it seems reasonable to look at the lease/license distinction from the consumer law perspective rather than purely as an aspect of the law relating to real property'.

[58] As arguably Mrs Mountford herself: see above n 39. On the certainty of term requirement, and ways in which its rigours can be circumvented *de lege lata*, see additionally the references and discussion in n 40 above.

[59] On the consumer context, see above n 57 and the accompanying text.

III. Legal Substance Over Factual Appearance

The next category, that which may be called 'legal substance over factual appearance', sits somewhere between the 'content over name' type situation just considered and the 'economic substance over legal form' idea which will be dealt with in the next section. Indeed, no hard and fast lines can be drawn on either side. The picture is much more that of a continuum, with each category consisting of a number of core cases and a broad penumbra seamlessly shading into the next category. Indeed, one could even regard 'content over name' as a sub-category under the broad and multi-faceted heading 'legal substance over factual appearance'. They are here separated out for convenience only.

What this contribution means by 'legal substance over factual appearance' is that the law – for good reasons internal to itself – sometimes analyses transactions or relationships differently to what one might expect in the light of their outward manifestation. To use a very basic example, although a man, woman and children may be happily living together for many years, this alone does not legally make them husband and wife or parent and child. And while there is in many jurisdictions an evidential 'presumption of paternity', maintaining that a birth-mother's husband at the relevant point in time is to be considered the father of the child, this presumption can be rebutted and another man's biological and thus legal paternity established.[60]

Moving from family law into the law of obligations (more specifically, into the law of restitution), a question on which much ink has been spilt is whether and when one person can be enriched 'at another's expense' where the transfer of value apparently took a different or merely indirect route.[61] Some legal systems solve this problem through a definition of 'performance' which allows them to accommodate certain three-party scenarios with relative ease.[62] If a customer instructs his bank to pay money to one of his creditors in order to discharge a debt, then the execution of this transaction would be treated as a performance by the bank to its customer and at the same time a performance by the customer to his creditor, even though the only actual flow of money was between the bank and the recipient (or the recipient's bank). Between the bank and the ultimate recipient, on the other hand, the legal link is only indirect on this model. That the legal analysis

[60] The recent UK decision in *Re Baronetcy of Pringle of Stichill* [2016] UKPC 16, [2016] 1 WLR 2870, arguably went too far in privileging (biological) substance over the legal ascription of parentage: B Häcker, 'Honour Runs in the Blood' (2017) 133 *LQR* 36, especially 40–41.

[61] In the leading textbook known as *Goff & Jones*, for instance, the discussion of this question regarding personal claims in 'multiple-party cases' takes up a full 35 pages: C Mitchell, P Mitchell and S Watterson, *Goff & Jones: The Law of Unjust Enrichment*, 9th edn (London, Sweet & Maxwell, 2016) paras 6.10–6.105.

[62] For a comparison of German and English law, see G Dannemann, *The German Law of Unjustified Enrichment and Restitution: A Comparative Introduction* (Oxford, Oxford University Press, 2009) 21–24, 30–35, 50–60; B Häcker, 'Fog on the Channel? Six Comparative Lessons in Unjust Enrichment' (2017) 25 *Restitution Law Review* 61, 69–71.

consciously deviates from the transaction's outward appearance is owed to the specific setup of the parties' relationships.

Although English law has not (yet?)[63] embraced anything akin to such a notion of 'performance', the same phenomenon of prioritising the legal substance of a value transfer over its factual appearance can be made out here. The recent case of *Investment Trust Companies (in liq) v Revenue and Customs Commissioners*[64] examined the matter in respect of VAT which had been paid by the claimants to investment managers for the provision of their management services and which the latter had duly passed on to the revenue. When it emerged that no VAT should in fact have been charged, the claimants sought (in essence) to recover directly from the revenue that part of the tax which they could not recover via the managers.[65] There was a question over whether a mere 'causal link' or 'economic connection' between the claimant's payment and the defendant's receipt of money might be sufficient to satisfy the 'at the expense of' criterion, as had been suggested by the first instance decision and the Court of Appeal.[66] The Supreme Court, however, took a much narrower approach and tightened up the inquiry significantly, by effectively insisting that the defendant should have received the relevant enrichment 'directly' from the claimant.[67] Yet within this rigid outer corset, it admitted that the law treats certain transfers as 'direct' although, at first sight, they may look to be intermediated. Giving the unanimous judgment of the Supreme Court, Lord Reed said:[68]

> [47] There are … situations in which the parties have not dealt directly with one another, or with one another's property, but in which the defendant has nevertheless received a benefit from the claimant, and the claimant has incurred a loss through the provision of that benefit. *These are generally situations in which the difference from the direct provision of a benefit by the claimant to the defendant is more apparent than real.*
>
> [48] One such situation is where the **agent of one of the parties is interposed** between them. In that situation, the agent is the proxy of his principal, by virtue of the law of agency. The series of transactions between the claimant and the agent, and between the agent and the defendant, is therefore legally equivalent to a transaction directly between

[63] An increasing number of authors appear to be favouring a concept of 'performance' or 'conferral': R Stevens, 'The Unjust Enrichment Disaster' (2018) 134 *LQR* 574; A Burrows, '"At the Expense of the Claimant": A Fresh Look' (2017) 25 *Restitution Law Review* 167.

[64] Also known as *The Commissioners for Her Majesty's Revenue and Customs v The Investment Trust Companies (in liq)* [2017] UKSC 29, [2018] AC 275 ('*ITC*').

[65] The reasons why the claimants were unable to recover all of the tax paid via the managers need not detain us here. It was partly on account on the fact that the managers had deducted 'input tax' before paying the VAT received from the claimants ('output tax') over to the revenue, and partly down to a three-year limitation period in s 80 of the Value Added Tax Act 1994 (UK).

[66] See *Investment Trust Companies (in liq) v Revenue and Customs Commissioners* [2012] EWHC 458 (Ch), [2012] STC 1150; [2015] EWCA Civ 82, [2015] STC 1280.

[67] *ITC* [2017] UKSC 29, [2018] AC 275 [32]–[51]. This approach has very recently been reaffirmed in *Prudential Assurance Co Ltd v Revenue and Customs Commissioners* [2018] UKSC 39, [2018] 3 WLR 652 [68].

[68] *ITC* [2017] UKSC 29, [2018] AC 275 [47]–[50] (emphases added).

> the claimant and the defendant. Similarly, where the **right to restitution is assigned**, … the claimant stands in the shoes of the assignor, and is therefore treated as if he had been a party to the relevant transaction, and the defendant's enrichment had been directly at his expense. Another situation is where … an **intervening transaction is found to be a sham** … Since the sham is created precisely in order to conceal the connection between the claimant and the defendant, it is disregarded when deciding whether the latter was enriched at the former's expense … There have also been cases … in which a **set of co-ordinated transactions** has been treated as forming a single scheme or transaction for the purpose of the 'at the expense of' inquiry, on the basis that to consider each individual transaction separately would be unrealistic. There are also situations where the **defendant receives property from a third party into which the claimant can trace an interest**. Since the property is, in law, the equivalent of the claimant's property, the defendant is therefore treated as if he had received the claimant's property.
>
> [49] A different type of situation is typified by the case where the **claimant discharges a debt owed by the defendant to a third party**. Although it is the third party creditor who receives the payment from the claimant, the defendant is directly enriched, since the payment discharges his debt: the enrichment is not the payment which the third party receives, but the discharge which the defendant receives.
>
> [50] It has often been suggested that there is a general rule, possibly subject to exceptions, that the claimant must have directly provided a benefit to the defendant. The situations discussed in the two preceding paragraphs can be reconciled with such a rule, *if it is understood as encompassing a number of situations which, for the purposes of the rule, the law treats as equivalent to a direct transfer, in the sense that there is no substantive or real difference.*

His Lordship here explained why the designated 'exceptions' to the 'directness' requirement are, on a proper analysis of their legal substance, not exceptions at all. The agent's payment is ascribed to the principal by virtue of the law of agency. By dint of the law on assignment (where such assignment is possible), the assignee steps into the assignor's exact position. As a general rule, the law disregards shams,[69] and a concerted effort to co-ordinate a string of related transactions in order to achieve a particular outcome as part of a larger scheme may, in law, have to be treated as a single overall transaction.[70] On the (admittedly controversial) theory of tracing expounded in *Foskett v McKeown*,[71] property rights are simply 'transmitted' (as they are) from one asset to another, so receipt of a traceable substitute cannot in law be treated any differently from receipt of the original. Finally, where the claimant pays a third party and thereby discharges the defendant's debt,

[69] Lord Reed (*ITC* [2017] UKSC 29, [2018] AC 275 [48]) referred to *Relfo Ltd (in liq) v Varsani* [2014] EWCA Civ 360, [2015] 1 BCLC 14 especially [121], as an example.

[70] Lord Reed (*ITC* [2017] UKSC 29, [2018] AC 275 [61]) illustrated this by reference to *Banque Financière de la Cité SA v Parc (Battersea) Ltd* [1999] 1 AC 221 ('*Banque Financière*') and *Menelaou v Bank of Cyprus Plc* [2015] UKSC 66, [2016] AC 176 ('*Menelaou*'). In the former case, Lord Steyn had said (*Banque Financière* [1999] 1 AC 221, 227) that '[t]o allow the interposition of [a third party] to alter the substance of the transaction would be pure formalism'. As far as the tax law context is concerned, the so-called 'Ramsay principle' comes to mind: see below, n 105.

[71] *Foskett v McKeown* [2001] 1 AC 102.

the law of restitution looks not at the flow of money, but at the immediate effect the payment has on the legal position of the defendant who finds himself relieved of the third party's claim.

Another example where 'legal substance' takes precedence over factual appearance relates to cases where parties have mis-expressed their intention[72] in a document that purports to record their transaction. In the common law, this is the realm of the doctrine of rectification. In the civil law tradition, courts instead operate with the time-honoured principle that *falsa demonstratio non nocet* – a false description does no harm. The latter is a maxim of construction (the document is simply read to contain the words that were meant to be in it rather than those that actually are), while the former is an equitable remedy allowing the court to put a pen through words included inadvertently or by mistake and replacing them with the words that were actually intended and/or agreed (by one or several parties, as the case may be). This is not the time to explore the legal intricacies of the law of rectification, nor how much common ground there is between that remedy and the civilian interpretative approach.[73] Yet it is worth pondering a little over an area of rectification that is in danger of taking 'substance over form' a step too far.

Marley v Rawlings is a 2014 English case dealing with the rectification of wills.[74] Essentially, what happened is that the draft wills of a husband and wife had been mixed up, so that each spouse executed the document that ought to have been signed by the other. The mistake only came to light after the death of both. The Supreme Court felt just about able to correct the blunder and allowed rectification of the husband's will under section 20 of the Administration of Justice Act 1982 (UK) on the basis that what had happened could be counted as a 'clerical error'.[75] The interesting aspect of the decision for present purposes lies in an obiter dictum by Lord Neuberger, with whom all the other Justices agreed. His Lordship said:[76]

> [27] Rectification is a form of relief which involves 'correcting a written instrument which, by a mistake in verbal expression, does not accurately reflect the [parties'] true

[72] Whatever their legally relevant intention may be: see comment at the end of n 73 immediately below.

[73] There is a famous German case concerning what both parties intended to be a sale of 'whale meat', erroneously described as *Haakjöringsköd* (Norwegian for 'shark meat'): RG (8.6.1920) RGZ 99, 147. A comparison with *Frederick E Rose (London) Ltd v William H Pim Junior & Co Ltd* [1953] 2 QB 450 would seem to suggest that English law takes a more objective approach to the parties' legally relevant intentions than German law (where the mere subjective meeting of the minds was enough).

[74] *Marley v Rawlings* [2014] UKSC 2, [2015] 1 AC 129 ('*Marley*').

[75] Headed 'Rectification', s 20 of the Administration of Justice Act 1982 (UK) provides as far as is relevant here:

> '(1) If a court is satisfied that a will is so expressed that it fails to carry out the testator's intentions, in consequence —
>
> (a) of a clerical error; or
> (b) of a failure to understand his instructions,
>
> it may order that the will shall be rectified so as to carry out his intentions.'

[76] *Marley* [2014] UKSC 2, [2015] 1 AC 129 [27]–[28] (emphasis added).

> agreement' … It is available not only to correct a bilateral or multilateral arrangement, such as a contract, but also a unilateral document, such as a settlement … However, it has always been assumed that the courts had no such power to rectify a will…
>
> [28] *As at present advised, I would none the less have been minded to hold that it was, as a matter of common law, open to a judge to rectify a will in the same way as any other document: no convincing reason for the absence of such a power has been advanced.* However, it is unnecessary to consider that point further, as Parliament has legislated on the topic, in section 20 of the 1982 Act.

This, it is submitted, oversteps the mark.[77] It is one thing for judges to hold that the legal substance or true content of a document is otherwise than its wording suggests where the form of the document is a matter of party choice or (perhaps) a non-constitutive evidentiary requirement;[78] but it is quite another to rectify a document which the legislator requires to be in a particular form. This is because the process of rectification inserts words into the document that the party or parties concerned have – for whatever reason – not cast into the correct form.

The Wills Act 1837 (7 Will 4 and 1 Vict c 26) expressly states that '[no] will shall be valid unless' it is signed and witnessed as prescribed,[79] and this means that none of its individual provisions can be valid without signature and attestation by witnesses. Courts are only allowed to take cognisance of the testator's words which have found their way into the properly executed document,[80] unless they are specifically empowered by the legislator to disregard formalities in certain circumstances. South Australia, for instance, was the first of a substantial number of common law jurisdictions to introduce a judicial 'dispensing power' by statute.[81] A slightly different yet related mechanism is the so-called 'substantial compliance' doctrine, which originated in Queensland and has since spread far beyond the

[77] The argument which follows is elaborated in greater detail in B Häcker, 'What's in a Will? – Examining the Modern Approach Towards the Interpretation and Rectification of Testamentary Instruments' in B Häcker and C Mitchell (eds), *Current Issues in Succession Law* (Oxford, Hart Publishing, 2016) 131, especially 153–64.

[78] Hence arguably for trusts respecting land under s 53(1)(b) of the Law of Property Act 1925 (UK).

[79] Headed 'Signing and attestation of wills', s 9 of the Wills Act 1837 (7 Will 4 and 1 Vict c 26) (in its current form) reads:

> 'No will shall be valid unless—
>
> (a) it is in writing, and signed by the testator, or by some other person in his presence and by his direction; and
> (b) it appears that the testator intended by his signature to give effect to the will; and
> (c) the signature is made or acknowledged by the testator in the presence of two or more witnesses present at the same time; and
> (d) each witness either—
>   (i) attests and signs the will; or
>   (ii) acknowledges his signature, in the presence of the testator (but not necessarily in the presence of any other witness),
>
> but no form of attestation shall be necessary.'

[80] Of course, there may be some leeway in the meaning courts attribute to these words: Häcker, above n 77, 133–39.

[81] Wills Amendment Act (No 2) 1975 (SA).

Gold Coast.[82] In England, the power to rectify wills contained in section 20 of the Administration of Justice Act 1982 (UK) is a more limited move in the same direction.[83] It is not a superfluous statutory replication of a much broader innate judicial power to rectify wills, but the crucial authorisation of courts first to disregard the formalities hurdle, discover what the testator actually wanted to say and then to mould the testator's intended wording into the appropriate form.

The point is not confined to the law of succession. About 30 years ago, the English formality requirements governing contracts for the sale of land changed. What had thitherto been a merely evidentiary stipulation, that such agreements be recorded in writing and signed by the party against whom enforcement was sought,[84] was turned into a constitutive requirement of validity by section 2(1) of the Law of Property (Miscellaneous Provisions) Act 1989 (UK).[85] This meant that *even if* an innate judicial power to rectify contracts for the sale of land had previously existed,[86] it could not have survived the legislative reforms of 1989. This is why it was absolutely essential for Parliament, through an act of (implied) statutory authorisation, specifically to recognise the practice of rectifying such contracts.[87] The Law Commission Report pursuant to which the 1989 Act was passed sees and acknowledges this link.[88] Any doubts that may have been thrown on it by the case of *Tootal Clothing Ltd v Guinea Properties Management Ltd*[89] have since been alleviated by a number of subsequent Court of Appeal decisions.[90]

The upshot is that, whenever a certain form is required by statute, this necessarily constrains (or ought to constrain) judicial appeals to the 'legal substance' of a given transaction, and rectification of instruments can only occur if and to the

[82] Succession Act 1981, s 9(a) (Qld) as originally enacted; now amended and replaced by s 18. The 'substantial compliance' idea goes back to a proposal by JH Langbein, 'Substantial Compliance with the Wills Act' (1975) 88 *Harvard Law Review* 489.

[83] In particular, it does not allow the testator's signature to be dispensed with: see Häcker, above n 77, 153.

[84] See s 4 of the Statute of Frauds 1677 (29 Car 2 c 3) and subsequently s 40(1) of the Law of Property Act 1925 (UK).

[85] The Law of Property (Miscellaneous Provisions) Act 1989, s 2(1) (UK) reads: 'A contract for the sale or other disposition of an interest in land can only be made in writing and only by incorporating all the terms which the parties have expressly agreed in one document or, where contracts are exchanged, in each.'

[86] As suggested by *Craddock Brothers v Hunt* [1923] 2 Ch 136, but *cf* Younger LJ's strong dissent.

[87] The Law of Property (Miscellaneous Provisions) Act 1989, s 2(4) (UK) reads: 'Where a contract for the sale or other disposition of an interest in land satisfies the conditions of this section by reason only of the rectification of one or more documents in pursuance of an order of a court, the contract shall come into being, or be deemed to have come into being, at such time as may be specified in the order.'

[88] Law Commission, *Transfer of Land: Formalities for Contracts for Sale etc. of Land* (Law Com 164, 1987) para 5.6 (at 20: 'If rectified, the document will satisfy the proposed requirement of writing and thus there will be a valid contract') and the recommendation in para 6.4 (at 23: 'Contracts failing to comply with the formalities we recommend would be void and not merely unenforceable. The doctrine of part performance would therefore cease to have effect in contracts concerning land, but other remedies and doctrines would remain available … in particular … rectification …').

[89] *Tootal Clothing Ltd v Guinea Properties Management Ltd* (1992) 64 P & CR 452.

[90] See especially *Grossman v Hooper* [2001] EWCA Civ 615, [2001] 3 FCR 662; *Keay v Morris Homes (West Midlands) Ltd* [2012] EWCA Civ 900, [2012] 1 WLR 2855.

extent that the legislator permits. Without it, the courts' own manoeuvring space is restricted to the applicable rules of construction. When imposing constitutive statutory formality requirements, the legislature should therefore always give careful thought to the question of whether it wants to provide courts with a concomitant power to rectify affected instruments.

IV. Economic Substance Over Legal Form

The category here called 'economic substance over legal form' differs from the previous category in that a particular legal shape or structure (the 'legal form') is acknowledged to exist, but for particular purposes there are good reasons for departing from it and adopting a non-technical economic perspective. This economic perspective lies at the heart of the 'substance over form' doctrine as conventionally understood in the business context. According to the authoritative guidance on accounting policies issued by the International Accounting Standards Board,[91] a company's or other organisation's financial statements have to 'reflect the economic substance of transactions … and not merely the[ir] legal form'.[92]

A good example of a court putting on such economic spectacles and leaving the technical form of a transaction to one side is the landmark Australian case of *Andrews v ANZ Banking Group Ltd*.[93] The High Court there decided to extend the penalty clause jurisdiction to payments which were not technically triggered by a breach of contract, but could instead be regarded as forming part of the contractual consideration. A 'penalty' was (re)defined thus:[94]

> In general terms, a stipulation *prima facie* imposes a penalty on a party ('the first party') if, as a matter of substance, it is collateral (or accessory) to a primary stipulation in

[91] International Accounting Standard (IAS) 8: *Accounting Policies, Changes in Accounting Estimates and Errors* (last amended in 2018 with effect from 1 January 2020).

[92] ibid [10] (in full, emphasis added): 'In the absence of an IFRS [= International Financial Reporting Standard] that specifically applies to a transaction, other event or condition, management shall use its judgement in developing and applying an accounting policy that results in information that is:

(a) relevant to the economic decision-making needs of users; and
(b) reliable, in that the financial statements:
  (i) represent faithfully the financial position, financial performance and cash flows of the entity;
  (ii) *reflect the economic substance of transactions, other events and conditions, and not merely the legal form;*
  (iii) are neutral, ie free from bias;
  (iv) are prudent; and
  (v) are complete in all material respects.'

[93] *Andrews v Australia and New Zealand Banking Group Ltd* [2012] HCA 30, (2012) 247 CLR 205 ('*Andrews*').

[94] *Andrews* [2012] HCA 30, (2012) 247 CLR 205 [10]. In drafting this definition, the High Court relied on *Waterside Workers' Federation of Australia v Stewart* (1919) 27 CLR 119, 128–29, 131; *Acron Pacific Ltd v Offshore Oil NL* (1985) 157 CLR 514, 520; and – for the latter part – on *Rolfe v Peterson* (1772) 2 Bro PC 436, 442, 1 ER 1048, 1052; *Dunlop Pneumatic Tyre Co Ltd v New Garage and Motor Co Ltd* [1915] AC 79, 86.

> favour of a second party and this collateral stipulation, upon the failure of the primary stipulation, imposes upon the first party an additional detriment, the penalty, to the benefit of the second party. In that sense, the collateral or accessory stipulation is described as being in the nature of a security for and *in terrorem* of the satisfaction of the primary stipulation.

The Court was clearly concerned not to 'elevate form over substance' and to get a judicial hold on what might be considered 'in substance … disguised penalties'.[95] This is not the place to discuss the proper scope of the penalty clause jurisdiction, to evaluate post-*Andrews* developments Australia,[96] or to consider the UK Supreme Court's decision to go down an entirely different route.[97] But the example helps illustrate two things. Firstly, that 'economic substance over legal form' reasoning *can* apply even within the realm of the law itself, typically (but not necessarily) within different sub-fields. Secondly, it hints that different legal systems may well diverge in their willingness to adopt the economic perspective and to prioritise it over the strict 'legal' one, which is nevertheless the typical starting point of the analysis.

Two areas where we often encounter such issues are insolvency law and tax law. That is because both are inherently more interested in the economic reality of transactions and asset allocation than in strict legal attributions. Take title reservation (so-called *Romalpa*)[98] clauses as an example. These allow a seller of goods to retain his title to the goods until the buyer pays their full purchase price. Legally speaking, the parties have agreed to make the passing of title conditional on payment,[99] so that the seller's rights are nominally unchanged; but economically speaking, it could be said that the title that remains vested in him functions as a mere security interest. Some jurisdictions draw from this the conclusion that the seller cannot assert his retained title in the buyer's insolvency unless he has registered it as security interest on the relevant Personal Property Securities Register.[100] However, English law in particular takes a rather conservative approach to the re-characterisation of transactions.[101] It does not generally treat retention of title clauses as creating a registrable charge.[102]

[95] *Andrews* [2012] HCA 30, (2012) 247 CLR 205 [13] (referring to *Jobson v Johnson* [1989] 1 WLR 1026) and [28] (referring to the applicants' argument).

[96] See especially *Paciocco v Australia and New Zealand Banking Group Ltd* [2014] FCA 35, (2014) 309 ALR 249; [2015] FCAFC 50, (2015) 236 FCR 199; [2016] HCA 28, (2016) 258 CLR 525.

[97] *Cavendish Square Holdings BV v Makdessi, ParkingEye Ltd v Beavis* [2015] UKSC 67, [2016] AC 1172.

[98] Named after the case of *Aluminium Industrie Vaassen BV v Romalpa Aluminium* [1976] 1 WLR 676.

[99] As they are free to do under ss 17 and 19 of the Sale of Goods Act 1979 (UK) or the corresponding provisions in similar statutes.

[100] Statutory registration regimes (so-called Personal Property Security Acts or PPSAs) exist in Australia, Canada, and New Zealand. See also art 9 of the US Uniform Commercial Code.

[101] The leading cases on re-characterisation are *Re George Inglefield Ltd* [1933] Ch 1; *Welsh Development Agency* [1992] BCLC 148.

[102] See especially *McEntire v Crossley Brothers Ltd* [1895] AC 457 especially 462; *Clough Mill Ltd v Martin* [1985] 1 WLR 111; *Armour v Thyssen Edelstahlwerke AG* [1991] 2 AC 339 especially 351–54. (Note that the first was an Irish and the third a Scottish appeal.)

The second area, tax law, raises similar issues.[103] Although tax law tends to take existing legal classifications as its starting point and is thus to an extent 'dependent' upon ordinary private law, it is also often said to be 'autonomous' of the rest of the law, in the sense that it may need to re-characterise transactions in order to capture their economic essence. Jurisdictions differ in respect of the degree to which such autonomy of tax law is recognised.[104] In some countries, such as the UK, where lawyers are traditionally sceptical about resorting to 'economic substance over legal form'-type reasoning,[105] the 'tax tail' can occasionally end of wagging the 'private law dog'.[106] Within systems more amenable to looking at private transactions through the 'economic substance' pair of spectacles, the pendulum has in the past tended to swing back and forth between a 'dependent' and an 'autonomous' understanding of tax law.[107] According to a saying about US revenue law, which is renowned for being particularly prone to the economic viewpoint,[108] 'substance controls over form, except, of course, in those cases in which form controls'.[109]

A few examples (drawn from different systems) of tax law putting 'economic substance over legal form' will suffice here.[110] They will lead us onto the next point.

[103] See, eg, F Zimmer, 'IFA General Report: Form and Substance in Tax Law' in International Fiscal Association (ed), *Cahiers de Droit Fiscal International* (The Hague, Kluwer Law International, vol 87a, 2002) 19–70.

[104] For a brief overview, see the various country reports contained in 'Part One' of HJ Ault and BJ Arnold (eds), *Comparative Income Taxation: A Structural Analysis*, 3rd edn (Alphen aan den Rijn, Kluwer Law International, 2010), in each chapter under the headings 'Respect for Legal Form'/'Respect for Civil or Private Law Form' and 'Anti-Avoidance Doctrines and Rules'.

[105] The case law has evolved over the years. The most significant decisions are *Inland Revenue Commissioners v Duke of Westminster* [1936] AC 1; *WT Ramsay Ltd v Inland Revenue Commissioners* [1982] AC 300; *Furniss (Inspector of Taxes) v Dawson* [1984] AC 474; *Craven (Inspector of Taxes) v White* [1989] AC 398; *MacNiven (Inspector of Taxes) v Westmoreland Investments Ltd* [2001] UKHL 6, [2003] 1 AC 311; *Barclays Mercantile Business Finance Ltd v Mawson (Inspector of Taxes)* [2004] UKHL 51, [2005] 1 AC 684; *UBS AG v Revenue and Customs Commissioners* [2016] UKSC 13, [2016] 1 WLR 1005. J Tiley, 'The United Kingdom' in HJ Ault and BJ Arnold (eds), *Comparative Income Taxation: A Structural Analysis*, 3rd edn (Alphen aan den Rijn, Kluwer Law International, 2010) 166 points out that English judges do not usually think of the problem as being about 'respecting' (or not respecting) legal form; they see the issue simply as a problem of interpreting the relevant tax legislation.

[106] It is interesting to note, for instance, that much of the case law and discussion concerning the meaning of the phrase 'disposition of an equitable interest' in s 53(1)(c) of the Law of Property Act 1925 (UK) has been generated by disputes over stamp duty.

[107] Illustrating this for Germany: W Schön, 'Germany' in HJ Ault and BJ Arnold (eds), *Comparative Income Taxation: A Structural Analysis*, 3rd edn (Alphen aan den Rijn, Kluwer Law International, 2010) 88.

[108] See, eg, JR Repetti, 'The United States' in AJ Ault and BJ Arnold (eds), *Comparative Income Taxation: A Structural Analysis*, 3rd edn (Alphen aan den Rijn, Kluwer Law International, 2010) 887–90.

[109] See, eg, MJ McMahon, 'Random Thoughts on Applying Judicial Doctrines to Interpret the Internal Revenue Code' (2001) 54 *Southern Methodist University Law Review* 195, 195; DJ Glassman, '"It's Not A Lie If You Believe It": Tax Shelters and the Economic Substance Doctrine' (2006) 58 *Florida Law Review* 665, 670.

[110] Many (though not all) of these examples have an underlying anti-avoidance concern, which is why the present discussion should be understood against this backdrop. For a prize-winning detailed comparative examination of the way in which tax avoidance is conceptualised and handled in Germany,

If A, B and C agree that A will transfer an asset to B, for B then to transfer it directly on to C, tax law may treat the transfer as though it had been made directly from A to C, even where the relevant private law recognises the two transactions as separate.[111] By the same token, where an asset is transferred by A to B for a merely nominal consideration or a disproportionately low price, contract law may not inquire into the adequacy of the consideration, but tax law will often regard the transfer as a (partial) gift.[112] Thirdly, in the business context of financial instruments, whether a person's contribution towards a company is classified as 'debt' or 'equity' under a given regime may well depend on whether the question is being asked for private, corporate or tax law purposes.[113] Lastly, the notion of 'beneficial ownership' or 'beneficial entitlement' does not necessarily mean the same in the tax context as it does in ordinary private law.[114] While private lawyers working in common law systems generally equate the 'beneficial owner' with the person who has an equitable interest under a trust, national (and a fortiori international)[115] tax law tends to take a different and less technical view.[116] On the one hand, 'beneficial ownership' for taxation purposes can be mediated not only by means of a trust, but also through other forms of 'legal representation', such as agency or a nominee relationship, and even through a corporate holding structure.[117] On the other hand, an equitable entitlement under a trust will not

France, the UK and the United States, see the forthcoming monograph by C Osterloh-Konrad, *Die Steuerumgehung* (Tübingen, Mohr Siebeck, 2019).

[111] Example based on BFH (13.19.1993) BFHE 172, 520, NJW 1994, 2248. Contrast BFH (18.7.2013) BFHE 242, 158, NJW 2014, 174. English law *might* regard such a case as one where a string of related transactions set up to achieve a particular purpose should be treated as a single overall transaction, but it would probably justify this conclusion by reference to the 'legal' substance of the scheme: see above, text accompanying n 70.

[112] While some civilian systems such as the German recognise so-called 'mixed gifts' (ie, part sale, part gift) as a private law concept, the common law generally draws a bright line between gratuitous transactions and those for value, with a peppercorn worth of consideration taking a transaction out of one category and into the other. However, UK tax and insolvency law takes a more nuanced view of the matter: see, eg, HM Revenue & Customs, 'Inheritance Tax Manual' (*Gov.UK*, 20 March 2016, last accessed 15 March 2019), www.gov.uk/hmrc-internal-manuals/inheritance-tax-manual/ihtm14316: 'A sale for less than full consideration, which is not merely a bad bargain, is a gift, the property disposed of by way of gift being the undervalue'; Insolvency Act 1986 (UK), ss 238 and 423: transactions at an undervalue treated in the same way as gifts.

[113] See, eg, W Schön, 'The Distinct Equity of the Debt-Equity Distinction' (2012) 66 *Bulletin for International Taxation* (IBFD Bulletin) 490, especially 494–96.

[114] For a recent study comparing different national systems and the OECD Model Tax Convention, see A Meindl-Ringler, *Beneficial Ownership in International Tax Law* (Alphen aan den Rijn, Wolters Kluwer, 2016).

[115] See, eg, *Indofood International Finance Ltd v JP Morgan Chase Bank NA London Branch* [2006] EWCA Civ 158, [2006] STC 1195, where the Court of Appeal emphasised that the term 'beneficial owner' in a double tax treaty was to be given an international fiscal meaning not derived from the domestic law of the contracting states.

[116] See, eg, *Bupa Insurance Ltd v Commissioners for Her Majesty's Revenue and Customs* [2014] UKUT 262 (TCC) [53] ('*Bupa*'): '[W]e consider that "beneficial entitlement" is not synonymous with an "equitable entitlement", as understood as a matter of English Private Law'.

[117] See, eg, *Mount Royal/Walsh Inc v The 'Jensen Star'* (1989) 99 NR 42, 47: '[T]he expression "beneficial owner" serves to include someone who stands behind the registered owner in situations where the latter functions merely as an intermediary, like a trustee, a legal representative, or an agent';

mark the beneficiary out as being the 'beneficial owner' of the trust assets unless he is able to exercise a sufficient degree of control and/or participate in the income derived from them.[118] True that common law systems vary as regards the extent to which they try to assimilate the tax definition of 'beneficial ownership' to the private law 'trust' paradigm, both geographically speaking and over the course of time.[119] And admittedly, many historical drafters of tax statutes will have had the private law concept in mind when using the language of 'beneficial ownership'.[120] Yet there is considerable force in what Dickson J said in the Supreme Court of Canada's decision in *Minister of Revenue (Ontario) v McCreath*: 'I do not believe that the niceties and arcana of ancient property law should be fastened upon with mechanical rigidity to determine the effect of a modern taxation statute whose purpose is plain'.[121]

Given that English courts are, on the whole, amongst the most reluctant when it comes to divorcing 'economic substance' from legal form and acknowledging that the former may sometimes triumph over the latter,[122] it is all the more remarkable that they should have allowed the line between property rights at common law and equitable entitlements in respect of such rights to become blurred at the very heart of private law itself.

Traditionally, it was taken for granted that the beneficiary under a trust could not sue in tort for wrongful interferences with the trust assets because, as far as the common law was concerned, the proper person to bring the action was the holder of the legal title. Of course, any damages recovered by the latter would be subject to the same trust. The only way in which the beneficiary could get involved was by forcing the trustee to act or by bringing the action in his name.

Bupa [2014] UKUT 262 (TCC) [53]: '[W]e consider, that "beneficial entitlement" is a wider concept than "equitable ownership" (in … respect [of the applicable group relief provisions] …). It is trite that one company has no proprietorial interest, as a matter of equity, in the assets of a subsidiary, let alone in the assets of a sub-subsidiary'.

[118] Discretionary trusts, in particular, can be problematic. What is crucial for tax law purposes is who, factually, has control over the relevant assets and disposes of the income. See *Bupa* [2014] UKUT 262 (TCC) [61]: '[E]quitable ownership may be (but will not always) be [sic] sufficient to confer "beneficial ownership" … In other words, it is the "more than a mere legal shell" test which applies in each and every case to ascertain whether there is a "beneficial" right of ownership or entitlement, which rights in equity may or may not satisfy, depending on whether they confer a right to deal with and enjoy the fruits of the asset.'

[119] Compare, for instance, the English case of *Ayerst (Inspector of Taxes) and C&K (Construction) Ltd* [1976] AC 167 with the Australian decision in *Commissioner of Taxation v Linter Textiles Australia Ltd (in liq)* [2005] HCA 20, (2005) 220 CLR 592.

[120] An interesting question (which cannot be pursued here) arises in respect of tax cases which – based on this assumption – have come to be understood as seminal rulings on substantive trusts or succession law, such as *Commissioner of Stamp Duties (Queensland) v Livingston* [1965] AC 694; *Vandervell v Inland Revenue Commissioners* [1967] 2 AC 291; *Re Vandervell's Trusts (No 2)* [1974] Ch 269.

[121] *Minister of Revenue (Ontario) v McCreath* (1976) 67 DLR (3d) 449, [1977] 1 SCR 2, 15. See also Lord Wilberforce's statement in *Gartside v Inland Revenue Commissioners* [1968] AC 553, 617 that 'to transfer a meaning from one context to another may breed confusion'.

[122] Indeed, a number of recent appellate decisions are openly dismissive of 'the somewhat fuzzy concept of economic reality': *Menelaou v Bank of Cyprus Plc* [2013] EWCA Civ 1960, [2014] 1 WLR 854 [62] (Moses LJ), cited with approval in *ITC* [2017] UKSC 29, [2018] AC 275 [64].

In *The Aliakmon*,[123] the claimants were the buyers of goods to whom the risk in them had passed, but not yet title. When the goods were damaged by the defendants' negligence, the buyers brought an action based on their contractual position and/or their (alleged)[124] equitable interest in the goods. Lord Brandon explained why the House of Lords unanimously rejected the claim:[125]

> [I]n order to enable a person to claim in negligence for loss caused to him by reason of loss of or damage to property, he must have had either the legal ownership of or a possessory title to the property concerned at the time when the loss or damage occurred, and it is not enough for him to have only had contractual rights in relation to such property which have been adversely affected by the loss of or damage to it.
>
> There may be cases where a person who is the equitable owner of certain goods has also a possessory title to them. In such a case he is entitled, by virtue of his possessory title rather than his equitable ownership, to sue in tort for negligence anyone whose want of care has caused loss of or damage to the goods without joining the legal owner as a party to the action ...[126] If, however, the person is the equitable owner of the goods and no more, then he must join the legal owner as a party to the action, either as co-plaintiff if he is willing or as co-defendant if he is not.[127] This has always been the law in the field of equitable ownership of land and I see no reason why it should not also be so in the field of equitable ownership of goods.

When courts in the past enabled beneficiaries to succeed in a tort action, they tended to do so with a view to some *legal* proprietary interest (such as a 'possessory title') which the beneficiary was – rightly or wrongly[128] – said to enjoy *in addition* to his equitable interest.[129] Yet in the 2010 case of *Shell UK Ltd v Total UK Ltd*,[130] the Court of Appeal held that someone's 'beneficial' or 'equitable ownership' of land is in principle enough to sustain a negligence action even in the absence of any relevant 'possessory title'.[131] The case was a fall-out of the fire and explosions that destroyed parts of the Buncefield oil storage facility in December 2005.

[123] *Leigh & Sillavan Ltd v Aliakmon Shipping Co Ltd (The Aliakmon)* [1986] AC 785 ('*The Aliakmon*').

[124] It is doubtful whether a so-called 'vendor-purchaser constructive trust' of the type recognised by *Walsh v Lonsdsale* (1882) 21 Ch D 9 in the context of land law can ever arise in the sale of goods context: see *The Aliakmon* [1986] AC 785, 812 (Lord Brandon's discussion of the 'second proposition').

[125] *The Aliakmon* [1986] AC 785, 809, 812.

[126] His Lordship here referred to *Healey v Healey* [1915] 1 KB 938 ('*Healey*'). The same interpretation of *Healy* was adopted by Mummery LJ in *MCC Proceeds Inc v Lehman Bros International (Europe)* [1998] 4 All ER 675, 689, but *cf* S Douglas, *Liability for Wrongful Interferences with Chattels* (Oxford, Hart Publishing, 2011) 42 for an argument that '[t]his interpretation of the case is clearly wrong'.

[127] This is known as the '*Vandepitte* procedure', named after the case of *Vandepitte v Preferred Accident Insurance Corp of New York* [1933] AC 70.

[128] For a discussion in the land law context, see above n 44. It is submitted that *if* a licensee obtains a fee simple by dint of being in possession of a plot of land, then a beneficiary under a trust who is in physical control of the trust property should also obtain a fee simple (or title in the case of goods) by virtue of his possession.

[129] See above n 126 and *International Factors v Rodriguez* [1979] QB 351, especially 359 (Buckley LJ), but *cf* the critical analysis by Douglas, above n 126, 41.

[130] *Shell UK Ltd v Total UK Ltd*, sub nom *Colour Quest Ltd v Total Downstream UK Plc* [2010] EWCA Civ 180, [2011] QB 86 ('*Shell*').

[131] See especially *Shell* [2010] EWCA Civ 180, [2011] QB 86 [128]–[150].

Total UK Ltd, the defendants, were vicariously responsible for the negligence which had caused the disaster. The claimants, Shell, were part of a group of oil companies using the depot to store oil before providing it to their customers at the nearby London airports. They sustained large losses as a direct result of the incident. The problem was that legal title to the affected land and pipelines did not vest in the oil companies themselves, but in two non-trading vehicle 'service companies'. These held all assets on trust for the beneficiaries (including Shell) by whom they were entirely controlled.[132] And while the vehicle companies could of course claim compensation for the physical damage caused by the explosions, they had not suffered any consequential economic loss since they were not involved in the onward sale of oil. The trade was all done by the beneficiaries themselves, for whom the loss was pure economic loss.

This very special scenario, in which the primary claimant sustains no loss, or only a small part of the loss which could reasonably be expected to flow from the negligent act, while a closely connected third party shoulders its brunt on account of some 'internal' arrangement with which the defendant has nothing to do, might well have been a good opportunity for English law to introduce (or rather: extend)[133] the so-called 'doctrine of transferred loss'.[134] This need not necessarily have resulted in a direct claim by Shell; it could simply have allowed the trustee company to assert the consequential loss sustained by the trading beneficiaries. However, partly motivated by 'substance over form' concerns and partly constrained by precedent, the Court of Appeal decided to go down a different route. It held that 'Shell can recover as beneficial owner for their economic losses',[135] provided it joined the legal owner in the proceedings.[136] The following two passages from Waller LJ's judgment illustrate quite how strong the lure of the 'economic substance' argument was:[137]

> [132] On the face of things, it is legalistic to deny Shell a right to recovery by reference to the exclusionary rule. It is, after all, Shell who is (along with BP, Total and Chevron) the 'real' owner, the 'legal' owner being little more than a bare trustee of the pipelines.

[132] Query whether Shell might thus actually have been in possession of the premises via the agency of the vehicle companies (contrary to the judges' findings that Shell was not in possession).

[133] *cf Owners of Cargo Laden on Board the Albacruz v Owners of the Albazero (The Albazero)* [1977] AC 774; Robert Goff LJ's failed attempt to generalise a version of the principle in *Leigh & Sillavan Ltd v Aliakmon Shipping Co Ltd (The Aliakmon)* [1985] QB 350; the 'narrow ground' of the *St Martin's Property* appeal in *Linden Gardens Trust Ltd v Lenesta Sludge Disposal Ltd* [1994] 1 AC 85; and, most recently, the discussion in *Swynson Ltd v Lowick Rose LLP (in liq)* [2017] UKSC 32, [2018] AC 313, especially [14]–[17], [52]–[54], [101]–[108].

[134] This is usually discussed in connection with contractual claims, but there is no reason why it should not, in principle, also extend to tortious liability. For a comparative study in the contractual context, see H Unberath, *Transferred Loss: Claiming Third Party Loss in Contract Law* (Oxford, Hart Publishing, 2003).

[135] *Shell* [2010] EWCA Civ 180, [2011] QB 86 [152].

[136] *Shell* [2010] EWCA Civ 180, [2011] QB 86 [142]. The reference to 'joining the legal owner in the proceedings' is no doubt an attempt to satisfy the procedural requirements referred to in *The Aliakmon* (see above n 127 and the text thereto).

[137] *Shell* [2010] EWCA Civ 180, [2011] QB 86 [132], [143] (emphasis added).

> [143] We must confess to being somewhat influenced ... by what Lord Goff of Chieveley in *White v Jones* [1995] 2 AC 207, 259–260 called 'the impulse to do practical justice'. It should not be legally relevant that the co-owners of the relevant pipelines, for reasons that seemed good to them, decided to vest the legal title to the pipelines in their service companies and enjoy the beneficial ownership rather than the formal legal title. Differing views about the wisdom of the exclusionary rule are widely held but however much one may think that, in general, there should be no duty to mere contracting parties who suffer economic loss as a result of damage to a third party's property, *it would be a triumph of form over substance to deny a remedy to the beneficial owner of that property when the legal owner is a bare trustee for that beneficial owner*.

Yet it is hard to accept that a defendant should owe a beneficiary a common law duty of care in respect of a particular asset on the sole basis that the beneficiary is 'linked' to the asset in a way which – *ex hypothesi* – the common law takes no notice of (precisely because that 'link' is mediated by the trustee whose fiduciary obligations are recognised only in equity). Refusing to blur the line between equity and the common law does not automatically entail 'denying' a remedy to the beneficiary, as the 'transferred loss' argument mentioned above shows. What is does mean is that (unless the beneficiary can establish a vested common law property right of his own, eg, through holding a possessory title to the trust assets in question)[138] the defendant's liability ought to be based on *one and the same cause of action* as regards both the trustee and the beneficiary, and that recovery of the trustee's and the beneficiary's losses ought to be coordinated (since, in law, they are one). The Court of Appeal's purely procedural solution of forcing the beneficiary to join the trustee in or to the proceedings is unsatisfactory. It fails to achieve any substantive linkage between the claims. If a separate duty of care were truly owed to a 'beneficial owner of property' alongside that owed to the 'legal owner', then it would indeed be very hard to see why the 'beneficial owner' should not be able to bring a free-standing action. The upshot is that the *Shell* decision is well-meaning, but lacks rigour. Worse than that, it opens the floodgates to all manner of technically self-standing tort actions by 'beneficial owners', with the potential for an unwarranted duplication of claims. At the same time, it seriously distorts the nature of the relationship(s) between a trustee, the beneficiary and the 'trust property'.[139] Luckily, *Shell* does not seem to have had much of an aftermath. The case was settled shortly before the Supreme Court was to hear an appeal, and other decisions have not flocked to follow it. Were they to do so, the Court of Appeal's dismissive reference to 'legalistic' reasoning could end up doing a great deal of collateral damage to English private law.

[138] See above, nn 128 and 132.

[139] The case has been heavily criticised on this and other grounds: see, eg, N Macklam, 'Colour Quest Ltd v Total Downstream UK Plc: The Nature of a Beneficiary's Interest under a Trust' [2010] *Conveyancer and Property Lawyer* 265; A Rushworth and A Scott, 'Total Chaos?' [2010] *Lloyd's Maritime and Commercial Law Quarterly* 536, especially 541–42; PG Turner, 'Consequential Economic Loss and the Trust Beneficiary' (2010) 69 *CLJ* 445; J Edelman, 'Two Fundamental Questions for the Law of Trusts' (2013) 129 *LQR* 66, especially 67–75; W Swadling, 'In Defence of Formalism', this volume, ch 5.

V. 'Substantivism' Over (Doctrinal) Formalism

The final category we need look at before moving on to the special context of comparative law concerns the way in which lawyers analyse, talk about and indeed 'discover' or 'develop'[140] law. It is more a matter of general approach than of specific area or issue. The attitude here called legal 'substantivism' can be contrasted with the more 'formalistic' approach which many people would describe as more 'doctrinal'. Just as the word 'legalistic' may be used pejoratively, so the attribute of being 'doctrinal' or – worse still – 'dogmatic' can be an insult. 'Substantivists' pride themselves in paying close attention to the merits of each case or rule rather than sticking unthinkingly to some schematic solution.

In principle, there is a lot to be said for the concerns underlying 'substantivism'. The worst excesses of formalistic legal reasoning are commonly referred to by the German word *Begriffsjurisprudenz* – a purely conceptual jurisprudence. The term was coined by Rudolph von Jhering[141] and employed to criticise what he perceived as an overly elaborate strand of private law scholarship, divorced from real life, which dominated the legal landscape in Germany during the second half of the nineteenth century.[142] The counter-reaction, peaking in the 1920s, called itself *Interessenjurisprudenz* ('interest jurisprudence')[143] and emphasised that the ultimate goal of law was to reconcile or resolve conflicting interests and to make value judgements.[144] Law was not an abstract system of norms and concepts, one logically following from the other, with rules deducible with mathematical precision and easily applicable to a given set of facts. Rather, according to this view, the judge had to be seen as:[145]

> not merely … an automated machine, into which the facts [of a given case] and [relevant] legal norm[s] are absorbed and from which then spouts the judgment without any own assessment on the part of the judge. Instead, [the judge] himself is a creator of applicable norms, an assistant to the legislator, albeit a subordinate one.

[140] Professor Eric Descheemaeker's inaugural lecture at the Melbourne Law School, delivered on the eve of the Obligations IX conference, contains fascinating and extremely perceptive comparative musings on the common law understanding of courts 'developing' the law: E Descheemaeker, 'To Think Against Oneself: A Stranger's Journey Through the Common Law' [52]–[67] (as yet unpublished, but on file with the author).

[141] Rudolph von Jhering, *Scherz und Ernst in der Jurisprudenz* (Leipzig, Breitkopf und Härtel, 1884) 337, 245, speaking of a '*juristischer Begriffshimmel*' ('heaven of legal concepts').

[142] So-called 'Pandectism' as developed by Georg Friedrich Puchta and perhaps most prominently espoused by Bernhard Windscheid.

[143] See especially P Heck, 'Gesetzesauslegung und Interessenjurisprudenz' (1914) 112 *Archiv für die civilistische Praxis* (AcP) 6; idem, *Begriffsbildung und Interessenjurisprudenz* (Tübingen, Mohr, 1932).

[144] It later evolved into what is known as *Wertungsjurisprudenz*, usually associated with the work of Karl Larenz.

[145] Heck, 'Gesetzesauslegung und Interessenjurisprudenz', above n 143, 22 (my translation).

In significant respects, this salutary reaction against the rigid formalism of nineteenth-century methodology is a direct sibling to American Legal Realism.[146] The latter, of course, made the pendulum swing too far the other way. In due course, it came to epitomise precisely the opposite extreme. Not long before the realists' scholarship was called a 'jurisprudence of despair', which 'sees no escape from an arbitrary rationalism save into a hopeless nihilism', such that it 'leaves the world without law'.[147] By comparison with this contemporary criticism, Peter Birks' assessment in the 1996 Western Australian Law Review was rather tame:[148]

> The realists and post-realists have done a good job of debunking legal science. In the United States where Jerome Frank and his intellectual successors did their most serious damage, it has never recovered and now lets in floods of law and economics in the hope of filling the broken vessel.

To HLA Hart, too, the realists' claim that 'rules are important [only] so far as they help you predict what judges will do'[149] amounts to a surrender of the entire legal order because it:[150]

> ignore[s] what rules actually are in any sphere of real life. It suggests that we are faced with the dilemma: 'Either rules are what they would be in the formalist's heaven and they bind as fetters bind; or there are no rules, only predictable decisions or patterns of behaviour.' Yet surely this is a false dilemma.

Hart avoids the dilemma by recognising that rules have an 'open texture'.[151] This, he explains:[152]

> means that there are, indeed, areas of conduct where much must be left to be developed by courts or officials striking a balance, in the light of circumstances, between competing

[146] Oliver Wendell Holmes Jr, a forerunner of the US Realist movement, famously observed that '[t]he life of the law has not been logic: it has been experience': OW Holmes, *The Common Law* (London, Macmillan & Co, 1882) 1. The influence of German scholarship in the US is traced by James E Herget, 'The Influence of German Thought on American Jurisprudence, 1880–1918' in M Reimann (ed), *The Reception of Continental Ideas in the Common Law World* (Berlin, Duncker & Humblot, 1993) 201; JE Grisé, M Gelter and R Whitman, 'Rudolf von Jhering's Influence on Karl Llewellyn' (2012) 48 *Tulsa Law Review* 93.

[147] P Mechem, 'The Jurisprudence of Despair' (1936) 21 *Iowa Law Review* 669.

[148] P Birks, 'Equity in the Modern Law: An Exercise in Taxonomy' (1996) 26 *University of Western Australia Law Review* 1, 4. For a markedly more positive assessment of Jerome Frank from the British perspective, see N Duxbury, 'Jerome Frank and the Legacy of Legal Realism' (1991) 18 *Journal of Law & Society* 175.

[149] KN Llewellyn, *The Bramble Bush: On Our Law and Its Study*, 3rd edn (New York, Oceana Publications, 1960) 14 – in this respect unchanged from the first edition which appeared in 1930: 'And *rules*, in all of this, are important to you so far as they help you see or predict what judges will do or so far as they help you get judges to do something. That is their importance. That is all their importance, except as pretty playthings'. Note that, from the 2nd edn (1951) onwards, the book contained a 'Foreword' by Llewellyn partially recanting this radical view.

[150] HLA Hart, *The Concept of Law*, 2nd ed (Oxford, Clarendon Press, 1961) 139. But *cf* the defence of realism against these and others of Hart's charges by EH Taylor Jr, 'H.L.A. Hart's Concept of Law in the Perspective of American Legal Realism' (1972) 35 *MLR* 606, especially 616–17 on the so-called 'prediction theory'.

[151] Hart, above n 150, especially 124–36, 139.

[152] ibid 135.

> interests which vary in weight from case to case. None the less, the life of the law consists to a very large extent in the guidance both of officials and private individuals by determinate rules which, unlike the applications of variable standards, do *not* require from them a fresh judgment from case to case … Here at the margin of rules and in the fields left open by the theory of precedents, the courts perform a rule-producing function …

We are used to courts doing this when they exercise a discretion, apply inherently vague standards such as that of 'reasonableness', or assess the 'proportionality' of a particular response. The open texture is then filled by the reasoning process judges employ (or at any rate choose to display) in reaching a particular conclusion.

On the whole, English law saw the pendulum settle into a relatively stable position mid-way between rigid 'formalism' and loose 'substantivism' during much of the twentieth century – disregarding perhaps the odd escapade by Lord Denning.[153] But in recent years there is a worrying trend towards understanding entire bodies of rules as open-textured, not merely at the margins, but at their very core. The case-by-case value judgement is thus factored into the heart of the rule produced; it *becomes* the new rule. Often this is not called 'exercising a discretion' (presumably because that would raise questions about the proper role of the courts), but something of similar undertone and effect.

A particularly popular term which has emerged is the so-called 'evaluative judgement' (frequently spelt 'judgment' rather than 'judgement'). Its growth may safely be described as exponential. A search for the term in Westlaw (UK) yields 416 hits.[154] All but two of these date from the year 2000 or later.[155] No thorough quantitative analysis has been conducted in compiling the present chapter, but flicking through the listed cases, many initially used the term in connection with the judicial review of someone else's decision – effectively allowing the decision-maker (such as a trustee or a public authority) some manoeuvring space.[156] It is similar where an appeal within the judicial system does not succeed because the trial judge has exercised his or her 'evaluative judgement' in a proper way.[157] But increasingly, appeal courts claim the scope of 'evaluative judgment' for themselves, either in finding or developing the law.

[153] A Burrows, 'Form and Substance: Fictions and Judicial Power', this volume, ch 2, text following n 2, notes that Lord Denning 'preferred substance over form' and contrasts him with the 'formalist' Lord Diplock.

[154] When the words 'evaluative judgment' and 'evaluative judgement' are typed – as alternatives – into the 'free text' search box (as at 9 July 2018).

[155] The remaining two cases date from 1972 and 1996 respectively.

[156] As far as public authorities go, the emergence of the term 'evaluative judg(e)ment' was in all likelihood prompted by the Human Rights Act 1998 (UK) coming into force, which largely replaced the standard of so-called '*Wednesbury* unreasonableness' with an inquiry into 'proportionality'.

[157] For a recent example concerning control of contractual terms under the Unfair Contract Terms Act 1977 (UK), see *First Tower Trustees Ltd, Intertrust Trustees Limited v CDS (Superstores International) Ltd* [2018] EWCA Civ 1396 [75]: 'Whether a clause passes the test of reasonableness is an evaluative judgment for the trial judge. An appeal court should be slow to interfere'.

One area where this is particularly evident is tort law. In *Normans Bay Ltd (formerly Illingworth Morris Ltd) v Coudert Bros*, Laws LJ said with reference to the *Fairchild* decision:[158]

> Authority supports the proposition that the resolution of causation issues, certainly in the law of tort, is by no means merely a fact-finding exercise; in many instances it is an *evaluative judgment, concerned to establish the extent to which a defendant should justly be held responsible for what has befallen the claimant.*

In the 2002 case of *Dubai Aluminium Co Ltd v Salaam*, a similar point was made by Lord Nicholls in response to the then newly established 'close connection' test for vicarious liability:[159]

> [25] This 'close connection' test focuses attention in the right direction. But it affords no guidance on the type or degree of connection which will normally be regarded as sufficiently close to prompt the legal conclusion that the risk of the wrongful act occurring, and any loss flowing from the wrongful act, should fall on the firm or employer rather than the third party who was wronged. It provides no clear assistance on when … an incident is to be regarded as sufficiently work-related, as distinct from personal …
>
> [26] The crucial feature or features, either producing or negativing vicarious liability, vary widely from one case or type of case to the next. Essentially the court makes an evaluative judgment in each case, having regard to all the circumstances and, importantly, having regard also to the assistance provided by previous court decisions. In this field the latter form of assistance is particularly valuable.

However, looking back, the case law since then has done little to provide guidance or establish a degree of predictability within an open-textured rule. Quite the contrary. It is now frankly acknowledged at the highest judicial level that '[t]o search for certainty and precision in vicarious liability is to undertake a quest for a chimaera'.[160] And that is no surprise. The *Lister* test started out as one inquiring 'whether the [employee's] torts were so closely connected with his employment that it would be fair and just to hold the employers vicariously liable',[161] but its 'close connection' criterion has meanwhile been almost completely whittled away,[162] leaving the criteria of 'fairness and justice' as the main focal points for debate in future cases.[163] Some guide!

[158] *Normans Bay Ltd (formerly Illingworth Morris Ltd) v Coudert Bros* [2004] EWCA Civ 215 [64] (emphasis added), referring to *Fairchild v Glenhaven Funeral Services Ltd* [2002] UKHL 22, [2003] 1 AC 32.

[159] *Dubai Aluminium Co Ltd v Salaam* [2002] UKHL 48, [2003] 2 AC 366 [25]–[26], referring to *Lister v Hesley Hall Ltd* [2001] UKHL 22, [2002] 1 AC 215 ('*Lister*').

[160] *Mohamud v Wm Morrison Supermarkets plc* [2016] UKSC 11, [2016] AC 677 [54] (Lord Dyson MR) ('*Mohamud*').

[161] *Lister* [2001] UKHL 22, [2002] 1 AC 215 [28] (Lord Steyn).

[162] In *Mohamud* [2016] UKSC 11, [2016] AC 677, for instance, the requirement that the relationship between tortfeasor and employer must have provided more than the 'mere opportunity' for committing the tort was effectively abandoned. See SSH Chan, 'Hidden Departure from the Lister Close Connection Test' [2016] *Lloyd's Maritime and Commercial Law Quarterly* 352.

[163] At any rate on the interpretation of English law propounded by the High Court of Australia in *Prince Alfred College Incorporated v ADC* [2016] HCA 37, (2016) 258 CLR 134 [43], [67]. Critical: D Ryan, 'From Opportunity to Occasion: Vicarious Liability in the High Court of Australia' (2017) 76 *CLJ* 14, 15–17.

The English law of restitution for unjust enrichment has in recent years suffered from the same vagueness.[164] It has too often brushed aside established legal patterns as 'formalistic' and instead embraced 'substantivist' reasoning. Indeed, 'substantivism' has occasionally become a substitute for precise legal thinking. The controversial decision in *Menelaou* is just one example.[165] *Pitt v Holt* is another,[166] and it is one which highlights the contrast between serious doctrinal analysis of the facts of a case and an unstructured appeal to its merits. In *Pitt*, the question (put simply) was whether a voluntary disposition by deed could be set aside on the ground that the person making it had laboured under a mistake regarding the tax implications of the settlement thereby created. This could have been answered in the affirmative by holding that, where a transaction involves no contractual bargain needing to be protected, any causal mistake is a ground of restitution.[167] It could also have been answered in the negative, by insisting that mistakes relating to no more than the *reasons* for entering into a transaction (so-called 'motivational mistakes') do not warrant gifts and similar dispositions being disturbed. But the Supreme Court chose to go down a different route. Referring to the case of *Gibbon v Mitchell*,[168] where Millett J had held that a voluntary deed would be set aside for mistake only if the mistake was 'as to the effect of the transaction itself and not merely as to its consequences or the advantages to be gained by entering into it',[169] Lord Walker said:[170]

> To confirm the *Gibbon v Mitchell* test as formulated by Millett J would in my view leave the law in an uncertain state … It would also be contrary to the general disinclination of equity to insist on rigid classifications expressed in abstract terms. Equity, unlike many continental systems, has not adopted Roman law's classification of mistakes: error in negotio (the nature of the intended transaction), error in corpore (the subject matter of the transaction), error in persona (the identity of the other party to the transaction) and error in substantia (the quality of the subject matter). The *Gibbon v Mitchell* test, at any rate if applied narrowly, would cover only the first of these categories. But in some situations errors in other categories may be just as basic and just as serious in their consequences.

[164] Although the new 'range of factor' test established in *Patel v Mirza* [2016] UKSC 42, [2017] AC 467 ('*Patel*') to govern illegality is an interesting case in point, it will not be discussed here (but *cf* the comment in n 173). As Lord Neuberger acknowledged, '[t]here is … some attraction in the point that the need for certainty in this area is diminished by the fact that parties to an arrangement which is illegal have less cause for complaint if the law is uncertain' (at [158]).

[165] *Menelaou* [2015] UKSC 66, [2016] AC 176. One justification given for why Melissa's appeal was dismissed was that her case (allegedly) 'represent[ed] a triumph of form over substance, or, to use the words of Lord Steyn in *Banque Financière* … "pure formalism"' (at [99]). Yet the outcome could have been supported more conventionally: R Stevens, 'The Unjust Enrichment Disaster' (2018) 134 *LQR* 574, 598–99.

[166] *Pitt v Holt, Futter v Futter* [2013] UKSC 26, [2013] 2 AC 108 ('*Pitt*').

[167] See B Häcker, 'Mistaken Gifts after *Pitt v Holt*' (2014) 67 *Current Legal Problems* 333.

[168] *Gibbon v Mitchell* [1990] 1 WLR 1304 ('*Gibbon*').

[169] *Gibbon* [1990] 1 WLR 1304, 1309.

[170] *Pitt* [2013] UKSC 26, [2013] 2 AC 108 [123].

So instead of seeking to categorise mistakes and their seriousness in accordance with what they relate to, hard as that may be, the Supreme Court plunged the law into even greater uncertainty and decided that 'the true requirement is simply for there to be a causative mistake of sufficient gravity'.[171] This is how the 'sufficient gravity' criterion is fleshed out:[172]

> [126] The gravity of the mistake must be assessed by a close examination of the facts, whether or not they are tested by cross-examination, including the circumstances of the mistake and its consequences for the person who made the vitiated disposition. Other findings of fact may also have to be made in relation to change of position or other matters relevant to the exercise of the court's discretion ... The injustice (or unfairness or unconscionableness) of leaving a mistaken disposition uncorrected must be evaluated objectively, but with an intense focus ... on the facts of the particular case ...
>
> [128] ... The court cannot decide the issue of what is unconscionable by an elaborate set of rules. It must consider in the round the existence of a distinct mistake (as compared with total ignorance or disappointed expectations), its degree of centrality to the transaction in question and the seriousness of its consequences, *and make an evaluative judgment whether it would be unconscionable, or unjust, to leave the mistake uncorrected.* The court may and must form a judgment about the justice of the case.

In short, a claimant can seek restitution of a gift or other voluntary disposition induced by mistake if the mistake was sufficiently serious – which is the case whenever the court, in light of all the circumstances, feels that restitution is warranted ... (!)

There are many more examples of the recent 'substantivist' tendency to treat values like 'justice' and 'fairness' as building blocks to be factored directly into legal rules, rather than regarding them as *desiderata* which legal rules should live up to.[173] Luckily, some cases also stem the tide. The *ITC* case discussed above[174] is one of them. Lord Reed there observed:[175]

> A claim based on unjust enrichment does not create a judicial licence to meet the perceived requirements of fairness on a case-by-case basis: legal rights arising from unjust enrichment should be determined by rules of law which are ascertainable and consistently applied.

[171] *Pitt* [2013] UKSC 26, [2013] 2 AC 108 [122].

[172] *Pitt* [2013] UKSC 26, [2013] 2 AC 108 [126], [128]. The one passage with more concrete, category-based hints is labelled '*additional guidance* to judges in finding and evaluating the facts of any particular case' (*Pitt* [2013] UKSC 26, [2013] 2 AC 108 [122]): 'the test will *normally* be satisfied only when there is a mistake either as to the legal character or nature of a transaction, or as to some matter of fact or law which is basic to the transaction.' (All emphases added).

[173] See, eg, the Supreme Court's reformulation of the illegality doctrine as an open-textured and flexible balancing exercise in *Patel* [2016] UKSC 42, [2017] AC 467, especially Lord Toulson's statement at [120] that 'the application of a formal approach [was] capable of producing results which may appear arbitrary, unjust or disproportionate'.

[174] In the text accompanying nn 63–71.

[175] *ITC* [2017] UKSC 29, [2018] AC 275 [39].

So how should we all, scholars and judges alike, strike the right balance between hair-splitting doctrinal legal formalism and open-textured, value-orientated 'substantivism'? How do we avoid taking for granted rules and concepts which may long have lost touch with reality and applying them unthinkingly? But, on the other hand, how do we control our urge to substitute our own judgement of what is right and wrong for what the existing law declares to be so?

It seems to me that, as lawyers, we must begin by erring on the formalistic side. We *have to* 'split hairs' and we have to engage fully with what is already there – with all its pitfalls and complexities. But that is only a starting point. We need not switch off our moral compass, and indeed we ought not to do so. If, as academics, we feel that the law has taken a wrong turn or is in a mess, we should flag this. Sometimes, we may be able to reassemble the existing body of statutes and case law in a manner which supports our view of what the law *should be*, and then we argue that – properly interpreted – the law is already as we suggest. Where this is not possible, we can criticise the law and call for its reform.

Judges are of course able to develop the law more pro-actively. If they feel that the outcome which a formalist application of existing rules and concepts would seem to dictate is unacceptable, unjust or unfair, they may be able to distinguish the case or sometimes even overrule an old authority. But, in doing so, they should formulate the new rule which emerges from their decision (as far as possible) without direct reference to concepts such as 'justice' or 'fairness'. And the new rule should (again, as far as possible) be capable of generalisation. One might say it ought to comply with the idea underlying the first formulation of Kant's categorical imperative: 'act only according to that maxim through which you can at the same time will that it become a universal law'.[176]

The idea of coming at a legal problem from the formalist angle before making careful 'substantivist' adjustments to the outcome is not new by any means. Recall only what Maitland said about the historical relationship between law and equity:[177]

> Equity had come not to destroy the law but to fulfil it. Every jot and every tittle of the law was to be obeyed, but when all this had been done something might yet be needful, something that equity would require.

And equity itself would in due course mould the circumstances where it intervened into principled riders on the common law rules, whose foundational value was thereby impliedly affirmed.

Occasionally, it is worth reminding ourselves that this is the right way around. Rather than showing disdain for formalism, we need to build on its strengths and use our 'substantivist' intuition to improve and augment the law. In doctrinal

[176] I Kant, *Groundwork of the Metaphysics of Morals* (trans and ed by M Gregor and J Timmermann, rev edn, Cambridge, Cambridge University Press, 2012) 34 (italics removed).

[177] FW Maitland, *Equity, Also the Forms of Action at Common Law: Two Courses of Lectures* (ed by AH Chaytor and WJ Whittaker, Cambridge, Cambridge University Press, 1909) 17.

discourse, 'substance over form' should not be brandished as an argument. Both strands of reasoning ought instead to be harmoniously interwoven within the fabric of our law.

VI. A Comparative Epilogue: Function Over Form

Before concluding, it is worth adding a comment specifically from the angle of comparative law. Traditional comparative law methodology has its own version of the 'substance over form' maxim, namely the call to prioritise 'function over form'. Students of comparative law are advised not to be deceived by looks: instead of comparing rules and institutions which have the same outward appearance, name, or form, they should dig deeper and identify rules and institutions which perform the same 'function' within the different systems under consideration.

This 'functional' or 'functionalist' approach to comparative law is summarised thus in the leading textbook of *Zweigert & Kötz*:[178]

> The basic methodological principle of all comparative law is that of *functionality*. From this basic principle stem all the other rules which determine the choice of laws to compare, the scope of the undertaking, the creation of a system of comparative law, and so on. Incomparables cannot usefully be compared, and in law the only things which are comparable are those which fulfil the same function.

More specifically in respect of the process of comparison this means:[179]

> It goes without saying that a comparative analysis will bring out the differences between the actual solutions … But one does not gain much by simply listing the similarities and differences one discovers … The process of comparison at this stage involves adopting a new point of view from which to consider all the different solutions. The objective report which sets out the law of a particular jurisdiction will give a comprehensive portrayal of its legal solution to a particular problem, but it does so 'on its own terms', with its particular statutory rules or decisions, its characteristic conceptual form, and in its systematic context … But when the process of comparison begins, each of the solutions must be freed from the context of its own system and, before evaluation can take place, set in the context of all the solutions from the other jurisdictions under investigation. Here too we must follow the principle of functionality: the solutions we find in the different jurisdictions must be cut loose from their conceptual context and stripped of their national doctrinal overtones so that they may be seen purely in the light of their function, as an attempt to satisfy a particular legal need.

In principle, this has a lot to be said for it. The further apart and more diverse legal systems are, the greater the danger that someone not fully steeped in all of them

[178] K Zweigert and H Kötz, *An Introduction to Comparative Law*, T Weir trans, 3rd edn (Oxford, Oxford University Press, 1998) 34.
[179] ibid 43–44.

will otherwise overlook some crucial feature or be fooled by a merely superficial similarity. Terminological resemblances are particularly treacherous. For instance, while the word 'guarantee', to the common law mind, describes a personal security right of an accessory nature, ie, a secondary liability, civilian lawyers commonly use the term (German: *Garantie*, French: *garantie*, Italian: *garanzia*) to refer to a primary liability which is legally independent of the debt being secured, hence more in the nature of a common law indemnity.[180]

However, even within mainstream comparative law, functionalism has been criticised for being one-dimensional in its external epistemic perspective: brushing the socio-cultural embeddedness of the law under the carpet[181] and being blind to significant insights which could usefully be gleaned from looking inside the 'black box' constituted by each legal system.[182] The less risk there is of the comparative inquiry being impeded by 'false friends' or the researcher's lack of familiarity with the legal landscape, the smaller the need for particular solutions to be 'cut loose from their conceptual context and stripped of their national doctrinal overtones'. At some point, the balance tips, and the advantages of privileging 'function over form' are outweighed by the disadvantages of conceptual blindness.

This is an important point to absorb as common lawyers around the world increasingly begin to understand their dialogue as a form of 'comparative law'. It is right and good that the comparative endeavour amongst ever more divergent common law systems should be so understood rather than hankering after the colonial myth of there being 'one common law'. But this new 'comparative common law' is special and should not simply be cast into the traditional European or less traditional global mould of comparative law. It is therefore submitted that 'function over form' is, for the most part,[183] *not* a suitable methodology to adopt. Instead, comparative common lawyers have the advantage of already sharing a basic conceptual apparatus and structure. The skeleton is there, and it is (still) fleshed

[180] The accessory form of personal security is called *Bürgschaft* (German), *cautionnement* (French), *fideiussione* (Italian).

[181] See the overview and assessment (with further references) by R Michaels, 'The Functional Method of Comparative Law' in M Reimann and R Zimmermann (eds), *The Oxford Handbook of Comparative Law* (Oxford, Oxford University Press, 2006) 339, especially 341, 351, 354, 362, 365.

[182] The black box metaphor is coined by H Kötz, 'Abschied von der Rechtskreislehre?' [1998] *Zeitschrift für europäisches Privatrecht* (ZEuP) 493, 505. It likens legal systems to intricate pieces of machinery, the inside life of which the functionalist deliberately refrains from exploring. Instead, he or she feeds in a particular 'social problem' at one end, and the various machines spew out the different national 'solution' at the other.

[183] There will be exceptions. Indeed, one of the classic examples used to illustrate the helpfulness of traditional functionalism is one where there is a rift even within the common law tradition. European-style land registration systems (as, eg, the Australian Torrens system and the modern English system) find a functional equivalent in the prevalent US system of private 'title insurance' companies offering protection against unknown third-party rights. In practice, it is said, these companies' records will be nearly as accurate a mirror of title as those of a state-run land register: Zweigert and Kötz, above n 178, 39. See, most recently, G Mjeku 'Documenting Interests in Land: The American and British Systems', www.ssrn.com/abstract=3200697 (last accessed 9 December 2018).

out in roughly the same way throughout the common law world. Moreover, a shared language – English – and a by and large shared understanding of technical terms, with all their complex underlying connotations, makes it relatively easy for common lawyers to focus on the divergence of black-letter rules and case trends.[184] So while common lawyers *should* regard themselves as true comparative lawyers, they are a special species. Differently to mainstream comparativists, comparative *common* lawyers should be slow to prioritise function over form.

[184] On the shared rules and language aspect, see B Häcker, 'Divergence and Convergence in the Common Law – Lessons from the Ius Commune' (2015) 131 *LQR* 424, 446–47.

4

Form, Substance and Recharacterisation

PEY-WOAN LEE*

I. Introduction

At common law, a court may 'recharacterise' a contract when it is satisfied that the transaction it embodies is substantially different from the label assigned to it by the parties. This process of recharacterisation is well-established in many legal spheres including those of employment, trusts, property, taxation and secured financing. Whether a transaction should be recharacterised is routinely said to depend on its 'substance'. Typically, this refrain is made to underscore the point that a court will not be bound by the label or form selected by the parties. However, precisely what constitutes 'substance' is less clear. Generally, a party seeking to recharacterise a transaction may do so on one of two grounds: first, that the transaction was a sham and hence unenforceable; or secondly, that on a true construction of the document, the transaction belongs to a category different from that identified by the parties. So expressed, these techniques engender the impression that recharacterisation – the location of 'substance' – is largely a matter of doctrinal analysis free from value judgment. But a closer inspection will reveal that the process is more textured and fine-grained.

This chapter examines the jurisprudence of recharacterisations in the areas of tenancy, employment, trusts and financing arrangements.[1] It argues that the characterisation of a transaction is always a question of law informed by policy considerations. Specifically, recharacterisations are concerned with *avoidances* so the central question is whether and to what extent parties are legally permitted to 'contract out' of a statutory regime or the legal incidents of a relationship. As such, the process of recharacterisation is neither reducible to the application

* I am deeply grateful to Professors Lusina Ho and Kelvin Low for their invaluable comments on an earlier draft. My gratitude extends also to the participants at Obligations IX conference for their helpful comments and encouragement. All errors are my responsibility.

[1] Questions of characterisation are also common in tax disputes but that is an area better left to specialist treatment.

of narrow legal doctrines nor merely an exercise in contractual interpretation. As will be observed, English courts generally incorporate policy considerations in this discourse but are accustomed to presenting them as ancillary (rather than primary) justifications in their reasoning. Only in legislative contexts such as those protecting tenants or employees where the policy underpinnings are unambiguous is a court likely to base a decision squarely on the pursuit of the legislative goal. In other cases, they are wont to retreat to the sanctuary of rules and doctrines. On the whole, therefore, the English judicial method in this context is more formal than substantive.[2] This predilection is not objectionable or detrimental where the relevant substantive concerns are balanced and embedded in the formal rules. But formal reasoning may descend into formalistic reasoning if the rules so harden as to eclipse important substantive concerns. This chapter contends that this risk subsists in recharacterisation cases. To minimise that risk, it is critical that judges articulate the interplay of values, policies and doctrines resulting in a particular characterisation. Similarly, courts should develop the broad techniques of recharacterisation (viz, shams and construction) more flexibly to make room for the evaluation of substantive reasons.

II. The Nature of Recharacterisation

Questions of characterisation arise in a wide variety of contexts. The characterisation of a particular issue in a dispute may, for example, determine which system of law is applicable to resolve that dispute.[3] The remedial consequence of a breach of obligation may depend on whether the obligation is 'fiduciary' in character.[4] Or a term of a contract may be unenforceable if it were properly characterised as a 'penalty'.[5] This chapter is concerned with characterisation in a narrower context, viz, situations where the characterisation of a transaction has been expressed in written form but which is challenged on the ground that the form is not reflective of its substance.

At the outset, it is necessary to clarify that the process of characterisation is distinguished from that of interpretation or construction.[6] The latter is concerned with ascertaining the meaning of words and language so as to determine their application to a set of facts whereas the former seeks to identify the legal category of a transaction in order to determine its legal effects. However, characterisation

[2] PS Atiyah and RS Summers, *Form and Substance in Anglo-American Law: A Comparative Study of Legal Reasoning, Legal Theory, and Legal Institutions* (Oxford, Clarendon Press, 1987).

[3] *Macmillan v Bishopsgate (No 3)* [1996] 1 WLR 387.

[4] *Hospital Products Ltd v United States Surgical Corporation* (1984) 156 CLR 41.

[5] *Cavendish Square Holding BV v Makdessi*; *ParkingEye Ltd v Beavis* [2015] UKSC 67, [2016] AC 1172.

[6] G McMeel, *The Construction of Contracts: Interpretation, Implication and Rectification*, 3rd edn (Oxford, Oxford University Press, 2017) para 1.20.

and interpretation are also intertwined in that characterisation is premised on an accurate understanding of the intended effects of the conduct constituting the transaction. In other words, a transaction can only be characterised if the conduct making up the transaction has first been construed. Where the transaction is effected by a written document, the construction of the document will, of course, precede categorisation.

This inter-relation of construction and characterisation is summed up by Lord Millett in *Agnew v Commissioner of Inland Revenue*, a case concerned with the characterisation of charges, as a two-stage process:

> At the first stage it must construe the instrument of charge and seek to gather the intentions of the parties from the language they have used. But the object at this stage of the process is not to discover whether the parties intended to create a fixed or a floating charge. It is to ascertain the nature of the rights and obligations which the parties intended to grant each other in respect of the charged assets. Once these have been ascertained, the court can then embark on the second stage of the process, which is one of categorisation. This is a matter of law. It does not depend on the intention of the parties. If their intention, properly gathered from the language of the instrument, is to grant the company rights in respect of the charged assets which are inconsistent with the nature of a fixed charge, then the charge cannot be a fixed charge however they may have chosen to describe it.[7]

On this account, characterisation comprises: first, an interpretive stage to establish the intended rights and obligations as a matter of fact; and secondly, an analytical or evaluative stage where the court decides how those rights and obligations ought to be classified as a matter of law. Differentiating between these distinct stages is important as the evaluative nature of the second stage is often overlooked or concealed. In order to decide if an act or transaction falls within a particular legal category, the court is first required to distill the 'objective criterion' that defines that particular category.[8] That process of abstraction invariably requires an appraisal of the values pertinent to the issue in question. Writing extra-judicially, Chief Justice Allsop explains the process as 'one where a *value judgment* is made by reference to ascribed meaning, found facts, an expressed principle or rule and the relevantly organised values that are to be brought to bear for the task'.[9] Thus, a court that has to decide if a particular relationship is fiduciary in nature would first have to identify the values that define such relationships. That defining value – protecting those vulnerable to abuse by reason of reposing trust, confidence and power in another – is gleaned not by syllogistic reasoning or logical interpretation alone but also by an appreciation of the characteristics and policy underpinnings

[7] *Agnew v Commissioner of Inland Revenue* [2001] UKPC 28, [2001] 2 AC 710 [32] ('*Brumark*').

[8] *Welsh Development Agency v Export Finance Co Ltd* [1992] BCLC 148, 160 ('*Welsh Development*'). Eg, the criterion applicable to tenancy relationships is that of 'exclusive possession', the employer's 'control' in the case of employment relations, and the 'divestment of ownership' in the context of trusts.

[9] J Allsop, 'Characterisation: Its Place in Contractual Analysis and Related Enquiries' (2017) 91 *Australian Law Journal* 471, 471 (emphasis added).

of accepted categories of fiduciaries (such as trustees, agents and directors).[10] An exercise in characterisation therefore encompasses but is more than, and distinct from, mere interpretation.[11] The failure to keep the two processes apart may sometimes obscure the true justifications of a particular characterisation.

For *recharacterisation*, the evaluative function of the process bears an additional dimension as courts are essentially tasked to decide the legitimacy of attempts to avoid particular legal classifications and their attendant legal consequences. Or, to take an alternative perspective, it is a process that *delimits contractual or individual freedom*. For that reason, the process of recharacterisation inevitably involves the assessment of the social, moral or economic aims of a particular legal regime. Specifically, courts would have to weigh the value of self-determinacy against the interests protected by the legal regime that is being circumvented. That tension is not resolved by simply uncovering the factual meaning of parties' conduct (for example, interpretation) but requires the reasoned prioritisation of competing interests. Recharacterisation thus encapsulates a normative inquiry as to what legal consequences *ought* to be, and not merely what they are.

Seen in this light, recharacterisation functions as a judicial tool for policing illegitimate avoidances.[12] That explains why the exercise would often require departures from the usual rules of contractual or documentary construction. Where the contractual or written form is itself the means by which parties seek to circumvent a particular legal regime, the court must be able to look past that form to ascertain what the real transaction is in order to decide how *that* transaction should be characterised. It must have access to evidence extrinsic to the written contract or document, including the parties' subjective intention and subsequent conduct,[13] for otherwise it would be 'led by the nose into the artificial task of defining the legal rights and obligations of the parties by reference to their proved documents and related conduct alone'.[14]

[10] ibid 474.

[11] Allsop cites the classification of contractual terms as an instance of such conflation: ibid 478–80. In that context, the question whether a term is a condition, warranty or innominate term is said to depend on parties' intention as discerned from the contract taking into account the contract's 'nature, purpose and circumstances' (*Bunge Corporation New York v Tradax Export SA, Panama* [1981] 1 WLR 711, 717). But while the discovery of 'parties' intention' is customarily thought to be a matter of interpretation, courts would in fact have to evaluate the importance of the term and the seriousness of its breach to decide if it is a condition or an innominate term (see *Torvald Klaveness A/S v Arni Maritime Corp* [1994] 1 WLR 1465, 1476 where Lord Mustill observed that '[the] classification of an obligation as a condition or an "innominate" term is largely determined by its practical importance in the scheme of the contract'). The classification of terms, therefore, is necessarily 'framed by an understanding of the context (including commercial context) and imperatives of a given contract or type of contract. It is from that understanding that the relevant values are drawn' (ibid 481).

[12] See, in relation to shams, M Stewart, 'The Judicial Doctrine in Australia' in E Simpson and M Stewart (eds), *Sham Transactions* (Oxford, Oxford University Press, 2014) para 3.56. See also *Re Watson* (1890) 25 QBD 27, 33.

[13] *Hitch v Stone* [2001] EWCA Civ 63, [2001] STC 214 [65]–[66].

[14] *Raftland Pty Ltd as Trustee of the Raftland Trust v Commissioner of Taxation* [2008] HCA 21, (2008) 238 CLR 516 [151].

III. Formal and Substantive Reasoning

Understanding recharacterisation in this way makes clear that the courts' reference to 'substance' in this context is but a shorthand for the composite analysis that it undertakes. Such an analysis looks past the parties' labels to take into account the interpretation of the written document, the nature of the transaction or relationship that parties are purporting to create, the policy concerns residing in the relevant legal or legislative context and the extent to which it is permissible to 'contract out' of that legal or regulatory framework.[15] To the extent that such an approach requires the court to articulate the policy reasons for a particular characterisation, this emphasis on 'substance' may be seen as instances of substantive reasoning. According to Patrick Atiyah and Robert Summers, substantive reasoning is characterised by the use of 'moral, economic, political, institutional or other social consideration' to justify an outcome.[16] It is contrasted with formal reasoning, which bases a decision on legally authoritative precepts, such as legal rules, to exclude from consideration other countervailing substantive reasons.[17] However, the discussion below will suggest that English courts have not, in cases of recharacterisation, always equated 'substance' with substantive reasoning. Instead, they do often, in keeping with the general preference for formal reasoning, apply formal rules and doctrines to ascertain the 'substance' of a transaction. This is not in itself problematic because frequently, the rule and doctrine being applied is itself founded on adequate substantive reasoning. But formal reasoning may degenerate into formalistic reasoning, which is detrimental, when there is 'a failure to take substantive considerations into account *when they ought to be taken into account*'.[18] This may occur when formal reasoning so dominates as to conceal or suppress policy concerns germane to the issue at hand.

IV. Recharacterisation Techniques

In *Welsh Development Agency v Export Finance Co Ltd*,[19] Staughton LJ identified two recharacterisation techniques. The first is to establish the written document as a 'sham' that does not represent the parties' true position. Absent evidence of sham, the second route is to characterise the transaction by interpreting the written document to ascertain the nature and effects of its terms. A key distinction between the two techniques is that the first 'external' route allows the court to

[15] Without so expanding, the term 'substance' is a type of 'meaningless reference' as it does not, by itself, provide any specific basis for drawing a particular conclusion: J Stone, *Legal System and Lawyers' Reasoning* (London, Stevens & Sons Ltd, 1964) 241.
[16] Atiyah and Summers, above n 2, 1.
[17] ibid 2.
[18] ibid 29.
[19] *Welsh Development* [1992] BCLC 148.

look to extrinsic evidence to prove the existence of a *separate* agreement that is not reflected by the written contract, whilst the second 'internal' route considers principally the parties' agreement 'on the basis that the parties intended to be bound by its terms, *and nothing else*'.[20] The latter, in so far as it requires only proof of internal inconsistency, is commonly thought to be a matter of contractual interpretation.[21]

Although 'sham' reasoning has been employed in a wide range of contexts, its precise scope and rationale remain unsettled. Modern expositions invariably begin with Diplock LJ's dictum in *Snook v London and West Riding Investments Ltd*,[22] which confined 'shams' to situations where parties enter into a false transaction with the common intention to mislead a third party. So defined, the concept is of very limited application. Quite apart from the high threshold for proof of dishonest collusion, courts are unwilling to make findings of sham that have the effects of castigating parties as dishonest and undermining commercial certainty.[23] As a result, courts confronting blatant instances of avoidance have on occasion had to either extend the concept to include cases where only one party acted with the intention to mislead, or developed adjacent principles (such as 'pretences') to recharacterise the transaction in question. In other contexts, courts have adhered to a narrow concept of 'sham' but also applied the 'internal' route more robustly to police avoidances. On the whole, the judicial approach to 'shams' is mixed: it is more flexible and substantive in contexts (such as tenancy and employment) where the strength of the legislative policy warrants a robust response, but more formal and restrictive in cases (such as those in trusts and financing) where legal certainty is prioritised above other concerns.

The 'internal' route of recharacterisation is employed when there is no apparent discordance between the form of the transaction and the parties' actual practice but the legal incidents of the transaction do not in fact correspond to those of the named category. Because its focus is on the terms of the document or contract, this technique may sometimes be construed as a mere interpretative exercise centred on the parties' contractual intention. As explained,[24] this is a reductive view of recharacterisation since the process is in fact interpretive *and* evaluative.

[20] *Welsh Development* [1992] BCLC 148, 187 (emphasis added).

[21] 'Once the documents are accepted as genuinely representing the transaction into which the parties have entered, its proper legal categorization is a matter of construction of the documents': *Orion Finance Ltd v Crown Financial Management Ltd* [1996] 2 BCLC 78, 84 (Millett LJ) ('*Orion*').

[22] *Snook v London and West Riding Investments Ltd* [1967] 2 QB 786, 802 ('*Snook*'): '[sham] means acts done or documents executed by the parties to the "sham" which are intended by them to give to third parties or to the court the appearance of creating between the parties legal rights and obligations different from the actual legal rights and obligations (if any) which the parties intend to create. But one thing, I think, is clear in legal principle, morality and the authorities … that for acts or documents to be a "sham," with whatever legal consequences follow form this, all the parties thereto must have a common intention that the acts or documents are not to create the legal rights and obligations which they give the appearance of creating' (footnotes omitted).

[23] *National Westminster Bank plc v Jones* [2001] EWCA Civ 1541, [2001] 1 BCLC 98 [59] ('*Westminster Bank*').

[24] See above, Section II.

Conceiving the process as one of construction or interpretation alone may also result in formalistic reasoning if it misleads the court to place excessive weight on the language chosen by parties (or, in the case of statutory interpretation, the literal meaning of a statute). Fortunately, English courts have (in the contexts considered below) generally avoided this pitfall by incorporating substantive reasoning into the 'construction' process. Nevertheless, the risk of formalistic reasoning subsists as formal reasoning remains dominant, such that substantive reasons are usually cited only as secondary reasons for a preferred characterisation.

V. Tenancy Agreements

In this context, English courts have employed recharacterisation techniques principally to counteract illegitimate avoidances of tenancy protection legislation. Typically, they are situations where landlords sought to disguise leases as licences to avoid statutory controls on rent or security of tenure. Although these devices have largely receded with the deregulation of the private rental market from the 1980s,[25] the cases decided in this context remain important examples of the situations in which recharacterisations are appropriate.

In the leading case of *Street v Mountford*,[26] the House of Lords characterised an agreement granting exclusive possession as a lease even though it was labelled as a licence. As the sole factual criterion for distinguishing between a lease and a licence is that of exclusive possession, the agreement is a lease once that criterion is satisfied; the parties could not alter that legal characterisation simply by giving it a different name. In the famous words of Lord Templeman, 'The manufacture of a five-pronged implement for manual digging results in a fork even if the manufacturer, unfamiliar with the English language, insists that he intended to make and has made a spade'.[27]

Street was arguably a decision reached via the internal route as it was not alleged that the agreement involved a sham.[28] The fact of exclusive possession was conceded,[29] and the court's only task was to decide if that operative feature was consistent with the agreement's stated form. Nevertheless, Lord Templeman made clear that the court would have been equally 'astute to detect and frustrate sham devices and artificial transactions whose only object is to disguise the grant of a tenancy and to evade the Rent Acts'.[30] In practice, however, shams in the

[25] S Bright, H Glover and J Prassl, 'Tenancy Agreements' in E Simpson and M Stewart (eds), *Sham Transactions* (Oxford, Oxford University Press, 2013) paras 6.52–6.54.

[26] *Street v Mountford* [1985] AC 809 ('*Street*').

[27] *Street* [1985] AC 809, 819.

[28] Bright analysed *Street* as a 'labelling' case that fell within the ambit of the internal route: see S Bright, 'Avoiding Tenancy Legislation: Sham and Contracting Out Revisited' (2002) 61 *CLJ* 146, 159.

[29] *Street* [1985] AC 809, 823.

[30] ibid, 825.

Snook sense are rare in this context as tenants would not usually have shared in the landlord's evasive intention. More commonly, the landlord would have sought to include in the agreement provisions denying exclusive possession, which the tenant accepted either without understanding or without belief that they would be enforced. In *Antoniades v Villiers*,[31] a landlord letting a single room to a couple sought to create a licence by including in the agreements a clause (Clause 16) that allowed him (or his nominee) to enter and share the room with the couple. The House of Lords held that Clause 16 was a 'pretence' rather than a genuine reservation of power to share occupation with the tenants.[32] A critical factor that led to this finding was the observation that the premises was too small for sharing between strangers.[33] Given that the couple were seeking a quasi-matrimonial home, there was 'an air of total unreality' in the terms seeking to negate the grant of exclusive possession.[34] The agreements in question therefore created a lease and the tenants were protected under the Rent Acts.

Antoniades was seen by some commentators to have extended 'shams' beyond that conceived in *Snook* because there was no finding in that case that the tenants had shared in the landlord's intention not to rely on Clause 16.[35] Instead, it was emphasised that tenants typically had no real choice in the inclusion of such clauses because '[a] person seeking residential accommodation may sign a document couched in any language in order to obtain shelter'.[36] Moreover, the pretence that was operative in *Antoniades* also differed from *Snook* shams in that it related only to a particular term of the contract rather than the validity of the agreement as a whole.

Subsequent courts that found the *Snook* constraints obstructive welcomed the flexibility inherent in the broader notion of 'pretence'. In *Bankway Properties Ltd v Pensfold-Dunsford*, Arden LJ explained *Antoniades* as an application of the doctrine of pretence, a 'variant' of the *Snook* sham.[37] This doctrine, according to Arden LJ, applies where the court has to resolve an issue by discovering 'the substance and reality of the transaction entered into by the parties'.[38] For that purpose, it may look at all relevant circumstances, including subsequent conduct,

[31] *Antoniades v Villiers* [1990] 1 AC 417 ('*Antoniades*').

[32] *Antoniades* [1990] 1 AC 417, 463.

[33] ibid.

[34] *Antoniades* [1990] 1 AC 417, 467.

[35] Bright also observed that 'Lord Templeman was seeking [in *Antoniades v Villiers*] to develop a flexible doctrine, free from the constraints of the *Snook* definition of sham, that would apply whenever an agreement has been artificially structured so as to be tantamount to contracting out of the Rent Acts'. See S Bright, 'Beyond Sham and into Pretence' (1991) 11 *OJLS* 136, 139–40. See further B MacFarlane and E Simpson, 'Tackling Avoidance' in J Getzler (ed), *Rationalizing Property, Equity and Trusts: Essays in Honour of Edward Burn* (London, LexisNexis, 2003) 152.

[36] *Antoniades* [1990] 1 AC 417, 458.

[37] *Bankway Properties Ltd v Pensfold-Dunsford* [2001] EWCA Civ 528, [2001] 1 WLR 1369 [43] ('*Bankway*'). The distinction between 'pretence' and 'sham' was accepted by the Court of Appeal in the earlier cases of *Aslan v Murphy (Nos 1 and 2)* and *Duke v Wynne* [1990] 1 WLR 766, 770–71.

[38] *Bankway* [2001] EWCA Civ 528, [2001] 1 WLR 1369 [43].

but proof of a common intention to deceive is not needed.[39] Applying the doctrine to the facts, Arden LJ struck down as a pretence a rent review clause that purported to increase the rent to more than five-fold after two years.[40] It was not a genuine provision for fixing rent but a mere 'device' to enable the landlord to repossess the leased premises otherwise than in accordance with the statutory scheme of the Housing Act 1988 (UK).[41]

The decisions in *Antoniades* and *Bankway* are clear instances of substantive reasoning, motivated by the desire to give effect to relevant legislative policies. In *Antoniades*, Lord Templeman prefaced his discussion with the declaration that 'Parties to an agreement cannot contract out of the Rent Acts; if they were able to do so the Acts would be a dead letter because in a state of housing shortage a person seeking residential accommodation may agree to anything to obtain shelter'.[42] This ready acceptance of an implicit prohibition against 'contracting out' underscores the primacy of the legislative objective – the protection of a vulnerable class. It affirmed, as did Arden LJ in *Bankway*,[43] that the disparate bargaining powers (then) inherent in landlord and tenant relationships warranted closer scrutiny of, and interference with, contractual arrangements. The broad latitude within which landlords could draft and dictate contractual terms necessitated that courts be equipped with an equally responsive tool to detect more subtle and indirect ways of circumventing statutory protection for tenants. A narrow sham doctrine in the *Snook* sense did not adequately meet this purpose.

Those who are uncomfortable with the uncertainty that resides in such an approach have, unsurprisingly, agitated over the difficulty of justifying these 'anomalous' cases in doctrinal terms.[44] On one view, they may be seen as manifestations of the general principle that courts may disregard terms conceived for purely avoidance motives, viz, where they were incorporated into the contract for no purpose other than to avoid a particular mandatory regulatory regime.[45]

[39] ibid, [44].

[40] Pill LJ, however, analysed the issue using the 'internal' route. He found that the terms of the lease evinced a clear intention to create an assured tenancy and thereby to grant long-term security. The rent review clause, which has the effect of precipitating early termination, was 'inconsistent with and repugnant' to that main purpose and ought therefore be ignored: *Bankway* [2001] EWCA Civ 528, [2001] 1 WLR 1369 [66]–[70]. For a criticism of this reasoning, see Bright, above n 28, 166.

[41] *Bankway* [2001] EWCA Civ 528, [2001] 1 WLR 1369 [55]. Her Ladyship based this conclusion on three findings: the absence of any evidence that the parties had even negotiated the rent-review clause; that the increased rent well exceeded the market rate and was clearly beyond the means of the defendants or other persons likely to rent in the same location; and that the landlord had taken no action to demand the higher rent when it could have done so: see *Bankway* [2001] EWCA Civ 528, [2001] 1 WLR 1369 [53], [54], [60].

[42] *Antoniades* [1990] 1 AC 417, 458. His Lordship also cited (463) *Street* as authority for reasserting the principle that parties cannot contract out of the Rents Act.

[43] *Bankway* [2001] EWCA Civ 528, [2001] 1 WLR 1369 [45], citing Lord Simon in *Johnson v Moreton* [1980] AC 37, 66–67.

[44] Bright, Glover and Prassl, above n 25, 110.

[45] *Antoniades* [1990] 1 AC 417, 462, 463. Bright thus explicated the case as having laid down the rule that 'if a non-exclusive occupation clause is inserted as a pretence and is not intended to be relied upon, that this is an attempt to contract out of the Rent Acts and so cannot be allowed'. See Bright, above n 35, 141.

But this explanation is unsatisfactory as it is well established that an avoidance motive is not, by itself, a sufficient reason for striking down a contract or a term.[46] An alternative explanation is that pretence is simply a wider concept of sham in that a contract or an obligation could be regarded as 'not genuine' if there was no intention to enforce or rely on it.[47] Yet this, too, is flawed since contracting parties may always legitimately form an intention of non-enforcement for reasons of benevolence rather than deception or contrivance.[48] Once the requirement for common intention (to deceive) is abandoned, it is also unclear what threshold conduct would justify the finding of a 'non-genuine' term.[49]

These concerns reflect the anxiety that is commonly experienced when substantive reasons are prioritised over formal ones. The flexibility that enables courts to respond to varying avoidance tactics inevitably undermines predictability. To some degree, such instability may be mitigated if courts react consistently to a recurrent fact pattern so that a formal rule is eventually recognised to govern that situation, but even so, the rigid application of such a rule regardless of context could lead to questionable outcomes. In *Swan v Uecker*,[50] the Supreme Court of Victoria held that a tenant had 'sublet' the rented premises when he offered it for short-term occupation through Airbnb. Under Victorian residential tenancy law, subletting without the landlord's consent is a ground upon which the landlord may evict the tenants. Notwithstanding that the Airbnb agreement was labelled as a licence, Croft J found it constituted a lease because its terms granted exclusive possession to Airbnb guests. This was a surprising outcome as it runs counter to the common perception that such short-term home-sharing arrangements are no more than mere licences. At its heart, the case is concerned with a tenant's security of tenure, whether eviction rights should be restrictively construed, and the extent to which a tenant's right to quiet enjoyment extended to a right to participate in the sharing economy.[51] By adopting a formalistic approach that focused narrowly on the test of 'exclusive possession', the Court effectively sidestepped these substantive concerns and arrived at an inadequately-considered outcome. The surprising outcome highlights the centrality of policy considerations even in cases where the issue hinges on an apparently stable rule (such as the 'exclusive possession' test).

[46] Thus, Megarry J observed in *Miles v Bull* [1969] 1 QB 258, 264 that 'a transaction is no sham merely because it is carried out with a particular purpose or object. If what is done is genuinely done, it does not remain undone merely because there was an ulterior purpose in doing it'. See also McFarlane and Simpson, above n 35, 158.

[47] Bright, above n 28, 157, citing Neuberger J in *National Westminster Bank plc v Jones* [2001] EWCA Civ 1541, [2001] 1 BCLC 98 [45].

[48] McFarlane and Simpson, above n 35, 160–61.

[49] Bright, Glover and Prassl, above n 25, 114.

[50] *Swan v Uecker* [2016] VSC 313, (2016) 50 VR 74.

[51] See the criticisms of B Swannie, 'Trouble in Paradise: Are Home Sharing Arrangements "Subletting" under Residential Tenancies Legislation' (2016) 25 *Australian Property Law Journal* 183.

VI. Employment Agreements

Like tenants, employees constitute a vulnerable group that is statutorily protected against exploitation and unfair treatment. A person who qualifies as an 'employee' will therefore enjoy particular protections such as the right to redundancy payments and the right not to be unfairly dismissed,[52] while a 'worker' is entitled (inter alia) to minimum wage and protections for working overtime.[53] In practice, employers who wish to avoid these additional burdens may, in a contract of appointment, explicitly exclude the indicia of employment so as to ensure that the relationship falls outside the ambit of the relevant statutory protections. Where, however, there is evidence that such attempts are a matter only of form and bear no relation to reality, the question would arise as to whether the agreement is in truth one of employment.

Traditionally, courts have been reluctant to look behind the parties' written contracts in the employment context.[54] Close adherence to contractual orthodoxy meant that parol evidence is generally inadmissible in construing the contract of appointment. Hence, a contract that explicitly excludes salient features of employment (such as control or the obligation to provide personal service) would be given effect to even if there were evidence that the term was not enforced.[55] Moreover, the *Snook* doctrine is not usually of assistance in this context since the contracts are typically drafted by the employer and signed by the putative employee on a 'take-it-or-leave-it' basis so the latter can hardly be said to have been complicit in the employer's 'deception'.

More recently, however, a new approach emphasising substance over form has evolved in recognition of the power imbalance inherent in employment relations. In *Consistent Group Ltd v Mrs Kalwak*,[56] Elias J upheld a tribunal decision that a group of Polish workers who had contracted with an employment agency ostensibly as 'sub-contractors' were in fact employees. Although the contract contained various explicit denials of employment relations (by, for example, providing for the right to refuse work and to provide substitute service), these provisions were shams as they did not reflect reality. Explaining why it was crucial to look behind written contracts to discern the parties' true agreement, Elias J astutely observed:

> The concern to which tribunals must be alive is that armies of lawyers will simply place substitution clauses, or clauses denying any obligation to accept or provide for work in

[52] Employment Rights Act 1996 (UK), ss 135, 94.

[53] National Minimum Wage Act 1998 (UK); Working Time Regulations 1998 (SI 1988/1833) (UK).

[54] See ACL Davies, 'Employment Law' in E Simpson and M Stewart (eds), *Sham Transactions* (Oxford, Oxford University Press, 2013) paras 10.25–10.30.

[55] See, eg, *Express & Echo Publications Ltd v Tanton* [1999] ICR 693, 697, where a finding of an employment relationship by the Employment Appeal Tribunal was overturned because the Tribunal judge placed too much weight on 'what actually happened' rather than what the legal obligations were.

[56] *Consistent Group Ltd v Mrs Kalwak* EAT/0535/2006 ('*Consistent*').

> the employment contracts, as a matter of form, even where such terms do not begin to reflect the real relationship.[57]

These observations point to the real risk of employers depriving workers and employees of their statutory protection simply by creating a documentary fiction of self-employment.

Elias J's decision was reversed on appeal,[58] but his reasoning was subsequently endorsed in *Firthglow Ltd v Szilagyi*.[59] In this case, the English Court of Appeal held that a claimant who had contracted as a 'partnership' was in fact employed by the defendant. Under the arrangement, the claimant (Szilagyi) was required to form a partnership with another, and the partnership in turn contracted to supply services to the defendant, Protectacoat. The service agreement provided, inter alia, that Protectacoat was under no obligation to provide the partnership with work. The undisputed purpose of these arrangements was to ensure that Szilagyi would not become an employee of Protectacoat. Eventually, a dispute arose and the arrangements were terminated.

Szilagyi brought proceedings in the Employment Tribunal for unfair dismissal. A preliminary issue that arose was whether the Tribunal had jurisdiction to hear the case, which turned on whether Szilagyi was an employee of the company. The Court of Appeal affirmed the Tribunal's decision that an employment relationship existed because both the partnership and service agreements were shams. Smith LJ, who delivered the principal judgment, was emphatic that 'the test for a sham must be sensitive to the context'.[60] Her Ladyship accepted that a broader test (than *Snook*) is justified in the employment context where contractual terms are not usually negotiated but dictated by the employer.[61] So, rather than insist on a common intention to deceive a third party,[62] the right approach is simply to consider whether the written contract represents the parties' true intentions. What that means is that 'If the evidence establishes that the true relation was, and was intended to be, different from what is described in the document, then it is that relationship and not the document or the document alone which defines the contract'.[63] Applying these principles to the facts, the Court was satisfied that an employment relationship existed between the parties. No true partnership existed between Szilagyi and his assistants since they did not operate a common business for profit.[64] The parties' actual conduct further confirmed that Protectacoat had

[57] *Consistent* EAT/0535/2006 [57].
[58] *Consistent Group Ltd v Mrs Kalwak* [2008] EWCA Civ 430, [2008] IRLR 505.
[59] *Firthglow Ltd (trading as Protectacoat) v Szilagyi* [2009] EWCA Civ 98, [2009] ICR 835 [54] ('*Firthglow*').
[60] *Firthglow* [2009] EWCA Civ 98, [2009] ICR 835 [42].
[61] ibid, [52].
[62] ibid [53].
[63] ibid [56].
[64] ibid [63].

significant control over Szilagyi,[65] and that mutuality of obligations was implicit in their agreement.[66]

Together, the approach of Elias J in *Consistent* and that of Smith LJ in *Firthglow* marked a trend towards greater worker-protection that has since been vindicated by the Supreme Court in *Autoclenz Ltd v Belcher*.[67] *Autoclenz* concerned a claim by a group of valeters that they were 'workers' entitled to minimum wage under relevant wage protection regulations.[68] The valeters were engaged by the respondent company (Autoclenz) to provide car cleaning services. Although the contracts described the valeters as self-employed independent contractors and contained the usual rights to substitute and refuse work, the UK Supreme Court held that the claimants were workers for the purposes of the National Minimum Wage Regulations 1999 (UK). Delivering the sole judgment of the Court, Lord Clarke unhesitatingly adopted the wider notion of 'sham' advocated by Elias J in *Consistent*.[69] In his view, the *Snook* definition was 'too narrow',[70] and not the only route by which the courts may disregard a term of the written contract.[71] That employment relations are distinguished by unequal bargaining power justifies greater skepticism in assessing the genuineness of the written terms. Lord Clarke summed up this 'purposive approach' as follows:

> [T]he relative bargaining power of the parties must be taken into account in deciding whether the terms of any written agreement in truth represent what was agreed and the true agreement will often have to be gleaned from all the circumstances of the case, of which the written agreement is only a part.[72]

Autoclenz now stands as high authority for the proposition that a court may recharacterise a contract on the basis of sham analysis even if the conditions of *Snook* are not satisfied. It is a clear instance of substantive reasoning at work, where the Court readily departed from standard contractual doctrines (by admitting evidence of the parties' subsequent conduct and disregarding the signature rule[73]) in order to give effect to legislative policy. Alan Bogg has sought to rationalise such departure as a special *contractual* doctrine that is 'attuned to the distinctiveness of the personal employment contract'.[74] On that view, the identification of 'true agreement' in *Autoclenz* could be explained as a type of contextual interpretation based on an expanded view of the principles set out in *Investors Compensation*

[65] ibid [59].
[66] ibid [67].
[67] Davies, above n 54, para 10.31; *Autoclenz Ltd v Belcher* [2011] UKSC 41, [2011] 4 All ER 745 ('*Autoclenz*').
[68] Viz, National Minimum Wage Regulations 1999 (UK) and Working Time Regulations 1998 (UK).
[69] *Autoclenz* [2011] UKSC 41, [2011] 4 All ER 745 [29].
[70] ibid [28].
[71] ibid [23].
[72] ibid [35].
[73] *L'Estrange v F Graucob Ltd* [1934] 2 KB 394.
[74] A Bogg, 'Sham Self-Employment in the Supreme Court' (2012) 41 *Industrial Law Journal* 328, 331.

Scheme v West Bromwich Building Society.[75] That would involve 'a more aggressive form of contextualism in the context of personal employment contracts',[76] that allows courts recourse to evidence of 'how the parties conducted themselves in practice and what their expectations of each other were'.[77] By this means, Bogg sought to bring *Autoclenz* back within the fold of doctrinal (and formal) analysis but its effect is to elide the distinct processes of interpretation and characterisation with the risk of reducing the test of characterisation to one of parties' intention and suppressing the proper analysis of substantive, policy considerations.

Rather than force-fitting the decision within the strictures of contractual doctrines, *Autoclenz* is better defended on substantive grounds. The Court was not there concerned with the construction of contract per se but with the broader issue of avoidance.[78] The issue at hand was not simply what the terms of the contract meant, but whether the employer could legitimately devise a 'fake' self-employment to evade its statutory obligations. That inquiry necessarily requires the court to discern the parties' true agreement in order to establish if an evasive scheme exists in the first place, and (if it does) then to determine if the scheme is permissible having regard to the legislative policies. The latter is inevitably a normative inquiry which the court must undertake within the confines of legislative objectives.

VII. Trusts

Given the widespread use of the trust as an asset-protection mechanism, it is unsurprising that attempts are occasionally made to invalidate trust settlements as 'shams' devised to shield assets from creditors, former spouses and tax authorities. Increasingly, these settlements are structured as discretionary trusts, so that the settlor could be said to have no proprietary interest in the trust assets even if he is named as a potential beneficiary. In this context, as in others, the courts have employed the *Snook* definition of sham. A trust document is a sham if it is not intended to have the legal effects that it purports to create. A classic instance is *Abdel Rahman v Chase Bank (CI) Trust Company Limited*,[79] where the Royal Court of Jersey was prepared to invalidate a trust settlement that reserved significant

[75] ibid 336–39; *Investors Compensation Scheme v West Bromwich Building Society* [1998] 1 WLR 896. cf the argument of Bright, Glover and Prassl in the tenancy context that the *ICS* principles cannot explain the pretence 'doctrine' as they are only applicable when ambiguity subsists in the contractual terms: see Bright, Glover and Prassl, above n 25, para 6.36.

[76] Bogg, above n 74, 339.

[77] *Autoclenz* [2011] UKSC 41, [2011] 4 All ER 745 [30], citing Smith LJ in *Autoclenz Ltd v Belcher* [2008] EWCA Civ 1172, [2010] IRLR 70 [53].

[78] As Davies cogently observes, courts are justified in taking a more astute approach in tackling 'fake' self-employment arrangements as they are, in substance, attempts to contract out mandatory employment regulations: Davies, above n 54, para 10.43.

[79] *Abdel Rahman v Chase Bank (CI) Trust Company Limited* [1991] JLR 103 ('*Abdel Rahman*').

powers to the settlor,[80] because the settlor had 'exercised dominion and control over the trustee in the management and administration of the settlement … [and] treated the assets comprised in the trust fund as his own and the trustee as though it were his mere agent and nominee'.[81] The settlement was a sham 'in the sense that it was made to appear to be a genuine gift when it was not'.[82]

Unlike tenancy and employment agreements, trusts may be constituted unilaterally but that has not persuaded courts to adopt a wider concept of sham than that defined in *Snook*. Despite some dicta to the contrary,[83] the prevailing view appears to be that a trust that is prima facie validly constituted can only be struck down as a sham upon proof that the settlor and trustee(s) shared a *common* intention to mislead another,[84] although a reckless indifference as to the genuineness of the transaction could count as requisite intention.[85] Conaglen has defended the strict application of *Snook* in this context.[86] He argues that *Snook* shams are manifestations of a doctrine distinct from that of construction, which 'permits the court to step outside the normal process of construction, and to consider evidence of the subjective intention of the parties which show that the arrangements that they put in place were a façade or disguise'.[87] On this view, it is the intention to deceive that lies at the heart of sham reasoning.[88] For that reason, courts are justified to depart from the objective approach to construction and look, instead, to the parties' subjective state of mind.

This explanation has influenced the jurisprudence on sham trusts in New Zealand,[89] and one can see the obvious force of the suggestion that shams have much to do with deliberate attempts to present a misleading front. Nevertheless, it does not logically or necessarily follow that shams as defined in *Snook* bears the

[80] The settlement was stated to be discretionary but provided, inter alia, that the settlor may without the consent of the trustee appoint up to one-third of the trust fund and its income over a 12-month period; that the trustee could at its absolute discretion pay or apply the whole or part of the capital of the trust fund to the settlor or for his benefit and in so doing *shall* have regard exclusively to the settlor's interests; that the powers to invest, to change the law of the settlement, to delegate and to change trustees were all to be exercised either with the sanction of the settlor or in accordance with his instruction: see *Abdel Rahman* [1991] JLR 103, 140–46.

[81] *Abdel Rahman* [1991] JLR 103, 147.

[82] ibid.

[83] See, eg, *Midland Bank plc v Wyatt* [1997] 1 BCLC 242, 245; *Minwalla v Minwalla* [2004] EWHC 2823 (Fam), [2005] 1 FLR 771 [53]–[55]; *Carmen v Yates* [2004] EWHC 3448 (Ch), [2005] BPIR 476 [218]; *Ali v Bashir* [2014] EWHC 3853 (Ch) [26].

[84] See *Shalson v Russo* [2003] EWHC 1637, [2005] 2 WLR 1213 [190]; *A v A* [2007] EWHC 99 (Fam), [2007] 2 FLR 467 [38]–[40]; *JSC Mezhdunarodniy Promyshlenniy Bank v Sergei Viktorovich Pugachev* [2017] EWHC 2426 [150] ('*Pugachev*'). cf *Painter v Hutchison* [2007] EWHC 758 [114]–[115] where Lewison J confined the requirement for common intention to cases of bilateral trusts.

[85] *In re Esteem Settlement* [2003] JLR 188 [58]; *A v A* [2007] EWHC 99 (Fam) [52]; *Pugachev* [2017] EWHC 2426 [150], [435].

[86] M Conaglen, 'Sham Trusts' [2008] 67 *CLJ* 176; M Conaglen, 'Trusts and Intention' in E Simpson and M Stewart (eds), *Sham Transactions* (Oxford, Oxford University Press, 2013).

[87] Conaglen, 'Trusts and Intention', above n 86, 125.

[88] Conaglen, 'Sham Trusts', above n 86, 186–87.

[89] *Official Assignee v Wilson* [2008] NZCA 122, [2008] 3 NZLR 45 ('*Wilson*').

status of a 'doctrine' that is of universal application.[90] As we have just seen in the context of tenancy and especially that of employment, courts have been prepared to adopt broader notions of 'sham' where the context justifies doing so. While it is true that *Snook* shams would often be the most flagrant examples of illegitimate avoidances, it is not obvious that the *Snook* criteria are the only criteria relevant for detecting shams in all contexts. Nor is it always the case that an agreement or a term would be disregarded only because it does not reflect reality.[91] Ultimately, the question whether a transaction should be set aside as a sham is assessed not only by legal doctrines but also by the intensity of the substantive policy reasons relevant to the context.

For trusts, the key policy consideration that has shaped judicial preference for a restrictive conception of shams is the need to preserve commercial certainty. As Robertson J acknowledged in *Official Assignee v Wilson*: 'A court will only look behind a transaction's ostensible validity if there is good reason to do so, and "good reason" is a high threshold, since a premium is placed on commercial certainty'.[92] This 'premium' on commercial certainty is especially needed to protect two specific groups – the trustee and the beneficiaries – who would in all likelihood act in reliance on the trust. A formal, doctrinal approach to sham reasoning would protect honest trustees from liability,[93] as well as the beneficiaries' security of receipt.[94]

But whilst important, commercial certainty does not exhaust the policy considerations relevant to trusts law. An obvious countervailing concern is the need to deter abuses of trust structures, which in recent years has sparked the judicial recognition of 'illusory trusts'. In *Clayton v Clayton*,[95] the Supreme Court of New Zealand accepted (obiter) that a trust that is honestly intended by the settlor (and hence not a sham) may still fail as an 'illusory trust',[96] either because

[90] MacFarlane and Simpson, above n 35, 139.

[91] See the interesting Canadian case *1524994 Ontario Ltd v Canada* [2007] FCJ No 234 [20] where the Ontario Federal Court of Appeal held that an arrangement contrived to circumvent the strict rules regulating insurable audiological services must be regarded as representing the true economic reality for taxation purposes even though the arrangement was in fact a contractual fiction intended to misrepresent a legal relationship. The principle, Décary JA explained, is that 'Where a taxpayer has created a fiction and has lived by it, his fiction has become its real economic world, for better and for worse, plus GST'.

[92] *Wilson* [2008] NZCA 122, [2008] 3 NZLR 45 [52].

[93] This concern was, eg, implicit in *A v A* [2007] EWHC 99 (Fam) [79], [86] where Munby J emphasised that 'there is not a shred of evidence to justify a finding of "sham" against "four professional men"'. See also A See, 'Revisiting Sham Trusts: Common Intention, Estoppel and Illegality' [2018] *Conveyancer & Property Lawyer* 31, 36.

[94] As evidenced, eg, by Rimer J's reasoning for insisting on 'common intention' in *Shalson v Russo* [2003] EWHC 1637, [2005] 2 WLR 1213 [190]: 'One might as well say that an apparently outright gift made by a donor can subsequently be held to be a sham on the basis of some unspoken intention by the donor not to part with the property in it. But if the donee accepted the gift on the footing that it was a genuine gift, the donor's undeclared intentions cannot turn an ostensibly valid disposition of his property into no disposition at all. To set that sort of case up the donee must also be shown to be a party to the alleged sham.'

[95] *Clayton v Clayton* [2016] NZSC 29, [2016] 1 NZLR 551 [123] ('*Clayton*').

[96] Though the Court rejected the 'illusory' label since it has no value except to describe a trust that has failed: see *Clayton* [2016] NZSC 29, [2016] 1 NZLR 551 [123], [129]. See also *Pugachev* [2017]

the settlor had reserved so much power to himself that he could not be said to have divested sufficient control to constitute a trust, or the breadth of the powers vested in the settlor calls into question the irreducible core of the trustee's duties set out in *Armitage v Nurse*.[97] The question whether a trust fails on this ground is a matter of construction of the trust deed. So, unlike a sham, an 'illusory' trust is 'not about deception, but self-contradiction that is apparent on the face of the trust deed'.[98] In *JSC Mezhdunarodniy Promyshlenniy Bank v Sergei Viktorovich Pugachev*,[99] Birss J in the English High Court adopted this reasoning to invalidate several discretionary trusts. The significant features of this case were that the settlor was not only a named beneficiary under the discretionary trusts but also their protector. In his capacity as protector, he could exercise extensive powers,[100] selfishly for his own benefit, the effect of which was to 'allow him to retain complete control over the assets he had settled in the trusts'.[101] Consequently, the trust deeds did not have the effect of divesting the settlor of the beneficial ownership of the trust assets.

Pugachev is controversial as its correctness has been doubted.[102] Specifically, it has been criticised for suggesting that a trust may fail by reason of extensive settlor control even if the trustee remains accountable to the beneficiaries,[103] and continues to exercise real discretion in the administration of the trust.[104] Such an approach conflates the distinct concepts of power and property,[105] and threatens to unsettle even trusts that reserve wide powers to settlors for legitimate reasons.[106] But even if one accepts these criticisms as cogent, it does not necessarily follow that

EWHC 2426 [169]. This chapter will, however, continue to use the term as a convenient shorthand for a trust that fails by reason of the excessively wide powers reserved by the settlor.

[97] *Armitage v Nurse* [1998] Ch 241. See *Clayton* [2016] NZSC 29, [2016] 1 NZLR 551 [124]. The case concerned a dispute over the division of matrimonial property. A large part of Mr Clayton's property was settled under various trusts and Mrs Clayton sought to argue that these assets were 'relationship property' to which she was entitled under the Property (Relationships) Act 1976 (NZ). The Supreme Court disposed of the issue on the ground that the trust assets fell within the definition of 'relationship property' by reason of the general power of appointment vested in Mr Clayton. As such, it did not have to determine the true rationale of 'illusory trusts': see *Clayton* [2016] NZSC 29, [2016] 1 NZLR 551 [127].

[98] L Ho, '"Breaking Bad" – Settlors' Reserved Powers' in R Nolan, K Low and HW Tang (eds), *Trusts and Modern Wealth Management* (Cambridge, Cambridge University Press, 2018) 45.

[99] *Pugachev* [2017] EWHC 2426.

[100] The protector had the power to veto all major decisions regarding investment, distribution of income or capital and variation of the deed, had the right to appoint new beneficiaries, to appoint a successor in the event that he is barred by a (legal) disability from acting, and was free to remove a trustee who did not act in accordance with his wishes: see *Pugachev* [2017] EWHC 2426 [236]–[244].

[101] *Pugachev* [2017] EWHC 2426 [245].

[102] See J Davies, 'New Developments in Settlor Reserved Powers' [2018] *Conveyancer and Property Lawyer* 175; J Brightwell and L Richardson, '*Mezhprom v Pugachev*: Bold New Approach or Illusory Development?' (2018) 24 *Trusts & Trustees* 398.

[103] cf *Re AQ Revocable Trust* [2010] Bda LR 26.

[104] And so is not a mere agent or nominee.

[105] *Re Armstrong* (1886) 17 QBD 521, 531.

[106] G Hogan, 'Case Note: *Mezhprom Bank v Pugachev* [2017] EWHC 2426 (Ch)' (2018) 24 *Trusts & Trustees* 212, 214–15.

the case was wrongly decided. Rather, these doctrinal lapses point to the substantive reasons that underpin the decision. So, despite Birss J's attempt to couch his reasoning in formal (doctrinal) terms (by invoking the authority of *Clayton* and stressing the objective, interpretive nature of the inquiry),[107] his Lordship's interpretation of the trust deeds was ultimately coloured by the perception that the settlor had established the trusts principally to ring-fence his assets against creditors.[108] This context featured prominently in his Lordship's analysis of the settlor-protector's powers. In deciding that the settlor-protector's powers were personal (evidencing control) rather than fiduciary (negating control) in nature, Birss J was categorical that a court should not lend its assistance to an 'unscrupulous person',[109] who tried to conceal his beneficial ownership of property by using a trust deed to vest unfettered powers on himself as protector so as to defeat the claims of creditors.[110]

To sum up, the current English approach to recharacterisation in the area of trusts is marked by a discernibly formal approach to the sham 'doctrine', while a more intricate interplay of form and substance is observable in the nascent development of illusory trusts. A court confronting an alleged illusory trust will typically utilise formal reasoning as the starting point to keep faith with precedents and promote legal certainty but is willing to employ substantive reasoning to bridge the gap when it perceives existing rules to be deficient in deterring the abuse of trust structures as an avoidance device. Overall, however, judicial preference for formal reasoning would mean that substantive reasons are accorded only a subsidiary role in rationalising particular outcomes. In *Pugachev*, Birss J's attempt to present the outcome as an application of an exercise in 'construction' premised on strong judicial authority,[111] did not ultimately conceal the judge's concern for protecting creditors, but it is conceivable that the leaning in favour of formal reasoning may occasionally undermine a decision by obscuring pertinent policy considerations.

VIII. Financing Arrangements

Attempts to recharacterise financing agreements are typically made to secure priorities in the event of the debtor's insolvency. Although it is clear that such transactions may be set aside upon proof of *Snook* shams,[112] the 'internal' route

[107] *Pugachev* [2017] EWHC 2426 [166]–[168].

[108] There was evidence that the settlor had engaged the services of a consultancy firm specifically to defend his assets against Russian creditors and that the settlor's powers as protector were designed to be judgment proof: see *Pugachev* [2017] EWHC 2426 [23], [275].

[109] *Pugachev* [2017] EWHC 2426 [182].

[110] ibid [187].

[111] And such reasoning is therefore formal in appearance: see M Bennett, 'Trusts law – Form over Substance or Substance over form?' (Obligations IX Conference, Melbourne, July 2018).

[112] See, eg, *Re Watson* (1890) 25 QBD 27.

or 'construction' method is more commonly employed as parties entering into financing agreements *do* usually intend to perform the terms agreed.[113] In so far as this approach is understood as a process of objective interpretation aimed at discovering the 'intention of the parties', it is formal in appearance. In general, however, this approach has not (but with notable exception)[114] resulted in formalistic reasoning as English courts are often cognizant of the policy factors at play.

The leading cases of *Brumark* and *In re Spectrum Plus Ltd*, on the characterisation of company charges usefully illustrate this policy-informed process.[115] Both cases attest to the important principle that the categorisation of a charge is a question of law not dictated by parties' contractual labels. In *Brumark*, the Privy Council held that a purported 'fixed' charge over uncollected book debts was a floating charge as the chargor was at liberty to use the proceeds of the debts. The decision confirmed that contracting parties are *not* free to make whatever agreements they like.[116] *Brumark* was followed a few years later by *Spectrum Plus*. Adopting Lord Millett's exposition of legal categorisation,[117] the House of Lords held that a mislabelled 'fixed' charge over book debts was in substance a floating charge as the chargor could freely draw on the proceeds of the receivables. The parties' declared intention or label may be relevant but is not conclusive.[118] While the reasoning in both cases proceeded largely on a formal basis by identifying the chargee's control as the defining feature of a fixed charge, the Courts clearly also took into account policy factors militating against an exclusively contractual approach. In *Spectrum Plus*, Lord Scott highlighted the need to keep in mind the legislative imperative to preserve preference creditors' priority over the floating chargee in the event of insolvency as the common law develops the concept of 'floating charge'.[119] Likewise, Lord Walker observed, after noting the parallel with the lease/licence distinction drawn in *Street*, that there is 'public interest' in 'ensuring that preferential creditors obtain the measure of protection which Parliament intended them to have'.[120]

Transactions involving title financing are another fertile ground that breeds problems of characterisation. Hire purchase, sale and leasebacks and retention of titles are common examples of such transactions. Unlike cases on charges, the judicial approach to this category of transactions has sometimes been criticised for placing too much weight on parties' express intention (and hence formalistic).

[113] D Neuberger, 'Company Charges' in E Simpson and M Stewart (eds), *Sham Transactions* (Oxford, Oxford University Press, 2013) para 9.04.

[114] See *PST Energy 7 Shipping LLC v OW Bunker Malta Ltd* [2016] UKSC 23, [2016] AC 1034, discussed below, text accompanying nn 129–37.

[115] *Brumark* [2001] UKPC 28, [2001] 2 AC 710; *In re Spectrum Plus Ltd* [2005] UKHL 41, [2005] 2 AC 680 ('*Spectrum Plus*').

[116] Overruling *In re New Bullas Trading* [1994] 1 BCLC 485.

[117] *Spectrum Plus* [2005] UKHL 41, [2005] 2 AC 680 [141].

[118] ibid [80], [119], [141].

[119] ibid [98].

[120] ibid [141].

Welsh Development is a case in point. There, the English Court of Appeal had to decide if a complex receivables financing arrangement that was structured as a sale should be recharacterised as a secured loan. The Court upheld the parties' characterisation. In its reasoning, the Court reiterated the need to look at the 'substance' of the agreement but went on to locate 'substance' largely in the 'language' of the agreement.[121] Indeed, the deference to form seemed complete when Dillon LJ approvingly cited Lord Wilberforce in *Lloyd's & Scottish Ltd v Cyril Lord Carpet Sales Ltd* to the effect that '[it] would be a strange doctrine of "looking for the substance" or "looking through the documents" which would produce a contractual intention so clearly negated by the documents and by oral evidence'.[122] 'Substance' is therefore equated with parties' intention,[123] so their choice of legal category would (save in the rare case of a sham) generally prevail.[124]

Prioritising form over substance is not, however, formalistic or objectionable if there are good substantive reasons so to do. In this context, the main reason for respecting the selected form is the recognition that parties should generally be free to finance their trades through sales.[125] That this was a highly germane consideration in *Welsh Development* is evident in Dillon LJ's observation that:

> The crux of this point, as I see it, is that the parties were entitled to choose the way in which Parrot would raise finance. There was nothing illegal about it. It could be raised either by borrowing or by the sale of assets, whether goods or book debts.[126]

As such, a genuine finance sale would not usually be recharacterised as a loan simply because it has the economic effects of a loan.[127] Courts would only countenance recharacterisation if there are sound policy reasons to justify the reallocation of contractual risks.[128]

[121] *Welsh Development* [1992] BCLC 148, 161–62.

[122] *Welsh Development* [1992] BCLC 148, 168; *Lloyd's & Scottish Ltd v Cyril Lord Carpet Sales Ltd* [1992] BCLC 609, 615.

[123] See A Berg, 'Recharacterisation after Enron' [2003] *Journal of Business Law* 205, 218.

[124] Or, as Millett LJ summed up in *Orion* [1996] 2 BCLC 78, 85: 'The legal classification of a transaction is not, therefore, approached by the court in vacuo. The question is not what the transaction is but whether it is in truth what it purports to be. Unless the documents taken as a whole compel a different conclusion, the transaction which they embody should be categorised in conformity with the intention which the parties have expressed in them.'

[125] See also F Oditah, 'Financing Trade Credit: *Welsh Development Agency v Exfinco*' [1992] *Journal of Business Law* 541, 541–43. The commercial reasons that may justify a sale structure would include the trader's borrowing limits, its gearing ratio, whether consents are required for creating further debt or security, restrictions by way of cross-default or negative pledge provisions in existing debt instruments, whether off-balance results are desired and whether registration would damage the trader's credit.

[126] *Welsh Development* [1992] BCLC 148, 168.

[127] As Lord Devlin said *Chow Yoong Hong v Choong Fah Rubber Manufactory* [1962] AC 209, 216–17: 'If in form [the transaction] is not a loan, it is not to the point to say that its object was to raise money for one of them or that the parties could have produced the same result more conveniently by borrowing and lending money.'

[128] In *Welsh Development*, a relevant counter policy argument arose from the concern that sale structures with recourse could, as a form of off-balance sheet financing, render the trader's financial statements misleading and unreliable. Ralph LJ considered this argument but ultimately decided that

From this cursory account, it will appear that the judicial technique employed in this context is a prima facie formal one: the characterisation of a transaction is determined by construing the document to determine if its intended effects are consistent with the features of a particular legal category. In practice, however, courts do take into account policy factors that may favour one construction over another though such considerations are usually presented as subsidiary or supplemental justifications for outcomes derived by the process of objective construction. Often, this 'blended' approach would allow courts to adequately weigh and mediate divergent policy interests. Yet, the (often unconscious) subordination of substantive reasons implicit in such an approach may, on occasion, so stifle or obscure relevant social or economic goals as to render a decision insensible in its context.

A poignant example is found in the perplexing decision of *PST Energy 7 Shipping LLC v OW Bunker Malta Ltd*.[129] In this case, the owners of the *Res Cogitans* had contracted to purchase bunkers from the OWB group ('OWB') subject to a retention of title ('ROT') clause. OWB, in turn, obtained the bunker from other suppliers who physically delivered the bunkers to the vessel. When OWB became insolvent, the owners (fearing it might be liable twice over to both OWB and the physical suppliers) sought declarations that it was not liable to pay OWB the price of the bunkers. It argued that since the transaction was a sale subject to the Sale of Goods Act 1979 (UK) ('SOGA'), OWB could only maintain an action for price under section 49 SOGA if the property in the bunkers had first vested in the owners. On the facts, this condition was not satisfied since the property in the bunkers had been consumed without property having first passed to the owners under the ROT clause.[130] To avoid the awkward result argued by the owners (that they do not have to pay for the consumed bunkers), the UK Supreme Court recharacterised the supply contract as a sui generis licence to consume bunkers for the propulsion of vessels.[131] That meant, significantly, that the transaction was *not* a contract for the sale of goods to which the SOGA applied. However, while this preserved the seller's rights to sue for price on the sui generis contract, the decision is astounding in overturning the widely-held assumption that the SOGA governed sales of goods subject to ROT clauses. Given that ROT clauses are widely adopted on the (implicit if not express) understanding that the buyer could use, consume or sell the goods before payment is due, to exclude such contracts from the ambit

the redress of any such concern lies in the province of the legislature rather than the judiciary: see *Welsh Development* [1992] BCLC 148, 178–79.

[129] *PST Energy 7 Shipping LLC v OW Bunker Malta Ltd* [2016] UKSC 23, [2016] AC 1034 ('*The Res Cogitans*').

[130] A line of reasoning previously affirmed in *FG Wilson (Engineering) Ltd v John Holt & Co (Liverpool) Ltd* [2013] EWCA Civ 779, [2014] 1 WLR 2365.

[131] The Court reasoned that since the contract specifically contemplated that the bunkers could be consumed before payment was due without any property passing in the bunkers consumed, the contract did not meet the definition of a 'sale' under s 2(1) of the SOGA, viz, a contract by which a seller *transfers or agrees to transfer the property in the goods* to the buyer for a money consideration: see *The Res Cogitans* [2016] UKSC 23, [2016] AC 1034 [26]–[28].

of the SOGA is virtually to deprive the Act of all practical relevance.[132] Outside the SOGA framework, it is also uncertain how this new category of sui generis contracts would be interpreted.[133] Ironically, therefore, *The Res Cogitans* has, in vindicating the seller's rights, also greatly destabilised the law on contracts subject to ROT clauses. In large part, this unfortunate outcome is the result of an excessively formal analysis. 'Title fundamentalism',[134] combined with a narrow view of 'contractual interpretation', have the unwitting effect of excluding from the court's view the policies that underpin the historical development of ROT clauses. As a ubiquitous feature of modern trade, ROT clauses serve a useful function in facilitating credit financing by securing the seller's interests in the event of the buyer's insolvency. On that view, such clauses are a mechanism that reorders proprietary interests in the limited context of insolvency but were not intended to alter the nature of the underlying transaction as a sale, nor to prevent the seller from suing for price when the buyer is solvent.[135] Sales on credit that envisage the consumption of goods before property passes and payment is due have become widespread precisely because they strike a fair balance between the buyer's need for credit and the seller's need for security.[136] Against this backdrop, the recharacterisation in *The Res Cogitans* is puzzling: it is difficult to see why credit sales on ROT terms should be excluded from the SOGA when they do not offend the policies of the Act. Had the Court given more explicit consideration to the legitimate economic functions of the ROT clause, it might well have adopted alternative analyses[137] that recognise the transaction as a sale.

IX. Conclusion

At the heart of recharacterisation lies the question of self-determination: to what extent are parties free to prescribe the legal consequences of their acts by adopting particular forms and terms? The foregoing analysis demonstrates that English courts have largely addressed that question through a composite process of interpretation and evaluation. Construing the constitutive contract or document sets the stage for determining its legal effects, but its legal character is ultimately

[132] L Gullifer, '"Sales" on Retention of Title Terms: Is the English Law Analysis Broken?' (2017) 133 *LQR* 244, 259; KFK Low and KCF Loi, 'Bunkers in Wonderland: A Tale of How the Growth of Romalpa Clauses Shrank the English Law of Sales' [2018] *Journal of Business Law* 229, 247–48.

[133] Discussed in M Bridge, 'The UK Supreme Court Decision in *the Res Cogitans* and the Cardinal Role of Property in Sales Law' [2017] *Singapore Journal of Legal Studies* 345. See also Gullifer, above n 132, 256–60; Low and Loi, above n 132, 249–52.

[134] See, eg, 'the high degree of importance attaching to property matters in the law of sale': see Bridge, above n 133, 348.

[135] Gullifer, above n 132, 252–53.

[136] ibid 246–50.

[137] Eg, by implying the term that property in the goods passed to the buyer immediately before consumption: see Gullifer, above n 132, 260–61; Low and Loi, above n 132, 252–53.

determined by weighing competing values and social goals. But while English courts recognise the composite nature of the analysis, they have customarily placed greater weight on formal rather than substantive reasons with the result that the latter are usually considered more obliquely or incidentally. This chapter has argued that there is a need for more explicit articulation of policy influences in recharacterisation cases. That is not to abandon settled rules and doctrines, but it does mean that courts should intentionally and scrupulously examine the policy underpinnings of a particular legal category to decide if the parties' characterisation should prevail. The honest and open consideration of such factors is particularly important for developing new rules and doctrines (such as 'illusory trusts') or where recharacterisation threatens (as did *The Res Cogitans*) to unsettle a longstanding and widely adopted practice. Even in contexts where the rules of characterisation appear settled by reference to a particular concept or test (such as 'exclusive possession'), the concept or test would still have to be applied with acute sensitivity to the underlying social objectives. Finally, if recharacterisation is essentially a judicial response to improper avoidances, then the judicial weaponry would have to be flexible and responsive to context, so that a one-size-fits-all approach – such as a universal 'doctrine' of sham – that applies across diverse contexts would generally be inappropriate.

5

In Defence of Formalism

WILLIAM SWADLING

It is an increasingly common habit among some judges (and academics[1]) to dismiss without argument rules of which they disapprove as 'formalistic', 'technical', or even 'legalistic'. Instead, the reader is entreated to have regard to the 'substance' or 'reality' of the situation. The thesis of this chapter is that this appeal to substance over form must be treated with caution. Through the detailed examination of two cases drawn from the law of obligations, it will be demonstrated that, while sometimes valid, the distinction between form and substance can, when improperly applied, lead to both wrong results and a disregard of the rule of law.

I. Form and Substance Arguments

There are at least three types of argument which seek to differentiate form from substance. The first is historical, and concerns the long-abolished forms of action. It states that the form of action may bear little relation to the substance of the claim, and that the substance should prevail. The second is concerned with the form as opposed to the substance of the transaction, for example, leases dressed up to look like licences or mortgages masked as sales. Here courts do not allow the language used to hide a completely different bargain. As will be demonstrated, appeals to substance over form in both these cases is perfectly legitimate. A third sense, however, is where only rules of substantive law are in play. Where a rule of substantive law gives a result of which the judge (or academic) does not approve, it is dismissed as 'formalistic' or 'technical' and another rule of substantive law, one said to reflect the 'substance' or 'reality' of the matter, is adopted. It is this third sense of substance over form which will be argued is illegitimate.

[1] Birks, eg, once attempted to dismiss the argument that there is no enrichment at the claimant's expense when a thief steals money from his victim's pocket as 'technical': P Birks, 'Property and Unjust Enrichment: Categorical Truths' [1997] *New Zealand Law Review* 623, 654.

II. Forms of Action

The modern law is organised around the substance of the claim – contract, tort, company, property, and so on. But this is a relatively recent phenomenon. As is well known, until the middle of the nineteenth century, the common law was organised around forms of action.[2] These were formulae, sets of words, which, if substantiated by the claimant, brought him success in his claim. There were different forms of action for different types of claim. Crucially, the different forms of action had different procedural rules, some being more claimant-friendly than others. All were abolished at various points in the nineteenth century,[3] but, as Maitland astutely observed: 'The forms of action we have buried, but they still rule us from their graves'.[4] Take, for example, the law of restitution (including both restitution of unjust enrichment and restitution for wrongs), where recovery was, according to the most popular form of action, dependent on the implication of a promise or even a contract to pay.[5] A number of decisions, however, illustrate how form was not allowed to affect the substance of the claim.[6]

Most claims for restitution were originally brought using the action of debt. However, for procedural reasons,[7] restitutionary claimants preferred to sue using the more modern action of *indebitatus assumpsit* ('being indebted, the defendant promised to pay'), a species of the action on the case. So, for example, someone who paid money by mistake would bring a sub-species of *indebitatus assumpsit*, *indebitatus assumpsit* for money had and received, the pleadings alleging, first, that the defendant owed the claimant a certain sum because of money paid to the defendant on the claimant's behalf, second, that the defendant had subsequently promised to pay that money over to the claimant, and third, that the defendant, intending to deceive and defraud the claimant, was now refusing to do so. Of course, none of this was true in the case of money paid by mistake: the money

[2] See, eg, the structure of T Bullen, C Dodd, and C Clifford, *Bullen and Leake's Precedents of Pleadings and Rules Related to Pleadings*, 5th edn (London, Stevens & Sons, 1868).

[3] First, for personal (as opposed to real) actions, the Uniformity of Process Act 1832 (2 Will 4 c 39) imposed a single uniform process. Next, the Common Law Procedure Act 1852 (15 and 16 Vict c 76) removed the need to mention any particular form of action in the writ and at the same time removed the need to plead fictions. Finally, with the enactment of the Judicature Acts 1873–75 (36 and 37 Vict c 66)–(38 and 39 Vict c 77), it was only necessary for the claimant to plead facts sufficient to give rise to his or her cause of action.

[4] FW Maitland, *The Forms of Action at Common Law* (Cambridge, Cambridge University Press, 1909) 296.

[5] Which explains why the subject for many years went by the names of 'Implied', 'Quasi', and even 'Constructive' Contract.

[6] This has not always been the case. The worst example is probably *Sinclair v Brougham* [1914] AC 398, where it was held that it was not possible to sue on a contract implied by law unless a consensual contract to that effect would have been binding. This erroneous belief in the power of the forms of action was not finally dispelled until the late-twentieth century. Although the result in the case may well be justified in that a successful claim in unjust enrichment would have stultified the purpose of the ultra vires rule then existing, this was purely a matter of luck.

[7] Principally because in the action of debt the defendant was able to 'wage his law' whereas in the newer 'action on the case' fact finding was made by juries.

had not been received on the claimant's behalf but for the defendant himself; the defendant had never promised to repay the money; and the defendant had no intention to deceive and defraud the claimant. Yet the action was still allowed, the pleadings being acknowledged to be fictitious, a mere matter of form.[8]

Thus, in *City of London* v *Goree*,[9] (not a claim in unjust enrichment) *indebitatus assumpsit* was used to recover customary wharfage dues. The defendant objected to the form of action on the ground that he had not promised to pay the duty, but the Court held that 'it being agreed that debt lieth, a fortiori an indebitatus'.[10] All that mattered was that there was a debt – the promise was implied by law. Similarly, in *Lamine* v *Dorrell*,[11] a case of restitution for wrongs, *indebitatus assumpsit* was brought in respect of the proceeds of a tortious sale of debentures. To fit his claim within an action promissory in form, the claimant alleged that the defendant received the money from the sale as his agent. The defendant's objection that he sold them as his own was dismissed by Powell J:

> It is clear the plaintiff might have maintained detinue or trover for the debentures; but when the act that is done is in its nature tortious, it is hard to turn that into a contract, and against the reason of assumpsits. But the plaintiff may dispense with the wrong, and suppose the sale made by his consent, and bring an action for the money they were sold for, as money received to his use.[12]

The idea of the claimant 'dispensing with the wrong' later became known as 'waiver of tort', and, as will shortly be seen, gave rise to much confusion.

A similar appeal to the form of the action was famously rejected in *Moses v Macferlan*.[13] Moses endorsed over to Macferlan four promissory notes, made out to Moses by Jacobs, for 30s each in value, it being agreed that Macferlan would sue Jacobs for the money direct and not Moses on the notes. Macferlan did, however, successfully sue Moses in a Court of Conscience, courts set up for the speedy recovery of small debts, which refused to admit evidence of the collateral agreement between the parties. Moses brought *indebitatus assumpsit* to recover the £6 he had to pay Macferlan, who maintained that it was 'impossible to presume any contract to refund money, which the defendant recovered by an adverse suit'.[14] The argument was rejected by Lord Mansfield:

> If the defendant be under an obligation, from the ties of natural justice, to refund; the law implies a debt, and gives this action, founded in the equity of the plaintiff's case, as it were upon a contract ('quasi ex contractu', as the Roman law expresses it).[15]

[8] There are many more examples throughout private law. One was the allegation of finding in trover, which could not be traversed. Another was the fictitious grant of a lease of land so that actions to try freehold title could be brought in ejectment, thus avoiding trial by battle inherent in the writ of right.

[9] *City of London* v *Goree* (1675) 3 Keble 677, 84 ER 947 ('*Goree*').

[10] *Goree* (1675) 3 Keble 677, 678, 84 ER 947, 948.

[11] *Lamine* v *Dorrell* (1705) 2 Ld Ray 1216, 92 ER 303 ('*Lamine*').

[12] *Lamine* (1705) 2 Ld Ray 1216, 1216, 92 ER 303, 303.

[13] *Moses v Macferlan* (1760) 2 Burr 1005, 97 ER 676 ('*Moses*').

[14] *Moses* (1760) 2 Burr 1005, 1008, 97 ER 676, 678.

[15] *Moses* (1760) 2 Burr 1005, 1009, 97 ER 676, 678.

Once again, the form of action was not allowed to affect the substance of the claim.

Perhaps the most famous rejection of an appeal to form over substance came in the decision of the House of Lords in *United Australia* v *Barclays Bank Ltd.*[16] Interestingly, this was a twentieth-century case, decided long after the forms of action had been abolished. A cheque made out to the claimants, United Australia Ltd, was fraudulently endorsed over by United Australia's secretary to MFG Trust Ltd, a company controlled by the secretary himself. MFG presented the cheque to Barclays for collection and received the amount collected. In dealing with the cheque without the consent of United Australia, Barclays committed the tort of conversion. However, instead of suing Barclays, United Australia brought *indebitatus assumptsit* for money had and received[17] against MFG. This action, however, was discontinued before it came to trial, and MFG was now in liquidation. When United Australia later sued Barclays, the latter argued that the earlier claim against MFG involved a 'waiver' of MFG's tort and therefore a forgiveness of the wrong, which could not now be undone, even against a third party, Barclays.

The argument was rejected by the House of Lords. The language of the form of action did not reflect its substance, which was an action based on the wrong: there was no forgiveness of anything. As Lord Atkin explained:

> The action of indebitatus assumpsit for money had and received to the use of the plaintiff … was … supported by the imputation by the Court to the defendant of a promise to pay. The fiction was so obvious that in some cases the judge created a fanciful relation between the plaintiff and the defendant. Thus in cases where the defendant had wrongly sold the plaintiff's goods and received the proceeds it was suggested in some cases, not in all, that the plaintiff chose to treat the wrongdoer as having sold the goods as his agent and so being under an implied contract to his principal to repay … But the fiction is too transparent. The alleged contract … never was made and never could be made. The law, in order to do justice, imputed to the wrongdoer a promise which alone as forms of action then existed could give the injured person a reasonable remedy. But while it was just that the plaintiff in such cases should be able to recover the money in the possession of the other party, he was not bound to exercise this remedy: in cases where the money had been received as the result of a wrong he still had the remedy of claiming damages for tort in actions for trespass, deceit, trover, and the like. But he obviously could not compel the wrongdoer to recoup him his losses twice over. Hence he was restricted to one of two remedies: and herein as I think arose the doctrine of 'waiver of the tort'.[18]

[16] *United Australia* v *Barclays Bank Ltd* [1941] AC 1 ('*United Australia*').

[17] Given the abolition of the forms of action almost 100 years before, it is surprising to see claims still formulated in this way. However, the practice continues today, as, eg, in *Lipkin Gorman v Karpnale Ltd* [1991] 2 AC 548, 552, perhaps because litigants have no other convenient form of words to use, the language of damages being considered inappropriate.

[18] *United Australia* [1941] 1 AC 1, 27–28.

The fiction, Lord Atkin famously continued, should not affect the substance of the matter:

> These fantastic resemblances of contracts invented in order to meet requirements of the law as to forms of action which have now disappeared should not in these days be allowed to affect actual rights. When these ghosts of the past stand in the path of justice clanking their mediaeval chains the proper course for the judge is to pass through them undeterred.[19]

The substance of the matter was that the claimant had not excused MFG's conversion of the cheque by seeking to recover from it the proceeds it received. The tort had two alternative remedies. In choosing one rather than the other, the claimant was not excusing the wrongful conduct but relying on it.

The forms of action were a peculiarity of the common law. However, we also see a similar use of fictions to expand the law in equity. One famous example is the use of the language of constructive trusts. Take, for example, the case of a right transferred by mistake. The common law had no jurisdiction to order anything but the payment of its value: there was no ability to obtain specific restitution at common law.[20] However, courts of equity could order specific restitution by branding the defendant a constructive trustee for the plaintiff, who could then invoke the *Saunders v Vautier*[21] jurisdiction to petition the court for an order for the defendant to execute the 'trust'. However, as Brunyate explained, the constructive 'trust' was nothing more than:

> a remedial device by which a person can recover property to the present or future benefit of which he is equitably entitled. It is only by a fiction called a trust. The Court does not suppose that the constructive trustee has actually been holding or managing property for the cestui que use, but by a fiction it deems that he has been so doing, in order that the cestui que use may recover the property from him.[22]

This explains the famous statement of Pound that 'An express trust is a substantive institution. Constructive trust, on the other hand, is purely a remedial institution … [There is not] the substance of a trust'.[23]

Likewise, in cases where a defendant is sued for assisting a breach of trust or the receipt of rights dissipated in breach of trust, he is often described as a 'constructive trustee'. This is once again a matter of form, not substance. As Millett LJ explained in *Paragon Finance Plc v D B Thakerar & Co*:

> Such a person is not in fact a trustee at all, even though he may be liable to account as if he were. He never assumes the position of a trustee, and if he receives the trust property at all it is adversely to the plaintiff by an unlawful transaction which is impugned by the

[19] ibid 29.

[20] In the same way that the common law could not order the specific performance of a contract or the specific delivery of converted chattels.

[21] *Saunders v Vautier* (1841) Cr & Ph 240, 41 ER 482.

[22] J Brunyate, *Limitation of Actions in Equity* (London, Stevens & Sons, 1932).

[23] R Pound, 'The Progress of the Law, 1918–1919 Equity' (1920) 33 *Harvard Law Review* 420, 420–21.

> plaintiff. In such a case the expressions 'constructive trust' and 'constructive trustee' are misleading, for there is no trust and usually no possibility of a proprietary remedy; they are 'nothing more than a formula for equitable relief'.[24]

The obvious problem with such language is the impression it creates in the unwary that, despite this warning, the defendant really is a trustee, and that imposing 'constructive trusteeship' on him imposes the onerous obligations of trusteeship. Indeed, in *Re Montagu's Settlement Trust*,[25] Megarry J fell into this trap,[26] holding that a recipient of rights received in breach of trust could only be liable if there was a high degree of fault, conduct amounting to a 'want of probity'. He rejected the argument of the claimant that notice, constructive or imputed, of the dissipation was enough, on the ground that this was not appropriate to decide 'whether or not a person is to have imposed upon him the personal burdens and obligations of trusteeship'.[27] Of course, no such burdensome obligations were sought to be imposed; the defendant was not being sued for breach of trust. As Lord Sumption more recently said of the knowing recipient:

> His possession is … at all times wrongful and adverse to the rights of both the true trustees and the beneficiaries. No trust has been reposed in him. He does not have the powers or duties of a trustee, for example with regard to investment or management … It is true that he may be accountable for any profit that would have been made or any loss that would have been avoided if the assets had remained in the hands of the true trustees and been dealt with according to the trust. There may also, in some circumstances, be a proprietary claim. But all this is simply the measure of the remedy. It does not make him a trustee.[28]

Fortunately, Megarry J's thinking in *re Montagu's Settlement Trusts* is the exception, not the rule, with courts generally seeing through these equitable fictions.[29]

Why are such appeals to substance over form innocuous? So far as the common law is concerned, the reason why it was legitimate for courts to extend the reach of the forms of action by fictionalising various parts was that, because of a political compromise between the King and the barons, the common law early on put a brake on the issue of new writs. If the common law was to develop,

[24] *Paragon Finance Plc v D B Thakerar & Co* [1999] 1 All ER 400, 409. His Lordship is here citing Ungoed-Thomas J in *Selangor United Rubber Estates Ltd v Cradock (No 3)* [1968] 1 WLR 1555, 1582.

[25] *Re Montagu's Settlement Trust* [1987] Ch 264.

[26] So described by Lord Millett in *Dubai Aluminium Co Ltd v Salaam* [2002] UKHL 48, [2003] 2 AC 366 [142].

[27] *Re Montagu's Settlement Trust* [1987] Ch 264, 272–73. The requirement of a high degree of fault may well be justified, though for the reason that such claims are in fact ones for inconsistent dealing: see W Swadling, 'The Nature of "Knowing Receipt"' in PS Davies and J Penner (eds), *Equity, Trust and Commerce* (2017) 303–30.

[28] *Williams v Central Bank of Nigeria* [2014] UKSC 10, [2014] AC 1189 [31].

[29] See generally, WJ Swadling, 'Substance and Procedure in Equity' (2016) 10 *Journal of Equity* 1, 10–12. The exception is the erroneous notion that the constructive trust takes rights out of an insolvent estate with the result that they are not available for distribution to secured and unsecured creditors, as, eg, in *Chase Manhattan Bank NA v Israel-British Bank (London) Ltd* [1981] Ch 105.

if it was not to be stuck in a time-warp, a way had to be found to break the impasse, and that was the adoption of fictions. The tactic would not have worked, however, if the fictions could have been traversed, and it was that which led to the victory of substance over form. For equity, fictions were necessary to give the court jurisdiction to grant relief not otherwise available at common law. Once again, however, the use of fictions was not allowed to distort the substance of the law.

III. Form of Transaction

The law often gives protection to particular classes of persons to a transaction, usually those at some disadvantage in the bargaining process. In order to avoid that protection, the dominant party may insist that any document signed be dressed up to look like a non-protected transaction.[30] In such cases, courts are willing to bypass the 'form' of the transaction and look instead to its 'substance'.[31]

A well-known example comes from the law of mortgages. For centuries, courts of equity gave mortgagors an extra-contractual right to redeem their loan and recover their security. Moreover, this extra-contractual right could not be contracted away.[32] Unsurprisingly, mortgagees sought to evade this right by dressing the transaction up as a sale. The courts of equity, however, were not deceived, and would look to the substance of the matter, not its form.[33] So, for example, if a transaction was expressed in the form of a conveyance with an option to repurchase the subject-matter of the conveyance in a year's time, it would still be seen as a mortgage, with the mortgagor having a right to redeem even after the year had passed.

Likewise, the protection of the Bills of Sale legislation was held in *Re Watson*[34] not able to be avoided by a transaction being clothed with the appearance of a sale. Lord Esher MR said:

> I do not deny that people may evade an Act of Parliament if they can, but, if they attempt to do so by putting forward documents which affect to be one thing when they really mean something different, and which are not true descriptions of what the parties to them are really doing, the Court will go through the documents in order to arrive at the

[30] For the approach of the courts to this question, see generally *Welsh Development Agency v Export Finance Co Ltd* [1992] BCC 270.

[31] This is a different process to the divide between form and function seen in some legal systems. So, eg, a retention of title clause in a sales contract is seen in some jurisdictions as having the function of giving the seller security in the event of the buyer's default and so is subject to the rules on security interests, as for example happens under art 9 of the Uniform Commercial Code. This is not, however, the view taken by English courts and will not be discussed further here.

[32] *Salt v Marquess of Northampton* [1892] AC 1.

[33] As, eg, in *England v Codrington* (1758) 1 Eden 169, 28 ER 649; *Barnhart v Greenshields* (1853) 9 Moo 18, 14 ER 204; *Douglas v Culverwell* (1862) 4 De G F & J 20, 45 ER 1089.

[34] *Re Watson* (1890) 25 QBD 27. See also *Re Walden* (1878) 10 Ch D 76.

> truth. So when the transaction is in truth merely a loan transaction, and the lender is to be repaid his loan and to have a security upon the goods, it will be unavailing to cloak the reality of the transaction by a sham purchase and hiring.[35]

A modern example of this phenomenon comes from the law of leases. By statute, tenants of certain types of land are given a right to a fair rent and security of tenure. Not surprisingly, landlords sought to evade these tenant-sided rules by drafting their agreements as 'licences' rather than leases. Such a tactic was, however, decisively rejected by the House of Lords in *Street v Mountford*.[36]

Mr Street wanted to hire out two furnished rooms in a house to which he had a fee simple title to Mrs Mountford. Wishing to avoid giving her a Rent Act protected tenancy, he drew up a contract which described the agreement as a 'non-assignable licence' and contained the following term: 'I [the licensee] understand that a licence in the above form does not and is not intended to give me a tenancy protected under the Rent Acts'. No-one else was to share the rooms with Mrs Mountford and the agreed 'licence fee' was £37 per week. After moving in, Mrs Mountford applied to a tribunal to have the rent reduced. Mr Street unsuccessfully sought a declaration that the tribunal had no jurisdiction because Mrs Mountford had only a licence. Lord Templeman said:

> If the agreement satisfied all the requirements of a tenancy, then the agreement produced a tenancy and the parties cannot alter the effect of the agreement by insisting that they only created a licence. The manufacture of a five-pronged implement for manual digging results in a fork even if the manufacturer, unfamiliar with the English language, insists that he intended to make and has made a spade.[37]

There are many other situations where this sort of thinking is displayed. One comes from the law of trusts, where documents purporting to declare a trust are executed but the court finds it to be a sham. In *Midland Bank v Wyatt*,[38] a husband and wife held a title to a house beneficially as joint tenants. The husband set up a new business and, on his solicitor's advice, both husband and wife executed a document declaring that the title was henceforth held on trust for the wife and the two daughters of the family. When the claimant bank later sought a charging order against the title, the husband duly produced the 'declaration' of trust. DEM Young QC, sitting as a deputy judge of the High Court, held that it was a sham:

> I do not believe Mr Wyatt had any intention when he executed the trust deed of endowing his children with his interest in Honer House, which at the time was his only real asset. I consider the trust deed was executed by him, not to be acted upon but to be

[35] *Re Watson* (1890) 25 QBD 27, 37.

[36] *Street v Mountford* [1985] AC 809 ('*Street*').

[37] *Street* [1985] AC 809, 819. The conclusion of the House of Lords that the agreement constituted a lease is challenged by Birke Häcker on the ground that there was no certainty of term: B Häcker, '"Substance Over Form" – Has the Pendulum Swung Too Far?', this volume, ch 3. However, the point seems to have been conceded by the claimant, who argued solely on the basis that it was the intention of the parties which was determinative: *Street* [1985] AC 809, 816.

[38] *Midland Bank v Wyatt* [1995] 1 FLR 696 ('*Midland Bank*').

> put in the safe for a rainy day … as a safeguard to protect his family from long-term commercial risk should he set up his own company. As such I consider the declaration of trust was not what it purported to be but a pretence or, as it is sometimes referred to, a 'sham'.[39]

These cases are also innocuous, for the simple reason that one party to the transaction is trying through misrepresentation to evade the consequences of the law. The protection given to mortgagors, to tenants, and to creditors should not be able to be sidestepped by casting a transaction in a form which does not match its substance. A deliberate intention to deceive should not be countenanced by the court.

IV. Form vs Substance Disguising Substance vs Substance

We now come to the third sense of appeals to substance over form, though crucially no issue of form is now involved. Instead, an appeal to a rule of substantive law is rejected on the ground that it is variously 'formalistic', 'legalistic', 'technical', 'not in accordance with the economic reality', or one ignoring the 'substance' of the matter. This tactic allows the author to introduce a different rule of substantive law, one he or she prefers. We will look in detail at two cases where this has happened in England, the tort case of *Shell UK Ltd v Total UK Ltd*, and the unjust enrichment case of *Menelaou v Bank of Cyprus UK Ltd*, though there are many more. It will be argued that this is a misuse of the dichotomy precisely because no dichotomy is involved.

A. *Shell UK Ltd v Total UK Ltd*[40]

Oil-pipelines at an oil refinery were damaged through the negligence of the defendant's employee. Titles to the pipelines were held on trust for Shell UK Ltd and three other oil companies. Because of the damage, Shell, who had a contractual licence to do so,[41] was unable to ship its fuel through the pipelines to clients and thereby suffered economic loss. In English law, a claim for negligently inflicted 'pure' economic loss is generally barred, a rule known as the 'exclusionary rule'. An exception is, however, made for those who can link their loss to damage to

[39] *Midland Bank* [1995] 1 FLR 696, 707. Other well-known contexts include employment, contract, and taxation.

[40] *Shell UK Ltd v Total UK Ltd* [2010] EWCA Civ 180, [2011] QB 86 ('*Shell*'). See also the excellent discussion of J Edelman, 'Two Fundamental Questions for the Law of Trusts' (2013) 129 *LQR* 66, 67–76.

[41] Beneficiaries of trusts have no right to the physical enjoyment of the subject-matter of the right held for them on trust.

their 'property'. Thus, if Shell had held the title to the pipelines themselves, they could have recovered their economic loss. The question was whether the fact that it was held for them on trust meant that they had no claim.

At first instance, David Steel J held that this was fatal to Shell's claim.[42] His decision was, however, reversed by the Court of Appeal, which held that a 'beneficial owner' could sue provided the trustee was joined to the action. Waller LJ, giving the judgment of the Court which also comprised Longmore and Richards LJJ, said:

> Total, who has admittedly damaged the pipelines owned by UKOP Ltd and WLPS Ltd, submits that it owes no duty to Shell who has a contractual right to have its fuel loaded into, carried and discharged from the pipelines. If Shell were a complete stranger to the transaction that would be understandable but Shell is not a complete stranger. It is the (co-) beneficial owner of the pipelines and the contract to use the pipeline is only an incident of its beneficial ownership (albeit a necessary incident, since it is a co-owner of the pipelines with others who also wish to use it). On the face of things, it is *legalistic* to deny Shell a right to recovery by reference to the exclusionary rule. It is, after all, Shell who is … the 'real' owner, the 'legal' owner being little more than a bare trustee of the pipelines.[43]

Waller LJ said that it should not be relevant that:

> the co-owners of the relevant pipelines, for reasons that seemed good to them, decided to vest the legal title to the pipelines in their service companies and enjoy the beneficial ownership rather than the formal legal title. Differing views about the wisdom of the exclusionary rule are widely held but however much one may think that, in general, there should be no duty to mere contracting parties who suffer economic loss as a result of damage to a third party's property, it would be a *triumph of form over substance* to deny a remedy to the beneficial owner of that property when the legal owner is a bare trustee for that beneficial owner.[44]

The decision of the House of Lords *in Leigh & Sillavan Ltd v Aliakmon Shipping Co Ltd*,[45] which had denied recovery to a 'beneficial owner' of goods damaged through negligence, was distinguished on the ground that the trustee had not there been joined to the action.[46]

There are three problems which this appeal to substance over form conceals. First, the nature of the rights of a beneficiary of a trust do not amount to 'beneficial' or 'equitable ownership' of the subject-matter of the right held for them on trust. Second, where a claim is brought by a beneficiary against a tortfeasor who damages the subject-matter of the right held on trust, joinder of the trustee does not alter the liability of the defendant. And third, a direct claim by a beneficiary is only possible in certain special circumstances, none of which were present on the facts of this case. All are issues of substance, not form.

[42] *Colour Quest Ltd v Total Downstream UK Plc* [2009] EWHC 540 (Comm), [2009] 2 Lloyd's Rep 1.
[43] *Shell* [2010] EWCA Civ 180, [2011] QB 86 [132] (emphasis added).
[44] ibid [143] (emphasis added).
[45] *Leigh & Sillavan Ltd v Aliakmon Shipping Company Ltd* [1986] AC 785 ('*The Aliakmon*').
[46] *Shell* [2010] EWCA Civ 180, [2011] QB 86 [131].

i. Beneficial/Equitable Ownership

The decision of the Court of Appeal was predicated on the understanding that Shell, as the beneficiary of a trust, was a 'beneficial' or 'equitable' owner of the damaged pipeline. This is a common misconception. It is often said that the beneficiary of a trust has something called 'beneficial' or 'equitable' ownership of the trust 'property', whilst 'legal' ownership is vested in the trustee.

In truth, the rights of the beneficiary are of a different order altogether; there is no duplication of rights. Beneficiaries have no right to possession of the subject-matter of the right held by the trustee where it relates to a physical thing, or to the exercise of the rights held by the trustee. The rights of the beneficiary of a trust are instead to an account of the exercise of the rights of the trustee. They do not have some 'equitable' or 'beneficial' version of the rights held for them on trust. The point is illustrated by *Schalit v Joseph Nadler*,[47] where the landlord of a lease of land declared that he held his rights on trust for a corporation. The corporation later sought to exercise the remedy of distraint, one available to landlords for non-payment of rent by their tenants. The Court held that it could not do so and that the distraint was therefore tortious:

> The right of the cestui que trust whose trustee has demised property subject to the trust is, not to the rent, but to an account from the trustee of the profits received from the demise … The cestui que trust has no right to demand that the actual bank-notes received by the trustee shall be handed over to him or that a cheque for rent drawn to the trustee shall be indorsed over. What he can require is that the trustee shall account to him, after taking credit for any outgoings or other payments properly chargeable, for the profits received from the trust property.[48]

The same point can be seen in *MCC Proceeds v Lehman Bros*,[49] a case not discussed in *Shell*,[50] where bearer shares were held on trust for the claimant. As holders of the shares, the trustees had a right to exclusive possession of the share certificates. In breach of trust, they pledged the shares to the defendant as security for a loan. The beneficiary brought an action for conversion of the share certificates. The claim was rejected by the Court of Appeal. The trustee had a right to possession of the share certificates, not the claimant, and so the latter could not maintain conversion.[51] To the same effect is *Parker-Tweedale v Dunbar Bank Plc (No 1)*,[52] where a trust beneficiary was not able to sue a mortgagee for negligence in the sale

[47] *Schalit v Joseph Nadler* [1933] 2 KB 79 ('*Schalit*').

[48] *Schalit* [1933] 2 KB 79, 83.

[49] *MCC Proceeds v Lehman Bros* [1998] 4 All ER 675 ('*MCC Proceeds*').

[50] It was, however, cited by counsel for the defendant, Lord Grabiner QC.

[51] The Court also put paid to the heretical view of Sir David Cairns in *International Factors Ltd v Rodriguez* [1979] QB 351, 357–58, that the Judicature Acts 1873–75 (36 and 37 Vict c 66)–(38 and 39 Vict c 77) effected a 'fusion' of law and equity, allowing beneficiaries to bring claims at common law: *MCC Proceeds* [1998] 4 All ER 675, 690–91 (Mummery LJ), 698 (Pill LJ), 700–01 (Hobhouse LJ).

[52] *Parker-Tweedale v Dunbar Bank Plc (No 1)* [1991] Ch 12 ('*Parker-Tweedale*').

of mortgaged trust rights, and *Atlasview Ltd v Brightview Ltd*,[53] where beneficiaries of a trust of shares sought to bring an unfair prejudice action under section 459 of the Companies Act 1985 (UK). Such an action was only available to members of a company. Not surprisingly, the action was dismissed on the ground, inter alia, that the claimants were not members.

That the beneficiary does not have some form of ownership of the rights held for him or her on trust is also illustrated by the rule that they are unable to sue for their personal losses where the trustee commits a breach of trust. All they can claim is that the trustee reconstitutes the trust fund: 'the measure is the actual loss which the acts or omissions have caused to the trust estate'.[54] That the beneficiaries sue in a representative rather than a personal capacity is further illustrated by the fact that claims to reconstitute the fund can be brought by those only entitled to a future interest.[55] Even someone with a mere contingent interest can sue. It is probably also the case that a single member of a class of discretionary objects can sue. Although there seems to be no case-law on the point, it is undoubtedly the case that such a person can bring a claim to secure the trust fund and their rights in it. By the same token, a member of the class should also be able to bring a claim for reconstitution of the fund. Moreover, claims to reconstitute the fund can be brought by one trustee against another, which clearly demonstrates that the breach of trust action is not concerned with the protection of any 'ownership' interest of the beneficiary.[56]

Nor is the notion that the trust beneficiary has 'beneficial' ownership while the trustee has 'legal' ownership explained on the ground that a right previously held absolutely by the settler is subdivided when settled on trust.[57] Take the case of a self-declaration of trust of shares. When one asks what rights the settlor in his new capacity of trustee no longer has, the answer is, none. Prior to his self-declaration, and depending on his class of shareholding, he had a right to vote in company meetings, a right to receive dividends if a dividend was declared, and to a right to share in the dissolution of the company. After the declaration of trust, he still has those rights. Of course, he must now *exercise* those rights with the interests of his

[53] *Atlasview Ltd v Brightview Ltd* [2004] EWHC 1056 (Ch), [2004] 2 BCLC 191.

[54] *Fales v Canada Permanent Trust Co* [1977] SCR 302, 320 (Dickson J).

[55] *Clowes v Hilliard* (1876) 4 Ch D 413, 415 (Sir George Jessel MR).

[56] See generally, L Tucker, N Le Poidevin and J Brightwell, *Lewin on Trusts*, 19th edn (London, Sweet & Maxwell, 2017) paras 39.071–39.080, where the whole topic is discussed in terms of *locus standi*.

[57] This was the view put forward by Lord Diplock in *Ayerst v C & K Construction Ltd* [1976] AC 167, 177: 'Upon the creation of a trust … the full ownership in the trust property was split into two constituent elements, which became vested in different persons: the "legal ownership" in the trustee, what came to be called the "beneficial ownership" in the cestui que trust.' Some textbooks also take this view: see, eg, J McGhee (ed), *Snell's Equity*, 33rd edn (London, Sweet & Maxwell, 2014) para 21.002; G Virgo, *Principles of Equity and Trusts*, 3rd edn (Oxford, Oxford University Press, 2018) paras 1.4.7, 3.2. The notion of 'division' is also suggested in the language of 'asset partition' used by some to describe, inter alia, what happens when rights are settled on trust, eg, H Hansmann and R Kraakman, 'The Essential Role of Organizational Law' (2000) 110 *Yale Law Journal* 387. What is really meant, however, is that the rights in question are 'ring-fenced', ie, not available to claims by creditors of the trustee. Despite the language of partition, there is no 'division' of anything.

beneficiary in mind, but that is a different thing altogether. Another way of looking at it is to ask what rights the beneficiary now has. He has a right against the trustee that the trustee account for the rights he holds for the beneficiary's benefit. But this is a new right, not something that existed before. It cannot therefore be a product of any 'division' of rights.

We see the correct view of the matter stated in a number of Australian decisions, which hold that the rights of the settlor/trustee remain the same throughout, and that the beneficiary is given new rights to hold the trustee to account for his exercise of those rights. We are not, in other words, dealing with a zero-sum game, where the total number of rights before and after the declaration is the same. As McLelland J said:

> [There is imprecision in the notion] that absolute ownership of property can properly be divided up into a legal estate and an equitable estate. An absolute owner holds only the legal estate, with all the rights and incidents that attach to that estate. Where a legal owner holds property on trust for another, he has at law all the rights of an absolute owner but the beneficiary has the right to compel him to hold and use those rights which the law gives him in accordance with the obligations which equity has imposed on him by virtue of the existence of the trust. Although this right of the beneficiary constitutes an equitable estate in the property, it is engrafted onto, not carved out of, the legal estate.[58]

There is no subtraction of rights. The trustee has all the rights the settler had. The only difference is that someone else, either the beneficiary in the case of a person trust or the Attorney-General in the case of a charitable trust, has the power to compel him to use those rights in a certain way.

In *Shell*, it was the trustee's right to exclusive possession of the pipeline which gave them the ability to sue in negligence, both for physical damage to it and for consequential economic loss; the beneficiary had no such right, even in equity, and no appeal to substance over form could change that. However, on the view of the Court of Appeal, a declaration of trust of a right to land or goods will have the effect of increasing the number of persons to whom duties of care are owed by third parties from only the right-holder himself to what could be hundreds or even thousands of trust beneficiaries.

There is one final point. Not surprisingly, trustees, though able to sue for their own losses, are unable to sue for those suffered by their beneficiaries, for still the beneficiaries will have had no rights infringed by the tortfeasor. To meet this point Waller LJ said:

> It is well established that a trustee can sue in contract and recover damages for the loss suffered by the beneficial owner at any rate if the other party to the contract knew that the first party was a trustee: see *Pan Atlantic Insurance Co Ltd v Pine Top Insurance Co Ltd*

[58] *Re Transphere Pty Ltd* (1986) 5 NSWLR 309, 311, indirectly cited with apparent approval by Lord Mance in *Akers v Samba* [2017] UKSC 6, [2017] AC 424 [50].

> [1988] 2 Lloyd's Rep 505; affirmed [1989] 1 Lloyd's Rep 568, which Total did know in the present case.[59]

Although there is authority for the proposition that those holding contractual rights on trust can sue for the losses of their beneficiaries,[60] the cases are controversial in that the trust is one imposed by the court purely to avoid problems of privity, which would obviously be self-defeating if the trustee was unable to recover the beneficiary's loss. They do not reflect orthodox trust law.

ii. Joinder of Trustee Does Not Alter What Can be Recovered

It will be recalled that the decision of the House of Lords to deny liability in respect of a claim by a beneficiary of a trust in *The Aliakmon* for negligent damage to goods, a title to which was held on trust for the claimant, was distinguished by Waller LJ in *Shell* on the ground that the trustee had not there been joined to the action. The question is what difference this could possibly make. As already seen, beneficiaries of trusts cannot sue for their own losses consequent on damage to the trust *res*; nor can trustees recover such losses on the beneficiaries' behalves.

To understand the requirement of joinder, we must remember that the trustee is always able to sue in tort those who interfere with the right he is holding on trust. Moreover, in certain circumstances,[61] a trust beneficiary can bring an action in his own name in respect of the infringement of the rights held by the trustee. However, it is clear that the bringing of the action by the beneficiary in his own name does not alter the substance of the claim. It is the trustee's loss for which the beneficiary sues, and what is enforced are duties owed to the trustee, not the beneficiary. As Nourse LJ said in *Parker-Tweedale*:

> It is important to emphasise that when a beneficiary sues under the exception he does so in right of the trust and in the room of the trustee. He does not enforce a right reciprocal to some duty owed directly to him by the third party.[62]

The claim, in other words, is purely derivative.

Moreover, it is the derivative nature of the beneficiary's action which explains the requirement of joinder of the trustee, for if he was not joined, he would not be bound by any judgment given and free to bring claims of his own against the tortfeasor. As Viscount Cave LC has said:

> That an equitable owner may commence proceedings alone, and may obtain interim protection in the form of an interlocutory injunction, is not in doubt; but it was always the rule of the Court of Chancery, and is, I think, the rule of the Supreme Court, that, in

[59] *Shell* [2010] EWCA Civ 180, [2011] QB 86 [138].
[60] *Robertson v Wait* (1853) 8 EX 299, 155 ER 1360; *Lloyd's v Harper* (1880) 16 Ch D 290.
[61] Below, text accompanying nn 66–68.
[62] *Parker-Tweedale* [1991] Ch 12, 19–20.

> general, when a plaintiff has only an equitable right in the thing demanded, the person having the legal right to demand it must in due course be made a party to the action … If this were not so, a defendant after defeating the claim of an equitable claimant might have to resist like proceedings by the legal owner, or by persons claiming under him as assignees for value without notice of any prior equity, and proceedings might be indefinitely and oppressively multiplied.[63]

Indeed, the joinder rule only makes sense when seen as preventing double recovery.[64] If the beneficiary is suing for his own loss, as was the case in *Shell*, there would be no point in joining the trustee. As Lord Collins has said:

> The purpose of joinder has been said to ensure that they are bound by any judgment and to avoid the risk of multiplicity of actions … But joinder also has a substantive basis, since the beneficiary has no personal right to sue, and is suing on behalf of the estate, or more accurately, the trustee.[65]

The joinder rule is not therefore to be dismissed, as Waller LJ seems to do, as a mere matter of procedure or 'form'. Although there was no joinder in *The Aliakmon*, it would have made no difference had there been, for the claim was for the beneficiary's loss, not that of the trustee.

iii. Was this a Case Where the Beneficiary was Able to Bring a Derivative Action?

The final point to note is that it is not automatically the case that a beneficiary can sue in his own name in respect of an interference with the rights held by his trustee; he can only do so in special circumstances, those which, according to *Lewin*:

> tend to disable the trustees from suing (as where their acts and conduct with reference to the trust fund are impeached), or circumstances rendering it difficult or inconvenient for the trustees to sue, as where there is a conflict between their interest and duty.[66]

[63] *Performing Right Society Ltd v London Theatre of Varieties Ltd* [1924] AC 1, 14 (footnotes omitted). The same rule applies to shareholders' derivative actions, where it is well established that the company must be joined. As Chitty LJ explained in *Spokes v Grosvenor and West End Railway Terminus Hotel Co Ltd* [1897] 2 QB 124, 128–29: 'To such an action as this the company are necessary defendants. The reason is obvious: the wrong alleged is done to the company, and the company must be party to the suit in order to be bound by the result of the action and to receive the money recovered in the action. If the company were not bound they could bring a fresh action for the same cause if the action failed, and there were subsequently a change in the board of directors and in the voting power. Obviously, in such an action as this is, no specific relief is asked against the company; and obviously, too, what is recovered cannot be paid to the plaintiff representing the minority, but must go into the coffers of the company.'

[64] A proposition acknowledged in *Shell* [2010] EWCA Civ 180, [2011] QB 86 [141] itself, though seemingly not properly understood.

[65] *Roberts v Gill & Co* [2010] UKSC 22, [2011] 1 AC 240 [62] (footnotes omitted). Although the decision of the Supreme Court was made after judgment in *Shell* was handed down, the same point is discussed by Arden LJ in the Court of Appeal: *Roberts v Gill & Co* [2008] EWCA Civ 803, [2009] 1 WLR 531 [14], citing and approving the same passage of *Lewin on Trusts* which subsequently received the *imprimatur* of the Supreme Court on appeal. Unfortunately, the decision of the Court of Appeal, like many other relevant cases, was not cited in *Shell*.

[66] Tucker, Poidevin and Brightwell, above n 56, para 43.008.

As *Lewin* goes on to point out, there must be 'exceptional circumstances which embrace a failure … by the trustees in the performance of a duty to the beneficiaries to protect the trust estate'.[67] If such exceptional circumstances are absent, then only the trustee can sue. However, if he refuses to do so, and only a bare trust is involved,[68] which was the case in *Shell*, the beneficiary may bring a derivative claim. On the facts of *Shell*, however, there appears to have been no refusal by the trustee to sue. Nor were there any exceptional circumstances of the type just discussed. Once again, however, these important restrictions on the availability of a derivative action were sidestepped by an appeal to substance over form.

B. *Menelaou v Bank of Cyprus UK Ltd*[69]

The second case to be examined is the decision of the Supreme Court in *Menelaou v Bank of Cyprus UK Ltd*. Like *Shell*, it was a case in which an appeal to substance over form concealed nothing more than a preference for one set of substantive law rules over another.

The claimant was Melissa Menelaou. Her parents, Mr and Mrs Menelaou, were registered as proprietors of a fee simple title to a house known as Rush Green Hall, which title had been twice charged to the Bank of Cyprus to secure a loan of £2.2 million. The parents decided to sell their title and buy a smaller property, title to which, for tax planning reasons, was to be vested in Melissa, though on trust for herself and her two younger siblings. The parents found a purchaser for their title, who agreed to pay £1.9 million. Contracts were exchanged and a deposit of £190,000 paid by the purchaser to the parents' solicitors, Boulter & Co, some members of which were close family relations of Mr Menelaou. The parents subsequently found another property to buy, Great Oak Court. Contracts of sale were exchanged between the vendor and Melissa alone in respect of this title.[70] The agreed purchase price was £875,000, and a deposit of £87,500 was paid on exchange, the money being taken from the £190,000 deposit paid by the intending purchaser of Rush Green Hall and held by Boulters.

The Bank of Cyprus, which had also engaged Boulters to act for them in the transactions, later reluctantly agreed with the Menelaou parents not to insist on payment to them of the whole of the £1.9 million from the sale of Rush Green Hall, which in any event would have left £300,000 outstanding, but to allow £875,000 to be used to buy Great Oak Court, £275,000 to be paid to Melissa's older sister to

[67] ibid.

[68] A refusal to sue in the case of a special trust will not of itself entitle any beneficiary to bring a derivative action: *Sharpe v San Paulo Railway Co* (1873) LR 8 Ch App 597, 610; *Yeatman v Yeatman* (1887) 7 Ch D 210.

[69] *Menelaou v Bank of Cyprus UK Ltd* [2015] UKSC 66, [2016] AC 176 ('*Menelaou*').

[70] *Menelaou v Bank of Cyprus UK Ltd* [2012] EWHC 1991 (Ch) [4] ('*Bank of Cyprus*').

be used as a deposit on another property, and only the remaining £750,000 to be paid to them in partial discharge of the secured loans. In exchange, the parents promised the bank a charge over the new property for their remaining indebtedness of £1.145 million (plus accruing interest). Before receiving any charge, the bank released its charges over Rush Green Hall so that the two sale and purchase transactions could go ahead. The balance of the purchase price of Rush Green Hall was then paid to Boulters, who in turn paid £787,500 to the vendor of Great Oak Court, £275,000 to Melissa's older sister, and £750,000 to the bank.

Since the title to Great Oak Court was to be vested in Melissa, it was for her to execute the charge in favour of the bank. It was here that the problem arose, for Melissa knew nothing of the proposed charge and so signed nothing. Instead, her signature on the charge document was forged, possibly by her brother, and certainly with the connivance of Boulters. When Melissa later sought to have the charge removed, which application was unopposed, the bank counterclaimed for a declaration that it was subrogated in equity to the unpaid vendor's lien[71] of Melissa's counter-party to the contract of sale of Great Oak Court, and an order for sale. The claim for subrogation was made on two alternative grounds: first, that the money used to pay the £875,000 purchase price had been held on trust for the bank by Boulters, what will be called the 'orthodox' subrogation claim; and second, if there was no such trust, that Melissa was unjustly enriched at the bank's expense and the appropriate remedy to reverse that unjust enrichment was subrogation to the same lien, what will be called the 'unjust enrichment' subrogation claim.[72]

The bank's counterclaim was initially dismissed.[73] David Donaldson QC, sitting as a deputy judge of the High Court, rejected the orthodox subrogation claim on the ground that the money used to discharge the lien was in fact held by Boulters on trust for Mr and Mrs Meneloau, not the bank.[74] Although a trust of the proceeds of sale would have arisen in favour of the bank had the sale not had their authority, 'there was nothing to qualify … the straightforward position that in receiving the sale proceeds of Rush Green Hall Boulters was acting as agent for Mr and Mrs Menelaou and held all the monies for them alone'.[75] Indeed, given that Mr and Mrs Menelaou's debt to the bank was not discharged in respect of the amount involved, it is difficult to see how the trial judge's conclusion on this point could have been anything other than correct.

[71] Which itself arises by operation of law: *Barclays Bank Plc v Estates & Commercial Ltd* [1997] 1 WLR 415, 419 (Millett LJ).

[72] This, of course, assumes that subrogation is not necessarily a remedy for unjust enrichment. It also leaves unanswered the question of the causative event triggering the 'orthodox' subrogation claim.

[73] *Bank of Cyprus* [2012] EWHC 1991 (Ch).

[74] In all cases up to this point, the person successfully claiming subrogation to the security had at least been the source of the funds used to discharge the secured debt, as, eg, in *Butler v Rice* [1910] 2 Ch 277. Indeed, a claim to subrogation was rejected by the Court of Appeal because this requirement was not satisfied in *Banker's Trust Co v Namdar* [1997] NPC 22.

[75] *Bank of Cyprus* [2012] EWHC 1991 (Ch) [17].

As to the alternative claim for subrogation on the basis of unjust enrichment, the trial judge held that though Melissa had been enriched by 'the gratuitous acquisition of a fee simple title to [Great Oak Court], albeit subject to a trust in favour of her siblings',[76] the enrichment was not at the expense of the bank because it came not from them but from the vendor of Great Oak Court. It was not enough that but for the agreement of the bank to release its charges over Rush Green Hall, Melissa would not have received the right. Moreover, the decision to release the charges had been made before the receipt of the forged charge over Great Oak Court, so there was not even a 'but for' link. This problem was not overcome, said the trial judge, by appeals to 'economic or any other kinds of reality'.[77] Given his rejection of the subrogation claim, the trial judge did not need to determine the question whether to grant an order for sale.

His decision was, however, reversed by the Court of Appeal,[78] the Court declaring that the bank was subrogated to the unpaid vendor's lien for the sum of £875,000 plus interest (amounting to some £3,855 per calendar month),[79] payable when the title was sold. Only the second route to subrogation to the unpaid vendor's lien, unjust enrichment, was discussed, and only the question of subrogation was decided.[80] Floyd LJ held that though the trial judge was undoubtedly right to say that Melissa was enriched, and that the enrichment was unjust, he was wrong to decide that the enrichment was not at the bank's expense. There need be no transfer of value; it was enough that had the bank not agreed to release its charges over Rush Green Hall, the proceeds of sale could not have been used to pay for Great Oak Court.[81] The 'economic reality' was that the bank provided or released the money.[82] To refuse a remedy here, he said, would be 'mere formalism'.[83] Tomlinson LJ agreed that mere causality was enough to satisfy the 'at the expense of' requirement, saying that he could not see how the present facts could 'sensibly be described as anything other than a transfer of value between the Bank and Melissa in whose name the purchase of Great Oak Court was made'. That, he said, gave effect to the 'reality of the transaction', whereas the conclusion of the trial judge was 'pure formalism'.[84] Moses LJ likewise held that 'but for' causation was enough to satisfy the at the expense of requirement, though interestingly he said he had no need to 'invoke the somewhat fuzzy concept of economic reality, which, like reliance on common sense … sometimes suggests that the author knows the

[76] ibid [22].
[77] ibid.
[78] *Menelaou v Bank of Cyprus UK Ltd* [2013] EWCA Civ 1960, [2014] 1 WLR 854.
[79] See the judgment of Master Matthews in the subsequent proceedings for an order for sale: *Menelaou v Bank of Cyprus UK Ltd* [2016] EWHC 2656 (Ch), [2017] EGLR 8 [35].
[80] The question whether there should be an order for sale would need to be remitted to a trial judge. This was eventually decided in the affirmative: *Menelaou v Bank of Cyprus UK Ltd* [2016] EWHC 2656 (Ch).
[81] *Menelaou v Bank of Cyprus UK Ltd* [2013] EWCA Civ 1960, [2014] 1 WLR 854 [42].
[82] ibid [37].
[83] ibid.
[84] *Menelaou v Bank of Cyprus UK Ltd* [2013] EWCA Civ 1960, [2014] 1 WLR 854 [57]–[58].

result he seeks to achieve but is unable to articulate his reasons'.[85] In his view, Floyd LJ had amply demonstrated how the discharge of the liability of the vendors of Great Oak Court was at the Bank's expense, though seemingly without noticing Floyd LJ's own appeal to the 'fuzzy concept'.

The decision of the Court of Appeal was upheld by the Supreme Court.[86] Once again, only the second route to subrogation to the unpaid vendor's lien, unjust enrichment, was pursued. As with the Court of Appeal, there were multiple appeals to substance over form. Lord Clarke (with whom Lords Neuberger, who also gave a concurring judgment, Kerr and Wilson agreed) said that it was undoubtedly the case that Melissa was enriched by the receipt of the fee simple title to Great Oak Court and that the enrichment was unjust. As to the 'at the expense of' question, he said that it was not in dispute that if the bank had received all of the money from the sale of Rush Green Hall and then re-advanced it, it would be entitled to succeed, and it was 'pure formalism' to suggest that it made a difference that this did not happen. It was enough that the 'value of the property to Melissa was considerably greater than it would have been but for the avoidance of the charge and the bank was left without the security which was central to the whole arrangement'.[87] What mattered was not whether there was a direct transfer of value but a 'sufficient causal connection', which requirement was satisfied here.[88] As to the remedy sought by the bank, Lord Clarke said that subrogation to the unpaid vendor's lien would reverse Melissa's unjust enrichment by ensuring that the bank not only had a personal claim against her but also an equitable interest in Great Oak Court, as it would have done had the scheme gone through as planned.[89]

As with *Shell*, there are a number of problems which this appeal to substance over form conceals. Specifically, there are issues over: the identification of the enrichment; whether that enrichment, whatever it was, was at the bank's expense; the identification of an unjust factor; and the appropriateness of subrogation to the unpaid vendor's lien as a remedy to reverse Melissa's unjust enrichment.

i. Enrichment of Melissa

The first difficulty is that there is no clarity whatsoever in the judgments of the Supreme Court as to the precise way in which Melissa was enriched. For Lord Clarke, there was 'no doubt' that Melissa was:

> enriched when she became the owner of Great Oak Court, which she was given by her parents, albeit on the basis that she would hold it for the benefit of herself and her

[85] *Menelaou v Bank of Cyprus UK Ltd* [2013] EWCA Civ 1960, [2014] 1 WLR 854 [62], citing Lord Hoffmann, 'Common Sense and Causing Loss', *Lecture to the Chancery Bar Association* (15 June 1999).

[86] *Menelaou v Bank of Cyprus UK Ltd* [2015] UKSC 66, [2016] AC 176.

[87] ibid [24].

[88] ibid [27].

[89] ibid [50].

> two younger siblings. As it was correctly put on behalf of the bank, her obligation to pay the purchase price of Great Oak Court to the vendor was discharged.[90]

This passage is ambiguous, with Melissa's enrichment possibly being the fee simple title, her interest under the trust, or the discharge of her liability under the contract of sale. In Lord Neuberger's concurring judgment, Melissa is described as 'plainly' enriched 'because she received the freehold of Great Oak Court … for nothing'.[91] However, his Lordship went on to say that 'the relevant enrichment' may be Melissa's receipt of 'the freehold free of any charge, instead of receiving it subject to a charge to secure her parents' indebtedness to the bank'.[92] We thus have four possible candidates for Melissa's enrichment: the freehold; her interest under the trust of the freehold; the freehold free of a charge in favour of the bank; and the discharge of her obligation under the contract of sale.

The enrichment could not, however, have been the fee simple title, for that is not what she was ordered to give up. In the case of unjust enrichment, the remedy is inextricably tied to the enrichment, with the order of the Court being that the defendant give up that enrichment, either *in specie* or through the payment of money, to the claimant. Since Melissa was not ordered to give up the freehold to the bank, it cannot be said that the freehold was her enrichment. So too with her interest under the trust, which she was likewise not ordered to transfer to the bank. Nor could it have been the freehold free of any charge to the bank securing the parents' indebtedness, for the remedy to reverse that would have been the creation by the Court of a charge in favour of the bank for that sum. Thus, despite not being mentioned by Lord Neuberger, and referred to only ambiguously by Lord Clarke, the relevant enrichment, given the nature of the remedy granted, can only have been the discharge of Melissa's liability under the contract of sale. But that leads to the odd result that had the recipient of the title been a stranger to the contract of sale, there would have been no remedy against them.[93] Yet Lord Neuberger, for no convincing reason, said that the outcome would be the same in such a case.[94] Moreover, the complete disjunction between enrichment and remedy is once again demonstrated by the fact that were Melissa's parents to pay off their debt to the bank, this could in no way diminish Melissa's so-called 'enrichment' of the discharge of her own liability under the contract of sale.

ii. At the Expense of the Bank

Whether Melissa's enrichment was at the expense of the bank was the most contentious point of the case. In the typical unjust enrichment case, the defendant's

[90] ibid [20].

[91] ibid [62].

[92] ibid.

[93] On the facts of the case itself, it would render Melissa's older sister, who received £275,000 from the proceeds of sale to enable her to place a deposit on a house also liable, though for exactly what is difficult to say.

[94] *Menelaou* [2015] UKSC 66, [2016] AC 176 [71]–[72].

enrichment is at the claimant's expense because it was transferred from claimant to defendant. To take a very simple example, if A transfers title to a $50 note to B by mistake, B's enrichment is at A's expense because the right which A previously had is now vested in B. The difficulty is in seeing a transfer of anything from the bank to Melissa.

As we have seen, given the nature of the remedy, the only plausible candidate for her enrichment was the discharge of Melissa's liability under the contract of sale. It will also be recalled that the reason why an 'orthodox' subrogation analysis failed was that the money used to discharge this liability was not that of the bank but money held on trust for Melissa's parents. Despite this, Lord Clarke held that it was 'plainly' the case that Melissa's enrichment was at the bank's expense:

> The bank was central to the scheme from start to finish. It had two charges on Rush Green Hall which secured indebtedness of about £2.2m. It agreed to release £785,000 for the purchase of Great Oak Court in return for a charge on Great Oak Court. It was thus thanks to the bank that Melissa became owner of Great Oak Court, but only subject to the charge. Unfortunately the charge was void … In the result Melissa became the owner of Great Oak Court unencumbered by the charge. She was therefore enriched at the expense of the bank because the value of the property to Melissa was considerably greater than it would have been but for the avoidance of the charge and the bank was left without the security which was central to the whole arrangement.[95]

The obvious problem here is that we are once again thrown back on the difficulty that the enrichment is no longer the discharge of Melissa's liability under the contract of sale but the difference between the value of a charged and uncharged fee simple. Yet that was not the enrichment Melissa was ordered to give up, so that the necessary link between enrichment and remedy has disappeared.

Lord Clarke went on to say that had the bank received all the proceeds of sale of Rush Green Hall and then re-advanced the money required for the purchase of Great Oak Court, it would be entitled to succeed whether or not the re-advance was to the Menelaou parents or to Melissa. It was therefore 'pure formalism' to insist that it had to be the bank's money which was used to discharge the contractual liability before subrogation to the unpaid vendor's lien could arise.[96] Yet the fact that a transaction might have been structured in a different way is not normally something of which the court will take cognisance. So, for example, in the tax context, it is often the case that a more favourable result would be achieved for a taxpayer had he arranged his affairs differently, yet that is never a defence to a claim for tax due on the arrangements he actually made. Settlements can of course be undone, but only through an application for rescission, which, according to the Supreme Court in *Pitt v Holt*, requires a causative mistake so serious as to make it unconscionable to refuse relief.[97] Yet, as will be seen below, it is not even possible to say that the bank made a mistake.

[95] ibid [24].

[96] ibid [33], endorsing the view of Tomlinson LJ in the Court of Appeal (*Menelaou v Bank of Cyprus UK Ltd* [2013] EWCA 1960, [2014] 1 WLR 854 [57]–[58]).

[97] *Pitt v Holt* [2013] UKSC 26, [2013] 2 AC 108 [128] ('*Pitt*').

Moreover, the simple 'but for' test adopted by Lord Clarke captures too much. It would, for example, cover any increase in the value of the fee simple received by Melissa, and any profits she might have made by letting it out. Indeed, on the Court's reasoning, even if the charge had been validly granted, a claim to be subrogated to the unpaid vendor's lien would still succeed because the bank's release of the charge would still have been a 'but for' cause of Melissa's enrichment. Indeed, it is easy to imagine hypothetical examples of 'but for' enrichments where no-one would wish to allow a claim. Oft-cited cases are the owner of a rare stamp who mistakenly destroys it, the consequence of which is a rise in the value of the defendant's same type of stamp, the apartment owner who mistakenly leaves his heating on whilst on holiday and thereby heats his upstairs neighbour's flat, and the landowner who mistakenly cuts down trees on his own land, thereby improving the views of his neighbour.[98] All involve 'causative enrichments', yet it is doubtful that even this Supreme Court would have allowed claims in such cases. Appeals to substance over form gives us no guidance why these claims would be denied while that in *Menelaou* succeeded.

iii. Unjust Factor

As we have seen, there was no discussion of the precise reason why Melissa's enrichment was unjust in the Court of Appeal; it was simply seen as self-evident. In the Supreme Court, the point was finally addressed, albeit only briefly, with Lord Clarke talking in terms of both mistake and failure of basis.[99]

However, neither mistake nor failure of basis work on the facts. When the bank released the charges, they made no mistake. They instead made a misprediction as to the occurrence of a future event, viz, that they would be granted a charge over the title to Great Oak Court. However, as the Privy Council made clear in *Dextra Bank & Trust Company Ltd v Bank of Jamaica*,[100] and confirmed in the decision of the Supreme Court in *Pitt*,[101] mispredictions do not count as unjust factors. The reason is that they point to no false data in the claimant's head, no vitiation of

[98] See the examples given by Lord Reed in the subsequent case of *Investment Trust Companies v HMRC* [2017] UKSC 29, [2018] AC 275 [53]–[58] ('*Investment Trust Companies*'), discussing the notion of 'incidental benefits'. Although this decision held that the 'at the expense of' requirement was not satisfied by a mere but for test of causation, and restored the need for a direct transfer of value from claimant to defendant, *Menelaou* was not overruled, no doubt because counsel did not ask the Court to do so. Instead, the case was said to involve a series of co-ordinated transactions which were equivalent to a direct transfer: *Investment Trust Companies* [2017] UKSC 29, [2018] AC [61]–[66]. Exactly how that was the case, beyond the fact that the transactions were but for causally related, and, more importantly, how it justified the result, was not, unfortunately, explained.

[99] *Menelaou* [2015] UKSC 66, [2016] AC 176 [21]–[22]. Lord Neuberger spoke of Melissa's enrichment, which at this point is described as the 'receipt of the freehold uncharged instead of subject to the charge', being unjust because she received it as a gift from her parents. This, however, identifies no unjust factor at all: *Menelaou* [2015] UKSC 66, [2016] AC 176 [69]–[71].

[100] *Dextra Bank & Trust Company Ltd v Bank of Jamaica* [2001] UKPC 50, [2002] 1 All ER (Comm) 193 [29].

[101] *Pitt* [2013] UKSC 26, [2013] 2 AC 108 [104].

consent in the decision-making process leading up to transfer. That was undoubtedly the case here. Failure of basis fares no better, for the basis has to be found in the agreement between claimant and defendant,[102] and Melissa of course knew nothing of her parents promising the bank a charge over the title. Although there could be said to be a failure of basis viz a viz her parents, there was none as regards Melissa.

iv. Remedies

The usual response to a successful claim in unjust enrichment is for the court to order the defendant to pay the value of the enrichment to the claimant. Lord Clarke would have been happy to make such an award had it been sought, though subject to the qualification put forward by Lord Neuberger,[103] that 'in so far as the quantification would result in an unfair or oppressive sum, the court could adjust the sum to avoid any unfairness or oppression'.[104] Lord Neuberger, by contrast, had misgivings about subjecting Melissa to a personal claim for £875,000, the reason being that the freehold might later decline in value.[105] To him, it was 'hard to identify a more appropriate remedy' than subrogation to the unpaid vendor's lien because it 'would accord to the bank, and impose on Melissa, a right very similar to, although rather less in value than, that which the bank should have had'.[106]

The approach of both Lord Clarke and Lord Neuberger to this issue is problematic in two respects. First, it is difficult to see how any personal award could be adjusted to avoid 'unfairness or oppression'. No guidance is given as to how this might be done and it seems illegitimate to deny a deserving claimant a remedy on the ground of hardship to the defendant. It is certainly not something encountered elsewhere in the law of unjust enrichment. Although a defendant might have a defence of change of position, the mere fact that a successful claim might be unfair or oppressive is simply irrelevant. Second, Lord Neuberger's reference to the value of the freehold demonstrates that he is here seeing the enrichment as the freehold, but, as noted above, that cannot be right, for it once again breaks completely the indissoluble link between enrichment and remedy. Moreover, it goes against his Lordship's own preference at a different point in his judgment for seeing Melissa's enrichment as the (equally untenable) value of the freehold free of the charge in favour of Melissa's parents.[107]

[102] *Guardian Ocean Cargoes Ltd v Banco de Brasil SA* [1991] 2 Lloyd's Rep 68.
[103] *Menelaou* [2015] UKSC 66, [2016] AC 176 [81].
[104] ibid [54].
[105] Lords Kerr and Wilson preferred to leave the question of any personal claim against Melissa open: *Menelaou* [2015] UKSC 66, [2016] AC 176 [141].
[106] *Menelaou* [2015] UKSC 66, [2016] AC 176 [79].
[107] ibid [71].

V. Conclusion

It has been shown that there are at least three senses of 'form and substance' known to our law. Whilst looking through form to substance is perfectly legitimate where questions of the form of action or the form of transaction are concerned, it is inappropriate for judges to invoke this language when confronted with arguments over substantive law. As both *Shell* and *Menelaou* illustrate, judicial appeals to form and substance in this third context can lead to wrong decisions being made. Simply describing a rule as 'formalistic', 'technical' or 'legalistic' provides no guidance. It is nothing more than a rhetorical device allowing judges to summarily dismiss settled rules of substantive law, whilst at the same time substituting new and generally vaguer rules without the need to articulate reasons why the old rules are unsatisfactory or the new ones better. This is not to say that judges should not develop the common law. It is instead a criticism of their method, more particularly, that it defies the rule of law, which, at the very least, requires that formalism, which in this context means the application of rules rather than judicial discretion, and the articulation of reasons for decisions, be defended. Something more is required when a rule is to be dispensed with than its condemnation as 'formalistic'.

6

Private Law and the Form of Reasons

ROBERT STEVENS

"Art is nothing without form"

Gustave Flaubert

I. Form Before Substance

Tolstoy's *War and Peace* could not have been a sonnet. *Hey Jude* by Lennon and McCartney could not have been a five-act opera. The form of something controls what its substance can be.

This is true in law in general, and of private law in particular. Its form dictates the kinds of substantive reasons that can justify it.

We lose sight of the distinctiveness of private law, and of what justifies it, because of the way in which we are taught it. Perhaps it is a peculiarity of common law systems and its causes of action to see law as a system of liability spells, with defences being a set of counter chants. Invoke the right words and the judge will make the order. The most extreme form of this liability-spells phenomenon is found in the area of the 'economic' torts, that I first studied 25 years ago. Being vaguely on the side of the workers, I had chosen to study 'Labour Law' as one of my options on the Oxford Jurisprudence BA. In order to understand the various statutory immunities for trade unions from civil action in trade disputes (and the withdrawal of those immunities where the union has failed to take various procedural steps such as ballots) it is first necessary to understand the economic torts. My regular tutor in 'Tort Law' (sic) did not teach the area, and so I was sent to a different tutor at another college. I was then presented with reading lists of staggering length, and expected to learn by rote the various formulae for relief that there were (and are).

These formulae seemed to have no rhyme nor reason to them. In this they resembled other areas of law that I had been taught, such as equitable estoppel and constructive trusts, where the student was expected to take a leap of faith, accept that the rules existed, and then through a feat of memory remember the case names that stood for each element of each separate magic spell. Back then, being less world-weary and with a better memory than now, I happily complied with the task expected of me. Around two weeks after the exams had taken place, however, most of what I had forced into my skull through an effort of will had disappeared.

The general approach in reasoning about how these liability formulae *ought* to work was, and largely still is, to throw at an issue all the reasons one could think of in favour or against a particular result in the hope that one or more of them might stick, much as does a weak advocate in court. So, holding the defendant liable would reduce the incidence of this kind of thing in the future, or an expansion of liability might cause defendants to overreact inhibiting certain kinds of useful activity and so on. The advantage of this kind of approach is that it does not require the student (or scholar) to delve very deep into any particular 'purist' theory of justice, but instead has the exciting quality of leaving every possible rational reason for or against a result in play.

In this chapter, I shall argue in favour of a more structured, or formal, method for understanding private law and the kinds of reasons that can justify the various rights, privileges, powers and immunities that make it up. It is in three unequal parts.

First, I shall consider the nature of private law, and argue that the civil recourse, the ability to sue, is not central to it. Rights are.

Secondly, I shall argue, with examples, the main proposition that the kind of reasons that can justify the rules of private law must be of the requisite form.

Thirdly, in the longest part, I shall seek to establish that the predominant academic approach to the law of restitution does not conform with the required form of justifications, and that this has led the courts, in England but not Australia, into error.

II. Rights and Powers, Duties and Liabilities

Professor Weinrib, who has done more than anyone to attempt to restore formalism to its proper place in private law, identifies 'the basic feature of private law [as being]: a particular plaintiff sues a particular defendant'.[1] Similarly, Professors John Goldberg and Ben Zipursky have sought to elevate civil recourse, the power to sue, into being a theory of the law of torts specifically, and perhaps private law in general.[2] This emphasis on civil recourse is mistaken.

First, and most obviously, civil recourse is not confined to private law. There is much litigation by individuals to enforce public duties, for example, where a

[1] E Weinrib, *The Idea of Private law* (Oxford, Oxford University Press, rev edn, 2012) 63.

[2] See, eg, BC Zipursky, 'Rights, Wrongs and Recourse in the Law of Torts' (1998) 51 *Vanderbilt Law Review* 1; JCP Goldberg and BC Zipursky, 'Seeing Tort Law from the Internal Point of View: Holmes and Hart on Legal Duties' (2006) 75 *Fordham Law Review* 1563.

public body's decision is subject to judicial review. In practice, much of public law concerns a particular claimant suing a particular defendant.

Second, the duties of private law are not dependent upon their enforceability (although enforceability is dependent upon there being pre-existing duties).

This may be shown by the many unenforceable private law duties that there are, and their legal consequences. So, under the Statute of Frauds 1677 (29 Cha 2 c 3), 'noe action shall be brought … unlesse the Agreement upon which such Action shall be brought or some Memorandum or Note thereof shall be in Writeing'.[3] One way of showing that the *obligations* created by agreements that do not fulfil this formality requirement exist as a matter of law despite the inability to enforce them, is the effect of performance. Ordinarily, a benefit that is conferred for no reason may be recovered, the classic example being a mistaken payment. Where a benefit is conferred under an unenforceable contract, whether the payment of a sum of money or another kind of benefit, it cannot be recovered, unless the condition under which it is earned under the bargain is not satisfied. In other words, the conditions for restitution are identical for enforceable and unenforceable agreements. The recipient's enrichment is justified by the valid, but unenforceable, agreement into which the parties have entered. Similarly, a third party who procures the breach of an unenforceable contract is liable for a tort under the principle in *Lumley v Gye*,[4] which again shows that the unenforceable contract is not a nullity. Recourse is also not a necessary feature of the duties within the law of torts. Those with special immunities from suit, such as the Queen in the UK, the Federal Government in the US, or the postal service in Australia,[5] still owe the same duties as others and this has legal consequences, even though they cannot be sued.

Even if we closed all the courts, and civil recourse were completely abolished, this would not alter the existence of private law and its duties. The position would then be analogous to that which currently exists in public international law, which imposes certain duties upon states to act in certain ways, but where enforceable redress is not available where they do not comply. Where recourse is missing, the *moral* imperative of obeying the law is, if anything, stronger. If the law is not respected it loses its ability to act as a method of guidance. Absent recourse, our only way of encouraging others to obey the law is to obey it ourselves.

If it is not civil recourse that differentiates private from public law, what does? One common answer is that public law concerns the relationship between citizen

[3] Section 4. The Statute of Frauds has far more significance in the US than in England. In the US, it continues to apply to contracts for the sale of goods with a value over US$500 (Uniform Commercial Code § 2-201). In England, whilst the requirement of form still applies to contracts of guarantee, it was otherwise largely repealed by the Law Reform (Enforcement of Contracts) Act 1954 (UK). Although there are still formalities requirements in Australian states (see, eg, Instruments Act 1958 (Vic), s 126) the Statute of Frauds (amended) itself only lives on in Western Australia.

[4] *Lumley v Gye* (1853) 2 El & Bl 216, 118 ER 749.

[5] Australian Postal Corporation Act 1989 (Cth), s 34(1).

and state, whereas private law concerns the relationships between individuals. On this approach, the duty of a police officer not to detain me against my will is a matter of public law, the duty of a private citizen not to commit the crime of murdering another is part of private law. The tortious liability of public bodies would belong in books on public law on this approach (and some public lawyers do indeed seem to think this is part of their subject).[6]

An alternative, and it is suggested more profitable, distinction is to look at the *form* of duties created. The criminal law duties not to commit murder, engage in insider dealing or break the speed limit are, in an important sense, public duties. This is not because they do not concern the interests of others (clearly the duty not to commit murder exists because of the interests of others in not being killed). Almost all legal duties, public or private, exist because of the interests of other people. Rather they are archetypal public duties because they are not owed to identifiable individuals who have control over those duties. This control does not take the form of the ability to enforce them. There are public prosecutors capable of enforcing sanctions for the breach of criminal law duties, but they are not the right-holders. In fact, there is no individual who can either consent to the non-performance of the duty ('it is ok for you to commit insider trading today') or to release the obligor from duty altogether ('you have permanent leave to park wherever you like on the streets of Melbourne').

Private law duties by contrast are distinguished by the fact that at the other end of the duty is an individual with control over it. Right-holders can consent to another walking on his land, punching him on the nose, calling him an axe murderer, or to the late delivery of the goods he has contracted to be carried. If they are owed sums of money they may release the debtor altogether from fulfilling his obligation.

It is in this sense that private law is distinct. It is the area of law where individuals have control over the duties owed to them. A *common* additional form of that control is the ability to sue to enforce them, but as we have seen this is not a defining feature. Where an individual has such control, they have a 'claim-right', but the prefix 'claim' to describe rights 'properly so-called' was an unfortunate choice by Hohfeld.

A nice illustration of this formal distinction between private and public law is the difference between private and public nuisance. Private nuisance is a (private) wrong in relation to a right to land. Those whose reasonable enjoyment of their right to land is disturbed suffer a tort. It is a private wrong because the right-holder (the landowner) can consent to the activity, so that no wrong is thereby committed. Public nuisance is a public wrong committed by impacting upon the 'comfort and convenience' of the public. A classic example is the unauthorised obstruction

[6] See, eg, P Craig, *Administrative Law*, 7th edn (Sweet & Maxwell, London, 2012) ch 30.

of the highway. There is no individual who can consent to conduct of this kind so as to prevent it from being wrongful. Private nuisance, like private law generally, has no standing requirements to determine who can sue. Private law has a general principle of privity that has nothing specifically to do with contract law. Right-holders are those who can sue and, unlike in public law, it does not matter whether they have any interest in the outcome (as, for example, a trustee usually will not). Public nuisance, like public law more generally, has standing requirements to restrict the class of the public who can bring an action, in this case confined to those who suffer 'special damage'.

The account given above is sometimes called a 'choice' theory of rights.[7] This is often contrasted, and seen as being in competition with, an 'interest' theory of rights. In fact, we are just using 'rights' in two different senses, and one is no more correct than the other.[8]

So, sometimes, as above, we use rights as conclusions. To say 'Freda has a legal (claim-) right that Barry does not do X' is a conclusion, not a reason for the duty Barry is under. The one and only necessary and sufficient reason why such a right exists as a matter of the positive law is that the relevant authority has posited that rule. That authority (a legislature or court) may have done so for a good reason, a bad one, or no reason at all. The distinction between private and public duties is not based upon the underlying reason for the duties they create (which in some cases may be the same) but rather upon their *form*.

On other occasions, we use 'rights' not as conclusions but as a term for particular kinds of reasons that feature other people. So, when we refer to a 'right to privacy' we are referring to an interest that individuals have that may provide a justification for the imposition of a duty on others. Rights in this sense are the start of the analysis, not its conclusion. Does my right to privacy entail the conclusion that you are under a duty not to publish the truth about my disgusting personal habits, or does your right to freedom of speech outweigh this? These interests are not what Hohfeld meant when he spoke of 'claim-rights'. Rights in this latter sense are not specific to private law at all. Most legal duties are other regarding in this sense and may be said to concern our 'rights'.

An illustration of the difference may be the 'rights of animals'. Dogs do not have claim-rights in the private lawyer's sense. They can however be the subject matter of our reasons for acting or not acting in a particular way, and those can legitimately justify legal duties. It is wrong in law and morality to torture animals (and probably in morality to eat them) because of their interests. In this latter sense animals can have rights, and as a result they are protected in various ways in the law as it stands.

[7] HLA Hart, *Essays on Bentham: Studies in Jurisprudence and Political Theory* (Oxford, Clarendon Press, 1982) 183.

[8] See R Stevens, 'The Conflict of Rights' in A Robertson and HW Tang (eds), *The Goals of Private Law* (Oxford, Hart Publishing, 2009).

III. Right-Shaped Reasons

Although I consider Weinrib to have been mistaken in his placing the ability to sue at the centre of private law, his more important insight was in relation to the kind of reasons that can legitimately justify private rights.

Duties of right are necessarily owed to other people in a way that duties of virtue or public duties need not be. This form imposes a constraint upon the kind of reasons that can, as a matter of justice, justify them. They must be reasons that tie this particular right-holder to this particular duty-bearer. They must be reasons that are bilateral in form, applying to both parties.

Three illustrations may be given.

The first, familiar to torts theorists, is the inadequacy of the reasons commonly given at the start of textbooks on the law of torts that seek to justify the imposition of liability. So, it is often said, that imposing liability for injuries caused by careless drivers serves the goal of deterring prospective defendants from antisocial conduct of this kind. Allowing the injured victim of careless driving to sue serves the useful goal of ensuring those who suffer injury through no fault of their own obtain compensation to counterbalance their loss.

One problem with seeking to justify the law of torts generally, or the tort of negligence specifically, through the goals of deterrence and compensation is that these justifications do not relate the claimant to the defendant in any way. If we took these justifications seriously, it may be better to operate a clearing house system instead, where all the negligent drivers paid a fine into a central fund, and all those who had suffered injury had a claim on that fund. Such a system would look superior to the one we have now because we could tailor the fine on the negligent to obtain the level of deterrence required, and quantify the compensation awarded to the degree of need. These reasons are not bilateral in the way that right-shaped reasons need to be.

Almost all policy arguments in favour of the torts system (such as loss spreading, risk allocation, or enterprise liability) suffer from the same flaw. They fail to account for the system of rights, because they are not right-shaped. If we take them seriously, which requires exceptional intellectual honesty such as that possessed by the late Patrick Atiyah, they lead to proposals for the abolition of private law in whole or in part, as has happened in relation to liability for personal injuries caused by accidents in New Zealand.

A more complex example is the arguments for (and against) the creation of a constructive trust over the proceeds of a bribe received by a fiduciary (typically an agent). No doubt the fiduciary is personally liable to account for the value of the bribe, but must he also hold it on trust? The most common (but not sole) reason why a claimant wishes to assert that he has such a proprietary claim is to obtain priority over unsecured creditors in the event of the fiduciary's bankruptcy. It is therefore tempting to cut to the chase, and to ask, as some commentators have, whether the claimant is more substantively deserving of priority on insolvency than other creditors?

A combination of two (substantive) arguments can be given as to why the principal may be thought deserving of such preferential treatment.

First, he has not voluntarily extended credit. Lenders on an unsecured basis, or suppliers of goods on a credit basis who have not retained title, may be thought undeserving of protection because they are aware of the risk they are running. They will (presumably) have reflected that level of risk in the price charged, and can (often) protect themselves through diversification (ie, being owed money by many different parties, not all of whom will be unable to pay). Second, although there are other unsecured creditors who are involuntary, most importantly tort victims, the betrayed principal may be thought particularly deserving compared to them because the wrong he has suffered has swelled the general pool of assets available for distribution to unsecured creditors. Allowing him a priority will only therefore remove a proportion of the assets that ought not, in justice, to be available for the general body of creditors. Tort victims who claim for their consequential loss may be involuntary creditors but they have not swelled the assets, and so are less deserving. So the argument goes.

The problem with arguments of this kind is that they do not relate the claimant to any particular thing or right in the agent's estate. They are the kind of reasons that insolvency lawyers are familiar with for justifying giving employees preferential treatment on a corporation's bankruptcy. They are arguments for *priority* rather than arguments for proprietary at all as they do not relate the claimant to any particular asset of the defendant's. If we truly accepted them we would accord the claimant priority regardless of his ability to identify any asset in the defendant's estate to which his claim related (ie, it would be unnecessary to trace). However, if we did that, the illegitimacy of allowing such a result would become apparent. The order of distribution in modern insolvency codes is found in legislation. All of these codes afford some deserving creditors priority over others (most usually the tax authorities and employees). It is illegitimate for courts to create new categories of priority for persons who are not accorded it under the legislation.

By contrast, we might try to justify the result that the agent holds the bribe on constructive trust by relying upon the *form* of the trust, and giving reasons for rights of that form. Say, arguendo, we accepted that a trust is defined as constituted by the duty of a trustee to a beneficiary not to use identifiable rights for his own benefit. Is such a relationship created when an agent is bribed?

> *D* is employed as *P's* purchasing agent for widgets. *X* bribes D with a jade chess set to buy widgets from him, which *D* subsequently does. *D* has now gone into bankruptcy.

What should *D* be obliged to do upon receipt of the bribe? Given that she is a fiduciary, a person obliged to subordinate her interests to those of her principal, should she be free to keep the chess set itself, and merely account for its value? Or should she be additionally obliged not to use the (right to) the chess set for her own benefit, at her principal's option? I would suggest that the latter is correct, and so the UK Supreme Court was correct to conclude that a trust arises in such circumstances.[9]

A third example is that it should not be possible to confer rights upon others without either their acceptance, or the option to renounce. One might intuitively think that there can be no objection to giving people more rights than they choose. It may be objectionable to be able to impose duties upon me without my consent, but what is the objection to my acquiring further rights? Surely, the more rights the merrier?

If you wish to make a gift of a camel to me, should you be able to do so by leaving one on my doorstep, or more usually by completing a deed of conveyance? Ownership of a camel may carry with it onerous legal obligations (eg, to feed and stable it), or even where these are absent, the right-holder may feel morally obliged to take steps that he is now the person best placed to undertake. It may be that the law should treat the right as conditionally conferred, with an option in the (potential) right-holder to reject it with retrospective effect as is the position under a unilateral deed of conveyance. The option of complete rejection should, however, always be open until acceptance.

Is a contractual right to, say, be paid $1 million sensibly comparable to a right to an even-toed ungulate? Should acceptance be necessary? An individual may not even wish such a right. It may be that it places him in a higher tax bracket, or removes benefits that we would otherwise be entitled to, either from the state or from a private settlement. It may be that I have taken a vow of poverty, and to confer such a right upon me offends my religious beliefs. An offer *and* an acceptance are necessary because both together create the necessary bilateral relationship for the creation of a right. In principle, it is correct that others should not be able to confer rights upon me without my consent.

It follows from this that I think the English Contracts (Rights of Third Parties) Act 1999 (UK) goes too far in allowing for the creation of rights in third parties without, on its face, allowing for their rejection. Just as it should not be possible to confer rights upon others through the act of promising alone, without the acceptance of the promise, it should not be possible to do so with respect of a third party. A promise alone should not, in principle, be sufficient for the creation of a right.

It is important here to distinguish between obligations of *virtue* and obligations owed as a matter of *right*. Virtuous people keep their promises. Indeed, a vow, which only takes place in our heads, ought to be kept. Good people are resolute. No acceptance by the beneficiary is required for obligations of this form. The conferral of *rights* is an altogether different matter.[10]

[9] *FHR European Ventures LLP v Cedar Capital Partners LLC* [2014] UKSC 45, [2015] AC 250 but see the more flexible, and less formal, approach of the Australian Federal Court in *Grimaldi v Chameleon Mining NL (No 2)* [2012] FCAFC 6, (2012) 200 FCR 296.

[10] For a long form denial of this distinction, see J Gardner, *From Personal Life to Private Law* (Oxford, Oxford University Press, 2018).

IV. Other Kinds of Reasons

Not all of private law directly concerns which rights we have, however, and so not all of the reasons in play need to be of the same bilateral kind. Three examples follow.

Limitation periods are justifiable on policy grounds. They are not centrally related to what is fair as between claimant and defendant. They enable us all to close the books, knowing that after a certain point we cannot be sued for things that happened in the past. There is no necessarily correct answer as to how long a limitation period should be (three, five, seven years?) and it is more important that there is a certain rule than that the line is drawn in one place or another. Limitation periods are, quite properly, the province of the legislature, and may be contrasted with the court-created doctrine of laches which does look to considerations of what is fair as between claimant and defendant (has the defendant been induced to rely upon no claim being brought? Was the claimant's delay excusable?) in determining its application.

Limitation periods properly concern *recourse* not *rights*. They justify the barring of a power to claim, not the extinguishing of rights. So, if a duty, the enforcement of which is barred by a limitation period is performed, it cannot be recovered, and in private international law much ink has been spilled on the question of whether the appropriate law to apply to a limitation period should also be that which governs the underlying right, or whether it should be a matter of procedure for the forum.

A judge-created rule that has similarly nothing to do with the rights between the parties, but rather the court's willingness to provide recourse, is the doctrine of illegality. The traditional understanding of this rule was given by Lord Mansfield in *Holman v Johnson*:

> If, from the plaintiff's own stating or otherwise, the cause of action appears to arise ex turpi causa, or the transgression of a positive law of this country, there the Court says he has no right to be assisted. It is upon that ground the Court goes; not for the sake of the defendant, but because they will not lend their aid to such a plaintiff. So if the plaintiff and defendant were to change sides, and the defendant was to bring his action against the plaintiff, the latter would then have the advantage of it; for where both are equally in fault, potior est conditio defendentis.[11]

This is a doctrine based upon the coherence of the law, a claimant or defendant cannot rely upon his own illegal conduct in making out a claim if he wants the assistance of the legal system. Again, this has nothing to do with the rights as between the parties, and it may be for this reason that the courts have struggled with the doctrine of illegality. The entire effect and point of the doctrine of illegality is to require the court to do something other than what justice requires as

[11] *Holman v Johnson* (1775) 1 Cowp 341, 343, 98 ER 1120, 1121.

between the parties. For this reason, judges have sought to evade its logic: judges by training and inclination are in the business of trying to do what is just as between the parties before them. So, in England the *locus poenitentiae* exception was employed beyond its legitimate limits to evade the rule,[12] and more recently the traditional understanding has been supplanted altogether in England by a more 'flexible' approach. The court is asked to answer the impossible question of whether denying a claim (or a defence?) would be 'disproportionate' by weighing the incommensurables of the legal system's coherence and the injustice to the individual litigant.[13] It will no doubt be a rare case where this nonsensical weighing does not come down in favour of ignoring the illegality.

It may be doubted whether other common law systems will be tempted to follow England's path-breaking lead in allowing those who bribe public officials for honours to litigate to recover them when they are not forthcoming, or to require judges to decide whether the terms of the bribe were for a CBE or OBE.[14] However in *all* common law systems the effect of the operation of the doctrine of illegality is at the civil recourse level. It does not alter the rights that there are as between the parties, but rather their ability to enforce them, and this is reflected in the justification for the rule. The effect on a contract of illegality is that it cannot be enforced, not that there is no agreement. It is, therefore, a mistake when considering its operation within the law of negligence to think that illegality is a matter of whether a 'duty of care' is owed,[15] as in all other areas of private law it properly concerns recourse only.

A third example, of relevance to the detailed consideration of the law of unjust enrichment that forms the third part of this paper, is the doctrine of *volenti non fit iniuria*. Although it is not clear on the current state of the case law, this defence has two aspects. The first is where the defendant is responsible for creating the objective impression of consent. If I walk into a boxing ring wearing gloves, aim a blow at my opponent and am hit back, I cannot be heard to complain that I did not subjectively consent to any resultant blow. The second is the case of subjective consent. If I subjectively consent to you walking on my land, no wrong is done to me. This form of the defence is wholly 'claimant-sided'. My consent prevents there from being a wrong to me, and this defence, as with others, need not be bilateral in form.

[12] *Tribe v Tribe* [1996] Ch 107: the illegal purpose, hiding wealth in case of bankruptcy, had been fulfilled. It was not part of the illegal purpose that the transferor went into bankruptcy.

[13] *Patel v Mirza* [2016] UKSC 42, [2017] AC 467 ('*Patel*').

[14] *Parkinson v College of Ambulance Ltd* [1925] 2 KB 1 was disapproved by Lord Neuberger in *Patel* [2016] UKSC 42, [2017] AC 467 [150] but may still be good law, see Lord Toulson at [118].

[15] *Miller v Miller* [2011] HCA 9, (2011) 242 CLR 446. This is part of a more general phenomenon of seeing the 'duty of care' as being a 'control device' for restricting liability for negligence, rather than as a real legal duty owed to another. The suggestion that we have a law of outlawry conferring privileges to injure those engaged in illegal conduct is repugnant. Rather illegality provides an immunity from suit.

V. Lack of Reason and Restitution

An example:

> *C*, mistakenly believing that he owes *D* £1 million, pays him this sum in cash. *C* subsequently discovers his error and seeks restitution from *D*.

This is often treated as a central example of a claim in unjust enrichment. Clearly there is no contractual entitlement to repayment; nor has the defendant committed any wrong. All legal systems everywhere, of which I am aware, allow a claim for restitution in such a case. Why?

An explanation that has been put forward is that the claimant's consent to the defendant's enrichment (or possibly of the transfer of the proprietary right to the cash) is vitiated by the mistake that has been made.[16] This is said to be one of a sequence of claims where the claimant's consent to the defendant's enrichment is impaired, qualified or absent, justifying restitution.

This explanation will not do. The problem with a 'claimant-sided'[17] account is that it provides no explanation as to why the defendant should be obliged to do anything at all. *C*'s mistake was nothing to do with him. By what mechanism can another's actions impose obligations upon me to which I do not consent?

One common answer is to point to other examples of claims of strict liability. If, for example, I pick up your umbrella, honestly and reasonably believing it to be my own, I am liable for conversion: it will not avail me that I was wholly blameless in my actions. But, in such a case, the defendant is being held liable both for the violation of a right of another, and for his own actions for which he is responsible. The problem with the standard explanation for the recovery of the mistaken payment based upon the claimant's vitiation of consent is not that liability is strict but that a new obligation is being imposed for which the defendant is in no way responsible.

Another suggestion is that it is unobjectionable to require the defendant to repay because this will leave him no worse off than if the mistake had never been made in the first place. This is not a *positive* explanation for imposing liability, but merely a *negative* one, explaining why an obligation explicable on another basis may be morally unobjectionable. We are still wanting an explanation as to how the claimant's mistakenly enriching the defendant can, without more, justify the imposition of an obligation.

Just as with those who in the context of negligence invoke the (defendant-sided) consideration of 'deterrence' and the (claimant-sided) consideration of 'compensation', the mistake on the claimant's side and the gain on the defendant's side cannot justify a right in the former to restitution from the latter. Again, even

[16] P Birks, *An Introduction to the Law of Restitution* (Oxford, Clarendon Press, rev edn, 1989) 147; *Swynson Ltd v Lowick Rose LLP* [2017] UKSC 32, [2018] AC 313 [22] (Lord Sumption).

[17] P Birks, *Restitution: The Future* (Sydney, Federation Press, 1992) 27.

if we believed in these justifications, why not have a clearing-house system into which all mistaken payees must pay, and upon which all mistaken payors had a claim? Such a system would have the advantage that individual payors were not vulnerable to having their claims wiped out by the misfortune of their counter-party's bankruptcy.

Another example:

> *C* and *D* each own one of only two examples of a rare collectible stamp worth thousands of pounds. *C*, by mistake, destroys his stamp, which causes *D*'s stamp to more than double in value. *D* sells his stamp. *C* seeks restitution from *D* of the enrichment *D* has made at his expense.[18]

Some accounts of the law of unjust enrichment appear to justify imposing an obligation upon *D* in such a case.[19] The elements of the four-stage test for unjust enrichment appear to have been made out. *D* is undoubtedly factually better off as a result of *C*'s error. There is some dispute as to whether *D*'s enrichment must correlate with a loss suffered by *C*, but here there is no doubt that there is at least considerable overlap between the two, and so *D*'s enrichment is at *C*'s expense, at least to that extent. The mistake *C* has made is not one as to his liability to pay, but confining recovery to that category of mistake has long been deprecated. After all, if the justification for the claim is the vitiation of the claimant's consent, that does not vary according to the kind of mistake made. Absent any defence, such as change of position if *D* has given away his realised gain, there appears to be no answer to the logic of there being a claim in this case.

If we accept that no claim should succeed, and no legal system anywhere allows one in such a case, something has gone wrong with the theory.

It is suggested that the root of the problem is that the reasons proffered are of the wrong *form*. Just as with the deterrence/compensation theory of the law of torts, it has sought to combine factors concerning the claimant with those concerning the defendant in isolation from one from another. Defects in or conditions present in the state of mind of the claimant cannot justify imposing an obligation on another. A factual improvement in the defendant's position is not enough either, even if it fortuitously coincides with a consequential gain on the part of the claimant. When these independent elements are combined they do no good. They are not the right shape.

The central positive claim of this chapter is that this bilateral relation in the case of the mistaken payment is created through two necessary conditions that are bilateral in form.

First, there must have been a performance rendered from the claimant accepted by the defendant. This performance between them is what is reversed, not any

[18] cf D Friedmann, 'Restitution of Benefits Acquired Through the Appropriation of Property or the Commission of a Wrong' (1980) 80 *Columbia Law Review* 504, 532 fn 144.

[19] C Mitchell, P Mitchell and S Watterson, *Goff & Jones: The Law of Unjust Enrichment*, 8th edn (London, Sweet & Maxwell, 2011) chs 6–7 but see now C Mitchell, P Mitchell and S Watterson, *Goff & Jones: The Law of Unjust Enrichment*, 9th edn (London, Sweet & Maxwell, 2016) paras 6.09, 6.26–6.29.

consequential factual improvement of the defendant's position. This performance (the payment made, the service received) is the doing of both of them, for which they are each responsible. The terminology of 'enrichment' is apt to obscure this and mislead us. We are never in such cases reversing a realised gain or a saved expense.

Second, there must have been no reason, or an absence of basis, for this performance. This is not a unilateral consideration that applies to one party alone, but rather it applies to both. It is an objective matter, not determined by the state of mind of one of the parties.

It may be instantly retorted that there are many kinds of claim currently gathered together in the books on restitution and the law of unjust enrichment that do not satisfy one or both of these conditions, but where restitution is allowed. All that space allows to be said here is that those cases succeed, where justified, for entirely different reasons. So, for example, where one party discharges an obligation properly borne by another, she may have a claim against him for the costs of discharge. This involves no performance from one party to another, and no inquiry as to whether there was a justifying reason for it. It is no more an objection to the analysis presented here that it does not explain that kind of case than that it does not account for the entire law of contract or torts either.

A. Performance

The focus of the remainder of the chapter will be on what is meant when we say there is 'no reason' for a performance, and why this matters. However, some consideration of the idea of performance is necessary.[20]

Performance has three elements. First, what the claimant is seeking to reverse is his *doing*. So:

> *C* pays *X* £1,000 by mistake. *X*, delighted by this windfall, pays £200 to *D*, a charity.
>
> Although *D* has accepted a payment of £200, this payment was not made by *C*.

Similarly, inaction, such as the mistaken failure to exercise a valuable power or initiate proceedings in time, thereby leaving the lucky defendant factually better off as a result, should not suffice. Where an executory contract is set aside there is also no performance to reverse.

Second, the action rendered must have been intended by *C* to have been *for D*. So:

> *C* cuts down the hedge that neighbours his land with *D* in order to improve his view. *D* thinks the work is being done for his benefit, when it is not, and stands by admiring the work.

[20] For more detail see R Stevens, 'The Unjust Enrichment Disaster' (2018) 134 *LQR* 574.

Although *D* may have benefitted from the work, and by standing by might be taken to have accepted it, the work was not done *for* him, and so its value is irrecoverable. Notice that it should not matter whether *C* was mistaken in cutting the hedge.

Third, the performance must have been *accepted* by *D*. Pollock CB's aphorism that 'One cleans another's shoes; what can the other do but put them on?'[21] reflects what the law is and ought to be. There should be no claim available even where, as things turn out, the cleaning leaves the defendant better off than he otherwise would be. The bilateral nature of the necessary relation has caused some to prefer the word 'transaction',[22] but where a contract is set aside it is the performance rendered under it that must be reversed.

To suffice, a performance cannot be made unilaterally: a performance rendered by the claimant must have been accepted by the defendant. Returning to the core case of the mistaken payment, the payment of a sum of money can only be made if accepted by the recipient.

This meets the objection that the defendant is not responsible for the state of affairs that requires correction. It is not the case, and cannot be, that the justification for recovery is wholly 'claimant-sided'. Such an approach would be immoral. We would be using the defendant as a means to an end, requiring him to correct a state of affairs that was not his doing.

We cannot distinguish 'enrichment' and 'at the expense of' as separate elements of this kind of claim: they are the same thing looked at from one side or the other. The same justifying reason for restitution, the performance for which there is no reason, applies to both parties concurrently. The elements of the claim form a single normative sequence and cannot be separated one from another.

If the law were concerned with the *consequences* of performance, the relevant time for quantification of gain would be the time of trial. Just as in determining consequential loss in the law of damages, it would make no sense to ignore facts that have occurred in the interim in quantifying any consequential gain. This is not the positive law nor should it be. If the relevant 'enrichment' is the performance, that must be quantified at the time it is rendered; it cannot diminish or increase after that time. Where the performance takes the form of a service, it is the service itself that we are reversing, and this is measured by its market value, not the realised gain or saved expense of the defendant.[23] Where the performance takes the form of a payment, it is the payment that is reversed, and not any consequential gain, which may be higher or lower, that the defendant obtains from it.[24]

[21] *Taylor v Laird* (1856) 25 LJ Ex 329, 332.

[22] *Her Majesty's Revenue and Customs v Investment Trust Companies* [2017] UKSC 29, [2018] AC 275 [48] ('*ITC*').

[23] *Benedetti v Sawiris* [2013] UKSC 50, [2014] AC 938.

[24] It follows that the defence of change of position cannot be based upon any notion of 'disenrichment'. See the important work of E Bant, *The Change of Position Defence* (Oxford, Hart Publishing,

A defendant who receives a performance from a claimant does so either on the basis that it is made for some justified reason, or that it is not. If the recipient knows from the outset that there is no justifying reason for the performance (eg, it is not a gift, payment of a debt owed etc), then he must make restitution. If the recipient initially believes that there is a good reason for the performance, or does not care, and the claimant can now show that there was not (eg, he shows that he paid under a mistake as to liability) then again, the defendant must make restitution.

The difference between a performance and a transfer of property, or anything else, and that it is the former that matters, is illustrated by the following example:

> *C1* mistakenly believes that he owes *D* £1,000. *C1* requests *C2* to pay *D* this sum on his behalf. *C2* pays *D* this sum in cash. *C2* would not have done so if he too had not also mistakenly believed that he owed *C1* this sum.

Who has a claim against *D*?

The law is[25] (and ought to be) that *C1* has a claim against *D*. C2 may have a claim for reimbursement from *C1*, but no claim against *D*. Why?

The only transfer that has occurred is between *C2* and *D*. *C2* has transferred both possession of the physical notes and the right to them to *D*. However, the performance *to D* has not been rendered by *C2*. *C2* intended and did make his performance *for C1*: he did the action on his behalf and at his request. This action by *C2* is attributed to *C1* because it was both authorised by *C1* and done by *C2* on his behalf. *C1* rendered a performance to *D* because that was his objective in the performance of the act of payment that was done on his behalf. It is the payment from *C1* to *D* that must be reversed, although in this example *C1* has done this without divesting himself of any right.

Where therefore we rescind a contract for misrepresentation, duress or anything else, a payment or the provision of a service,[26] rendered under it, must be reversed. The genus to which both belong is that of a performance, not a transfer of a thing or a right.

B. The Role of Unjust Factors

If the law is, as claimed, truly concerned with whether there was an absence of reason for the performance, why do the leading cases in the common law world ask whether the claimant is mistaken in rendering performance,[27] if the

2009) and S Kiefel, 'Lessons from a "Conversation" About Restitution' (2014) 88 *ALJ* 176. Change of position is purely defendant-sided: it protects the innocent from being left worse off.

[25] *Aiken v Short* (1856) 1 H & N 210, 156 ER 1180; *MacDonald Dickens & Macklin v Costello* [2011] EWCA Civ 930, [2012] QB 244. See analogously in the context of the provision of a service *Lumbers v W Cook Builders Pty Ltd* [2008] HCA 27, (2008) 232 CLR 635.

[26] *Whittington v Seale-Hayne* (1900) 82 LTR 49.

[27] See, eg, *David Securities Pty Ltd v Commonwealth Bank of Australia* (1992) 175 CLR 353.

explanation does not lie in the 'vitiation' of the consent of the claimant to the payment made?

The 'unjust factor' of mistake plays three quite distinct roles within the law of unjust enrichment. The first two categories concern where the mistake either *negatives* or *nullifies* the reason for performance. The difference between negativing and nullifying is the difference between establishing that none of the possible valid reasons for a performance exist, and invalidating or setting aside what would otherwise constitute a good reason. It is the same difference as that identified by Lord Atkin in relation to whether there was a valid contract where the parties were mistaken.[28]

An example:

> *C*, a life insurance company, pays $1,000 to *D* not realising that the policy had lapsed because the deceased had failed to pay the premium.

How does a claimant establish that there is no valid reason for the payment? Iacobucci J in *Garland v Consumers' Gas Co* stated that the Canadian approach was as follows:

> First, the claimant must show that no juristic reason from an established category exists to deny recovery. By closing the list of categories that the plaintiff must canvass in order to show an absence of juristic reason, [Professor Lionel] Smith's objection[29] to the Canadian formulation of the test that it required proof of a negative is answered. The established categories that can constitute juristic reasons include a contract, a disposition of law, a donative intent, and other valid common law, equitable or statutory obligations.[30]

This cannot be correct as a matter of practice. The claimant in the case of the simple mistaken payment could not be expected to show that there was no contract, no gift, no moral obligation, no court judgment, and no statute that provided a good reason for the payment to be made. This is especially so as, despite what is stated, Iacobucci J's list is not in fact closed.

Rather, by showing that the payment was made under a mistake as to liability he negatives, or disproves, the existence of all of these potential explanations at once. For this purpose, any mistake will do. That this is correct is demonstrated by the subsequent decision of the Supreme Court of Canada in *BMP Global Distributions Inc v bank of Nova Scotia*.[31] This concerned a bank's right to recover payments made under a forged cheque. The focus was upon whether the payment

[28] *Bell v Lever Brothers Ltd* [1932] AC 161, 217 (Lord Atkin) ('*Bell*').

[29] LD Smith, 'The Mystery of "Juristic Reason"' (2000) 12 *Supreme Court Law Review* (2d) 211, 212–13.

[30] *Garland v Consumers' Gas Co* 2004 SCC 25, [2004] 1 SCR 629 [44] (footnotes omitted).

[31] *BMP Global Distributions Inc v Bank of Nova Scotia* 2009 SCC 15, [2009] 1 SCR 504 ('*BMP Global Distributions*').

had been made by mistake and, once it was shown that it had been, no further analysis of the want of any other validating reason was needed.

Peter Birks in his final work stated:

> A pyramid can be constructed in which, at the base, the particular unjust factors such as mistake, pressure and undue influence become reasons why, higher up, there is no basis for the defendant's acquisition, which is then the master reason why, higher up still, the enrichment is unjust and must be surrendered.[32]

This is incorrect both in a case such as *Kelly v Solari*,[33] which is the basis for the simple insurance example and in *BMP Global Distributions Inc v Bank of Nova Scotia*. In both the mistake is not the reason why the payment is unjustified. Rather, it is the easiest way of establishing this fact. In almost all cases where mistake is used to negative the existence of any possible basis, the mistake will be as to the existence of a legal or moral obligation on the claimant to the defendant (or another)[34] to perform – usually termed 'liability mistakes'. The mistake establishes that the claimant thought there was a good reason for the payment and there was not. That he did so thinking he was liable to do so negatives the existence of any donative intent. An explanation for the performance rendered has been provided other than the presence of a good reason to render it. Although it is sometimes said that mistake and other unjust factors 'vitiate consent',[35] in a case such as *Kelly* this is not so, there is nothing to vitiate or set aside.

The account presented here fits more accurately with the traditional understanding of the judges in the cases as to the role of mistake. So, in *Kelly*, Parke B said:

> [If the money] is paid under the impression of the truth of a fact which is untrue, it may, generally speaking, be recovered back, however careless the party paying may have been, in omitting to use due diligence to inquire into the fact. *In such a case the receiver was not entitled to it, nor intended to have it.*[36]

Birks interpreted this statement as providing two reasons for recovery: absence of entitlement and lack of consent.[37] Properly interpreted there is but one. There must be no reason for the payment. That the payment was made under a mistake as to liability shows that there was no entitlement to the payment. It is not relied upon in order to show that any 'transfer' was 'vitiated'.

Quite different is where the claimant seeks to show that a contract or gift that he has performed is nullified by a mistake.

[32] P Birks, *Unjust Enrichment*, 2nd edn (Oxford, Oxford University Press, 2005) 116. See also T Baloch, 'The Unjust Enrichment Pyramid' (2007) 123 *LQR* 636.

[33] *Kelly v Solari* (1841) 9 M & W 54, 152 ER 24 ('*Kelly*').

[34] See, eg, *Barclays Bank Ltd v WJ Simms Son & Cooke (Southern) Ltd* [1980] QB 677.

[35] Birks, above n 16, 147; Mitchell, Mitchell and Watterson, *Goff & Jones*, 8th edn, above n 19, 1–22; cf A Burrows, *The Law of Restitution*, 3rd edn (Oxford, Oxford University Press, 2011) 203.

[36] *Kelly* (1841) 9 M & W 54, 58, 152 ER 24, 26 (emphasis added).

[37] Birks, above n 32, 116.

An example:

> *C* agrees to provide *D* with financial services in return for a share in a business. *C* discovers that *D* had misrepresented material facts to him before entering into the deal. *C* now seeks to rescind and recover the value of the service provided.

The objective bilateral conditions for the creation of an enforceable contract right (offer/acceptance, consideration etc) have been fulfilled. The subjective error in *C's* head, for which *D* is responsible, entitles him to be excused, and to rescind, or avoid the contract. The basis of the performance that once exists is therefore retrospectively invalidated, or nullified. Where we seek to nullify a valid contract or gift the category of mistakes that suffice is not, and has never been, confined to liability mistakes.

A more restricted class of mistakes will nullify a contract where neither party is responsible for a shared mistake.

Another example:

> *C* agrees to hire a music hall from *D* for a hire of $10,000 per month for three months, payment in advance. Unbeknownst to the parties, the music hall had burned to the ground an hour before they entered into their agreement.

Agreements, like the words that are used to make them, have limits. In some cases, agreements run out and are not (objectively) interpreted as covering the situation the parties now find themselves in. This is usually so in cases of the unforeseen non-existence of the subject matter of the agreement.[38] If the fire had occurred two hours later the agreement, that there undoubtedly is, would have been frustrated.[39] The agreement cannot be interpreted as covering the state of affairs that now exists, and so cannot provide a justification for any performance rendered under it. Again, any old mistake will not do, and in order to give a label to the idea that the agreement does not cover the facts as they are now known to be, we label the requisite mistake a 'fundamental' one.

More difficult are cases where the contract is possible to perform, but its entire purpose has been frustrated or fallen away. This has happened extremely rarely, the most famous cases being the 'Coronation' cases, where again it did not matter whether the agreement was made before[40] or after[41] the unforeseen illness of the king.

The same pattern of a limited class of mistakes that operate to nullify a voluntary transaction is found in the area of gifts, although here the law is less clear and well-developed.

C gives $1,000 cash to his niece *D* as a birthday present, not realising that she has just married a man that he privately detests.[42] Should the mistake be sufficient

[38] See, eg, *Couturier v Hastie* [1856] 5 HLC 673, 10 ER 1065.
[39] *Taylor v Caldwell* (1863) 3 B & S 826, 122 ER 309.
[40] *Griffith v Brymer* (1903) 19 TLR 434.
[41] *Krell v Henry* [1903] 2 KB 740.
[42] A Tettenborn, *The Law of Restitution in England and Ireland*, 3rd edn (London, Cavendish Publishing, 2001) 76.

to nullify the gift? The requirements of a valid gift of cash all seem to be satisfied (ie, intention to give this thing to this person, acceptance, and delivery or a deed of conveyance). The mistake does not render performance impossible, but rather partially frustrates its purpose. As with the case of a contract, the correct answer should be, and is, 'it depends'. In the contractual context, it would not suffice that one of the many motivations for making a contract, each of which may have been necessary, is frustrated. We require the entire purpose of the agreement to fall away. Why then did *C* make the gift to his niece? If, as will usually be the case, he did so for several reasons, some of which still obtain at the time the performance was rendered, no recovery should be permitted.

Professor Burrows has argued that any mistake will do for purposes of invalidating a gift and that restitution should be available in such a case.[43] The UK Supreme Court in *Pitt v Holt*,[44] following a line of earlier authority, rejected such a wide approach to setting aside a deed of gift. In *Pitt*, a discretionary trust was set up in such a way as to be liable to inheritance tax, when it could easily have been structured so as to avoid it. Could the trust be set aside? This turned upon the centrality of this mistake to the gift that was sought to be set aside. As the entire purpose of the settlement had been to achieve the most tax-efficient disposition possible, the Court (somewhat generously) found that it was 'unconscionable', and could be set aside.

When a transfer is made by a will, an even more restricted approach is taken to the kinds of mistake that count. So, a mistake as to the legal effect of the words used is not enough to enable a will to be set aside[45] and it may only be rectified, today in England under the Administration of Justice Act 1982 (UK), section 20 and in Victoria under the Wills Act 1997 (Vic), section 33, in cases of clerical error or failures to understand the testator's instructions.

In order to understand what kinds of mistake should count, and which should not, it is necessary to have a theory of contract, gifts and wills and when they are and ought to be valid. Whenever the mistake fulfils the role of nullifying a contract, gift or will it does not take the form of a mistake as to liability to perform.

In relation to voluntarily created obligations of all kinds (under deeds, contracts, wills) mistakes are not the only way of demonstrating that, despite appearances, there is no responsibility for the putatively valid obligation. Duress, undue influence and incapacity are all methods of invalidating an obligation that

[43] A Burrows, above n 35, 217. Against *Deutsche Morgan Grenfell Group plc v IRC* [2006] UKHL 49, [2007] 1 AC 558 [87] ('*Deutsche Morgan*') (Lord Scott); S Hedley, *A Critical Introduction to Restitution* (London, Butterworth, 2001) 106–07; TH Wu 'Restitution for Mistaken Gifts' (2004) 20 *Journal of Contract Law* 1; S Meier and R Zimmermann, 'Judicial Developments of the Law, Error Iuris, and the Law of Unjust Enrichment – A View from Germany' (1999) 115 *LQR* 556.

[44] *Pitt v Holt* [2011] EWCA Civ 197, [2012] CH 132 ('*Pitt*').

[45] JR Martyn et al, *Theobald on Wills*, 17th edn (London, Sweet & Maxwell, 2010) para 3.016; *Morrell v Morrell* (1882) 7 PD 68, 70–71; *Collins v Elstone* [1893] P 1; *Re Horrocks* [1939] P 198; *Re Morris* [1971] P 62, 79.

would otherwise be created by nullifying responsibility for it. However, where the obligation is created other than voluntarily, as for example where it is created by a court judgment or a tax statute, defects in the consent of the payee are neither here nor there. Mistake, duress and undue influence cannot set aside obligations that are imposed independently of the obligor's manifestations of consent. If these obligations are set aside for other reasons, as where a court judgment is successfully appealed, or a tax statute declared unconstitutional, restitution of performances rendered under them should follow, but not because of anything to do with the state of mind of the payor.

The third role for 'mistake' is that it shows that the claimant has not consented to the state of affairs he now seeks to correct. An example:

> *D* claims that *C* owes him $1,000 and demands it from him. *C* is certain that he does not owe this sum but pays anyway.

Even if it can be shown that the money is not owing, so that there is no objective reason for the payment having been made, there is no injustice to *C* in refusing to reverse the payment. Just as with *volenti non fit iniuria* in the law of torts, *C's* subjective consent means that there is no reason for the law to come to his aid. The subjective state of mind of the claimant again provides a reason for barring the enforcement of a right, not for its creation. Just as in the law of torts however, the claimant's mistake shows that there was no such consent, so that the reason for recovery still obtains.

A nice illustration of the principle that a claimant cannot recover back a payment that he knows he is making for no reason is *CTN Cash and Carry Ltd v Gallagher Ltd*.[46] A buyer paid a sum of money to his supplier. This sum was not owed. They paid because of threats to discontinue supplies. The suppliers made the threats in the honest belief that the sum was owed. A threat to discontinue the conferral of a benefit, as opposed to a threat to cause harm, cannot constitute duress.

This is an example of money paid where the claimant knows there is no good reason to do so. Absent duress (or mistake, undue influence or incapacity) recovery was rightly denied.

That the performance rendered must be intentional leaves no role for the suggestion by academics of 'unjust factors' such as 'ignorance' or 'powerlessness'.[47] Such 'unjust factors' seem required under the vitiation of consent theory because in such cases the consent to the enrichment is entirely absent, and so they follow a fortiori from the case of mistake. No case in England or Australia has recognised the existence of such reasons for restitution. We may also dispense with such 'unjust factors' as 'legal compulsion' and 'moral compulsion' as neither establish that a performance has been rendered for no reason, but rather the reverse.

[46] *CTN Cash and Carry Ltd v Gallagher Ltd* [1994] 4 All ER 714.

[47] J Edelman and E Bant, *Unjust Enrichment* (Oxford, Hart Publishing, 2016) ch 12.

By contrast there ought to be, and are, other ways of demonstrating that a performance has been rendered for no reason without relying upon defects in the consent of the person rendering it. If, for example, an agent (usually a director) purports to enter into a contract on behalf of his principal (her company), but lacks the actual or ostensible authority to do so, and then performance is rendered by the principal under the purported contract, restitution should follow as being demonstrably made for no reason. The reason for the invalidity of the contract, want of authority, is unrelated to the state of mind of the claimant. Similarly, if a tax levy is ultra vires, a public authority's payments made under it ought to be recoverable, regardless of the absence of any demand from the public authority. Lack of reason alone will suffice.

C. The Role of Justifying Reasons

Until relatively recently, academic textbooks on the law of restitution wholly ignored the role of justifying reasons. Where it could be shown that payment had been made mistakenly where there was no liability, or a contract rescinded for duress, or a tax paid following an ultra vires demand, there was no justifying reason for what had been done. The removal of the so-called mistake of law bar, coupled with the view that any mistaken payment was prima facie recoverable on the basis of the claimant's vitiated consent, required an explanation as to why this did not follow where there was some justifying reason for the performance.

Current textbooks recognise that the presence of an *obligation* to render performance may bar recovery, but provide no explanation as to how this can be so. So, *Goff & Jones* states that 'the defendant can escape liability if another legal rule entitles him to keep the benefit, and this rule overrides the rule generated by the law of unjust enrichment which holds that the defendant should make restitution.'[48] It is however unclear how the right to restitution can be overridden by the obligation to pay if it is created by the defendant's vitiation of consent. How does one obligation override the other? Professor Burrows claims that sometimes they will and sometimes they will not, but provides us with no (convincing) account as to how or why this should be so.

Justifying reasons are not confined to legally enforceable obligations to perform. If I perform an unenforceable contract, or make a gift to you, restitution should not follow despite the absence of any legal obligation to have done so. We cannot therefore explain the role of justifying reasons by reference to any principle of subsidiarity of unjust enrichment to other areas of law, preventing circularity of action, set off and so on.

This lack of focus on justifying reasons caused some of the older cases to be unfairly criticised, as not fitting with vitiation of consent theory. The most notable

[48] Mitchell, Mitchell and Watterson, *Goff & Jones*, 8th edn, above n 19, para 2.01.

feature of the much maligned *Bilbie v Lumley*,[49] the case usually treated as introducing the so-called mistake of law bar, is that it is rightly decided.

The claimants' insurers had paid £100 under a contract for the insurance of a ship. The insured had not disclosed to them the sailing time of the ship. The claimants alleged that they had made a mistake as to their liability to pay, the defendant's non-disclosure being enough to constitute a defence to any action that had been brought.

This error of law was not enough on its own to show that there was no good reason for the payment. If the claimants had sought to set aside the contract for non-disclosure, *returning the premiums received*, then restitution of the insurance payout should have been awarded. No recovery of payments made under a still extant and valid contract should however be awarded. There is a large difference between a mistake as to whether you are obliged to pay, and mistakenly failing to take steps to avoid an obligation to pay.

At the time of *Bilbie* it was unclear whether a fully executed contract could be avoided for non-disclosure,[50] but absent rescission, no recovery should be allowed based only upon the fact that the claimant had made an error of law in paying.

Further in relation to those claims where the basis of the claim is *not* the lack of any reason for the performance rendered, its presence is irrelevant. Two examples follow. First:

> *D* ships his pet dog with *C Carriers* from Oxford to York. Upon arrival *D* fails to collect the animal. *C Carriers* incurs expense in feeding and caring for the dog until it is collected the following week.

If *C* had disposed of the dog or failed to feed it, *D* would have had a claim against him for its loss. As a voluntary bailee, *C* has come under a positive duty to *D* to care for the beast. There is a perfectly good reason why the performance was rendered. However, *because C* was exceptionally compelled by law to incur this expense on *D*'s behalf, as a quid pro quo, he is entitled to reimbursement. It is *C's* (exceptional) obligation to perform that justifies his right to reimbursement.

Second:

> *D* agrees to supply *C* with 10 guards to protect his office buildings per month for three years, at a price of $100,000 per month, payable annually in advance. After the first year, *C* discovers that by an oversight no guards had been provided in the month of June. *C* does not wish to terminate the contract.

C should be entitled to restitution of the $100,000 paid for the guards in the month of June. It was a condition of this sum being earned under the agreement that the guards were in fact provided. As the performance had been agreed to be

[49] *Bilbie v Lumley* (1802) 2 East 469, 102 ER 448 ('*Bilbie*'). *Deutsche Morgan* [2006] UKHL 49, [2007] 1 AC 558 although much more complex is essentially the same, and so wrongly decided.

[50] A bar to rescission removed in the context of misrepresentation in the UK by the Misrepresentation Act 1967 (UK), s 1(1)(b), but left tantalisingly unreformed in Australia.

conditional, and that condition had failed, restitution should follow. This relevant condition is not found in the minds of one or other of the parties. What they think is irrelevant. It does not matter that the agreement is unenforceable, for want of form,[51] lack of certainty, or any other reason. The claim is not to enforce the agreement or claim damages under it. It should be also irrelevant that the contract has not been avoided or terminated, and to think these are a necessary condition of recovery is to repeat the '*Chandler v Webster*[52] fallacy' rejected before the war.[53] The majority of the High Court of Australia in *Roxborough v Rothmans Pall Mall Australia Ltd*[54] correctly rejected any such limitation on analogous facts.

Some commentators have suggested that it should be a condition of recovery that a contract is terminated before restitution should be permitted.[55] It is difficult to understand why this should be so on any view. Termination brings obligations of future performance to an end. In the example, if the contract had been terminated, the obligations to provide future guards and future payments would no longer arise. It does not operate so as to retrospectively invalidate prior obligations of performance. This is to confuse termination with avoidance.

The mere fact of termination also cannot, therefore, mean that there was no good reason for performances already rendered under the contract. There was: that is what the claimant was obliged to do. The nature of a claim for 'failure of consideration' is not dependent upon there being no such reason for performance. It is instead based upon the performance rendered having been agreed to be conditional. Indeed, such a claim pre-supposes the presence of a good reason for the performance rendered: the agreement.

D. What is a Good Reason for a Performance Rendered?

As we have seen, the easiest examples of a good reason for a performance are those that are legally obligatory and enforceable. So, payments under contracts, wills, court judgments, tax statutes and so on are not recoverable, regardless of whether mistakenly made.

As we have also seen, legal obligations do not cease to be such simply because they are unenforceable. The distinguishing feature of legal obligations that are unenforceable and those that are a nullity (ie, that do not exist) is that once it is

[51] *Pavey & Matthews Pty Ltd v Paul* (1987) 162 CLR 221.
[52] *Chandler v Webster* [1904] 1 KB 493.
[53] *Fibrosa Spolka Akcyjna v Fairbairn Lawson Combe Barbour Ltd* [1943] AC 32.
[54] *Roxborough v Rothmans Pall Mall Australia Ltd* [2001] HCA 68, (2001) 208 CLR 516 (Kirby J dissenting).
[55] Mitchell, Mitchell and Watterson, *Goff & Jones*, 8th edn, above n 19; J Beatson and G Virgo, 'Contract, Unjust Enrichment and Unconscionability' (2002) 118 *LQR* 352.

performed it cannot be recovered. So, payments made after the expiry of a limitation period, or a contract that is unenforceable for want of a formality requirement cannot be recovered.

More difficult as a matter of the positive law because underdeveloped (although not problematic in principle) is the performance of 'natural' or 'moral' obligations. We need here to again draw the distinction between matters of virtue and matters of right. The question of how I ought, as a virtuous person, to behave is a different question from the rights you have against me. So, virtuous passers-by will pick up a baby that is drowning in an inch of water, but the baby has no right to be picked up.

An example:

> *C* agrees to pay *D* half of his winnings should he win the lottery. Having done so, and believing that gratuitous promises are enforceable, *C* pays *D*.

Has *D* a right to be paid? If we take the view that consideration goes to enforceability (as I would) then the answer is yes. Here, *D* has a right to be paid, albeit an unenforceable one, and no restitution should be enforced.

By contrast, a man who makes a large gift to his niece on her wedding day acts as *virtue* requires of him, although the niece has no right to the money. If his gift can be set aside, because for example he was subject to duress or he was making a sufficiently serious mistake, the mere fact that he had behaved as a virtuous person *should* have done cannot alone provide a supporting reason for the payment.

Once we accept that a justifying reason need not be a legally enforceable obligation, the decision in *Brisbane v Dacres*,[56] also nowadays usually dismissed as wrong, becomes justifiable.

Masters of ships during the Napoleonic wars could, as now, be ordered by their superiors to do anything lawful. Where they were ordered to carry a large amount of public money, a gratuity was paid to them of half of one per cent the value. By convention, one third of that sum was then paid over by the master of the vessel to the admiral under whom he served. In *Montagu v Janverin* an admiral had brought an action to claim his third when it had not been paid, and Mansfield CJ had refused to enforce the custom.[57] The question that arose in *Brisbane* was whether a payment that had been made to an admiral under the customary convention could then be recovered.

The decision that it could not appears justifiable. It is one thing to hold that a convention cannot be enforced, quite another to decide that it provides no justification for payments made under it. Those who make a conventional contribution at the end of a church service should not be able to get their money back on the basis that one of the reasons they had been so generous was that they were making an error of law.

[56] *Brisbane v Dacres* (1813) 5 Taunt 143, 128 ER 641.
[57] *Montagu v Janverin* (1811) 3 Taunt 442, 128 ER 175.

E. Better Fit

I have so far provided a number of examples where the account here gives a better 'fit' with both the positive law as it is, and as it ought to be, than the alternative of seeking to explain the law in terms of the 'vitiation', 'qualification' or 'absence' of the claimant's consent to the defendant's enrichment. Here are some more examples, most of which are well known.

F. 'Deemed' Mistakes

> *C* pays *D* $100,000 because obliged to do so under a tax statute. The tax statute is repealed with retrospective effect.

The positive law is a matter of fact just like any other fact. It is simply a matter of the rules posited by those with the authority within a legal system to do so. Mistakes about what the positive law requires are mistakes of fact. What justice requires of us is not (simply) a matter of fact. No amount of facts (including cases and statutes) can, alone, tell us what the position as a matter of justice is. You cannot extract an 'ought' from an 'is' alone.

According to 'vitiation of consent' theory, a mistake grounds a right to recover a mistaken payment on the basis that it caused the transfer to the defendant. In the above example this is impossible to establish. *C* made no error at the time the payment was made. We can, in a looser sense, describe *C* as mistaken, as the reason she had for making the payment no longer applies, but this does not fit with the theory of why such mistakes count. If we accept, as we should, that restitution should follow in this case, this cannot be explained in terms of the claimant's 'vitiation' of consent.[58]

Identical are those cases where the retrospective change in the positive law occurs because of judicial decision.

> *C* pays *D* $100,000 because the decision in *X v Y* states that in the circumstances she finds himself in, she is obliged to do so. *X v Y* is overturned with retrospective effect by *Q v R*.

Again, the positive law, the facts upon which *C* based her decision to pay, once were one thing and are now something else. There was nothing wrong with the data in her head at the time the payment was made, and consequently no 'vitiation' of her consent to pay. Again, this is of no concern as this is not why the claimant's mistake establishes that restitution should be awarded. *C* can show that she paid because she thought she was obliged to do so, and not for no reason or any other possible reason. In the absence of such an obligation, restitution should follow.

[58] See *Commissioner of State Revenue v Royal Insurance Australia Ltd* (1994) 182 CLR 51.

Again, it is not an abuse of language to describe *C* as mistaken, but to allow recovery, as we should, is not consistent with vitiation of consent theory.

G. No Causal Connection Necessary

Vitiation of consent theory is based on the idea that the defect in the consent of the claimant *caused* the defendant's enrichment. Usually, this will be so. The mistake is the reason why the payment is made.

However, this is not always so. The 'unjust factor' may nullify what would otherwise be a good reason justifying the claimant's performance, but need not cause the performance itself to be rendered. Some examples follow.

> *C*, a 14-year-old boy, contracts to buy in-game bonuses from *D*, a mobile phone game app developer. After payment has been made *C*, at the instigation of his furious father, seeks restitution from *D* of the (extortionate) price paid.

If the law says in such a case that the contract between *C* and *D* is a nullity, and not merely unenforceable, because of *C*'s lack of capacity due to his age, restitution should follow. It does not matter whether *C*'s age had any causal contribution to the payment (eg, if he would have made precisely the same foolish bargain if he had been 18 and his age made no contribution whatsoever).

Similarly:

> *C* settles a large amount of property on *D*, a religious order of which he has recently become a member. *C* is in thrall to the charismatic religious leader of *D*. Payments have been made under the settlement, that *C* now wishes to recover.

Again, if the settlement can be set aside because of undue influence, payments made under it should be capable of being recovered. It should not (and does not) matter whether the same settlement would have been made independently of any undue influence.

H. Rescission

The operation of the law of rescission is a further illustration of the inexactness of vitiation of consent theory.

> *C* agrees to buy a ship from *D*. During the negotiations, *D* has misrepresented the size of the propellers of the vessel. This forms part of *C*'s decision-making process to go ahead. Six months later, *C* pays the price, at which point he no longer cares one way or the other about the propellers. Having now discovered the misrepresentation, he avoids the deal.

In a legal system that permits rescission in such circumstances, restitution should follow. It should not matter that the mistake played no part in the decision to perform, so long as it is sufficient to nullify the reason that would have justified that performance.

This pattern is always found within the law of rescission, which is a one stage process. If a contract is set aside for misrepresentation, duress, undue influence or any other reason, restitution of the performance rendered always follows. We do not ask a claimant to plead and prove that the misrepresentation, duress or undue influence that was operative at the time the bargain was entered into, was *also* present at the time the performance that it is sought to reverse was made. The latter is irrelevant because the state of mind of the claimant at the time of performance is irrelevant.

I. Birks' Account

My copy of the first edition of Peter Birks' last work, *Unjust Enrichment*, is inscribed by the author. He has written 'You were right, a life's work up in flames'. This refers back to a BCL seminar in the previous year. These had followed the same pattern that they had for decades, mainly a trawl through the various so-called unjust factors (mistake, duress, undue influence, ignorance, legal compulsion etc). In discussing the decision of the Court of Appeal in *Guinness Mahon & Co Ltd v Kensington and Chelsea RLBC*,[59] where the Court had seemed to base its decision upon an absence of consideration (ie, lack of juristic reason) for the payment, I had joked that if that were correct all of Peter's previous work needed to be discarded. Now I am a Professor of Law, I would deprecate such mockery by a junior colleague. In fact, Birks did not, at the last, reject his earlier account, and this has caused confusion.

In this final work, he sought to argue that the English law of unjust enrichment had fundamentally changed as a result of a 'cataclysm': a series of cases concerning void interest rate swaps in the 1990s. He argued that (almost)[60] all of the law he had previously described in one way was now better understood in a new way. He did not claim that his earlier account was wrong, or that it had a poor fit with the positive law as it then was, but on the basis that the positive law had been changed by the judges.

This was always a far-fetched claim. Judges are not legislators. Although it is not unknown for them to engage in the wholesale re-writing of an area of law[61] this is rarely a legitimate exercise of their power. To have done so *sub silentio* would have been very surprising. To have done so whilst expressly disavowing any intention to effect any such change would be utterly extraordinary. In common law jurisdictions outside of England, such as Australia, that had never had the equivalent of the swaps litigation, the idea that their law needed to be radically

[59] *Guinness Mahon & Co Ltd v Kensington and Chelsea RLBC* [1999] QB 215.

[60] The exception was the area covered in civilian law by the *action negotiorum gestio contraria* as these are claims for compensation for expenditure – see Birks, above n 32, 22–23 – which Birks had previously sought to explain as a claim for restitution based upon 'moral compulsion'.

[61] See, eg, *Patel* [2016] UKSC 42, [2017] AC 467.

reconfigured was even less plausible. Further, even in England, the leading case following the swaps litigation was inconsistent with Birks' new account.[62] The new version looked dramatically different from the old. This made it too easy to dismiss what he had written.

Further, Birks' new account did not resemble the law in any civilian system. They do not seek to group together cases concerned with the discharge of another's obligation, receipt of things to which another has a better right, or reversal of performances which have been agreed are conditional, as all are concerned with the reversal of a performance that has been rendered for no juristic reason. Further, in those systems, unjust enrichment always gives rise to a personal claim to the payment of a sum of money, never the creation of proprietary rights. Birks sought to invoke a single principle covering all of this area, on the basis of a change the judges expressly said they were not making. That others were not convinced, despite the veneration many of us had for its author, was unsurprising.

The picture I present here has some similarities too, but also some profound differences from, the last work of Peter Birks.

First, I have renounced the naturalistic meaning of enrichment that Birks employed. If what we are reversing is the performance by the claimant accepted by the defendant, to describe this as an 'enrichment' is misleading in everyday language. It would be safer to return to the label 'restitution' for the subject.

Second, although I have employed the idea of an absence of juristic reason, that is also found in civilian systems, I have argued, consistently with those systems, that it is *only* ever relevant where there has been a performance for which there is no basis. It has no application to cases concerning: a failure of consideration, discharge of another's obligation, receipt of a thing to which another has a superior right, expenses legally compelled to be incurred on another's behalf, knowing receipt of trust property and a host of other cases appearing in books travelling under the restitution or unjust enrichment banner.

Third, I have argued that this not only should be the law, but always has been. It is, and always has been, a superior account, both descriptively and normatively, of the law of mistake, duress, undue influence and so on in common law systems than is one based upon giving recovery based upon defects and qualifications in the state of mind of the claimant at the time of 'transfer.

VI. Australian Conservatism, English Radicalism

Since the turn of the millennium the High Court of Australia has adopted a conservative approach to the law of restitution, steadfastly refusing to accept

[62] *Kleinwort Benson Ltd v Lincoln City Council* [1999] 2 AC 349.

the omnibus unjust enrichment framework.[63] Even the staunchest critic of this approach accepts that the Court has not, in fact, decided any cases incorrectly.[64]

Until recently, the UK's Supreme Court had been far less cautious, accepting that there is a unified subject enabling reasoning by analogy across it, whilst adopting Birks' four stage test for unjust enrichment with alacrity, and seeking to employ it directly in deciding cases. The result[65] has been cases that either have to be explained on different grounds from those given by the Court (*Lipkin Gorman v Karpnale Ltd*,[66] *Menelaou v Bank of Cyprus*,[67] *International Energy Group Ltd v Zurich Insurance Plc*[68]) or are, more seriously, wrongly decided (*Banque Financière de la Cité v Parc (Battersea) Ltd*,[69] *Deutsche Morgan*,[70] *Sempra Metals Ltd v Commissioners of Inland Revenue*[71]). This heroic expansionist era may have been halted by the speech of Lord Reed in *Her Majesty's Revenue and Customs v Investment Trust Companies*.[72] It took a Scottish public lawyer to remind English private lawyers that the four-stage questions 'are no more than broad headings for ease of exposition' and 'are not themselves legal tests'.[73] The old learning could not be simply dismissed and the recognition of an area of law called restitution did not present 'a tabula rasa, entitling them to disregard or distinguish all authorities predating *Lipkin Gorman*'.[74]

Judges should not be dangerous radicals. The English error, at a level of high principle, has been caused by insufficient attention to the form of reasoning required in private law.

[63] *Farah Constructions Pty Ltd v Say-Dee Pty Ltd* [2007] HCA 22, (2007) 230 CLR 89; *Lumbers v W Cook Builders Pty Ltd* [2008] HCA 27, (2008) 232 CLR 635; *Bofinger v Kingsway Group Ltd* [2009] HCA 44, (2009) 239 CLR 269. All of these cases are clearly correctly decided. See also Kiefel, above n 24.

[64] A Burrows, 'The Australian Law of Restitution: Has the High Court lost its way?' in E Bant and M Harding (eds), *Exploring Private Law* (Cambridge, Cambridge University Press, 2010) 67–85.

[65] For consideration of these English cases see Stevens, above n 20.

[66] *Lipkin Gorman v Karpnale Ltd* [1991] 2 AC 548.

[67] *Menelaou v Bank of Cyprus* [2015] UKSC 66, [2016] AC 176.

[68] *International Energy Group Ltd v Zurich Insurance plc* [2015] UKSC 33, [2016] AC 509.

[69] *Banque Financière de la Cité v Parc (Battersea) Ltd* [1999] 1 AC 221.

[70] *Deutsche Morgan* [2006] UKHL 49, [2007] 1 AC 558.

[71] *Sempra Metals Ltd v Commissioners of Inland Revenue* [2007] UKHL 34, [2008] AC 561.

[72] *ITC* [2017] UKSC 29, [2018] AC 275.

[73] ibid [41].

[74] ibid [40].

7

The Formality of Contractual Obligation

LIAM MURPHY*

I. Form and Substance

I argue in this chapter that all of contract law is formal in content. I first develop and defend the sense of content formality that I have in mind and then turn to argue that contract law is formal in that sense. Even if I am unpersuasive on the second claim, I hope that the notion of formality I develop will seem illuminating. It is striking that content formality, my focus, is hardly at all mentioned in the several rather exhaustive discussions of form and substance in the law of obligations to be found in this volume.

My starting point is the account of content formality introduced by Patrick Atiyah and Robert Summers in *Form and Substance in Anglo-American Law*, along with their account of interpretive formality for the sake of contrast.[1] I will also draw on Lon Fuller's celebrated discussion of formality in contract in his 1941 article 'Consideration and Form'.[2] Like Fuller, I will use US enforceability doctrine for my main examples.

A legal rule has greater content formality, according to Atiyah and Summers, to the extent that it is shaped by fiat and/or the extent to which it is under- or over-inclusive with respect to its objectives.[3] An obvious example of a rule shaped by fiat would be the rule still found in several US states that contracts under seal are subject to an extended statute of limitations period of 20 years.[4] An example of a rule over-inclusive with respect to its objective is the Statute of Frauds

* Thanks to members of the audience at the Obligations IX conference in Melbourne for helpful discussion. The support of the Filomen d'Agostino and Max E. Greenberg Research Fund of the New York University School of Law is gratefully acknowledged.

[1] PS Atiyah and RS Summers, *Form and Substance in Anglo-American Law: A Comparative Study of Legal Reasoning, Legal Theory, and Legal Institutions* (Oxford, Clarendon Press, 1987).

[2] L Fuller, 'Consideration and Form' (1941) 41 *Columbia Law Review* 799.

[3] Atiyah and Summers, above n 1, 13.

[4] See, eg, 42 Pa C S § 5529(b)(1).

requirement of the Uniform Commercial Code that applies to contracts for the sale of goods valued at $500 or more.[5] This is over-inclusive because it renders unenforceable some actual and well-considered exchange agreements. Atiyah and Summers note that it is not always easy to tell whether a rule has high content formality, because it is not always easy to see what the purposes of the rule are.[6] This is a crucial point that I will spend some time with. Atiyah and Summers' own account of content formality is inadequate, however. Before turning to develop an alternative account of content formality, it will be helpful to consider interpretive formality in some detail, in order to bring the distinctiveness of content formality into clearer focus.

Interpretive formality is a matter of the resources that may legitimately be used in interpreting a rule – there is high interpretive formality if the interpreter is limited to the semantic content of the rule and is not permitted to read it in light of its understood purposes, or in light of other substantive concerns such as background principles of law or morality. Atiyah and Summers rightly note that 'Legal systems vary greatly in the degree to which they permit interpreters to go behind the verbal expression of the law and thus engage in reasoning that is more substantive than formal in deciding what the law itself *is* in the first place'.[7] One of the main arguments of their book is that the US allows for much more substantive interpretation by judges than does England. Ben Chen and Jeffrey Gordon in Chapter 16 of this volume argue persuasively that there has been some convergence over the last 30 years, in part due to the rise of textualist statutory interpretation in the US.[8] It nonetheless remains true that interpretation of contract law's common-law rules in state and federal courts in the US is strongly substantive, sometimes startlingly so.[9] As for statutes, the most important one for contract law, the Uniform Commercial Code (UCC), itself stipulates that it 'must be liberally construed and applied to promote its underlying purposes and policies' and it goes on helpfully to list them.[10]

Now content formalism and interpretive formalism interact in obvious ways. An interpreter from any jurisdiction will feel more comfortable engaging in substantive interpretation the less apparently formal the content of the rules he or she is interpreting. It is not hard to justify substantive interpretation of section 2-302 of the UCC, which provides that a court may limit enforcement of

[5] UCC § 2-201.

[6] Atiyah and Summers, above n 1, 14.

[7] ibid, 15.

[8] B Chen and J Gordon, 'Interpretive Formalism in the Law of Obligations: Thirty Years After Form and Substance', this volume, ch 16.

[9] I'm thinking in particular of certain law professors turned judges on the 7th Circuit Court of Appeals. See the opinion of Judge Easterbrook in *Pro CD v Zeidenberg* 86 F 3d 1447 (1996), or that of Judge Posner in *Walgreen v Sara Creek* 966 F 2d 273 (1992).

[10] UCC § 1-103. The purposes are: (1) to simplify, clarify, and modernize the law governing commercial transactions; (2) to permit the continued expansion of commercial practices through custom, usage, and agreement of the parties; and (3) to make uniform the law among the various jurisdictions.

an unconscionable contract without offering any guidance on what unconscionability is. In fact many of the rules of Article 2 of the UCC, the Sales article, have evident low content formality. The word 'reasonable' appears a great deal. The substantive surface content of many of the rules of Article 2 makes it easier to comply with the Code's injunction that it be interpreted substantively.

So the more substantive the apparent content of the rule, the easier to justify substantive interpretation. Nonetheless, substantive interpretation of rules with high apparent content formality is certainly possible. In 1765, in the case of *Pillans and Rose v Van Mierop and Hopkins*,[11] it was held that a written gratuitous promise for commercial purposes among merchants was legally enforceable despite the lack of consideration. Lord Mansfield wrote this: 'I take it, that the ancient notion about the want of consideration was for the sake of evidence only: for when it is reduced into writing, as in covenants, specialties, bonds, etc., there was no objection to the want of consideration.'[12] What Mansfield is doing here is interpreting substantively a rule that he takes to have formal content. The rule must have formal content, he reasoned, since no consideration was required for sealed instruments, and seals obviously have no substantive purpose. So the purpose of the consideration requirement can only be evidentiary. In the case of a written commercial promise between merchants, however, there is plenty of other evidence already, and so, interpreting the rule according to its evident purpose, the requirement of consideration could be waived. Good reasoning, but Mansfield was overturned by the House of Lords about ten years later on the simple ground that English law in fact required consideration for all agreements that were not under seal (specialties); it did not distinguish written commercial agreements among merchants from other unsealed agreements.[13]

What the House of Lords said, in effect, was that English judges were not to interpret the rule of consideration substantively in the way that Lord Mansfield had done. Even if he was right about the best way to understand the rule's content, his job was to interpret it formally, paying no attention to its underlying purpose. There is of course much to discuss here. Not only do legal systems vary greatly in how far they permit judges to engage in substantive interpretation, there is considerable scholarly controversy about how far they should permit judges to engage in substantive interpretation. In the US for most of the twentieth century, a broadly legal realist consensus prevailed in the academy, finding its way into the courts and, through Chief Reporter Professor Karl Llewellyn, into the UCC. Today, by contrast, the dominant approach in US legal theory is the economic analysis of law, and within that broad school of thought many favour a more formalist approach than has been the norm for the past 100 years. Important as it is, I will leave the normative debate about how far judges can legitimately engage in substantive interpretation to one side. My interest in this chapter is in

[11] *Pillans v Van Mierop* (1765) 3 Burr 1663, 97 ER 1035 ('*Pillans*').
[12] *Pillans* (1765) 3 Burr 1663, 1669, 97 ER 1035, 1038.
[13] *Rann v Hughes* (1778) 4 Bro PC 27, 2 ER 18.

understanding contract law, which is a very different question from that of how judges should decide contracts cases. In attempting to understand contract law, my perspective is that of the legal theorist. Judges need to understand the law to make good decisions, but when resolving a case before them they are constrained, to some extent at least, by rule-of-law and efficiency considerations. Similarly, a legal expert called upon to state his or her view about the content of current law, even though he or she is a private citizen with no formal institutional role, may nonetheless affect the outcome of cases and the development of the law, and should therefore be properly mindful of the potential practical effects of his or her statements.

The ethics and politics of interpretive formality as they apply to judges and legal experts do not apply to a legal theorist. What then does determine the proper way for a theorist to interpret the law? What does it mean for a theorist to offer an understanding of the content of legal doctrine? In particular, to what extent is a theorist constrained to fit the legal materials as they are found rather than offer a vision of an ideal legal order? And what does it mean to fit the materials as they are found – to be true to the semantic content of the rules? Or is it also appropriate to consider the underlying purposes?

We can distinguish three broad camps of legal theories of an area of law, reflecting three different approaches to theoretical interpretation of law. What we might call descriptive legal theory aligns with a kind of interpretive formalism. It is the view that the theory should fit the semantic content of the existing materials. Textbooks do this, though most, especially in the US, also engage in substantive interpretation, especially when it comes to offering an account of the overall structure of an area of law. At the opposite extreme from descriptive theory, there is normative legal theory, an approach that treats existing legal materials merely as useful sources of possibly good ideas; the aim of normative legal theory is to provide an account of the best kind of legal order for a particular area of life. Much of the economic analysis of law now takes this form, and I have mostly engaged in normative legal theory myself, though not of the economic variety.[14]

But in this chapter I am interested in understanding contract law as it is, in order to advance a claim about its formality. Normative legal theory is not really an attempt to understand any particular legal order at all. And purely descriptive legal theory doesn't seem likely to help us understand the formality of contract law because its commitment to interpretive formality means that we will be stuck at the surface level of legal doctrine, unable, for example, to ask whether the rule of consideration is for the sake of evidence and therefore formal in its content, or not.

What we need is an approach that precisely allows us to look behind the surface semantic content of the doctrine to reflect on the rationales of the rules.

[14] See L Murphy, 'The Practice of Promise and Contract' in G Klass, G Letsas and P Saprai (eds), *The Philosophical Foundations of Contract Law* (Oxford, Oxford University Press, 2014).

The contracts scholar Stephen Smith uses the label 'interpretive theory' for this kind of theory.[15] The theorist engaged in interpretive theory is attempting to uncover the normative foundations of some area of the law and, at least in my case, in this chapter, reflecting on how those normative foundations get expressed (more formally, more substantively?) in the content of the legal rules.

So that's the project: to offer an interpretive theory of contract law that aims in particular to uncover the degree of content formality of its rules.

II. Consideration and Form

Let me return now to the notion of content formality, and return also to Lord Mansfield, reading him, now not as a judge, but as an interpretive legal theorist.

The purpose of the rule requiring something given in exchange for a promise is evidentiary, Mansfield concluded. How could there be a substantive reason to care about consideration, if a purely formal device, like a seal, could dispense with the requirement? We could understand Mansfield as saying that though the rule says there must be an exchange, we shouldn't think that that means that exchanges matter, that there is some intrinsic reason *not* to enforce gratuitous promises. The purpose of the rule is not to be found by taking the requirement at face value. Put otherwise, we could say that Mansfield argued that the rule of consideration does not state its own rationale. For if it did the point of the rule would be that exchanges are more worthy of legal enforcement than gratuitous promises.

I suggest that we understand substantive legal rules as those that do state their own rationale. Karl Llewellyn wrote that the best rules 'carry their reason on their face';[16] in saying this, I take him to be stating his preference for substance over form. It is tempting to say that a substantive rule wears its rationale on its face. That has a good ring to it, but it would seem to imply that it was always clear from the face of the rule what its rationale was. As already mentioned, however, it can be hard to determine what the rationale of a rule is, and therefore hard to tell whether the rule is formal or substantive in content.[17] So my definition is that a substantive legal rule states its own rationale, with the understanding that it can be hard to tell whether that is in fact the case for any particular rule. Atiyah and Summers' definition of content formality in terms of arbitrariness and under- and over-inclusiveness doesn't seem to get to the heart of the matter, even though it may be a generally accurate descriptive statement about formal rules.

Sometimes it is obvious that a rule does or does not state its own rationale, and sometimes it isn't. The UCC requirement that enforceable agreements for the sale

[15] S Smith, *Contract Theory* (Oxford, Oxford University Press, 1993) 4.

[16] KN Llewellyn, *The Common Law Tradition: Deciding Appeals* (Boston, Little Brown and Co, 1960) 335, quoted by Atiyah and Summers, above n 1, 15 n 12.

[17] I am grateful here to Fred Wilmot-Smith.

of goods priced at $500 or more require a written memorandum obviously has some rationale other than that a written memorandum matters in itself for such agreements. So that one's formal. But with the requirement of consideration it is possible to go either way. Mansfield's argument depended on an assumption of overall coherence in the law; he would not have been able to reach the conclusion that the point of the rule was evidentiary just by looking at the rule.

If a rule does not state its own rationale, an obvious question to ask is precisely why it requires something that does not, in itself, matter. Why would a legislator or other law-maker create a rule like that? Here we can turn to Fuller and his celebrated discussion of the variety of functions of form. One of the functions of form he identified is the evidentiary. But he also introduced two other functions of form, the cautionary and the channelling functions. The cautionary function is clear enough. Even the promise to hand over a peppercorn could add a sense of seriousness that may hinder rash promising. By the channelling function Fuller has in mind that formalities can allow us to know with some certainty what the legal effects of our actions are. Here the seal, traditionally dispositive of enforceability, seems to serve the channelling function well, along of course with both the cautionary and evidentiary.

This enriching of our understanding of form via Fuller allows us to see that Mansfield's argument neglected an important alternative. It is true that a letter may do as good a job on the evidence front. Perhaps too his restriction of his decision to commercial cases involving merchants indicated that he was aware of the cautionary function, since perhaps promises in such a context are rarely rash. But what of the channelling function? If a form is to have a channelling function, it must be strictly enforced; it won't do to lift the formal veil.

The range of thought about consideration in the US is instructive here. At one extreme, we have Oliver Wendell Holmes declaring in 1881 that 'consideration is a form as much as a seal'.[18] At the other extreme, one hundred years later, with the role of the seal all but abolished as far as enforceability is concerned, we have the Restatement (Second) of Contracts embracing a substantive interpretation of the requirement of an exchange or bargain. Under Restatement doctrine, bargains have to be real for there to be consideration – not just in the sense that a promise given in return for a promise must not be illusory, but in the sense that the parties were really seeking what the other was offering. It must be the case that at least one reason why each side did what they did is that they were seeking what the other side did. This means that purely nominal or sham bargains will not satisfy the rule.[19] Since that is so, US law, at least Restatement law, appears to have a substantive rather than a formal doctrine of consideration. It really matters, in itself, that there be a bargain, a real bargain in the sense of mutual inducement.

[18] OW Holmes, *The Common Law* (New York, Dover, 1991) 273.
[19] *Restatement (Second) of Contracts (1981)* §71. Comment *b* expressly rejects nominal consideration.

We have then three options for consideration: a strict form with a channelling function, a non-channelling form that serves the evidentiary and cautionary functions only, and a substantive rule that expresses the proposition that exchanges are more worthy of legal enforcement than gratuitous promises. Which interpretation is right, and why?

III. Interpretive Constraints

This brings us to a fundamental issue for interpretive legal theory. Which criteria should guide our interpretation?

Two criteria are fairly straightforward and uncontroversial. First, the interpretation must fit the surface level of the legal rules reasonably well. That is, the interpretation must be compatible with what the rule says. All three interpretations of the consideration requirement satisfy this criterion. Second, the interpretation must show the law, or an area of law, to be tolerably coherent as a whole. As we saw, this criterion was decisive in Mansfield's argument for a formal interpretation of consideration in the age of sealed instruments.

A third criterion of interpretation, in addition to fit and coherence, also seems inescapable. It is what in a different context Ronald Dworkin called the dimension of justification.[20] Of two interpretations that equally well fit the doctrine, and equally show it to be coherent, we will generally prefer the account that shows it in its best light, morally and pragmatically speaking. There are of course exceptions; sometimes the best explanation of an area of law reveals an entirely immoral goal, such as racial subordination. What we are really looking for is the interpretation that is most plausible as an account of the underlying purpose. Benjamin Cardozo once wrote that in contract interpretation, 'Intention not otherwise revealed may be presumed to hold in contemplation the reasonable and probable'.[21] The same should go for our efforts to figure out the underlying normative goals of an area of law.

As an additional criterion, it is sometimes proposed that the interpretation must vindicate the kind of reasoning that participants in the legal practice, especially judges, actually engage in. Smith calls this the requirement of transparency.[22] This would be a criterion of considerable potential bite. It would rule out *ab initio* the economic analysis of law, since apart from a few law professors who join the bench, judges typically do not reason about the law from the point of view

[20] R Dworkin, *Law's Empire* (Cambridge, MA, Harvard University Press, 1986). Smith, above n 15, 13–24, calls this the criterion of 'morality'. The context is not the same as Dworkin is presenting a theory of how to determine the content of the law in force. I am engaged not in that inquiry, but in the theorist's effort to understand the normative foundations of contract law.

[21] *Jacob and Youngs v Kent* 230 NY 239, 242.

[22] Smith, above n 15, 24–25.

of economic efficiency. But it is surely a mistake to demand that the normative structure of an interpretive theory must mirror the way judges actually reason or should reason. It is entirely possible, and in fact plausible, to believe that judges should be constrained by a high level of interpretive formality that is simply not required of the legal theorist. It is entirely possible, in particular, that the right way to understand a body of law and its ideal application by judges and other legal decision makers should come apart. An economic or other instrumental account of the point of contract law could recommend the creation of an artificial normative order, with its own internal structure of rules and principles, tailor-made to advance certain social goals that are not referred to in the content of the rules. A natural analogy is the rules of a game. The point of the rules might be to make the game challenging and fun, but that doesn't mean that they must be applied with those goals in mind. Of course, a good interpretation will make sense of and explain the merits of the reasoning that legal-decision makers engage in, otherwise we would not have made sense of the legal rules. But that is a far cry from demanding that a theorist trying to understand the law should be limited to the kind of considerations properly taken into account in adjudication and other forms of legal decision-making.[23]

The point can be taken further, beyond the difference between the role of the legal decision-maker and the theorist. Thus in private law theory much is often made of the bilateral structure of private law, and it is often said that an account of an area of private law that does not do justice to this structure is for that reason defective. But again, it is one thing to *explain* that bilateral structure, to make good sense of it, it is another to assume that the best way to understand private law is to treat that structure as a matter of substance, rather than form. So though, as should go without saying, to make sense of a body of law we need to be able to explain why its rules have the content that they do, there is no requirement that an interpretation treat that structure as substantively significant.

As a perfect example of the kind of reasoning I here reject, consider Robert Stevens' chapter in this volume. Stevens explains that what is distinctive about private law duties is that they are correlated with rights, and the right holder has 'control' over the duty. It is up to me to decide whether to enforce the contract with you that you have breached.[24] I fully agree with this account of the distinctive normative structure of private law. But he goes on:

> This form imposes a constraint upon the kind of reasons that can, as a matter of justice, justify them. They must be reasons that tie this particular right holder to this particular duty bearer. They must be reasons that are bilateral in form, applying to both parties.[25]

[23] Felipe Jiménez helpfully distinguishes between a reflective and an explanatory demand of transparency. I agree with him that the latter is all that we should accept. See F Jiménez, *The Pluralism of Contract: A Theory of Contract Law*, JSD dissertation, NYU School of Law, 2018.
[24] R Stevens, 'Private Law and the Form of Reasons,' this volume, ch 6, Section III.
[25] ibid.

From this premise, Stevens goes on to reject, among other examples, instrumental justifications of accident law in terms of the goals of deterrence and compensation. 'These reasons are not bilateral in the way that right-shaped reasons need to be'.[26] The problem with all this is that Stevens gives us no argument at all in defence of his premise. Why should we accept this constraint on the kind of argument that could justify a particular legal normative order? This dogmatic and rigid attachment to legal form strikes me as a kind of fetishism. Stevens rightly notes that if we treat the formal structure of private law normative orders as having instrumental significance only, we may conclude that parts of private law should be abolished.[27] That this, for him, is apparently a *reductio* seems to support the charge of fetishism.

To return to my own argument, we have three criteria for interpretive legal theory as I am understanding it: fit, coherence, and justification. Let's apply them to our three readings of the consideration doctrine: Holmes' strict form with a channelling function, Mansfield's soft form serving only the evidentiary and cautionary functions, and the substantive bargain theory of the Restatement of Contracts. Holmes' strict form account seems poor on the level of justification because channelling requires general knowledge of legal effect. Fuller rightly emphasises the point that von Jhering made in *The Spirit of Roman Law* that the extreme formality of Roman Law was supportable only because of the ready availability of free legal advice.[28] For a form to have a channelling function, its effect must be known.

The substantive account of the Restatement seems poor on the level of justification too because no one has ever been able to explain why bargains are, as a matter of substance, more worthy of enforcement than gratuitous promises. The Scholastic quality of the brilliant, but to my mind, misguided argument Peter Benson offers by way of a substantive rational for the rule strikes me as providing evidence that none is likely to be found.[29] And so I venture that Mansfield has it right at least as far as justification goes: the rule is best seen as softly formal, serving evidentiary and cautionary functions. Seriously made promises, whether bargained for or not, are equally worthy of enforcement. It's just that evidentiary and cautionary issues arise for gratuitous promises more frequently than for exchange promises.

Unfortunately, this best account of the rule at the level of justification is a poor fit with US law, where precedent and the Restatement explicitly reject the idea that the rule is formal. US law does require a real bargain. This is unfortunate not only for being unmotivated, it has led to serious problems. By the early-twentieth century it had become clear that some gratuitous promises that looked good so far as evidence and caution were concerned were being left unenforced.

[26] ibid.
[27] ibid.
[28] Fuller, above n 2, 802.
[29] P Benson, 'The Idea of Consideration' (2011) 61 *University of Toronto Law Journal*, 241–78.

Rather than deal with this by embracing nominal consideration or dispensing with the requirement of consideration in some contexts, US law responded with a second substantive doctrine of enforceability, that of promissory estoppel.

A few words about the peculiar career of promissory estoppel in the US are worthwhile for further illustrating the issue of form and substance as I am understanding it. Promissory estoppel is pretty much an invention of the first Restatement of Contract, from 1933. Section 90 had it, roughly, that reasonably expected reliance rendered a gratuitous promise enforceable. This idea took off, and led in the academy to Grant Gilmore's celebrated 1974 book, *The Death of Contract*.[30] A popular school of thought emerged, which Patrick Atiyah was part of, that contract should be seen as a branch of tort, providing a remedy for the wrong of inducing reliance by promise and letting the losses fall with the promisee. This reliance school of thought assumed that promissory estoppel would become the dominant route to enforceability, that the bargain requirement would fall by the wayside, that purely executory agreements would begin to be regarded with suspicion, and, most importantly, that the remedy of expectation damages would be replaced with that of reliance damages.

All this reflects a substantive interpretation of the doctrine of promissory estoppel. A rule that says that promises that induce reasonably expected reliance are enforceable seems to have as its clear purpose the prevention of reasonably expected reliance losses, and the remedy of reliance damages is at hand to do just that. Coherence demands reliance and not expectation damages. In most states, however, expectation damages have routinely been awarded for promissory estoppel claims.

To achieve coherence, there is an alternative to changing the remedy: we could offer a different account of the purpose of the doctrine. And indeed, another school of thought had all along denied that the doctrine was all about compensation for reasonable detrimental reliance. Promissory estoppel can be understood as a formal rule, where the promisee's reliance provides evidence that the promise was made. Serious gratuitous promises are, substantively speaking, worthy of enforcement, relied upon or not. And to enforce a promise is to enjoin the promisor to perform or pay damages that are ideally just as good for the promisee.[31] So there is no problem with expectation damages since the point of the promissory estoppel doctrine really has nothing substantively to do with compensation for

[30] G Gilmore, *The Death of Contract* (Columbus, Ohio State University Press, 1974).

[31] See S Thel and E Yorio, 'The Promissory Basis of Section 90' (1991–92) 101 *Yale Law Journal*, 111. Samuel Williston, the Reporter for the first Restatement, embraced expectation damages for promissory estoppel cases. In discussion of §90 at the American Law Institute, he said this:

> Either the promise is binding or it is not. If this promise is binding it has to be enforced as it is made … I could leave this whole thing to the subject of quasi contracts so that the promisee under those circumstances shall never recover on the promise but he shall recover such an amount as will fairly compensate him for any injury incurred; but it seems to me you have to take one leg or the other. You have either to say the promise is binding or you have to go on the theory of restoring the status quo. (S Williston, *Proceedings April 29 1926, ALI Proceedings*, vol 4, App, 103–04).

detrimental reliance. Whether or not that is a plausible reading on the grounds of fit, which seems doubtful, antagonism to expectation damages as a remedy in promissory estoppel cases has waned considerably in recent decades.

IV. The Formality of Contractual Obligation

To take stock: I have introduced an idea of content formality according to which a rule is formal if it does not state its own rationale. And I have indicated the criteria I believe an interpretive legal theorist should use in investigating the relative formality of an area of law, using enforceability doctrine for illustration. It is time, finally, to turn to my claim that all of contract law is formal. Leaving aside the complexities of US enforcement doctrine, the proposition that agreements made ought to be kept and will be enforced if they are not seems to be stated on the surface of contract doctrine everywhere. We talk of contractual obligation, the rights of promisees, the duty of the promisor to perform contractual terms in good faith, and so on.[32] This seems to show that the most fundamental rules of contract law in fact do state their own rationale – the rationale that people should perform their serious promises and agreements. If people don't do that, the law will make them do so, either by injunction or an award of money damages ideally just as good for the promisee as performance. The goal of contract law seems precisely to be to enforce contractual obligations. The core principles of the promisor's obligation to perform and the promisee's correlative right to performance seem to be about as substantive as you can get.

But in fact we cannot get to the point and rationale of contract law by looking at the surface of the core rules and reading them straight. It is true that the surface of the doctrine has it that promisees have contractual rights, which correlate with obligations on the part of promisors. This deontological structure of the legal doctrine naturally suggests that it is aiming to reflect real natural moral rights and obligations that people have. But I believe that this is a mistake. Those legal rights and obligations exist only internally to the legal normative order, which must be justified instrumentally and as a whole; the rights and obligations have no independent intelligibility.

So I am against a substantive interpretation of contractual rights and obligations according to which the legal rules mirror and enforce real moral duties. Though such an interpretation does very well by the criteria of fit and coherence, it is ineligible because of its total failure in the dimension of justification. This is

[32] *Restatement (Second) of Contracts*: §1 'Contract Defined. A contract is a promise or a set of promises for the breach of which the law gives a remedy, or the performance of which the law in some way recognizes as a duty.' *Ahmed Angullia Bin Hadjee Mohamed Salleh Angullia v Estate & Trust Agencies (1927) Ltd* [1938] AC 624, 635 (PC, appeal taken from Singapore) held that an executor never has a duty to break an enforceable contract because breach is an unlawful act.

for the simple reason that there are no natural promissory obligations and duties. Promissory morality is, as David Hume argued in the eighteenth century, an artificial rather than a natural part of morality – in the sense that we cannot make sense of it without reference to valuable conventional practices. There is no promissory obligation without a prior social practice that comprises rules specifying that promises made should be kept.

Of course, much discussion is required to defend this Humean position. Any argument for natural moral promissory duties and rights, duties and rights that could exist absent a conventional social practice and that contract law could simply mirror, would need to be confronted. I attempt such a defence of the Humean view elsewhere,[33] but here I am simply going to assume for the sake of argument that there is no such thing as a natural, non-artificial, promissory morality.

So we grant that the morality of promise and fidelity to agreements requires the existence of a conventional social practice. We have such a practice, and it is supported and made more secure by the legal institution of contract law. We have the social practice and the legal order because they are socially valuable. They expand people's options by making possible cooperative behaviour that would not otherwise occur, with resulting benefits for all of us.

Now the fact that a conventional normative order is socially beneficial does not mean that its rules have genuine deontological force; that they are, in other words, real moral duties. It is, of course, a very important fact that the practice of promise and the institution of contract law are socially valuable. If informal social enforcement and formal legal enforcement of the practice of making and keeping agreements is to be justified, it had better (among other requirements) do some good.[34] But justification for enforcing a conventional normative order and the genuine moral force of its rules are two different matters.

This does not mean that individuals can regard with moral indifference the health of a socially beneficial practice. The fact that a practice or institution is socially beneficial means that we should be disposed to promote and protect it, and not undermine it. This is very important. But that we should support and not undermine the normative orders of promise and contract doesn't mean that we have an obligation always to comply with their rules.

Violations of the rules of the practice of promise and contract law do, it is true, on occasion cause actual material harm to individuals – the material harm of detrimental reliance is the clearest case. There might be a natural moral rule that one should not encourage reliance and then leave losses to lie where they fall. But since contractual obligation does not require detrimental reliance, we should

[33] I make my case in L Murphy, 'The Artificial Morality of Private Law: The Persistence of an Illusion' (unpublished ms 2018).

[34] In G Gaus, *The Order of Public Reason* (Cambridge, Cambridge University Press, 2011) Gerald Gaus makes the important point that legitimacy is a requirement not only of state enforcement, but of conventional morality.

leave cases where non-performance causes reliance losses to one side. We need to focus on pure cases of promissory noncompliance, those where no reliance has occurred. In such cases, non-performance causes no material harm. What are misleadingly called expectation losses are not in themselves actual material losses; they are losses only relative to contractual obligation and right, as established by the rules of the legal normative order. And in question is precisely what reason we have to follow those rules.

It's my view that the moral tie between individuals and the rules of the practice of promise and contract law is exhausted by the duty, already mentioned, to protect and promote the health of the practice and the legal institution. Probably anyone with that goal will develop a disposition generally to keep promises and honour contracts, unusual circumstances aside. But having that goal is also compatible with noncompliance with the rules, since sometimes breach of promise or contract will not tend to undermine the practice, and in fact will do no harm at all. The rules, in particular the fundamental rule of contractual obligation, are nominal or formal rules. For there is no such thing as contractual or promissory obligation, morally speaking, that the legal rules could be mirroring. The law of contract does not enforce real moral duties. It enforces the beneficial social practice of making and keeping promises and agreements. The point of enforcing the rules is entirely to make possible the achievement of the social goods that justify the practice.

V. Form as Instrument

This is why I say that all of contract law is formal; that, in particular, contractual obligation and right are formal. The most fundamental rules of contract law do not state their rationales. So they are not substantive, but formal. In saying this, I have gone beyond Fuller's short list of the functions of form. But what binds Fuller's three functions together is just that they are purposes not stated in a rule's semantic content. The basic idea I have been working with, that formal rules cannot be understood in terms of the intrinsic importance of what they require, means that the functions of form can include any kind of instrumental purpose. Form and substance in legal content turns out to be most usefully understood as a matter of whether what a rule requires is of intrinsic or instrumental significance. Many legal rules, especially in the criminal law, and the constitutional law of fundamental rights, where that exists, are substantive. The rules of contract law, however, are entirely instrumental, and therefore formal.

To say that the rules of contract are formal because instrumental is not to criticise them. Nor is it inevitably to fall into some kind of objectionable reductionism. To defend an instrumental view is not to join the camp of economic analysis. There are many social goods other than economic efficiency, including social justice, the promotion of autonomy for its own sake, and so on, that the practice of promise and contract law may serve.

It is also worth emphasising that the fact that the rules of contract law are formal for being instrumental does *not* mean that legal decision-makers should give the content of the rules no force in their reasoning and always reason instrumentally. Contract law is a wonderfully complex, elegant, and mostly coherent body of doctrine. When I teach it, I teach the rules as real rules. Legal decision-makers can obviously also reason from the rules, without always looking behind them to the instrumental purposes they serve. Perhaps Mansfield the judge was wrong to look behind the rule of consideration in the way that he did. Perhaps, but perhaps not. That contract law is a coherent legal order that can mostly be applied on its own terms does not mean that judges should never have an eye to its underlying instrumental rationale. But either way, the point is that it is entirely possible to treat the rules of contract law as providing genuine reasons in the right context (the context of adjudication, or teaching, or giving expert advice) while fully understanding that, in truth, they do not provide any reasons on their own, but only virtue of their being part of a beneficial social practice.

VI. Conclusion

I have offered an interpretive theory of contract that gives it a purely instrumental justification and has it that, as a result, the law of contract is formal throughout. If that theory, true as it may be, is not going to determine how judges, educators, or legal experts should reason about the content of contract law, is it really all that important? It is, and not just because it is of intrinsic importance to understand major social institutions such as contract law. This conclusion of legal theory has political importance as well. For it is very important that in our political discourse we understand the normative order of promise/contract as the instrument it is. We go badly astray if we treat the rules of the social practice promise and contract law as substantive in content.

To bring this out, I will close with a word about the idea of freedom of contract. On the conventionalist formalist view I have been defending, there is no such right. Which contracts should be enforced is a question to be figured out when designing the rules of the legal order. The practice of making and keeping agreements, and its legal enforcement, is good and worth having to the extent that it does some good. In my view promises both gratuitous and bargained-for are equally worthy of enforcement, but there is no reason to think a priori that agreements of any content are equally worthy of enforcement. Of course, it is a sound rule of thumb, and perhaps the fundamental reason why private ordering is a good idea, that the people best able to figure out what is in their interests are the individuals who might be parties to agreements. But the rule of thumb is just that. If there are good reasons for thinking that enforcing some categories of agreements does more harm than good, there is no reason based in contractual right for the state to enforce them. Going so far as to ban agreements might have the effect of making certain conduct impossible in practice, which may infringe liberty rights. But even banning certain agreements does not infringe a right to freedom of contract, as there is no such thing.

This is not how most people think about it, it seems to me. Though perhaps no one believes in a right to sell yourself into slavery, the idea of a right to freedom of contract is alive and well. Consider debates over sexual or reproductive services, or the sale of body parts. Most people do not think that whether certain kinds of agreements should be legally enforceable or unenforceable turns solely on the value of the results of enforcing versus not enforcing. The supposed right to freedom of contract, even if it is not absolute, is given weight in moral argument. There is a presumption in favour of enforceability that is grounded not just in the observation that things generally go better when people make up their own minds; instead, it is said that a decision not to enforce requires establishing that enforcement would involve very serious harm, serious enough to overcome the infringement of people's right to freedom of contract.

For people who believe in genuine moral contractual rights and obligations, then, there is a special moral hurdle to be overcome if, for example, minimum wage laws, or occupational health and safety laws, are to be justified. Whether or not constitutional courts are striking down such legislation on the grounds of infringement of a right to freedom of contract,[35] the thought that there is such a right certainly distorts the deliberations of legislators and legal experts everywhere.

I make these points to bring out the fact that the proper understanding of contract law, and private law generally, is of great political significance. Even if judges and other legal-decision makers should never think about the instrumental rational for contract law and always interpret its rules formally, all of us should be clear about contract law's content formality when thinking about social policy and legal change.

[35] *Lochner v New York* 198 US 45 (1905) (striking down maximum working hours for bakery employees).

8

Two Forms of Formalism

DAN PRIEL

I. Introduction

This chapter is an attempt to investigate the philosophical foundations of doctrinal scholarship. Such an inquiry may seem surprising. From the outside, those who do not engage in doctrinal scholarship often see it as a pedestrian enterprise of collecting the cases and arranging them, a kind of menial labour that's perhaps necessary but is of limited intellectual interest;[1] from the inside, doctrinal scholars sometimes present themselves as uninterested in, perhaps even positively opposed to, philosophical ruminations.[2] They see themselves as 'practical' scholars who aim to help the courts reach better decisions, and they do that by a careful reading of the cases seeking to derive from them a coherent set of rules and principles already found in them, a task for which there is no need for any serious knowledge of history, economics, psychology, or philosophy.[3] And indeed doctrinal works typically avoid, or at most treat cursorily, what they perceive to be 'academic' discussions of 'high theory'.[4]

But as Daniel Dennett once said in a different context, 'there is no such thing as philosophy-free science; there is only science whose philosophical baggage is taken on board without examination'.[5] And what is true of science is true also of other intellectual pursuits. It is with this belief in mind that I set out to examine the philosophical assumptions of doctrinal scholarship, and in doing that also the normative foundation of legal doctrine itself. This chapter seeks to identify and distinguish between two approaches to legal doctrine which have been

[1] T Becher and PR Trowler, *Academic Tribes and Territories: Intellectual Enquiry and the Culture of Disciplines*, 2nd edn (Milton Keynes, Open University Press, 2001) 31.

[2] See F Cownie, *Legal Academics: Cultures and Identities* (Oxford, Hart Publishing, 2004) 69–72.

[3] See A Burrows, *Understanding the Law of Obligations: Essays on Contract, Tort, and Restitution* (Oxford, Hart Publishing, 1998) 113; G Jones, '"Traditional" Legal Scholarship: A Personal View', in P Birks (ed), *What Are Law Schools for?* (Oxford, Oxford University Press, 1996) 9.

[4] See the remarks of AWB Simpson, 'Contract: The Twitching Corpse' (1981) 1 *OJLS* 265, 266–67.

[5] DC Dennett, *Darwin's Dangerous Idea: Evolution and the Meanings of Life* (London, Penguin Press, 1995) 21; *cf* OW Holmes, 'The Path of the Law' (1897) 10 *Harvard Law Review* 457, 478.

described as 'formalistic'. I will distinguish between what I call 'conceptualism' and 'doctrinalism' and analyse the way in which they are different from each other. I will then proceed to evaluate both. My conclusions with respect to conceptualism are negative, as it seems to be based on indefensible assumptions. My evaluation of doctrinalism is a different matter. I find that doctrinalism provides a fairly robust answer to many theoretical legal-political concerns. However, I argue that doctrinalism is vulnerable to challenges of legitimacy and of instability. I conclude not with a definitive answer on doctrinalism, but with an attempt to point out different ways of dealing with its weaknesses and the costs that come with them.

II. Conceptualism and Doctrinalism

A. What the Two Approaches Have in Common

There is a familiar distinction between 'internal' legal scholarship, one that 'takes law seriously', and 'external' legal scholarship, one that takes greater interest in ideas coming from other disciplines and seeks (to varying degrees) to use ideas coming from economics, philosophy, sociology, psychology, literary theory, or even neuroscience, to explain, justify, or challenge the law.[6] It is common to describe the former approach as 'formalist' and the latter as 'realist'. But in fact this internal/external divide hides from view two very different approaches to legal scholarship, two approaches that on the usual classification are taken by their proponents to be 'internal', but which are, so I will argue, in important respects very different from each other. One approach, I will call it 'conceptualism', sees itself as internal to types of relations among individuals, and uses its analysis of these relations as the basis for legal analysis. The other approach, 'doctrinalism', focuses its attention on the products of legal officials, and considers proper legal analysis to be internal to that.

Before we examine their differences – and they are significant – it is worth considering in what sense the two approaches came to be seen as belonging to a single category, why these two rather different views have often been analysed together, why even members of these two groups often seem to think of them as complementary, even if not quite the same.

I think the fundamental idea that unites conceptualism and doctrinalism is that law is in some important sense autonomous from other disciplines,

[6] This distinction is found, eg, in S Hedley, 'Looking Outward or Looking Inward? Obligations Scholarship in the Early 21st Century' in A Robertson and HW Tang (eds), *The Goals of Private Law* (Oxford, Hart Publishing, 2009) 193, 195–99; SA Smith, *Contract Theory* (Oxford, Oxford University Press, 2004) ch 1; P Cane, *Anatomy of Tort Law* (Oxford, Hart Publishing, 1997) 206–13; C McCrudden, 'Legal Research and the Social Sciences' (2006) 122 *LQR* 632, 633–34.

which means that the law has its own solutions to certain problems. Law is not just a technique of getting people to do (or not do) whatever society wants them to do; it has its own answers to what it is that people should (or should not) do. That makes appeal to other disciplines at best unnecessary and possibly confusing. Another way of putting it is that proponents of both views are jointly committed to the idea that to use the legal form inexorably pushes one to a certain substance. It is this view that makes the idea of law's autonomy possible, and it is this view that joins these two approaches in opposition to a common – and these days, mighty – enemy: interdisciplinary approaches to the study of law. To the formalist of either strand, other approaches, perspectives, or disciplines may provide observations *about* law (that it tends to contribute to economic growth, that it favours the rich and powerful), but they cannot contribute to the study *of* law.

The link between formalism and law's autonomy should not come as a surprise: formalists of both stripes have explicitly embraced it.[7] But it may still seem a bit odd, for legal autonomy is primarily a claim about the relationship between law and non-law, between law and other things that are 'outside' the law. The word 'formalism', by contrast, seems to be a claim about what goes on within the law: about legal analysis and reasoning, and more specifically about the ways legal 'forms' (whatever those are) matter 'inside' the law. One task of this chapter will be to explain this relationship between legal autonomy (the law/non-law interface) and the place of 'forms' within the law. As I will attempt to show, conceptualism and doctrinalism have a different answer to this question.

I will return to these questions later. For the moment, the idea of autonomy suffices for understanding what brings the conceptualism and doctrinalism together. I turn now to what sets them apart.

B. The Two Approaches Contrasted

As mentioned, the doctrinalist and the conceptualist often join forces in resisting incursions from other disciplines, both insisting on the significance of the 'internal point of view'. But at heart they are quite different and they pursue their goal of explaining legal practice in quite different ways. An imprecise but often accurate proxy for telling them apart is looking at an author's footnotes. The doctrinalist will cite lots of cases, and he or she will mostly cite cases; the conceptualist, on the other hand, will have relatively few citations to cases, which he or she will use to illustrate ideas said to be implicit in the law. Even when conceptualists discuss

[7] See, eg, EJ Weinrib, *The Idea of Private Law*, 2nd edn (Oxford, Oxford University Press, 2012) ch 8; Burrows, above n 3, 113; see also J Steyn, 'Does Legal Formalism Hold Sway in England?' (1996) 49 *Current Legal Problems* 43, 44.

cases, however, more often than not they are presented as *illustrations* of principles whose soundness is explained and justified completely independently of the cases. This seemingly small difference between the two approaches could be dismissed as inconsequential, at most reflecting an author's writing style. On the contrary, I believe it reflects a deep divide between two different approaches, one that tells us something about how the doctrinalist and the conceptualist think of law and the basis of its authority. The doctrinalist starts with the cases, from which by way of induction, he or she seeks some general principles; the cases for him or her are thus constitutive of the law. The conceptualist sees law as an abstract idea of reason that cases in a particular time and place may or may not exemplify. The conceptualist's project is thus deemed internal to the abstract idea, not to its often defective worldly manifestation.

At the risk of misusing two well-worn philosophical labels, I suggest that the doctrinalist is the law's empiricist while the conceptualist is its rationalist. And if we push this distinction even more perilously further to the association of empiricism with English early modern philosophy and rationalism with philosophy coming from the European continent, the traditional doctrinalist will typically be less interested in importing ideas from civil law systems and may even insist that there are fundamental differences between the common law and civil law; the philosophical rationalist, on the other hand, will tend to be more universalistic in his or her views about the foundations of law and will therefore more likely draw on civilian ideas and methods.[8] The conceptualist will do so both because true ideas about law are universal, but perhaps also because civilian scholars have more often adopted the same general picture that is so central to conceptualist thinking.

The rationalist label is also helpful because it explains how the conceptualist seeks to identify certain truths of practical rationality from which particular legal rules are derived. Proponents of this view do not typically think that reason provides a determinate answer to every outstanding legal question and so allow for some legal novelty, either legislative or judicial. But such legal creations happen only at the margin. The general contours of the law are stable and unchanging. The doctrinalist sees things very differently. For him or her, the ultimate origin of the authority of law does not lie with pure reason but with acceptability. That is why for doctrinalists the reason of the law is artificial (manufactured, technical), a set of principles, ideas and maxims, which are not available to all reasonable creatures, but requires long study. These general principles in turn feed back into the articulation of legal rules to particular cases.[9] This idea resonates with a conception

[8] See D Priel, 'The Philosophies of the Common Law and their Implications: Common Law Divergences, Public Authority Liability, and the Future of a Common Law World' in A Robertson and M Tilbury (eds), *The Common Law of Obligations: Divergence and Unity* (Oxford, Hart Publishing, 2016) 233, 237–40.

[9] See GJ Postema, 'The Philosophy of the Common Law' in JL Coleman and SJ Shapiro (eds), *The Oxford Handbook of Jurisprudence and the Philosophy of Law* (Oxford, Oxford University Press, 2002) 588, 592–95.

of authority quite different from the conceptualist's: not abstract and unchanging pure reason, but the concrete and shifting working out of lawyers' custom or artifice. This 'custom' typically retains concepts that are part of lay moral discourse (fault, cause, blame and so on), but which acquire a semi-technical meaning in legal practice.

Figure 1 is a simplified diagrammatic presentation of these two approaches.

Figure 1 Conceptualism (left) and doctrinalism

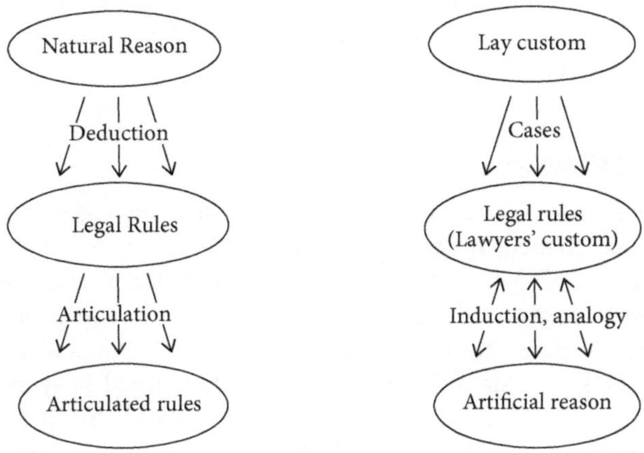

I hope it is clear that conceptualism and doctrinalism as presented here are ideal-types. In reality, there will often be cross-currents and less than pure specimens. Especially doctrinalists, who are typically less self-consciously philosophical (or more self-consciously pragmatic), will sometimes draw on ideas coming from conceptualists, either to justify their engaging in doctrinal scholarship or in providing a theoretical basis on which they built their more detailed case-based investigations. It is notable, however, that these attempts to fuse the two often only partially work.[10]

Sticking to ideal-types, I consider below eight features that set conceptualists and doctrinalists apart. These differences are not coincidental; they are systematic and, at bottom, reflect different philosophical outlooks. They lead to competing views of the authority of law,[11] and on occasion they yield differences in practice.

[10] Peter Birks's work is probably the most serious attempt to fuse the two approaches. From the perspective presented in this chapter, his greatest theoretical effort – some will say his greatest theoretical achievement – has been to provide a convincing synthesis between them, such that proponents of both approaches could feel, with some justification, that he belonged to their camp. Nevertheless, in my view, Birks' deeper commitments lie with the conceptualists.

[11] See D Priel, 'Conceptions of Authority and the Anglo-American Common Law Divide' (2017) 65 *American Journal of Comparative Law* 609.

i. The Declaratory Theory of Law

The conceptualist is committed to the apparent 'fairy tale' that law is discovered, not made. They are the last holdouts of the declaratory theory.[12] For them, the foundational legal categories are part of reality that lawyers seek to discover. Only at a relatively low level of resolution is there some flexibility in legal categorisation. By contrast, doctrinalists do not see any theoretical reason to accept the declaratory theory, and judges – who by inclination or habituation are more commonly doctrinalists than conceptualists – have largely abandoned it.[13] Doctrinalists typically think that there are serious limits to what a judge can do, but those are institutional and political, not conceptual.

ii. Validation of the Account

As already briefly mentioned, for the doctrinalist it is the cases from which the classifications are created; for the conceptualist, the cases at most demonstrate them. In a recent book Allan Beever, who is clearly on the conceptualist side, has stated that, '[w]hen asked a difficult legal question, the common lawyer, if she is a [doctrinalist], thinks either of cases or statutes and, if she is a [conceptualist], ponders principles and ideas'.[14] Birks, it is true, has urged lawyers not to look skyward to abstract justice, but downwards to the cases,[15] but it is notable that compared to works of doctrinalists his books were relatively sparse in their citation to cases. More importantly, he sought ultimate support for his views not in the cases, but in reason itself. It is notable that he found the ultimate justification for the principle of unjust enrichment not in the cases, but in its intuitive self-evidence.[16]

[12] See P Birks, 'Mistakes of Law' (2000) 53 *Current Legal Problems* 205, 217–18; A Beever, 'The Declaratory Theory of Law' (2013) 33 *OJLS* 421. For a slightly different formulation, see M Stone, 'On the Idea of Private Law' (1996) 9 *Canadian Journal of Law and Jurisprudence* 235, 259: 'corrective justice is meant to exhibit a characteristic sort of reason *already* captured in the ongoing activity of argument and judgment directed towards the situation to which modern liability rules are a judicially evolved response'.

[13] J Reid, 'The Judge as Law-Maker' (1972) 12 *Journal of the Society of the Public Teachers of Law* 22, 22; see also *State Government Insurance Commission v Trigwell* (1979) 142 CLR 617, 650 (the declaratory theory 'should not be regarded seriously'); A Burrows, 'Form and Substance: Fictions and Judicial Power', this volume, ch 2.

[14] A Beever, *Forgotten Justice: The Forms of Justice in the History of Legal and Political Theory* (Oxford, Oxford University Press, 2013) 206.

[15] P Birks, *An Introduction to the Law of Restitution* (Oxford, Clarendon Press, rev edn, 1989) 19.

[16] See P Birks, *Unjust Enrichment*, 2nd edn (Oxford, Oxford University Press, 2005) 6–7. Contrast this with the very different approach taken in A Burrows, *The Law of Restitution*, 3rd edn (Oxford, Oxford University Press, 2011) 35, where scepticism about unjust enrichment is answered by appeal to 'the judicial opinion in England'. (Does he therefore accept that the critique of unjust enrichment is correct in Australia?)

iii. The Attitude Toward Discretion and Policy

Conceptualists are hostile to discretion and think of policy (and politics) as the antithesis of law. To look to any of those when considering legal questions is to commit a category error. Discretion is particularly pernicious because it is like an open invitation to turn to these irrelevant considerations.[17] Doctrinalists are less dogmatic about the matter. Courts, after all, rely on 'policy' all the time, and so as faithful followers of the courts, they cannot ignore policy. However, doctrinalists concerned for maintaining the autonomy of law insist that policy is nothing more than what one can find in the cases.[18]

iv. Taxonomy and its Significance

It is the law's initial messiness that is the doctrinalist's raison d'être; for conceptualists, the law's *alleged* messiness is derived from a philosophical mistake, the error of confusing the cumulative efforts to *identify* the law's pre-existing order (also known as 'legal cases') for the law itself. This difference implies quite different views about taxonomy.

For conceptualists taxonomy is significant because it is an attempt to describe pre-existing reality. It is thus crucial for identifying true legal classification, and by implication the correct way of deciding cases. Birks' constant invocation of the map metaphor is not accidental: The map-maker aims to give an accurate method of finding one's way around an independently-existing reality.[19] Courts are participants in this enterprise, but none of their judgments on the matter can determine reality. For Birks, for example, unjust enrichment will remain an independent legal category even if all courts rejected this view.

Doctrinalists think taxonomy is valuable because it is an effort to *impose* order onto a mass of cases. Taxonomy is useful, but it is much more a conclusion of an argument than a discovery. Doctrinalists, unlike conceptualists, thus see classification as an artificial human construction,[20] and are more likely to acknowledge that it requires appeal, even if implicit, to some non-legal considerations. Taxonomical work is thus to some extent about *persuasion*, about showing that a particular taxonomy is better than another. What makes one taxonomy superior is that it

[17] See A Beever, 'Policy in Private Law: An Admission of Failure' (2006) 25 *University of Queensland Law Journal* 287.

[18] P Wright, 'Public Policy' in *Legal Essays and Addresses* (Cambridge, Cambridge University Press, 1939) 66, 95; R Grantham and D Jensen, 'The Proper Role of Policy in Private Law Adjudication' (2018) 68 *University of Toronto Law Journal* 187, 207.

[19] P Birks, 'Equity in the Modern Law: An Exercise in Taxonomy' (1996) 26 *University of Western Australia Law Review* 1, 8–9, P Birks, 'Introduction' to P Birks (ed), *English Private Law* (Oxford, Oxford University Press, 2000) xxxv, xlvi.

[20] Contrast D Jensen, 'The Problem of Classification in Private Law' (2007) 31 *Melbourne University Law Review* 516, 523 (legal taxonomy is artificial) with P Birks, 'Rights, Wrongs, and Remedies' (2000) 20 *OJLS* 1, 3, 19 (lawyers must pay attention to the law's 'own taxonomy', and maintaining the right taxonomy guarantees 'rationality').

makes more sense of existing cases, or it makes dealing with new ones easier. Though this inevitably forces doctrinalists to rely on normative considerations that they do not always acknowledge, the judgment is 'pragmatic' rather than 'metaphysical'.

Doctrinalism also differs from conceptualism in the role it gives judges in the taxonomical enterprise. The conceptualist view is grounded in ideas of theoretical authority, of expertise about an aspect of reality. As such, whether a given judge has it is a contingent matter. Indeed, a committed conceptualist might argue that given that judges do not have the time to dedicate themselves to taxonomical questions, most of them are in a worse position than the academic when it comes to discovering legal reality. In the doctrinalist view, the source of judges' authority on taxonomical questions is practical. Legal taxonomy is fundamentally a human creation, and not everyone has the same power to shape it. Given their positions, with their power to shape the law, judges are in a completely different status compared to others on matters of classification. Their judgments are not mere observations on the order of legal things, rather their pronouncements determine this order. To be sure, the work of academics may sway others to think (or rethink) the organisation of law, but on their own, their work has no authority. However intellectually impressive, until adopted by judges, such works are purely 'academic'.

It also follows from this view that history and path dependence matter for classification. What may be the correct classification in one place (for example, in civilian systems) may not fit the law in other places (for example, common law systems).[21]

v. The Significance of Coherence

Both approaches give some place to coherence, although what is meant by that term is different. For the doctrinalist the coherence is imposed upon the materials by the lawyers who organise and rationalise them. It is for this reason that the coherence imposed is typically fairly local. Local coherence is instrumentally valuable – it makes the law easier to understand, it provides clear guidance and thus helps in rule-following.

Since legal categories are a human construction, it is simply a fact about the world that legal coherence is a relatively local matter. This is a reflection of the fact that most human efforts at increasing legal coherence have been limited to particular legal domains. This does not mean that it is impossible to construct a globally coherent legal system, but the practical benefits from such a gargantuan effort are likely to be small. Moreover, whatever value one finds in coherence, it is only one value that has to be measured against other goals the law may seek to promote, values that are often reflected in 'policy'. By contrast, for conceptualists

[21] *cf* R Stevens, *Torts and Rights* (Oxford, Oxford University Press, 2007) 341–47.

coherence is 'built into' the law from the start: True (natural) law is the product of reason and reason is perfectly coherent. The incoherence one finds in the law is a reflection of the human failure to discover true legal reality, not a problem with the law itself. For some conceptualists, the coherence of the law is universal because they see a perfectly coherent morality (or a certain part of it) as a blueprint for law. Law, properly understood, is coherent, because morality is coherent.

An interesting implication of this difference is the attitude toward categorical overlaps. Conceptualists generally think that reality abhors overlapping or conflicting classification, and tend to think that particular events fall under a singular classification. Starting with the assumption that the scholar works out a pre-existing taxonomy along the lines of the Linnaean biological taxonomy, such overlaps look as suspect as that of a biological species that belongs to more than one biological family.[22] By contrast, for doctrinalists, categorical overlaps are not problematic as such, and given the history of the development of legal categories, are quite likely. The problem with categorical overlaps is ultimately practical, namely that it risks confusion. Other than that, there is nothing inherently problematic about such overlaps.

vi. The Standard of Correctness

The conceptualist is committed to the idea that it is a fundamental error to derive an ought from an is; the doctrinalist is committed to the almost opposite view that the most assured way to identify a community's oughts, is through an examination of its practices. For the doctrinalist the ultimate mark of the correctness of law is its acceptability. Acceptability by whom? The relevant community for doctrinalists is typically that of fellow lawyers, an important fact which explains how the law can remain autonomous.[23] Conceptualists, on the other hand, dismiss acceptability as a relevant source of law: The law is the product of reason. Custom and practice are facts, and as such are, on their own, of no normative force.

vii. The Normative Force of History

As part of the general distinction between 'internal' and 'external' approaches to law and legal scholarship, there is a distinction between 'doctrinal' legal history and 'social' legal history. The former tracks the development of legal doctrine and legal institution in relative isolation from social history. Some legal historians

[22] P Birks, 'Unjust Enrichment and Wrongful Enrichment' (2001) 79 *Texas Law Review* 1767, 1781; Birks, 'Equity in the Modern Law: An Exercise in Taxonomy', above n 19, 7 ('The law cannot tolerate, or should not be able to tolerate, torts named so as to intersect … [And] the same problem which bedevils tort bedevils the whole law'). Contrast this view with Burrows, above n 3, ch 2, who defends the possibility of concurrent liability.

[23] What I call 'traditional legal realists' also think correctness is measured by acceptability, but they typically turn to the wider community, thus adopting a more 'open' standard. See S IV(d).

adopting this stance have even argued that social history has had relatively little effect on the development of law.[24] By contrast, internal legal history matters: It has normative force. One cannot give a full account of why a certain legal answer is right or wrong independently of a process of historical development. One could cite a case that stands for a certain legal rule, but to know whether the case is actually true (that is was not 'wrongly decided') requires looking at its place within the history of past cases.

By contrast, conceptualists' accounts are fundamentally ahistorical, because history is devoid of normative significance: The fact that people have done something in the past is not in itself any reason to keep on doing it.[25] The justification of a legal rule is its internal normative force, which can be grasped by considering the rule alone. The way the rule came about is neither here nor there.

viii. Formalist, in What Way

For the doctrinalist, the 'forms' in formalism are legal categories, and they seek to have precise, well-articulated categories that provide clear answers to legal questions. The opposite of formalism in this sense is rough justice, unguided intuitions on the specific facts of a case (the identity of the plaintiff, the background of the defendant), 'substantive justice' in the sense of unmediated reaction to a case on which legal categories are imposed as ex post rationalisations. What makes one a lawyer as opposed to a moralist is that upon hearing a factual scenario one strips from it all legally irrelevant information and places it in the relevant legal category ('this is a contract', 'this is a trust'), and finds out, on the basis of existing legal rules, what follows from that classification. When one does that, one is not expressing one's view, but simply applying the law. The ideal underlying this view is that different people, with different backgrounds and having different political orientations, when confronted with a factual scenario, will be able to reach the same legal outcome. Thinking like a lawyer means being able to ignore one's personal views on the matter, something that the autonomy of law assists with. In short, for the doctrinalist the 'forms' in formalism are legal categories (contract, tort, trust, and so on), and the reason to take them seriously is political, or if you prefer metapolitical.[26]

The conceptualist shares many of these ideas, but at bottom he is a formalist in a different sense. As I understand it, for the conceptualist what is central are not legal categories but kinds of relations or interactions between individuals.

[24] The most prominent defender of this view is Alan Watson, eg, in *The Evolution of Western Private Law* (Baltimore, Johns Hopkins University Press, expanded edn, 2001); see also P Karsten, *Head versus Heart: Judge-Made Law in Nineteenth Century America* (Chapel Hill, University of North Carolina Press, 1997) 300, *passim*.

[25] A Beever and C Rickett, 'Interpretive Legal Theory and the Academic Lawyer' (2005) 68 *MLR* 320, 330.

[26] P Birks, 'Book Review' (2003) 119 *LQR* 156, 159.

These are perceived as central even for intelligibility of the rights and obligations of people towards each other even before, or outside, the law.

Ultimately, the conceptualist's view of law is part of a far more comprehensive view about the true order of nature. Alongside all the physical stuff, the world contains certain categories pertaining to human relations, and those are no less real than the physical aspects of the world. The world thus has a certain natural order, which can be discovered by the power of reason. That order is known as 'natural law'. One is a formalist in this sense to the extent that one *acknowledges* certain 'forms' of human *relations* or interactions (for example the relation that exists between 'doer' and 'sufferer').[27] The reason why one can, and should, turn to Kant for valuable lessons about the nature of twenty-first century common law is because he discovered some truths about moral reality.

The two versions of formalism can thus speak of the autonomy and objectivity of law in a way that looks superficially similar but is in fact quite different. For conceptualists the objectivity in question is the same objectivity that we speak about when talking about the objectivity of physical reality. And that separate reality of the legal domain also explains law's autonomy: Law belongs to a separate metaphysical order. For the doctrinalist the objectivity in question is tied to the place of law within a given community and the role of lawyers and judges within it. The objectivity of law is the product of human effort and its autonomy is a kind of political achievement that needs to be constantly guarded.

C. The Two Approaches Illustrated

In discussions on formalism, these differences are not often adequately acknowledged. Perhaps it is thought that these are two fairly similar ways of attacking the same problem ('start with the cases and build your way up to the principles' as opposed to 'start with general principles and work your way through to particulars', both leading to the same conclusions). But the occasional alliance between conceptualists and the doctrinalists cannot hide their fundamental differences.

Though sometimes hidden, at times these differences come into clear view. One instance when this happened was when Allan Beever and Charles Rickett published a scathing review of a book by Stephen Waddams.[28] When the review was first published, it puzzled many of its readers.[29] The book it so harshly criticised

[27] EJ Weinrib, 'The Special Morality of Tort Law' (1989) 34 *McGill Law Journal* 403, 412 ('corrective justice is internal to the relationship of doer and sufferer: it is the morality applicable when this relationship is considered on its own, without being oriented toward some extrinsic ideal.').

[28] Beever and Rickett, above n 25, which reviewed S Waddams, *Dimensions of Private Law: Categories and Concepts in Anglo-American Legal Reasoning* (Cambridge, Cambridge University Press, 2003). Though far more mild-mannered in tone, a similar critique of Waddams' views is J Weinrib, 'What Can Kant Teach Us about Legal Classification' (2010) 23 *Canadian Journal of Law and Jurisprudence* 203.

[29] As evidenced in responses to this review, which suggested that it was 'ungenerous[]' towards Waddams, that Beever and Rickett's 'extraordinarily fierce' critique of the book 'must come as

seemed a rather unlikely target for such an attack. It did not try to explain private law with the aid of abstruse mathematical formulae and economic jargon; it was not a book that presented private law as a tool for elite oppression or male domination; it did not even suggest that all private law was just public law in disguise. Waddams based his conclusions not on some postmodernist rejection of the possibility of meaning, or by deconstructing all categories. This was a book mild in tone and conclusions, written by a mainstream doctrinal scholar; it displayed deep familiarity with, and great respect for, law and legal doctrine. Moreover, Waddams' overall conclusions, that cases do not fit into neatly-parcelled categories, and that private law cannot be explained in terms of a single overarching idea like corrective justice are, in historical terms, not revolutionary.[30] Even these conclusions were qualified: Though the law is not perfectly organised, it is equally wrong to think it is completely chaotic.[31]

Why then was this book subjected to such a vitriolic attack?[32] The puzzle is largely resolved once we see the fundamental rift between conceptualism and doctrinalism and we understand that Waddams' book was a doctrinalist's critique of conceptualism, and that Beever and Rickett's review was a conceptualist rejoinder. From a conceptualist perspective, doctrinalism already gives in too much. The conclusion that the law is not a total mess is for the doctrinalist an empirical finding, and as such a contingent fact that could be shown to be false. Even worse, the doctrinalist, even if he or she does not engage in interdisciplinary scholarship and even dismisses it as non-legal, may encourage such a hostile takeover. Exactly because he or she has no theory (or, more accurately, is *perceived* not to have one) to explain the normative foundations of the law apart from the lawyers' own understanding of legal materials, he or she invites the challenge that he or she is a mere collector of cases, nothing but a reporter.[33] This absence of a theory, combined with the admission that the law (despite the best

something of a surprise to those who have actually read the book'. See, respectively, J Dietrich, 'What Is "Lawyering"? The Challenge of Taxonomy' (2006) 65 *CLJ* 549, 550; S Hedley, 'The Shock of the Old: Interpretivism in Obligations' in C Rickett and R Grantham (eds), *Structure and Justification in Private Law: Essays for Peter Birks* (Oxford, Hart Publishing, 2008) 205, 210–11.

[30] For many references to similar ideas see PS Atiyah, *Pragmatism and Theory in English Law* (London, Stevens & Sons, 1987) 8–13.

[31] Waddams, above n 28, 232–33.

[32] One aspect of the review cannot pass without comment, although it is somewhat incidental to my argument. Beever and Rickett, above n 25, 322, write: 'Waddams' fundamental error is to assume that there is "simple dichotomy in legal analysis between description and prescription"'. This is no mere slip as this point is repeated two more times in the review (ibid 321, 335). There is no gentler way of saying this, but the words as quoted are a fabrication of Waddams' actual views. What Waddams actually said in the passage quoted is: 'It has *not* been possible … to maintain a simple dichotomy in legal analysis between description and prescription'. Waddams, above n 28, 222 (emphasis added). This is worth keeping in mind when reading A Beever, 'Engagement, Criticism, and the Academic Lawyer' (2017) 27 *New Zealand Universities Law Review* 1111, 1123 with its appeal to charity and 'constructive engagement' in reviewing academic legal books.

[33] See A Beever, *The Law of Private Nuisance* (Oxford, Hart Publishing, 2013) 2, where he refers disparagingly to the work of some legal scholars' as 'journalistic', because they are content to merely report what courts have said.

doctrinalist efforts) remains disorganised, may suggest that something external to the law – moral or political theory, economics, evolutionary psychology – will salvage the wreckage.

Having clarified the differences between the two views, in the next two sections, I turn to evaluating them.

III. Conceptual Legal Autonomy

Conceptualism is premised on the idea that the separation of law and other categories of knowledge, as well as the separation among legal categories within the law, corresponds to a pre-existing, rationally discoverable, order of reality. It is thus broadly classified as 'rationalist'. Those who defend rationalism in philosophy argue that one can know a priori that something cannot be red and green all over at the same time, that one can know that 7+5=12. Only a few venture slightly beyond that.[34] Even these relatively modest claims are highly contested. By contrast, legal conceptualists make much bolder claims both about the world, and our way of coming to know it. Entire areas of morality and law can be constructed out of – or discovered by – the power of reason alone. Terms like 'wrong' and 'fault' thus have universal, 'enduring' meaning, true regardless of what the world happens to be; there is a way of finding out those meanings; and these terms describe types of relations, as well as reasons for holding some people liable to others for their actions, regardless of any positive law. Conceptualists then further argue that despite the independence of this framework of any positive law, it is only by following this framework that we may come to have a coherent positive law.[35]

These are truly remarkable claims, which require remarkably powerful argument to be convincing. I do not think conceptualists have done enough to acknowledge the problems with such views,[36] but my discussion below does not examine the conceptualists' views at this level. Instead, I focus on the central notion of formalism – disciplinary autonomy – as understood by conceptualists, and seek to show why it cannot be sustained.

Underlying conceptualism is the idea that, like all other genuine disciplines, law has its own methods and answers to the question it faces, and it is only those that matter for lawyers. This idea is, of course, intimately related to the idea of autonomy that I singled out as central to both versions of formalism. As I suggested

[34] See, eg, L BonJour, *In Defense of Pure Reason: A Rationalist Account of A Priori Justification* (Cambridge, Cambridge University Press, 1998); JR Brown, 'Peeking into Plato's Heaven' (2004) 71 *Philosophy of Science* 1126.

[35] See EJ Weinrib, 'The Juridical Classification of Obligations' in P Birks (ed), *The Classification of Obligations* (Oxford, Clarendon Press, 1997) 37, 42–44.

[36] For some reasons to doubt these ideas see D Priel, 'The Justice in Unjust Enrichment' (2014) 51 *Osgoode Hall Law Journal* 813, 821–37.

above, this idea ties together the question of the relationship between law and non-law, and the role of categorical thinking within the law.

The basic idea seems to be this: Different categories of knowledge are distinct, and the one uniquely appropriate for private law is corrective justice. It is for this reason that other perspectives, no matter how interesting their insights may be for understanding private law, should play no role in reforming the law. It is against this background that one can make some sense of the claim that any approach other than conceptualism amounts to admitting that law is 'intellectually bankrupt'.[37] If we fail to heed this warning, law:

> will become, at best, the handmaid of some other discipline or series of disciplines, and legal academics will be replaced by academic economists, political philosophers, and the like, who merely interpret case law and other legal material through the lenses of their own disciplines. Perhaps even worse than this, academic lawyers will become the handmaids of judges, and will see their role as being merely to summarise judicial decisions in clear and accessible ways, perhaps coupled with criticism based on little more than raw intuition.[38]

They key to maintaining law as an academic discipline is ensuring that it has its own resources, both substantive and methodological, for resolving its own questions. Indeed, this passage reveals an animosity toward doctrinalists, who are no less guilty than their interdisciplinary colleagues in selling out the academic discipline of law, for they erroneously think that judges have authority to say what the law is.

But is this the only path to academic respectability? In his entertaining essay 'The Convergence of the Law School and the University' economist Paul Samuelson wrote that 'an anthropologist who has spent forty years, as I have, observing the strange practices of American universities can testify that, until recently, the same zip code often used to be about all the law school and the university had in common'.[39] And what was true in 1975 of American universities, was true (a fortiori?) of universities in the rest of the English-speaking world. The convergence Samuelson has spoken about has to do exactly with the fact that academic lawyers opened up to other disciplines and began collaborating with them. Rather than law schools' autonomy being the source of academic respectability, it was the reason why law schools languished at the periphery of the university. If matters are different now, this is so precisely because academic lawyers have become more engaged with the rest of the university, often adopting their research methods.

Why did it happen? Part of the change has to do with a general trend toward removing disciplinary boundaries. Beever and Rickett's view reflects an approach

[37] Beever and Rickett, above n 25, 333.
[38] ibid 337; see also above n 34.
[39] PA Samuelson, 'The Convergence of the Law School and the University' (1975) 44 *American Scholar* 256, 258.

in which every 'science' (understood roughly to mean 'a body of organised knowledge') is defined by its ability to be self-contained and self-validating. Kant gave a clear description of this view:

> Every science is a system in its own right; and it is not sufficient that in it we construct according to principles, and so proceed technically, but we must also set to work architectonically with it as a separate and independent building. We must treat it as a self-subsisting whole, and not as a wing or section of another building – although we may subsequently make a passage to or fro from one part to another.[40]

Weinrib expresses a very similar view (surprisingly, without reference to his intellectual idol): different disciplines have 'different perspectives' and '[e]ach of these perspectives has its own validity, rests on its presuppositions, and operates within its own disciplinary boundaries'. Therefore, any discussion of law must take into account 'law's distinctiveness as a mode of normative discourse', a distinctiveness that 'excludes other perspectives, but does not deny their authority within their own spheres'.[41]

In another essay Beever has attempted to explain this idea by comparing law to music. Proper music analysis must study 'music as such' or 'music as itself' rather than the effects of music; similarly, proper legal analysis must study law itself, not its effects.[42] Whatever one thinks of studying the effects of music, the analogy is fallacious because it presupposes precisely what it seeks to prove, namely that law is one of those things that (presumably like music) should not be studied in terms of its effects. In other words, the question that Beever begs with this analogy is whether the study of law should be analogised to the study of music (as itself) or to (say) to the study of engines or software. I will just say that music is an art form, engines are tools; and law is much more often thought of as a tool than an art form, suggesting that an analogy with engines may be more apposite.

The suggestion that an academic discipline can exist only if it has a unique method of acquiring knowledge does not fare much better. Taken seriously, it would imply that most scientific disciplines are 'intellectually bankrupt'. Biology is a recognised academic discipline because of its subject-matter (and not some unique methodology), and it does not have complete autonomy from other disciplines. It is hard to see why the same cannot be true of law. The view that for a discipline to exist it must have a unique methodology is unconvincing also in another sense. The conceptual analysis that conceptualists think is properly

[40] I Kant, *Critique of Judgment* (Oxford, Oxford University Press, 1790) 209 (para 68; Ak 5:381).

[41] EJ Weinrib, *Corrective Justice* (Oxford, Oxford University Press, 2012) 325.

[42] A Beever, 'Formalism in Law and Music' (2011) 61 *University of Toronto Law Journal* 213, 231–32. The next step is then to argue that those who favour a functionalist analysis of law 'allege, for instance, that the duty of care is a smokescreen for policy that has no content … How can one study something that has no content?' (ibid 232). To say that the 'duty of care' label is a cover (or even a smokescreen) for policy considerations is not the same thing as saying it has no content.

internal to the study of law is very similar to a method used by some philosophers. It is hard to see why conceptual analysis is a more distinctively legal methodology than any others denounced as non-legal. Just as in the case of the methodologies conceptualists criticise, what distinguishes philosophers' conceptual analysis from the lawyers' is the subject-matter, not method. It is for this reason, after all, that many defenders of conceptualism can find inspiration in the works of Kant, who was not a lawyer. In other words, the suggestion that certain methodologies are 'internal' to the law ends up looking completely arbitrary.

Even assuming conceptual analysis is an appropriate method for attaining legal knowledge, it is unclear why the choice of rules should be based *only* on that knowledge. Truths about the world are not themselves 'legal', 'chemical', 'economic', or 'psychological': these are human categories imposed upon reality that itself does not contain them. Subject to certain qualifications (to be addressed in a moment) the content of our law should be based on truths. If a truth is *relevant* to making a better decision, it matters little whether they have been arrived at using 'lawyers' methods' or by other means. The community subject to a certain legal rule will take little solace from the fact that judges ignored certain relevant information in favouring a certain rule over another, just because those truths could not be attained by means considered 'legal'. They would rightly complain that if those truths are relevant for informed decisions about the content of the law, then those methods should be *made* legal. The only way to understand the claim that each discipline should be confined to its 'own sphere' is to deny this, ie, it is to claim that truth is relative to a discipline: there is a legal truth about certain events and there is an economic truth about it, and these may be different and incommensurable. That is a thoroughly relativist claim about knowledge. (The alternative, even more absurd, is that there are no possible economic truths about law.)

Consider an analogy: the subject of human psychology is not considered part of engineering. In most academic divisions these are independent disciplines, using different methods and studying different subjects. Taking seriously the conceptualist argument, it follows that engineers must ignore findings about human psychology, because they belong to a different discipline. Yet, knowledge about humans, with all their foibles and limitations, is central to successful engineering.[43] If this is true for engineers, it is true for lawyers too. To make this point more concrete: if it is a true fact that, say, expanding vicarious liability tends to make employees more careless, it is a true fact about the world, about the humans subject to law. It is, if labels are necessary, a psychological or sociological truth, and it is one that cannot be discovered by the methods sanctioned by conceptualists. To say that *merely* because it was not arrived at by way of proper legal analysis (whatever that means) it should have no role in deciding legal questions,

[43] D Norman, *The Design of Everyday Things* (New York, Basic Books, rev edn, 2013) 6–10, *passim*.

is to hold that lawyers must ignore some true information because of the way it was found.[44]

All this is relevant for evaluating conceptualists' bugbear, 'policy', and their campaign to eliminate it from the law:

> The danger is that, as an appeal to policy becomes a more frequent practice, academic lawyers will appeal to policy rather than attempt to refine their understandings of private law so that they are no longer inadequate. If this occurs, then, with respect to the private law, academic lawyering will no longer exist as a discipline. As Geoffrey Samuel recently, and rhetorically, asked: 'can it seriously be argued that "policy" is anything less than a *passerelle* to other knowledge disciplines?' Accordingly, the concern is that academic private lawyers will come to rest content with understandings of the law that are manifestly inadequate and will not attempt to improve on them, but will instead prefer to explain away the inadequacies by reference to policy, which is merely a veiled reference to other disciplines. On this view, academic private lawyers will have abandoned the primary task of the academic lawyer, which is to treat the law as an academic discipline.[45]

Policy is not an appeal to other 'knowledge disciplines'. At times it is an appeal to certain value judgments that typically prefer one group of people over others: this is the sort of policy consideration relied upon when in borderline cases preference is given to the innocent over the careless, to those with shallow pockets over those with deep pockets and so on. These are decisions of distributive justice, not appeals to other disciplines (although such judgments too often are grounded in facts). Whenever such decisions are made, however, the contrast is not between policy and no-policy, it is between one value judgment over another. More often, however, when lawyers talk about 'policy' they refer to estimates about the likely consequences of adopting one rule over another, which conceptualists think have no place in the law. For a single individual to act without considering the consequences of her actions is usually the mark of irrationality: those incapable of adequately assessing the consequences of their actions (small children, people suffering from certain mental illnesses) are for this reason relieved from legal responsibility. Yet somehow, in the domain of private law, ignoring the consequences of decisions that potentially apply to millions is the mark of moral uprightness and legal rigour.

[44] There is an important exception to the idea that generally speaking, one should seek to design one's laws on the basis of more accurate information. Information acquisition is costly, and since it is generally subject to the law of diminishing returns, there is a point at which the costs of gathering more information outweigh the benefits of doing it. There may also be valid moral limits to the acquisition of relevant information (for example, we may choose to limit the acquisition of potentially useful information due to concerns over privacy). Whatever weight is given to such considerations, they have little to do with any alleged conceptual division between different knowledge disciplines.

[45] Beever and Rickett, above n 25, 335–36 (quoting G Samuel, 'English Private Law: Old and New Thinking in the Taxonomy Debate' (2004) 24 *OJLS* 335, 343). I note in passing that the recruitment of Samuel is surprising. Samuel's essay is critical of Birks' views, and can be understood as a critique of the conceptualist approach more generally. Samuel has also published a highly laudatory review of Waddams' book. See G Samuel, 'Can the Common Law Be Mapped?' (2005) 55 *University of Toronto Law Journal* 271.

It is not surprising that courts have for centuries considered the consequences of their decisions.[46] It is worth noting, however, that judicial decisions looking to other 'knowledge disciplines' are by no means limited to 'policy'. Virtually all the facts that judges rely upon in deciding cases are the product of other 'knowledge disciplines', simply because law is not a 'knowledge discipline'.[47] When speaking of 'law' we may refer to a profession, to a practice, to a set of rules (which can be learned by methods that are not uniquely legal). Whatever is the sense used, law in itself is only a very indirect way of knowing what the world is like. In short, whenever lawyers rely on factual information, they appeal to other 'knowledge disciplines'. For the same reasons that in the course of tort litigation lawyers turn to those with the relevant expertise to inform them about the likely earning prospects of a single individual who was seriously injured in an accident, they should turn to experts when the prediction pertains to the consequences of adopting a rule.

And here is where the problem may lie. Lawyers are not trained to gather information, and they are particularly uninformed about making predictions about the consequences of alternative rules. This creates the possibility that lawyers will succumb to familiar biases: cherry picking the studies that fits their preconceptions, discounting facts they disagree with, misinterpreting the results of studies, and so on. These risks of error are by no means special to lawyers, they are the result of well studied cognitive biases that affect all humans. Despite their prevalence, it is wrong to think that there is no way to overcome them. Moreover, when lawyers refuse to turn to experts, it does not mean they will not rely on such considerations, it is more likely they will rely on a less informed version of them. For example, the claim that Britain suffers from a 'compensation culture' made it to a House of Lords decision,[48] despite being almost certainly the product of a sensationalist media.[49] The right solution, however, is not to call on courts to ignore relevant data, it is to help improve the quality of data they get and their ability to evaluate it.

Finally, it hardly needs saying that there should be no limitation on lawyers or judges relying on relevant information, from whatever 'knowledge discipline',

[46] Waddams, above n 28, *passim*, especially ch 10; *cf* L Hoffmann, 'The COMBAR Lecture 2001: Separation of Powers' (2002) 7 *Judicial Review* 137, 142 ('It is curious how many people seem to think that the question of what things cost should not be mentioned in polite judicial society').

[47] Incidentally, Samuel would presumably agree. See G Samuel, 'Is Legal Knowledge Cumulative?' (2012) 32 *Legal Studies* 448, 474–78.

[48] See Lord Hobhouse's remarks about 'an unrestrained culture of blame and compensation' in *Tomlinson v Congleton Borough Council* [2003] UKHL 47, [2004] 1 AC 46 [81]. These comments led to an unusual rebuke from the Court of Appeal. See *Corr v IBC Vehicles* [2006] EWCA Civ 331, [2007] QB 46 [63] (Ward LJ).

[49] See K Williams, 'State of Fear: Britain's "Compensation Culture" Revisited' (2005) 25 *Legal Studies* 499; A Morris, 'Spiralling or Stabilising? The Compensation Culture and Our Propensity to Claim Damages for Personal Injury' (2007) 70 *MLR* 349. More generally on the paucity of empirical data informing policy decisions see A Blackham, 'Legitimacy and Empirical Evidence in the UK Courts' (2016) 25 *Griffith Law Review* 414; K Burns, 'Judges, "Common Sense" and Judicial Cognition' (2016) 25 *Griffith Law Review* 319.

for the sake of maintaining law as an academic discipline. If legal methods are inadequate for gathering all the relevant information for making good decisions on what the law should be, then new methods should be adopted. And if this implies the end of law as an academic discipline, so be it. But the worry seems unwarranted. After all, by the standard set by Beever and Rickett one must conclude that much of public law (where law constantly mixes with policy, politics, political theory and empirical evidence) is not law. And yet the academic study of public law seems to be thriving. At most, then, the end of law as an academic discipline means adding private law to the discipline to which public law belongs.

The view that seeks to protect the academic respectability of law by closing it off from information coming from other disciplines has the exact opposite effect. This view implies the knowing embrace of the possibility that it will lead to the adoption of rules that have a negative impact on society when compared with alternative rules, because that helps maintain law as an academic discipline. This is not just acknowledging but actually endorsing Bentham's (or Dickens's) claim that lawyers shaped the law with their own interests in mind. This claim is not just intellectually bankrupt, it is also morally perverse.

IV. Doctrinal Legal Autonomy

A. Doctrinal Autonomy as a Justification for Judicial Lawmaking

The conclusion of the preceding discussion is, I think, quite negative. But the difference between conceptualism and doctrinalism means that criticism of the former need not imply similarly negative conclusions about the latter. Common lawyers have always prided themselves on their pragmatic attitude, not metaphysical exactitude. It is not in philosophical ruminations about the boundaries between different bodies of knowledge, but in the realities of legal practice that we should look for their reasons for maintaining law as an autonomous discipline.

I want to offer an explanation of doctrinalist legal autonomy in terms of the role of judges as junior lawmakers in a democracy. The conceptualist answer to this question is essentially about truth discovered by reason. To the extent that judges succeed in discovering moral truth, they are not making law, but simply telling us how, regardless of the law, we ought to treat each other. This answer is not available to doctrinalists, who do not claim that the law reflects some metaphysical truths, but it is easy to see why doctrinalists need the ethos of conceptualism, and it is why doctrinalists are often drawn to it. In the end, however, the unresolved tensions between the two views cannot be overcome. Doctrinalism needs a different theory of legitimacy.

To be able to justify their role, judges need to be able to provide justifications for legal decisions that do not rest on 'political' considerations. So understood, autonomous legal doctrine is a set of argumentative and decision-making techniques that provide judges to develop the law, but can be seen as politically neutral. Therefore, this approach need not insist on some metaphysical separation between law and politics, only that the legal principles it relies on are sufficiently mainstream that they can be accepted as politically uncontroversial.[50] For example, private property is not politically neutral. If Proudhon's 'property is theft' is the product of a political ideology, the same must be true of its opposite. Nevertheless, it is so uncontroversial within the legal community that it can be accepted as unproblematic, as apolitical, within legal discourse. Without question, there will be the occasional case that will test the boundaries of the mainstream understanding. Such a case may even bring to the fore some hitherto hidden disagreements about what private property 'is' (ie, what forms of private property are justified) that have no bearing on the outcome in the run-of-the-mill case. For the most part, however, cases can be decided without delving too deeply into foundational questions.

For the doctrinalist, then, a question is deemed political not in virtue of its subject-matter, but due to its epistemic status. Specifically, a question is political when there is little factual information and much disagreement about it. Doctrinalism can thus serve as a response to the need for judges to decide under such constraints, one that looks epistemically responsible and (therefore) politically legitimate. The conceptualist epithet of doctrinalism as mere journalistic reportage of judicial decisions misses the very point of this approach. It is a way of generating answers to specific questions, as well as more general legal principles, without any apparent overarching philosophy. Such an approach may even explain the unsophisticated way judges use policy. Since this approach takes law to be justified because it is understandable and acceptable to the relevant community (and as such less contentious), this approach may favour imprecise data or policy speculations, over more accurate but 'counterintuitive' information.[51] It is, if you wish, a metapolitical non-neutral approach (a version of Burkean conservatism) in the service of political neutrality, as long as courts remain within the boundaries of political mainstream.

I think there is no question that doctrinalism is superior to conceptualism. Conceptualism enjoys a degree of success within the legal academy, but it is virtually non-existent as part of legal practice; by contrast, doctrinalism is (still)

[50] *cf* D Priel, 'The Indirect Influence of Politics of Tort Liability of Public Authorities in English Law' (2013) 47 *Law and Society Review* 169, 191–94.

[51] *cf Clements v Clements* 2012 SCC 32, [2012] 2 SCR 181 [9]–[11]; *Wilsher v Essex Area Health Authority* [1988] AC 1074, 1090). In both cases, the courts insisted that causation in the law is a common-sense judgment, which does not require scientific exactitude.

in reasonably good health. The practice suggests a method with a proven track record for resolving legal disputes, as well as other questions.[52] It fits well with ideas of separation of powers, the rule of law, objectivity, detached and impartial adjudication, a distinction between law and politics, and the related distinction between judicial and legislative forms of law-making. That is a considerable achievement. One significant theoretical advantage of this view is that it does not require accepting the implausible suggestion that law is separate from politics in some metaphysical sense. On the contrary, the assumption is that law is political, only grounded in the political mainstream, and contains various techniques aimed to keep it within that mainstream by limiting the kind of arguments one can make in the law.[53]

There are doctrinal devices such as justiciability that are quite clearly invoked by doctrinalists with the aim of maintaining the separation of law from politics. Of particular interest in this context are two doctrinal devices central to private-law doctrinalism: The assumption of normative equality between the parties, and the breaking down of a legal problem into its constituent 'elements'. Starting with the latter, I argue that both are techniques used to limit judges' straying into illegitimate political domains.

B. Formalism from within: Technical Legal Doctrine

The hallmark of doctrinalism is the breaking down of a claim into 'elements', as opposed to a holistic evaluation of the case. These elements are ideally fairly technical and relatively easy to establish; in other words, they are ideally more 'rules' than 'standards'. The decision whether someone is liable to another is thus an answer to a series of questions that stand in the way of – and ideally completely replace – thinking about the case as a whole. If the non-lawyer comes to the case with an unstructured 'intuitive' judgment, the trained lawyer is the one who has learned to put these intuitions in check. On this view, holistic adjudication is prone to the influence of subjective views and unconscious biases. By breaking down a case to small doctrinal elements, each of which ideally can be determined by means of a technical assessment, the judge is given a method for resolving a case in a way that guarantees judicial objectivity. If followed properly, different people, who might have different intuitive reactions to the case as a whole, will be led

[52] See CE Lindblom, 'The Science of "Muddling Through"' (1959) 19 *Public Administration Review* 79. This essay generated much critical discussion, which I am not going to consider here.

[53] Critiques pointing out that legal doctrine rests on political assumptions should thus not be seen as a challenge to doctrinalism. Still, this does not necessarily make such critiques unimportant: mainstream views are not necessarily correct, and they often come to be seen as not just widely acceptable but as natural or even essential. Exposing the political foundations of law is valuable to the extent that it challenges the inclination to conflate the politically familiar with the inevitable.

by the law toward a similar answer. So understood, the 'technicality' of the law derided as 'formalistic', is not a bug, but a feature.[54]

It is here that we see the link between the idea of law's autonomy (ie, a clear divide between what's inside and what's outside the law) and categorical thinking (ie, a clear demarcation of different classifications within the law). Clear categorical thinking and the closedness of the legal domain are both mutually reinforcing bulwarks against the intrusion of personal politics or subjective moral intuitions into the law; they are two complementary strategies with a similar aim. The key to doctrinalism, the sense in which it is 'formalist', is that the decision in particular cases is not made on the basis of an evaluation of all specific facts of a given case, but only on those that are relevant for placing a case within a recognised category, a particular legal 'form' (contract, trust, libel). Whether one falls into a category is itself to be determined 'formally'. Having a winning case should not depend on being able to tell a moving story that stirs the decision-maker's emotion, nor should it be based on an unmediated intuition that his claim was deserving. It is the ability to fit the facts of a case into a precisely recognised legal category.

Why, then, is doctrinalism so often ridiculed? What I see as the main concern over doctrinalism can be presented in the form of a dilemma: doctrinalism is bad if it works, and it is bad if it doesn't. If doctrinalism works, it leads to 'mechanical jurisprudence', adjudication that is insufficiently insensitive to social context, too enamoured of legal doctrine for its own sake. Rather than serving some further social goal, law becomes a fetish. If doctrinalism does not work, ie, if it cannot control judges' discretion, then continuing with it results in an elaborate charade. Experienced lawyers learn how to play the doctrinal game, to find the openings that allow them to manipulate the categories in such a way that they can get to any conclusion they want. It is easy enough to hack the doctrinalist method, to produce decisions of impeccable doctrinal form, but which in substance really are just politics in disguise. When that happens doctrinalism serves not as a device for restraining decision making in circumstances of epistemic deficiency, but as a cover for the real (political) reasons judges decide cases. Doctrinalism thus helps give the law a semblance of neutrality (and thus of non-political authority) that it does not deserve.

It seems to me that most critics of doctrinalism adopt the second possibility, and say: if that is the case, let us remove the cover and discuss the real considerations that drive the decision more openly. Such a view is, of course, disastrous for doctrinalism. It is therefore clear why doctrinalists want to resist this view, the second horn of the dilemma, and so must offer an adequate response to the first one. They need not deny some loose connection between the legal rules and abstract moral intuitions, but the more elaborate the law becomes, the weaker that link becomes.

[54] *cf Holt v Markham* [1923] 1 KB 504, 513 where Scrutton LJ rejected 'that vague jurisprudence which is sometimes attractively styled "justice as between man and man"', as it inevitably leads to 'well-meaning sloppiness of thought'.

Formality (in the doctrinalist sense) thus serves as a key to peremptoriness.[55] The rationale for doctrinalism on this view is not guidance or publicity: the public have no real opportunity to know the law, and making it more 'technical' inevitably makes it less knowable. Rather, it is an approach that directs the judge's attention away from the intuitive or emotional reaction one has to the case as a whole; it forces (or at least encourages) the judge to focus on particular, doctrinal details in the hope that doing so would minimise the potential effect of biases. In terms of the rule of law, this approach makes the law predictable to the small community of lawyers who work in the field.

This approach thus solves the doctrinalist dilemma by opting for something closer to (though not identical with) mechanical jurisprudence. It does not require thinking of law as amoral. It will accept that legal concepts probably have their origin in prevailing notions of right and wrong, and will maintain that such influence never completely disappears. Even in a doctrinalist legal system, there will exist pressures for reducing significant and persistent tensions between law and morality. Acknowledging that, however, is different from occasional divergences between the two, which are on this view inevitable, a price worth paying for maintaining the separation of law from politics. As long as such cases are not too frequent, such divergences can be seen as evidence that the system is working. It is only a slight exaggeration to say that it is a happy day for the doctrinalist when he or she finds herself morally conflicted about what he or she considers the legally correct outcome of a case. For when this happens, she can be sure that she follows the rigours of (objective) law, refusing to let her subjective moral intuitions take control. There is no better proof that one is 'thinking like a lawyer', that one is following the law, than reaching a legal outcome one finds morally problematic. When that happens, one can be sure that the judge is not 'manipulating' doctrine for the sake of reaching a desired outcome.

The doctrinalist will give a similar response to another problem that is also a product of doctrinalism: Breaking down legal claims into fairly technical constituent elements makes it easier to organise one's activity around the rules. To use a more familiar terminology, it allows for exploiting loop holes. (In a way, this is just a special case of the problem of divergence just mentioned.) The committed doctrinalist will not necessarily see anything wrong with this. Even when a problem exists, the right approach will be to call on the legislature to deal with the problem, rather than try to fix it themselves. Maintaining the autonomy of law implies that there will be some problems that doctrinalism will admit are serious but that it cannot fix.

[55] This view implies some connection between legal positivism and a version of formalism, something positivists strenuously deny. As the text implies, I think such a link exists, but exploring the topic more carefully will have to wait for another occasion.

C. Formalism from without: Normative Equality

The previous subsection considered how one form of legal analysis is motivated by substantive concerns over legitimacy. The breaking down of law into ever finer categories can thus be seen as an anti-politics technique. It is notable that it became prominent around the time that the common law became secondary to legislation.[56] In this subsection, I consider the other aspect of legal autonomy, that of limiting the information a lawyer will consider relevant.

The question I consider here is whether there can be an argument for limiting the judge from looking into some *relevant* information. The response is such a limit will be justified when relying on some relevant information is more likely to lead judges astray. How can this be? Given judges' training and the constraints on judicial decision-making, it makes sense for judges to make decisions on the basis of limited information, if there is some information that they are unlikely to evaluate accurately, or if it is information that is likely to draw them to rely on their subjective worldviews.

Of all information that is excluded because of its potential deleterious effects on decision-making, I examine here just one issue, that of wealth differences between the parties.[57] This problem is worth examining not just because of its intrinsic significance, but also because the assumption of equality between the parties to a private law dispute was a direct target of charges of mechanical jurisprudence when first made.[58] As we will see, adopting this assumption was not a coincidence.

The starting point is that doctrinalism recognises some idea of equality, the one captured by the slogan 'treating like cases alike'.[59] The attraction of this idea of fairness is that it seems politically neutral: If two people are in a similar situation, it is in some sense 'unfair' to treat them differently, regardless of what it is you are doing to them. One can thus commit to following a past case without having to commit to the truth of the value underlying the original decision. This idea of equality is considered an aspect of the rule of law, one that is often mentioned together with the slogan that everyone is equal before the law.

But as many commentators have pointed out, the formula that requires treating like cases alike is empty, because it does not tell us which cases are similar.[60]

[56] J Baker, 'Reflections on "Doing" Legal History' in A Musson and C Stebbings (eds), *Making Legal History: Approaches and Methodologies* (Cambridge, Cambridge University Press, 2012) 7, 9; S Stern, 'The Analytical Turn in Nineteenth-Century Legal Thought', www.ssrn.com/abstract=1856146.

[57] D Kennedy 'Form and Substance in Private Law Adjudication' (1976) 89 *Harvard Law Review* 1685, 1737–40, 1745, has also pointed out connections between form (rules versus standards) and substantive ideals (individualism versus altruism). He focuses on the predictability of rules and its congruence with an ideology of non-intervention. Though related, my analysis is different. 'Altruistic' goals can be achieved with rules (think about rule-based progressive taxation), but it is more difficult to achieve by the judiciary. Doctrinalists fear the risks of wide judicial discretion are not worth taking for the (possible) benefits of addressing problems inequality poses to private law doctrine.

[58] See R Pound, 'Mechanical Jurisprudence' (1908) 8 *Columbia Law Review* 605, 609–10, 615–16.

[59] See Burrows, above n 3, 16, 127.

[60] See, eg, C Webb, 'Treating Like Cases Alike: Principle and Classification in Private Law' in A Robertson & HW Tang (eds), *The Goals of Private Law* (Oxford, Hart Publishing, 2009) 215.

It depends on a judgment not provided by the formula itself of what factors are relevant to making a judgment of similarity. The solution proposed to this problem toward the end of the nineteenth century, the time when doctrinalism became dominant, was that the common law has general rules that apply in the same way to all. In the famous Diceyean formulation it implies 'the equal subjection of all classes to the ordinary law of the land administered by the ordinary Law Courts'.[61] This had the effect of minimising considerations of unfairness arising from differences in the bargaining power,[62] or (what was Dicey's main concern) subjecting the state to rules different from those applicable for the general public.

This was a time when academic lawyers sought to show that a rigorous study of law was possible, that law was a worthy subject for academic study.[63] And similar to the simplifying assumptions of perfect rationality which were adopted by economists to make mathematical modelling easier,[64] it is tempting to say that assuming the parties to a private law dispute were equal considerably simplified legal analysis. The difficulties posed by inequality could be summarised under two headings: lack of relevant information, and difficulty in carving out an adequate response to the problem using the limited tools of the common law. The first problem is easy to state: questions about the effect of power imbalances depend on factual information about the existence of inequality and its effects. These are not matters that are readily available for judges.

The second problem is this: in the case of equal parties, the law needs one solution. Inequality, by contrast, comes in degrees, and as such it is plausible that the level of inequality may play a role in the legal response. The law can provide such a differentiated response depending on the level of inequality, but it is the kind that typically is much easier to achieve through legislation. Tax law, for example, contains detailed legislative schemes imposing different tax rates depending on one's wealth. Vague standards like 'unreasonable' or 'unconscionable' provide a partial solution, but even here, the response is typically binary: the transaction was unconscionable or not; the defendant's behaviour was unreasonable or not. Keeping private law largely in the hands of the courts made it unlikely that these areas of law would see similar developments.

[61] AV Dicey, *Lectures Introductory to the Study of the Law of the Constitution* (London, Macmillan, 1885) 215.

[62] See, eg, W Swain, 'Reshaping Contractual Unfairness in England 1670–1900' (2014) 35 *Journal of Legal History* 120, 139–42; see also Lord Diplock's historical remarks in *Macaulay v A Schroeder Music Publishing Co Ltd* [1974] 1 WLR 1308, 1315.

[63] Dicey himself contributed to this effort. See AV Dicey, *Can English Law Be Taught at the Universities?* (London, Macmillan, 1883).

[64] ED Beinhocker, *The Origins of Wealth: The Radical Remaking of Economics and What It Means for Business and Society* (Boston, Harvard Business School Press, 2006) 31–33, 47. The analogy with the development of economics is possibly telling here for another reason. In both areas a simplifying assumption became an ideological touchstone, one that had to be maintained even against considerable evidence to the contrary.

D. The Choice

Economic, social, and political changes that took place during the twentieth century made the problem of inequality within private law more significant. Corporations grew larger and more powerful, democratic pressures enhanced concerns over inequality, the state became a more powerful participant in social and economic life. Some response to these changes was needed. In the context of legal doctrine what was needed was a *strategy* that addressed and balanced the two aspects of doctrinal autonomy identified in this section. The three responses I consider reflect a different balancing.

i. Solution 1: Maximum Predictability

This solution asserts that in the face of the twin problems of insufficient information and judges' limited ability to craft adequate solutions, it is best to maintain technicality with all the benefits that come with it, especially predictability. Such an approach will thus be critical of extensive use of words like fairness, justice, equity, and unconscionability in the common law. To the extent that these words are found in the law, they should be 'translated', as much as possible, into doctrine that avoids such terminology.[65]

One of the most notable strategies used by proponents of this approach is the late 'discovery' of a robust distinction between private and public law. Not historically dominant in the common law,[66] the distinction has recently assumed a central role.[67] Corresponding to it is another distinction between law and regulation. In this divide, regulation is merely public policy dressed in the garb of legal form; law has its own governing principles and a distinct mode of reasoning.[68] Maintaining these distinctions makes it easier to say that certain values, or certain concerns, as a conceptual matter, do not belong in (private) law. In this way, the doctrinalist can limit the 'intrusion' of considerations and values found in public law discussions into the domain of private law.

This solution may acknowledge its limitations, but will ultimately conclude that they are less significant than the alternatives. It provides lawyers with relatively well-formed means for solving legal disputes in ways that are clear and explicable to others. In terms of the two problems identified above, this approach avoids the

[65] For a critical discussion of such efforts see BR Reiter, 'The Control of Contract Power' (1981) 1 *OJLS* 347, 358–62; R Bigwood, 'Undue Influence: Impaired Consent or Wicked Exploitation' (1996) 16 *OJLS* 503.

[66] See R Pound, 'The Development of American Law and Its Deviation from English Law' (1951) 67 *LQR* 49, 57 ('Public law was not recognised in the common-law world as an important systematic category until recently. To Blackstone it was no more than a branch of the private law of persons').

[67] For a discussion of the strategic role that the private law/public law divide has played in formalists' work see D Priel, 'The Political Origins of English Private Law' (2013) 40 *Journal of Law and Society* 481.

[68] J Gava and J Greene, 'Do We Need a Hybrid Law of Contract? Why Hugh Collins Is Wrong and Why It Matters' (2004) 63 *CLJ* 605, 612–13.

problem of inadequate information by ignoring the question, thereby also avoiding the need to develop legal doctrine that will take levels of inequality seriously. With concerns over inequality growing, this approach has proven inadequate.

ii. Solution 2: Turn to (Community) Standards

Unable to develop detailed, technical rules to address the problems arising from inequality, courts turned to vague standards. In contract law, it was in doctrines like unconscionability or undue influence, and the more contentious idea of inequality of bargaining power, all of which assumed greater prominence in the course of the twentieth century. In tort, it was the increasing prevalence of policy considerations in the decision on whether to impose duty of care in negligence, where instead of an attempt at a careful evaluation of empirical evidence, courts rely on vague concepts like 'fair, justice, and reasonable'. Inequality of power is arguably also in the background of recent developments in tort liability of public authorities and vicarious liability.

Opting for standards is a rational, perhaps inevitable, response in the face of the constraints that judges face. Lacking in information, and unable to carve detailed technical solutions, judges can feel their way to an answer using vague terms that allow them to decide each case based on their inarticulate sense of the particular case. But it is a limited response: adopting this choice does little to address the problem of low information and provides only a limited solution to the need to provide a response that is sensitive to the level of inequality.

For some, this approach is dangerous.[69] Vague standards are 'mushy' and give judges almost unbounded discretion. From the perspective of the analysis offered here, these concepts are perceived as dangerous because they undermine doctrinalism from within. As much as courts and commentators tried to give these doctrines further specificity and precision, in relying on them they brought into the law what legal doctrine was meant to avoid, namely the holistic judgment about the case as a whole, and the loose, subjective evaluation of the relative merit of the parties' behaviour. It is an invitation for judges to turn back to subjective intuitionism. Moreover, as reliance on such concepts has grown, judges were tempted to rely more and more on terms like 'good faith' or 'unjust enrichment' as overarching norms that could be relied upon to override the perceived rigours of doctrine.

Despite all this, there is no denying that such an approach has been popular with many judges. Perhaps feeling more of the pressure for 'doing justice' in particular cases, courts embraced such concepts in the course of the twentieth century. But the problems with this approach, specifically the concern that judgments will reflect the subjective preferences of individual judges, become significant when

[69] For examples of this attitude see C Rickett, 'Unconscionability and Commercial Law' (2005) 24 *University of Queensland Law Journal* 73, 81–85; Birks, 'Equity in the Modern Law: An Exercise in Taxonomy', above n 19, 17, 64.

even judges acknowledge on occasion that their views may not be representative of those of the entire population.[70]

The legal realists have offered the most worked-out example of the adoption of this approach, as well as an attempt to provide a normative answer to its potential problems. This may come as a surprise to some, because the prevailing image of legal realism is as the view that law is largely epiphenomenal, something that judges simply use as a cover for their personal opinions. In fact, the realists are better understood as trying to provide a satisfactory response to the problem of indeterminacy, and specifically to the problem of legitimacy that comes with the use of concepts that are open to subjective interpretation. Here, I will focus only on the answer provided by one strand among the legal realists, one that elsewhere I called 'traditional legal realism', whose most notable representative was Karl Llewellyn.[71] Traditional legal realists did not seek to abandon legal doctrine, nor did they dismiss its significance. Instead, they thought that the problems with the indeterminacy of law, especially when using vague terms like 'unconscionable', could be solved by turning to dominant community values. This approach thus bills itself as more 'democratic' in that it is supposed to reflect not the judge's subjective preference, but those of his or her community. In this way, this approach can provide an answer to the challenge of legitimacy.

Figure 2 is an attempt to explain the difference between doctrinalism and traditional legal realism.

Figure 2 Doctrinalism (left) and traditional legal realism

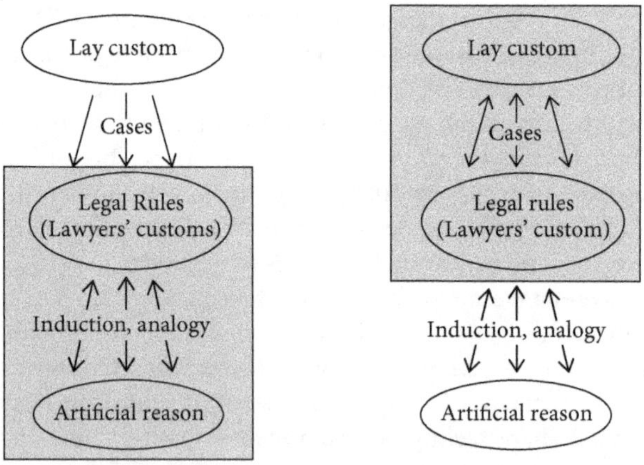

[70] See, eg, *Sienkiewicz v Greif (UK) Ltd* [2011] UKSC 10, [2011] 2 AC 229 [172] (Lady Hale).

[71] Llewellyn's most complete statement is found in his *The Common Law Tradition: Deciding Appeals* (Boston, Little Brown, 1960), but the ideas are found in many of his earlier writings. A different type of legal realism, which I call 'scientific legal realism', offers a different solution to this problem, one that resembles the third solution I discuss below. For more on the divide among the realists see D Priel, 'The Return of Legal Realism' in MD Dubber and C Tomlins (eds), *The Oxford Handbook of Legal History* (Oxford, Oxford University Press, 2018) 457, 464–69.

As Figure 2 shows, both approaches are made up of similar building blocks. That is because both can trace their origins to what has been called classical common law theory. The different shaded areas are meant to reflect a difference in focus, with traditional legal realism being an attempt to keep the law in touch with community values in a way that doctrinalism does not. Whereas traditional legal realism seeks legitimacy from the wider population, and considers a legal decision 'right' to the extent that it resonates with the entire community, doctrinalism prefers keeping the law more 'technical' (for the reason spelled out above), and seeks acceptability by the standards of a small group of lawyers. Melvin Eisenberg gave a clear example of the realist approach when he stated that courts should base their decisions on 'moral standards that claim to be rooted in aspirations for the community as a whole', rather than 'those moral standards the court thinks best', and further suggested that everyday conversations and newspapers are valid sources for courts to rely on in search of community values.[72]

In seeking this form of community approval, such an approach attenuates the search for technical solutions and ever more refined legal categories as the main mechanism for guaranteeing that the judge's personal influences do not overtake his or her knowledge of the law. In terms of the problems of information and the need for a graded solution, this response assumes that the judge who is properly attuned to community values will be able to correctly apply vague terms to particular cases.

Plainly, however, this approach rests on assumptions that may be more romantic aspirations than real: The assumption is not just that judges have the ability to discern prevailing community values, but that such shared values exist. Moreover, while the legal realists were not enemies to legal doctrine, it is not a huge step from this view to the conclusion (now often attributed to the legal realists) that doctrine is a waste of time. Those who wish to avoid this conclusion, will understandably be wary of the whole approach.

iii. Solution 3: Legislation

Presenting the two previous options helps identify the missing third possibility, viz, the one that tries to take account of all relevant considerations on the basis of better information while keeping the law 'technical', thereby both reducing the potential influence of personal judgment, and providing solutions that are sensitive to levels of inequality. There is a familiar law-making technique that can achieve all that. Legislation is (ideally) based on a more robust assessment of facts, and it can be designed in such a way that provides graded solutions to problems of inequality without resorting to vague standards. This is why tax law is primarily the work of legislation.

[72] MA Eisenberg, *The Nature of the Common Law* (Cambridge, MA, Harvard University Press, 1987) 15–17.

Tax legislation also provides a good illustration of the problem with this model: it encourages lobbying efforts to create different rules that favour particular groups. Hayek's claim that only laws that apply equally to all is consistent with the rule of law is unconvincing,[73] but it is true that it is more difficult to lobby for exceptions to general rules when no exceptions are recognised. Though we tend to think of private law as still primarily the work of courts, specific areas (for example, the law relating to fraud and misleading information in the securities market), demonstrate that specific and more technical legislation is clearly possible.

It is impossible to answer a priori which of the three solutions is best. In part, the answer depends on an evaluation of the relative strengths and weaknesses of each approach in any given context. The strength of the first approach lies in its relative predictability and relative imperviousness to politicisation, but it is hampered by the fact that it ignores relevant considerations. By taking more relevant considerations into account, the second approach may have some epistemic advantages, but it introduces uncertainty and may be more prone to the infiltration of personal biases (which may, in the case of an unrepresentative judiciary, mean class biases). The third approach has the potential of overcoming the shortcomings of both approaches, but to do it well is costly and time-consuming.[74] And it seems more likely to be exploited by interest groups than the other approaches.

Given the uncertainties about these factors, the decision in a given situation may well depend on competing jurisprudential views about what law is (for). Those who see the law as primarily a matter of providing clear guidance to action will tend to prefer the first approach; those who see law as primarily a matter of justice, especially justice in individual cases, will tend to favour the second approach. Presented in this way, however, it is surprising that doctrinalists are not more supportive of more detailed, technical, legislation in this area. The answer, it seems, reflects the lingering influence of conceptualism, the view that private law reflects a unique domain, where judges have special access to its truths.[75] This chapter suggests that doctrinalists should be open to giving legislation in private law a more serious try.

V. Conclusion

I have argued that formalism comes in two forms. Conceptualism, despite its vaunted philosophical grounding, is both a poor representation of legal reality and is normatively unappealing. Little wonder that it finds very little support in

[73] FA Hayek, *The Road to Serfdom* (Chicago, University of Chicago Press, 1944) ch 6.

[74] D Howarth, *Law as Engineering: Thinking about What Lawyers Do* (Cheltenham, Edward Elgar, 2013) 73–87.

[75] See Birks, 'Equity in the Modern Law: An Exercise in Taxonomy', above n 19, 97, who acknowledges that this view reflects a 'democratic bargain', which he justifies by the judges' special expertise in this field.

the courts. Doctrinalism, on the other hand, is a much more powerful view, one that fits quite neatly within a certain political environment. Its real-world success is not a coincidence. I have then further articulated different versions of the doctrinalist positions, showing their different strengths and weaknesses. Though in practice each legal system displays aspects of all, the different approaches reflect rival assessments of why law is valuable.

Given that there is little data about these choices, the evaluation of these different approaches is itself coloured by value judgments. Those judgments are not made in the abstract, as the different approaches may be attuned to different socio-political contexts. In less abstract terms, given the American political system, there may be some reasons to prefer the legal realist approach in the US, while rejecting it elsewhere. Such a conclusion will disappoint those seeking more definitive answers on the appropriate approach to legal doctrine. As I have attempted to show, this is a jurisprudential and political question, and in these domains definitive answers are rare.

9

Form and Substance in Equity

BEN McFARLANE

I. Introduction

The argument of this chapter is that the distinction between form and substance is crucial to understanding and justifying the distinction between common law and equity and, more fundamentally, the distinction between two different types of legal rule.[1] The terms 'form' and 'substance' are used here in a particular sense: 'form' refers to the type of legal relation arising from the parties' dealings and the application of particular rules to those dealings; 'substance' refers to the effect in practice of such dealings and rules. The argument here is not based on the notion that 'equity looks to the substance not the form'.[2] In fact, this chapter asserts something close to the opposite: the key to understanding much equitable intervention in the law of obligations lies in paying very close attention to the form of the legal relations involved.

Three main points will be made. First, in seeking to understand and justify many equitable rules,[3] it is crucial to see such rules as controlling, in favour of one party, B, the enforcement or acquisition of a right by another party, A.[4] Equity, in that specific sense, functions as second-order or meta-law.[5] Second, this means

[1] 'Legal rule', and 'legal relation', will be used here to encompass both common law and equitable rules.

[2] As noted by J Heydon, M Leeming and P Turner (eds), *Meagher, Gummow and Lehane's Equity: Doctrines and Remedies*, 5th edn (Sydney, LexisNexis, 2015) para 3.145, this is 'another wording' of the maxim that 'equity looks to the intent, rather than to the form'. See too J McGhee (ed), *Snell's Equity*, 33rd edn, (London, Sweet & Maxwell, 2015) paras 5.013–5.014.

[3] This chapter does not consider all equitable rules; in particular, remedial rules are beyond its scope.

[4] See too B McFarlane and R Stevens, 'What's Special About Equity? Rights About Rights' in D Klimchuk, I Samet and H Smith (eds), *Philosophical Foundations of the Law of Equity* (Oxford, Oxford University Press, 2019). As stated by Lord Cairns in *Hughes v Metropolitan Railway Co* (1877) 2 App Cas 439, 448 ('*Hughes*'): 'the first principle upon which all Courts of Equity proceed [is that] … the person who otherwise might have enforced those rights will not be allowed to enforce them where it would be inequitable having regard to the dealings … between the parties.'

[5] For equity as operating in a second-order, or meta way see, eg, H Smith, 'Equitable Defences as Meta-Law' and R Stevens, 'Set-Off and the Nature of Equity' in P Davies, S Douglas and J Goudkamp (eds), *Defences in Equity* (Oxford, Hart Publishing, 2018).

that certain equitable rules often seen as having an effect very similar to that of particular common law rules must in fact be carefully distinguished from their supposed common law 'equivalents'.[6] Third, once certain rules (whether originating in equity or not) are identified as regulating, in B's favour, the enforcement or acquisition of a right by A, this has consequences for how those rules might be justified.[7] A focus on form is thus a necessary preliminary to a consideration of the substantive justifications of particular rules.

These three points, taken together, can be seen as emphasising the importance of means (form) as well as ends (substance). Often, an equitable claim is of value because it allows a party to secure many of the practical benefits associated with a similar common law claim. If, for example, A holds a property right on trust for B, it might be thought that B's right is in many ways 'as good as' ownership of the relevant property, so that B is the 'real' owner of that property. B's vulnerability to a purchaser from A invoking the defence of bona fide purchase of a legal estate for value without notice might be seen as the major weakness of B's position but, where B has an equitable interest in land which can be protected by an entry in the register, even that difference may disappear. An equitable lease, for example, arising under the doctrine in *Walsh v Lonsdale*,[8] is thus often regarded as being 'as good as' a legal lease.[9] The very success of equity in securing such benefits for B may lead us to regard B's equitable right as simply a somewhat watered-down version of a common law original. This then raises the difficult question of why any legal system should have two different sets of rules governing the acquisition of very similar rights. The argument of this chapter, however, is that similarities in the practical outcomes of particular rules should not blind us to the different ways in which such rules achieve those outcomes.[10] Looking to the form in this sense is important for both practical and conceptual reasons. Practically, the fact that

[6] See, eg, the discussion of equitable estoppel below, text accompanying nn 77–83. For a discussion of the important differences between an equitable assignment of a right and the transfer of a right, see, eg, CH Tham, 'The Nature of Equitable Assignment and Anti-Assignment Clauses' in J Neyers, R Bronaugh, and S Pitel (eds) *Exploring Contract Law* (Oxford, Hart Publishing, 2009); J Edelman and S Elliott, 'Two Conceptions of Equitable Assignment' (2015) 131 *LQR* 228; McFarlane and Stevens, above n 4.

[7] See, eg, the discussion of the mistaken transfer of rights below, text accompanying nn 71–73.

[8] *Walsh v Lonsdale* (1882) 21 Ch D 9.

[9] See, eg, *R v Tower Hamlets, ex parte Von Goetz* [1999] 1 QB 1019, 1023, where Mummery LJ described the right of a party with an equitable lease as 'for all practical purposes, an interest as good as a legal interest'.

[10] The chapter thus picks up on a point made by Maitland in relation to the trust. In 'Trust and Corporation', Maitland stated that: 'I believe that for the ordinary thought of Englishmen "equitable ownership" is just ownership pure and simple, though it is subject to a peculiar, technical and not very intelligible rule in favour of bona fide purchasers': see D Runciman and M Ryan (eds), *Maitland: State, Trust and Corporation* (Cambridge, Cambridge University Press, 2003) 94. In that essay (first published in German: F Maitland, 'Trust und Korporation' (1905) 32 *Grünhut's Zeitschrift für das Privat- and Öffentliche Recht* 1) and in F Maitland, *Equity: A Course of Lectures*, AH Chaytor and WJ Whittaker (eds) 2nd edn (Cambridge, Cambridge University Press, rev by J Brunyate, 1909), however, Maitland identified important further differences between the rights of a beneficiary and those of an unencumbered owner.

two particular rules (eg, as to the effect of legal property rights, and as to the effect of equitable interests) often lead to the same outcome does not mean that those rules will *always* do so. Conceptually, it helps us to see that the law as a whole has a number of different resources, and can thus respond to problems in more nuanced and varied ways: where an innocent pre-contractual misrepresentation has been made by A to B, for example, it is possible to find that the contract is valid, but that, by allowing B a power to rescind the contract, A's enforcement of A's rights under the contract can be controlled in favour of B. Further, rules that thus control the acquisition or enforcement of rights may have distinct justifications: they may be necessary, for example, to prevent other rules operating to cause an injustice.

It would be no surprise if equity were to be particularly associated with this function of controlling, in B's favour, the acquisition or enforcement of A's rights. It accords both with the notion of equity as a supplementary, or secondary, system, and with the ancient idea that equity can operate to correct problems caused by the generality of primary rules.[11] Two warnings should, however, be noted. First, it is not argued here that rules controlling the acquisition or enforcement of rights are recognised only by equity; second, it is not argued that equity consists only of such rules. The key distinction made here is not between common law and equity as such, but rather between primary rules that define the parties' rights, and secondary rules that control, in favour of B specifically, A's acquisition or enforcement of rights. There is no reason, either historically or in the present law, why the common law cannot also recognise such secondary rules.[12] The ability of equity, historically, to recognise primary rules is a more difficult question, but it is clear that there are modern cases in which equity has gone beyond its traditional function of controlling the acquisition and enforcement of rights.[13] As a result, it is not argued here that the function can explain *all* of modern equity. It is rather argued that it is at least important in understanding many areas in which equity has an impact on the law of obligations. Space precludes consideration here of all such examples, but three will be considered: in Section III, the effect of a trust on the obligations of third parties; in Section IV, restitutionary claims based on

[11] See D Klimchuk, 'Equity and the Rule of Law' in L Austin and D Klimchuk (eds), *Private Law and the Rule of Law* (Oxford, Oxford University Press, 2014), discussing Aristotle's account in *Nichomachean Ethics* (in J Barnes (ed), *The Complete Works of Aristotle*, JO Urmson and WD Ross trans (Princeton, Princeton University Press, vol 2, 1984) 1796) of the 'equitable' as 'a correction of law where it is defective owing to its universality'.

[12] As noted below, text accompanying nn 82–83, common law rules of waiver are an example of rules that regulate in B's favour the enforcement of a right by A. A common law power to rescind a contract entered into as a result of duress or fraud is a further example, although its pedigree has been doubted: see W Swadling, 'Rescission, Property, and the Common Law' (2005) 121 *LQR* 123.

[13] The development of breach of confidence to include misuse of private information and other breaches of privacy (such breaches often being referred to as 'torts': see, eg, *TLT v Secretary of State for the Home Dept* [2018] EWCA Civ 2217, [2018] 4 WLR 101 [15], [18], [26] (Gross LJ)) provides one example: see further J Goldberg and H Smith, 'Wrongful Fusion: Equity and Tort' in J Goldberg, H Smith, and P Turner (eds), *Equity and Law: Fusion and Fission* (Cambridge, Cambridge University Press, 2019).

mistaken transfers; in Section V, equitable estoppel. First, however, it is necessary briefly to explain how the view put forward here relates to the traditional view that equity looks to substance not form.

II. Substance and Form in Equity: An Initial Example

Lord Romilly MR, in *Parkin v Thorold*, stated that 'Courts of Equity make a distinction in all cases between that which is matter of substance and that which is matter of form'.[14] So even if a contract makes 'positive and unambiguous' provision that property is to belong to the mortgagee if a debt is not repaid on time, a Court of Equity 'treats the substance of the contract to be a security for the repayment of money advanced, and that portion of the contract which gives the estate to the mortgagee as mere form'.[15] If, as in *Parkin* itself, a court finds that a term of a contract allowing A to gain or retain property is intended to operate as security for the performance of a duty, the court can characterise A's interest in the property as a security right, and prevent it being used by A for other purposes. This remains true today even for a contract concluded by well-advised commercial parties: the clear terms of a contract can, it seems, be disregarded by a court where those terms would allow a party to take advantage of a security right to gain the borrower's property even when the borrower is able, in substance, to perform the secured duty.[16]

It is important in such cases to distinguish between two stages of the court's reasoning. First, there is a question as to the construction of the contract: has B transferred a right to A, or given A a new right, by way of security? At this stage, of course, a court of equity need not be taken in by a party's attempt to present a transaction in a particular light, if in fact the objectively manifested intentions of the parties lead to a different conclusion. This point can be presented as depending on a preference for substance over form, but such a preference is clearly not distinctive to equity. In *Parkin* itself, Lord Romilly MR stated that: 'A contract is undoubtedly to be construed alike both in equity and at law'[17] and there is no shortage of common law examples where a court has looked beyond a particular party's characterisation of a transaction in order to establish the parties' rights.[18] Further, whether at law or in equity, the limits on the court's characterisation come from the objectively manifested intentions of the parties and so, for example, neither

[14] *Parkin v Thorold* (1852) 16 Beav 59, 66, 51 ER 698, 701 ('*Parkin*').

[15] *Parkin* (1852) 16 Beav 59, 69, 51 ER 698, 702.

[16] See, eg, *Cukurova Finance International Ltd v Alfa Telecom Turkey Ltd* [2013] UKPC 20, [2016] AC 923, especially [125]–[126] (Lord Neuberger).

[17] *Parkin* (1852) 16 Beav 59, 66–67, 51 ER 698, 701.

[18] See, eg, *Street v Mountford* [1985] AC 809, discussed by B Häcker, '"Substance Over Form": Has the Pendulum Swung Too Far?', this volume, ch 3; *Orion Finance v Crown Financial Management* [1996] 2 BCLC 78; and the discussion in *Welsh Development Agency v Export Finance Company* [1992] BCLC 148, 186.

equity nor common law can look beyond a clear expression of such intentions.[19] There is no relevant 'substance' beyond establishing such intentions, and courts do not look at 'substance' in the sense of the wider function or practical effect of the transaction. For example, it may be clear to all that a transaction has been structured as a lease or a hire-purchase agreement, or as a sale subject to retention of title, in order to serve the same economic function as giving A a security right; but if the transaction has genuinely taken such a form, then, absent a statutory direction to the contrary, equity and common law courts will not apply rules (such as those requiring registration) that would apply to a security right such as an equitable charge.[20]

So, whilst the initial stage of the court's reasoning (construction of the contract) might be said to involve a preference for substance over form, that characterisation is potentially misleading, first because it does not show anything distinctive about equity as opposed to common law, and second because the preference is not for substance in a general sense of the function or effect of the transaction, but is simply for giving effect to the parties' objective intentions. The second stage of the court's reasoning in a case such as *Parkin* is of more significance to the argument made in this chapter. Once the parties' rights have been established through construction of the contract, it is possible then that a particular principle will control, in B's favour, the way in which A may exercise A's rights. The point in *Parkin*, for example, is that once A's right is characterised as a security right, A's assertion of that right against B can be controlled to ensure that A does not use it for a different purpose. The form of equity's intervention consists of controlling A's exercise of a particular right: in this case, the right is controlled because of the basis on which A acquired it. There is an element of 'substance', of course, in the operation of the equitable rule: where the right secured is a duty of B to make payment to A, B is allowed to redeem by making a late payment of the secured sum, provided A's interests and costs are also met. In 'substance', in such a case, B can be said to have performed the primary duty even if the precise requirements of that duty have not been met. It is important to note, however, the limited role played by 'substance' and how the justification for equitable intervention is the existence of a specific reason to control the exercise of A's right.

The operation of the equitable jurisdiction to relieve against forfeiture thus provides an example of equitable intervention that takes the specific form of controlling, in favour of B, the assertion of a right by A. The High Court of Australia's analysis of the rule against penalties in *Andrews v Australia and New Zealand Banking Group Ltd*[21] is consistent with such a view of equitable intervention and indeed uses it as a justification for the much-debated rule

[19] See, eg, *Union Eagle Ltd v Golden Achievement Ltd* [1997] AC 514; *Byrnes v Kendle* [2011] HCA 26, (2011) 243 CLR 253.

[20] See, eg, *Lloyds & Scottish Finance v Cyril Lord Carpets Sales* [1992] BCLC 609; *Associated Alloys Pty Ltd v ACN 001 452 106 Pty Ltd* [2000] HCA 25, (2000) 202 CLR 588.

[21] *Andrews v Australia and New Zealand Banking Group Ltd* [2012] HCA 30, (2012) 247 CLR 205 ('*Andrews*').

against penalties. In contrast, the Supreme Court in *Cavendish Square Holding BV v Makdessi*[22] preferred to emphasise the common law basis of the modern rule against penalties. The point here is not to express a view on whether the rule should best be understood, either historically[23] or in its current operation, as a common law or equitable rule,[24] but rather to note how the equitable emphasis in *Andrews* depends on a particular conceptualisation of the rule, which in turn fits with the analysis of this chapter. So, in *Andrews*, '[i]t is the availability of compensation which generates the "equity" upon which the court intervenes' as, given the contested stipulation is 'in the nature of security',[25] it would be an abuse if A could insist on asserting that right beyond the extent required to provide compensation for the non-occurrence of the primary, secured outcome. Where a term is thus identified as a penalty, a court can control A's assertion of the right to ensure that A does not use the right to make a disproportionate gain, or to inflict a disproportionate loss on B. In some cases, therefore, a court may allow A to enforce the right, but only to a limited extent.[26] In contrast, in *Cavendish*, the Supreme Court did not regard the penalties doctrine as limiting the assertion of an acknowledged right of A, but rather saw it as denying A and B the power to create in A a particular type of contractual right. On that view, a penal stipulation seems to be simply void: there is no primary right to be controlled, and the doctrine can be seen, like the doctrine of illegality, as a limit on the parties' powers to create contractual rights. As a result, there is no possibility of the court's permitting limited enforcement of the penalty.

Clearly then, important practical differences flow from the different characterisations of the penalties rule adopted in Australia and in England. It is not the case, however, that the Court in *Andrews*, unlike that in *Cavendish*, was willing to ignore the actual form of the parties' legal relations in order to respond to a broader practical reality: indeed, the analysis in *Andrews*,[27] like that in *Cavendish*,[28] makes clear that if the parties choose to arrange a transaction so that, eg, a payment must be made by B to A not as a result of the failure of a stipulation, but rather as a fee

[22] *Cavendish Square Holding BV v Makdessi* [2015] UKSC 67, [2016] AC 1172 ('*Cavendish*').

[23] For a convincing account of the equitable origin and nature of the rule, see P Turner, '*Lex Sequitur Equitatem:* Fusion and the Penalty Doctrine' in J Goldberg, H Smith, and P Turner (eds) *Equity and Law: Fusion and Fission* (Cambridge, Cambridge University Press, 2019).

[24] Or, indeed, whether there are two separate rules, one deriving from common law and one from equity, which was the basis on which Gordon J proceeded in *Paccioco v Australia and New Zealand Banking Group Ltd* [2014] FCA 35, (2014) 309 ALR 249. Certainly, the *Andrews* decision is not the last word in Australia, as the High Court's decision in *Paccioco v Australia and New Zealand Banking Group Ltd* [2016] HCA 28, (2016) 258 CLR 525 ('*Paccioco*') plays down possible differences between the Australian position and that in England following *Cavendish*. For discussion, see N Tiverios, 'A Restatement of Relief against Contractual Penalties (I) and (II)' (2017) 11 *Journal of Equity* 1 and 185.

[25] *Andrews* [2012] HCA 30, (2012) 247 CLR 205 [10]–[11].

[26] See, eg, the approach of Deane and Dawson JJ in *AMEV-UDC Finance Ltd v Austin* (1986) 162 CLR 170.

[27] *Andrews* [2012] HCA 30, (2012) 247 CLR 205 [80]–[92].

[28] *Cavendish* [2015] UKSC 67, [2016] AC 1172. Although note the somewhat unclear reference to a 'disguised penalty' at [258] (Lord Hodge) and to a 'disguised punishment' at [77] (Lords Sumption and Neuberger).

for some additional benefit conferred by A, then the penalties doctrine does not apply. Nor does the difference between an equitable and a common law analysis mean, in itself, that the Australian courts have more discretion or flexibility when deciding if an impugned term is a penalty: the test in each case is whether the effect of the term is disproportionate to the legitimate interests of A.[29] Rather, the practical differences flow from the particular form which intervention takes: is it a case, as is the *Andrews* view, of controlling, in favour of B, the enforcement of A's right; or is it a case, as is the *Cavendish* view, of simply denying the parties the power to create a particular remedial regime? The crucial question is thus as to the form of the rule, rather than as to its derivation from either equity or common law.

III. Trusts and Third Parties

It was contended in Section II above that regarding the penalties rule as 'equitable' is linked to conceiving of the rule as having a particular form: it allows the court to control, in favour of one party, another party's enforcement of a right. It will be argued in this section that understanding the obligations imposed by trusts on third parties similarly depends on seeing the right of the beneficiary of a trust as having a particular form: the beneficiary does not have a right to the trust property itself, but rather benefits from rules that control another's acquisition or enforcement of rights.

A. Obligations of Third Parties Interfering with Trust Property

In *Shell UK Ltd v Total UK Ltd*,[30] a large explosion, resulting in part from the carelessness of the defendant, X, damaged fuel storage and pipeline facilities used by B, causing B to suffer financial loss as a result of its inability to supply customers. The difficulty for B was that legal title to the relevant property was held by trustees (T) on trust for B, and not by B itself. Such was the legal form of the parties' arrangements, arrived at when B, along with other companies, co-operated to establish the facilities. It was held at first instance that, as B had no legal ownership or possessory title to the property, the loss it had suffered as a result of the damage was purely economic loss and so the general 'exclusionary rule' applied, meaning that X was not liable for having carelessly caused such loss.[31] The Court of Appeal, in contrast, allowed B's claim for substantial damages. It avowedly looked beyond

[29] See *Cavendish* [2015] UKSC 67, [2016] AC 1172 [22], [28], [31]–[32] (Lords Neuberger and Sumption) and *Paccioco* [2016] HCA 28, (2016) 258 CLR 525 [29], [57]–[58] (Kiefel J).

[30] *Shell UK Ltd v Total UK Ltd* [2010] EWCA Civ 180, [2011] QB 86 ('*Shell*').

[31] The first instance decision is reported as *Colour Quest Ltd v Total Downstream Ltd* [2009] EWHC 540 (Comm), [2009] 2 Lloyd's Rep 1.

the legal form of the parties' arrangements to the substance of the position, stating that:

> it is legalistic to deny [B] a right to recovery by reference to the exclusionary rule. It is, after all, [B] who is (along with [the other three beneficiaries]) the 'real' owner, the 'legal' owner being little more than a bare trustee of the pipelines.[32]

The decision in *Shell* has met with much disapproval[33] and has some potentially unwelcome practical effects: for example, if a large number of beneficiaries are making use of property in different ways, is X, following one act of carelessness, liable for all of the foreseeable economic loss of each of those beneficiaries? Certainly, where a stranger carelessly damages the trust property, the orthodox position is that this is a wrong against the trustee rather than against the beneficiary.[34] It is true that a beneficiary of a trust may enjoy the major practical benefits associated with the trust property and, indeed, will often receive the property itself at some point.[35] Yet this does not mean that, during the currency of the trust, we should simply regard the beneficiary as having the same rights as an unencumbered owner of the property (or even a slightly weaker version of such rights). To do so would be to ignore the *form* of legal relations involved in a trust. Title to the trust property is vested in the trustee and the intervention of equity consists of recognising a duty on the trustee that relates specifically to the trust property. Equity does not ask: 'Who is the owner of the property?' and then give a different answer to that provided by common law.[36] Rather, equity accepts that T, the trustee, holds title to the property, but at the same time recognises that T is under a duty to the beneficiary, B, and that duty limits (in favour of B) the ways in which T may exercise T's rights to the trust property.

The 'proprietary' nature of B's right then comes from the fact that equity is also prepared to control, in B's favour, the exercise or enjoyment of the same right[37] by a successor in title to T's right, if that successor's conscience is affected at the time he or she holds that right.[38] This is easy to explain if we focus on equity's role

[32] *Shell* [2010] EWCA Civ 180, [2011] QB 86 [132].

[33] See, eg, K Low, 'Equitable Title and Economic Loss' (2010) 126 *LQR* 507; P Turner, 'Consequential Economic Loss and the Trust Beneficiary' [2010] *CLJ* 445; J Edelman, 'Two Fundamental Questions for the Law of Trusts' (2013) 129 *LQR* 66.

[34] See, eg, *The Lord Compton's Case* (1587) 3 Leo 197, 74 ER 629; *Leigh and Sillavan Ltd v Aliakmon Shipping Co Ltd (The Aliakmon)* [1986] AC 785; Restatement (Third) of Trusts (2003) §§ 107–08.

[35] As pointed out by, eg, J Penner, 'The (True) Nature of a Beneficiary's Proprietary Interest Under a Trust' (2014) 27 *Canadian Journal of Law and Jurisprudence* 473, 485.

[36] Maitland, *Equity: A Course of Lectures*, above n 10, Lecture II, memorably claimed that such a contradiction between common law and equity would give rise to 'civil war and utter anarchy'.

[37] Or to a right that counts as a product of T's initial right (as where, eg, T grants a lease of trust property to the third party).

[38] See, eg, the analysis of Lloyd LJ in *Independent Trustee Services Ltd v GP Noble Trustees Ltd* [2012] EWCA Civ 195, [2013] Ch 91 [75]–[81]. The importance of the third party's conscience being affected is confirmed by the language used by Lord Sumption in *Akers v Samba Financial Group* [2017] UKSC 6, [2017] AC 424 [89]. See too S Agnew and B McFarlane, 'The Paradox of the Equitable Proprietary Claim' in B McFarlane and S Agnew (eds) *Modern Studies in Property Law: vol 10* (Oxford, Hart Publishing, 2019).

in controlling T's assertion of a right: the successor in title to T acquires a right and so the form of legal relations as between B and T may be replicated, to at least some extent, as between B and the successor in title. There is, therefore, no reason to assume that a stranger, who simply interferes with the trust property without acquiring any right, is under any immediate duty to the beneficiary. Indeed, the rules as to the acquisition of an interest under a trust would be difficult to explain if such duties arose: for example, registration is generally a requirement for the acquisition of a legal property right in land,[39] whereas no such publicity is needed for the acquisition of an equitable interest in land.

The better view, it is suggested, is that the duties owed by third parties to an owner of property are not changed if the owner then declares a trust of the property.[40] Such a declaration does of course change the previous legal relations as between the trustee and the party who is now the beneficiary, and any damages recovered by the trustee from a third party interfering with the property, for example for the cost of repairs to the property, would then also be held on trust. Such damages are proceeds of the right held on trust and if the trustee were to refuse, in breach of his duty to the beneficiary, to bring a claim, then the beneficiary can join an action against the trustee with the trustee's action against the stranger.[41] The need for joinder of the trustee is not an empty formality, however, as it is, crucially, the *trustee's* right that is enforced against the stranger.[42] This means, for example, that consequential loss suffered only by the beneficiary as a result of the damage to the property should not be recoverable.

One difficulty with the Court of Appeal's reasoning in the *Shell* case is that it sees the claim against X as in fact the claim of B, the beneficiary of the trust (thus allowing for recovery of B's consequential loss) whilst also insisting on joinder of the trustee,[43] seemingly regarding such joinder as merely a mechanism to prevent double recovery by B. This misunderstands the purpose of the joinder. A further, more significant difficulty with the Court's reasoning is that, having correctly characterised the losses suffered by B as purely economic loss, it found that B could rely on an exception to the 'exclusionary rule' preventing recovery of such losses, as: '[b]eneficial ownership of the damaged property goes well beyond contractual or non-contractual dependence on the damaged property and does indeed constitute a special relationship of the kind required'.[44] The problem, of course,[45] is that the

[39] See, eg, Land Registration Act 2002 (UK), ss 4, 27; Transfer of Land Act 1958 (Vic), s 40.

[40] See too P Matthews, 'The Compatibility of the Trust with the Civil Law Notion of Property' in L Smith (ed), *The Worlds of the Trust* (Cambridge, Cambridge University Press, 2013), noting that T retains his or her general entitlement to the trust property.

[41] Employing the *Vandepitte* procedure, named for *Vandepitte v Preferred Action Insurance Co* [1933] AC 70.

[42] This also explains why legislative provision is required to protect beneficiaries in a case where a limitation period has expired against trustees of land, and why that protection consists of preserving the estate of the trustees: Limitation Act 1980 (UK), s 18(3).

[43] *Shell* [2010] EWCA Civ 180, [2011] QB 86 [144]

[44] *Shell* [2010] EWCA Civ 180, [2011] QB 86 [134].

[45] See too B McFarlane, 'Avoiding Anarchy? Common Law v Equity & Maitland v Hohfeld' in J Goldberg, H Smith, and P Turner (eds), *Equity and Law: Fusion and Fission* (Cambridge, Cambridge

special relationship required for the recovery of pure economic loss must be a relationship between the claimant and the defendant (in *Shell*, therefore, between B and X), whereas the existence of the trust simply shows there is a particular relationship between B and *the trustee*, T.[46]

This flaw in the reasoning in *Shell* can be connected to a failure to scrutinise the form of legal relations involved in a trust, leading to an under-estimation of the rights of the trustee and an exaggeration of the rights of the beneficiary. It is tempting to say that the rights of a trustee are in some sense diminished as compared to the rights of an unencumbered owner of property. We might say, for example, that a trustee is not free to use the property for his or her own benefit, and so, for example, does not have the power to take a renewal of a lease held on trust;[47] we might also say that it is then the beneficiary who has the right to the benefit of, or value of, the trust property. This overlooks the fact that the existence of the trust imposes duties on the trustee only *as regards* the beneficiary: as regards all other parties, the trustee remains free to assert the rights that come with holding the property. A classic example of this point is the decision in *Burgess v Wheate*:[48] when a beneficiary died without heirs, so that there was no longer anyone with a right correlating to the trustee's duty, the trustee was then free to use the property for his own benefit; it was not the case that the beneficial interest instead passed to another under the rules on escheat. The point here is that, in recognising the beneficiary's rights, equity is not carving out any distinct interest and thus reducing the interest of the trustee; rather, the trustee's right remains, but is now encumbered by a duty owed to the beneficiary.[49] At the level of practical effect, the trust, in substance, may allocate value as between trustee and beneficiary; but at the level of legal form, it involves no such division.[50]

B. Obligations of Recipients of Trust Property

The specific question to be examined here concerns the circumstances in which D (a third party receiving trust property from the trustee) can come under a liability

University Press, 2019). Note that the Supreme Court gave permission for an appeal against the Court of Appeal's decision in the *Shell* case, but the appeal was settled. Even if X had succeeded on the point as to the negligence claim, B was also pursuing a claim against X based on public nuisance.

[46] The position is different where D has expressly or impliedly assumed responsibility to B (as may occur where, eg, D, knowing of the trust in B's favour, contracts with T to perform a service for the benefit of B: see, eg, *Chappell v Somers & Blake* [2003] EWHC 1644, [2004] Ch 19).

[47] See, eg, *Keech v Sandford* (1726) Sel Cas T King 61, 25 ER 223.

[48] *Burgess v Wheate* (1759) 1 Black W 123, 96 ER 67 ('*Burgess*'). See P Matthews, '*Burgess v Wheate*' in C Mitchell and P Mitchell (eds), *Landmark Cases in Equity* (Oxford, Hart Publishing, 2012).

[49] The actual result in *Burgess* was modified by statute in 1884. See now Law of Property Act 1922 (UK), s 148, Administration of Estates Act 1925 (UK), ss 45(1)(d), 46(1)(vi). The reasoning as to the nature of the trust, however, may remain relevant: see, eg, Brennan J in *DKLR Holding Co (No 2) Pty Ltd v Commissioner of Stamp Duties* (1982) 149 CLR 431, 474.

[50] See N Jones, 'Trusts in England After the Statute of Uses: A View from the Sixteenth Century' in R Helmholz and R Zimmerman (eds), *Itinera Fiduciae: Trust and Treuhand in Historical Perspective* (Berlin, Duncker & Humblot, 1998) 190.

to B, the beneficiary of the trust. Let us first assume that the transfer is not one that the trustee has authority to make under the terms of the trust (and so does not overreach B's right) and also that D is not a bona fide purchaser for value of the trust property (and so is not thus immune from a claim of B). It is clear that if D is aware of the fact that the transfer was in breach of trust, and still holds the trust property (or a right that can be identified as its product), D comes under a duty not to use that right for his or her own benefit, and so must account to B for it. If D still has that property when B's claim is determined, D can be ordered to transfer that property to a new trustee, or, in an appropriate case,[51] to B; if D no longer has that property, because he or she disposed of it after becoming aware of the initial breach of trust, D is liable to account to B as a constructive trustee.[52] Such liability is often referred to as arising in knowing receipt, although D's knowledge need not coincide with the receipt, as long as it arises whilst D still has the trust property or a right identifiable as its product.

It has been argued, for example by Birks,[53] that a strict liability restitutionary claim, subject to the standard defences such as change of position, should also be available to B against D. Such a claim would be useful to B in the case where, although D disposed of the trust property and any traceable product of it before becoming aware of the breach of trust, D nonetheless retains a benefit from the receipt of the trust property and would not be able to rely on a change of position as a complete defence to B's claim. This might occur, for example, where D innocently disposed of the trust property in order to make an expenditure which D would have made in any case. One of Birks' contentions was that equity should follow the common law in recognising such a restitutionary claim, as it makes little sense to deny it to a beneficiary, given it is available to an unencumbered holder of a right transferred without authority.[54] It might also be said that it is the beneficiary, rather than the trustee, who has the right to the value of the trust property, and so any enrichment of the recipient is at the beneficiary's expense.[55]

The preceding analysis reveals a difficulty in these arguments and thus a justification for the current denial of such a strict liability claim across the common law world.[56] It may be true that, as a matter of practical reality, the existence of a trust can secure to the beneficiary the enjoyment or value of the trust property.

[51] As when the initial trust is simply a bare trust in favour of B.

[52] For a description of the process of taking an account, as a means of enforcing such a liability, see Lewison J in *Ultraframe (UK) Ltd v Fielding* [2005] EWHC 1638 (Ch), [2006] FSR 17 [1513].

[53] See, eg, P Birks, *Unjust Enrichment*, 2nd edn (Oxford, Oxford University Press, 2005) 156–58. See too D Nicholls, 'Knowing Receipt: The Need for a New Landmark' in WR Cornish et al (eds), *Restitution: Past, Present and Future: Essays in Honour of Gareth Jones* (Oxford, Hart Publishing, 1998) 321; the decision of the New South Wales Court of Appeal in *Say-Dee Pty Ltd v Farah Constructions* [2005] NSWCA 309 ('*Say-Dee*'); J Edelman and E Bant, *Unjust Enrichment*, 2nd edn (Oxford, Hart Publishing, 2016) 288–91.

[54] See, eg, Birks, above n 53, 156–58.

[55] *Say-Dee* [2005] NSWCA 309 [233]. See too JB Ames 'Purchaser for Value Without Notice' (1887) 1 *HLR* 1.

[56] See, eg, *Bank of Credit and Commerce International v Akindele* [2001] Ch 437; *Farah Constructions Pty Ltd v Say-Dee Pty Ltd* [2007] HCA 22, (2007) 230 CLR 89; *Citadel General Insurance Co v Lloyds*

Nonetheless, it is not true, as a matter of the parties' legal relations, to say that the beneficiary has an abstract right to the value of the trust property: B's enjoyment depends on B's ability to control a specific right held by another and, where third parties are concerned, that ability is limited to cases where the third party holds a relevant right with knowledge of the initial breach of trust. The transfer of the trust property from the trustee to D does not involve any transfer of a right from B to D. The point is a similar one to that made in Section III.A in relation to *Shell*: the existence of the trust means that the trustee is under a duty to the beneficiary in relation to the trust property, but it does not otherwise change the position of the trustee as regards third parties. Whatever the terms of the trust, the trustee does have the power, as holder of the trust property, to make a valid transfer of that property.

This means that the argument for a strict liability restitutionary claim faces two linked problems. First, the right acquired by the recipient, D, is acquired from the trustee, not the beneficiary: there is no distinct 'right to enjoyment' which D purports to acquire from B. This clearly distinguishes the case from that where, for example, the claimant makes a mistaken payment to the defendant. Second, there is a difficulty in locating an 'unjust factor': B has not exercised any power at all, or made any transfer which B could seek to reverse, and so there is no flawed transfer to which B can point. Of course, the transfer by T to D may involve a breach of trust, and be unauthorised under the terms of the trust, but it is hard to see why that in itself should give rise to a strict liability restitutionary claim.[57] The substance (in the sense of practical effect) of T's transfer in breach of trust may indeed be that B has lost out, and D has gained, without B having consented to such a state of affairs, but it is the form of the parties' legal relations that must rather be considered in determining if a claim can be made. This raises a broader point about restitutionary claims, which will be considered in Section IV below.

C. Rights of an Insolvent Beneficiary to Set Aside a Transaction between the Trustee and a Third Party

The analysis above is consistent with the Supreme Court's decision in *Akers v Samba*,[58] which also considers the impact of a trust on a third party. The Court's

Bank Canada [1997] 3 SCR 805. The position in the US is less clear: it is assumed in the Restatement (Third) of Restitution (as in the First and Second Restatements) that a strict liability restitutionary claim is available in such a case (§ 17, comment c, illustration 9) but no authority is cited.

[57] If the recipient retains the trust property or its traceable proceeds at a point when he acquires knowledge of the breach of trust, he will then be under a duty to the beneficiary in relation to the property, and such a duty can be enforced either by an equitable 'proprietary' claim (see, eg, *Agip (Africa) Ltd v Jackson* [1990] 1 Ch 265, 290 (Millett J) ('*Agip*')), or by an action in knowing receipt. Neither claim though is available against the recipient who, although retaining a benefit from the receipt, disposed of the trust property and any traceable proceeds before acquiring knowledge of the breach (see, eg, *Agip* [1990] 1 Ch 265, 290 (Millett J)).

[58] *Akers v Samba* [2017] UKSC 6, [2017] AC 424 ('*Akers*'). For a fuller discussion of the relevance of this decision to the nature of equitable rights, see McFarlane and Stevens, above n 4.

analysis proceeded on the assumption that T had purported to declare himself a trustee for B, a Cayman Islands company, of shares in a Saudi company and to have Cayman law govern the trust. After a winding-up presentation had been presented in the Cayman Islands against B, T had transferred the shares to D. It appeared that, under Saudi law, D would therefore receive good title to the shares free from any claim of B. B's liquidators, however, relied on section 127 of the Insolvency Act 1986 (UK), which states that, in a winding up by the court, 'any disposition of the company's property … made after the commencement of the winding up is, unless the court otherwise orders, void'.

For present purposes, there are two significant aspects to the reasoning of the Supreme Court. First, it was accepted that the Court could uphold the validity of a trust of shares even if it were the case that Saudi law, as the *lex situs* of the shares, had no concept of the trust, or of a division between legal and equitable entitlements.[59] The explanation consistently provided by the authorities is that the recognition of a trust does not, in itself, undermine the position under the *lex situs*, as it does not deny that T has a proprietary entitlement, but simply recognises that T is under a duty to B in relation to T's assertion of that entitlement.[60] The relationship of English law to the *lex situs* provides a modern parallel to the relationship of equity to common law in the early development of the use, and then the trust. There is a sense in which the common law recognised T as simply an unencumbered holder of a property right. As Maitland noted,[61] equity did not contradict or undermine the common law, as it did not deny that T held that property right, but rather imposed a duty on T in relation to it. On this view, the reason why Cayman law can recognise a trust of Saudi shares without undermining the *lex situs* also explains why a court of equity can recognise a trust of English land without undermining the common law.[62] Second, it was held that a transfer of the trust property by T to D, even where it leads to the loss of B's beneficial interest, is not a disposition of that interest within the meaning of section 127. There is thus a clear difference between the transfer (eg, by a director) of a right vested in a company and the transfer by a trustee of a right held on trust for a company.[63] The practical effect of each transaction – the loss of a company's right – may be the same, but the legal analysis differs as each transaction has a distinct formal structure. As Lloyd LJ had noted in an earlier case, a transfer by T to D, where D is a bona fide purchaser of the legal estate for value without notice, 'is as effective as it would be if [the trustee] could vest the beneficial title in the purchaser' but does not in truth involve any such transfer of beneficial title.[64] D acquires title to the

[59] See, eg, Lord Mance: 'the English courts have regularly stated their willingness to enforce in personam trusts in respect of property abroad': *Akers* [2017] UKSC 6, [2017] AC 424 [24].

[60] The same analysis applies to other equitable property rights, such as the equity of redemption: see, eg, *British South Africa Co v De Beers Consolidated Mines Ltd* [1910] 2 Ch 502, 513–14.

[61] Maitland, *Equity: A Course of Lectures*, above n 10, 17.

[62] This reasoning also supports the decisions of the English courts and the European Court of Justice in *Webb v Webb* [1991] 1 WLR 1410; *Webb v Webb* [1994] ECR I-1717, [1994] QB 696.

[63] As noted by, eg, Lord Mance in *Akers*: [2017] UKSC 6, [2017] AC 424 [53]–[55].

[64] *Independent Trustee Services Ltd v GP Noble Trustees Ltd* [2012] EWCA Civ 195, [2013] Ch 91 [106].

property from T and is free to use that property for D's own benefit, but this is not because previously separate legal and beneficial interests have been re-united. It is rather because D has acquired a right from T and, given the bona fide purchase, there is no grounds on which equity can impose a restriction, in B's favour, on D's use of that right.[65] There is, therefore, no disposition from B to D.[66]

IV. Mistaken, But Valid, Transfers of Rights

The argument of this chapter is that equitable intervention in favour of B has a characteristic form: it involves controlling the assertion of a right held by another, A. Whilst such intervention may, in practice, give B many of the advantages that go with other forms of legal relation, it is a mistake to equate the position in equity with those other forms of legal relation. So, as discussed in Section III, where a right is held on trust for the beneficiary, the beneficiary enjoys many of the practical advantages that come from holding such a right, but it is a mistake to regard the beneficiary as in fact holding that right. It has also been seen that this formal point does have substantive effects, particularly when regarding the obligations owed by third parties. Such an analysis can be linked to the historical development of equity as a secondary system: it provides a means to control rights established by the primary system of common law rules. As noted in Section II, when considering the rule against penalties, a debate as to whether a rule is best seen as equitable or not may sometimes be a debate as to whether the rule has such a secondary nature. Certainly, the form taken by such secondary rules can also be seen in areas which are not necessarily considered to be principally the domain of equity: this can be seen by examining some core aspects of the law of restitution.

In the first article in the very first edition of the Harvard Law Review, James Barr Ames considered a puzzle that is still debated today: where a claimant, C, makes a mistaken transfer of a right to D, why is it that, even if the transfer is valid, C's mistake may give rise to a claim by C to recover from D the value of the right transferred? This will be referred to here as the 'mistaken transfer' case and the claim recognised as a 'personal restitutionary claim'. Ames argued that an analogy with the receipt of trust property may assist in understanding that claim. Where the trustee holds a right on trust and then transfers that right to a recipient

[65] *Akers* [2017] UKSC 6, [2017] AC 424 [51] (Lord Mance) and [88] (Lord Sumption). See too *Pilcher v Rawlins* (1865) LR 7 Ch App 259, where B's inability to bring a claim against D in such a case is seen as depending on a lack of equitable jurisdiction to reach D.

[66] This point, decisive in *Akers*, had not in fact been considered in the courts below, nor in oral argument before the Supreme Court, but was noted by the Justices only after that point, so that written submissions were invited: see *Akers* [2017] UKSC 6, [2017] AC 424 [9]. Although this point is not mentioned by the Supreme Court in *Akers*, its analysis accords precisely with the interpretation of the phrase 'disposition of an equitable interest' given by the House of Lords in *Vandervell v IRC* [1967] 2 AC 291 when considering s 53(1)(c) of the Law of Property Act 1925 (UK). There, similarly, the transfer of legal title to shares by T to D (in that case, with the permission of B) did not involve any disposition of B's beneficial interest to D.

(not a bona fide purchaser for value of the legal estate without notice) in breach of trust, the fact that the recipient has indeed acquired the right is not inconsistent with a holding that, if his conscience is affected by knowledge of the trust, he may come under a personal liability to the beneficiary as a constructive trustee. One broad way of understanding that result would be to say that the transaction between the trustee and the recipient was effective to transfer a right, but that it did not transfer the *value* of that right from the beneficiary to the recipient. A similar analysis might then be said to apply to the mistaken transfer case: the imposition of liability on the defendant is not inconsistent with the finding that the right was indeed transferred, as it can be said that, as a result of the mistake of the claimant, the value of the right has not been validly transferred. Or, in Ames' words: 'a court of equity will compel the surrender of an advantage by a defendant whenever, but only whenever, upon grounds of obvious justice, it is unconscientious for him to retain it at another's expense'.[67]

Ames' argument repays careful consideration.[68] The difficulties with it are clear from the analysis in Section III above. First, in the case of the trust, the beneficiary (B) has no abstract entitlement to value. Indeed, as against parties other than B, the trustee (T) has the same general liberty as an unencumbered owner to use the trust property for his or her own benefit, and to that extent, has an entitlement to the value of the trust property. In order to deny D, the recipient from T, such a liberty as against B, it is necessary to find a specific reason why D is under a duty to B: for example, because D acquired knowledge of the initial trust whilst still holding the trust property or its traceable proceeds. Second, there is of course a difference between the claim made by B against a recipient who retains trust property and the claim asserted by a mistaken transferor. The former case involves B's assertion that D has or had a specific right, and is under a duty to B in relation to that right; whereas the mistaken transferor simply asserts that the recipient be ordered to pay a sum of money.

Ames' analysis may nonetheless be helpful. First, it is worth noting that his language of unconscientious retention, drawn from some foundational English cases,[69] has been echoed more recently by Australian courts.[70] Second, a link

[67] Ames, above n 55, 3.

[68] For Ames's general influence on the development of the law of restitution, see A Kull, 'James Barr Ames and the Early Modern History of Unjust Enrichment' (2005) 25 *OJLS* 297.

[69] See, eg, *Moses v Macferlan* (1760) 2 Burr 1005, 1012, 97 ER 676, 680 (Lord Mansfield): 'This kind of equitable action, to recover back money, which ought not in justice to be kept, is very beneficial, and therefore much encouraged. It lies only for money which, ex aequo et bono, the defendant ought to refund.' See too *Clarke v Shee & Johnson* (1774) 1 Cowp 197, 199, 98 ER 1041, 199–200 (Lord Mansfield): 'This is a liberal action in the nature of a bill in equity; and if, under the circumstances of the case, it appears that the defendant cannot in conscience retain what is the subject matter of it, the plaintiff may well support this action' and Parke B in *Kelly v Solari* (1841) 9 M & W 54, 58, 152 ER 24, 26: it is 'against conscience' to retain money paid in the mistaken belief that the recipient is entitled to it 'though a demand may be necessary in those cases in which the party receiving may have been ignorant of that mistake'.

[70] See, eg, *Australian Financial Services v Hills* [2014] HCA 14, (2014) 253 CLR 560 [65]–[76], and the thorough exposition of Gummow J in *Roxborough v Rothmans of Pall Mall Australia Ltd* [2001] HCA 68, (2001) 208 CLR 516.

can be made at a more abstract level between the protection of the beneficiary against a recipient from the trustee and the protection of the mistaken transferor of a right. In the first case, the secondary nature of B's claim is clear: B accepts that the recipient, D, holds a particular right, but argues that D is under a duty to B in relation to that right. The mistaken transferor's claim can also be seen as secondary, in the sense that the primary rules (which dictate that the transfer is valid, despite the mistake) are respected, but a claim is still asserted. Indeed, it can be argued that, like B's claim, the claim of the mistaken transferor provides a means of regulating the consequences of D's acquisition of a right.[71] On this view, the existence of the personal restitutionary claim helps to justify the operation of the rules which mean that the transfer of the right is valid, notwithstanding the transferor's mistake.[72] There may be good reasons, particularly when considering certainty for third parties, for the law to stipulate that an apparent transfer is valid and that the recipient does indeed hold the right in question; but those reasons do not necessarily prevent the existence of the restitutionary claim. To the extent then that the restitutionary claim regulates the consequences, as between claimant and defendant, of the defendant's acquisition of a right, it can be seen as performing the role associated in this chapter with equity. So, whether or not one agrees with the historical claim in the first part of Cardozo's assertion that the action for money had and received is 'equitable in origin and function', it is possible to agree with the second part of that assertion.[73]

V. Equitable Estoppel

The analysis so far has picked out rules that regulate, in favour of B, either A's assertion, or A's acquisition, of a right. In relation to the trust, a consideration of the form of legal relations also cast doubt on the idea that a beneficiary of a trust should be seen as an 'equitable owner' as this falsely suggests that the beneficiary's rights are equivalent to, or simply a weaker version of, those of a common law owner. Similar care must be taken with the concept of equitable estoppel.

There is a form of equitable estoppel which is indeed identical to the common law doctrine of estoppel by representation as it prevents the party bound, A, from making a particular assertion. This form of estoppel regulates the assertion not only of facts, but also of mixed matters of fact and law, and can thus be a means of regulating A's assertion of a right. To that extent the doctrine, recognised both

[71] See, eg, *Cressman v Coys of Kensington (Sales) Ltd* [2004] EWCA Civ 47, [2004] 1 WLR 2775 [24], where Mance LJ noted that, far from being a defence to the restitutionary claim, the fact that a registration scheme vested a right in the defendant was a pre-condition of that claim.

[72] See, eg, B McFarlane, 'Unjust Enrichment, Rights and Value' in D Nolan and A Robertson (eds), *Rights and Private Law* (Oxford, Hart Publishing, 2012) 579, 591, 606. See too J Mee, 'Justifying Restitutionary Liability for Mistaken Payments' (Obligations IX Conference, Melbourne, July 2018).

[73] *Atlantic Coast Line Railroad Co v Florida*, 295 US 301 (1935) 309.

in common law and at equity,[74] can be a means of regulating a party's assertion of a right;[75] although it is not primarily focused on controlling the acquisition or exercise of rights, and does so only as a by-product of its evidential role in preventing the assertion of particular matters. Such a doctrine, of course, whilst it may be very useful to B in practice, cannot, in itself, operate as an independent means by which B can make a claim. Nor, as recognised in equity as well as at common law,[76] can the doctrine apply where A has simply made a representation or promise as to A's future conduct: a preclusionary doctrine, whilst it can operate to prevent A denying that such a representation or promise was made, cannot determine the legal effects of such a representation or promise.[77]

When other forms of equitable estoppel are considered, however, the link to the preclusive estoppel by representation survives in name only. First, consider promissory estoppel. *Hughes*[78] has been instrumental in the development of the modern law of promissory estoppel. The decision provides a clear example of equity's second-order role in acknowledging the existence of a right, but then controlling the exercise of that right. A was prevented from exercising a contractual right to forfeit B's lease, as such a forfeiture would have allowed A to benefit from B's failure to complete repairs within a particular time, even though A had encouraged B to believe that B's inaction during a period when the parties were negotiating as to B's possible surrender of the lease would *not* lead to forfeiture of the lease. A did not thereby lose the contractual right; rather, A was prevented from asserting that right before the expiry of an additional period, so that the period in which negotiations had taken place did not count against B in assessing whether the repairs had been completed in time. As B was not claiming that A had lost the initial contractual right, there was no need for B to show that the parties' contract had been varied; B was instead protected through equity's control of A's assertion of the contractual right. Indeed, the relevant principle can be seen as responding to a possible defect in the general contractual rules controlling A's acquisition of the power to forfeit the lease: whilst the condition for A's acquisition of the right (B's failure to complete repairs in the contractually agreed six-month period) had arisen, that condition consisted of particular action or inaction by B, and it would be unjust for A to be free to enforce the right where B's decision to adopt that course of conduct was based on A's encouragement to B that A would *not* acquire or enforce the right. Certainly, A's action would seem to consist

[74] It is today more commonly associated with common law, but for examples of its application in equity, see, eg, *Hunt v Carew* (1649) Nels 46, 21 ER 786; *Hunsden v Cheney* (1690) 2 Vern 150, 23 ER 703 and see the helpful discussion in Heydon, Leeming and Turner, above n 2, para 17.180, pointing out that the 'origins of estoppel by representation lay in Chancery'.

[75] See, eg, *Pickard v Sears* (1837) 6 Ad & E 469, 112 ER 179.

[76] See, eg, *Jorden v Money* (1854) 5 HLC 185, 10 ER 868, which was an appeal from a court of Chancery.

[77] As noted by Gaudron J in *Waltons Stores (Interstate) Ltd v Maher* (1988) 164 CLR 387, 459 ('*Waltons Stores*').

[78] *Hughes* (1877) 2 App Cas 439, above n 4.

of precisely the sort of opportunistic taking advantage of a legal rule which equity, on one view,[79] characteristically aims to prevent.

The reasoning in *Hughes* is thus characteristically equitable, in as much as it regulates, in B's favour, A's acquisition or enforcement of a right. It is, however, hardly a classic case of estoppel, and no mention was made of that term in the case itself. Certainly, the principle applied differs markedly from estoppel by representation, as it is based not on a representation as to an existing state of affairs but on A's encouraging B to believe something about A's future conduct. As later noted by Lord Denning MR, the main way in which the *Hughes* principle resembles estoppel by representation is in the fact that it cannot, by itself, operate as an independent cause of action:[80] it is not a means by which A comes under a duty to B. This is simply a consequence of the nature of the principle, which seeks to prevent the unconscionable assertion of a right of A. Similarly, in *Legione v Hateley*,[81] an equitable estoppel would have operated to prevent A taking advantage of a power to terminate the contract arising on B's failure to provide the purchase price at the agreed time. The closest common law cousin of such a doctrine is not estoppel by representation, but is rather the doctrine of waiver.[82] Indeed, the *Hughes* principle can be seen as closer to waiver (in that it shares the form of modifying A's ability to enforce a right) than to estoppel by representation.

In some jurisdictions, of course, equitable estoppel has also come to function as an independent cause of action.[83] This happened first, it seems, in the 'classic example of proprietary estoppel, [A's] standing by whilst [A's] neighbour [B] builds on [A's] land believing it to be his property, [which] can be characterised as acquiescence'.[84] This acquiescence principle can apply even where B is unaware of A's failure to act and so it does not seem to require any actual or implied representation to have been made by A to B. The use of estoppel language – again notable by its absence from the cases first recognising the principle[85] – is therefore misleading.[86] Indeed, from an early period, courts allowed the principle not only to give B an immunity against a potential claim of A, but also to impose a duty or liability

[79] See, eg, Smith, above n 5.

[80] *Central London Property Trust Ltd v High Trees House Ltd* [1947] KB 130, 134 ('*High Trees*').

[81] *Legione v Hateley* (1983) 152 CLR 406.

[82] This is also true of the (slightly different) doctrine applied in the *High Trees* case, which prevents D from enforcing a right against C where D has accepted a substitute performance as a discharge of that right: for discussion, see B McFarlane, 'Understanding Equitable Estoppel: From Metaphors to Better Laws' (2013) 66 *Current Legal Problems* 1.

[83] See, eg, Australia (eg, *Waltons Stores* (1988) 164 CLR 387) and jurisdictions within the US (see, eg, Restatement (Second) of Contracts, § 90).

[84] *Fisher v Brooker* [2009] UKHL 41, [2009] 1 WLR 1764 [62] (Lord Neuberger). See, eg, Sir John Romilly MR in *Duke of Beaufort v Patrick* (1853) 17 Beav 60, 74–75, 51 ER 954, 960 ('*Duke of Beaufort*'): 'he who stands by and encourages an act, cannot afterwards complain of it, or interfere with the enjoyment of that which he has permitted to be done.'

[85] Such as, eg, *Duke of Beaufort* (1853) 17 Beav 60, 51 ER 954; *Lord Cawdor v Lewis* (1835) 1 Y & C Ex 427, 160 ER 174 ('*Lord Cawdor*').

[86] For considerations of possible justifications of the principle see I Samet, 'Proprietary Estoppel and Responsibility for Omissions' (2015) 78 *MLR* 85.

on A, which might be satisfied only by A's transferring property, or paying money, to B.[87] Even if thus operating as a cause of action, however, the principle retains an element of a second-order function, as it addresses a particular danger arising from the existence of a system of legal entitlements: it protects B against the risk of A's abusing B's mistaken belief as to B's existing entitlements.[88]

A more significant use of equitable estoppel as a cause of action has occurred in cases where B reasonably relies on A's promise in such a way that B would suffer a detriment were A wholly free to renege on that promise. It is clear in both England[89] and Australia[90] that such a cause of action can arise where A's promise is to give B a right in relation to A's land, but English courts have been more reluctant than their Australian counterparts to extend the principle to other promises.[91] There are two questions which must be separated when considering such extensions of equitable estoppel. First, there is a question as to outcomes (or, it might be said, substance): is there a good reason for recognising a principle whereby A can have a duty to perform a non-contractual promise (or, at least, a liability to ensure B is not made worse off by reliance on that promise) where B would otherwise suffer a detriment as a result of B's reasonable reliance on A's promise? Second, there is a question as to means (or, it might be said, form): if there is a good reason for recognising such a principle, should it be enforced through the doctrine of promissory estoppel? The problem of course is that 'estoppel' is wholly inapt as a label, as the defendant is not being estopped from asserting anything. Indeed, for those who think there is good reason for first-order intervention in such cases, the link to promissory estoppel is unfortunate as it allows opponents of such a principle[92] to cast doubt on it not by

[87] See, eg, *Duke of Beaufort* (1853) 17 Beav 60, 51 ER 954; *Lord Cawdor* (1835) 1 Y & C Ex 427, 433, 160 ER 174, 176: 'It is admitted to be a proper subject for equitable interference, where one party stands by and allows another to spend money upon his lands without giving him notice of his title ... Whether the relief be a perpetual injunction, or an allowance by way of compensation, or a lease, must be determined by the result of the hearing.'

[88] N McBride, *The Humanity of Private Law: Part I: Explanation* (Oxford, Hart Publishing, 2018) 232 analyses the different strands of proprietary estoppel as doctrines which share the aim of preserving the legitimacy of private law, stating for example that, in the acquiescence case, a claim arises to prevent A 'bring[ing] private law into disrepute in the eyes of [B], who stands to lose out as a result of [A's] inconsistent treatment of him'. There is of course significant overlap between the aim identified by McBride of preserving the legitimacy of the law, and the second-order function identified in this chapter, but McBride's concept is broader and is used by him to explain, eg, why an objective standard of care is applied in the tort of negligence (ibid 202–04). The basis of the second-order function identified in this chapter is closer to that suggested by S Smith, 'A Duty to Make Restitution' (2013) 26 *Canadian Journal of Law and Jurisprudence* 157, 170, when describing certain liabilities as 'not responses to failures by defendants; they are responses to imperfections in the legal system itself'.

[89] See, eg, *Thorner v Major* [2009] UKHL 18, [2009] 1 WLR 776 ('*Thorner*').

[90] See, eg, *Sidhu v Van Dyke* [2014] HCA 19, (2014) 251 CLR 505.

[91] In *Thorner* [2009] UKHL 18, [2009] 1 WLR 776 [61], Lord Walker states that it is the relation of A's promise to some identified land that justifies B's claim. The principle does however seem to have been applied more broadly (eg, in cases concerning intellectual property rights, such as *Motivate Publishing FZ LLC v Hello Ltd* [2015] EWHC 1554 (Ch) [55]–[61]). For discussion see B McFarlane and P Sales, 'Promises, Liability, and Detriment: Lessons from Proprietary Estoppel' (2015) 131 *LQR* 610.

[92] See, eg, the analysis of K Handley both judicially (eg, *Saleh v Romanous* [2010] NSWCA 274, (2010) 79 NSWLR 453) and in *Estoppel by Conduct and Election* (London, Sweet & Maxwell, 2006) para 13.008.

challenging its own merits, but rather by pointing out the differences between the principle and the type of second-order regulation of rights that is characteristic of equity and is evidenced by the decision in *Hughes*. Certainly, the use of the estoppel label may lead a judge to misunderstand the nature of the claim.[93]

In *Waltons Stores*, Brennan J answered the second question positively by finding no relevant distinction between a 'change in legal relationships effected by a promise which extinguishes a right and a change in legal relationships effected by a promise which creates one'.[94] The analysis in this chapter points to exactly the opposite conclusion – there *is* a difference between a principle that controls the acquisition or assertion of an existing right (such as the principle in *Hughes*) and one that instead imposes a new duty or liability. That difference is recognised at common law: for example, the rules applying to waiver of contractual rights differ from those applying to variation of a contract.[95] When a principle has a second-order nature, this opens up new possibilities for its justification: its explanation may be connected to the rules applying to the primary rights regulated by the second-order principle.[96]

The instability of Brennan J's contention can be seen in the subsequent development of the law of promissory estoppel in Australia: when it operates as a means to impose a new duty or liability on A, the requirement that the doctrine applies only to 'a change in legal relationships' has been challenged and, in some cases, departed from.[97] The legal relationship requirement makes sense when promissory estoppel performs its more established, second-order role of regulating the acquisition or assertion of rights, but it is very hard to justify when the impetus for intervention is the first-order concern of enforcing a promise, or of preventing B from suffering a detriment as a result of reliance on such a promise. For example, A's promise to enter into a contract to provide a service for B falls into the scope of Brennan J's formulation, whereas A's more direct promise simply to provide that service for B does not.

As a matter of substance, such a distinction is very hard to defend. Interestingly, however, it would be one means of preserving a (weakened) second-order form for equitable estoppel, even when operating as a cause of action. The argument would have to be that the existence of certain legal powers (such as the power to transfer a right, or to enter a contract), whilst advantageous overall, carries certain risks: a party may abuse such a power by, for example, causing another to suffer a detriment through reasonable reliance on a promise that such a power will be exercised. A second-order rule can then control the risk inherent in the powers

[93] As appears to have occurred, in the context of proprietary estoppel, in Lord Scott's judgment in *Cobbe v Yeoman's Row Management Ltd* [2008] UKHL 55, [2008] 1 WLR 1752 [14].

[94] *Waltons Stores* (1988) 164 CLR 387, 425.

[95] Most notably, consideration is not required: see, eg, *Hickman v Haynes* (1875) LR 10 CP 598.

[96] As noted in relation to personal restitutionary claims by, eg, McFarlane, above n 72.

[97] See, eg, *W v G* (1996) 20 Fam LR 49; *ACN 074 971 109 Pty Ltd (as Trustee for the Argot Unit Trust) v National Mutual Life Association of Australasia Ltd* [2008] VSCA 247, (2008) 21 VR 351. For a full survey see A Robertson, 'Three Models of Promissory Estoppel' (2013) 7 *Journal of Equity* 226, 240–43.

established by the primary legal rules, by offering some protection to the relying party; just as a second-order rule allowing a personal restitutionary claim may control the risk inherent in those same legal powers by offering some protection to a party who mistakenly exercises them.[98] Indeed, one might support this analogy between equitable estoppel and certain restitutionary claims by pointing to the similar language sometimes used by the courts in such cases[99] and also to the fact that, in each case, the rules seem to impose a liability, rather than an immediate duty,[100] on the defendant.

VI. Conclusion

The notion that equity looks to substance not to form can create a false opposition: attention to the form of legal relations is in fact a crucial step in considering the justification of particular substantive outcomes. In the examples discussed in this chapter, the application of a particular formal analysis has favoured specific practical results. The basic claim made here is that, in many cases, the importance and distinctiveness of equitable rules lies in the fact that such rules regulate, in favour of a specific claimant, the enforcement or acquisition of a right of the defendant. This means, first, that equitable rules often produce different effects from common law rules to which they are linked. This was seen by considering the trust, where it was argued that there are significant formal differences between the legal relations involved in an equitable interest on the one hand and a legal property right on the other. Those formal differences have important substantive effects when considering the obligations of third parties. For example, it was argued that the existence of a trust does not impose on third parties an immediate duty to the beneficiary, nor does it give a beneficiary an abstract entitlement to value that can be asserted against third parties. Rather, such third parties are better understood as being under a liability: it is possible that their own enforcement of acquisition of particular rights (ie, the trust property or its traceable proceeds) may be controlled in favour of the beneficiary.

It was then argued that this second-order model, whilst reasonably clear in the case of trusts, is also relevant to other parts of the law of obligations. Indeed, as seen when considering restitutionary claims based on mistaken transfers of

[98] See McFarlane, above n 72, 591, 606 and Mee, above n 72.

[99] See, eg, the reference to unconscionability as an overarching concept, and the making of a direct comparison between restitution and equitable estoppel in both *Pitt v Holt* [2013] UKSC 26, [2013] 2 AC 108 [126]–[128] (Lord Walker) and *Australian Financial Services Ltd v Hills* [2014] HCA 14, (2014) 253 CLR 560 [65]–[76] (Hayne, Crennan, Kiefel, Bell and Keane JJ).

[100] For a liability-based analysis of the personal restitutionary claim see Smith, above n 88; for a liability-based analysis of equitable estoppel when operating as a cause of action, see B McFarlane, 'Equitable Estoppel: Neither One Thing Nor One Other' in S Degeling, J Edelman and J Goudkamp (eds), *Contract in Commercial Law* (Sydney, Thomson Reuters, 2016) 359.

rights, the model can apply in areas which are not always thought of as dependent on equitable intervention. The important point here is not as to the jurisdictional origin of the rules, but is rather as to their form. The second-order nature of the rules may help to resolve certain puzzles as to their justification. In particular, such rules can be seen as helping to mitigate the effects of primary rules (for example as to when the transfer or creation of a right is or is not valid) and thus limiting some of the risks that arise when the law recognises a power to transfer or create rights. Indeed, in relation to each of the restitutionary claim and equitable estoppel, it may be that the answer to the substantive question as to the appropriate scope of a cause of action depends on determining the formal function of the underlying principle. So, is the personal restitutionary claim arising in the case of a mistaken transfer of rights part of a broader primary principle imposing a prima facie duty on A in cases where A is enriched (in whatever form) at B's expense,[101] or is it better seen as a more limited secondary rule which exists to mitigate the risks created by the existence of legal powers to transfer or create rights, therefore applying to impose a liability on A only where such a power has been exercised by B?[102] Similarly, is the claim arising where B reasonably relies to his or her detriment on a promise by A part of a broader primary principle which may apply whatever the content of A's promise may be, or is it better seen as a more limited secondary rule which exists to mitigate the risks created by the existence of legal powers to transfer or create rights, and so applies only where A has promised to exercise such a power in B's favour? To answer such questions within the context of established judicial rules, whether such rules arose at common law or in equity, we must look to form as well as to substance.

[101] This was essentially Birks' argument (above n 53, ch 1), where the key feature of a mistaken payment is seen as the mistaken transfer of *value*, rather than as the mistaken transfer of a right.

[102] This second view is consistent with, eg, McFarlane, above n 72.

10

Modern Equity – At the Edge of Formal Reasoning?

MAN YIP*

I. Introduction

Equity, in its inception, was more inclined than the common law towards substantive reasoning – with reference to conscience, moral reasons and circumstances of the case.[1] Ecclesiastical Chancellors did not consider themselves bound by precedents.[2] These features of early equity may be explained by its historical function to supplement common law and mitigate its harshness.[3] The concern was with ensuring that justice was achieved in each case, particularly where the dispute could not be adequately dealt with by common law. Equity nevertheless progressively retreated towards formal reasoning – characterised by rules, fixed criteria and strict application of stare decisis principles – in conformity with the English vision of 'law' and the judicial function.[4]

Today, in Lord Neuberger's words, English equity is 'not only alive, but kicking – or being kicked'.[5] However, a number of recent equitable developments evidence signs of embracing fact-based reasoning, evaluative approaches or flexible criteria. This chapter has three goals: first, to identify these developments; second, to explain the cause for such developments; and finally, to reflect on the

* I would like to thank TM Yeo, Lusina Ho, Alvin See, Goh Yihan, John Mee, Peter Jaffey, Kelvin Low and Kenny Chng for helpful comments on earlier versions of this chapter. All errors and views remain my own.

[1] See JH Baker, *An Introduction to English Legal History*, 4th edn (Oxford, Oxford University Press, 2005) 102–04.

[2] FW Maitland, *Equity: A Course of Lectures*, AH Chaytor and WJ Whittaker (eds) 2nd edn (Cambridge, Cambridge University Press, rev by J Brunyate, 1936) 8.

[3] ibid 17, 19.

[4] Maitland, above n 2, 3–10.

[5] D Neuberger, 'Equity – The soul and spirit of all law or a roguish thing?' (Lehane Lecture, Supreme Court of New South Wales, Sydney, 4 August 2014) [6].

wider themes of equity's renewal and legal harmonisation. This chapter examines recent equitable developments through the lenses of 'form' and 'substance' as defined by Atiyah and Summers.[6]

The discussion consists of three main parts. Section II, which follows immediately after this introduction, highlights three symptoms of equity's struggle to maintain a strongly formal approach. First, courts have on occasions changed the law with greater boldness than before in disregarding contrary authorities. Second, in a number of instances, the courts have replaced 'hard and fast rules' with approaches that have an in-built flexibility. Such in-built flexibility is manifested in two forms: first, an open discretion model which is based on a multi-factorial, fact-specific analysis; and secondly, a residual discretion model which confers on courts the residual jurisdiction to override the primary 'hard and fast rule' or mitigate its effect. Third, the courts are increasingly relying on contextualist reasoning, most notably, by drawing a distinction between commercial and non-commercial cases. Contextualism is a rough model of the fact-specific approach, as well as a gateway to a different set of policy considerations (substantive reasons) to justify the court's conclusions.

Section III investigates the underlying causes of the symptoms. The discussion suggests three main causes of equity's recent retreat from formal reasoning: diversity, complexity and pragmatism. Traditional equitable rules were formulated on the basis of simple paradigms that do not apply naturally or easily in many modern disputes that straddle different areas of the law. Consequently, to avoid inconsistency between the different branches of the law, an obvious solution is to deploy fact-specific, evaluative tests that place the competing concerns at the forefront. The diversity of scenarios in which modern equitable principles apply further contributes to the need for some measure of flexibility in the rules. Finally, pragmatism, of various forms, permeates the judicial process. But differing from Atiyah, this chapter argues that judges are not merely pragmatic in the narrow sense of being concerned with doing justice in the particular case, but also in the wider sense of a concern with the 'possible impact of the decision in the future'.[7]

Finally, Section IV considers the broader themes of equity's renewal and legal harmonisation across the common law world. It argues that English equity's retreat from strong formal reasoning is part of its renewal process and English courts have the responsibility to ensure that this process will lead to greater clarity and certainty for the law in the end. It also examines the impact that this English trend may have on equity's renewal and harmonisation across England and Wales, Australia, Hong Kong and Singapore.

[6] PS Atiyah and RS Summers, *Form and Substance in Anglo-American Law: A Comparative Study of Legal Reasoning, Legal Theory, and Legal Institutions* (Oxford, Clarendon Press, 1987).

[7] PS Atiyah, 'From Principles to Pragmatism: Changes in the Function of the Judicial Process and the Law' (1980) 65 *Iowa Law Review* 1249, 1251.

II. Symptoms

No system of law will be purely formal, or purely substantive. The question is one of degree. The central question is whether modern English equity is increasingly more formal or increasingly more substantive, and in what ways this is shown in recent developments. It would be impossible to demonstrate the precise balance between form and substance; nor is that the aim of this chapter. My analysis shall be qualitative and in broad strokes, to provide a rough sketch of the emerging patterns.

I will start off by identifying three symptoms of modern equity's struggle to maintain a strongly formal approach. The analysis is primarily focused on English developments, the historical source of equitable principles and a contemporary reference point for other common law jurisdictions. Where appropriate, comparative reference to the developments in Australia, Hong Kong and Singapore will be made. Space constraints do not permit a comprehensive comparative review, but it should be made clear that the point of the exercise here is to extract 'outside insights' on whether English trends are unique. These three jurisdictions are selected for two reasons. First, whilst comparative review between English and Australian law is aplenty, little work has been done in comparing the developments in these jurisdictions with those in Hong Kong and Singapore. This chapter seeks to pave the way for deeper reflections in this area. Second, English and Australian developments are natural reference points for Hong Kong and Singapore, jurisdictions with a relatively small case load. Further, the appointment of English and Australian judges (or former judges) as Overseas Non-Permanent Judges in the Hong Kong Court of Final Appeal and as International Judges in the Singapore International Commercial Court builds an interesting legal eco-system between these four jurisdictions, which has yet to receive in-depth study. I will return to this point in Section IV.

A. Conflicting Authorities

The extent of deference to precedents and persuasive authorities as grounds for decision is indicative of a legal system's inclination towards formal reasoning.[8] It has been observed that the English legal tradition tends towards a strict application of the doctrine of precedent, so as to promote certainty and predictability in the law.[9] Reliance on the force of authority as a ground for decision may of course be a judicial technique to avoid dealing with the more complex justificatory reasons

[8] Atiyah and Summers, above n 6, 118–33.

[9] ibid; BV Harris, 'Final Appellate Courts Overruling Their Own "Wrong" Precedents: The Ongoing Search for Principle' (2002) 118 *LQR* 408.

or to imbue the conclusion with an air of authoritativeness, thereby rendering the decision more 'clarificatory' than inventive.[10]

Of particular interest here is the way in which English courts deal with conflicting authorities. On the observation of Atiyah and Summers, the traditional English approach is to 'strive to reconcile all or most of the cases cited to them, and explain why some are binding and will be followed, while the others are distinguishable and need not be followed, or, just occasionally, are wrong and ought to be overruled'.[11] In other words, the traditional English approach is to undertake an intensive interpretative exercise to reconcile or distinguish the authorities, even if performed awkwardly. In *Barlow Clowes International Ltd v Eurotrust International Ltd*,[12] the Privy Council's strained clarification that *Twinsectra Ltd v Yardley*[13] had not departed from the objective standard laid down in *Royal Brunei Airlines v Tan*[14] amply illustrates this judicial technique. By deploying an interpretative approach, the Privy Council 'corrected' the law through formal reasoning, and avoided engaging with policy considerations.[15]

Such was also the approach undertaken by the English Court of Appeal in *Sinclair Investments (UK) Ltd v Versailles Trade Finance Ltd*.[16] The case raised the then hotly-debated question of whether a bribe or secret commission received by a fiduciary should be treated as the principal's property. Notably, authorities and academic literature were split as to what the answer should be. In *Sinclair*, Lord Neuberger answered the question in the negative. In choosing between *Attorney General for Hong Kong v Reid*[17] (a Privy Council decision) and *Lister & Company v Stubbs*[18] (a previous Court of Appeal decision), he emphasised that the rule of stare decisis dictates that the Court of Appeal would generally follow its own previous decision, leaving the Supreme Court to overrule contrary authorities.[19] In any event, Lord Neuberger was confident that the Supreme Court would not choose to follow *Reid*, setting out seven premises for his view.[20] Notably, the force of precedent was one of the main grounds relied upon by Lord Neuberger:[21]

> [T]here is a consistent line of reasoned decisions of this court (two of which were decided within the last ten years) stretching back into the late 19th century, and one decision

[10] See, eg, *Fistar v Riverwood Legion and Community Club Ltd* [2016] NSWCA 81, (2016) 91 NSWLR 732; *Great Investments Ltd v Warner* [2016] FCAFC 85, (2016) 243 FCR 516. Both decisions relied on the force of precedent to justify their interpretation of *Farah Constructions Pty Ltd v Say-Dee Pty Ltd* [2007] HCA 22, (2007) 230 CLR 89 as not entirely ruling out strict liability receipt claims.

[11] Atiyah and Summers, above n 6, 129.

[12] *Barlow Clowes International Ltd v Eurotrust International Ltd* [2005] UKPC 37, [2006] 1 WLR 1476 [14]–[16].

[13] *Twinsectra Ltd v Yardley* [2002] UKHL 12, [2002] 2 AC 164.

[14] *Royal Brunei Airlines v Tan* [1995] 2 AC 378.

[15] TM Yeo, 'Dishonest Assistance: Restatement From The Privy Council' (2006) 122 *LQR* 171, 173.

[16] *Sinclair Investments (UK) Ltd v Versailles Trade Finance Ltd* [2011] EWCA Civ 347, [2011] 3 WLR 1153 [57]–[87] ('*Sinclair*').

[17] *Attorney General for Hong Kong v Reid* [1994] 1 AC 324 ('*Reid*').

[18] *Lister & Company v Stubbs* (1890) 45 Ch D 1.

[19] *Sinclair* [2011] EWCA Civ 347, [2011] 3 WLR 1153 [74]. See more recently, *Garcia v Marex Financial Limited* [2018] EWCA Civ 1468, [2018] 3 WLR 1412 [69] (Lewison LJ).

[20] *Sinclair* [2011] EWCA Civ 347, [2011] 3 WLR 1153 [77]–[84].

[21] ibid [88].

> of the House of Lords 150 years ago, which appear to establish that a beneficiary of a fiduciary's duties cannot claim a proprietary interest, but is entitled to an equitable account, in respect of any money or asset acquired by a fiduciary in breach of his duties to the beneficiary, unless the asset or money is or has been beneficially the property of the beneficiary or the trustee acquired the asset or money by taking advantage of an opportunity or right which was property that of the beneficiary.

However, two recent Supreme Court decisions demonstrate greater judicial candour in recognising the limits of case law in generating the 'right answer'. Lord Neuberger's remarkable tergiversation from his *Sinclair* decision in *FHR European Ventures LLP v Cedar Capitals Partners LLC*[22] marked a pragmatic approach. In *FHR*, Lord Neuberger, reviewing the same conflicting authorities, commented that 'it is not possible to identify any plainly right or plainly wrong answer to the issue … as a matter of pure legal authority'.[23] In fact, he said 'it would be unrealistic to expect complete consistency from the cases over the past 300 years' and the court should in such circumstances turn first to the arguments based on principle and practicality.[24] But even arguments based on principle – notwithstanding the voluminous academic literature – did not illuminate, according to the Court, rendering the 'simple answer' the correct answer.[25] Ultimately, it was a policy-based decision, dictated by a balance of justice between the innocent beneficiary and the errant fiduciary,[26] wider policy considerations concerning bribery as a social evil,[27] and the need to harmonise English law with the laws of other common law jurisdictions.[28] In light of these policy concerns, the contrary line of authorities was overruled.[29]

Similarly, in *AIB Group (UK) plc v Mark Redler & Co Solicitors*,[30] a controversial decision on equitable compensation for breach of trust, there was a conflict between older cases that supported awards based on traditional accounting rules[31] and more recent developments following *Target Holdings Ltd v Redferns*,[32] which applied a 'but-for' causation approach to the issue of liability. In *AIB*, Lord Toulson began his analysis by declaring that it was not 'necessary to set out a full historical account of all the case law cited in the literature reaching back to *Caffrey v Darby* (1801) 6 Ves 488'.[33] The question was quite simply whether *Target Holdings* 'should be affirmed, qualified or (as the bank would put it) reinterpreted'.[34]

[22] *FHR European Ventures LLP v Cedar Capitals Partners LLC* [2014] UKSC 45, [2015] AC 250 ('*FHR*').
[23] *FHR* [2014] UKSC 45, [2015] AC 250 [32]. At [46], Lord Neuberger reasoned that the authorities did not preclude the conclusion reached.
[24] *FHR* [2014] UKSC 45, [2015] AC 250 [32].
[25] *FHR* [2014] UKSC 45, [2015] AC 250 [32].
[26] ibid [41].
[27] ibid [42].
[28] ibid [45].
[29] ibid [50].
[30] *AIB Group (UK) plc v Mark Redler & Co Solicitors* [2014] UKSC 58, [2014] 3 WLR 1367 ('*AIB*').
[31] See further L Ho, 'An Account of Accounts' (2016) 28 *Singapore Academy of Law Journal* 849.
[32] *Target Holdings Ltd v Redferns* [1996] AC 421 ('*Target Holdings*').
[33] *AIB* [2014] UKSC 58, [2014] 3 WLR 1367 [47].
[34] ibid [49].

Whilst acknowledging that '[t]here are arguments to be made both ways',[35] he did not think that summarising the different threads of academic arguments would 'improve the clarity of the judgment'.[36] By disregarding the older cases and the academic literature, Lord Toulson essentially avoided having to deal with the full force of the contrary view. Lord Reed, using a slightly different technique, more blatantly avoided addressing the older cases. His analysis was focused on *Canson Enterprises Ltd v Boughton & Co*,[37] a Canadian Supreme Court decision on equitable compensation for breach of fiduciary duty and its consistency with *Target Holdings*, as well as the broader issue of coherence between common law and equity. He also conducted a selective and superficial review of developments in other jurisdictions since *Target Holdings* as some form of external benchmarking of the correctness of *Target Holdings*, allowing him to arrive comfortably at the conclusion that there is a 'broad measure of consensus across a number of common law jurisdictions' that both *Canson Enterprises* and *Target Holdings* were rightly decided.[38] Most notably, Lord Reed only discussed[39] Ribeiro PJ's speech in *Libertarian Investments Ltd v Hall*,[40] without any mention of Lord Millett NPJ's analysis, which articulated with great clarity the accounting principles and how they would apply to modern disputes. It should also not be missed that the claim in *Libertarian Investments* was for reparative equitable compensation to which causation was relevant.[41]

Nevertheless, the effect is that the older authorities supporting the application of accounting principles were overruled in *AIB*. Unlike *Target Holdings*, which might be criticised as having been decided *per incuriam*, the Supreme Court in *AIB* intentionally set English law on a new direction.[42] Lord Toulson said plainly that he did not think it was sensible 'to impose or maintain a rule that gives redress to a beneficiary for loss which would have been suffered if the trustee had properly performed its duties'.[43] The only exception Lord Toulson would make is if the case involved fraud, which in his view would engage other policy considerations.[44] Contrary to critics' views,[45] he did not think that English law took a wrong turn in *Target Holdings*;[46] the case simply marked a new beginning.

[35] ibid [62].
[36] ibid [47].
[37] *Canson Enterprises Ltd v Boughton & Co* [1991] 3 SCR 534 ('*Canson Enterprises*').
[38] *AIB* [2014] UKSC 58, [2014] 3 WLR 1367 [133]. *Caffrey v Darby* (1801) 6 Ves Jun 488, 31 ER 1159 was mentioned only twice (*AIB* [2014] UKSC 58, [2014] 3 WLR 1367 [88], [135]).
[39] *AIB* [2014] UKSC 58, [2014] 3 WLR 1367 [129]–[132].
[40] *Libertarian Investments Ltd v Hall* [2014] 1 HKC 368 ('*Libertarian Investments*').
[41] See analysis in L Ho and R Lee, 'Reparative Compensation for Deliberate Breaches of Trust' (2014) 130 *LQR* 542.
[42] Over 900 pages of academic writing had been brought to the Supreme Court's attention (*AIB* [2014] UKSC 58, [2014] 3 WLR 1367 [47]).
[43] *AIB* [2014] UKSC 58, [2014] 3 WLR 1367 [62].
[44] ibid.
[45] See, eg, J Edelman, 'An English Misturning with Equitable Compensation' in S Degeling and J Varuhas (eds), *Equitable Compensation and Disgorgement of Profit* (Oxford, Hart Publishing, 2017) ch 5.
[46] *AIB* [2014] UKSC 58, [2014] 3 WLR 1367 [68].

In both *FHR* and *AIB*, the Supreme Court was confronted with the task of clarifying a deeply confused area of the law mired in conflicting authorities. In both instances, the apex court took the quickest way out of the thicket because there was little to be gained by intensively scrutinising the conflicting lines of authorities that stretched far back in time. Instead, they anchored their decisions on substantive policy bases. In *FHR*, in particular, the Supreme Court, made no pretense that the correct answer can be derived from the conflicting authorities. This is not to say that the Supreme Court is no longer concerned with examining the case law. There are clearly occasions where the Supreme Court has 'changed' the law by rationalising the authorities.[47] In most circumstances, the doctrine of precedent functions as a constraint on the exercise of judicial law-making, ensuring that legal developments are incremental and non-arbitrary.[48]

B. In-built Flexibility

In the last two to three decades, the role of judicial discretion in equity has been the subject of ceaseless debate.[49] At the heart of the voluminous literature lies the question of whether discretionary remedialism can be justified. It is a big debate that touches on issues such as rule of law, certainty and administering individual justice. Amongst the opponents to remedial discretion, Birks was one of the most vociferous.[50] To be fair, the existence of remedial flexibility does not mean that equity is devoid of any firm rules and fixed principles. As Harding points out, the law on the creation and enforcement of an express trust is an example of determinate principles.[51] As a matter of case law developments, there have been instances of judicial reining in of indeterminacy in contemporary equity jurisprudence in the last three decades. For example, subsequent English courts[52] had refused to follow Lord Denning's 'new model' constructive trust in *Hussey v Palmer*.[53] Arden LJ's open-textured 'unconscionability' approach in *Pennington v Waine*[54]

[47] See, eg, *Pitt v Holt* [2013] UKSC 26, [2013] 2 AC 108 ('*Pitt*').

[48] JD Heydon, 'Limits to the Powers of Ultimate Appellate Courts' (2006) 122 *LQR* 399, 403.

[49] See, eg, P Birks, 'Proprietary Rights as Remedies' in P Birks (ed), *The Frontiers of Liability*, (Oxford, Oxford University Press, vol 2, 1994); S Gardner, 'The Element of Discretion' in P Birks (ed), *The Frontiers of Liability*, (Oxford, Oxford University Press, vol 2, 1994); J Edelman, 'Remedial Certainty or Remedial Discretion in Estoppel after *Giumelli*?' (1999) 15 *Journal of Contract Law* 179; J Edelman, 'Judicial Discretion in Australia' (2000) 19 *Australian Bar Review* 285; DM Jensen, 'The Rights and Wrongs of Discretionary Remedialism' [2003] *Singapore Journal of Legal Studies* 178; M Harding, 'Equity and the Rule of Law' (2016) 132 *LQR* 278.

[50] P Birks, 'Equity in the Modern Law: An Exercise in Taxonomy' (1996) 26 *University of Western Australia Law Review* 1; P Birks, 'Three Kinds of Objection to Discretionary Remedialism' (2000) 29 *University of Western Australia Law Review* 1.

[51] Harding, above n 49, 284.

[52] *Burns v Burns* [1984] Ch 317; *Grant v Edwards* [1986] Ch 638.

[53] *Hussey v Palmer* [1972] 1 WLR 1286.

[54] *Pennington v Waine* [2002] EWCA Civ 227, [2002] 1 WLR 2075 [64] ('*Pennington*').

also attracted trenchant criticism,[55] and the decision was later reinterpreted as being based on the concept of detrimental reliance[56] or to some degree reconcilable with the *Re Rose* doctrine.[57] The 'public conscience' approach towards illegality was rejected by the House of Lords in *Tinsley v Milligan* in favour of a rigid rule of technical reliance.[58] English courts continue to resist recognising the remedial constructive trust,[59] even though Canada, Australia and Singapore have embraced their respective models of this discretionary remedy.

Yet, even contemporary English law tolerates indeterminacy arising from more open-textured evaluation of the circumstances of the case. For example, both the remedial stage of proprietary estoppel[60] and the quantification stage under the common intention constructive trust[61] involve a measure of discretion. More worryingly, these are not isolated instances. Virgo, writing on the meaning and role of 'unconscionability' in modern equity jurisprudence, helpfully identifies two main strands of 'unconscionability'.[62] The first strand relates to the defendant's conscience by reference to his subjective or objective state of mind. The second strand relates to the court's conscience, and encompasses two sub-streams of cases: first, where the dictates of conscience are determined through principled decision-making; and secondly, where conscience is a judicial formula for purely discretionary decision-making.[63] It is the latter sense of judicial conscience that is dangerous. Whilst Virgo's illuminating taxonomy provides a fresh analytical lens through which to view and understand modern developments, in practice, the different discretionary formulae which courts invent fall across a spectrum, and may be studied in a variety of ways. This part of the discussion examines the form through which strong discretion is being deployed in recent equitable innovations.

English decisions in the last five years evidence rekindled judicial enthusiasm for discretion and flexibility. In various areas, courts are increasingly replacing 'hard and fast rules' formulated in simple terms with approaches that incorporate flexibility. The in-built flexibility generally takes two forms: first, an open discretion model that is based on a multi-factorial, fact-specific evaluation; second, a residual discretion model which confers on courts residual discretionary jurisdiction

[55] See, eg, M Halliwell, 'Perfecting Imperfect Gifts and Trusts: Have We Reached the End of the Chancellor's Foot?' [2003] *Conveyancer and Property Lawyer* 192.

[56] *Curtis v Pulbrook* [2011] EWHC 167 (Ch), [2011] 1 BCLC 638 [43].

[57] *Zeital v Kaye* [2010] EWCA Civ 159 [40].

[58] *Tinsley v Milligan* [1994] 1 AC 340 ('*Tinsley*').

[59] *Bailey v Angove's Pty Ltd* [2016] UKSC 47, [2016] 1 WLR 3179 [28].

[60] See S Gardner, 'The Remedial Discretion in Proprietary Estoppel – Again' (2006) 122 *LQR* 492; J Mee, 'The Role of Expectation in the Determination of Proprietary Estoppel Remedies' in M Dixon (ed), *Modern Studies in Property Law*, vol 5 (Oxford, Hart Publishing, 2009) 389; T Tattersall, 'A Portable Palm Tree: Proprietary Estoppel in *Davies v Davies* (CA)' (2016) 30 *Trust Law International* 237.

[61] See *Stack v Dowden* [2007] UKHL 17, [2007] 2 AC 432 [69].

[62] G Virgo, 'Whose Conscience? Unconscionability in the Common Law of Obligations' in A Robertson and M Tilbury (eds), *Divergences in Private Law* (Oxford, Hart Publishing, 2016) ch 15.

[63] ibid 305–08.

to override the default rule or mitigate its effect. The distinction between the two models is only in form. In substance, both endorse the exercise of strong discretion.

i. Open Discretion Model

An open discretion model is readily illustrated with the Supreme Court's restatement of the test for setting aside a voluntary disposition on the basis of mistake in *Pitt v Holt*. The pre-*Pitt v Holt* law[64] required a mistake as to the effect of the transaction which is of sufficient gravity in the *Ogilvie v Littleboy* sense.[65] A mistake as to the consequence of the transaction, no matter how disastrous the impact on parties, would not suffice under the old test. Whilst the effect and consequence distinction appears a simple and determinate rule, the division between the two in practice is not always straightforward.[66] Nor is there good sense in barring all claims based on a mistake as to the consequences of the transaction.

In *Pitt v Holt*, Lord Walker reformulated the test as requiring a causative mistake of sufficient gravity which would render it unjust or unconscionable to leave the mistake uncorrected.[67] The rigid distinction between the effects and consequences of a transaction was abolished.[68] Lord Walker propounded a multifactorial test for the 'sufficient gravity' requirement:[69]

> The gravity of the mistake must be assessed by a close examination of the facts … including the circumstances of the mistake and its consequences for the person who made the vitiated disposition. Other findings of fact may also have to be made in relation to change of position or other matters relevant to the exercise of the court's discretion.

On whether it would be unjust or unconscionable to leave the mistaken disposition uncorrected, Lord Walker said that it would be an objective evaluation with 'intense focus' on the facts.[70] He conceded that 'unconscionability' cannot be decided by 'an elaborate set of rules' and would involve a 'judgment about the justice of the case'.[71] It has been pointed out before that Lord Walker's test of

[64] See the Court of Appeal decision: *Pitt v Holt* [2011] EWCA Civ 197, [2012 Ch 132] [210] (Lloyd LJ with whom Mummery and Longmore LJJ agreed).

[65] Laid down by Lindley LJ in *Ogilvie v Littleboy* (1897) 13 TLR 399, 400; affirmed in *Ogilvie v Allen* (1899) 15 TLR 294.

[66] See J Hilliard, '*Gibbon v Mitchell* Reconsidered: Mistakes as to Effects and Mistakes as to Consequences: Part I' [2004] *Private Client Business* 357, 362–63; J Hillard, '*Gibbon v Mitchell* Reconsidered: Mistakes as to Effects and Mistakes as to Consequences: Part 2' [2005] *Private Client Business* 31.

[67] *Pitt* [2013] UKSC 26, [2013] 2 AC 108 [124]–[125].

[68] *Pitt* [2013] UKSC 26, [2013] 2 AC 108 [123]. See also S Kempster, 'Who Said You Can't Legislate For Mistakes? – International Aspects of "The Rule in *Hastings-Bass*"' [2016] *Private Client Business* 248, 249.

[69] *Pitt* [2013] UKSC 26, [2013] 2 AC 108 [126].

[70] ibid.

[71] *Pitt* [2013] UKSC 26, [2013] 2 AC 108 [128]. See further PS Davies and S Douglas, 'Tax Mistakes Post-*Pitt v Holt*' (2018) 32 *Trust Law International* 3.

unconscionability in the context of rescission for mistake is mildly reminiscent of Arden LJ's approach to the constitution of trusts in *Pennington*.[72] Unsurprisingly, therefore, Lord Walker's test has not escaped rebuke for generating uncertainty[73] and endorsing a strong model of judicial discretion.[74]

More importantly, in contrast with Arden LJ's approach in *Pennington*, the *Pitt v Holt* test involved an assessment in the round in two interlinked stages: first, in determining the gravity of the mistake; and second, in deciding whether it would be unjust to leave the mistake uncorrected, a process that takes into account the gravity of the mistake. The discretion is very wide and uncertainty is thus compounded. The High Court decision in *Co-operative Bank Plc v Hayes Freehold Ltd*[75] illustrates the two-stage discretion-based process. In that case, a deed of surrender was entered into with the objective of surrendering both the head lease and the underlease so as to release all parties from their obligations thereunder. However, the surrender of the head lease turned out to be ineffective because the freeholder had not obtained the mortgagee's consent to the surrender as required under the terms of the mortgage. The bank, which was the head tenant, was left in the unenviable position of having to pay rent under the head lease while potentially losing the right to receive rent under the underlease. It thus sought to set aside the deed of surrender pursuant to the *Pitt v Holt* principles, on the basis that it mistakenly believed that the freeholder had the power to surrender the head lease. Rescission was, however, denied. The Court did not think that the mistake was sufficiently serious as the severity of the consequences was mitigated by the fact that the bank had an alternative remedy against its lawyer for negligent advice.[76]

The Court also did not think that it would be unconscionable to leave the mistake uncorrected for a number of reasons, including but not limited to the finding that the mistake was not sufficiently serious. Another reason was that the bank accepted the risk of the surrender of the head lease being ineffective. Further, the bank's recourse, in the event of the risk materialising, ought to be against the party responsible for avoiding that risk – that is, the legal advisors. Moreover, correcting the bank's mistake in the circumstances would prejudice the financial position of the guarantor of the underlessee's obligations under the underlease, as there would be little chance of recovering the released escrow monies.[77]

[72] M Yip, 'Further Reflections on the *Hastings-Bass* Rule, Rescission for Mistake and Rectification' (2014) 8 *Journal of Equity* 46, 55.

[73] E Bant, 'Constructive Trusts, Unconscionability and the Necessity for Working Criteria' (2014) 8 *Journal of Equity* 259, 282; Harding, above n 49, 287; R Lee, 'Correcting Mistakes in Trust Planning: A Comparative Post-*Pitt* Analysis' [2018] *Conveyancer and Property Lawyer* 45, 55.

[74] B Häcker, 'Mistaken Gifts After *Pitt v Holt*' (2014) 67 *Current Legal Problems* 333, 345.

[75] *Co-operative Bank Plc v Hayes Freehold Ltd* [2017] EWHC 1820 (Ch) ('*Co-operative Bank*').

[76] *Co-operative Bank* [2017] EWHC 1820 (Ch) [139].

[77] ibid [140].

The Court was ultimately concerned with the question of who ought to answer for the consequences of the mistake. Not correcting the mistake in this case would compel the bank to sue its legal advisors.[78]

Significantly, Lord Walker's reformulation in *Pitt v Holt* forces judges to articulate which transactions may be rescinded and for what reasons, and which may not. Courts can no longer hide behind the technical distinction between effects and consequences. The joint appeals in *Pitt v Holt* were concerned with tax-planning transactions that had gone wrong, a typical context in which the equitable tools of the *Hasting-Bass* principle, rescission and rectification were invoked pre-*Pitt v Holt*. The abrogation of the requirement of a mistake as to the effect of the transaction would mean that a transaction can be set aside on the basis of a mistake as to its fiscal consequences. But Lord Walker did not think that all such mistakes should be corrected. He introduced the controversial 'artificial tax avoidance' limitation which would enable courts to withhold rescission in cases where the transaction has been entered into for artificial tax avoidance. As he explained, 'there has been increasingly strong and general recognition that artificial tax avoidance is a social evil'.[79] Its merits aside,[80] the artificial tax avoidance limitation is evidence of judicial acceptance, at least at the Supreme Court level, of strong remedial discretion underlined by policy considerations and moral norms.

Another example is the 'range of factors' approach towards illegality enunciated by the majority in *Patel v Mirza*.[81] This saw the triumph of discretion and flexibility over 'hard and fast rules'[82] in the Supreme Court. Although not an exclusively equitable development – as the test applies in a number of areas of private law[83] – it is indicative of the judicial inclination towards policy-based and discretionary decision-making. Lord Toulson, delivering the majority judgment, rejected a 'mechanistic process'. He identified three categories of factors that are relevant to the court's exercise of discretion: the purpose of the prohibition, other relevant public policies, and proportionality.[84]

Lord Toulson also responded to concerns of uncertainty with the new test, highlighting in particular the fact that the experience of the other jurisdictions which have taken 'a relatively flexible approach' did not show that uncertainty generated serious problems.[85] Goudkamp, however, points out that the approaches

[78] The Court was of the view that the bank had acted reasonably: *Co-operative Bank* [2017] EWHC 1820 (Ch) [137].

[79] *Pitt* [2013] UKSC 26, [2013] 2 AC 108 [135].

[80] This policy-based consideration has been skirted around or avoided by courts in subsequent cases.

[81] *Patel v Mirza* [2016] UKSC 42, [2017] AC 467 ('*Patel*').

[82] In this context, the technical reliance principle in *Tinsley* [1994] 1 AC 340 was overruled by *Patel* (*Patel* [2016] UKSC 42, [2017] AC 467 [110]).

[83] cf *Henderson v Dorset Healthcare University NHS Foundation Trust* [2018] EWCA Civ 1841, [2018] 3 WLR 1651 [87]–[91]. In view that *Patel* raised contractual and unjust enrichment issues, the Court of Appeal held that the *Patel* test did not apply to a claim against another for negligence by an individual who killed her mother while undergoing a psychotic episode.

[84] *Patel* [2016] UKSC 42, [2017] AC 467 [101].

[85] ibid [113].

adopted in New Zealand, Canada and Australia[86] are not 'nearly as flexible as' the *Patel* 'range of factors' test.[87] Indeed, the Singapore Court of Appeal, whilst rejecting the technical reliance principle, has declined to adopt the English test precisely because of the degree of uncertainty it engenders in the judicial process.[88] Such a broad balancing approach, according to the Singapore Court, should be introduced by the legislature.[89] Yet, the emerging background picture is that the common law world favours a flexible and discretionary approach.[90] What divides them is the permissible ambit of discretion.

Whilst we are on developments that are not exclusively equitable, it may be worthwhile to mention that the reformed English rule on penalties in contract law, which had its origins in equity, admits an evaluative component.[91] The new rule focuses on whether the allegedly offensive contract provision relates to a secondary obligation which effect is *entirely disproportionate* to the legitimate interest sought to be protected. The Supreme Court clarified that the *Dunlop Pneumatic Tyre Co Ltd v New Garage and Motor Co Ltd*[92] tests are not rules, but considerations that indicate whether a clause is an unenforceable penalty provision.[93] 'Penalty' is not an absolute standard.[94] The renewed Australian penalty rule, after *Paciocco v Australia and New Zealand Bank Group Limited*,[95] whilst differing from the English rule in its scope of application, similarly embraces an open-textured inquiry as to whether the stipulated consequences are entirely 'out of proportion' with the commercial interests of the party seeking to rely on the clause.[96]

Returning to equitable developments, but venturing beyond English law, Australian law and Singapore law have long embraced their respective models of remedial constructive trusts. In each jurisdiction, the remedial constructive

[86] See the recent High Court of Australia decision: *Gnych v Polish Club Ltd* [2015] HCA 23, (2015) 255 CLR 414.

[87] J Goudkamp, 'The End of an Era? Illegality in Private Law in the Supreme Court' (2017) 133 *LQR* 14, 17.

[88] *Ochroid Trading Ltd v Chua Siok Lui (trading as VIE Import & Export)* [2018] SGCA 5, [2018] 1 SLR 363 [120] ('*Ochroid*').

[89] *Ochroid* [2018] SGCA 5, [2018] 1 SLR 363 [121].

[90] Hong Kong law currently still applies the reliance principle in *Tinsley* (see *Tse Chun Wai v Leung Kwok Kin Joseph trading as Joseph Leung & Associates* [2017] 4 HKLRD 563 [64]) by reason of stare decisis (bound by the earlier Hong Kong Court of Appeal decision in *Kan Wai Chung v Hau Wun Fai* [2016] 5 HKC 585). The Hong Kong Court of Final Appeal has yet to review the position post-*Patel* but see: *Chung Tin Pui v Li Pak Sau* [2017] HKEC 2103 (unreported) (applied *Patel* test); *Li Po Lai v Tai Wo Finance Ltd* [2017] HKEC 2329 [27]–[35] (considered what the outcome would have been had the *Patel* test applied); *Arrow ECS Norway AS v M Yang Trading Ltd* [2018] HKCU 1479 [28] (commented that the *Patel* position would be reviewed in due course).

[91] *Cavendish Square Holdings BV v Makedessi; Parkingeye Ltd v Beavis* [2015] UKSC 67, [2016] AC 1172 ('*Cavendish*').

[92] *Dunlop Pneumatic Tyre Company Ltd v New Garage and Motor Company Ltd* [1915] AC 79.

[93] *Cavendish* [2015] UKSC 67, [2016] AC 1172 [22].

[94] ibid [31] (Lords Neuberger and Sumption), [225], [248] (Lord Hodge).

[95] *Paciocco v Australia and New Zealand Bank Group Limited* [2016] HCA 28, (2016) 258 CLR 525.

[96] See further M Yip and YH Goh, 'Convergence Between Australian Common Law and English Common Law: The Rule Against Penalties in the Age of Freedom of Contract' (2017) 46 *Common World Law Review* 61.

trust is a discretionary device which allows the court to award relief, proprietary or personal, in accordance with the circumstances of the case. Hong Kong law, which conventionally and faithfully follows English footsteps, has not presently recognised this type of constructive trust.[97] The discretionary component of the Singaporean model remains unclear, so a meaningful assessment is premature.[98] As for the Australian model, recent decisions have emphasised that proprietary relief would only be awarded when it is necessary and appropriate to do so.[99] Although the elements of necessity and appropriateness do not sufficiently clarify when proprietary relief would be available,[100] in the specific context of proprietary relief for bribes received in breach of fiduciary duty, the Full Court of the Federal Court of Australia said that it would depend on what type of relief would be sufficient to achieve 'practical justice' in the case, highlighting that relevant considerations would include third party interests and the fiduciary's insolvency.[101] It is crystal clear that the Australian model, in the context of fiduciary breaches, adopts a discretionary, evaluative approach, instead of relying on fixed and determinate rules.[102]

ii. Residual Discretion

A residual discretion model relies on residual judicial discretion to override or mitigate the effects of the application of the primary rule. This model differs from the ordinary operation of discretion in equitable remedies such as specific performance, as the latter involves decision-making that is guided by (relatively more) fixed principles. The residual discretion model, in contrast, contemplates a wider ambit of discretion.

An illustration of the residual discretion model is the exceptional award of equitable allowances to fiduciaries who are liable to account for their profits. The primary rule is that a fiduciary's liability to account for profits made in breach of fiduciary duty is strict.[103] The strict primary rule is subject to the court's discretion to award an equitable allowance for the fiduciary's skill and effort in generating

[97] However, claims based on the Australian version (*Baumgartner v Baumgartner* (1987) 164 CLR 137) have been brought before the lower courts in domestic property disputes: *Ip Man Shan Henry v Ching Hing Construction (No 2)* [2003] 1 HKC 256, 286; *Cheung Hon Hung v Siu Wai Chun* [2014] HKEC 1447 [76].

[98] See further M Yip, 'Singapore's Remedial Constructive Trust: Lessons from Australia?' (2014) 8 *Journal of Equity* 77.

[99] *John Alexander's Clubs Pty Ltd v White City Tennis Clubs Ltd* [2010] HCA 19, (2010) 241 CLR 1 [128]; *Grimaldi v Chameleon Mining NL (No 2)* [2012] FCAFC 6, (2012) 200 FCR 296 [583] ('*Grimaldi*').

[100] E Bant and M Bryan, 'Constructive Trusts and Equitable Proprietary Relief: Rethinking the Essentials' (2011) 5 *Journal of Equity* 171, 192.

[101] *Grimaldi* [2012] FCAFC 6, (2012) 200 FCR 296 [583].

[102] Harding, above n 49, 289.

[103] *Keech v Sandford* (1726) Sel Cas T King 61, 25 ER 223. See strictness of the rule: *Regal (Hastings) Ltd v Gulliver* [1967] 2 AC 134, 153, 155 (Lord Wright).

the profits in *exceptional circumstances*.[104] To date, the jurisprudential basis of the allowance award,[105] the conditions for its availability[106] and the principles of assessment[107] are far from clear. Recent English authorities simply described the award as being available exceptionally[108] and subject to the court's exercise of wide discretion based on the circumstances of the case.[109] The award has been denied on the basis of the fiduciary's blameworthiness in respect of the breach of duty and post-breach conduct,[110] as well as to avoid interfering with the company's administration.[111]

A more recent example of the residual discretion model is the remedy of account of profits against a dishonest accessory for assisting a breach of fiduciary duty/trust. In *Novoship (UK) Ltd v Nikitin*,[112] the English Court of Appeal held that a dishonest accessory is liable to account for profits he or she made which have a sufficiently direct causal connection with his or her assistance,[113] but such relief may be exceptionally withheld at the court's discretion.[114] A possible ground on which to withhold relief, as applied by the Court of Appeal in *Novoship*,[115] is that the account would be disproportionate to the particular form and extent of wrongdoing. Where such disproportion exists, the gain-based award is 'not automatic'.[116] The difference in treatment between the fiduciary and the accessory was justified by the Court of Appeal on the basis that the latter actor, unlike the former, did not voluntarily undertake to act for the principal's interests.[117] But this only accounts for why a distinction ought to be made which could be satisfied by the introduction of a causation requirement for the accessory's liability to account. It does not explain why residual discretion ought to be introduced as a final remedial gatekeeping mechanism. The concept of proportionality is remarkably elastic and affords a

[104] *Boardman v Phipps* [1967] 2 AC 46.

[105] For a counter-restitution account, see P Birks, *An Introduction to the Law of Restitution* (Oxford, Clarendon Press, 1989) 420. cf *Re Berkeley Applegate (Investment Consultants) Ltd* [1989] Ch 32, 36–37.

[106] Under English law, honesty appears to be a condition (*Guinness plc v Saunders* [1990] 2 AC 663, 700–01 (Lord Goff) ('*Guinness*')), although the award may still be granted if the fiduciary's conduct is not completely blameless (*O'Sullivan v Management Agency Ltd* [1985] QB 428, 467–68; *Cobbetts LLP v Hodge* [2009] EWHC 786 (Ch), [2010] 1 BCLC 30 [115] ('*Cobbetts*')). cf Australian law: *Warman International Ltd v Dwyer* (1995) 182 CLR 544.

[107] D Whayman, 'Equitable Allowances or Restitutionary Measures for Dishonest Assistance and Knowing Receipt' (2017) 68 *Northern Ireland Legal Quarterly* 181, 188–89.

[108] *Global Energy Horizons Corp v Gray* [2015] EWHC 2232 (Ch) [212] ('*Global Energy*').

[109] *Cobbetts* [2009] EWHC 786 (Ch), [2010] 1 BCLC 30 [115].

[110] *Global Energy* [2015] EWHC 2232 (Ch) [213].

[111] *Guinness* [1990] 2 AC 663, 696.

[112] *Novoship (UK) Ltd v Nikitin* [2014] EWCA Civ 908, [2015] QB 499.

[113] *Novoship* [2014] EWCA Civ 908, [2015] QB 499 [115].

[114] ibid [119].

[115] Disgorgement was considered disproportionate because the profits were generated from an opportunity which the principal deliberately chose to forgo.

[116] *Novoship* [2014] EWCA Civ 908, [2015] QB 499 [119]. cf *Ancient Order of Foresters in Victoria Friendly Society Ltd v Lifeplan Australia Friendly Society Ltd* [2018] HCA 43, (2018) 92 ALJR 918 [14]–[16].

[117] *Novoship* [2014] EWCA Civ 908, [2015] QB 499 [104]–[107].

wide ambit of discretion. Further, *Novoship* provides little guidance as to the other grounds on which relief may be withheld. All things considered, it is arguable that the motivation for incorporating residual discretion for an accessory's liability to account for profits – as with Harding's proposed justification for allowance awards – is to give 'to people what they deserve'.[118] There is thus symmetry in the gain-based remedial regimes applicable to the fiduciary and the accessory.

More broadly, the discretionary jurisdiction to award an equitable allowance to an errant fiduciary, and the residual discretion to withhold a disgorgement award against the dishonest accessory, operate to override the primary rule or mitigate the effect of its application.[119] Both regimes employ fact-specific, open-textured approaches.

The developments discussed in this section bring to mind James Allsop CJ's extra-judicial comment on an important aspect of doctrinal development and legal thinking: the futile struggle to define the indefinable.[120] Yet, Lord Neuberger has (extra-curially) affirmed a modern judge's responsibility to 'render the law as clear and simple as possible', warning against the danger of trying to 'reach a fair result in every case' by changing or distorting the law.[121] The two exhortations reveal a tension between the aim of providing legal clarity and simplicity and the reality that determinacy may not be achievable in all instances.

C. Context Sensitivity

In *Stack v Dowden*, Baroness Hale famously remarked that '[i]n law, "context is everything" and the domestic context is very different from the commercial world'.[122] This has led to the English development of the dichotomous treatment of property ownership disputes, differentiating between situations in which the property is purchased primarily for domestic consumer use and those in which the property is purchased primarily for investment purposes.[123] The subsequent Privy Council decision in *Marr v Collie*, however, retreated from the *Stack* developments, identifying the central inquiry as one being concerned with parties' intentions.[124]

The *Marr v Collie* episode aside, context-based reasoning continues to flourish in equitable jurisprudence in two main ways. First, the commercial/domestic

[118] M Harding, 'Justifying Fiduciary Allowances' in A Robertson and Tang HW (eds), *The Goals of Private Law* (Oxford, Hart Publishing, 2009) 342.

[119] See M Yip and J Lee, 'The Commercialisation of Equity' (2017) 37 *Legal Studies* 647, 666–67.

[120] J Allsop, 'Singapore Academy of Law Distinguished Speaker Lecture 2017 – "The Doctrine of Penalties in Modern Contract Law"' (2018) 30 *Singapore Academy of Law Journal* 1, 3.

[121] Neuberger, above n 5, [30].

[122] *Stack v Dowden* [2007] UKHL 17, [2007] 2 AC 432 [69] ('*Stack*').

[123] *Laskar v Laskar* [2008] EWCA Civ 347, [2008] 1 WLR 2695.

[124] *Marr v Collie* [2017] UKPC 17, [2018] AC 631, noted M George and B Sloan, 'Presuming Too Little About Resulting and Constructive Trusts?' [2017] *Conveyancer and Property Lawyer* 303.

distinction[125] operates as a gateway device to the applicable analysis. This can be readily observed in English developments beyond *Stack*. Lord Toulson's approach in *AIB* is arguably another example of context-specific reasoning, notwithstanding his explicit disavowal of the same.[126] On his approach, equitable compensation for breach of a commercial bare trust arising out of a contract would be the same as if damages for breach of contract had been sought.[127] This approach has been subsequently considered by lower courts.[128] In *Pitt v Holt*, regarding the proper formulation of the *Hastings-Bass* principle, Lord Walker acknowledged (in obiter) the merits of applying the 'would not' test for family trusts and the less stringent 'might not' test for pension trusts in view of pension scheme members' contractual merits.[129] As he explained, rigid rules are inimical to the search for 'the best practical solution' in different situations.[130]

Secondly, the context may subtly influence the principles applied by the courts, even if there is no explicit acknowledgement of distinguishing between the commercial and non-commercial contexts. On the issue of inferring a trust in the commercial setting, there is some suggestion in English and Australian authorities that the search is for the contractual intention, instead of the settlor's intention.[131] Further, *Korda v Australian Executor Trustees (SA) Ltd* left open what is the proper role for considerations of 'commercial necessity' – which were applied by the Court of Appeal but rejected by the High Court – in ascertaining trust-making intention in the commercial context. Such considerations are clearly irrelevant to the inference of an express trust in the family context. The only guidance was provided by Keane J, who commented that 'considerations of commercial necessity may afford assistance in discerning the objective intentions of the parties where the language of their written agreement is not explicit', but noted that that was not the case in *Korda*.[132] Keane J's remarks cohere with the contractual approach to the implication of terms based on the 'business efficacy' test.[133] Further, on the way in which Australian law has addressed issues arising from conflicts in commercial trusts, Beazley J noted extra-judicially that:

> The tension is between, on the one hand, the desire for flexibility and for the accommodation of commercial expectations, and the contractarian model that reflects those

[125] The use of 'commercial' here includes cases arising in the contractual context.

[126] Yip and Lee, above n 119, 655–56.

[127] *AIB* [2014] UKSC 58, [2014] 3 WLR 1367 [71].

[128] See *Purrunsing v A'Court & Company (a firm)* [2016] EWHC 789 (Ch), [2016] 4 WLR 81 [42]; *Wessley v White* [2018] EWHC 1499 (Ch) (*AIB* applied). See also the formalistic attempt to restrict the scope of *AIB* in *Various Claimants v Giambrone and Law (A Firm)* [2017] EWCA Civ 1193 [63].

[129] *Pitt* [2013] UKSC 26, [2013] 2 AC 108 [92].

[130] ibid.

[131] English law: see *Co-operative Group Ltd v Birse Developments Ltd (in liquidation)* [2014] EWHC 530 [85]–[88]. Australian law: see *Korda v Australian Executor Trustees (SA) Ltd* [2015] HCA 6, (2015) 255 CLR 62 [53] (French CJ), [72] (Hayne and Kiefel JJ), [108] (Gageler J) ('*Korda*'). See M Yip, 'The Commercial Context in Trust Law' [2016] *Conveyancer and Property Laywer* 347, 351–52.

[132] *Korda* [2015] HCA 6, (2015) 255 CLR 62 [138].

[133] P Crutchfield, RG Craig and EJ Batrouney, '*Korda Australian Executor Trustees* [2015] HCA 6: Imputed Trusts in a Commercial Context – Australia Clarifies its Approach' (2016) 22 *Trusts & Trustees* 384, 391.

> desires, and on the other hand, the idea that there are certain fundamental and mandatory consequences that inhere in particular relationships.[134]

Even for Singapore law, which generally resists embracing a commercial/domestic distinction,[135] commercial considerations have been applied by the Court of Appeal in restricting commercial actors' scope of recipient liability in equity.[136]

Two motivations underline this emerging judicial recourse to a commercial/domestic distinction, whether explicitly or implicitly. First, the commercial/domestic distinction is a very rough form of fact-specific inquiry. At the most basic level, the courts are evaluating the circumstances of the case, including the background against which the dispute arose. Context-sensitivity in this form enables the courts to better interpret the parties' conduct and declarations in light of the norms of that context,[137] in order to determine what is a fair and just outcome. However, the judicial technique discussed above goes beyond a 'context-neutral, outcome-specific' approach.[138] The second motivation is to allow the courts, through the distinction, to reach for a different set of principles in a 'commercial' case that better reflect the policy interests of commerce or contract in general. Whilst the policy objectives are not always clearly articulated by the courts, simplicity, certainty and freedom of contract would be the prioritised considerations when courts adapt traditional equitable principles for application in a 'commercial' case.

Even the *Marr v Collie* episode, whilst signaling retreat from contextualist reasoning, supports the broader point put forward here that courts are increasingly more focused on assessing the facts of the case in their decision-making process. This shift also explains the decline of the equitable presumptions of resulting trust and advancement and the rigid *Shephard v Cartwright* rule.[139] A more fact-specific approach as embodied in the common intention constructive trust doctrine was thus favoured by the majority in *Stack*. But post-*Stack* cases, including cases from other common law jurisdictions such as Singapore,[140] demonstrate that the

[134] MJ Beazley, 'Conflicts in Commercial Trusts' (Annual Commercial and Corporate Law Conference, Supreme Court of New South Wales, 15 November 2016) [66].

[135] *Chan Yuen Lan v See Fong Mun* [2014] SGCA 36, [2014] 3 SLR 1048 [152] ('*Chan Yuen Lan*') (declined to follow *Stack* developments); *BOK v BOL* [2017] SGHC 316 [116] (declined to distinguish between voluntary dispositions and non-gratuitous dispositions in the context of rescission on the basis of 'unconscionability').

[136] *George Raymond Zage III v Ho Chi Kwong* [2010] SGCA 4, [2010] 2 SLR 589 [52]. See Yip and Lee, above n 119, 668.

[137] See, eg, the application of the *Pallant v Morgan* equity principles in the commercial context: *Farrar v Miller* [2018] EWCA Civ 172 [46]; *Generator Developments Ltd v Lidl UK GmbH* [2018] EWCA Civ 396 [78].

[138] See N Hopkins, 'Regulating Trusts of the Home: Private Law and Social Policy' (2009) 125 *LQR* 310.

[139] *Shephard v Cartwright* [1955] AC 431.

[140] *Tan Yok Koon v Tan Choo Suan* [2017] SGCA 13, [2017] 1 SLR 654 ('*Tan Yok Koon*'), noted A See, 'Transferor's Intention, Trustee's Undertaking and the Scope of Fiduciary Liability' (2018) 32 *Trust Law International* 50.

commercial/domestic distinction may be difficult to apply in a variety of situations where 'commercial and personal factors collide'.[141] It is also not unusual for family disputes to arise from events occurring over decades, the facts of which are hotly contested at trial. For these reasons, the simplistic tools of contextualist reasoning are not always sufficient to deal with complex human relationships.

III. Causes

Based on the discussion in Section II, it is fair to say that recent English equitable developments are showing signs of scaling back from strong formal reasoning. In particular, there is an emerging trend of replacing firm rules with evaluative approaches that allow the courts to openly consider the policy considerations arising from the specific circumstances of each case. Section III examines the possible causes of this development. The backdrop against which this change took place highlights its significance. Positivism in legal doctrine dominated English legal tradition in nineteenth and twentieth centuries.[142] More specifically, from the late-twentieth century, Birks and like-minded scholars began challenging traditional equitable methods and doctrines. Birks, in particular, advocated the importance and relevance of the law of unjust enrichment in recasting the law in more orderly and certain terms.[143] However, Birks' account of the law, notwithstanding its attractions and laudable aims, did not prevail, at least not in all respects.[144] I offer three interrelated causes of this phenomenon: diversity, complexity and pragmatism.

A. Diversity

Baker observed in *An Introduction to English Legal History*:

> In a celebrated case of 1615, Lord Ellesmere C explained that the reason why there was a Chancery was that men's actions are so diverse and infinite that it is impossible to make a general law which may aptly meet with every particular and not fail in some circumstances.[145]

[141] M Yip and J Lee, '"Less Than Straightforward" People, Facts and Trusts: Reflections on Context: *Favor Easy Management Ltd v Wu* [2012] EWCA Civ 1464' [2013] *Conveyancer and Property Lawyer* 431, 439. See, eg, *Favor Easy Management Ltd v Wu* [2012] EWCA Civ 1464.

[142] Atiyah and Summers, above n 6, 240–57; Allsop, above n 120, 8.

[143] See discussion in P Ridge, 'Modern Equity: Revolution or Renewal from Within?' in S Worthington, A Robertson and G Virgo (eds), *Revolution and Evolution in Private Law* (Oxford, Hart Publishing, 2018) 252–53.

[144] See further TT Arvind, 'Paradigms Lost or Paradigms Regained? Legal Revolutions and the Path of the Law' in S Worthington, A Robertson and G Virgo (eds), *Revolution and Evolution in Private Law* (Oxford, Hart Publishing, 2018) ch 4. Stevens notes recent Supreme Court decisions 'have retreated from a more expansive approach to the law of restitution' (see R Stevens, 'The Unjust Enrichment Disaster' (2018) 134 *LQR* 574).

[145] Baker, above n 1, 106.

Take the institution of the trust for example. It has grown beyond the space of family trusts and infiltrated the commercial arena, taking every shape and form, from a simple commercial bare trust to constituting a key feature of securitisation transactions and collective investment schemes.[146] Even within the family setting, the legal work is increasingly centred on 'private client work',[147] a comprehensive range of legal services offered to wealthy individuals that cut across trust law, company law, succession law, law of charities and immigration law. In England and Australia, the occupational pension schemes, concerned with the 'reconciliation of competing economic interests',[148] inject a new dimension to our understanding of a trustee's duties.[149] As such, we begin to see the law struggling to apply the same set of 'hard and fast rules' in all situations. This struggle accounts for the balancing approach adopted in *Schmidt v Rosewood Trust*[150] regarding an object's access to information relating to the trust; as well as the much criticised distortion of the irreducible core of trustee's obligations in *Citibank NA v MBIA Assurance SA*.[151] The point is this: there is increasing judicial recognition that one size does not fit all. Indeed, the contemporary uses of trust are not always chiefly about custodianship.[152] For example, debt securitisation transactions utilise the trust structure as a way to consolidate the right to enforcement of the note holders' rights in the hands of the note trustee, primarily for the protection of the note issuer.[153]

Moving beyond trusts to the fiduciary doctrine, conventional wisdom divides fiduciary relationships into two categories: recognised categories and ad hoc relationships.[154] Even this traditional division implicitly acknowledges that fixed categories alone would be unhelpful in predicting when fiduciary duties arise, given the variety of contexts in which one party may be said to have voluntarily undertaken to act for another.[155] As such, even though a trustee is the paradigmatic fiduciary, one cannot study other fiduciary relationships (especially non-custodial relationships) on the basis of the trust relationship. More generally, the different

[146] See P Rawlings, 'The Changing Role of the Trustee in International Bond Issues' [2007] *Journal of Business Law* 43.

[147] R Walker, 'The Changing Face of Trust Law' (2017) 31 *Trust Law International* 19, 21.

[148] ibid 22.

[149] See further SEK Hulme, 'The Basic Duty of Trustees of Superannuation Trusts – Fair to One, Fair to All?' (2000) 14 *Trust Law International* 130.

[150] *Schmidt v Rosewood Trust*, [2003] UKPC 26, [2003] 2 AC 709.

[151] *Citibank NA v MBIA Assurance SA* [2007] EWCA Civ 11, [2007] 1 All ER (Comm) 475.

[152] Even in respect of discretionary trusts, the modern practice is 'now in many respects far more akin to contract-like voluntary arrangements than to the gifting of determinable key beneficial property rights in respect of identified assets'. See J Palmer and C Rickett, 'The Revolution and Legacy of the Discretionary Trust' (2017) 11 *Journal of Equity* 157, 157.

[153] P Rawlings, 'Reinforcing Collectivity: The Liability of Trustees and the Power of Investors in Finance Transactions' (2009) 23 *Trust Law International* 14.

[154] G Virgo, *The Principles of Equity and Trusts*, 3rd edn (Oxford, Oxford University Press, 2018) 420–23.

[155] J Edelman, 'When Do Fiduciary Duties Arise' (2010) 126 *LQR* 302. Singapore law has abandoned the categorical approach in favour of a fact-based approach: see *Tan Yok Koon* [2017] SGCA 13, [2017] 1 SLR 654 [205]–[207].

contexts and ways in which actors interact – relating to the second point on complexity – would render it necessary for courts to be given a degree of flexibility in deciding the outcome.[156]

Similarly, the restitutionary paradigms upon which Birks built his taxonomy and doctrines – and which he in turn used to reshape private law (including equity) – may oversimplify the disputes that arise in reality.[157] Tang has forcefully argued that the 'stock stories' which Birks used 'are controversial in that either they do not reflect the typical context in which unjust enrichment claims arise or they are based on certain controvertible assumptions'.[158] Moreover, the stories are always based on simple and clear fact patterns. The disputes that end up in the court room, especially the apex courts, often arise from more complex stories and are complicated by parties' diverse versions of what actually happened.[159] Real life disputes frequently involve large sums of money and quite a number are situated in the commercial setting. Take for example the core story which Lionel Smith uses to advance his views on backwards tracing – it is based on the story of a trustee misappropriating trust monies for the repayment of his or her mortgage debt incurred for the purchase of a specific asset.[160] Smith's analytical focus was on the concrete steps in the transaction. The cases in which the 'backwards tracing' concept was invoked and succeeded are generally more complex.[161] *Relfo v Varsani*[162] and *Brazil v Durant International Corporation*[163] concerned fraud, money laundering and bribes. Moreover, these cases were not truly 'backwards tracing' cases[164] because the courts' focus did not lie with the causative sequence of events or the concrete steps involved in the asset transfers. The question is whether the assets which the claimants sought to claim could be said to be the traceable substitutes of the original assets.[165] The courts' analysis was thus focused on whether the apparently disparate events were part of a single scheme.[166] Hence, the practical utility of the concept of 'backwards tracing' is in combating illicit activities in which perpetrators would frequently employ sophisticated techniques to defeat the process of forward tracing. Notably, in *Relfo*, Arden LJ, in deciding whether one asset is a

[156] In *Patel* [2016] UKSC 42, [2017] AC 467 [107], Lord Toulson said: 'I would not attempt to lay down a prescriptive or definitive list because of the infinite possible variety of cases.' In *Cavendish* [2015] UKSC 67, [2016] AC 1172 [116], Lord Mance noted that the two appeals before the Supreme Court 'lie at the opposite ends of a financial spectrum'. See further *Pitt* [2013] UKSC 26, [2013] 2 AC 108 [92] (on the *Hastings-Bass* rule), [126] (on rescission for mistake).

[157] See Arvind, above n 144.

[158] Tang HW, 'Storytelling in the Law of Unjust Enrichment' in A Robertson and Tang HW (eds), *The Goals of Private Law* (Oxford, Hart Publishing, 2009) 458.

[159] See, eg, *Rashid v Munir* [2018] EWHC 1258 (QB) [19] ('*Rashid*').

[160] LD Smith, 'Tracing into the Payment of a Debt' (1995) 54 *CLJ* 290.

[161] cf *The Fish Man Ltd (in Liquidation) v Hadfield* [2017] NZCA 589, [2018] 2 NZLR 428.

[162] *Relfo v Varsani* [2014] EWCA Civ 360, [2015] 1 BCLC 14 ('*Relfo*').

[163] *Brazil v Durant International Corporation* [2015] UKPC 35, [2016] AC 297.

[164] R Nolan, 'Civil Recovery After Fraud' (2015) 131 *LQR* 8, 11; PG Turner, 'Tracing To and Fro' (2016) 75 *CLJ* 462, 465.

[165] ibid.

[166] T Cutts, 'Tracing, Value and Transactions' (2016) 79 *MLR* 381, 403.

substitute for another in seemingly separate transactions, employed a 'basket of factors' approach.[167]

Finally, simple stories do not always bear out the interplay between statute and common law in practice.[168] As such, the solutions proposed for simple problems may not be appropriate for scenarios where common law has been curtailed by or exists alongside statutory solutions. This point will be discussed in greater detail below.

B. Complexity

The diversity in human interactions, which evolves with time as society progresses, undoubtedly contributes to the complexity of disputes. But complexity also springs from other sources. Notably, the proliferation of statutory law to regulate spaces which were once occupied only by common law[169] results in a complex and evolving interface between statute and common law. In some instances, the courts feel compelled to adopt a more open-textured, evaluative approach in order to take into account statutory values. Conversely, the lack of legislative intervention in a complex area of the law ripe for reform may also force courts to adopt evaluative approaches that many consider only apt for statutory endorsement. The *Stack* developments in the family property ownership arena represented a clear judicial response to legislative inaction.[170] The disputes arising between unmarried cohabitees at the end of their relationship are not simply property claims. They are more broadly concerned with the *financial consequences* for the respective family members at the dissolution of these relationships. As academics, we may debate about whether the common intention constructive trust is a doctrine capable of being stretched to meet such socio-legal objectives.[171] The courts, on the other hand, are faced with real people and their less than straightforward problems. As Lady Hale reflected extra-judicially: 'Parliament may do nothing, but a judge must always do something, even if it is not at all clear what he or she should do'.[172] Lord Walker has also explained extra-judicially that a fact-specific

[167] *Relfo* [2014] EWCA Civ 360, [2015] 1 BCLC 14 [57]–[58].

[168] M Leeming, 'Theories and Principles Underlying the Development of the Common Law: The Statutory Elephant in the Room' (2013) 36 *The University of New South Wales Law Journal* 1002.

[169] See further W Gummow, 'Illegality and Statute in Hong Kong' (Hochelaga Lecture, Hong Kong, 15 December 2017); Beazley, above n 134, [41], [64]; TT Arvind, 'Obligations, Governance and Society: Bringing the State Back In' in A Robertson and M Tilbury (eds), *The Common Law of Obligations: Divergence and Unity* (Oxford, Hart Publishing, 2016) ch 12.

[170] See *Jones v Kernott* [2011] UKSC 53, [2012] 1 AC 776 [36] (Lady Hale and Lord Walker), [57] (Lord Collins); *Gow v Grant* [2012] UKSC 29, [2013] SC(SC) 1 [45]–[50] (Lady Hale).

[171] See, eg, S Gardner and K Davidson, 'The Future of *Stack v Dowden*' (2011) 127 *LQR* 13, 18; S Gardner and K Davidson, 'The Supreme Court on Family Homes' (2012) 128 *LQR* 178, 181.

[172] B Hale, 'Fifty Years of the Law Commissions: The Dynamics of Law Reform Now, Then and Next' in M Dyson, J Lee and S Wilson Stark (eds), *Fifty Years of the Law Commissions: The Dynamics of Law Reform* (Oxford, Hart Publishing, 2016) 24.

'whole course of dealing' approach is required as most homes are now purchased with mortgages and the unmarried cohabitees' contributions to the mortgage repayment would depend on 'wholly unpredictable matters' concerning their financial positions and sharing of parental responsibility throughout the course of their relationship.[173] An approach that looks at parties' intentions at the outset is unrealistic and inappropriate.

There are also instances where the Law Commission, after detailed research, recommends legal reform by way of judicial development of the law. The illegality defence in the areas of contract and unjust enrichment is one such example. After successive reports, the Law Commission ultimately proposed a very modest scope of reform, the law concerning concealment of interests under trusts,[174] which the government declined to take forward. As for the other areas of the law, the Law Commission concluded that statutory reform was unnecessary because the courts have been more willing to articulate the policy considerations in their reasoning in recent years and that clarity will be brought to the law if this trend continues.[175] The majority in *Patel* could be seen as agreeing with the Law Commission's conclusion. Indeed, the 'range of factors' approach in essence gives effect to the Law Commission's proposals.[176]

According to Henry E Smith, equity is 'part of a modular private law that manages complexity'.[177] In the context of our discussion, modern equity also takes on the function of managing complexity in areas which the legislature has refused to act. In *Patel*, Lord Toulson, citing Kirby J's pointed comments in *Clayton v The Queen*,[178] agreed that the courts must take on the responsibility of remedying the defects of the common law, instead of waiting for legislative intervention which might never come.[179]

C. Pragmatism

Nearly 40 years ago, Atiyah observed that there has been a 'profound shift' away from principles to pragmatism, reflecting a shift away from the desire to make law for future application to the desire to do individual justice.[180] Atiyah identified two characteristics of the law which demonstrate this shift. First, the courts'

[173] Walker, above n 147, 29.

[174] Law Commission, *The Illegality Defence*, Law Com No 320 (2010); Draft Trusts (Concealment of Interests) Bill (Draft Bill).

[175] Law Commission, *The Illegality Defence*, Law Com No 320 (2010) para 3.40.

[176] Goudkamp, above n 87, 20.

[177] HE Smith, 'Fusing the Equitable Function in Private Law' in K Barker, K Fairweather and R Grantham (eds), *Private Law in the 21st Century* (Oxford, Hart Publishing, 2017) 195.

[178] *Clayton v The Queen* [2006] HCA 58, (2006) 231 ALR 500.

[179] *Patel* [2016] UKSC 42, [2017] AC 467 [114].

[180] Atiyah, above n 7, 1251.

increasing reliance on rules with in-built flexibility and secondly, the emphasis on fact-finding in the judicial process. These two characteristics are also evident in the more recent equitable developments discussed in Section II. Aityah suggested that the shift stemmed from the courts' recognition that strict rules do not necessarily lead to better human conduct[181] and they thus prioritised upholding justice in the particular case over the more remote gains of improved human conduct in the long run. Atiyah's proposition deserves fuller consideration, at least in the province of equity.

Given the diversity and complexity of the situations in which equitable doctrines and principles are invoked in modern disputes, the question is how should courts 'change' the law to better respond to them. There are at least three options. The first option is to start with provisional firm rules and develop exceptions along the way. The *Tinsley* reliance principle (and its exceptions) is a good example. The second option is to develop a comprehensive, step-by-step framework of analysis. The six-step framework to deal with property ownership disputes laid down by the Singapore Court of Appeal in *Chan Yuen Lan*[182] illustrates this solution. But it is an approach that is rarely resorted to because it is difficult to lay down a detailed framework (which also deals with exceptional circumstances) at an early stage of legal evolution. The third option is to adopt fact-specific, evaluative approaches which give courts the flexibility to identify relevant factors in each case and work out incrementally whether more generalised rules are appropriate and how they should be formulated.[183] In Harding's words, 'judges, by repeatedly evaluating the facts of particular cases within a certain class in light of the demands of conscience, may over time come to a clearer understanding of those demands that in turn renders them more determinate'.[184] This is problem-solving by experience.[185]

To be clear, whilst part of the analysis under Section II clearly reflects the third option, this is not to say that modern equity has abandoned the first option entirely. The commercial/non-commercial distinction is an attempt at broadening the scope for flexibility through fixed criteria. But which option the courts should take up must depend on the nature of the problem before it. Firm rules and fixed criteria are most needed in activities which require forward-planning. Hence, the criteria for the valid creation of a legal arrangement should and are generally certain, for example, the requirements for creating an express trust. But there are situations in which the courts are called upon to clean up the mess arising from failed non-commercial dealings, most notably, in determining property

[181] ibid 1268–69.
[182] *Chan Yuen Lan* [2014] SGCA 36, [2014] 3 SLR 1048 [160].
[183] In particular, vague and overly generalised language should be avoided.
[184] Harding, above n 49, 288.
[185] See *Australian Financial Services and Leasing Pty Ltd v Hills Industries Limited* [2014] HCA 14, (2014) 253 CLR 560 [23] (French CJ) ('*Australian Financial Services*').

ownership between separated unmarried cohabitees. The focus is naturally on the course of dealings between the parties and the approach is appropriately more evaluative.[186] Similarly, for equitable accounting, the English High Court has recently affirmed that it is 'ultimately a question of determining the common intention of the parties which is inevitably a fact sensitive exercise',[187] citing from *Snell's Equity*: 'To the extent rules have developed, these are (non-binding) guidance or rules of convenience aimed at achieving justice between the co-owners'.[188] This is not to say that certainty is unimportant in such situations or that forward-planning is completely irrelevant. Based on legal advice, parties may decide whether to fight the legal battle and how best to move on from the separation. But these are peripheral issues that should not distract attention from the central problem: these cases involve parties formerly in a close and loving relationship who are now going separate ways and require the law to assist them in the division of their family home and likely their most valuable asset. Laying down firm rules on family property disputes which would apply upon the termination of the relationship is unlikely to influence parties' conduct while a relationship is merry and ongoing. Surely, selfless and non-calculative behaviour – which one can and should expect from familial dealings – is not to be discouraged whilst the parties are building a home together, even if they have not chosen marriage.

Equity also deals with cases involving abuse of power, advantage-taking and opportunism of different degrees. Firm rules are not needed to help the opportunists, the abusive and the oppressive to plan how best to carry out their endeavours.[189] What may be argued is that firm rules (which operate strictly against the wrongdoers) are required to effect deterrence[190] or at the very least, to send out a clear message that certain kinds of conduct would not be tolerated. But we also need to be discerning for two reasons. First, in many instances, equity acts in partnership with common law and/or statute in a number of ways. Equity must therefore take into account the position at law or in statute in determining its own stance, in particular, what supplementary role it should play. Indeed, this is entirely consistent with how equity has traditionally operated. Secondly, where remedial rules are concerned, they need not always be as strict as the liability rules if, for example, the case concerns a wrongdoer who has acted in good faith and whose efforts have benefited the principal.

[186] Another example would be disputes based on proprietary estoppel. In *Davies v Davies* [2016] EWCA Civ 463, [2016] P & CR 241 [38], Lewison LJ said that cases based on proprietary estoppel are 'fact sensitive' and no claim 'can be divided into watertight compartments'.

[187] *Rashid v Muir* [2018] EWHC 1258 (QB) [13].

[188] J McGhee (ed), *Snell's Equity*, 33rd edn (London, Sweet & Maxwell, 2015) para 20.084.

[189] See *Patel* [2016] UKSC 42, [2017] AC 467 [113].

[190] The effect of both specific and general deterrence has been doubted, though such doubts are generally expressed in the context of searching for an appropriate justification for awarding proprietary relief for breach of fiduciary duty (see K Barnett, 'Distributive Justice and Proprietary Remedies Over Bribes' (2015) 35 *Legal Studies* 302, 305–06).

IV. Renewal

A. English Courts' Responsibility

The judicial inclination towards fact-specific and evaluative approaches is not necessarily a permanent state of affairs. The pessimists may describe this trend as equity having lost its way or courts descending into irretrievable confusion. A more optimistic interpretation is that equity is undergoing the natural process of renewal (in the sense of reinvigoration) – reimagining how problems may be solved. It may be that some of these discretionary approaches will over time evolve to become firmer rules and fixed criteria; and some may provide the foundation for legislative reform. Not all solutions to modern problems need to be found in equity, but its tradition of tolerating discretion and 'guiding' criteria[191] enables courts to have a holistic overview of the issues arising in new contexts.

However, it is not an unreal danger that the proliferation of evaluative approaches may spawn internal reinforcement of the appropriateness of strong discretion, nebulous criteria, and ex post analysis on a case-by-case basis, thereby delaying or even preventing the natural refinement of these approaches into more concrete rules over time. Courts must therefore be guided by a strong sense of the mission of rendering the law more determinate and certain. In this connection, it is encouraging to note that the UK Supreme Court is not unaware of its general responsibility to develop 'more precise criteria' to replace legal tests articulated in 'vague and generalised language'.[192] In respect of equitable developments, in *Gavin Edmondson Solicitors Ltd v Haven Insurance Company Ltd*, a case concerning a solicitor's equitable lien, Lord Briggs said:

> I acknowledge that equity operates with a flexibility not shared by the common law, and that it can and does adapt its remedies to changing times. But equity nonetheless operates in accordance with principles. While most equitable remedies are discretionary, those principles provide a framework which makes equity part of a system of English law which is renowned for its predictability.[193]

In that case, Lord Briggs restrained the development of the law on a solicitor's equitable lien on the wider basis of protecting the solicitors from 'any unconscionable interference with their expectations in relation to recovery of their charges'.[194] Extra-judicially, Lord Briggs clarified that 'unconscionability' is merely an overarching requirement to restrain equitable intervention in spaces where

[191] *Australian Financial Services* [2014] HCA 14, (2014) 253 CLR 560 [23] (French CJ).

[192] *HMRC v Investment Trust Companies* [2017] UKSC 29, [2018] AC 275 [38]. Lord Reed's comments were made in relation to the requirement of 'at the expense of' in an unjust enrichment claim, although he did not consider it wise to 'attempt in this appeal to arrive at a more definitive statement' of the test.

[193] *Gavin Edmondson Solicitors Ltd v Haven Insurance Company Ltd* [2018] UKSC 21, [2018] 1 WLR 2052 [57] ('*Gavin Edmondson*').

[194] *Gavin Edmondson* [2018] UKSC 21, [2018] 1 WLR 2052 [57].

'they have no role at all to play';[195] he stressed the need to formulate clear and specific equitable principles. It is hoped that these reminders would bring about more determined judicial efforts, especially in the appellate and apex courts, to distil clearer principles in the future.

B. Harmonisation

We now turn to reflect on equity's renewal from a broader geographical context. Owing to the smaller case load, instances of equity's renewal in Hong Kong and Singapore are frequently inspired by the legal developments in other jurisdictions. In terms of private law developments, Hong Kong follows English law much more faithfully than Singapore law does,[196] although the appointment of Australian Non-Permanent Judges on the Hong Kong Court of Final Appeal may occasionally add a different complexion to that legal convention.[197]

Yet, English equity's renewal process may not necessarily generate harmonisation of equitable principles across the four jurisdictions, even though both English and Australian judges have separately spoken favourably of the goal of legal harmonisaton.[198] This is because 'every community establishes laws for its own purposes, and to suit the needs which they perceive'.[199] There are clearly cultural, historical and political distinctions between the four jurisdictions. The Australian legal environment, even in the private law domain, is far more regulated by legislation,[200] which results in a more complex interplay between statute and common law. The Australian courts are thus more tolerant of concurrent causes of action,[201] as well as being more attentive to statutes in developing the common law.[202] On the other hand, Hong Kong law's faithful adherence to English law demonstrates its confidence in English law as setting the legal

[195] M Briggs, 'Equity in Business' (The Denning Society Annual Lecture, Lincoln's Inn, London, 8 November 2018) [59].

[196] cf *Chang Pui Yin v Bank of Singapore* [2017] 4 HKLRD 458. In this case, the Hong Kong Court looked to Australian developments as the legislation under consideration was drafted based on an Australian statute.

[197] See *Big Island Construction (HK) Ltd v Wu Yi Development Ltd* [2015] HKEC 1232.

[198] *FHR* [2014] UKSC 45, [2015] AC 250 [45] (Lord Neuberger), *AIB* [2014] UKSC 58, [2014] 3 WLR 1367 [121] (Lord Toulson); *Hasler v Singtel Optus Pty Ltd* [2014] NSWCA 266, (2014) 87 NSWLR 609 [71] (Leeming JA).

[199] S Hedley, 'The Rise and Fall of Private Law Theory' (2018) 134 *LQR* 214, 216.

[200] See, eg, Contracts Review Act 1980 (NSW) which confers on courts the power to deal with 'unjust' contracts.

[201] See YH Goh and M Yip, 'Concurrent Liability in Tort and Contract: An Analysis of Interplay, Intersection and Independence' (2017) 24 *Tort Law Journal* 148.

[202] It is thus unsurprising that Gummow J's recommendation to Hong Kong in the area of illegality is to pay primary attention to statute. See W Gummow, 'Illegality and Statute in Hong Kong' (Hochelega Lecture, Hong Kong, 15 December 2017).

standards for its community,[203] notwithstanding the cultural differences between the two societies. As for Singapore, its legal system is required by the Application of English Law Act[204] to develop an indigenous law to suit the local conditions. Interestingly, not all departures from English law are derived from the need to cater for specific socio-cultural conditions. Recent Singapore decisions, in particular, have declined to follow English developments on the basis that English law is not sufficiently certain.[205] More generally, there is a growing sense that Singapore courts are determined that Singapore should develop its own law,[206] in part to further consolidate its position as the favoured dispute resolution forum. As such, even though Hong Kong and Singapore are culturally similar, the differences in their legal cultures and jurisdictional objectives would lead to the adoption of different principles in certain areas of the law.

Turning to the recent proliferation of fact-specific, evaluative approaches in English equity, one wonders what impact this trend may have on equity's renewal in Hong Kong and Singapore. As English authorities remain persuasive in these two jurisdictions, English developments may trigger a renewal process in Hong Kong law and Singapore law. For instance, both Hong Kong and Singapore courts have adopted the *Pitt v Holt* approach to rescission on the basis of mistake.[207] It may also be that the English renewal process signals that a change is in order, but the resultant change in the laws of Hong Kong or Singapore might proceed in a different direction. More generally, evaluative approaches may require courts to openly consider the policy interests that are relevant to their societies, prevailing societal norms, and developments in related areas of law. Over time, the same approaches may be refined along slightly different lines in each jurisdiction.

The final point is the significance of the appointment of foreign jurists on the Hong Kong Court of Final Appeal (HKCFA) and the Singapore International Commercial Court (SICC). It can scarcely be doubted that case law developments are heavily influenced by the training, experience and personalities of the judges.[208] These foreign judges will certainly enhance the influence of foreign law on local law developments, and to some degree indirectly increase the prospects of legal harmonisation.[209] But the degree to which foreign judges can fully

[203] Certainty and consistency with the rule of law are values which the Hong Kong judiciary holds dear in the era of 'one country, two systems'.

[204] Application of English Law Act 1993, Cap 7A, 1994 rev edn (Singapore).

[205] See, eg, *Turf Club Auto Emporium Pte Ltd v Yeo Boong Hua* [2018] SGCA 79 [281] (rejected the test laid out in *Morris-Garner v One Step (Support) Ltd* [2018] UKSC 20, [2018] 2 WLR 1353).

[206] Singapore law's most remarkable departure from English law was in its rejection of *Lister & Co v Stubbs* (1890) 45 Ch D 1 in the Singapore High Court decision of *Sumitomo Bank Ltd v Thahir Kartika Ratna* [1992] 3 SLR(R) 638.

[207] Hong Kong: *Estate of Chan Chung Han* [2016] HKEC 1117; Singapore: *BMM v BMN* [2017] SGHC 131, [2017] 4 SLR 1315.

[208] Yip and Lee, above n 119, 649–52.

[209] More uncommonly, however, a retired foreign judge's views may no longer represent the prevailing views of the current foreign court. See Lord Millett's speech (which endorsed the application of traditional equitable accounting rules in assessing equitable compensation for breach of trust) in *Libertarian*

appreciate local conditions in their application and development of local laws remains unclear.[210] Their understanding of local society, legal culture and values are crucial to the application of fact-specific, evaluative approaches in areas of the law where policy interests are to be openly considered. This is perhaps not a serious concern for the HKCFA Overseas Non-Permanent Judges who have the aid of their local colleagues. Further, as a matter of principle, appellate courts generally refrain from disturbing the trial court's findings of fact. But in the case of the SICC, an International Judge may be and has been appointed as the sole judge in disputes governed by Singapore law.[211] In non-commercial cases, where policy interests and societal values differ more markedly between societies, the SICC can decline to assume jurisdiction on the basis of its subject-matter jurisdiction. Even more interestingly, it may be that their role as judges in a specialist commercial court may colour the International Judges' view on how the law should develop – in particular, they may feel a greater need to promote commercial certainty and simplicity in the law. For instance, in *CPIT Investments Ltd v Qilin World Capital Ltd*, Vivian Ramsay IJ (mis)interpreted Singapore case law as indicating that 'a remedial constructive trust in Singapore law, as in other legal systems, is only to be imposed sparingly'.[212]

In *Telemedia*, Patricia Bergin IJ, citing *AIB* and not contrary Australian case law,[213] appeared enthusiastic to simplify the law on equitable compensation for breach of fiduciary duty:[214]

> Having regard to my findings it is not necessary to pursue that debate further other than to say that had it been necessary I would have preferred the view that there has to be some causal link between the breach and the loss for which compensation is awarded.

V. Conclusion

This chapter offers an in-depth analysis of recent English equitable developments through the analytical lenses of 'form' and 'substance'. The main observation is that there are clear signs of English equity scaling back strong formal reasoning.

Investments [2014] 1 HKC 368 [166]–[175]. cf *AIB* [2014] UKSC 58, [2014] 3 WLR 1367, discussed above under Section II.

[210] Some parallels may be drawn with the experience of the Privy Council: see P Mitchell, 'The Privy Council and the Difficulty of Distance' (2015) 36 *OJLS* 26.

[211] In *Telemedia Pacific Group Ltd v Yuanta Asset Management International Ltd* [2016] SGHC(I) 3, [2016] 5 SLR 1 ('*Telemedia*'), Patricia Bergin IJ was appointed as a single judge in the case. In this case, the parties agreed that the content of any applicable foreign law was identical with Singapore law and proceeded on that basis.

[212] *CPIT Investments Ltd v Qilin World Capital Ltd* [2017] SGHC(I) 5, [2017] 5 SLR 1 [199].

[213] *Agricultural Land Management Ltd v Jackson (No 2)* [2014] WASC 102.

[214] *Telemedia* [2016] SGHC(I) 3, [2016] 5 SLR 1 [517] (footnotes omitted). In *Winsta Holding Pte Ltd v Sim Poh Ping* [2018] SGHC 239 [193]–[194], without considering *Telemedia*, the Singapore High Court has also affirmed the correctness of *AIB* and held that a principal would have to prove that there is a 'but-for' causation between the breach of duty and the loss he or she suffered. cf *Tongbao (Singapore) Shipping Pte Ltd v Woon Swee Huat* [2018] SGHC 165.

The trend of embracing fact-specific, evaluative approaches is particularly of note. It is argued that the diversity and complexity of modern disputes combined with judicial pragmatism have prompted the emergence of this trend. It is also argued, with a note of optimism, that this trend may be interpreted as English equity undergoing a natural cycle of renewal. Importantly, going forward, English courts have the responsibility to rein in the indeterminacy of the law by making greater efforts in distilling clearer and more specific principles as they acquire deeper understanding of the issues through judicial experience. Building on the main observation proffered by this chapter, the analysis reflected on the impact that English equity's embrace of fact-specific, evaluative approaches would have on the reception of English law in Hong Kong and Singapore and legal harmonisation, in particular, having regard to the appointment of English and Australian jurists to the HKCFA and SICC. It is hoped that the insights in this chapter might pave the way for more thoughtful scholarship on the comparative review between English law and the laws of Hong Kong and Singapore, as these legal systems continue to diverge and converge over time owing to both internal and external factors.

11

The Form and Substance of Equitable Estoppel

ANDREW ROBERTSON

An important point of tension between form and substance in the law of obligations lies in the field of taxonomy. A core taxonomic question is whether the doctrinal form of the law accords with its substantive purpose, operation and effect. As a matter of form, the law might treat A and B as separate doctrines when, as a matter of substance, the two doctrines serve the same function and operate in circumstances that are so closely analogous that no purpose is served in distinguishing them. In those circumstances, recognising the unity of the two doctrines may simplify the law, avoid overlap or inconsistency, and provide a larger body of learning and experience to legal advisors, judges and scholars seeking to resolve difficult problems. Conversely, close analysis sometimes shows that the form the law is understood to take is too simplistic. What is in form a single doctrine is in substance more complex, addressing substantially different sets of concerns, each of which could be addressed more effectively by recognising its distinctiveness and defining more precisely its constituent elements or remedial effects. The lumping and splitting of legal doctrines are essentially exercises in ensuring that the form in which the law is presented – or the form the law is understood to take – properly reflects its substance.[1]

Taxonomic uncertainty has long been a feature of equitable estoppel. The unifiers had their heyday in a period roughly centred on the 1980s. The idea that motivated the unification movement was that, in this area of equity at least, form must not be allowed to trump substance, in the sense that legal classifications with arbitrary limits must not prevent justice from being done. In *Crabb v Arun District Council* Scarman LJ said he did not find the distinction between promissory and proprietary estoppel helpful: 'putting the law into categories', he said, is not of

[1] cf C Darwin (letter to JD Hooker) in F Darwin (ed), *Life and Letters of Charles Darwin: Volume II* (London, John Murray, 1887) 105: 'It is good to have hair-splitters and lumpers. Those who make many species are the "splitters", and those who make few are the "lumpers".'

the slightest assistance 'in solving the particular problem raised by a particular case'.[2] In *Amalgamated Investment & Property Co Ltd (in liq) v Texas Commerce International Bank Ltd*, Robert Goff J identified 'a tendency in the more recent authorities to reject any rigid classification of equitable estoppel into exclusive and defined categories' and agreed that 'it cannot be right to restrict equitable estoppel to certain defined categories'.[3] He considered the well-known statements of the doctrine of acquiescence,[4] the doctrine of encouragement,[5] and promissory estoppel[6] to be describing aspects of 'a wider doctrine of equitable estoppel'.[7] On appeal, Denning LJ approved the shift in emphasis from form to substance. He accepted that the separate doctrines of 'proprietary estoppel, estoppel by representation of fact, estoppel by acquiescence, and promissory estoppel' could 'now be seen to merge into one general principle shorn of limitations', which he found had been correctly applied by Robert Goff J in that case.[8]

While the notion of a unified principle of 'equitable estoppel' had its origins in England, it gained far more traction in Australia and New Zealand.[9] The leading Australian cases in that unifying movement were *Waltons Stores (Interstate) Ltd v Maher*[10] and *Commonwealth v Verwayen*.[11] In their focus on matters of substance, and in their insistence on prioritising substance over doctrinal form, the judgments in those cases provide a striking contrast with those of more recent decades. Lengthy passages are focused on exploration of the reasons underlying the principles recognised in the cases. A primary focus of the judgments is the idea that the law must develop so as to conform to the dictates of justice, which means that the form the law has been understood to take must not stifle its development or prevent justice being done in particular cases.

[2] *Crabb v Arun District Council* [1976] 1 Ch 179, 193.

[3] *Amalgamated Investment & Property Co Ltd (in liq) v Texas Commerce International Bank Ltd* [1982] 1 QB 84, 103–04 ('*Texas Bank*').

[4] *Ramsden v Dyson* (1866) LR 1 HL 129, 140–41 (Lord Cranworth LC) ('*Ramsden*'); *De Bussche v Alt* (1873) 8 Ch D 286, 314 (Thesiger LJ) and *Willmott v Barber* (1880) 15 Ch D 96, 105–06 (Fry J).

[5] *Ramsden* (1866) LR 1 HL 129, 170–71 (Lord Kingsdown).

[6] *Hughes v Metropolitan Railway Co* (1877) 2 App Cas 439, 448 (Lord Cairns LC) ('Hughes') and *Central London Property Trust Ltd v High Trees House Ltd* [1947] KB 130, 134 (Denning J).

[7] *Texas Bank* [1982] QB 84, 103.

[8] ibid 122. Denning LJ described the principle as follows:

> When the parties to a transaction proceed on the basis of an underlying assumption – either of fact or of law – whether due to misrepresentation or mistake makes no difference – on which they have conducted the dealings between them – neither of them will be allowed to go back on that assumption when it would be unfair or unjust to allow him to do so. If one of them does seek to go back on it, the courts will give the other such remedy as the equity of the case demands.

[9] As to the latter, see *Gillies v Keogh* [1989] 2 NZLR 327, 331: 'The tide is setting or has set, I think, against the view … that proprietary estoppel and promissory estoppel are entirely separate and take their origins from different sources.' (Cooke P) and *Wilson Parking New Zealand Ltd v Fanshawe 136 Ltd* [2014] NZCA 407, [2014] 3 NZLR 567, especially at 577 and 584 (applying a unified 'doctrine of equitable estoppel').

[10] *Waltons Stores (Interstate) Ltd v Maher* (1988) 164 CLR 387 ('*Waltons Stores*').

[11] *Commonwealth v Verwayen* (1990) 170 CLR 394 ('*Verwayen*').

In *Waltons Stores*, Brennan J agreed with Scarman LJ that it is not helpful to divide the cases into different categories: there are broader principles at play and the categories are 'not necessarily exhaustive of the cases in which equity will intervene'.[12] The underlying principle, he explained, is that it is unconscionable for one person to cause detriment to another by inducing an assumption about the legal relations between the parties, knowing the other will act on it, and then behaving inconsistently with it.[13] The object of the doctrine is to prevent that detriment.[14] Brennan J went on to set out what has proved to be an extremely influential numbered list of its elements, and then to explain why the principle was applicable to the facts of the case.[15] The broad, unified principle that emerged from *Waltons Stores* was further explained by Priestley JA in *Silovi Pty Ltd v Barbaro*, in a judgment that also went on to be highly influential in subsequent cases.[16] Priestley JA distilled from *Waltons Stores* the propositions that the principle of equitable estoppel encompasses estoppel by acquiescence, estoppel by encouragement and promissory estoppel, that it is a positive source of legal obligation (ie, a sword) arising from reliance on an assumption that an interest will be granted, a contract made or a promise performed, and that the remedy granted is that which is necessary to prevent detriment arising from unconscionable conduct.[17] In *Verwayen* most if not all of the Justices of the High Court recognised the unity of the promissory and proprietary strands of equitable estoppel.[18]

Today, however, the splitters are in the ascendant. A sharp distinction between promissory and proprietary estoppel has been maintained in England,[19] and recently reasserted in Australia.[20] The rejection of a unified principle of equitable estoppel in Australian law has been led by KR Handley, both in extra-judicial writing[21] and in the New South Wales Court of Appeal.[22] Within the category of

[12] *Waltons Stores* (1988) 164 CLR 387, 420.

[13] ibid 419–27.

[14] ibid 423, 427.

[15] ibid 428–29ff.

[16] *Silovi Pty Ltd v Barbaro* (1988) 13 NSWLR 466 ('*Silovi*').

[17] ibid 472 (Priestley JA, Hope and McHugh JJA agreeing, as supplemented by the judgment of Priestley JA in *Austotel Pty Ltd v Franklins Selfserve Pty Ltd* (1989) 16 NSWLR 582, 610–12).

[18] *Verwayen* (1990) 170 CLR 394, 409–17 (Mason CJ), 422–23 (Brennan J), 440 (Deane J), 453–54 (Dawson J), 487 (Gaudron J); cf Toohey J at 475–76 (recognising a substantive doctrine of promissory estoppel) and at 471 (noting that there is much to be said for 'one subsuming principle' of estoppel by conduct). A series of judgments in *Waltons Stores* (1988) 164 CLR 387, 451 (Deane J), *Foran v Wight* (1989) 168 CLR 385, 435 (Deane J) and *Verwayen* (1990) 170 CLR 394, 413 (Mason J) and 440 (Deane J) went further, recognising a principle that unified estoppel by representation of fact with the various strands of estoppel in equity.

[19] See, eg, the obiter discussion in *MWB Business Exchange Centres Ltd v Rock Advertising Ltd* [2016] EWCA Civ 553, [2017] QB 604 [50]–[65] (Kitchen LJ) ('*MWB Business Exchange Centres*') (overturned on unrelated grounds: *Rock Advertising Limited v MWB Business Exchange Centres Ltd* [2018] UKSC 24, [2018] 2 WLR 1603 ('*Rock Advertising*').

[20] See A Robertson, 'Three Models of Promissory Estoppel' (2013) 7 *Journal of Equity* 226, www.ssrn.com/abstract=2473402.

[21] KR Handley, *Estoppel by Conduct and Election*, 2nd edn (London, Sweet & Maxwell, 2016).

[22] Most notably in *Saleh v Romanous* [2010] NSWCA 274, (2010) 79 NSWLR 453 ('*Saleh*').

'proprietary estoppel' there appears to be a growing insistence on the separation of estoppel by acquiescence and estoppel by encouragement.[23] Ben McFarlane has provided powerful intellectual support for the splitting movement, arguing in a substantial body of scholarly work that what is known as 'equitable estoppel' in fact consists of five separate principles.[24]

This chapter seeks to question that growing consensus. It considers the case for the unity of equitable estoppel by identifying what might be understood to be its core principle, and then considering a series of questions which might help us to understand whether that core principle can be said to underlie 'equitable estoppel' as a whole. The answer, unfortunately, is 'not quite', but there is much to be learned from an exploration of the points of unity and disunity.

I. The Core Principle of Equitable Estoppel

A. The Principle

The broad principle which might be claimed to underlie equitable estoppel is as follows. Where:

(a) one person (the inducing party) plays a role in the adoption by another person (the relying party) of an assumption as to the existing legal rights of the relying party or the future conduct of the inducing party;
(b) the inducing party ought reasonably to expect that the relying party might act in reliance on the assumption in such a way that he or she will suffer detriment if the inducing party behaves inconsistently with that assumption;
(c) the relying party does act on the assumption in such a way; and
(d) it was reasonable for the relying party to adopt and act on the assumption in the way that he or she did,

then it is unconscionable for the inducing party to act inconsistently with the assumption, at least without taking steps to ensure that the relying party suffers no detriment as a result of the action he or she took in reliance on the assumption. The inducing party is therefore liable to do what is necessary to prevent the relying party from suffering detriment as a result of that change of position. Because the detriment resulting from action taken in reliance is typically non-pecuniary

[23] The current Australian position and issues are discussed in detail in *ADM v FDGK* [2018] NSWSC 442 [900]ff (Ward CJ in Eq).

[24] B McFarlane, 'Understanding Equitable Estoppel: From Metaphors to Better Laws' (2013) 66 *Current Legal Problems* 267; B McFarlane, 'Form and Substance in Equity', this volume, ch 9, text accompanying nn 74–100; B McFarlane, 'Equitable Estoppel as a Cause of Action: Neither One Thing Nor One Other' in S Degeling, J Edelman and J Goudkamp (eds), *Contract in Commercial Law* (Sydney, Thomson/Law Book, 2016); B McFarlane, *The Law of Proprietary Estoppel* (Oxford, Oxford University Press, 2014).

and not readily quantifiable, this usually, but not always, requires fulfilment of the assumption that was relied upon.[25]

B. Normative Foundation

The justification for the principle is that a party who induces an assumption in another person (as to the existing rights of that person or the future conduct of the inducing party) creates the risk of a certain kind of harm. The relying party stands to suffer harm if he or she acts or refrains from acting in reliance on the assumption and the inducing party then engages in inconsistent behaviour. Since the inducing party:

(a) played a role in inducing the assumption;
(b) should reasonably have expected the relying party to change his or her position in reliance on the assumption; and
(c) to a significant extent controls the risk of harm,

then the inducing party can be considered to bear sufficient responsibility for the relying party's plight that the inducing party ought to take (or ought to have taken) steps to minimise or avoid that risk, by:

(i) not inducing the assumption;
(ii) resiling from the assumption before it is relied upon;
(iii) qualifying the assumption to make its unreliability clear;
(iv) warning the promisee not to act on the assumption;
(v) acting so as to prevent the relying party from suffering detriment (eg, by giving notice of an intention to resile which is sufficient to allow the relying party to take action to avoid detriment); or
(vi) behaving consistently with the assumption.

Because of the inducing party's responsibility for creating the risk of detriment, good conscience requires the inducing party either to *prevent* the detriment – by discouraging reliance or behaving consistently – or to *answer for* the detriment if he or she behaves inconsistently.

The principle is particularly controversial in its application to assumptions about the inducing party's future conduct. The reason for that controversy is that in such circumstances the reliability of the assumption is almost entirely in the hands of the inducing party.[26] Reliance on the assumption therefore involves a particularly high degree of trust. The higher degree of trust reposed by the relying party on the inducing party in such situations may be considered to provide a

[25] A Robertson, 'The Reliance Basis of Proprietary Estoppel Remedies' (2008) 72 *Conveyancer and Property Lawyer* 295.

[26] A Robertson, 'Revolutions and Counterrevolutions in Equitable Estoppel' in S Worthington, A Robertson and G Virgo (eds), *Revolution and Evolution in Private Law* (Oxford, Hart Publishing, 2018) 161, 162.

strong reason for imposing responsibility on the inducing party, but may also be considered to provide a reason to blame the relying party for his or her fate. It has now been accepted at the highest level in England and Australia that the principle in question can, at least in some circumstances, generate liability where one person is led to adopt and act upon an assumption as to future conduct of another.[27] The question, is not, therefore, as to the existence of the principle, but as to its precise form and scope.

The notion that there is a broad, overarching principle of equitable estoppel along the lines suggested above rests on the idea of a unity between promissory estoppel and at least some of the proprietary estoppel lines of cases. There are numerous different views as to the precise taxonomy of equitable estoppel, but the primary questions they raise are as follows. The first question is whether promissory estoppel is distinct from the core principle identified above. That depends primarily on whether detriment is required for promissory estoppel, and on whether the essentially defensive nature of promissory estoppel marks it out as fundamentally different from the proprietary estoppels. Secondly, it is necessary to consider whether promissory estoppel is itself comprised of irreducibly dissimilar principles, as Ben McFarlane has argued. The third question is whether a promise is required for some types of equitable estoppel, but not others. If that is the case, then any categories of estoppel that require a promise (such as estoppel by encouragement) may be considered fundamentally different from those that do not (such as estoppel by acquiescence). The final question is whether the estoppel by acquiescence category might encompass cases that do not fall within the core principle. Those questions will be considered in turn.

A question that will not be considered in this chapter is whether estoppel by representation of fact can or should properly be considered to fall within a unified principle, along with estoppels relating to existing rights and estoppels relating to future conduct. While there is some support for that idea in the contemporary literature, there is little if any support for it in the contemporary case law.[28] The issues it raises could not adequately be addressed here.

II. Is Promissory Estoppel Distinct?

The idea that promissory estoppel is a distinct doctrine rests on one or both of two ideas: first, that detriment is not required for promissory estoppel and, secondly, that promissory estoppel is a purely defensive principle.

[27] In England, *Thorner v Major* [2009] UKHL 18, [2009] 1 WLR 776 ('*Thorner*'). In Australia, *Waltons Stores* (1988) 164 CLR 394 and, eg, *Giumelli v Giumelli* (1999) 196 CLR 101 ('*Giumelli*').

[28] Compare M Bryan, 'Unifying Estoppel Doctrine: The Argument for Heresy' (2013) 7 *Journal of Equity* 209 and E Bant and M Bryan, 'Fact, Future and Fiction: Risk and Reasonable Reliance in Estoppel' (2015) 35 *OJLS* 427, with J Hudson, 'The True Purpose of Estoppel by Representation' (2015) 32 *Journal of Contract Law* 275 and J Hudson, 'The Price of Coherence in Estoppels' (2017) 39 *Sydney Law Review* 1.

A. Is Detriment Required?

If there is a single principle underlying equitable estoppel, it is concerned with the prevention of the particular kind of detriment that arises from inconsistent conduct on one side and reliance on the other. The case for the unity of equitable estoppel therefore rests on the centrality of detrimental reliance to all constituent doctrines. The relatively weak role played by detrimental reliance in the foundational promissory estoppel cases provides some strength to the argument for disunity. Detrimental reliance was present in *Hughes*,[29] but was not emphasised in the speeches in the House of Lords, and does not provide the only possible explanation for the decision. In that case a landlord, having issued a notice to repair, entered into negotiations with a tenant for a possible purchase of the leasehold, knowing the tenant was deferring commencement of the repairs pending the outcome of the negotiations. The landlord's conduct 'justified and naturally led to' the tenant's impression that the notice was suspended.[30] The landlord was therefore held not to be entitled to treat a lease as forfeited on the basis of the tenant's non-compliance with a notice to repair. Lord Cairns LC famously said:

> It was not argued at your Lordships' Bar, and it could not be argued, that there was any right of a Court of Equity, or any practice of a Court of Equity, to give relief in cases of this kind, by way of mercy, or by way merely of saving property from forfeiture, but it is the first principle upon which all Courts of Equity proceed, that if parties who have entered into definite and distinct terms involving certain legal results – certain penalties or legal forfeiture – afterwards by their own act or with their own consent enter upon a course of negotiation which has the effect of leading one of the parties to suppose that the strict rights arising under the contract will not be enforced, or will be kept in suspense, or held in abeyance, the person who otherwise might have enforced those rights will not be allowed to enforce them where it would be inequitable having regard to the dealings which have thus taken place between the parties.[31]

Neither Lord Cairns nor any other member of the House of Lords clearly explained when it will be inequitable to enforce such legal rights, or why it was inequitable in this case for the landlord to exercise its legal rights. Forfeiture of a lease is of course detrimental to the tenant, but may also confer a windfall on the landlord. Either the detriment to the tenant or the windfall to the landlord might, in conjunction with other factors, justify the conclusion that it is inequitable to exercise a legal right to a forfeiture which the landlord had a hand in bringing about.

An important step in the development of promissory estoppel was the interpretation of *Hughes* by Bowen LJ in *Birmingham & District Land Co v London and North Western Railway Co.*[32] In that case the plaintiff was in possession of

[29] *Hughes* (1877) 2 App Cas 439.
[30] *Hughes* (1877) 2 App Cas 439, 451 (Lord Selbourne).
[31] *Hughes* (1877) 2 App Cas 439, 448.
[32] *Birmingham & District Land Co v London and North Western Railway Co* (1888) 40 Ch D 268 ('*North Western Railway Co*').

land under a building lease. The defendant initiated a railway scheme which would allow the defendant to take part of the land, and which therefore threatened to affect the building operations. The landlord's agent advised the plaintiff to stop the building operations until the railway scheme was resolved. The defendant subsequently bought some of the land subject to any rights the plaintiff might have. The terms of the building lease having expired, the central issue was whether the plaintiff had any rights in relation to the land. The Court of Appeal applied the principle from *Hughes*, holding that what had passed between the landlord's agent and the tenant 'raised an equity' against the landlord which would have prevented him from exercising the rights he would otherwise have had under the building lease, and 'would oblige the landlord to give the tenant a reasonable time to complete the building operations which had been stopped by his agent'.[33] Bowen LJ observed that the principle was not limited to cases involving forfeiture:

> It seems to me to amount to this, that if persons who have contractual rights against others induce by their conduct those against whom they have such rights to believe that such rights will either not be enforced or will be kept in suspense or abeyance for some particular time, those persons will not be allowed by a Court of Equity to enforce the rights until such time has elapsed, *without at all events placing the parties in the same position as they were before*.[34]

Bowen LJ saw the basis of the principle as the change of position made by the relying party in the belief that the inducing party would not enforce his or her rights or would keep them in abeyance for a particular period. The notion that the inducing party could enforce the rights in question if the parties were restored to their original positions makes it clear that detrimental reliance is at the heart of the principle. Unfortunately, Denning J did not share this view when he revived the principle in *Central London Property Trust Ltd v High Trees House Ltd*.[35] In that case Denning J expressed the view, by way of obiter dicta, that a landlord's promise to accept a reduced rent must be honoured if it was intended to create legal relations, was intended to be acted upon, and was in fact acted upon. The promise was said, in equity, to give rise to an estoppel in the sense that, while a breach does not generate a cause of action for damages, the courts will not allow the landlord to act inconsistently with it.[36] Denning J made no mention of detriment, although it is difficult to see the significance of the promisee acting on the promise if there was no detrimental change of position.

In Australia, it has never been in doubt that detrimental reliance is an essential element of promissory estoppel. In the first Australian case in which it was applied, on facts very similar to those in *High Trees*, King CJ recognised that

[33] *North Western Railway Co* (1888) 40 Ch D 268, 277 (Cotton LJ).
[34] ibid 286 (emphasis added).
[35] *Central London Property Trust Ltd v High Trees House Ltd* [1947] 1 KB 130, 134 ('*High Trees*').
[36] *High Trees* [1947] 1 KB 130, 134.

promissory estoppel rests on the same foundation as estoppel by representation.[37] He said: 'If the representee or promisee will suffer no detriment as a consequence of the other party resiling from his position and asserting his strict legal rights, it is difficult to see where the injustice of permitting him to do so would lie'.[38] To similar effect is the judgment of White J in that case, who observed that:

> In many later cases following the *High Trees* case, many judges in many courts have preferred to base themselves upon Bowen LJ's formulation with its implication of detriment rather than upon Lord Denning's statement of the principle which seems to imply that there is no need to show any consideration or detriment.[39]

In *Legione v Hateley*, Mason and Deane JJ also accepted that promissory estoppel rested on the same grounds as estoppel by representation and therefore will not operate unless the relying party has placed himself or herself in a position of 'material disadvantage'.[40]

In English law, there remains a question as to whether detriment is required. The issue was raised in argument but not resolved in *Collier v P & M J Wright (Holdings) Ltd*.[41] More recently, in *MWB Business Exchange Ltd v Rock Advertising Ltd*, Kitchin LJ described the principle of promissory estoppel in a way that left open the question of detriment:

> Drawing the threads together, it seems to me that all of these cases are best understood as illustrations of the broad principle that if one party to a contract makes a promise to the other that his legal rights under the contract will not be enforced or will be suspended and the other party in some way relies on that promise, whether by altering his position or in any other way, then the party who might otherwise have enforced those rights will not be permitted to do so where it would be inequitable having regard to all of the circumstances.[42]

The foremost defender of the idea that detriment is not required for promissory estoppel is Sir Guenter Treitel in the consideration chapter of *Chitty on Contracts*.[43] Treitel insists that what he prefers to call 'equitable forbearance' does not require detriment. Rather, it is said to be 'enough if the promisee has altered his position in reliance on the promise so that it would be inequitable to allow the promisor to act inconsistently with it'.[44] According to Treitel:

> It must be 'inequitable' for the promisor to go back on the promise. This requirement cannot be defined with anything approaching precision, but the underlying idea is that

[37] *Je Maintiendrai Pty Ltd v Quaglia* (1980) 26 SASR 101, 105 ('*Je Maintiendrai*'), citing *Grundt v Great Boulder Gold Mines Pty Ltd* (1937) 59 CLR 641, 674 (Dixon J).

[38] *Je Maintiendrai* (1980) 26 SASR 101, 106.

[39] ibid 111.

[40] *Legione v Hateley* (1983) 152 CLR 406, 435, 437.

[41] *Collier v P & M J Wright (Holdings) Ltd* [2007] EWCA Civ 1329, [2008] 1 WLR 643 [29]–[40].

[42] *MWB Business Exchange* [2016] EWCA Civ 553, [2017] QB 604 [61] (overturned on unrelated grounds: *Rock Advertising* [2018] UKSC 24, [2018] 2 WLR 1603).

[43] HG Beale (ed), *Chitty on Contracts*, 33rd edn (London, Sweet and Maxwell, 2018) ch 4.

[44] ibid para 4.095.

> the promisee must have acted in reliance on the promise … so that he can no longer be restored to the position in which he was before he took such action. If the promisee can be restored to that position, it will not be inequitable for the promisor to go back on the promise.[45]

If the notion of detriment adds anything to this, it would seem to be that the position in which the relying party finds himself or herself as a result of the action taken must be one in which he or she is perceptibly worse off than if no action had been taken. But if the relying party is no worse off, then it is difficult to see why it would be considered inequitable to resile from the position. The difficulty is compounded by Treitel's acknowledgement that it may be relevant that the relying party 'has not suffered any *prejudice* by acting in reliance on the promise … for in such circumstances it may not be "inequitable" for the promisor to go back on his promise'.[46]

Treitel gives three examples of situations in which the relying party acts on the promise but it is not inequitable for the inducing party to resile from it. First, it will not be inequitable to go back on a promise if the promisee can be restored to the position he or she occupied before any action was taken, or 'if the detriment consists of the payment of money to the promisor and the latter has offered to refund that payment'.[47] This is simply a case of the inducing party taking steps to prevent the relying party from suffering detriment, and therefore becoming free to resile from the induced assumption. The example therefore tends to confirm the centrality of detriment rather than undermine it. Secondly, Treitel notes that in *The Post Chaser* Robert Goff J held that it was not inequitable for a promisor to resile from a promise only two days after making it, because the promisee had 'not suffered any prejudice by acting in reliance on the promise' and was 'restored to exactly the position in which he had been before the promise was made'.[48] Again, here, there seems no difference between the concept of prejudice and the concept of detriment. Robert Goff J held in *The Post Chaser* that in the absence of any 'prejudice' by reason of action taken in reliance by the sellers on the buyer's intimation that it would not enforce its rights, 'a necessary element for the application of equitable estoppel is lacking'.[49] Thirdly, Treitel suggests that a change of circumstances may justify the promisor in resiling from the promise without giving any notice to the promisee.[50] This does not contradict the notion that detriment is an element of liability. Rather, the idea is that whether it is inequitable to resile is a broader question encompassing factors beyond the position of the relying party, and a promisor may in some circumstances be entitled to resile even in the face of detriment.

[45] ibid para 4.096.
[46] ibid para 4.095 (emphasis added).
[47] ibid para 4.096 fn 531.
[48] ibid para 4.096, discussing *Société Italo-Belge pour le Commerce et l'Industrie v Vegetable Oils (Malaysia) Sdn Bhd* (*The Post Chaser*) [1981] 2 Lloyd's Rep 695 ('*The Post Chaser*').
[49] *The Post Chaser* [1981] 2 Lloyd's Rep 695, 702.
[50] Beale, above n 43, para 4.096.

In *Kosmar Villa Holidays plc v Trustees*, Rix LJ noted that the need to establish unfairness in order to satisfy the 'inequitable' requirement of promissory estoppel 'probably means that the reliance of the representee has to constitute a detriment'.[51] The discussion of injustice in *Chitty on Contracts* seems to bear that out, even if a different label such as 'prejudice' or 'irrevocable change of position' is used. A case does not appear to have been made that there is a different principle of justice on which promissory estoppel might be founded. As a matter of substance, then, promissory estoppel seems to rest on the core principle of equitable estoppel.

B. Is Promissory Estoppel Purely Defensive?

A second reason promissory estoppel may be considered distinctive is on the ground that, unlike other forms of equitable estoppel, it does not in itself provide a cause of action. It is said to be essentially defensive, though it may be used by a plaintiff who has relied on a promise that a particular defence will not be set up.[52] The idea that promissory estoppel does not in itself generate liability is established in England by the decision of the Court of Appeal in *Combe v Combe*.[53] In Australia, the position is less clear.[54] Since *Waltons Stores*, promissory estoppel has successfully been relied upon as an independent basis of liability in several cases.[55] The Full Court and Court of Appeal of the Supreme Court of Victoria have, in numerous cases, applied a broad doctrine of equitable or promissory estoppel which can operate positively as an independent source of liability, to which the court gives effect through relief 'moulded to meet the justice of the case'.[56] Other Australian courts have taken a similar approach.[57] The New South Wales Court of Appeal has in recent years insisted, however, that promissory estoppel operates only as a restraint on the enforcement of rights and is negative in substance.[58]

[51] *Kosmar Villa Holidays plc v Trustees* [2008] EWCA Civ 147, [2008] Bus LR 931 [38].

[52] See, eg, Beale, above n 43, paras 4.099–4.102; cf Handley, above n 21, paras 13.007, 13.029 (on the essentially defensive nature of promissory estoppel) and at paras 13.030–13.036 (denying that promissory estoppel may provide an answer to a defence).

[53] *Combe v Combe* [1951] 2 KB 215 ('*Combe*').

[54] See Robertson, above n 20.

[55] Eg, *W v G* (1996) 20 Fam LR 49; *Lee Gleeson Pty Ltd v Sterling Estates Pty Ltd* (1991) 23 NSWLR 571; *Chanrich Properties Pty Ltd v Baulkham Hills Shire Council* [2001] NSWSC 229; *Gray v National Crime Authority* [2003] NSWSC 111; *ACN 074 971 109 Pty Ltd (as Trustee for the Argot Unit Trust) v The National Mutual Life Association of Australasia Ltd* [2008] VSCA 247, (2008) 21 VR 351 ('*Argot Unit Trust*'); *Yarrabee Chicken Company Pty Ltd v Steggles Ltd* [2010] FCA 394 (all discussed in Robertson, above n 20, 240–43).

[56] *Anaconda Nickel Ltd v Edensor Nominees Pty Ltd* [2004] VSCA 167, (2004) 50 ACSR 679 [44]. See also *Metropolitan Transit Authority v Waverley Transit Pty Ltd* [1991] 1 VR 181; *Commonwealth v Clark* [1994] 2 VR 333; *Fifteenth Eestin Nominees Pty Ltd v Rosenberg* [2009] VSCA 112, (2009) 24 VR 155; *Argot Unit Trust* [2008] VSCA 247, (2008) 21 VR 351.

[57] See the cases discussed in Robertson, above n 20, 240–43.

[58] Most notably in *Saleh* [2010] NSWCA 274, (2010) 79 NSWLR 453 [62]–[76] (Handley AJA, with whom Giles JA and Sackville AJA agreed). In *Ashton v Pratt* [2015] NSWCA 12, (2015) 88 NSWLR 281 a differently constituted Court of Appeal treated the issue as unresolved [138]–[140].

Waltons Stores has been interpreted as a case of estoppel by encouragement, the unusual feature of which was that the relevant promise was made *to the land owner* and was to *take*, rather than confer, an interest in land.[59]

To the extent that there is a limit on the offensive capacity of promissory estoppel, it is not grounded in any concerns about justice between the parties. What is distinctive about the scope of promissory estoppel in its traditional formulation is that it operates on an assumption that the inducing party will not exercise a right or power against the relying party. There is nothing about that fact pattern that requires, as between the parties, that the principle have only a preclusionary operation. It has been argued that, if a non-contractual promise to confer a proprietary right can give rise to liability by way of proprietary estoppel, there is no reason in principle why a non-contractual promise to confer a non-proprietary right should not also give rise to liability.[60] McFarlane and Sales have gone further, arguing that there is no reason in principle why *any promise* that could reasonably be understood to have been seriously intended by the promisor as one that was capable of being relied on by the promisee should not similarly give rise to liability.[61] Similarly, one could argue that there is no reason in justice why promissory estoppel should have only a defensive operation when proprietary estoppel is not so limited.

If the exclusively defensive nature of promissory estoppel is justified, it is on the basis that positive enforcement of such promises would create incoherence or conflict with the law of contract.[62] Analysis of this kind implicitly accepts that promissory estoppel is based on the same principle of justice as proprietary estoppel by encouragement, but insists that its effect must be limited for reasons of legal coherence. It is difficult to rebut claims about incoherence because incoherence is such a vague concept and any effects it might have are intangible. Moreover, views differ as to what level of tension between different parts of the law might render it incoherent. It is, however, very difficult to see why an offensive doctrine of reliance-based liability causes any difficulties for the law of contract. As argued elsewhere, the grounds of liability are different, the factual elements of the causes of action

[59] Handley, above n 21, paras 11.025–11.029, 13.038–13.043.

[60] D Jackson, 'Estoppel as a Sword' (1965) 81 *LQR* 223, 241–43; *Waltons Stores* (1988) 164 CLR 387, 425–26 (Brennan J).

[61] B McFarlane and P Sales, 'Promises, Detriment, and Liability: Lessons from Proprietary Estoppel' (2015) 131 *LQR* 610, especially at 621–25. McFarlane and Sales suggest that the failure of English law to develop in this direction may be a result of the fact that a strong case has not yet exposed the injustice of the current law, explaining why neither *Combe* [1951] 2 KB 215 nor *Baird Textile Holdings Ltd v Marks & Spencer Plc* [2001] EWCA Civ 274, [2002] 1 All ER (Comm) 737 did so. See also S Bright and B McFarlane, 'Personal Liability in Proprietary Estoppel' (2005) 69 *Conveyancer and Property Lawyer* 14; J Neyers, 'A Coherent Law of Estoppel?' (2003) 2 *Journal of Obligations and Remedies* 25, 31–33; D Nolan, 'Following in their Footsteps: Equitable Estoppel in Australia and the United States' (2000) 11 *King's College Law Journal* 202.

[62] Handley, above n 21, para 13.029; S Wilken and K Ghaly, *The Law of Waiver, Variation and Estoppel*, 3rd edn (Oxford, Oxford University Press, 2012) paras 8.09, 8.82; R Halson, 'The Offensive Limits of Promissory Estoppel' [1999] *Lloyd's Maritime and Commercial Law Quarterly* 256, 277.

are distinct, and the principles governing the granting of relief are different.[63] In the US, an offensive doctrine of promissory estoppel has co-existed for decades with the enforcement of contractual bargains, which it does not undermine but complements.[64] Moreover, if recognition of an offensive doctrine of promissory estoppel would create incoherence with the law of contract, it is difficult to see why the application of the principle of proprietary estoppel in cases such as *Thorner v Major*,[65] *Giumelli v Giumelli*[66] and *Sidhu v Van Dyke*[67] does not also do so. In any case, if promissory estoppel rests on the broad principle of justice outlined at the beginning of this chapter, but its scope of application is limited for reasons of legal coherence, then it remains in substance a manifestation of the unified principle.

III. Does 'Promissory Estoppel' Itself Encompass Distinct Principles?

Another possibility is that promissory estoppel is not a distinct principle in itself, but a category that encompasses or confuses principles that are fundamentally different from each other. Within what might broadly be called 'promissory estoppel', Lord Denning distinguished between cases involving promises that were intended to affect the legal relations between the parties, which were binding if acted upon, even in the absence of detriment, and cases in which no promise was made but one party led another to believe that contractual rights will not be enforced, in which case detrimental action or inaction was required.[68] More recently, Ben McFarlane has sought to distinguish three different strands of cases within the territory understood as 'promissory estoppel'.[69] The first is the promise/detriment principle, which is similar to the core principle under discussion here, but requires a promise that the promisee could reasonably understand as seriously intended by the promisor as capable of being relied on by the promisee.[70] That principle spans the categories of promissory estoppel and proprietary estoppel by encouragement, and also justifies liability in cases falling outside those categories. The second distinct principle McFarlane identifies is that applied in *High Trees*, and the third is that applied in *Hughes*. It is those second and third principles that are of interest here.

[63] Robertson above n 20, 248, drawing on *Waltons Stores* (1988) 164 CLR 387, 425–27 (Brennan J).
[64] Restatement (Second) of Contracts, § 90.
[65] *Thorner* [2009] UKHL 18, [2009] 1 WLR 776.
[66] *Giumelli* (1999) 196 CLR 101.
[67] *Sidhu v Van Dyke* [2014] HCA 19, (2014) 251 CLR 505.
[68] A Denning, 'Recent Developments in the Doctrine of Consideration' (1952) 15 *MLR* 1, 5–6 (noting that the distinction 'has not yet been drawn in the cases but … the actual decisions are all consistent with it').
[69] Principally in the works cited above, n 24.
[70] McFarlane and Sales, above n 61, 613.

A. The 'Acceptance of Substitute Performance Principle'

McFarlane argues that the principle recognised by Denning J in *High Trees* is not a manifestation of equitable estoppel, but an entirely unrelated principle, which is simply that where a person to whom a duty is owed accepts particular action by the obligee as performance of that duty, the duty is discharged.[71] The principle, McFarlane suggests, is not grounded in the right-holder's promise to discharge the duty, nor in any detrimental reliance by the obligee, but in the right-holder's consent to the discharge of the duty. The main obstacle to the acceptance of such a principle in a case like *High Trees* itself, where a reduced rent was accepted, is the rule in *Foakes v Beer*, which holds that a debt cannot be discharged by acceptance of a lesser sum.[72] McFarlane argues that *Foakes v Beer* can be understood on a different basis, and this would clear the path to the acceptance of substitute performance principle.[73]

Normatively, McFarlane's 'acceptance of substitute performance' principle has some attractions. Detriment can be difficult to establish in contract variation cases, especially those involving the payment of lesser sums,[74] so dispensing with that requirement in this category of cases may be considered desirable. The doctrine of consideration is becoming more accommodating towards contract variations, and these developments are proceeding on the assumption that business people expect contract variations to be enforceable, and on the basis that certainty in such transactions is desirable from a commercial point of view.[75] Where underperformance has been executed and accepted, the desirability of finality in transactions provides a strong additional reason to treat the duty as discharged. McFarlane's 'acceptance of substitute performance' principle might make the cases it covers more straightforward to decide since everything would turn on proof of acceptance. But it would make the law more complex. While executed contract variations would be governed by the substitute performance principle, unexecuted variations would continue to be governed by the doctrine of consideration and a residual principle of promissory estoppel (or what McFarlane calls the promise-detriment principle).

If the 'acceptance of substitute performance' principle were to be authoritatively recognised, it would not undermine any argument for the unity of equitable estoppel. That is because it would not limit the ambit of equitable estoppel. Rather, it would be an additional principle which has different elements and a different rationale and would simply overlap with promissory or equitable estoppel in a case where detriment could be established. In the case of an executory contract variation, the practical benefit rule now leaves little room for equitable estoppel to operate, particularly if practical detriment is accepted as a corollary of the practical

[71] McFarlane, 'Understanding Equitable Estoppel', above n 24, 281–82.
[72] *Foakes v Beer* (1884) LR 9 App Cas 605.
[73] McFarlane, 'Understanding Equitable Estoppel', above n 24, 282.
[74] See, eg, *Je Maintiendrai* (1980) 26 SASR 101.
[75] See, eg, *Rosas v Toca* 2018 BCCA 191.

benefit rule, as it was in *Musumeci v Winadell*.[76] The 'acceptance of substitute performance' principle would similarly obviate the need for equitable estoppel in the particular circumstances covered by the narrower rule.

B. The 'Encouragement-benefit Principle'

The second principle McFarlane identifies within the ambit of what is understood as promissory estoppel is the 'encouragement-benefit principle' based on *Hughes*:

> where A claims that particular conduct by B has given A a right, A may be prevented from enforcing that right if B's conduct was undertaken in reliance on a belief, encouraged by A, that A would not in fact acquire or enforce that right, or would do so only on terms.[77]

Like the 'acceptance of substitute performance' principle, the encouragement-benefit principle requires neither a promise by A nor detrimental reliance by B. Rather, the principle is concerned with the benefit received by A and the injustice of allowing A to take advantage of a right which was acquired by A – as a result of action or inaction by B – on the basis that A would not acquire or would not enforce such a right. It is focused on the injustice of the inducing party acquiring a benefit, rather than any injustice resulting from detrimental reliance. The effect of the principle is only to prevent A from asserting the right in question. Although *Hughes* has long been interpreted and understood as a foundational case on reliance-based liability, the speeches were somewhat opaque and can be understood to have been motivated either by the detriment suffered by the relying party or the benefit that accrued to the inducing party from the forfeiture of the lease. It is not uncommon in equitable estoppel cases, particularly those involving the improvement of land, for action taken in reliance on an assumption to result in detriment to the relying party and gain to the inducing party. More broadly, it is not uncommon for gain on one side and loss on another to provide alternative grounds for legal intervention. But if *Hughes* can be understood to be justified by a broader principle, it seems to add unnecessary complexity to an already-complex area of law to justify it by reference to a novel and more narrow principle.

As with the 'acceptance of substitute performance' principle, if the encouragement-benefit principle were to be generally accepted, that would not undermine the unity of equitable estoppel because it would simply be another separate principle that would operate alongside the core principle. It would not cut down the ambit of equitable estoppel, but would operate alongside it. In some circumstances, the encouragement-benefit principle and reliance-based liability in equitable estoppel might yield alternative causes of action. What is significant for the present analysis is not whether the encouragement-benefit principle, if it exists,

[76] *Musumeci v Winadell* (1994) 34 NSWLR 723.
[77] McFarlane, 'Equitable Estoppel as a Cause of Action', above n 24, 368.

undermines the unity of equitable estoppel, but whether the decision in *Hughes* can help us to understand whether a promise is a necessary element of reliance-based liability in equitable estoppel.

IV. Is a Promise Required in Some Categories But Not Others?

A central plank in the case for the disunity of equitable estoppel is the notion that a promise is required for some categories of case, but not for others. If this is correct, then equitable estoppel is not, as a matter of form, a single doctrine. The existence of a promise requirement in some categories but not others would also point strongly towards the conclusion that, as a matter of substance, equitable estoppel does not rest on a single principle. It would suggest that the different categories might have fundamentally different normative foundations. In his book *Estoppel by Conduct and Election*, KR Handley treats a promise as a threshold requirement of both promissory estoppel and estoppel by encouragement, and is supported in doing so by references in cases in both categories to the idea that a promise is required.[78] Central to McFarlane's redrawing of the boundaries within equitable estoppel is the existence of a promise-detriment principle, which is similar to the core principle described at the outset of this chapter, but requires a promise made by the inducing party to the relying party as a threshold requirement. A core plank in McFarlane's argument that equitable estoppel is a confused and confusing amalgam is the notion that a promise is required in some categories of case but not others.

A. The Normative Question

The case for a promise requirement has some normative strength. Section 90 of the Restatement (Second) of Contracts suggests that a promise is foundational to the equivalent principle in the laws of the US. There are subtle differences of opinion as to what precisely is required to constitute a promise, but the notion of a commitment is clearly at the heart of the idea.[79] The making of a promise provides a strong justification for reliance-based liability. An inducing party who can be understood to have made a commitment bears a greater responsibility than one who has merely induced an assumption that he or she will act in a particular way.[80]

[78] Handley, above n 21, paras 11.013–11.014 (estoppel by encouragement), 13.008 (promissory estoppel).

[79] The Restatement (Second) of Contracts, § 2(1) helpfully defines a promise as 'A manifestation of intention to act or refrain from acting in a specified way, so made as to justify a promisee in understanding that a commitment has been made'.

[80] See further S Smith, *Contract Theory* (Oxford, Oxford University Press, 2004) 244; S Smith, 'The Reliance Interest in Contract Damages and the Morality of Contract Law' [2001] *Issues in*

A relying party who acts on the faith of a commitment may be considered more deserving of the protection of the law than one who acts on a weaker indication as to either the rights of the parties or the inducing party's future conduct.

The case against a promise requirement is as follows:

(a) liability arising from conduct short of a promise can be justified in the way explained at the outset of this chapter;
(b) such liability is supported by decisions of respectable antiquity and of the highest authority;
(c) such liability is consistent with liability in negligence in analogous circumstances;
(d) the cases indicate that people do in fact not uncommonly rely on assumptions induced by non-promissory conduct; and
(e) the cases show that a promise is an artificial requirement.

If a promise is not required, then three elements are essential. The first is that the assumption must relate to the inducing party's future conduct, not his or her present intentions. It is well accepted that an assumption as to the inducing party's intentions will not found an estoppel, for the simple reason that it is understood that a person's intentions can change, and so it is not reasonable to act in reliance on such an assumption. It could also be said that no estoppel can arise from a statement of intention because, strictly, a statement of intention is a statement of present fact. If the inducing party changes his or her mind, then he or she does not behave inconsistently with the assumption: the fact was true when the assumption was induced and it is no longer true. The second crucial point is that it must be reasonable for the relying party to adopt the assumption and to take such action as he or she took to on the faith of it. McFarlane suggests that it is impossible to justify liability if the inducing party has not made a promise.[81] He cites Stephen Perry's example of a philosopher who takes an afternoon walk at the same time each day, inducing his neighbours to set their clocks by his progress.[82] It is telling that not only does this example not involve any substantial detriment incurred by the neighbours, but it is difficult to see how they could incur any real detriment. Assuming the neighbours somehow did act to their detriment on the faith of an assumption as to his future conduct, the philosopher clearly should not be liable even if he knew of the action they were taking. Any change of position on the faith of the philosopher's conduct would be unreasonable given the nature of the assumption and the fact that it was adopted on the basis of observation rather than communication between the parties. Thirdly, and relatedly, the inducing party can only be seen as responsible for the relying party's plight if the inducing party could

Legal Scholarship 1, 23; PS Atiyah and S Smith, *Atiyah's Introduction to the Law of Contract*, 6th edn (Oxford, Oxford University Press, 2005) 127.

[81] McFarlane, *The Law of Proprietary Estoppel*, above n 24, para 2.80.

[82] ibid, citing S Perry, 'Protected Interests and Undertakings in the Law of Negligence' (1992) 42 *University of Toronto Law Review* 247, 285.

reasonably have foreseen that the relying party might act on the assumption to his or her detriment.

McFarlane cites *Cook v Thomas* in support of the idea that reasonableness of reliance is insufficient and a promise is required. In that case a landowner's daughter and son in law received what the primary judge found was 'intended to be and was regarded by the [daughter and son in law] as an indication of [the landowner's] expectation and belief that if all proceeded smoothly [they] would be able to live at the farmhouse after her death'.[83] The primary judge found, as Lloyd LJ noted, that:

> 'It was not intended to be nor was it taken by the Defendants to be an assurance that the Claimant was committing herself' to leaving Tretawdy to them, *nor that she would not change her mind as to the destination of the property*.[84]

The claim could be said to have failed for want of a promise or assurance, but it was clear that the judge regarded the landowner's statement as no more than one of a present intention. Any assumption that the farm would be left to the defendants was not, therefore, one that could reasonably be adopted or relied upon. On no view of the law can an equitable estoppel arise from a statement of present intention.

B. Analogous Negligence Cases

Liability for non-promissory conduct inducing a foreseeable, detrimental change of position may be justified by analogy with railway gate and navigation-light cases in the law of negligence.[85] In *Mercer v South Eastern & Chatham Railway Companies' Managing Committee*, a railway company that adopted a practice of locking a level crossing gate when a train was approaching was held liable to a person who was struck by a train when the company failed to lock the gate.[86] Lush J said that the company ought to have contemplated that those who knew of the practice would draw an inference from the non-closure of the gate.[87] The company had, by its own non-promissory conduct, created a responsibility to passers-by in relation to its own future conduct, which it could avoid only by giving notice to prevent the inference from being drawn.[88] Reliance was reasonable and reasonably to

[83] *Cook v Thomas* [2010] EWCA Civ 227 [36] ('*Cook*'), discussed by McFarlane, *The Law of Proprietary Estoppel*, above n 24, para 2.93.

[84] *Cook* [2010] EWCA Civ 227 [36] (emphasis added).

[85] See A Robertson and J Wang, 'The Assumption of Responsibility' in K Barker, R Grantham and W Swain (eds), *The Law of Misstatements: 50 Years on from Hedley Byrne v Heller* (Oxford, Hart Publishing, 2015) 49, 71–73.

[86] *Mercer v South Eastern & Chatham Railway Companies' Managing Committee* [1922] 2 KB 549 ('*Mercer*').

[87] *Mercer* [1922] 2 KB 549, 554.

[88] ibid.

be expected. Lush J said that: 'In this case I think that the defendants gave a tacit invitation, and that it was in consequence of his acting upon that invitation that the plaintiff was injured.'[89]

Similarly, in *The Queen v Nord-Deutsche Versicherungs-Gesellschaft*, the Canadian Government was held liable for the consequences of its failure to maintain coastal navigation lights in their proper positions.[90] Mariners were held to be 'entitled to place reliance' on the lights.[91] And in *Indian Towing Co v United States* the Coast Guard was held liable to the owner of a tug that ran aground when the Coast Guard failed to maintain a lighthouse that it was under no obligation to provide.[92] In each of these cases the defendant created a risk of harm by engaging in non-promissory conduct that engendered reasonable reliance on the part of others, and then failed either to behave consistently, or to warn those who might act on the assumption that it would do so.

C. Making Good Representations Cases

The idea that a relied-upon assumption induced by conduct other than a promise can give rise to liability finds historical support in the making good representations cases.[93] In *Hobbs v Norton*, for example, a settlor purported to create an annuity in favour of his younger son charged on lands that were entailed.[94] Some 20 years after the father had died, the younger son sought to sell the annuity. The prospective purchaser asked the defendant – the older son who had inherited the land – whether his younger brother had good title and his father had been seized in fee at the time the settlement was made. The defendant indicated that there was some doubt about the validity of the annuity, but encouraged the plaintiff to proceed with the purchase on the basis that he had paid the annuity for 20 years, implying that he would continue to do so. The report records that the Lord Keeper 'decreed the payment of the annuity, purely on the encouragement Sir George gave Hobbs to proceed in his purchase'.[95] The inducing party made no promise in the sense of any commitment to make the payments, but clearly induced the assumption that the payments would be made regardless of the validity of the instrument, and did so with the apparent intention of inducing reliance.

[89] ibid.

[90] *The Queen v Nord-Deutsche Versicherungs-Gesellschaft* [1971] SCR 849 ('*Nord-Deutsche*').

[91] *Nord-Deutsche* [1971] SCR 849, 863.

[92] *Indian Towing Co v United States* 350 US 61 (1955).

[93] Another clear example is *Hammersley v De Biel* (1845) 12 Cl & F 45, 8 ER 1312, where the relevant statement was expressly intended to be acted upon, but was expressed as a statement as to what the inducing party 'proposes' and 'intends'.

[94] *Hobbs v Norton* (1682) 1 Vern 136, 23 ER 370 ('*Hobbs*'). See further A Robertson, 'Revolutions and Counterrevolutions in Equitable Estoppel' in S Worthington, A Robertson and G Virgo (eds), *Revolution and Evolution in Private Law* (Oxford, Hart Publishing, 2018) 161, 165–66.

[95] *Hobbs* (1682) 1 Vern 136, 137, 23 ER 370, 370.

D. Promissory Estoppel Cases

Two leading promissory estoppel cases lend support to the proposition that, in spite of its name, a promissory estoppel can arise in the absence of a promise. If *Hughes* continues to be treated as a promissory estoppel case, then it is noteworthy that there was nothing in the landlord's conduct in that case that could be construed as a commitment to acting in a particular way. As noted earlier, the landlord's conduct was said to have 'justified and naturally led to' the tenant's impression that the notice was suspended.[96] Similarly, no promise or commitment was made in *Waltons Stores*. Waltons had an urgent need for new premises for its department store. The Mahers made it clear that they would need to begin demolition and construction work very quickly in order to meet Waltons' deadline. The terms of the lease were agreed on both sides and the lease signed by the Mahers. Waltons knew the Mahers intended to proceed immediately with the construction work and failed to communicate the fact that they were reconsidering the transaction. Waltons' conduct led the Mahers to believe that that Waltons would sign the lease and proceed with the transaction but made no promise or commitment to that effect.[97] When sending documents incorporating a final round of amendments, Waltons' solicitor noted that he did not have instructions in relation to each of the amendments, but expected approval to be forthcoming. He said: 'We shall let you know tomorrow if any amendments are not agreed to.' That could hardly be understood as a promise made on behalf of Waltons to proceed with the transaction. The key factors establishing the estoppel were the urgent need to proceed with the transaction, a reasonable expectation on the part of Waltons that the Mahers would be acting on the assumption that the transaction was proceeding, and then knowledge that they were doing so, and a reasonable expectation on the side of the Mahers that they would be told of anything on Waltons' side that might prevent the transaction from proceeding.[98] The only accurate way to characterise the basis of the estoppel in that case is in the language of an induced assumption as to Waltons' future conduct.

E. Proprietary Estoppel Cases

Three leading proprietary estoppel cases support the notion that a promise is not required. In *Inwards v Baker*,[99] a father encouraged his son to build a bungalow on

[96] *Hughes* (1877) 2 App Cas 439, 451 (Lord Selbourne).

[97] Mason CJ and Wilson J *Waltons Stores* (1988) 164 CLR 387, 408 did attribute an 'implied promise' to Waltons, but did not do so to explain why Waltons was liable, but only to express their ultimate conclusion about the effect of Waltons' inaction in the orthodox language of promissory estoppel. They said: 'To express the point in the language of promissory estoppel the appellant is estopped in all the circumstances from retreating from its implied promise to complete the contract.'

[98] *Waltons Stores* (1988) 164 CLR 387, 407 (Mason CJ and Wilson J).

[99] *Inwards v Baker* [1965] 2 QB 29 ('*Inwards*').

the father's land in the expectation that the bungalow was to be the son's home for life or as long as he wished to remain. Many years later the trustees of the father's will sought to evict the son. The primary judge found for the trustees on the basis that the father had made no promise, and the need for a promise was a focus of the appeal. The Court of Appeal found it sufficient to raise an equity that the father had encouraged the expenditure in the expectation that the son could remain. Dankwerts LJ observed that it was not necessary to imply a promise to justify the intervention of equity.[100] McFarlane and Sales have suggested that the decision could be justified 'by reference to some other principles, such as waiver'. But that is not the basis on which the case was decided. Both Lord Denning MR and Dankwerts LJ relied on *Dillwyn v Llewelyn*,[101] *Plimmer v Wellington Corporation*[102] and *Ramsden v Dyson*.[103] Denning MR held that circumstances gave rise to an equity, that it was for the court to say how the equity was to be satisfied, and that it should be satisfied by holding that the defendant could remain in the house for as long as he wished.[104]

In *Crabb v Arun District Council*, Crabb owned land which was accessed via the Council's land, with a right of way, at point A. Crabb requested access at a second point (point B) to enable him to subdivide his land. At a meeting the council agreed in principle to provide access at point B.[105] Crabb gave evidence that the council had made a firm commitment to provide access at point B, but the primary judge found that in this respect he was 'rather over sanguine'.[106] The parties then proceeded to act in the belief that the right would be granted.[107] The council fenced the boundary, installing gates at both point A and point B. Crabb sold the front portion of his land without reserving any right of access to the rear portion. The council later removed the gate and demanded a substantial sum for access at point B. The primary judge held that there could be no 'equitable estoppel, promissory or proprietary … "in the absence of a definitive assurance by the representative of the council"'.[108]

In the Court of Appeal, Lawton LJ disagreed with the judge's interpretation of the evidence and found that the defendant had given a firm undertaking that Crabb would be granted access at point B. Lord Denning MR and Scarman LJ, on the other hand, found that Crabb came away from the relevant meeting with no more than 'a confident expectation' that he would be granted the right of access in due course. The council had, however, encouraged the continuation of that expectation by abstaining from giving any indication that they were 'standing on their

[100] *Inwards* [1965] 2 QB 29, 38.
[101] *Dillwyn v Llewelyn* (1862) 4 De G F & J 517, 45 ER 1285.
[102] *Plimmer v Wellington Corporation* (1884) 9 App Cas 699.
[103] *Ramsden v Dyson* (1866) LR 1 HL 129, 170 (Lord Kingsdown) ('*Ramsden*').
[104] *Inwards* [1965] 2 QB 29, 37.
[105] ibid 185 (Lord Denning MR).
[106] *Inwards* [1965] 2 QB 29, 185.
[107] ibid 186.
[108] ibid 187 (Lord Denning MR, quoting Pennycuick VC at first instance).

rights', and by installing the gates, and did so in the knowledge that Crabb planned to act on the expectation by subdividing his land. An equity therefore arose against the council which was satisfied by requiring it to grant a right of way. The case therefore provides strong support for the proposition that a promise, commitment or assurance is not needed to establish an equitable or proprietary estoppel. It was enough that the council had induced the adoption of an assumption as to its future conduct in the knowledge that it would be acted upon.

In *Thorner v Major*,[109] a promise or assurance was found to have been made, but the evidence supporting that conclusion suggests that the requirement was not rigorously applied. The relying party (David) worked very long hours for many years without remuneration and gave up real and significant alternative career prospects in the expectation that he would inherit Peter's farm. His expectations were disappointed when Peter revoked a will leaving the farm to David (probably because of a falling out with another beneficiary) and died intestate. The facts were set out in detail and with great clarity by the primary judge, so we can precisely identify the findings of primary fact on which the estoppel claim was based. The primary judge noted that Peter was not given to direct communication and there was none in this case. David initially worked in the hope of inheriting the farm, and later in the developing expectation of doing so. The 'watershed' moment was when, at a time David was considering other career opportunities, Peter handed David documents related to life insurance policies and said, 'that's for my death duties'. That 'marked the point at which David's hope of inheriting (born of … various hints …) became an expectation'.[110] The primary judge said:

> Given the clear picture which has emerged from the evidence of Peter as a man of few words, who generally maintained his privacy about his personal financial affairs (even David only learned after his death of the extent of his monetary resources), and who hardly ever spoke in direct terms, I am satisfied that in making such a remark, and handing such a document to David to keep, Peter was intending to indicate to David that he would be Peter's successor to Steart Farm, upon his death, and that David's understanding to that effect was correct. I find that this remark and conduct on Peter's part strongly encouraged David, or was a powerful factor in causing David, to decide to stay at Barton House and continue his very considerable unpaid help to Peter at Steart Farm, rather than to move away to pursue one of the other opportunities which were then available to him, and which he had been mulling over.

Subsequently, 'Peter made remarks to David in conversation which, though not saying so directly, carried with them the implication that David was to have continuing long-term involvement with Steart Farm'.[111] The primary judge found that:

> such remarks encouraged the expectation which David had formed (in the circumstances I have already explained) that he would be Peter's successor to Steart Farm, upon his death, and encouraged David to continue with his very considerable unpaid

[109] *Thorner* [2009] UKHL 18, [2009] 1 WLR 776.
[110] *Thorner v Curtis* [2007] EWHC 2422 (Ch) [94] ('*Curtis*').
[111] *Curtis* [2007] EWHC 2422 (Ch) [98].

> help to Peter there. I am also satisfied that it was reasonable for David to understand them and rely on them in that way.[112]

The primary judge held that he would, 'if necessary' regard Peter's conduct in the 'watershed' conversation as 'tantamount to an assurance to David'.[113] On the basis of the findings of primary fact, it is difficult to see this as anything more than a conclusion that Peter created an expectation on which it was reasonable for David to rely. In the House of Lords, at least Lord Hoffmann and Lord Walker held that a promise or assurance was required to support an estoppel of this kind, and Lord Hoffmann, Lord Walker, Lord Roger and Lord Neuberger held that any such requirement was satisfied.[114] With respect, when viewed in light of the facts, this must be viewed as an artificial requirement. Clearly Peter led David to expect that he would inherit the farm, and that reliance by David was reasonable and should reasonably have been expected by Peter, but it is difficult to see anything in the nature of an assurance or commitment in Peter's conduct.

F. Conclusions about the Need for a Promise

Whether a promise should be necessary to found an estoppel relating to future conduct is a difficult normative question. While there is some strength in the argument that a promise should be required, numerous leading cases arising in different contexts make it clear that responsibility for detrimental reliance on an assumption as to one's future conduct does not depend on the making of a promise or commitment. While one or two cases may be explained on other grounds or treated as errors, the judicial instinct to recognise the justice of such claims is sufficiently longstanding and widely held and applied as to call to be understood and explained.

V. Do All Estoppel by Acquiescence Cases Fall within the Core Principle?

The point at which the unity of equitable estoppel breaks down is in the acquiescence line of cases. 'Estoppel by acquiescence' appears to include two distinct principles: one based on the inducement of an assumption and detrimental reliance, the other based on mistake and the conferral of benefit. Estoppel by acquiescence has been described in various ways, but the core case is one in which one person improves another's land in the mistaken belief that he or she has some

[112] ibid.
[113] *Curtis* [2007] EWHC 2422 (Ch) [125].
[114] *Thorner* [2009] UKHL 18, [2009] 1 WLR 776 [2], [8] (Lord Hoffmann), [22], [25] (Lord Rodger), [55]–[56] (Lord Walker), [72], [77] (Lord Neuberger).

rights in it, while the landowner stands by and acquiesces in the improvements with knowledge of the mistake. Such cases fit within the core principle discussed in this chapter only if they involve a detrimental change of position taken in reliance on an assumption induced by the land owner. That is so whether the assumption is induced by positive conduct or standing by. Lord Eldon LC appears to have had reliance-based liability of this kind in mind in *Dann v Spurier*, when he said that:

> I fully subscribe to the doctrine of the cases, that have been cited; that this Court will not permit a man knowingly, though but passively, to encourage another to lay out money under an erroneous opinion of title; and the circumstance of looking on is in many cases as strong as using terms of encouragement … Still it must be put upon the party to prove that case by strong and cogent evidence; leaving no reasonable doubt, that he acted on that sort of encouragement.[115]

John Mee and Ben McFarlane have observed, however, that estoppel by acquiescence is sometimes expressed in terms that require neither inducement on the part of the person against whom the estoppel is claimed nor, therefore, any reliance on the part of the person claiming the benefit of the estoppel on the first party.[116] The most influential such formulation is the statement of Lord Cranworth LC in *Ramsden v Dyson* that:

> If a stranger begins to build on my land supposing it to be his own, and I, perceiving his mistake, abstain from setting him right, and leave him to persevere in his error, a Court of equity will not allow me afterwards to assert my title to the land on which he had expended money on the supposition that the land was his own.[117]

To the extent that the 'estoppel by acquiescence' line encompasses cases in which there is neither inducement on one side, nor action by B on the faith of A's conduct, then those cases rest on fundamentally different foundations from those underlying the principle discussed in this chapter. As John Mee has said, the reason for the court's intervention in such a case is not that one party has led another to his or her detriment on a mistaken assumption, but that one party has failed to act when he or she was aware that the other was acting under a mistake as to his or her rights.[118] The early cases indicate that standing by in such circumstances constitutes equitable fraud only if the party standing by stands to benefit from the action taken by the mistaken party.[119] In *Huning v Ferrers* the prospective heir of entailed land stood by while a tenant improved land held under an invalid lease, then sought ejectment of the tenant after his father's death. It was held that the son's conduct in 'suffering the Plaintiff to go on in the Repairs, *with a Design to reap the whole Benefit thereof* when his Father was dead, was such a Fraud and

[115] *Dann v Spurier* (1802) 7 Ves Jun 232, 235–36, 32 ER 94, 95–96.

[116] J Mee, 'Proprietary Estoppel, Promises, and Mistaken Belief' in S Bright (ed), *Modern Studies in Property Law*, vol 6 (Oxford, Hart Publishing, 2011) 175, 182; McFarlane, 'Understanding Equitable Estoppel', above n 24, 295–97.

[117] *Ramsden v* (1866) LR 1 HL 129, 140–41.

[118] Mee, above n 116, 182.

[119] K Low, 'Nonfeasance in Equity' (2012) 128 *LQR* 63.

Practice in him as ought to be discountenanced in this Court'.[120] The focus on benefit was also emphasised by both Lord Cranworth LC and Lord Wensleydale in *Ramsden*.[121] Lord Cranworth LC justified the intervention of equity on the basis that it 'would be dishonest … to remain wilfully passive … *in order afterwards to profit* by the mistake which I might have prevented'.[122] Lord Wensleydale said:

> If a stranger build on my land, supposing it to be his own, and I, knowing it to be mine, do not interfere, but leave him to go on, equity considers it to be dishonest in me to remain passive and afterwards to interfere *and take the profit*.[123]

The acquiescence principle based on mistake and the conferral of benefit has some similarity to the core principle discussed in this chapter, which is concerned with inducement and detrimental reliance. Both may be described as principles of 'equitable estoppel' because they are concerned with inconsistent conduct which can fairly be understood and be characterised as unconscionable. As a matter of substance, however, the principles are fundamentally different because the inconsistent conduct of the non-mistaken party is considered unconscionable for different reasons in the two classes of case. While it is in form a principle of equitable estoppel, in its underlying motivations the mistake-benefit principle may have more in common with rectification for unilateral mistake than with the core principle of inducement and reliance discussed in this chapter.[124]

VI. Conclusion

The taxonomy of equitable estoppel is a question about the form of the law which turns on issues of underlying substance. While promissory estoppel and proprietary estoppel by encouragement may in form be separate doctrines, recognising their substantive unity is an essential step in the rationalisation of this area of law and the development of a coherent regime of reliance-based liability in which like cases are treated alike. Estoppel by acquiescence, on the other hand, may be more complex than it appears and may usefully be broken down by reference to the principle of justice that animates each class of case falling within it. More than 30 years ago Paul Finn asked whether estoppels in equity have 'a unity of principle and purpose – a unity that should ordain the future development of our law'.[125] The analysis in this chapter has shown that it is at least as difficult to answer that question today as it was 30 years ago. Despite that difficultly, or perhaps because of it, it remains important and useful to continue to scrutinise the extent to which form reflects substance in this area of the law.

[120] *Huning v Ferrers* (1711) 1 Gilb Rep 85, 85, 25 ER 59, 60 (emphasis added).
[121] *Ramsden* (1866) LR 1 HL 129.
[122] *Ramsden* (1866) LR 1 HL 129, 141 (emphasis added).
[123] ibid 168 (emphasis added).
[124] Handley, above n 21, para 11.012 alludes to this.
[125] PD Finn, 'Equitable Estoppel' in PD Finn (ed), *Essays in Equity* (Sydney, Law Book Co, 1985) 59, 59.

12

Trends in Tort Law: Bad Form and Addictive Substance?

JAMES LEE*

I. Introduction

This chapter examines the form and substance of tort law reasoning in the UK Supreme Court ('UKSC').[1] I take a thematic approach to identify trends in tort decisions and show that the framework offered by Atiyah and Summers in their individual and collective works on form and substance[2] is particularly helpful. It is argued that we can and should understand contemporary developments through the lens of the form/substance analysis.[3]

Lord Neuberger, who retired as President of the UKSC in 2017, has promoted the centrality of policy in tort reasoning.[4] In the year after Lord Neuberger's

* I thank PC Woo & Co and the Faculty of Law at the University of New South Wales for the generous support of Research Fellowships for this project. The chapter was written while I was a Senior Visiting Fellow, Gilbert + Tobin Centre of Public Law, University of New South Wales, and earlier drafts presented at the University of Newcastle, King's College London and the Obligations IX conference. In addition to those who attended those presentations, I am grateful to Stephen Bailey, Andrew Burrows, Robert Chambers, Georgia Davis, Liam Elphick, Neil Foster, Paula Giliker, James Goudkamp, Simon Lee, Mark Lunney, Nicholas McBride, Colm McGrath, Dan Priel, Craig Purshouse, Andrew Robertson, Desmond Ryan and Judith Skillen for helpful comments on various points. My thinking on this subject has benefited from lecturing on Tort Law for the Judicial College of England and Wales and a lecture from Simeon Maskrey QC for our students at King's College London, although I stress that none of the views here represents the opinions of any of the participants in those sessions: all views, and any errors, are my own.

[1] Without intending to be comprehensive, I make some comparative reference to Australia and Canada where appropriate.

[2] Principally of course in PS Atiyah and RS Summers, *Form and Substance in Anglo-American Law: A Comparative Study in Legal Reasoning, Legal Theory, and Legal Institutions* (Oxford, Clarendon Press, 1987) ('*Form and Substance*'); but I also draw upon their separate writings on the theme as appropriate.

[3] And perhaps also its cousin, also analysed by Atiyah, of principle versus pragmatism: eg PS Atiyah, 'From Principles to Pragmatism: Changes in the Function of the Judicial Process and the Law' (1979–80) 65 *Iowa Law Review* 1249.

[4] D Neuberger, 'Implications of Tort Law decisions', Northern Ireland Personal Injury Bar's Inaugural Conference (County Down, 13 May 2017), www.supremecourt.uk/docs/speech-170513.pdf and D Neuberger, 'Some Thoughts on Principles Governing the Law of Torts', Singapore Conference on

retirement, the Court decided several important decisions which demonstrate an endorsement of this view, and the cumulative effect of the decisions is potentially transformative for the law of tort. The relevant Justices are strikingly transparent in their engagement with these policy considerations, both in their judgments and extra-curial observations: there is clear scepticism over the utility of declarations of general principle. My argument here focuses not so much on the substantive outcomes of the decisions, but on the character of the reasoning. The narrative points to a prevailing teleology in the Court's approach which is at odds with tort law principle and treats form as 'formalistic' in a pejorative sense.[5]

This chapter takes three areas as illustrations of this trend – duty of care, actionable damage, and vicarious liability. As will be seen, the developments in each of these areas match against the form-substance distinction in different ways. The duty cases have seen an attempt to re-establish the approach to duty within a formal structure of incremental development, deprecating resort to 'fair, just and reasonable' considerations, but there is a question as to how such substantive considerations may nevertheless be factored into the determination of the duty of care. In respect of actionable damage, I argue that the decision in *Dryden v Johnson Matthey Plc*[6] represents a substantive shift in reasoning, albeit presented as within a formal framework. Finally, recent decisions on vicarious liability offer the clearest and most open instance of the Court's preference for more substantive[7] reasoning over formal considerations.

Although to an extent these are perennial questions in tort (and the common law more generally), what I argue is distinctive about the current trend in the UKSC is the open embracing of indeterminacy in the formulation of the relevant tests. The closing sections assess the consequences of the turn in tort reasoning in terms of institutional implications for the courts and the common law. I thus seek to build on Atiyah and Summers' work, which assessed the institutional factors that explained what they understood to be the predominant style of reasoning in English law.[8] Here, I argue that there is a reflexive relationship between the style of reasoning and the institutional structures – a change in the former has consequences for the latter. In 1988, Atiyah and Summers wrote that '[m]odern American tort law is shot through with flexible rules and principles, while English law remains in general loyal to the idea of law as a set of formal rules'.[9] We shall

Protecting Business and Economic Interests: Contemporary Issues in Tort Law (www.supremecourt.uk/docs/speech-160819-03.pdf, later published as (2016) 23 *Torts Law Journal* 89, but references here are to the publicly accessible version). cf PS Atiyah, 'Judges and Policy' (1980) 15 *Israel Law Review* 346.

[5] See Section II below on Atiyah and Summers. See also RS Summers, 'Form and Substance in Anglo-American Law' (1987) 14 *Cornell Law Forum (Faculty edition)* 2, 3: 'In stating that the English system is more formal, we imply no evaluative judgment. Our primary thesis is descriptive. Thus we do not use the word formal pejoratively.'

[6] *Dryden v Johnson Matthey Plc* [2018] UKSC 18, [2018] 2 WLR 1109 ('*Dryden*').

[7] Or perhaps 'substantivistic': Atiyah and Summers, above n 2, 30. See Section II below.

[8] See, eg, Atiyah and Summers, above n 2, 37–40.

[9] ibid 86.

see that, assuming Atiyah and Summers' views of English law were correct at the time,[10] some 30 years later, the English law of tort has undergone, and is undergoing substantial and substantive change.

II. Opening Formalities

Before developing my argument, I make some preliminary observations to limit its scope. I do not attempt to identify a definitive start date, but the trend can be particularly seen since the Presidency of Lord Neuberger, with my interest primarily in case law since *Michael v Chief Constable of South Wales Police* at the start of 2015.[11] My analysis is not limited to the tort of negligence, although that is where some of the key action has been seen. Section III considers duty of care, with the important 2018 decisions in *Robinson v Chief Constable of West Yorkshire*,[12] *James-Bowen v Commissioner of Police of the Metropolis*,[13] and *Darnley v Croydon NHS Trust*[14] (as well as a pair of cases concerning pure economic loss).[15] Section IV examines the approach to actionable damage in negligence taken in *Dryden*.[16] Section V then looks at vicarious liability with *Cox v Ministry of Justice*,[17] *Mohamud v WM Morrison Supermarkets plc*,[18] and *Armes v Nottinghamshire County Council*.[19] Further reference is made to other tort cases to illustrate the patterns of reasoning that I identify,[20] and also to assess how the lower courts are dealing with developments and dicta from the Supreme Court.

I shall not interrogate the case law on the defence of illegality here, partly because I have done so in previous work[21] and others have ably and fully covered

[10] In 1992, Professor Summers noted some indications of change: R Summers, 'The Formal Character of Law' (1992) 51 *CLJ* 242, 243: 'First, there are signs over the past two decades that overall levels of legal formality in the English system may be in decline … England has been adopting more and more rules that are relatively open-ended and thus formally not very definitive.'

[11] *Michael v Chief Constable of South Wales Police* [2015] UKSC 2, [2015] AC 1732 ('*Michael*'). See S Tofaris and S Steel, 'Negligence Liability for Omissions and the Police' (2016) 75 *CLJ* 128.

[12] *Robinson v Chief Constable of West Yorkshire* [2018] UKSC 4, [2018] AC 736.

[13] *James-Bowen v Commissioner of Police of the Metropolis* [2018] UKSC 40, [2018] 1 WLR 4021.

[14] *Darnley v Croydon NHS Trust* [2018] UKSC 50, [2018] 3 WLR 1153 ('*Darnley*').

[15] *Steel v NRAM Ltd* [2018] UKSC 13, [2018] 1 WLR 1190 and *Banca Nazionale del Lavoro v Playboy Club London* [2018] UKSC 43, [2018] 1 WLR 4041.

[16] *Dryden* [2018] UKSC 18, [2018] 2 WLR 1109.

[17] *Cox v Ministry of Justice* [2016] UKSC 10, [2016] AC 660.

[18] *Mohamud v WM Morrison Supermarkets plc* [2016] UKSC 11, [2016] AC 677 ('*Mohamud*').

[19] *Armes v Nottinghamshire County Council* [2017] UKSC 60, [2018] AC 355.

[20] There are many more examples in the recent Supreme Court jurisprudence which is beyond the scope of this chapter to consider: see, eg, *Montgomery v Lanarkshire* [2015] UKSC 11, [2015] AC 1430 (on breach of duty in disclosure of risk cases); *Willers v Joyce (No 1)* [2016] UKSC 43, [2018] AC 779 (on malicious prosecution); *Commissioner of Police of the Metropolis v DSD* [2018] UKSC 11, [2018] 2 WLR 895 (a human rights claim brought by victims of a serial rapist against the police); *JSC BTA Bank v Khrapunov* [2018] UKSC 19, [2018] 2 WLR 1125 (conspiracy).

[21] See J Lee, 'The Etiquette of Law Reform' in M Dyson, J Lee and S Wilson Stark (eds), *Fifty Years of the Law Commissions – the Dynamics of Law Reform* (Oxford, Hart Publishing, 2016); J Lee,

it elsewhere,[22] including in this volume.[23] But in the major UKSC decision of *Patel v Mirza* (in which the Court was divided), Lord Sumption framed the debate as being between 'those judges and writers who regard the law of illegality as calling for the application of clear rules, and those who would wish to address the equities of each case as it arises'.[24] That view is an example of the theme of tension between formal and substantive approaches that cascades through the debates which will be seen in the tort cases below.

The trend in the cases has also been identified by Lord Neuberger extra-judicially: in one 'remarkable'[25] speech, his Lordship suggested that:

> when it comes to the field of torts, the area covered is so large, disparate and innately incoherent that the problem of identifying and consistently applying established principles is particularly acute. Issues of policy are particularly prone to arise in tort cases, and to call into question any principles which may initially appear to be justified, even uncontestable. I suggest that this is true of individual torts, in particular the most significant and wide-ranging tort, negligence.[26]

My concern is that Lord Neuberger here underplays the value of form when engaging with tort – like the boy who points out that the Emperor is naked rather than wearing new clothes in the fable, Lord Neuberger seems to suggest that to emphasise form over substance is to mask what is really going on. His Lordship further noted that in respect of individual torts, 'the notion that there are clear principles which can be applied with confidence is much more the exception than the rule'.[27] Pursuing this view to its logical conclusion, it leads to little respect for form. But I wish to defend the idea that a structured and principled approach is a legitimate aim for the law of tort.

There can be a tendency to use 'form' and 'principle' interchangeably, and the same with 'substance' and 'policy'.[28] Much depends upon what one means by policy and principle, and my aim here is to illuminate the character of the courts' reasoning: for that purpose, Atiyah and Summers' interrogation of form and substance is helpful for what it shows us about the nature of legal reasoning, especially in tort.

'The Judicial Individuality of Lord Sumption', (2017) 40 *University of New South Wales Law Journal* 862, 874–80; and J Lee, 'Illegality, Familiarity and the Law Commission' in S Green and A Bogg (eds), *Illegality after Patel v Mirza* (Oxford, Hart Publishing, 2018).

[22] See especially the other chapters in S Green and A Bogg (eds), *Illegality after Patel v Mirza* (Oxford, Hart Publishing, 2018).

[23] A Burrows, 'Form and Substance: Fictions and Judicial Power', this volume, ch 2; B Häcker, '"Substance over Form": Has the Pendulum Swung too Far?', this volume, ch 3 and M Yip, 'Modern Equity – At the Edge of Formal Reasoning?', this volume, ch 10.

[24] *Patel v Mirza* [2016] UKSC 42, [2017] AC 467 [226] ('*Patel*'). On discretion embedded within a tight structure of formal legal rules, see Atiyah and Summers, above n 2, 79.

[25] NJ McBride and R Bagshaw, *Tort Law*, 6th edn (Harlow, Pearson, 2018) preface, xxii.

[26] Neuberger, 'Some Thoughts on Principles Governing the Law of Torts', above n 4, para 5. Compare K Burns, '"In this Day and Age": Social Facts, Common Sense and Cognition in Tort Law Judging in the United Kingdom' (2018) 45 *Journal of Law and Society* 226.

[27] Neuberger, 'Some Thoughts on Principles Governing the Law of Torts', above n 4, para 12.

[28] J Plunkett, 'Principle and Policy in Private Law Reasoning' (2016) 75 *CLJ* 366.

The framework offered by Atiyah and Summers in their book was designed to be 'sufficiently flexible to accommodate the very great complexity of legal reasoning',[29] and to demonstrate the interaction between formal and substantive dimensions of such reasoning. Here, I adopt their definitions: a *substantive* reason 'is a moral, economic, political, institutional or other social consideration',[30] while a *formal* reason 'is a legally authoritative reason on which judges and others are empowered or required to base a decision or action'.[31] A formal reason 'usually excludes from consideration, overrides, or at least diminishes the weight of any countervailing substantive reason arising at the point of decision or action'.[32]

Their approach offers considerable nuance precisely because it rejects caricature of legal arguments: 'although it may sometimes be carried to excessive lengths which deserve criticism, legal formality cannot just be condemned out of hand'.[33] They go on to speak of the difference between formal (pointing to the appropriate reliance on form, which is not 'per se bad')[34] and reasoning termed 'formalistic' (as denoting excessive reliance on form).[35] Their concern was that formal arguments can be described pejoratively as formalistic when critics are really taking exception to the substantive result.[36] Instead, formalistic reasoning should be understood as consisting of 'various degenerate species of formal reasoning'.[37] In a similar vein, Atiyah and Summers helpfully distinguish between substantive reasoning and that which may be 'substantivistic',[38] a term that they 'use pejoratively to designate first-level substantive reasons beyond their appropriate scope or range'.[39] Substantivistic reasoning is in turn a degenerate form of substantive reasoning.

As a final preliminary point, it should also be clear that my focus is on the actual reasoning of the judges, rather than in the jurisprudential characterisation of legal reasoning in the abstract. In this, I seek to follow Atiyah, who wrote, appositely for the purposes of this chapter:

> It is high time that more attention was devoted by theorists of the judicial decision to the way in which judges actually reason in their opinions, and the kinds of legal

[29] Atiyah and Summers, above n 2, 408.

[30] ibid 1.

[31] ibid 2.

[32] ibid.

[33] PS Atiyah, 'Justice and Predictability in the Common Law' (1992) 15 *University of New South Wales Law Journal* 448, 452.

[34] Atiyah and Summers, above n 2, 420.

[35] ibid 28–30.

[36] In *Moulton v Texas* (2013) PD–1889–11, Cochran J filed a concurring opinion in the Court of Criminal Appeals of Texas because 'I believe that this area of law has become overly formalistic and divorced from its original purpose of giving notice to the defendant': 'formalistic' perhaps better captures the pejorative sense in which 'formalist' may be used.

[37] Atiyah and Summers, above n 2, 420.

[38] 'To coin an ugly word': ibid 30. See also RS Summers, 'The Formal Character of Law' (1992) 51 *CLJ* 242, 251: 'the level of a formal attribute may be too low … Numerous examples from my own system could be cited in which legal ordering has floundered or is floundering because of under-formality. (Perhaps we need "substantivistic" in our scheme of possible criticisms, if not also in our lexicon.)' See also Summers, above n 5, 6.

[39] Atiyah and Summers, above n 2, 30.

> justification they offer. Furthermore, studying what judges actually do offer by way of justification for their decisions reveals (surprise, surprise!) that judges in all countries do not reason in the same way.[40]

In what follows, I shall examine what the reasoning of the courts reveals about the form and substance of the English law of torts.

III. Duty of Care

> The passages I have quoted, like all attempts to formulate principles of law compendiously and exhaustively, may be open to some criticism, and their universality may require some qualification, but as enunciations of general legal doctrine I am prepared … to accept them as sound guides. [Lord Macmillan in *Donoghue v Stevenson*[41]]

Over 75 years after a divided House of Lords recognised the modern duty of care in *Donoghue*, the correct approach to establishing a duty in the tort of negligence remains controversial. In the cases below, we shall see that the Supreme Court has disapproved the view that the supposed '*Caparo* test' – considering proximity, reasonable foreseeability of damage and whether it is fair, just and reasonable to impose the duty[42] – is the starting point for the analysis of a duty of care, or that it offers some unifying guide. Instead, that test is only to be applied in novel cases, and the courts should not be too ready to conclude that a case is 'novel'. On one view, this approach amounts to a reassertion of formal reasoning over the risks of discretionary decision-making if the third limb of *Caparo* is used to deny or impose a duty. We shall though see that there are differences among the Justices as to how 'orthodox' the position is[43] and where the boundaries lie, not least because, as Professor Robertson has shown, 'policy' may be used to refer to both 'broad considerations of interpersonal justice and considerations of community welfare[, which] are very different types of considerations'.[44] Using 'form and substance' in the sense explained in the previous section is therefore useful for understanding the complexity here. A trio of 2018 decisions on general duty of care considerations speak to these issues – *Robinson*, *James-Bowen* and *Darnley* – and I consider them in both chronological and logical order before examining the overall state of the law.

[40] P Atiyah, 'Review of Policy Arguments in Judicial Decisions by John Bell' (1985) 33 *The American Journal of Comparative Law* 342, 344.

[41] *Donoghue v Stevenson* [1932] AC 562, 614.

[42] *Caparo v Dickman* [1990] 2 AC 605, 617–18 ('*Caparo*').

[43] *Robinson v Chief Constable of West Yorkshire Police* [2018] UKSC 4, [2018] AC 736 [39] ('*Robinson*').

[44] A Robertson, 'Policy-based Reasoning in Duty of Care Cases' (2013) 33 *Legal Studies* 119, 121. See also A Robertson, 'Justice, Community Welfare and the Duty of Care' (2011) 127 *LQR* 370, 377–78.

A. *Robinson v Chief Constable of West Yorkshire Police*

The leading decision is *Robinson v Chief Constable of West Yorkshire Police*.[45] Mrs Robinson, an elderly woman, was injured when police officers collided with her while trying to effect an arrest on a suspected drug dealer on a high street in the town of Huddersfield. She sued in negligence: the Court of Appeal[46] held that there was no duty owed to her because it would not be fair, just and reasonable to impose the duty.[47] Hallett LJ viewed the case as 'a paradigm example of why the courts are loath to impose a duty towards individual members of the public on the police engaged in their core functions'.[48]

On appeal, the Supreme Court unanimously held that a duty was owed, and that the Court of Appeal had been wrong to characterise it both as a novel situation and also as one which did not satisfy the requirement of proximity.[49] Lord Reed gave the leading judgment, noting at the outset:

> Most of those issues can be decided by applying long-established principles of the law of negligence. The fact that the issues have reached this court reflects the extent to which those principles have been eroded in recent times by uncertainty and confusion.[50]

The approach in *Robinson* thus fits with the framing of the debate in *Michael*[51] in 2015, where Lord Toulson for the majority stated that it was 'paradoxical' that Lord Bridge's speech in *Caparo* had 'sometimes come to be treated as a blueprint for deciding cases, despite the pains which the author took to make clear that it was not intended to be any such thing'.[52]

In *Robinson*, Lord Reed noted that it was 'ironic'[53] that the *Caparo* test had taken on such significance when Lord Bridge had observed in *Caparo* that 'proximity' and 'fairness' 'are not susceptible of any such precise definition as would be necessary to give them utility as practical tests, but amount in effect to little more than convenient labels'.[54]

Lord Reed's reassertion in *Robinson* is an attempt to rein in the use of *Caparo*, with the concern that regular consideration of policy leads to less predictable decision-making.

45 *Robinson* [2018] UKSC 4, [2018] AC 736.

46 *Robinson v Chief Constable of West Yorkshire Police* [2014] EWCA Civ 15 [38]–[51] (Hallett LJ) ('*West Yorkshire*').

47 Arnold J additionally held that the police had not assumed any responsibility to the claimant: *West Yorkshire* [2014] EWCA Civ 15 [67].

48 *West Yorkshire* [2014] EWCA Civ 15 [51].

49 Lord Reed noted, somewhat archly, that 'Hallett LJ considered that there was no proximity between Mrs Robinson and the police officers, notwithstanding that she had been injured when they fell on top of her': *Robinson* [2018] UKSC 4, [2018] AC 736 [18].

50 *Robinson* [2018] UKSC 4, [2018] AC 736 [3].

51 *Michael* [2015] UKSC 2, [2015] AC 1732.

52 ibid [106] (Lord Toulson).

53 *Robinson* [2018] UKSC 4, [2018] AC 736 [25].

54 *Caparo* [1990] 2 AC 605, 618.

The *Robinson* orientation of the approach to duty of care does not mean that the courts ignore policy considerations – they are either subsumed into the supposed 'form' of existing principle or driven to other areas of the negligence analysis.[55] Exactly how this is to be done clearly concerned Lord Hughes and Lord Mance, who concurred in the outcome but expressed some reservations as to the extent of Lord Reed's reasoning. Lord Hughes endorsed the general approach to *Caparo* and positive acts,[56] but also spoke to the 'vital policy considerations' limiting the circumstances in which the police will owe a duty of care in respect of the investigation and prevention of crime:[57] considerations which his Lordship has elsewhere described as 'powerful, repeated and carefully considered'.[58] For Lord Mance, there was 'a genuine policy choice'[59] open to the Court, and the Court should:

> recognise the direct physical interface between the police and the public, in the course of an arrest placing an innocent passer-by or bystander at risk, as falling within a now established area of general police liability for positive negligent conduct which foreseeably and directly inflicts physical injury on the public.[60]

As Lord Hughes said:

> the error of *Anns [v Merton]*[61] lay chiefly in its effective imposition of an often impossible burden on a defendant to demonstrate that public policy ought to negate the existence of a duty of care. The relevance of considerations of public policy, such as those so fully adumbrated in *Hill*, *Brooks* and *Smith*, and the fact that they may indeed demonstrate that a duty of care is not owed, remains unchanged by the different formulation in *Caparo*.[62]

Lord Reed responded by saying that although he did not suggest that such policy considerations 'should be consigned to history', he was concerned to emphasise that 'such discussions are not a routine aspect of deciding cases in the law of negligence, and are unnecessary when existing principles provide a clear basis for the decision'.[63]

Atiyah and Summers considered that 'English judges believe that it is possible to make policy decisions … in a neutral sort of way without seriously impinging on the general, formal, rule-oriented nature of the legal system'.[64] The contrasting

[55] See similarly S Arnell, '*Robinson v Chief Constable of West Yorkshire Police*: A Re-interpretation by the Supreme Court' [2018] *Juridical Review* 128 and sub-section III.C on *Darnley* below.

[56] *Robinson* [2018] UKSC 4, [2018] AC 736 [98]–[102].

[57] ibid [103].

[58] *Commissioner of Police of the Metropolis v DSD* [2018] UKSC 11, [2018] 2 WLR 895.

[59] *Robinson* [2018] UKSC 4, [2018] AC 736 [95].

[60] ibid [97]. See also Lord Mance in *Robinson* [2018] UKSC 4, [2018] AC 736 [86] on combat immunity as a conclusion that no duty is owed, rather than a separate principle.

[61] A reference to *Anns v Merton London Borough Council* [1978] AC 728 ('*Anns*').

[62] *Robinson* [2018] UKSC 4, [2018] AC 736 [113].

[63] ibid [69](1).

[64] Atiyah and Summers, above n 2, 268, continuing that such 'beliefs are important, however ill founded they may be, because they influence the judicial view of the proper function of courts of last resort, and hence also influence the way they decide cases'.

certainty of Lord Reed and uneasiness of Lords Mance and Hughes when it comes to the role of, or for, policy reasoning, can be understood by using Atiyah and Summers' analysis of the interplay between formal and substantive reasoning: 'a formal reason usually incorporates or reflects substantive reasoning. Thus it is an admixture of certain formal attributes on the one hand and substantive reasoning on the other'.[65] It is this reflexive character of reasoning, especially in tort, that must be appreciated: once substantive reasons are incorporated into precedent, they can in turn form formal reasons which take their place within the structure to be applied.

B. *James-Bowen v Commissioner of the Police of the Metropolis*

In *James-Bowen*, the Commissioner of the Metropolitan Police had settled a claim with a terror suspect who alleged that he had been assaulted by police officers during the course of his arrest and detention. The settlement included an admission of liability and an apology for the 'gratuitous violence' of the officers in question. The officers subsequently sued the Commissioner in negligence, arguing that they were owed a duty of care in respect of their economic welfare and their reputational interests, and that the Commissioner ought to have taken care with regard to those interests in the conduct of the litigation brought by the suspect.

Following the guidance in *Robinson*,[66] Lord Lloyd-Jones accepted that the case was 'very clearly one in which it is sought to extend a duty of care to a new situation', and so *Caparo* was to be applied.[67] Foreseeability of harm and proximity (the relationship was akin to employment) were taken as established.[68] It was therefore necessary to consider the 'fair, just and reasonable' stage of the analysis: an 'ingredient [which] will be of critical importance in a situation where it is proposed that a duty of care should be imposed in novel circumstances'.[69] Lord Lloyd-Jones went on:

> the proposed duty will be tested against considerations of legal policy and judgment will have to be exercised with particular regard to both the achievement of justice in the particular case and the coherent development of the law.[70]

His Lordship considered the potential for a conflict of interest as between the employees and employer if the duty were to be imposed, albeit that it was not

[65] ibid 2.

[66] *James-Bowen v Commissioner of Police of the Metropolis* [2018] UKSC 40, [2018] 1 WLR 4021 [22]–[23] ('*James-Bowen*').

[67] ibid [23], although his Lordship accepted (at [26]) that *Calveley v Chief Constable of the Merseyside Police* [1989] AC 1228, in which a duty owed to police officers against whom disciplinary proceedings had been taken was rejected, has an 'important bearing' on the case.

[68] *James-Bowen* [2018] UKSC 40, [2018] 1 WLR 4021 [22].

[69] ibid.

[70] ibid [23].

a conclusive factor: the 'competing underlying policy considerations'[71] must be examined, which indicated that no duty should be recognised. A range of further policy considerations pointed against recognising the duty,[72] and so the Court held that 'it would not be fair, just or reasonable to impose on an employer a duty of care to defend legal proceedings so as to protect the economic or reputational interests of his employee'.[73]

James-Bowen is relevant here as it is an example of a situation accepted by the Court as novel, and thus justifying the application of tripartite analysis, in a climate in which the UKSC has encouraged the courts not to be too ready to apply the *Caparo* considerations. When the *Caparo* considerations were applied, the claim failed.

C. *Darnley v Croydon NHS Trust*

That the Court is being restrictive in its approach to 'novelty' is shown by the third case in the 2018 duty trilogy: *Darnley v Croydon NHS Trust*. The claimant suffered a head injury and went to hospital. At the Accident and Emergency department, he was told by the civilian receptionist that it would be four to five hours before he was seen, whereas the true position was that he would be seen by a triage nurse within 30 minutes. After 19 minutes, the claimant and his friend left and he went to his mother's home. He then suffered a deterioration in his condition and was taken back to the hospital. He suffered severe disabilities which earlier treatment would have prevented, and sued the hospital in negligence. The first instance judge and the Court of Appeal (with Jackson and Sales LJJ in the majority) both rejected the claim, with Jackson LJ disapproving what he considered would be 'a new head of liability for [National Health Service] trusts'[74] and Sales LJ concerned about the imposition of any such duty leading to defensive practices on the part of the NHS.[75] The Supreme Court however allowed the appeal. Lord Lloyd-Jones again gave the judgment, holding that the Court was not presented with a novel situation.[76] His Lordship held that:

> the present case falls squarely within an established category of duty of care. It has long been established that such a duty is owed by those who provide and run a casualty department to persons presenting themselves complaining of illness or injury and

[71] ibid [29].

[72] His Lordship explored the policy considerations, including the availability of litigation, the encouragement of settlements, disruption of civil proceedings, the potential for satellite litigation and the implications for legal professional privilege (*James-Bowen* [2018] UKSC 40, [2018] 1 WLR 4021 [34]–[46]).

[73] *James-Bowen* [2018] UKSC 40, [2018] 1 WLR 4021 [32]; see also the conclusion at [47].

[74] *Darnley v Croydon Health Services NHS Trust* [2017] EWCA Civ 151, [2018] QB 783 [53] ('*Croydon Health Services*').

[75] *Croydon Health Services* [2017] EWCA Civ 151, [2018] QB 783 [88].

[76] *Darnley* [2018] UKSC 50, [2018] 3 WLR 1153 [15].

> before they are treated or received into care in the hospital's wards. The duty is one to take reasonable care not to cause physical injury to the patient.[77]

The authority relied upon by Lord Lloyd-Jones was *Barnett v Chelsea and Kensington Hospital Management Committee*,[78] which concerned a failure to admit and treat men presenting as ill at a casualty department.[79] That though was a different case from the recognition of a duty in respect of information given to the patient, as Lord Lloyd-Jones went on to recognise:

> While it is correct that no authority has been cited in these proceedings which deals specifically with misleading information provided by a receptionist in an A & E department causing physical injury, it is not necessary to address, in every instance where the precise factual situation has not previously been the subject of a reported judicial decision, whether it would be fair, just and reasonable to impose a duty of care. It is sufficient that the case falls within an established category in which the law imposes a duty of care.[80]

The implications of what is meant by 'novelty' are examined in sub-section E below. For Lord Lloyd-Jones, the majority of the Court of Appeal erred because their judgments 'elide[d] issues of the existence of a duty of care and negligent breach of duty'.[81] Instead, such concerns as there were about the difficulties for staff in A&E departments were better accommodated at the breach stage of the negligence analysis, rather than by rejecting a duty altogether.[82] It is, with respect, far from clear that breach can bear the weight assigned to it by *Darnley*: but the displacement of some of the considerations[83] identified by the Court of Appeal from the duty to the breach stage is intended to justify the conception of the facts as falling within an existing category.

D. Pure Economic Loss

The UKSC has been less expansionist where a duty of care arises in respect of pure economic loss. In both *Steel v NRAM Ltd*[84] and *Banca Nazionale del*

[77] ibid [16].

[78] *Barnett v Chelsea and Kensington Hospital Management Committee* [1969] 1 QB 428.

[79] The claim in that case failed on the basis of but for causation.

[80] *Darnley* [2018] UKSC 50, [2018] 3 WLR 1153 [16].

[81] ibid [21].

[82] ibid [21]–[27]. Lord Lloyd-Jones drew support from James Goudkamp's note on the Court of Appeal decision: J Goudkamp, 'Breach of Duty: A Disappearing Element of the Action in Negligence?' (2017) 76 *CLJ* 480.

[83] In England and Wales, an unintended consequence of this approach may be that the Social Action, Responsibility and Heroism Act 2015 (UK) comes into play. The Act requires, when determining the standard of care, the court to have regard to factors such as whether the defendant was acting 'for the benefit of society or any of its members' (s 2) or 'heroically by intervening in an emergency to assist an individual in danger' (s 4), which would presumably be relevant in the case of the NHS. For further consideration of the 2015 Act, see R Mulheron, 'Legislating Dangerously: Bad Samaritans, Good Society, and the Heroism Act 2015' (2017) 80 *MLR* 88 and J Goudkamp, 'Restating the Common Law? The Social Action, Responsibility and Heroism Act 2015' (2017) 37 *Legal Studies* 577.

[84] *Steel v NRAM Ltd* [2018] UKSC 13, [2018] 1 WLR 1190 ('*Steel*').

Lavoro v Playboy Club London,[85] the Court rejected attempts to extend the scope of assumption of responsibility to cover the situations in the instant cases. In *Steel*, a lawyer negligently[86] misrepresented the terms of a lending agreement to the lender; the lender then relied on that misrepresentation, despite having the means to know the real terms of the agreement, and suffered a loss as a result.[87] Lord Wilson noted that 'no authority has been cited to the court, nor discovered by me in preparing this judgment, in which it has been held that there was an assumption of responsibility for a careless misrepresentation about a fact wholly within the knowledge of the representee'.[88] To rely on such a representation was not reasonable: the defendant had therefore not assumed responsibility for the misrepresentation towards the claimant.

In the *Playboy Club* case, a bank gave a negligent reference for a client of the club's casino, but the request for the reference was made by another company, Burlington, which the club used for protecting customers from embarrassment when the Club inquired as to their creditworthiness. Lord Sumption recognised that the *Hedley Byrne*[89] assumption of responsibility principle was 'capable of development',[90] but there could be no voluntary assumption towards the Club when the bank 'had no reason to suppose that Burlington was acting for some one else, and they knew nothing of the Playboy Club'.[91]

The significance of these two cases for my analysis here is two-fold. First, they are two of only three of the recent cases discussed here where the defendant won before the Supreme Court, *James-Bowen* being the third: the other decisions have all gone in favour of the claimant.[92] Second, both *Steel* and *Playboy Club* involved the application of existing criteria – the assumption of responsibility – to deny the claim in what was a 'novel' situation in that there were features that distinguished the cases from prior authority. *Caparo* was itself a case involving an attempt to establish a duty of care in respect of pure economic loss.[93] What is not clear is why the Court seems to regard the pure economic loss cases which it chooses to hear as

[85] *Banca Nazionale del Lavoro v Playboy Club London* [2018] UKSC 43, [2018] 1 WLR 4041 ('*Playboy Club*').

[86] Indeed, Lord Wilson stated that Ms Steel was 'no doubt … usually a solicitor of the utmost competence but on this occasion she was guilty of gross carelessness': *Steel* [2018] UKSC 13, [2018] 1 WLR 1190 [12].

[87] *Steel* [2018] UKSC 13, [2018] 1 WLR 1190 [38].

[88] ibid.

[89] *Hedley Byrne & Co Ltd v Heller & Partners Ltd* [1964] AC 465.

[90] *Playboy Club* [2018] UKSC 43, [2018] 1 WLR 4041 [7].

[91] ibid [16]. Lord Mance, it should be conceded, took a narrower view.

[92] In 'Tort Law and the Alternatives: Some Anglo-American Comparisons' (1987) 36 *Duke Law Journal* 1002, Atiyah advanced the thesis that 'American Law is more proplaintiff than English Law': ibid 1020.

[93] *Caparo* was relied upon by Lord Wilson in *Steel* [2018] UKSC 13, [2018] 1 WLR 1190 [22]–[23] and in *Playboy Club* [2018] UKSC 43, [2018] 1 WLR 4041 [8]–[9] by Lord Sumption (Lord Mance considered it at [20]–[22].

more straightforward compared with the evolution in its approach to duty cases in the more general run of cases.

E. Novel Approach to Novelty?

The UKSC has affirmed what may be understood as tort orthodoxy, in insisting that the common law should proceed by incremental development: the court should start with whether the case falls within an established category, or is sufficiently closely analogous to justify an extension, and only in a novel case should the *Caparo* test be applied. So Lord Reed said in *Robinson*:

> It is normally only in a novel type of case, where established principles do not provide an answer, that the courts need to go beyond those principles in order to decide whether a duty of care should be recognised. Following *Caparo*, the characteristic approach of the common law in such situations is to develop incrementally and by analogy with established authority.[94]

In *Robinson* and *Darnley*, the duties were held to be within orthodox categories, while in the Court's view, the proposed duty in *James-Bowen* was genuinely novel. The Court has reaffirmed that the search for a general principle is a vain one. The disavowal of a general unifying principle that would justify the imposition of the duty of care might be thought to be an example of form over substance. But I would argue that, without clarity or predictability as to when a case will count as 'novel', lower courts will struggle: even after the recent cases it is 'nonetheless still not entirely clear when a type of case is novel'.[95] Some of the uncertainty can be attributable to the different senses in which 'novel' might be used. A parallel might be the translation of the English word 'new' in French: 'neuf' means new as in 'brand new', while 'nouveau' means 'new to me'. How novel is 'novel'?

This challenge is most obviously seen in *Darnley*, where Lord Lloyd-Jones stated that the case fell 'squarely within an established category of duty of care',[96] even though there was no direct authority on the point. In *Steel*, however, the absence of authority in support of recognising the duty was taken as good reason for holding that there was no such duty. Of course, two cases are rarely the same, and so the fact that an instant case presents a 'precise factual situation [which] has not previously been the subject of a reported decision' does not *necessarily* make the case eligible as 'novel', since the law proceeds by analogy. But the breadth of construction of 'established categories' offered by the UKSC means that we lack

[94] *Robinson* [2018] UKSC 4, [2018] AC 736 [27]. His Lordship continued 'The courts also have to exercise judgement when deciding whether a duty of care should be recognised in a novel type of case. It is the exercise of judgement in those circumstances that involves consideration of what is "fair, just and reasonable"'.

[95] S Tofaris, 'Duty of Care in Negligence: A Return to Orthodoxy?' (2018) 77 *CLJ* 454, 455.

[96] *Darnley* [2018] UKSC 50, [2018] 3 WLR 1153 [16].

clear criteria as to when a case is truly 'novel': and the intended reduced scope for *Caparo* means that this matters. In her dissent in the earlier case of *Michael*, Lady Hale observed that to argue that 'the development of novel categories of negligence should proceed incrementally by analogy with existing categories[,] begs the very question at issue'.[97]

It may be that one way to rationalise the cases is to say that the UKSC has been concerned to discourage the use of Caparo in cases involving direct infliction of physical injury, as in *Robinson* and arguably *Darnley*:[98] in the latter, Lord Lloyd-Jones observed that 'The damage complained of is physical injury and not economic loss. This is a distinct and recognisable situation in which the law imposes a duty of care'.[99] But, applying *Robinson*, in *Sumner v Colborne*,[100] the Court of Appeal regarded the absence of a direct authority (even with the existence of a broadly relevant one)[101] for the claimed duty as indicating that it was a 'novel situation'.[102] Whether the case would be decided in the same way after *Darnley* is open to question.

i. A Canadian Example

The challenge of the duty of care analysis can be seen in the division in the Supreme Court of Canada ('SCC') in the case of *Rankin's Garage v JJ*.[103] The claimant and his friend were teenagers who, after drinking alcohol and taking drugs, broke into the defendant's garage: the claimant's friend found an unlocked car with the keys inside and invited the claimant to join him on a joyride in the vehicle. The car crashed and the claimant was severely injured. The Court had to consider whether the commercial garage could owe a duty of care to the claimant in such circumstances: a majority held that no such duty was owed. What is interesting for present purposes is that the division between the Justices saw both the majority and the minority claim to be applying fundamental principle which led inexorably to their preferred conclusions.

The majority decision was delivered by Karakatsanis J, who began by observing that 'this case is easily resolved based on a straightforward application of existing

[97] *Michael* [2015] UKSC 2, [2015] AC 1732 [193].

[98] I am grateful to Andrew Burrows for discussion on this point.

[99] *Darnley* [2018] UKSC 50, [2018] 3 WLR 1153 [16] (Lord Lloyd-Jones).

[100] *Sumner v Colborne* [2018] EWCA Civ 1006, [2018] 3 All ER 1049 (the purported duty concerned vegetation on land adjacent to the highway which allegedly obstructed the view of drivers on the highway).

[101] *Yetkin v Mahmood* [2010] EWCA Civ 776, [2011] QB 827 ('*Yetkin*').

[102] *Yetkin* [2010] EWCA Civ 776, [2011] QB 827 [29] (Sir Stephen Richards); no duty was recognised because 'the factors militating against the existence of a duty of care are in my view very powerful' (at [31]). At the time of writing, there was no indication of any appeal in this case.

[103] *Rankin (Rankin's Garage & Sales) v JJ* 2018 SCC 19, [2018] 1 SCR 587 ('*Rankin's Garage*'). See also the pure economic loss case of *Deloitte & Touche v Livent Inc (Receiver of)* 2017 SCC 63, [2017] 2 SCR 855.

tort law principles. This requires analytical rigour and a proper evidentiary basis'.[104] Her view was that the lower court's finding of a duty of care conflated mere possibility with reasonable foreseeability. But reasonable foreseeability required a 'higher threshold than mere possibility':[105] the contrary approach 'would fundamentally change tort law and could result in a significant expansion of liability'.[106]

By contrast, for Brown J dissenting (with whom Gascon J agreed), the case did not involve novelty, but instead 'involve[d] the unremarkable application of a category of relationships that has long been recognized as imposing a duty of care',[107] which was an act of the defendant foreseeably causing harm to the claimant. Brown J continued:

> The majority's approach thereby risks rendering meaningless a long-established category of relationships which have been found to give rise to a duty of care and undermining the viability of the categorical approach altogether.[108]

It must be conceded of course that a formally different approach to duty is taken in Canada,[109] where the SCC has developed its own formula drawing upon *Anns*.[110] But *Rankin's Garage* further illustrates the challenges and inherent controversiality of determining whether there is a duty of care: there is no universal recognition of when a case is novel and when it falls within a long-established category, so that both sides can claim that first principles dictate diametrically opposed answers. The formal constraints of judicial reasoning struggle to accommodate the substantive concerns, and judges can vehemently disagree over whether a case falls within existing principle, and, even then, within *which* existing principle it falls.[111]

To conclude this section, the UK Supreme Court's attempt to impose structure and clarity may be appreciated, along with the general deprecation of reaching

[104] *Rankin's Garage* 2018 SCC 19, [2018] 1 SCR 587 [2].

[105] ibid [46]: 'The fact that something is possible does not mean that it is reasonably foreseeable. Obviously, any harm that has occurred was by definition possible.'

[106] *Rankin's Garage* 2018 SCC 19, [2018] 1 SCR 587 [46].

[107] *Rankin's Garage* 2018 SCC 19, [2018] 1 SCR 587 [69], quoting *Cooper v Hobart* 2001 SCC 79, [2001] 3 SCR 537 [36] ('*Cooper*').

[108] *Rankin's Garage* 2018 SCC 19, [2018] 1 SCR 587 [75].

[109] Robertson, 'Justice, Community Welfare and the Duty of Care', above n 44, 370: 'The English, Canadian and Australian courts appear to adopt widely divergent approaches to the assessment of novel or contentious duty of care issues', Robertson goes on to demonstrate their similarities in practical application; A Robertson, 'On the Function of the Law of Negligence' (2013) 33 *OJLS* 31, 47.

[110] *Anns* [1978] AC 728; *Cooper* 2001 SCC 79, [2001] 3 SCR 537.

[111] In passing, I note that in his 'Tort Law and the Alternatives: Some Anglo-American Comparisons' (above n 92), Professor Atiyah referred to an American case with a certain degree of similarity to *Rankin's Garage*, and doubted that (at the time) there would have been liability if the same facts had occurred in England at 1022 fn 91: 'When I was a visiting Professor at Duke Law School in the spring semester of 1985, I was struck by newspaper reports of a case in Durham, North Carolina in which the parents of a sixteen year-old child recovered damages of $3 million against the Duke Power Company for alleged negligence in failing to lock an electric substation into which the deceased child had entered'. From my own research, this would appear to be a reference to the facts in the tragic case of *Cole v Duke Power Co* 344 SE2d 130 (1986).

for the *Caparo* test as a panacea.[112] But the Court has not offered clear criteria for novelty and it is difficult for the lower courts[113] to work out when a claim 'counts' as novel. The difficult choices for the courts over the establishment and extent of a duty of care are not solved by relegating them to a different stage of the analysis.

IV. Actionable Damage

The next example of the Supreme Court's approach to tort is *Dryden*[114] on actionable damage in negligence. My argument in respect of this case is that it is best understood as an example of 'substantivist' reasoning operating within a supposed formalist framework. The judgment of the Court, delivered by Lady Black, ostensibly works within existing precedent and principle, but can be seen to involve the use of problematic reasoning.

In *Dryden*, the claimants sued in negligence after having been exposed to platinum salts during the course of their employment in factories that made catalytic converters. This exposure was in breach of duty owed by their employers. They had developed platinum sensitisation as a result of this exposure, and the issue was whether this condition amounted to actionable damage. The condition was itself asymptomatic but further exposure to platinum salts was likely to develop into an allergy, and it was accepted that an allergy would amount to actionable damage. Once the claimants were identified as having sensitisation, they were redeployed into other roles to prevent further exposure, or had their employment terminated. There was no risk of exposure to platinum salts in everyday life.[115]

The key authorities relied upon were *Cartledge v Jobling*[116] and *Rothwell v Chemical Insulating Co Ltd*.[117] In *Cartledge*, Lord Pearce said that 'it is a question of fact in each case whether a man has suffered material damage by any physical changes in his body', and that where such changes were symptomless, they may fall 'within the principle of de minimis non curat lex'.[118] But where 'unusual exertion or … the onslaught of disease' led to suffering, that indicated that the damage was substantial.[119] In *Rothwell*, the claimants had developed pleural plaques as the

[112] See the dissent of Lord Lloyd of Berwick in *The Nicholas H* [1996] AC 211, 230; See also TK Feng, 'Of Duty' (1996) 112 *LQR* 209, 215. Compare further C Witting, 'Duty of Care: An Analytical Approach' (2005) 25 *OJLS* 33 and J Stapleton, 'Duty of Care Factors: A Selection from the Judicial Menus' in P Cane and J Stapleton (eds), *The Law of Obligations: Essays in Celebration of John Fleming* (Oxford, Clarendon Press, 1998).

[113] Robertson has argued, based on an empirical analysis of case law, that reasoning with respect to duty of care cases varies as between first instance, intermediate and final appellate levels: Robertson, 'Policy-based Reasoning in Duty of Care Cases', above n 44, 137.

[114] *Dryden* [2018] UKSC 18, [2018] 2 WLR 1109.

[115] ibid [7].

[116] *Cartledge v Jobling* [1963] AC 758 ('*Cartledge*').

[117] *Rothwell v Chemical Insulating Co Ltd* [2007] UKHL 39, [2008] AC 281 ('*Rothwell*').

[118] *Cartledge* [1963] AC 758, 778–79.

[119] ibid.

result of exposure to asbestos: these were markers of exposure, but asymptomatic and not harmful in themselves. Their claims failed: 'damages are given for injuries that cause harm, not for injuries that are harmless'.[120]

Applying these authorities, both Jay J at first instance[121] and the Court of Appeal[122] held that the claims failed. As Sales LJ put it, 'platinum sensitisation is not harmful in itself in any relevant sense'.[123] The Supreme Court however held that the claimants had suffered actionable damage: Lady Black reached her conclusion on the following basis:

> What has happened to the claimants is that their bodily capacity for work has been impaired and they are therefore significantly worse off. They have, in my view, suffered actionable bodily damage, or personal injury, which, *given its impact on their lives*, is certainly more than negligible.[124]

The Court was persuaded by the submission made by counsel for the claimants that the position of the individual employee case was that, after the exposure, 'tomorrow I can't do what I can do today'.[125] Although their condition was symptomless, it was a 'physiological change' that had an effect on their 'capability':

> As Lord Pearce said in *Cartledge*, it is a question of fact in each case whether a man has suffered material damage by any physical changes in his body. It is a question of fact that must be determined in the light of the legal principles applicable to personal injury actions, and this case has provided a useful opportunity to clarify some of those principles. The process has led me … to differ from Jay J and the Court of Appeal and to conclude that the concept of actionable personal injury is sufficiently broad to include the damage suffered by these claimants, which is far from negligible.[126]

Lady Black did not claim to depart from previous authority here: it is a different judgment over the application of the law to the relevant facts, after a 'clarification' of the applicable principles. But that clarification seems to be a 'broadening' of the concept: in particular, as seen above, Lord Pearce was speaking in the context of physical changes which might not be noticeable in ordinary daily life but could be revealed by unusual exertion.

There are several different ways of looking at *Dryden*. At first sight, and on its own terms, the Supreme Court simply took a different view of the level of injury suffered by the claimants, and this was a disagreement over the application of existing law to the specific facts. However, although it purports to work within the

[120] *Rothwell* [2007] UKHL 39, [2008] AC 281 [47].

[121] *Greenway v Johnson Matthew* [2014] EWHC 3957 (QB) (when the lead claimant was a Daniel Greenway – Jay J also considered the application of principles relating to actionable damage in [177]–[181], [444]–[468]).

[122] *Greenway v Johnson Matthey* [2016] EWCA Civ 408, [2016] 1 WLR 4487 ('*Greenway*').

[123] *Greenway* [2016] EWCA Civ 408, [2016] 1 WLR 4487 [30].

[124] *Dryden* [2018] UKSC 18, [2018] 2 WLR 1109 [40] (emphasis added).

[125] Submission in argument by Robert Weir QC: video of argument in the case is available (for a limited period) on the UKSC website here: www.supremecourt.uk/cases/uksc-2016-0140.html.

[126] *Dryden* [2018] UKSC 18, [2018] 2 WLR 1109 [48] (footnote omitted).

framework of previous case law, it is better to view *Dryden* as part of the narrative identified in this chapter, for Lady Black's approach certainly fits the wider trend of reasoning. There is no particular endorsement of the *Rothwell* approach, and the reasoning is result-orientated reasoning backwards from the fact that the claimants have suffered loss of amenity and an ability to work, rather than working out that they have suffered an actionable injury from which they could then claim for consequential losses.[127] At best it is, as Morgan puts it 'a decision at the very limit of "personal injury"'.[128]

With the Court having held that the claimants had suffered actionable personal injury, it was thus unnecessary to consider the claimants' alternative claim to be able to recover for pure economic loss[129] (which was a key driver of their action).[130] An alternative, not considered by the Supreme Court, would be to conceive of the claimant's claim as being for 'preventive damages', in that loss was incurred as a result of the defendant's breach, as it was necessary for the claimants to take steps to prevent the development of injury.[131] Given how the appeal was resolved by the Supreme Court, however, the issue was not considered.[132]

The *Dryden* reinterpretation of the actionable damage requirement, so that it concerns whether overall the claimant is worse off, has expansive potential: there are already examples of claimants seeking to extend the concept of actionable damage yet further, although the courts have not been receptive. In one such case, Stewart J described an attempt to include fear within the scope of actionable personal injury as 'wholly impermissible on authority'.[133] Even those who welcome the outcome in *Darnley* recognise its innovation, with Professor Brodie describing the decision as a 'laudable common law reform'.[134] Atiyah and Summers observed this feature of some legal changes, in a passage that can be perfectly applied to the reasoning in *Dryden*:

> change is glossed over, if not obscured altogether, by the judicial tendency … to claim that a new decision does not really amount to a change at all. On the other hand, the judge may advance reasons of substance for what the law ought to be, and then render

[127] For a critique of similarly instrumental reasoning in another context, see J Lee, '*Yearworth v North Bristol NHS Trust*: Instrumentalism and Fictions in Property Law' in E Waring, S Douglas and R Hickey (eds), *Landmark Cases in Property Law* (Oxford, Hart Publishing, 2015).

[128] J Morgan, 'The Outer Limits of "Personal Injury"' (2018) 77 *CLJ* 461, 464.

[129] *Dryden* [2018] UKSC 18, [2018] 2 WLR 1109 [49]. Although we may note that the Court's generous approach to the claimants here contrasts with the more restrictive approach taken to the pure economic losses in the *Steel* and *Playboy Club* cases consider in Section III above.

[130] Morgan, above n 128, 464.

[131] D Nolan, 'Preventive Damages' (2016) 132 *LQR* 68. See also P Benson, 'The Basis and Limits of Tort Recovery for General Average Contribution Economic Loss' (2008) 16 *Torts Law Journal* 1.

[132] Regretted by Morgan, above n 128, 463.

[133] *Kimathi v The Foreign and Commonwealth Office* [2018] EWHC 1305 (QB) [22]. See also *Network Rail Infrastructure Ltd v Williams* [2018] EWCA Civ 1514, [2018] 3 WLR 1105 [74] (Sir Terence Etherton MR).

[134] D Brodie, 'Employers' Liability and Allocation of Risk' (2018) 47 *Industrial Law Journal* 431, 433. See also J Fulbrook, '*Dryden v Johnson Matthey*: Case Comment' [2018] *Journal of Personal Injury Law* C138, C140.

a decision stating that the law already is what it ought to be. The result is that it is often unclear whether the judges are spelling out the reasons of substance embedded in the formal law involved, or changing the law.[135]

Dryden thus ties into the theme of the Supreme Court taking a more generous view of either principles or their application to the facts in favour of claimants. Though presented as working within the formal framework of existing authority, Lady Black's judgment develops the law by relying on reasons of substance to broaden the scope of actionable damage.[136]

V. Vicarious Liability

Vicarious Liability (on which Atiyah wrote the seminal text)[137] has seen considerable development in the past two decades, principally in the wake of revelations about the 'widespread evil'[138] of institutional physical and sexual abuse. The traditional approach to establishing such liability requires three elements: the tortfeasor must have committed a tort,[139] the tortfeasor must have been in a relationship with the defendant capable of giving rise to liability (typically, but not limited to, employment), and the tort must have been committed in the course of that relationship (or be sufficiently connected to it). That basic framework continues to apply, but 'in a revamped form',[140] as the UKSC has considered the doctrine four times in the past six years, with a significant expansion in the scope of liability. The recent Supreme Court case law began with the decision in *Various Claimants v Catholic Child Welfare Society*,[141] in which Lord Phillips led the Court in revising the approach to the relationship stage of the inquiry, in which Lord Phillips identified five policy reasons justifying the imposition of vicarious liability as 'fair, just and reasonable'.[142]

i) The employer is more likely to have the means to compensate the victim than the employee and can be expected to have insured against that liability;
ii) The tort will have been committed as a result of activity being taken by the employee on behalf of the employer;

[135] Atiyah and Summers, above n 2, 148. See also P Mitchell 'Patterns of Legal Change' (2012) 65 *Current Legal Problems* 177, 179.

[136] Nor should this be taken to be an approach which is unsympathetic towards the claimants: my critique is directed at the reasoning in the case. See, eg, D Nolan 'Rights, Damage and Loss' (2017) 37 *OJLS* 255, 274.

[137] PS Atiyah, *Vicarious Liability in the Law of Torts* (London, Butterworths, 1969).

[138] *The Catholic Child Welfare Society v Various Claimants and The Institute of the Brothers of the Christian Schools* [2012] UKSC 56, [2013] 2 AC 1 [83] (Lord Phillips) ('*CCWS*').

[139] 'Vicarious liability is not in itself a tort. It is a legal rule which imposes liability for someone else's tort' *Sophocleous v The Secretary of State for Foreign and Commonwealth Affairs* [2018] EWCA Civ 2167 [17] (Longmore LJ).

[140] *Grubb v Shannon* [2018] SC GLA 13, 2018 SLT (Sh Ct) 193 [62].

[141] *CCWS* [2012] UKSC 56, [2013] 2 AC 1.

[142] ibid [35].

iii) The employee's activity is likely to be part of the business activity of the employer;
iv) The employer, by employing the employee to carry on the activity will have created the risk of the tort committed by the employee;
v) The employee will, to a greater or lesser degree, have been under the control of the employer.[143]

These policy reasons are not 'the same as criteria', but will 'overlap'.[144] Later in the judgment, Lord Phillips referred to that list of five factors as 'incidents of the relationship … that make it fair just and reasonable to impose vicarious liability'.[145] The expansive approach in *CCWS* has been taken forward by three more recent decisions.

Valuable scholarship delves in more detail into the policy choices in the law in this area,[146] and the problems with the way in which the law has developed. Goudkamp has written that 'no convincing justification for the current law has been identified',[147] while Giliker has argued that 'the broad test for vicarious liability, as developed in the UK, would seem [to] lack definitional certainty, is expanding from case to case and lacks a clear theoretical underpinning'.[148] I share such concerns as, even with the Supreme Court's recent decisions, certainty and clarity remain elusive.

My interest here is in what the reasoning in these cases tells us about the English courts' approach to tort law. This section proceeds in four parts: first, I analyse the subsequent UKSC decisions of *Cox v Ministry of Justice*,[149] *Armes v Nottinghamshire County Council*,[150] and *Mohamud v Morrisons*;[151] then I explore how the doctrine has been applied in the lower courts since those three decisions and the different Australian approach; and then finally the options for reform are considered. As will be seen, the embracing of open-textured tests poses a problem for the application of the law to the facts, a point borne out by the subsequent attempts to apply the Supreme Court jurisprudence.

[143] ibid.
[144] ibid [34].
[145] ibid [47].
[146] See, eg, D Ryan, '"Close Connection" and "Akin to Employment": Perspectives on 50 Years of Radical Developments in Vicarious Liability' [2016] *Irish Jurist* 239; C Beuermann, 'Vicarious Liability: A Case Study in the Failure of General Principles?' (2017) 33 *Professional Negligence* 179; P Morgan, 'Certainty in Vicarious Liability: A Quest for a Chimaera?' (2016) 75 *CLJ* 202; P Giliker, 'Making the Right Connection: Vicarious Liability and Institutional Responsibility' (2009) 17 *Torts Law Journal* 35; P Giliker, 'Analysing Institutional Liability for Child Sexual Abuse in England and Wales and Australia' (2018) 77 *CLJ* 506.
[147] J Goudkamp, 'Case Comment: *Various Claimants v Barclays Bank Plc*' [2017] *Journal of Personal Injury Law* C194, C196.
[148] Giliker, 'Analysing Institutional Liability for Child Sexual Abuse in England and Wales and Australia', above n 146, 532.
[149] *Cox v Ministry of Justice* [2016] UKSC 10, [2016] AC 660 ('*Cox*').
[150] *Armes v Nottinghamshire County Council* [2017] UKSC 60, [2018] AC 355 ('*Armes*'). *Cox* and *Mohamud* were heard together and decided on the same day in 2016, while *Armes* followed in 2017, but I consider *Armes* straight after *Cox* as it concerns the same stage of the vicarious liability analysis.
[151] *Mohamud* [2016] UKSC 11, [2016] AC 677.

A. Supreme Court Authorities

i. Relevant Relationship: Cox v Ministry of Justice

In *Cox*,[152] the claimant worked as a catering manager in a prison and supervised prisoners who were given duties in the kitchen. One prisoner spilled a sack of rice while carrying it to the kitchen and the claimant told the other prisoners to stop while she bent down to clean it up. Another prisoner ignored this instruction and tried to carry his sacks of rice past her: he dropped one of the sacks onto the claimant's back, causing her injury. It was accepted that the prisoner was negligent; the question for the Supreme Court was whether the prison could be held vicariously liable, given the absence of an employment relationship. Lord Reed, for the Court, held that she could establish a relevant relationship because the prisoner was carrying on 'activities assigned to him by the defendant as an integral part of its operation and for its benefit',[153] and 'the commission of the wrongful act [was] a risk created by the defendant by assigning those activities to the individual in question'.[154]

Lord Reed considered the judgment in *CCWS* and held that Lord Phillips had there 'aligned the criteria with the various policy justifications for its imposition'.[155] A relationship other than employment was capable of giving rise to vicarious liability if it satisfied the *CCWS* criteria (ie, the 'incidents' listed above), subject to the glosses by Lord Reed in *Cox*. Lord Reed then said:

> It may be said that the criteria are insufficiently precise to make their application to borderline cases plain and straightforward: a criticism which might, of course, also be made of other general principles of the law of tort … The court has to make a judgment, assisted by previous judicial decisions in the same or analogous contexts. Such decisions may enable the criteria to be refined in particular contexts.[156]

Furthermore, the criteria were not to be applied 'mechanically or slavishly'.[157] It was not desirable in the general run of cases to consider whether the recognition of vicarious liability was 'fair, just and reasonable'.[158] It may though be 'valuable to stand back and consider' such considerations 'where a case concerns circumstances which have not previously been the subject of an authoritative judicial decision'.[159] Lastly, Lord Reed made clear, revisiting a point in *CCWS*,[160] that the imposition of vicarious liability was not justified in principle merely because the

[152] *Cox* [2016] UKSC 10, [2016] AC 660. See also Burns, above n 26, 232.
[153] *Cox* [2016] UKSC 10, [2016] AC 660 [30].
[154] ibid [24].
[155] ibid [41].
[156] ibid [28].
[157] ibid [42].
[158] ibid [41].
[159] ibid [42].
[160] *CCWS* [2012] UKSC 56, [2013] 2 AC 1 [35](i) (Lord Phillips).

defendant had deeper pockets than the tortfeasor: 'the mere possession of wealth is not in itself any ground for imposing liability. As for insurance, employers insure themselves because they are liable: they are not liable because they have insured themselves'.[161]

ii. Relevant Relationship: Armes v Nottinghamshire County Council

In *Armes*,[162] the claimant had been in foster care arranged by the defendant local authority. She was placed successively with two couples, and was physically abused by the wife from one couple and sexually abused by the husband from the other couple. She sought to sue the authority, alternatively holding them vicariously liable for the torts of the foster parents, or liable for breach of a non-delegable duty owed to her directly. The Supreme Court rejected the recognition of a non-delegable duty,[163] but held that vicarious liability was established. Lord Reed again gave the lead judgment, observing that the approach from *CCWS* and *Cox* 'does not depart from the normative roots of the doctrine of vicarious liability, but provides guidance to assist in discerning circumstances in which the doctrine applies'.[164] Applying that approach, his Lordship held that an analysis of the statutory framework governing the council's administration of fostering justified the imposition of liability. A relevant element in the analysis was the 'ability to satisfy an award of damages': 'local authorities which engage them can more easily compensate the victims of injuries which are often serious and long-lasting'.[165] Since Lord Reed had stated in *Cox* that the depth of the defendant's pockets was not a principled justification for imposing liability, this express appeal to that consideration is somewhat surprising.

Indeed, Lord Hughes, dissenting, pointed out that Lord Reed had affirmed the limits of the 'deep pockets' rationale in *Cox*.[166] His Lordship described it as 'certainly possible, and maybe initially tempting'[167] to conclude that vicarious liability could be established in the case of the foster parents. However, the situation called for caution:

> Vicarious liability is strict liability, imposed on a party which has been in no sense at fault. … the extension of strict liability needs careful justification. Once one examines

[161] *Cox* [2016] UKSC 10, [2016] AC 660 [20].

[162] The claimant waived her right to anonymity when the case reached the Court of Appeal: *Armes (formerly NA) v Nottinghamshire County Council* [2015] EWCA Civ 1139, [2016] QB 739 [1].

[163] Imposing such a duty 'is too broad, and that the responsibility with which it fixes local authorities is too demanding': *Armes* [2017] UKSC 60, [2018] AC 355 [49]. My focus here is on vicarious liability, so I do not delve further into the non-delegable duties point, but see the work of Giliker, above n 146.

[164] Cox [2016] UKSC 10, [2016] AC 660 [57].

[165] ibid [63].

[166] *Armes* [2017] UKSC 60, [2018] AC 355 [77]: 'the first (deep pockets or insurance), as Lord Reed explained in *Cox* at para 20, cannot by itself be a principled ground for vicarious liability and tends to be circular.' There is some academic support for Lord Reed's approach on this issue – see AJ Bell, 'The Liability of Local Authorities for Abuses by Foster Parents' (2018) 34 *Professional Negligence* 38, 40.

[167] *Armes* [2017] UKSC 60, [2018] AC 355 [78].

> the nature of fostering, its extension to that activity does not seem to me to be either called for or justified, but, rather, fraught with difficulty and contra-indicated.[168]

This reasoning is compelling. Lord Hughes had sat in the Court of Appeal in *CCWS* (in which the Supreme Court also overturned the decision below); in that appeal, his Lordship similarly argued that 'the social utility of vicarious liability where it applies is not a justification for extending it whenever there may be social usefulness in doing so'.[169]

iii. Sufficient Connection: Mohamud v Morrisons

Mohamud concerned a vicious assault. The claimant went into a petrol station operated by the defendant's supermarket and asked to print a document from a USB stick. The defendant's employee, a Mr Khan, refused to assist Mr Mohamud, and racially abused him. Khan then came out from behind the kiosk counter and chased the claimant as he returned his car, dragging him away from the car and attacking him. Khan was certainly an employee, but the issue was whether his behaviour was either in the course of his working relationship, or sufficiently closely connected to it.

The Court of Appeal had held that Khan's conduct fell outside his employment. Treacy LJ held that 'the mere fact that the employment provided the opportunity, setting, time and place for the tort to occur is not necessarily sufficient … some factor or feature going beyond interaction between the employee and the victim is required'. Similarly Arden LJ said, 'Mr Khan's assault of the appellant did not arise out of what he had been employed to do. The assault should never have happened, but the employer is not to be held vicariously liable for it'.[170]

The Supreme Court, however, held that Morrisons was vicariously liable, with Lord Toulson giving the principal judgment. There was a two-stage test to be applied. First, the court must ask 'what functions or "field of activities" have been entrusted by the employer to the employee'[171] (which must be assessed broadly); and second, 'whether there was sufficient connection between the position in which he was employed and his wrongful conduct to make it right for the employer to be held liable'.[172] The closeness should not be measured as though on 'a scale of 1 to 10'.[173] Applying that approach, Lord Toulson held that Mr Khan's 'conduct in answering the claimant's request in a foul mouthed way and ordering him to leave was inexcusable but within the "field of activities" assigned to him. What happened thereafter was an unbroken sequence of events … [and] a seamless episode'.[174]

[168] ibid [91].
[169] *CCWS* [2012] UKSC 56, [2013] 2 AC 1 [36].
[170] *Mohamud v WM Morrison Supermarkets plc* [2014] EWCA Civ 116, [2014] 2 All ER 990 [61].
[171] ibid [44].
[172] ibid [45].
[173] ibid: that would be 'a forlorn exercise'.
[174] *Mohamud* [2016] UKSC 11, [2016] AC 677 [47].

According to Lord Dyson MR in his short concurring judgment, the changes in the case law 'have been prompted by the aim of producing a fairer and more workable test. Unsurprisingly, this basic aim has remained constant'.[175] Lord Dyson went further than Lord Toulson's point about some notional scale of closeness and endorsed the idea that this area of the law was bound to lack precision: 'To search for certainty and precision in vicarious liability is to undertake a quest for a chimaera. Many aspects of the law of torts are inherently imprecise'.[176] By a 'quest for a chimaera', Lord Dyson seems to have meant that it is a vain search for a mythological monster that cannot be found. However, there are, with respect, two problems with this chimaera metaphor: first, in Greek mythology the sighting of a chimaera was an omen of impending disaster; second, Bellerophon and Pegasus undertook a quest for the Chimaera and slew it,[177] so it is a search that can be successful.

B. Applying the Tests

The general approach of the Supreme Court across these decisions requires careful application of the law in the courts below, and has caused some difficulties.

i. Relevant Relationship

At the stage of whether there is a relevant relationship between the tortfeasor and the defendant, a marked area of uncertainty in the application of the *Cox/Armes* test concerns when, if ever, there may be vicarious liability for independent contractors.[178] That there could not be such liability had been a principle in the prior case law,[179] and was not directly engaged by the recent UKSC decisions. Since *Armes*, two Court of Appeal decisions have seemed to point in opposite directions.

In *Kafagi v JBW Group Ltd*,[180] a case concerning purported liability for the actions of bailiffs, Singh LJ considered *Cox* and *Armes* and observed:

> In recent years the courts have had to address the question whether there can be vicarious liability even where there is no relationship of employment in the strict sense but where there is something "akin to employment". However, it is important to note that this development has not undermined the conventional distinction between a contract

[175] ibid [56].

[176] ibid [54] (referring to Lord Nicholls' judgment in *Dubai Aluminium Co Ltd v Salaam* [2002] UKHL 48, [2003] 2 AC 366 [26]).

[177] Hesiod, *Theogony* (Cambridge, MA, Harvard University Press/William Heinemann, 1914) 320 and Homer, *Iliad* II.6.102.

[178] See (writing before *Cox* and *Armes*) J Morgan, 'Liability for Independent Contractors in Contract and Tort: Duties to Ensure that Care is Taken' (2015) 74 *CLJ* 109 and Atiyah, above n 137, pt VII.

[179] *Market Investigations Ltd v Social Security Minister* [1969] 2 QB 173; *Hall (Inspector of Taxes) v Lorimer* [1994] 1 WLR 209; *Biffa Waste Services Ltd v Maschinenfabrik Ernst Hese GmbH* [2008] EWCA Civ 1257, [2009] QB 725.

[180] *Kafagi v JBW Group Ltd* [2018] EWCA Civ 1157 ('*Kafagi*').

> of employment and a contract for services, which continues to be relevant in the vast majority of situations.[181]

Vicarious liability was not established. By contrast, in *Barclays Bank Plc v Various Claimants*,[182] it was held that the bank could be liable for a doctor who conducted medical examinations of applicants and employees on behalf of the bank and committed sexual assaults during the course of those examinations. Irwin LJ held that whether the tortfeasor could be defined as an independent contractor was no longer the test in the light of *Cox*,[183] even if it might offer a 'bright line' test:[184] 'If the Supreme Court had intended [the independent contractor test] to survive as such, it seems unlikely, given that formerly this was a decisive test, that the Court would have failed to say so'.[185] However, one might also say that it is odd that the Supreme Court did not expressly mention the distinction at all in *Cox*, the closest being a reference that vicarious liability would not extend to 'where a tortfeasor's activities are entirely attributable to the conduct of a recognisably independent business of his own or of a third party'.[186] As Irwin LJ noted in *Barclays*, he had agreed with Singh LJ's analysis in *Kafagi*. While the outcomes in the cases are not necessarily inconsistent, the two *approaches* are, with respect, not easy to reconcile, and that is a consequence of the breadth of the UKSC's guidance.[187]

ii. Close Connection

The cases applying *Mohamud* have seen the Court of Appeal follow the UKSC's lead in extending the scope of vicarious liability. In *Bellman v Northampton Recruitment*,[188] the claimant had been attacked by a director of the defendant company after the work Christmas party, when a smaller group including the claimant and director had gone elsewhere for further drinks after the party had ended. The altercation occurred after an argument relating to work. At first instance,[189] HHJ Cotter QC had applied *Mohamud*, noting 'continuing difficulties'[190]

[181] *Kafagi* [2018] EWCA Civ 1157 [21].

[182] *Barclays Bank Plc v Various Claimants* [2018] EWCA Civ 1670 ('*Barclays*').

[183] *Barclays* [2018] EWCA Civ 1670 [44], [47].

[184] *Barclays* [2018] EWCA Civ 1670 [61]. See also Giliker, 'Analysing Institutional Liability for Child Sexual Abuse in England and Wales and Australia', above n 146, 516–17. In any event, for Irwin LJ, 'as has now become tolerably clear from the fields of employment and taxation law, establishing whether an individual is an employee or a self-employed independent contractor can be full of complexity and of evidential pitfalls' (*Barclays* [2018] EWCA Civ 1670 [61]).

[185] *Barclays* [2018] EWCA Civ 1670 [44].

[186] *Cox* [2016] UKSC 10, [2016] AC 660 [29]. An example of vicarious liability being rejected because it was found that the tort was committed in the course of a third party's business is the decision of Cockerill J in *Razumas v Ministry of Justice* [2018] EWHC 215 (QB).

[187] Permission to appeal in the *Barclays* case was granted on 12 February 2019 (shortly before this collection went to press).

[188] *Bellman v Northampton Recruitment* [2018] EWCA Civ 2214 ('*Bellman (CA)*').

[189] *Bellman v Northampton Recruitment Ltd* [2016] EWHC 3104 (QB), [2017] ICR 543 ('*Bellman (QB)*').

[190] *Bellman (QB)* [2016] EWHC 3104 (QB), [2017] ICR 543 [46]: 'the boundaries of this form of strict liability have often proved difficult to identify.'

with vicarious liability doctrine, but concluded that there was 'insufficient connection' between Mr Major's position of employment and the assault. Indeed, His Honour viewed it as 'a world away' from the appropriate imposition of vicarious liability. 'Given the lack of certainty or precision in the test, previous cases, although all turning on different facts, do provide greater assistance than in other areas of law'.[191] The Court of Appeal though decided that vicarious liability was established: 'misuse of authority can occur out of hours or when the parties are off-duty, particularly by someone in a senior position'.[192]

The Court of Appeal went further in *WM Morrison Supermarkets v Various Claimants*,[193] in holding that the defendant supermarket could be vicariously liable for a data breach whereby personal information relating to thousands of Morrisons' employees was posted on a file sharing website. The motive of the tortfeasor was, by harming the employees, to cause damage to Morrisons, both financially and in terms of reputation.[194] The judge at first instance had been concerned that recognising vicarious liability in such a case 'may seem to render the court an accessory in furthering [the tortfeasor's] criminal aims'.[195] The solution to the problem, said the Court of Appeal, was to insure against losses caused by such behaviour. This was, apparently, 'not a reason for imposing liability, but the availability of insurance [was] a valid answer to the Doomsday or Armageddon arguments put forward'[196] by Morrisons as counting against a finding of vicarious liability in such circumstances. That rather opaque distinction demonstrates again the uncertainty over validity of the 'deep pockets' and insurance considerations in the wake of *Cox* and *Armes*.

iii. *The Australian Approach*

The High Court of Australia revisited the doctrine of vicarious liability[197] in *Prince Alfred College v ADC*,[198] another sexual abuse case. The HCA considered similar ground to *Mohamud*, and reviewed the English authorities, but developed

[191] *Bellman (QB)* [2016] EWHC 3104 (QB), [2017] ICR 543 [63].

[192] *Bellman (CA)* [2018] EWCA Civ 2214 [33].

[193] *WM Morrison Supermarkets v Various Claimants* [2018] EWCA Civ 2339 ('*Morrison v Various Claimants*'); although the case applies *Mohamud*, it is a coincidence that Morrisons was also the defendant in this case.

[194] *Morrison v Various Claimants* [2018] EWCA Civ 2339 [76].

[195] *Various Claimants v WM Morrison Supermarkets* [2017] EWHC 3113 (QB), [2018] 3 WLR 691 [198] (Langstaff J).

[196] *Morrison v Various Claimants* [2018] EWCA Civ 2339 [78].

[197] The law was thought to be uncertain after *New South Wales v Lepore* [2003] HCA 4, (2003) 212 CLR 511.

[198] *Prince Alfred College v ADC* [2016] HCA 37, (2016) 258 CLR 134 ('*Prince Alfred College*'); J Goudkamp and J Plunkett, 'Vicarious Liability in Australia: On the Move?' (2017) 17 *Oxford University Commonwealth Law Journal* 162.

a distinct approach based on whether the employee's role provided the 'occasion' for the wrongful conduct,[199] including consideration of any special role assigned to the tortfeasor, though this test was still a 'necessarily general' one.[200] The plurality observed that the 'identification of a general principle for vicarious liability has … eluded the common law for a long time'.[201] The Court expressly declined to follow the English and Canadian lines of cases, in particular disagreeing with the UKSC:

> such a test of vicarious liability [as in *Mohamud*], requiring no more than sufficiency of connection – unconstrained by the outer limits of the course or scope of employment – is likely to result in the imposition of vicarious liability for wrongful acts for which employment provides no more than an opportunity.[202]

The Justices also recognised the more generally expansive nature of the UKSC jurisprudence – if 'a general principle favours the imposition of liability it may be said to provide some level of certainty'[203] – and the Justices did not believe that it did or should reflect the common law in Australia. The Australian position is highly sceptical towards the breadth of the English test.

C. The Solution: A Return to Form?

In *Cox*, Lord Reed rejected the regular injection of 'fair, just and reasonable' considerations as being 'liable to lead to uncertainty and inconsistency',[204] but I would argue that vicarious liability demonstrates the high point of the UK Supreme Court's substantivistic tendencies, and the corollary is an increase in uncertainty, a point Atiyah and Summers recognised.[205] Professor Giliker has compellingly argued[206] that the present law is problematic, and Dickinson has suggested that rather than offer principled justifications, 'judges have relied … on a casserole of incommensurable policy reasons and general resort to notions of what is "fair" and "just" to support the doctrine'.[207]

Another feature which distinguishes the vicarious liability cases from the other authorities considered so far is the express engagement with external factors as

[199] *Prince Alfred College* [2016] HCA 37, (2016) 258 CLR 134 [83] (Plurality Opinion).
[200] *Prince Alfred College* [2016] HCA 37, (2016) 258 CLR 134 [130] (Gageler and Gordon JJ).
[201] *Prince Alfred College* [2016] HCA 37, (2016) 258 CLR 134 [44].
[202] ibid [83].
[203] ibid [45].
[204] *Cox* [2016] UKSC 10, [2016] AC 660 [41].
[205] Atiyah and Summers, above n 2, 23: 'acting on formal reasons may operate more certainly and more predictably (and they may be more efficiently self-applied) than always acting for substantive considerations.' See further ibid, 26.
[206] Giliker, above n 146.
[207] A Dickinson, 'Fostering Uncertainty in the Law of Tort' (2018) 134 *LQR* 359, 36.

a justification for a change to the liability framework. The evolution of business practices and the flexibility offered by the 'gig economy' were cited by Lord Reed in *Cox*,[208] and in *Mohamud* Lord Toulson pointed to the changes in economic enterprises.[209] Lord Toulson also spoke of:

> changes in social attitudes and the courts' sense of justice and fairness, particularly when faced with new problems such as cases of sexual abuse of children by people in a position of authority.[210]

Lord Toulson also presented vicarious liability as relying on a 'principle of social justice'.[211]

As with the duty of care in negligence, there is a lack of clarity as to when the potential costs of the imposition (or rejection) of liability can be taken into account by the courts. Lord Reed in *Cox* was not impressed by the speculation as to the possible financial consequences for prisons: 'like the Fat Boy in *The Pickwick Papers*, counsel sought to make our flesh creep'.[212] In both *Cox* and *Armes*, his Lordship responded to financial floodgate arguments by highlighting the costs (both societal and economic) of *not* recognising liability,[213] and we have seen in *Morrisons* that the Court of Appeal similarly dismissed 'Doomsday' arguments.

The Court of Appeal has repeatedly been found to have been too strict in its application of principle. At the time of their decision, though, *Mohamud* and *Armes* could both fairly have been considered cases beyond the reach of even a more generous approach to vicarious liability, hence the Court of Appeal's view in each case. But when the cases went to the Supreme Court, the claimants succeeded because the Justices broadened the reach of the tests still further. Subsequently, the Court of Appeal has responded by being more willing to find vicarious liability established.

The embracing of rules at a high level of abstraction is alarming: the common law proceeds incrementally, but the law should not collapse into a caricatured general principle that 'each case will turn on its own facts',[214] or that refinement can always be left to later cases. This is not to claim that substantive considerations are irrelevant to the process of judging in the field of vicarious liability, but rather

[208] *Cox* [2016] UKSC 10, [2016] AC 660 [29]. Compare the caution displayed by the dissent of Underhill LJ in the context of whether Uber drivers are workers for employment law purposes: *Uber v Aslam* [2018] EWCA Civ 2748 [164]–[167]: 'These are quintessential policy issues of a kind that Parliament is inherently better placed to assess than the Courts.'

[209] *Mohamud* [2016] UKSC 11, [2016] AC 677 [10].

[210] ibid. Compare Lord Dyson at [56].

[211] *Mohamud* [2016] UKSC 11, [2016] AC 677 [45]. See the critique by Dickinson, above n 205, 362, describing vicarious liability as 'no more than a blunt tool for giving effect to judicial instincts for social justice'.

[212] *Cox* [2016] UKSC 10, [2016] AC 660 [43].

[213] ibid [43]–[44] and *Armes* [2017] UKSC 60, [2018] AC 355 [69]–[70].

[214] *Prince Alfred College* [2016] HCA 37, (2016) 258 CLR 134 [131]. 'Applications of the approach must and will develop case by case. Some plaintiffs will win. Some plaintiffs will lose.' See Atiyah, above n 33.

that they should be offered within a better framework. As Atiyah and Summers put it, 'formal reasons are a very efficient means of planning and institutionalizing a general societal agenda for decision making':[215] the traditional requirements for establishing vicarious liability offered such a formal structure. In addition, such an approach may lead to the conclusion that the appropriate routes for redress are not to be found in extending the reach of vicarious liability.[216]

The appellant in the case of *Kafagi* appeared in person and submitted that there should be vicarious liability as 'this is only fair because "where you have control, you also have responsibility – where you enjoy the benefits, you must take the burdens that go with them"'.[217] One might be forgiven for thinking that recent cases suggests that this lay view is an accurate summary of the present law. It is hard to resist the conclusion that the expansive, substantive approach taken by the Supreme Court has led to a distinctly pro-claimant conception of vicarious liability.

Lord Phillips in *CCWS* said that the law of vicarious liability was 'on the move'[218] and Lord Reed in *Cox* that 'it has not yet come to a stop'.[219] The recent case law indicates that, with the preference for substantivistic reasoning over formal limitations, the law is at risk of being in perpetual motion.

VI. Institutional Implications for the Courts and the Common Law

The analysis so far has demonstrated that there are problematic features in recent UKSC decisions on tort. This penultimate section of the chapter reflects more broadly on the implications of these patterns of reasoning. Identification of the justifications underlying legal rules can lead to transparency, refined rules and a better awareness of their application: ideally, we would see form and substance each informing and improving the other. However, my argument is that the shift towards more substantive reasoning in tort law by the UKSC poses problems for certainty in the application of the law. Atiyah and Summers' project on form and substance advanced the analysis of judicial reasoning in Anglo-American law by highlighting how conceptions of the judicial role and different judicial methods

[215] Atiyah and Summers, above n 2, 432.

[216] 'Victims of wrongdoing are entitled to justice, but legal principle must be coherent.' A Gray, 'Liability of Educational Providers to Victims of Abuse: A Comparison and Critique' (2017) 39 *Sydney Law Review* 167, 197. See also (writing before the *Prince Alfred College* case) C Beuermann, 'Conferred Authority Strict Liability and Institutional Child Sexual Abuse' (2015) 37 *Sydney Law Review* 113 and A Silink and P Stewart, 'Tort Law Reform for Survivors of Institutional Child Sexual Abuse' (2016) 39 *University of New South Wales Law Journal* 553.

[217] *Kafagi* [2018] EWCA Civ 1157 [41].

[218] *CCWS* [2012] UKSC 56, [2013] 2 AC 1 [19].

[219] *Cox* [2016] UKSC 10, [2016] AC 660 [1]. Indeed, Underhill LJ has noted that 'we have now been told authoritatively more than once' that the law is on the move: *Unite the Union v Nailard* [2018] EWCA Civ 1203 [42] n 2.

shape legal doctrine as part of an ongoing iterative process. Atiyah also argued that the different traditions are 'partly influenced by a wide and reinforcing network of institutional and cultural factors'.[220] As Fleming wrote in reviewing *Form and Substance*, 'all legal cultures bear the imprint, most of all, of their institutional structures, some of them adventitious, others the product themselves of an evolving legal culture'.[221] In this section, I argue that these modern trends towards substantive over formal reasoning also challenge our understanding of the role of judges in developing the law.

At the time when Atiyah and Summers wrote, their view of English law was that it was highly formal, at least compared with American law. What is clear is that some of Atiyah and Summers' collective and respective assumptions about English law, and the law of tort more broadly, even if they were true at the time,[222] may no longer be accurate.

The first aspect goes to what is to be expected of the courts at their respective levels of authority. As the late Lord Rodger observed in a tort case:

> Part of the function of appeal courts is to try to assist judges and practitioners by boiling down a mass of case law and distilling some shorter statement of the applicable law. The temptation to try to identify some compact underlying rule which can then be applied to solve all future cases is obvious.[223]

Lord Rodger's comment was in the context of deprecating the search for a 'compact underlying rule' or 'any single touchstone'[224] for establishing a duty of care in cases of pure economic loss – his Lordship continued that 'appellate judges should follow the philosopher's advice to 'Seek simplicity, and distrust it''.[225] We have seen that the UKSC Justices have very much followed the idea that the *Caparo* test neither can nor should offer that single touchstone, that the test for actionable damage has been broadened in its application, and the formulation of general principles has also proved difficult in vicarious liability.[226] But the first part of Lord Rodger's quote is also significant – to what extent is the Supreme Court currently fulfilling its function of assisting judges and practitioners (and for that matter, litigants, students and academics)?[227]

English law's perceived formalism had the advantage for Atiyah and Summers that 'it can be faithfully and uniformly followed by lower court judges';[228] the UK

[220] Atiyah, above n 33, 461.

[221] J Fleming, 'Form and Substance in Anglo-American Law' (1988) 37 *International and Comparative Law Quarterly* 445, 446.

[222] For some scepticism on this point, see S Lee, 'Review of *Form and Substance in Anglo-American Law*' (1989) 105 *LQR* 147.

[223] *Customs and Excise Commissioners v Barclays Bank plc* [2006] UKHL 28, [2007] 1 AC 181 [51] ('*Barclays Bank plc*'). See also Atiyah and Summers, above n 2, 267ff on the Function of Courts of Last Resort.

[224] *Barclays Bank plc* [2006] UKHL 28, [2007] 1 AC 181 [53].

[225] ibid [52].

[226] See Section VI above.

[227] Though see Atiyah and Summers, above n 2, 357: 'It is very doubtful if many English judges see their opinions as addressed to university students or even professors.'

[228] Atiyah and Summers, above n 2, 339.

Supreme Court's recent turn in tort, with its attendant uncertainties, necessarily makes it more difficult for judges in lower courts to apply the authorities uniformly (without doubting their faithfulness). It is clear that the Supreme Court is taking its supervisory role in policing tort doctrine seriously in one sense, differing from the Court of Appeal on numerous counts. A noticeable point in the UKSC tort case law has been that it is both pro-claimant and pro-appellant – the Court of Appeal was reversed on the relevant points in each of *Robinson*, *James-Bowen*, *Darnley*, *Dryden*, *Mohamud* and *Armes*. Indeed, only *Cox* saw the lower court affirmed. And yet, I would argue that the Court of Appeal's decisions in each case constituted a faithful and defensible application of existing authorities at the time, barring a failure to anticipate the persistent expansion of tort liability advanced by the Justices. This ties into Atiyah's arguments about the need for predictability: 'it must always be remembered, however, that it is uncertainty that engenders most trials and appeals'.[229]

At present, predictability of the law risks being undermined, and nowhere is that clearer than in the case of vicarious liability. Lord Pearce observed over 50 years ago that the 'doctrine of vicarious liability has not grown from any very clear, logical or legal principle but from social convenience and rough justice'.[230] But, as I have tried to show, that does not mean that the courts, particularly the Supreme Court, should not seek to offer clear, structured guidance as to how the tests are to be applied now. Such predictability and certainty as there is only comes from the deduction that the courts are to continue towards the relentless expansion of liability.

As well as the implications for the courts, there are related issues for the institution of the common law in the present approach of the Supreme Court to tort. There is judicial recognition of this concern, as we have seen above in Lord Hughes' caution in *Robinson* and *Armes*. Similarly, in his concurrence in *Robinson*, Lord Mance noted:

> It would be unrealistic to suggest that, when recognising and developing an established category, the courts are not influenced by policy considerations … The courts are not a Law Commission, but, in recognising the existence of any generalised duty in particular circumstances they are making policy choices, in which considerations such as proximity and fairness, justice and reasonableness must inhere.[231]

Lord Reed responded to that concern in his lead judgment by saying:

> The courts are not policy-making bodies in the sense in which that can be said of the Law Commission or government departments. But the exercise of judgement about the potential consequences of a decision has a part to play when the court is asked to decide whether a novel duty of care exists, together with a consideration of existing principles and of the need for the law to develop coherently and incrementally.[232]

[229] Atiyah, above n 92, 1020 fn 80.
[230] *Imperial Chemical Industries Ltd v Shatwell* [1965] AC 656, 685.
[231] *Robinson* [2018] UKSC 4, [2018] AC 736 [84].
[232] ibid [69].

At its root, then, the debate here between the Justices is over the transparency of reasoning and the circumstances in which judges can develop the law, and the way in which they can do it (not least the limits on judicial decision-making, which must arise in specific cases).[233] But the references to the Law Commission[234] also allude to a wider issue about the limits of the courts' competence: they cannot engage in systematic reform of an area of the law, both because they lack the institutional resources to do so, and also because of their constitutional limits.[235]

The Chancellor of the High Court, Sir Geoffrey Vos, has expressed reservations in quite strong terms, suggesting in an extra-curial speech that 'the integrity of the common law could be at risk if we depart from its traditions'.[236] Sir Geoffrey continued:

> I think the integrity of the common law could be at risk if we depart from its traditions. I detect a greater willingness amongst modern judges to throw away the rule book. It is the job of the Supreme Court to develop the common law and sometimes even to depart from its own previous decisions. But such development and such departures need to be cautious and principled. They need to be responsive to changes in society and in business culture, and not simply based upon differences of opinion between successive generations of judges.[237]

The tale of tort cases examined here lends support to the Chancellor's views. In *Patel*, Lord Sumption described the common law as 'a body of instincts and principles which, barring some radical change in the values of our society, is developed organically, building on what was there before'.[238] But that capacity for development and evolution, recognised by both Lord Sumption and Sir Geoffrey Vos, also poses challenges in terms of the limits of renewal. We can point to the paradox of Theseus' ship, which has several formulations,[239] but we may take that by Plutarch:

> The ship on which Theseus sailed with the youths and returned in safety, the thirty-oared galley, was preserved by the Athenians down to the time of Demetrius Phalereus. They took away the old timbers from time to time, and put new and sound ones in their places, so that the vessel became a standing illustration for the philosophers in the mooted question of growth, some declaring that it remained the same, others that it was not the same vessel.[240]

[233] *Prince Alfred College* [2016] HCA 37, (2016) 258 CLR 134 [127].

[234] See Lee, 'The Etiquette of Law Reform', above n 21.

[235] I have addressed some of these themes more fully elsewhere: most recently in Lee 'Illegality, Familiarity and Law Reform', above n 21, and J Lee, 'Judging Reformers and Reforming Judges' (2019) 21 *European Journal of Law Reform* 15.

[236] G Vos, 'Preserving the Integrity of the Common Law' (Annual Lecture to Chancery Bar Association Annual Conference, London, 16 April 2018) para 4, www.chba.org.uk/for-members/library/annual-lectures/preserving-the-integrity-of-the-common-law.

[237] ibid.

[238] *Patel* [2016] UKSC 42, [2017] AC 467 [226].

[239] For instance, in a variation which does not apply here: Thomas Hobbes postulated a second ship constructed by the repairman using all of the planks from Theseus' original ship.

[240] Plutarch, *Plutarch's Lives*, B Perrin trans (Cambridge, MA, Harvard University Press/William Heinemann, 1914) 1.

The same question may be applied for tort: when does the replacement of tests one by one, or gradual evolution in their application[241] amount to such significant change that the overall integrity of this area of the law has itself changed? One must not press this metaphor so far as to become wooden itself,[242] but I would argue that the cumulative effect of the changes seen in duty of care, actionable damage and vicarious liability is that the law of tort as a whole is not the same as it was before.

This concern is underlined by the attitude of Lord Neuberger seeming openly to deny that the law of tort has intellectual coherence or that principles are anything more than the distillation of policy. There are dangers in that view, with respect: it leads to a general scepticism which is not conducive to consistent and coherent judging. As McBride and Bagshaw have noted, responding[243] to Lord Neuberger, 'there may be an element of self-fulfilling prophecy about [those] remarks':[244] 'the more judges think along [substantive or substantivist] lines, the more it will come to be the case that it is correct to think along these lines'. It is thus both self-fulfilling and self-perpetuating: indeed, it is a habit that can become an addiction. Nevertheless, as is argued here, the law of tort should be a principled area of the law and a greater appeal to and reliance upon form is likely to lead to more certain and coherent outcomes.

Lords Mance and Hughes both retired in the summer of 2018, and thus two of the Justices whom we can identify (based on their judgments) as having reservations about this development in the law of tort are no longer on the Court.[245] Two of the Justices whose appointments to the Court were announced to the Court were amongst those who featured in more restrictive Court of Appeal decisions subsequently overturned by the Justices: Lady Arden in *Mohamud*, and Lord Sales in *Dryden* and *Darnley*. There are of course differing adjudicative structures and working practices for the Court of Appeal and Supreme Court, so I do not wish to overplay the point, but it is worth noting the previous views of two of the new Justices. 'Another thing which is required in a more formal and more predictable legal system is a higher degree of self-discipline on the part of the decision-makers'.[246]

At the time of their writing in *Form and Substance*, Atiyah and Summers considered that 'legislative reform of the common law is, in modern times,

[241] '[The] institutional framework of the common law allows for gradual development of the law over time. There is a feedback loop from the general legal culture to courts through commentary and development of legal analysis and critique': P Sales, 'The Common Law: Context and Method' (2019) 135 *LQR* 47, 55.

[242] In *Mohamud* [2016] UKSC 11, [2016] AC 677 [40], Lord Toulson quoted Immanuel Kant as justification for there being an unavoidable risk that an employee might misuse his position: 'Out of the crooked timber of humanity, no straight thing was ever made.'

[243] Writing after *Armes* but before the 2018 decisions which have continued the trend.

[244] McBride and Bagshaw, above n 25, xxiii.

[245] Albeit that, as I have noted elsewhere, Lord Hughes was more willing to develop the law judicially in the area of criminal law: Lee, 'Judging Reformers and Reforming Judges', above n 235, 19–24.

[246] Atiyah, above n 33, 460.

frequent in England',[247] which reassured the judges that they could 'often assume that reform will be forthcoming'[248] if they did not act themselves. They attributed to this a 'basic difference in the methodology of law reform' compared with American states,[249] and even went as far as to say that 'the modern technique for legal change in England is overwhelmingly legislative'.[250] Sir Philip Sales has written of the institutional dynamics, noting 'the subtle interplay' between the possibility or probability of legislative reform and judicial willingness to develop the law,[251] while Lady Hale has noted that 'there are problems with relying on *either* the judges or Parliament to develop or reform the law'.[252] Thirty years on from Atiyah and Summers' views, we can see that the Supreme Court no longer believes in those assumptions about English law, at least in tort, and the Justices are willing to contribute to law reform.

VII. Conclusions

The analysis here has shown that recent English authorities pose a challenge for how we reason within, and about, the law of tort. Any one decision, or perhaps even any one doctrine, may in isolation be explicable on the basis of specific circumstances. And, as we have seen, these engage what are to an extent eternal questions about the development of the law.[253] But I have identified a distinctive trend in tort law reasoning of the UKSC, which, drawing on Atiyah and Summers' contributions to our understanding of form and substance, can be framed as moving tort law further towards the substantive end of the spectrum. What is especially unusual is the consistent embracing of indeterminacy as though it were a virtue. I have argued that this trend is not only relevant to competing visions of tort, but also goes to our visions for the courts and for the common law.

In the field of unjust enrichment, McLachlin J (as she then was) once observed that:

> There is a tendency on the part of some to view the action for unjust enrichment as a device for doing whatever may seem fair between the parties. In the rush to substantive justice the principles are sometimes forgotten.[254]

[247] Atiyah and Summers, above n 2, 140.

[248] ibid, 141.

[249] ibid.

[250] ibid, 148.

[251] Sales, above n 241, 56. Compare Lee 'Illegality, Familiarity and the Law Commission', above n 21, A Burrows, 'Post-Legislative Scrutiny, Legislative Drafting and the "Elusive Boundary"' M Dyson, J Lee and S Wilson Stark (eds), *Fifty Years of the Law Commissions – the Dynamics of Law Reform* (Oxford, Hart Publishing, 2016) and B Hale, 'Legislation or Judicial Law Reform: Where should Judges Fear to Tread?' (Society of Legal Scholars Annual Conference, Oxford, 7 September 2016), www.supremecourt.uk/docs/speech-160907.pdf.

[252] Hale, above n 251, 8 (emphasis added).

[253] J Reid, 'The Judge as Law Maker' (1972–73) 12 *Journal of the Society of Public Teacher of Law* 22, 26: 'People want two inconsistent things; that the law shall be certain, and that it shall be just and shall move with the times.'

[254] *Peter v Beblow* [1993] 1 SCR 980, 988.

That dictum has recently been endorsed in the same context by Lord Reed, who denied that there was 'a judicial licence to meet the perceived requirements of fairness on a case-by-case basis'.[255] The law of tort should be no different. The various areas considered here, from across the spectrum of tort law, reveal the UK Supreme Court's preference for 'substance' over 'form', and increasingly for 'substantivism' over 'formalism'. The work of Atiyah and Summers is a valuable lens through which to analyse what is becoming a tort law jurisprudence of both bad form and addictive substance.

[255] *Revenue and Customs v The Investment Trust Companies* [2017] UKSC 29, [2018] AC 275 [39] ('*ITC*'). Lord Reed further noted that 'the courts should not be reinventing the wheel' in unjust enrichment: *ITC* [2017] UKSC 29, [2018] AC 275 [40]. See also B Hale, 'Reflecting on the Legacy of Chief Justice McLachlin' (University of Ottawa, 10 April 2018) 7–8 www.supremecourt.uk/docs/speech-180410.pdf.

13

Form and Substance in the Tort of Deceit

JASON W NEYERS*

I. Introduction

In their classic work, *Form and Substance in Anglo-American Law*, Atiyah and Summers contend that the American legal system is highly substantive and is therefore generally focussed on examining the 'moral, economic, political, institutional or other social considerations' that exist for a legal rule.[1] In contrast, they assert that the English legal system is highly formal and is generally focussed on the legal authoritativeness of a rule, a process which 'usually excludes for consideration, overrides or at least diminishes the weight of, any countervailing substantive reason'.[2] In Atiyah and Summers' view, this priority of form over substance takes several forms in the English legal system. For example, they contend that the English tend to be more rigorous in their application of the concept of stare decisis and with ranking sources of law in terms of their authoritativeness, thereby displaying more 'Authoritative Formality' than their American counterparts.[3] Additionally, Atiyah and Summers contend that the English tend to accept a greater amount of arbitrariness, or under- or over-inclusiveness in relation to a rule's purpose when applying statutes and doctrine, and therefore there is a high degree of 'Content Formality' to English law.[4] Finally, they contend that the English tend to focus more 'on the literal meaning of words, or on the narrow confines of normative

* This research was funded in part by an Insight Grant from the Social Sciences and Humanities Research Council of Canada. I thank Allan Beever, Andrew Botterell, James Goudkamp, Joanna Langille, Nick McBride, John Murphy, Donal Nolan, Stephen Pitel, Arthur Ripstein, Zoe Sinel and Ben Zipursky for their comments on earlier drafts of this chapter and Taylor Schmidt and Artur Adamian for their research assistance. The usual disclaimer applies.

[1] PS Atiyah and RS Summers, *Form and Substance in Anglo-American Law: A Comparative Study of Legal Reasoning, Legal Theory, and Legal Institutions* (Oxford, Clarendon Press, 1987) 1.

[2] ibid 2.

[3] ibid 12–13.

[4] ibid 13–14.

conduct' to be interpreted thereby displaying an 'Interpretative Formality' that is not as present in American law (which tends to prefer a search for the 'underlying purposes and rationales' of a given text).[5]

My argument is that the conventional understanding of damage in the English law of deceit – the one to be found in leading English treatises – displays many of the elements of formality expounded upon by Atiyah and Summers, as would be expected if the overall thesis of their book is sound.[6] Additionally, and perhaps more controversially, I will argue that this high degree of formality has caused this orthodox understanding of damage to become 'formalistic', a term of opprobrium used by Atiyah and Summers to indicate a 'degenerate species' of formality that is too far divorced from substance and substantive reasoning.[7] This formalistic view has prevented English scholars from providing compelling justifications for the results of leading deceit cases on damages and thereby from unearthing the core principle animating the tort.

To make these arguments, the chapter is divided into seven sections, the first of which is the introduction. In Section II, I set out the conventional English conception of damage in the tort of deceit. In Section III, I examine the conceptual and coherence problems with this loss-based understanding of the tort and in Section IV, I examine the inability of the conventional conception to explain leading deceit damages cases. In Section V, I examine a leading theory of deceit propounded by John Murphy and, finding it wanting, in Section VI, I present an alternative view of the tort of deceit and demonstrate that this alternative understanding can coherently explain the leading deceit damages cases identified in Section III. Section VII is a short conclusion.

II. The Conventional English Conception of Deceit

The classic statement of the elements of deceit comes from Viscount Maugham's restatement of the tort in *Bradford v Borders*.[8] As his Lordship made clear, a successful claimant would have to prove the following:

> First, there must be a representation of fact made by words or, it may be, by conduct … On the other hand, mere silence, however morally wrong, will not support an action of deceit. Secondly, the representation must be made with a knowledge that it is false. It must be wilfully false, or at least made in the absence of any genuine belief that it is true. Thirdly, it must be made with the intention that it should be acted upon by the plaintiff, or by a class of persons which will include the plaintiff, in the manner which resulted

[5] ibid 15.

[6] Unfortunately, it does not appear that Atiyah and Summers explicitly addressed deceit in *Form and Substance*: Atiyah and Summers, above n 1.

[7] Atiyah and Summers, above n 1, 28.

[8] *Bradford v Borders* [1941] 2 All ER 205. For a modern application, see *Hayward v Zurich Insurance Company plc* [2016] UKSC 48, [2017] AC 142 ('*Hayward*').

> in damage to him. If, however, fraud be established, it is immaterial that there was no intention to cheat or injure the person to whom the false statement was made. Fourthly, it must be proved that the plaintiff has acted upon the false statement and has sustained damage by so doing.[9]

The conventional English understanding of these elements is that the requirement of damage means that the tort of deceit is concerned with loss (in the sense of being factually worse off). As is stated by the authors of *Markesinis & Deakin's Tort Law*: 'Loss is an essential element of the tort'.[10] Similarly, the authors of *Clerk & Lindsell* state:

> The tort involves a perfectly general principle: where a defendant makes a false representation, knowing it to be untrue … and intends that the claimant should act in reliance on it, then in so far as the latter does so and *suffers loss* the defendant is liable.[11]

As the 'great majority of cases',[12] especially the early formative cases such as *Derry v Peek* and others,[13] dealt with the acquisition of shares or the entering into other types of financial contracts, loss is largely understood as having a pecuniary focus under the conventional view.[14] As is stated in *McGregor on Damages*, the 'principal, and generally the only, recovery in deceit is for pecuniary loss'.[15] As a result, the tort of deceit is included in textbooks on the economic torts,[16] is frequently discussed in general torts textbooks in chapters or sections dealing with the protection of economic interests,[17] and often finds its way into discussions of pure economic loss in the common law.[18] Murphy summarises the position as follows: 'According to conventional wisdom, deceit is an economic tort concerned

[9] *Bradford v Borders* [1941] 2 All ER 205, 211 (footnotes omitted).

[10] S Deakin, A Johnston and B Markesinis, *Markesinis and Deakin's Tort Law*, 7th edn (Oxford, Oxford University Press, 2012) 469. See also: P Mitchell and C Witting, 'Deceit and Misrepresentation' in K Oliphant (ed), *The Law of Tort*, 3rd edn (London, LexisNexis Butterworths, 2015) para 28.11: 'The claimant must suffer loss as a result of acting on the fraudulent misrepresentation'.

[11] A Tettenborn, 'Deceit' in M Jones (ed), *Clerk & Lindsell on Torts*, 22nd edn (London, Sweet & Maxwell, 2018) para 18.01 (emphasis added) (footnotes omitted).

[12] J Edelman (ed), *McGregor on Damages*, 20th edn (London, Sweet & Maxwell, 2018) 1651, 1653.

[13] *Derry v Peek* (1889) 14 App Cas 337, 343 ('*Derry*'). See also: *Smith v Chadwick* (1884) 9 App Cas 187 ('*Smith*'); *Peek v Gurney* [1873] LR 6 HL 377; *Edgington v Fitzmaurice* (1885) 29 Ch D 459 and the discussion in J Cartwright, *Misrepresentation, Mistake and Non-Disclosure*, 4th edn (London, Sweet & Maxwell, 2017) para 5.36.

[14] E Peel and J Goudkamp, *Winfield and Jolowicz on Tort*, 19th edn (London, Sweet & Maxwell, 2014) 331 (loss recovered is 'usually financial'); Tettenborn, above n 11, para 18.40 (loss 'recovered in deceit cases is normally pecuniary loss').

[15] Edelman, above n 12, 1653.

[16] See, eg, H Carty, *An Analysis of the Economic Torts*, 2nd edn (Oxford, Oxford University Press, 2010) ch 9. See also P Burns and J Blom, *Economic Torts in Canada*, 2nd edn (Canada, LexisNexis, 2016) ch 7.

[17] See, eg, N McBride and R Bagshaw, *Tort Law*, 6th edn (Harlow, Pearson Education, 2018) ch 20; C Witting, *Street on Torts*, 15th edn (Oxford, Oxford University Press, 2018) ch 14; Deakin, Johnston and Markesinis, above n 10, ch 5.

[18] See, eg, JA Jolowicz, 'The Law of Tort and Non-Physical Loss' (1972) 12 *Journal of Society Public Teachers of Law* 91; A Burrows, *Remedies for Torts and Breach of Contract*, 3rd edn (Oxford, Oxford University Press, 2005) 253ff.

with the protection of purely economic interests; and its gist is usually portrayed as being the infliction of economic loss'.[19]

This loss-based view of deceit is evidence of the interpretative formality elucidated by Atiyah and Summers which tends to favour a literal interpretation of words over something more substantive.[20] The process of interpretation that is employed by English scholars, perhaps implicitly in many instances, is something like this. Because the tort of deceit evolved from the action on the case, claimants must prove that they suffered damage.[21] As damage and loss are synonymous[22] and used interchangeably by many judges,[23] there is every reason for damage and loss to be equated and for deceit to be seen as a loss-based tort. Moreover, given that most cases deal with commercial fact patterns, the 'narrow confines' interpretative technique described by Atiyah and Summers suggests to English scholars that the heart of the tort of deceit has to do with economic or pecuniary loss rather than with more far-flung or abstract issues such as autonomy or rights that might cut across the law of torts.[24]

III. Conceptual and Coherence Problems with the Conventional Understanding

While there is widespread agreement as to economic or pecuniary loss being a key element in the tort of deceit, there is some disagreement among English scholars as to what function 'loss' is playing in the tort. On the one side, there are those who view the requirement of loss as completing the tort – in other words nothing wrong has occurred, no right has been violated, until someone has suffered loss as a result of relying on a fraudulent misrepresentation.[25] On the other side, are those who argue that loss does not go to tortiousness but rather merely to actionability – in other words a wrong has occurred and the tort is complete at some time before the suffering of loss. Relying on cases like *Briess v Woolley* and *Diamond v Bank of London and Montreal Ltd*,[26] scholars in this camp (notably Robert Stevens) contend that the tort is complete when the misrepresentation is acted

[19] J Murphy, 'Misleading Appearances in the Tort of Deceit' (2016) 75 *CLJ* 301, 316.

[20] Atiyah and Summers, above n 1, 15.

[21] See, eg, Witting, above n 17, 360 ('Being an action on the case, there is no cause of action in deceit unless the claimant proves that he sustained loss or damage'). See also C Sappideen and P Vines (eds), *Fleming's The Law of Torts*, 10th edn (Australia, Lawbook Co, 2011) para 28.60.

[22] See, eg, Oxford University Press, 'damage, n' (*Oxford English Dictionary Online*, July 2018) www.oed.com.

[23] See D Nolan, 'Rights, Damage and Loss' (2017) 37 *OJLS* 255, 270 for examples.

[24] Atiyah and Summers, above n 1, 15.

[25] See, eg, *Latkter v General Guarantee Finance Ltd* [2001] EWCA Civ 875 ('*Latkter*') and the discussion in PM Eggers, *Deceit: The Lie of the Law* (London, Informa Law, 2009) paras 8.109–8.116.

[26] *Briess v Woolley* [1954] AC 333 ('*Briess*'); *Diamond v Bank of London and Montreal Ltd* [1979] QB 333 ('*Diamond*').

upon by the claimant but only becomes actionable when the claimant proves that he or she suffered loss.[27] As Lord Tucker said in *Briess*:

> The tort of fraudulent misrepresentation is not complete when the representation is made. It becomes complete when the misrepresentation … is acted upon by the representee. Damage giving rise to a claim for damages may not follow or may not result until a later date, but once the misrepresentation is acted upon by the representee the tortious act is complete …[28]

Both views are problematic. The first view, as Nolan argues, is conceptually impossible:

> The structure of my argument could not be simpler. It rests on two independent claims, from the truth of which the conclusion follows as a matter of logic. The claims are: (i) that a wrong (in other words, the violation of a right) occurs in a moment of time; and (ii) that whether or not a person has suffered loss as a result of another's conduct cannot be determined at any given moment in time. It follows that the causing of loss cannot be a wrong, and hence that a right not to suffer loss is impossible.[29]

In addition to relying on the famous Taoist/Buddhist story (of the farmer, his horse and his son) and the existence of a 'confused and confusing case law' on limitation periods for the suffering of pure economic loss,[30] in defence of his second more controversial claim, Nolan also relies on a vivid and compelling example provided by Ernest Weinrib:

> Recall that the working definition of loss that we are using is "an abstract concept of being worse off", such that the suffering of a loss amounts to a "detrimental difference" to the person who suffers it. So the question we need to ask is whether it can be determined at any given moment in time that A's conduct has made B 'worse off'. Intuitively, we may feel that it is. Suppose, for example, that A's negligent driving causes an accident in which B's leg is broken. Can we not then say with some confidence at the time of the accident that A's conduct has left B worse off? In short, the answer is no … it is never possible to say at any particular moment in time that A's conduct has left B worse off, because we can never know whether later events will affect the impact that A's conduct had on B's welfare. In the car accident case, for example, what if at the time of the

[27] See R Stevens, *Torts and Rights* (Oxford, Oxford University Press, 2007) 89; R Stevens, 'Rights and Other Things' in D Nolan and A Robertson (eds), *Rights and Private Law* (London, Hart Publishing, 2014) 115, 128–29. See also: GHL Fridman, *Torts* (London, Waterlow, 1990) para 17.16; RFV Hueston and RA Buckley, *Salmond and Heuston on the Law of Torts*, 21st edn (London, Sweet & Maxwell, 1996) 370 fn 11; Nolan, above n 23, 266.

[28] *Briess* [1954] AC 333, 353 cited with approval in *Hayward* [2016] UKSC 48, [2017] AC 142 [24].

[29] Nolan, above n 23, 262. For a similar view, see Stevens, 'Rights and Other Things', above n 27, 119: 'A wrong, or injury, occurs at a moment of time … D commits a civil wrong in relation to C whenever he breaches a duty to C not to do *x*. It is consequently meaningless to talk of a right not to be caused loss. If loss is suffered, it is a consequence of a breach of duty; it cannot go to the definition of what D is under a duty to do or not do'.

[30] Nolan, above n 23, 254, 263–64. For a discussion of this case law and for judicial acknowledgement of these difficulties, see J O'Sullivan, 'The Meaning of "Damage" in Pure Financial Loss Cases: Contract and Tort Collide' (2012) 28 *Journal of Professional Negligence* 248; R Walker, 'Pure Economic Loss: The Problem of Timing' (2012) 20 *Torts Law Journal* 77; *Law Society v Sephton* [2006] UKHL 22, [2006] 2 AC 543 [10] (Lord Hoffmann).

> accident B was driving to the airport to catch a plane that crashed on take-off, killing all those on board, so that B would almost certainly have been killed if A had not driven negligently? In this scenario, we might *think* in the immediate aftermath of the accident that A's conduct had made B worse off, but a later event (the plane crash) would falsify that belief.[31]

Unlike the tortiousness view, Nolan claims that the second 'actionability view' is conceptually possible. As he points out, although there cannot be a right not to be caused pecuniary loss:

> there is nothing to stop the law from making the *actionability* of a wrong depend on whether at a given moment it looks as if the wrong has caused the claimant loss. Indeed, there are familiar examples of the law limiting the actionability of a wrong in this way, such as the rule that to sue in deceit you must show that the deceit has caused you loss …[32]

Although this second view is conceptually possible, it has a different problem – it is radically incoherent. To be coherent, a theory must be able to explain the legal rules and limitations attaching to the use of that doctrine – its starting and ending, its effects, and its remedy – as mutually interrelated. Thus, a coherent theory must explain its subject as constituting a unitary whole, rather than merely being 'an aggregate of conceptually disjunct or inconsistent elements that … happen to be juxtaposed'.[33] Put most simply, to be coherent, the reason for imposing liability must also be the reason for limiting liability and on this metric the actionability account of loss is not up to the task.[34] This incoherence can be seen most clearly when one examines the reasons given by Stevens in *Torts and Rights* for the actionability requirement in deceit. As he argues:

> The right that each of us has not to be lied to is similarly only actionable upon proof of consequential loss. This may be related to slander in the sense that it is considered that words are, in some sense, less important than actions. It would, of course, be unacceptable for the law to make actionable all of the minor deceptions that we practise upon one another.[35]

When viewed in this way, the actionability view is incoherent since the justification for the liability (actual reliance) is being arbitrarily cut off by the unrelated requirement that the claimant suffer consequential loss in order to delimit liability or avoid a floodgates problem.[36]

[31] Nolan, above n 23, 263 relying on EJ Weinrib, 'Right and Advantage in Private Law' (1989) 10 *Cardozo Law Review* 1283, 1283–84.

[32] Nolan, above n 23, 266 (footnotes omitted).

[33] EJ Weinrib, 'Legal Formalism: On the Immanent Rationality of the Law' (1988) 97 *Yale Law Journal* 949, 968–69.

[34] See W Seavey, 'Mr Justice Cardozo and the Law of Torts' (1939) 39 *Columbia Law Review* 20, 34.

[35] Stevens, *Torts and Rights*, above n 27, 89.

[36] As Murphy points out (above n 19, 317) this reasoning also seems incongruous with Stevens' overall project: 'floodgates concerns have no place in Stevens's theory of tort law. Indeed, he goes to very great lengths in his monograph, *Torts and Rights*, to discredit the role of policy-based reasoning in tort law. And floodgates considerations are nothing if not a type of policy concern' (footnotes omitted).

I find it telling that this disagreement over the function of loss and the obvious flaws with each explanation has not spurned more movement in the English academic literature to resolve these tensions and to suggest a coherent and conceptually possible interpretation of deceit. It is evidence, in the words of Atiyah and Summers, of the English acceptance of a high degree of content formality in law. To the traditional English scholar or lawyer, if the law of deceit is not conceptually stable or lacks coherence in straying away from the fundamental core of the tort, then this is not shocking and might even be expected. It is an acceptable cost of running a formal legal system since many legal rules are arbitrary or under- or over-inclusive, especially as one moves away from the core of their application to the penumbra.

Thus, it seems that the English tendency to accept interpretative and content formality has blinded English scholars to the conceptual and coherence problems with the conventional pecuniary loss view of damage in the tort of deceit. If these problems were not enough, this view of the tort also has some remarkable problems of fit. For example, it cannot easily explain the results of prominent deceit damages cases that one finds referenced in the standard treatises. One might be able to countenance the conceptual or coherence problems of the conventional view if it provided a high degree of fit with the case law, but what good is a theory that cannot explain the leading cases? Thus, this lack of fit is the final nail in the metaphorical coffin that allows us to say that conventional understanding has morphed from one that is merely formal to one that is formalistic (in the pejorative sense described earlier) and hence too far removed from the underlying substantive reason for the tort's existence. In order to continue on our path of unearthing the conceptual core of the tort of deceit, in the next section I will outline the cases that are problematic, and then, in the section that follows, examine a recent suggestion that a right to decision-making autonomy explains the contours of the tort as we find it.

IV. The Conventional Understanding and Problems of Fit

Four leading English cases on damages for deceit are *Mafo v Adams*,[37] *Smith Kline & French Laboratories Ltd v Long*,[38] *Clef Aquitaine SARL v Laporte Materials (Barrow) Ltd*,[39] and *OMV Petrom Sa v Glencore International AG*.[40] They expose the difficulties that the pecuniary loss-based conception has in accommodating their results and reasoning. I have chosen these cases as they are regularly found

[37] *Mafo v Adams* [1970] 1 QB 548 ('*Mafo*').

[38] *Smith Kline & French Laboratories Ltd v Long* [1989] 1 WLR 1 ('*Smith Kline & French*').

[39] *Clef Aquitaine SARL v Laporte Materials (Barrow) Ltd* [2001] QB 488 ('*Clef Aquitane*').

[40] *OMV Petrom Sa v Glencore International AG* [2016] EWCA Civ 778, [2017] 3 All ER 157 ('*OMV Petrom*').

in textbook discussions of the tort and are spaced out temporally to avoid the criticism that these particular cases might mark a short-lived (mis-)understanding of the conventional view rather than presenting a more pervasive problem of fit.

A. *Mafo v Adams*

In this case, the claimant was the lessee of a flat in a house owned by the defendant.[41] The flat was a protected tenancy under the then existing legislation. The defendant wished the claimant to move out of the flat (possibly so that the defendant could sell the house without it being subject to the protected tenancy). In order to induce the claimant to move out, the defendant had his ex-wife, who was unknown to the claimant, pretend to be the landlord of another property. The claimant went to that other property, found it quite appealing and purportedly entered into a 'lease' of it. Four days later, the claimant packed up his belongings from the flat and took them to the new property. When he arrived, he was unable to gain entry since the property was owned by another party and there was, in reality, no lease. The claimant then stayed with a friend for several weeks rent free until he was able to find fresh accommodation. The cost of the new accommodation was not more than what he had paid for his protected tenancy (though perhaps less commodious).

As such, the question for the Court of Appeal was whether the claimant could recover even though he could not be said to have suffered any pecuniary loss (any 'specific special damage').[42] If the conventional view of the tort were correct and if one thereby thought that pecuniary loss was the gist of deceit then one would have expected the claim to fail.

Instead, the Court held that the claimant could recover since, as Sachs LJ held, the 'cause of action became complete upon it being shown that the defendant secured by means of that fraud something of value, that is to say, possession of the flat … by fraudulently inducing the plaintiff to surrender it'.[43] Similarly, Widgery LJ stated that claimant could recover since 'he was deprived of the tenancy of a flat protected by the Rent Acts, and in the circles in which these parties move possession of such a flat is one of the most significant rights of property that any of them ever see in their lives'.[44]

As the cause of action was complete (even without proof of special damage), the Court awarded the claimant £100 for the loss of his protected tenancy and for the inconvenience and unpleasantness of the move.

[41] The facts are found at *Mafo* [1970] 1 QB 548, 552–53.
[42] ibid 552.
[43] ibid 554.
[44] ibid 557.

B. *Smith Kline & French*

In this case, the claimant was a manufacturer of pharmaceuticals who was anxious to develop a market for its product, Tagamet tablets, outside of the UK. The defendant was the managing director of a company called Swift.[45] As the result of a fraudulent misrepresentation by the defendant that Swift was intending to sell the claimant's tablets in Central African countries, the claimant supplied 16,800 packs to Swift. Swift then entered into liquidation leaving £157,028 of the total £951,888 debt for the packs unpaid. The claimant sued the defendant in deceit. The claimant conceded that it produced the tablets for free and could have supplied whatever quantity of tablets was necessary to meet demand in its territories. The claimant also conceded that if it had known the truth it would never have supplied Swift with the packs as it was prohibited from selling its products in the Netherlands (the location where the defendant had actually sold the tablets).

At trial, the claimant's claim for damages was dismissed on the basis that it had suffered no actual pecuniary loss as the defendant's deceit had not deprived it of any sales. As counsel for the defendant put it in the Court of Appeal, the defendant's actions had left the claimant with a 'windfall' of 'nearly £800,000', the only loser being the Dutch associate company that had lost sales in the Netherlands due to Swift's undercutting.

The Court of Appeal unanimously allowed the appeal and awarded the claimant the unpaid £157,028. Slade LJ, speaking for the Court, held that:

> the deceit of the defendant … had had the result of permanently depriving the plaintiffs of their goods. To place them in the position in which they would have been in if the deceit had not been perpetrated … [one] must … attempt fairly and properly to ascertain the value of the goods in question. In the absence of any authority compelling a contrary conclusion, I think the fair and proper test to apply is that which we would have applied if the defendant had deprived the plaintiffs of their goods by converting them – in other words, the market value and not the cost of replacing them.[46]

Once again, the result seems inconsistent with the pecuniary loss view of the tort of deceit. As Burrows notes in *Remedies for Torts and Breach of Contract*, according to the conventional view, the 'wrong result' was reached in *Smith Kline* as the 'award would only have been correct if the claimant would have sold the tablets at the same price to someone else'.[47]

[45] The facts are found at *Smith Kline & French* [1989] 1 WLR 1, 3–4.

[46] ibid 10.

[47] Burrows, above n 18, 260. In *Smith New Court Securities Ltd v Scrimgeour Vickers (Asset Management) Ltd* [1997] AC 254, 282 ('*Smith New Court*') Lord Steyn noted Burrows' criticism of *Smith Kline & French* but chose not to examine the 'correctness of that comment'.

C. *Clef Aquitaine*

In this case, the claimant was a company that proposed entering into a long-term distributorship agreement for France with the defendant.[48] The claimant was worried about UK companies buying the defendant's materials for less than the contract price, reselling them in France, and thereby undercutting the claimant's business. The defendant assured the claimant that the contractual list prices were the same prices that the defendant charged all its best UK customers. The claimant entered into the contract and for approximately 15 years operated its distributorship at a profit. In the course of a contractual dispute with the defendant, the claimant found out that the defendant had lied and in fact sold the materials much more cheaply (10–25 per cent less than the claimant was paying) to some of its biggest UK customers. It sued in deceit and claimed as damages the difference between the profits it actually made and the profits that it would have made had it been supplied at the cheaper prices.

The defendant argued that the claimant's case should fail since it could not prove any loss which was necessary to make the deceit actionable and to give these damages was to confuse the contractual and tortious measure of damages.[49]

The Court did not agree and found for the claimant. As Simon Brown LJ noted:

> [T]here is no absolute rule requiring the person deceived to prove that the actual transaction into which he was induced to enter was itself loss-making … It will sometimes be possible, as it was here, to prove instead that a different and more favourable transaction … would have been entered into but for the fraud, and to measure and recover the plaintiffs' loss on that basis.[50]

In their article, *Reforming Damages for Misrepresentation*, Jill Poole and James Devenney are highly critical of *Clef Aquitaine*, which they rightly claim is inconsistent with the conventional view of the tort of deceit.[51] To apply the loss-based view properly, they contend that courts should be careful to distinguish between:

1. the pecuniary loss that must be present for the tort to be actionable (the gist of deceit); and
2. the rules that are used to establish the extent of the defendant's responsibility for the claimant's change of position after it has been found that the tort is actionable.

Poole and Devenney compellingly claim that the mistake of the Court in *Clef Aquitaine* was to use the second set of rules related to remoteness (for example, responsibility for the speculative loss of extra profits) to establish the existence

[48] The facts are found at *Clef Aquitaine* [2001] QB 488, 490–92.
[49] ibid 493.
[50] ibid 500.
[51] J Poole and J Devenney, 'Reforming Damages of Misrepresentation: The Case for Coherent Aims and Principles' [2007] *Journal of Business Law* 269.

of the gist of the tort.[52] As they state: 'A loss which turns on hypotheticals which did not in fact happen can hardly, without more, be classified as "actual loss"'.[53] Similarly, the authors of *Winfield & Jolowicz* argue that the result in the case and its concept of the gist of deceit 'seems almost to elide the difference between the two measures of damages' in contract and tort.[54]

D. *OMV Petrom*

The facts of *OMV Petrom* were complicated but might fairly be simplified as follows.[55] The claimant was an oil importer and refiner. Over a period of three years, the claimant was supplied with 80 cargos of crude oil by the defendant. The crude oil was sold as established brands that the claimant preferred for use in its refineries. Approximately 40 per cent of the supplied cargos were not in fact established brands, but were instead custom mixtures of crude that were cheaper to produce and to supply than the established brands. As the custom mixtures had similar chemical characteristics and yields to those of the established brands, the fraud was not discovered by the claimant when they tested the cargos or refined the oil. Over the years, the oil was refined without issue and sold on to the claimant's customers at full price. The fraud was only discovered a decade later when a whistleblower, who used to work for the defendant during the relevant time period, came forward.

The claimant argued that had it known the truth it would have rejected the cargo and bought the established brands from other suppliers at the price it paid the claimant (which was the market price at the dates of delivery).[56] The trial judge awarded the claimant approximately £40 million in damages which was the difference between the price that the claimant had paid and the market value of the custom blends at the date of delivery. The low market price of the custom blends was justified by two reasonable fears that market participants would have had: first, that the custom blends would provide lower yields than the established brands; and secondly, that these blends might damage equipment and machinery while being refined.

In the Court of Appeal, the defendant argued that the trial judge's award overcompensated the claimant and that the claimant's damages should be limited to

[52] ibid 292–96.

[53] ibid 287. See also J Devenney, 'Re-Examining Damages for Fraudulent Misrepresentation: Towards a More Measured Response to Compensation and Deterrence' in L Di Matteo, K Rowley, Q Zhou and S Santier (eds), *Commercial Contract Law: Transatlantic Perspectives* (Cambridge, Cambridge University Press, 2013) 416, 429–30.

[54] Peel and Goudkamp, above n 14, 332. For an explanation as to why this is not the case, see below, text accompanying nn 96–97.

[55] The facts are found at *OMV Petrom* [2016] EWCA Civ 778, [2017] 3 All ER 157 [3]–[16]. This summary/simplification relies on that helpfully provided by A Summers and A Kramer, 'Deceit, Difference in Value and Date of Assessment' (2017) 133 *LQR* 41, 41–42.

[56] *OMV Petrom* [2016] EWCA Civ 778, [2017] 3 All ER 157 [11], [33].

any proven consequential pecuniary losses (such as a loss of yield or equipment damage traceable to the use of the lesser quality custom blends).[57] The Court of Appeal unanimously upheld the trial judge's award on the basis that the fraudster-defendant should not benefit from the fact that none of the expected deleterious consequences actually transpired.[58]

As Andrew Summers and Adam Kramer point out, the result in *OMV Petrom* is hard to square with a theory that the purpose of the tort of deceit is to compensate for pecuniary loss.[59] As they argue, the proper award:

> requires a comparison with what would have happened but for the breach, and based on the available evidence, this involved the purchase of different oil at the same … price. The correct comparison is therefore between the consequences of receiving bespoke blended oil (the breach position) as against receiving branded oil (the non-breach position).[60]

Therefore, 'the proper award should have been compensation for all actual losses proven to have been suffered' by use of the custom blends which 'because the claimant chose to resist investigation of post-acquisition events' were zero.[61] As they concluded: 'The claimant had taken the high risk approach of seeking jackpot damages without pleading its actual losses' and therefore 'it should have paid the price for this approach and recovered no damages at all'.[62]

E. Summary

It seems clear from the foregoing that the conventional English conception of damage in the tort of deceit is an inadequate interpretation of the tort as we find it. It is either conceptually impossible or radically incoherent and cannot explain the leading cases on damages that are found in the standard textbooks and treatises. Thus, in order to find our way out of this formalistic cul-de-sac it is necessary to look again at the substance of the tort of deceit. In the next section I therefore examine a recent suggestion that the core of the tort of deceit is the protection of decision-making autonomy.

V. A Right to Decision-making Autonomy?

Seeing that the conventional view of deceit's focus on pecuniary loss cannot explain many important features of the law, John Murphy, in his important article

57 ibid [33]–[36].
58 ibid [40].
59 Summers and Kramer, above n 55.
60 ibid 44.
61 ibid 46.
62 ibid.

Misleading Appearances in the Tort of Deceit has recently developed a view of the tort centred on protecting a right to decision-making autonomy.[63] Interestingly, in doing so he was building upon the work of American academics Goldberg, Zipursky and Sebok who, in the American style outlined by Atiyah and Summers, offered a more substantive and less formal analysis of deceit – one that looked past its judicially stated elements to the reasons for the existence of those elements.[64] After Anglicising their work to take into account the important doctrinal differences between the jurisdictions and the more stable body of English precedent on the matter, caused no doubt by the higher authoritative formality of the English legal system,[65] Murphy argues that the 'gist of deceit is an interference with the victim's decision-making autonomy that occurs by virtue of one of the established types of misinformation (laid down in *Derry v Peek*) and which results in a recognized form of harm'.[66]

Although in many respects a vast improvement upon the conventional English view,[67] Murphy's theory is problematic for three reasons. First, as a general matter, autonomy as a right appears to be too wide a concept to explain the law, as there are many ways that people can frustrate what others want to do that do not lead to legal liability (such as cornering the market by buying a rare stamp first or refusing to allow water to percolate onto neighbouring property).[68] Moreover, the existence of the law of duress, which requires the pressure exerted to be illegitimate,[69] and the requirement in the tort of intimidation that unlawful means be threatened in order to compel the victim,[70] are both inconsistent with the existence of a right to decision-making autonomy in private law. In other words, if we have such a right, why are only independently illegitimate or unlawful interferences with it actionable?

Secondly, the tort of deceit does not truly appear to be designed to protect a right to decision-making autonomy. As Alexander and Sherwin point out:

> [The law does not] correspond to moral theories that emphasize the effect of deception on the victim's autonomy ... [and] it seldom addresses injuries one might associate with autonomy. If autonomy were the focus of legal concern, one would expect regulation of

[63] Murphy, above n 19.

[64] See JCP Goldberg, AJ Sebok and BC Zipursky, 'The Place of Reliance in Fraud' (2006) 48 *Arizona Law Review* 1001; JCP Goldberg and BC Zipursky, 'The Fraud on the Market Tort' (2013) 66 *Vanderbilt Law Review* 101.

[65] Goldberg, Sebok and Zipursky's original statement of principle undergirding the tort is as follows: '[T]he core of the legal wrong that has historically been labelled "fraud" or "deceit" is the wrong of interfering with a particular interest of the victim, namely her interest in making certain kinds of choices in certain settings free from certain forms of misinformation' (Goldberg, Sebok and Zipursky, above n 64, 1011).

[66] Murphy, above n 19, 321.

[67] See the discussion below, text accompanying nn 99–102.

[68] See, eg, *Mayor of Bradford v Pickles* [1895] AC 587.

[69] See *Universe Tankships Inc of Monrovia v International Transport Workers Federation* [1983] 1 AC 366; *R v Attorney General for England and Wales* [2003] UKPC 22, [2003] EMLR 24.

[70] See *Rookes v Barnard* [1964] AC 1129. As Carty, above n 16, 112 states: 'Although the ingredient of threats gives the tort its name, the essence of the tort is the use of unlawful means.'

> fraud in sexual relations, which is in essence an affront to autonomy. One would also expect to see … civil remedies that vindicated an interest in freedom from manipulation, with or without accompanying economic harm … [C]ourts do not regularly protect a free-standing autonomy-based right not to be deceived. Instead, they prohibit deception as a means of causing harm to independently recognized interests, such as the interests in bodily integrity, property, physical liberty, and reputation.[71]

A recent example of what Alexander and Sherwin have in mind is provided by the decisions of the Ontario courts in the *PP v DD* litigation.[72] In that litigation, it was alleged that the defendant had lied to the claimant about taking birth control during a romantic relationship that lasted for less than two months. The defendant became pregnant and gave birth to a daughter, who paternity testing confirmed was the claimant's child. The claimant sued for $4 million in compensatory damages alleging that he 'was deprived of the choice of falling in love, marrying, enjoying married life, and when he and his wife thought "the time was right" [of] having a baby'.[73] The motions court struck out his claim as disclosing no reasonable cause of action since it was plain and obvious that this was not a type of damage that was actionable in the tort of deceit.[74] The Court of Appeal affirmed the decision noting that claims of involuntary parenthood had never been recognised as amounting to damage at common law.[75] The result in *PP v DD* is very surprising if the purpose of the tort of deceit is to protect a right to decision-making autonomy since clearly the claimant's autonomy had been violated, in a substantial way, if his allegations were true.

The third problem with Murphy's analysis is that a right to decision-making autonomy does not meaningfully link with the requirement of damage (understood as some form of loss). Why does one need an additional concept of damage if the heart of the tort is the autonomy? Phrased differently, what role is damage playing in furthering a right to decision-making autonomy? Thus, Murphy is on the horns of a dilemma. Either he can construct a coherent view of the tort of deceit based around the protection of decision-making autonomy but at the price of jettisoning the concept of damage and hence his theory's fit with the law;[76] or he can maintain a semblance of fit by positing a right and then arbitrarily cutting back that right to meet the requirements of the cases. Murphy chooses the latter option, which unfortunately causes his theory to be incoherent (much like the theory of Stevens).[77] As Murphy explains, 'the infringement of the claimant's right to decision-making autonomy is key; and the need to prove consequential

[71] L Alexander and E Sherwin, 'Deception in Morality and Law' (2003) 22 *Law and Philosophy* 393, 432.

[72] *PP v DD*, 2016 ONSC 258, 129 OR (3d) 175; affirmed *PP v DD*, 2017 ONCA 180, 409 DLR (4th) 691.

[73] *PP v DD*, 2016 ONSC 258, 129 OR (3d) 175 [6].

[74] See especially *PP v DD*, 2016 ONSC 258, 129 OR (3d) 175 [45]–[46].

[75] See *PP v DD*, 2017 ONCA 180, 409 DLR (4th) 691 [37]–[54].

[76] Recall Alexander and Sherwin's criticism of autonomy-based theories quoted above, text accompanying n 69.

[77] See the discussion above, text accompanying nn 31–35.

loss is very much a secondary aspect of the tort. Put more accurately, the need to show consequential loss is a mere condition of actionability, but not an element of the tort *strictu sensu*'.[78] Unfortunately, one cannot derive or construct a coherent and compelling interpretation of a cause of action in this fashion, which means that an explanation built around the protection of decision-making autonomy cannot be a good replacement for the conventional model of the tort centred on pecuniary loss.

VI. Rights and Deceit: A Different View

There is another way to understand the tort of deceit and that is as a tort which protects rights rather than one which is focused on preventing pecuniary loss or simple interferences with autonomy.

One could be forgiven for thinking that looking at deceit from the perspective of rights might not be fruitful. Murphy's right to decisional autonomy was criticised above, and as Jenks pointed out, as early as 1910, it seems impossible to fit deceit into a scheme 'which classifies torts according to the rights or interest which they infringe; for apparently, damage of any kind caused by fraud gives rise to an action'.[79] However, the secret to the tort of deceit – the secret that eluded Jenks but which is immanent in his comment – is that the tort does not protect just one right but rather it protects all of our rights (to things, to money, to contracts, to our bodies) from non-consensual dispossession as a result of another's fraud.[80] In this way, it is similar to the tort of negligence which can protect a multitude of rights from damage (in negligence's case damage caused by the imposition of an unreasonable risk of injury).[81] Further, this multi-right ability is confirmed by the law which allows the tort of deceit to be used to protect rights to bodily integrity,[82] property,[83] contractual performance,[84] and parental rights in relation to children.[85] As Ripstein notes, what is 'at issue is not … being lied to, but rather … being deprived of what you have through deceit'.[86]

What then of the fundamental requirement of damage?[87] On this view, the damage requirement of the tort of deceit is not to be understood as pecuniary loss

[78] Murphy, above n 19, 323.

[79] E Jenks, 'On Negligence and Deceit in the Law of Torts' (1910) 26 *LQR* 159, 166.

[80] See Alexander and Sherwin quoted above, text accompanying n 69.

[81] For a rights-protecting view of negligence, see A Beever, *Rediscovering the Law of Negligence* (Oxford, Hart Publishing, 2007).

[82] See, eg, *Langridge v Levy* (1837) 2 M & W 519, 150 ER 863; *Burrows v Rhodes* [1899] 1 QB 816.

[83] See, eg, *Mullett v Mason* (1866) LR 1 CP 559; *Smith Kline & French* [1989] 1 WLR 1; *Mafo* [1970] 1 QB 548.

[84] See, eg, *Firbank's Executors v Humphreys* (1886) 18 QBD 54.

[85] *F v Wirral Metropolitan Borough Council* [1991] 1 Fam 69.

[86] A Ripstein, *Private Wrongs* (Cambridge, MA, Harvard University Press, 2016) 50 fn 32.

[87] As was stated by Lord Halsbury LC in *Derry* (1889) 14 App Cas 337, 343: 'To quote the language now some centuries old in dealing with actions of this character, "fraud without damage or damage without fraud" does not give rise to such actions.'

or a simple interference with autonomy but rather as the claimant's non-consensual dispossession of his or her rights in consequence of the defendant's fraud. Thus the damage which is the gist of the tort of deceit occurs at the moment when the representee acts on the representation and thereby gives up control of a right or otherwise dispossesses him or herself of it.[88] Once there has been a dispossession, the cause of action is complete and the claimant may sue for substitutive damages represented by the difference between the market value of the right given away and the market value of what was received (the 'normal measure' in deceit according to *McGregor*)[89] and for any proven additional consequential losses flowing directly from that dispossession.[90]

As Stevens persuasively argues in *Torts and Rights*, in order to understand private law liability, 'it is necessary to distinguish between damages awarded as a substitute for the right infringed and consequential damages [given] as compensation for loss to the claimant … consequent upon this infringement'.[91] Substitutive damages are assessed objectively, calculated at the moment of the right infringement and awarded even if no economic loss is suffered by the claimant. In contrast, damages for consequential losses are 'specific or special to the claimant and must be proven', are assessed at the time of judgment and are subject to limitations, such as remoteness and mitigation, 'which do not apply to the substitutive award'.[92]

When Stevens' theory of 'damages' is applied to a tort that conceives of 'damage' as the dispossession of a right, the leading deceit cases are easily explainable and their results are no longer problematic from the perspective of substantive legal reasoning. For example, in *Mafo v Adams*, the claimant suffered damage when he was dispossessed of his protected tenancy through the fraud of the defendant. The Court awarded him £100 which was given partially in substitute for the loss of this tenancy, whose value was difficult to calculate in the absence of a functioning market for such rights, and partially as a consequential award for the physical inconvenience of the move and its aftermath caused by the fraud.[93] In response to the defendant's argument that £100 award was excessive given that no economic losses were proven, the Court argued that the sum was a 'a reasonable quantification of the damages due … for the above injuries'.[94]

[88] See *Mafo* [1970] 1 QB 548, 554; *Smith* (1884) 9 App Cas 187, 195–96.

[89] Edelman, above n 12, 1654, 1663.

[90] *Smith New Court* [1997] AC 254; *Doyle v Olby (Ironmongers) Ltd* [1969] 2 QB 158.

[91] Stevens, *Torts and Rights*, above n 27, 60. For criticism of Stevens' theory of substitutive damages, see A Burrows, 'Are "Damages on the *Wrotham Park* Basis" Compensatory, Restitutionary or Neither?' in D Saidov and R Cunnington (eds), *Contract Damages: Domestic and International Perspectives* (Oxford, Hart Publishing, 2008) 165; J Edelman, 'The Meaning of Loss and Enrichment' in R Chambers, C Mitchell and J Penner (eds), *Philosophical Foundations of the Law of Unjust Enrichment* (Oxford, Oxford University Press, 2009) 211; A Dyson and A Kramer, 'There Is No "Breach Date Rule": Mitigation, Difference In Value And Date Of Assessment' (2014) 130 *LQR* 259. For a response to many of these criticisms, see Stevens, 'Rights and Other Things', above n 27, 121–33.

[92] Stevens, *Torts and Rights*, above n 27, 60.

[93] *Mafo* [1970] 1 QB 548, 554 (Sachs LJ).

[94] ibid.

Similarly, in *Smith Kline & French*, the claimant suffered damage when it was fraudulently dispossessed of its drugs which had a readily ascertainable market price. It was therefore given the market value of the drugs, minus the value of what the defendant had already paid, in recognition of this dispossession as substitutive damages. As the claimant purposefully failed to prove any consequential losses,[95] no damages for this head of recovery were given.

In *Clef Aquitaine*, the claimant suffered damage when it was fraudulently dispossessed of its money in return for the defendant's goods. Unlike in *Smith Kline*, the Court in *Clef Aquitaine* could not easily ascertain a market price for the goods given the fact that the defendant was a monopoly supplier.[96] Thus, no damages were calculated in substitution of the right. Instead, the Court took an easier route and awarded damages for the consequences of the dispossession, these consequences being that the claimant would have used its money to purchase the defendant's goods at a cheaper price. Furthermore, the Court found that this head of damage was not too remote under the directness test applied for the tort of deceit.[97]

Finally, in *OMV Petrom* the claimant suffered damage when it was fraudulently dispossessed of its money in return for custom blends of oil instead of the name brands the defendant represented it would be receiving. It was therefore given substitutive damages calculated by the difference between the market price of the oil received and the amount it paid for the oil at the time of delivery – approximately £40 million. As the claimant choose not to prove any consequential losses, such as damage to its refinery equipment or a loss of profit on subsequent sales, no damages for this head of recovery were given.

Now at this point one may wonder: how is this different from the actionability theories offered by Stevens and Murphy? The differences are subtle but still meaningful and can be summarised as follows. On the actionability view, the tort is complete when the misrepresentation is acted upon by the claimant.[98] The right that the tort protects is therefore some form of freedom from manipulation or decisional autonomy. Because there are endless ways that one could act on a misrepresentation and much lying in the world,[99] and because it is trite law that deceit is not actionable per se, there must exist an additional hurdle in order to keep liability under control and to make their theories fit the law. This is the function of the concept of 'damage' and the damage requirement imposed is that the claimant must suffer a recognised form of 'loss'. To be fair, these scholars view 'loss' as more than mere pecuniary disadvantage and therefore their theories are an improvement, from the perspective of fit, on the conventional pecuniary loss view.

[95] *Smith Kline & French* [1989] 1 WLR 1, 5.

[96] *Clef Aquitaine* [2001] QB 488, 512 (Ward LJ).

[97] See above, text accompanying nn 50–53.

[98] Recall *Briess* [1954] AC 333, 353; *Diamond* [1979] QB 333.

[99] Recall Stevens, *Torts and Rights*, above n 27, 89: 'It would, of course, be unacceptable for the law to make actionable all of the minor deceptions that we practise upon one another.'

As Stevens argues, 'Loss is however given a broad meaning, so that a purchaser of a flat who has been deceived as to whether it included a roof terrace can recover for his disappointment and inconvenience, as well as for any financial loss.'[100] Similarly, Murphy states that 'it is a mistake to contend … that this tort is exclusively concerned with the protection of economic interests and that it ought to be regarded as a thoroughbred economic tort'.[101] As he continues, just as:

> negligence makes available a remedy to those who suffer physical harm by virtue of their reliance on another's misrepresentation, so too, on existing authority, does the tort of deceit cover such injuries. It also responds to the suffering of mental distress, and even mere discomfort.[102]

Unfortunately, this expansion of the concept of loss does not stop these theories from being incoherent since this requirement still imposes a limit on the scope of liability in the tort that stands in no relation to the deceit's rationale (as they understand it).

On the view presented in this section, the tort is complete when the claimant has acted on a fraudulent misrepresentation by dispossessing him or herself of a right. Because it is the non-consensual dispossession of a right that justifies the tort's existence, it is the only type or form of reliance that is protectable using the tort of deceit. Phrased differently, any other action or reliance taken as a result of another's lie are just not tortious under the tort of deceit. Thus if I fraudulently trick you so that you do not avail yourself of a certain opportunity but in failing to do so you do not actually give up anything that you already have, this would not constitute the tort.[103] Because deceit has such a narrow or austere focus, an additional damage requirement in the form of suffering loss, pecuniary or otherwise, is not needed to cut it back arbitrarily. Therefore, in this area of the law, the requirement that claimants should suffer damage means only that they should have dispossessed themselves of a right due to another's fraud. This does not dispense with the need for damage – it merely defines damage as a certain type of interference with a right as opposed to the suffering of some sort of loss. On this view, damages for physical injury, mental distress, or discomfort are awarded in deceit not because they are 'damage' but rather because they are consequential on that 'damage' (ie claimants giving up that which they already had), as they were in the case examples given by Stevens and Murphy. Thus, the theory herein presented is coherent since there is a 'unitary whole' to the tort of deceit,[104] namely the existence of the claimant's rights and their wrongful dispossession, which ensures that the reasons

[100] ibid citing *Shelley v Paddock* [1980] QB 348 ('*Shelley*').

[101] Murphy, above n 19, 321.

[102] ibid 321–22, citing *Allen v Ellis & Co* [1990] 1 EGLR 170 (physical harm); *Shelley* [1980] QB 348 (mental distress); *Mafo* [1970] 1 QB 548 (discomfort).

[103] See, eg, *Gale v Savings & Investment Corp* (1960) 26 DLR (2d) 466 ('*Gale*') (failing to purchase alternative insurance policy on the basis of a fraudulent misrepresentation as to coverage is not damage since one cannot lose that which they never had).

[104] Weinrib, above n 33, 968–69.

for imposing liability in one case, are the same reasons limiting or negating liability in another.[105]

Nor should this view of the tort be controversial from a fit perspective since in English law there appears to be only *one* reported case since 1845 whose actual result is inconsistent with this view,[106] and some Commonwealth authority supporting the position that causing other forms of reliance is just not tortious even when pecuniary loss is suffered.[107] Moreover, the view herein presented is perfectly consistent with the leading cases dealing with the date that a cause of action in deceit accrues,[108] so long as 'acted upon' is understood as a dispossession of a right. The same cannot, however, be said about the conventional view which requires the addition of the cumbersome and incoherent distinction between tortiousness and actionability in order to explain the law.[109]

VII. Conclusion

Writing recently in the *Oxford Journal of Legal Studies*, Donal Nolan argued that in:

> law we ought not to be prisoners of history, but instead should strive to progress our discipline, so that the law of the future is better than the law of the past. It follows that we must be prepared either to refine or to discard doctrines that are no longer fit for purpose.[110]

As an example of a doctrine ripe for change he gave the 'old distinction between wrongs actionable per se and wrongs actionable only on proof of damage'. As he noted, the meaning of the word 'damage' across the legal system has been 'slippery'.[111] It has variously been used to refer to a deleterious interference with a right, pecuniary loss and 'nothing at all, as in the tort of private nuisance, where the concept of damage is synonymous with (and so adds nothing to) the central idea of a substantial interference with the use and enjoyment of land'.[112]

[105] Seavey, above n 34, 34.

[106] *Barley v Walford* (1846) 9 QB 197 (claimant may sue for refraining from making silk products on faith of the defendant's fraudulent misrepresentation that the pattern was legally registered and unavailable for the claimant's use).

[107] *Gale* (1960) 26 DLR (2d) 466.

[108] Recall *Briess* [1954] AC 333, 353; *Diamond* [1979] QB 333.

[109] See Eggers, above n 25, paras 8.109–8.111 discussing the difficulty in making cases like *Briess* and *Diamond* cohere with the conventional view. As he states at para 8.110: if *Briess* 'is correct, one need not wait in order to determine whether the induced transaction was itself loss-making. This, however, is unlikely, being contrary to the necessity of proving both fraud and damage to constitute the tort of deceit. Thus, it has also been suggested that, in such cases, the cause of action arises subsequently upon damage being sustained [in *Latkter* [2001] EWCA Civ 875] … The position remains uncertain, however, given that the Court of Appeal in *Latkter* was not referred to Lord Tucker's dictum in *Briess v Woolley*' (footnotes omitted).

[110] Nolan, above n 23, 274–75.

[111] ibid 275.

[112] ibid 275 (footnotes omitted).

My argument is that in relation to the tort of deceit, the requirement of damage should be viewed as the non-consensual dispossession of a right previously held by the claimant (ie, an example of a deleterious interference with a right).

Understanding deceit in this way explains the leading cases on damages outlined above – cases that cannot be accommodated by the conventional pecuniary loss-based view of the tort. In addition, this rights-based view of the tort overcomes the conceptual and incoherence problems that abound if the suffering of loss is viewed as an element of tortiousness and/or actionability. The theory is conceptually possible because it is feasible for the claimant to point to the moment in time when the tort occurs, namely the time at which the claimant becomes dispossessed of his or her rights. It is also coherent since there is a 'unitary whole' to the tort of deceit that is centred around the claimant's rights and their wrongful dispossession. Thus with a little less formality in relation to interpretation and content, and with an eye fixed on its substance, the tort of deceit can be rescued from its current formalistic fate and integrated into the 'leading theoretical understanding' of the English law of wrongs, namely the rights-based interpretation of the law of torts.[113]

[113] Murphy, above n 19, 302.

14

Form and Substance in the Law of Punitive Damages

JAMES GOUDKAMP AND ELENI KATSAMPOUKA*

I. Introduction

Punitive damages, which are awarded to punish and deter, are the common law's most controversial remedy.[1] Consistently with their contested nature, there is no consensus as to the principles by which this remedy should be governed. Radically different approaches reflecting a diversity of judicial philosophies are taken throughout the common law world. The modest goal of this chapter is to promote understanding regarding punitive damages by comparing the relevant law in several jurisdictions with that of each other. Our focus is on Australia, Canada, England and the US.[2] Those jurisdictions have been selected for analysis because they are major common-law jurisdictions and because they all have an extensive and distinctive jurisprudence regarding punitive damages.

To facilitate our comparison, we employ the concepts of formal and substantive reasoning as those concepts were adumbrated by Atiyah and Summers in their path-breaking *Form and Substance in Anglo-American Law*.[3] A formal reason, Atiyah and Summers contended, 'is a legally authoritative reason on which judges … base a decision … and such a reason usually excludes from consideration … any countervailing substantive reason arising at the point of decision.'[4] By contrast, a substantive reason, Atiyah and Summers wrote, 'is a moral, economic, political,

* We are grateful to Václav Janeček, Jason Neyers, Andrew Robertson and Chaim Saiman for their comments on drafts of this chapter as well as to the Onassis Foundation and the Foundation for Education and European Culture for providing financial support.

[1] 'Exemplary damages are a controversial topic, and have been so for many years': *Kuddus v Chief Constable of Leicestershire Constabulary* [2001] UKHL 29, [2002] 2 AC 122 [50] (Lord Nicholls) ('*Kuddus*').

[2] In this chapter, we use the term 'England' to refer to all parts of the UK save for Scotland, which does not recognise punitive damages.

[3] PS Atiyah and RS Summers, *Form and Substance in Anglo-American Law: A Comparative Study of Legal Reasoning, Legal Theory and Legal Institutions* (Oxford, Clarendon Press, 1987).

[4] ibid 2.

institutional, or other social consideration'.[5] Atiyah and Summers recognised two basic types of substantive reasons: 'goal reasons' (ie, a rule being justified by the beneficial effects it is predicted to have in serving a social goal) and 'rightness reasons' (ie, a rule being justified morally because it is considered to be fair as applied to someone's past actions).[6]

Atiyah and Summers specifically addressed punitive damages and regarded the relevant law as powerfully supporting their overarching thesis that English law is highly formal whereas the law in the US is decidedly substantive and, in each case, excessively so. However, they dealt with the subject of punitive damages relatively briefly, and their treatment is now rather dated. In these circumstances, bringing Atiyah and Summers' distinction between formal reasoning and substantive reasoning to bear on the contemporary law of punitive damages in a more sustained way, and with reference to additional jurisdictions, promises to be worthwhile.

In Section II of this chapter, we argue that English law has adopted an extraordinarily formal approach to punitive damages since the landmark decision in *Rookes v Barnard*.[7] In Section III, we contend that Australian law takes a far more substantive approach to punitive damages relative to English law. The decision of the High Court of Australia in *Uren v John Fairfax & Sons Pty Ltd*,[8] which played an important role in Australian courts breaking free from the yoke of the Privy Council, is an outstanding illustration of a decision that is based on substantive reasons. Nevertheless, pockets of formal reasoning remain in the Australian law of punitive damages. In Section IV, attention is turned to the position in the US. Due to the dizzying diversity of approaches to punitive damages taken across the US, the rules articulated by the *Restatements of Law* published by the American Law Institute are regarded as representing the approach in the US. So understood, and speaking very broadly, the law concerning punitive damages in the US is similar to that in Australia in so far as the balance between formal and substantive reasoning is concerned. In Section V, we examine the Canadian law of punitive damages and argue that it is far more substantive than the corresponding law in England and (to a lesser but nonetheless meaningful degree) Australia and the US. Canadian courts have consistently paid close attention to the underlying justifications of civil punishment in deciding the questions regarding punitive damages. From the rejection of *Rookes* in *Paragon Properties Ltd v Magna Envestments Ltd* to the affirmation that punitive damages can be awarded in respect of breach of contract in *Whiten v Pilot Insurance Co*,[9] Canadian judges have been motivated by considerations of purpose and justice in shaping the law in this area.

[5] ibid 1.
[6] ibid 5.
[7] *Rookes v Barnard* [1964] AC 1129 ('*Rookes*').
[8] *Uren v John Fairfax & Sons Pty Ltd* (1966) 117 CLR 118 ('*Uren*').
[9] *Paragon Properties Ltd v Magna Envestments Ltd* (1972) 24 DLR (3d) 156 ('*Paragon*'); *Whiten v Pilot Insurance Co* 2002 SCC 18, [2002] 1 SCR 595 ('*Whiten*').

II. England

Over the last two centuries, the English law of punitive damages has drifted between formal and substantive approaches. However, in modern times, it epitomises a highly and, in our opinion, excessively, formal approach. The relevant English developments can be divided into four periods. The first runs from 1763 to 1963 during which time English law generally took a substantive approach to punitive damages. The second period covers developments between 1964 and 1992. The most important event in that period was the decision in *Rookes*, which committed English law to a highly formal approach by establishing the 'categories test'. During the third period – 1993–2000 – formalism intensified with the recognition in *AB v South West Water Services Ltd* of the pre-1964 test.[10] The fourth and final period covers developments from 2001 to date, during which time it appears that the relevant English law is gradually returning to a more substantive approach.

A. Substance in the Beginning (1763–1963)

Precisely when English law recognised the award of punitive damages is obscured by the mists of time. However, the term 'exemplary damages' – which is coterminous with the label 'punitive damages' – first appeared in English jurisprudence in 1763 in *Wilkes v Wood* and *Huckle v Money*. The claimant in *Wilkes*, who was a Member of Parliament, brought proceedings in trespass to land following a search of his house. Pratt LCJ said that the 'damages [awarded we]re designed not only as a satisfaction to the injured person, but likewise as a punishment to the guilty'.[11] The Lord Chief Justice also explained that their purpose was 'to deter from any such proceeding for the future, and [to prove] the detestation of the jury to the action itself'.[12] *Huckle* concerned a false imprisonment action brought by a man who had been detained by a messenger of the King. Pratt LCJ noted that the jury 'ha[d] done right in giving exemplary damages' because the messenger's conduct 'was a most daring public attack made upon the liberty of the subject … [and] the 29th chapter of Magna Charta … [which] pointed against arbitrary power, was violated'.[13]

In the era of *Wilkes* and *Huckle* through to the end of our first period, the availability of punitive damages was determined according to substantive considerations. Generally speaking, the jurisdiction to award the remedy existed whenever the defendant's conduct merited punishment and there was a need to deter similar behaviour in the future. For example, in *Williams v Settle* Sellers LJ

[10] *AB v South West Water Services Ltd* [1993] QB 507 ('*AB*').
[11] *Wilkes v Wood* (1763) Lofft 1, 18–19, 98 ER 489, 498 ('*Wilkes*').
[12] *Wilkes* (1763) Lofft 1, 19, 98 ER 489, 498–99.
[13] *Huckle v Money* (1763) 2 Wils KB 205, 207, 95 ER 768, 769 ('*Huckle*').

considered that an award of punitive damages was justified because it would 'hold the defendant up as an example to the community … [T]hey may act as a deterrent to others who are willing to supply to the press information which they know is going to be used in a manner which will be so hurtful and distressing to the people involved'.[14] His Lordship added that effective relief could not otherwise be given because this was a 'flagrant infringement of the right of the plaintiff, and it was scandalous conduct and in total disregard not only of the legal rights of the plaintiff regarding copyright but of his feelings and his sense of family dignity and pride'.[15]

Dumbell v Roberts provides another clear example of substantive reasoning. It involved a false imprisonment claim. The Court recognised deterrence as the underlying justification for the award of punitive damages and concluded that the more high-handed the defendant's conduct the greater the need for deterrence. Scott LJ said:

> [I]n so far as they represent the disapproval of the law … for improper interference with personal freedom [damages] may be 'punitive' … given by way of punishment of the defendant or as a deterrent example … The more high-handed and less reasonable the detention is, the larger may be the damages; and, conversely, the more nearly reasonable the defendant may have acted and the nearer he may have got to justification on reasonable grounds for the suspicion on which he arrested, the smaller will be the proper assessment. The whole of the facts will … be taken into account … in order to arrive at a proper figure.[16]

B. Formalism in the Ascendancy: The 'Categories Test' (1964–1992)

In what is still the leading English case on punitive damages,[17] *Rookes v Barnard*, which was decided in 1964, Lord Devlin confined the jurisdiction to award punitive damages to just three categories of case. These categories are cases: (1) involving oppressive, arbitrary or unconstitutional conduct by government servants; (2) in which the defendant sought to make a profit after paying compensation; and (3) in which statute authorised the award of punitive damages. The 'categories test' is an example of extreme commitment to formalism since, unless a case falls within one of the three narrowly defined groups of cases, punitive damages will be unavailable irrespective of how strongly the reasons for granting punitive damages may call for an award thereof. Thus, Atiyah and Summers observed with reference to

[14] *Williams v Settle* [1960] 1 WLR 1072, 1081 ('*Williams*').

[15] *Williams* [1960] 1 WLR 1072, 1082.

[16] *Dumbell v Roberts* [1944] 1 All ER 326, 330.

[17] *Rookes v Barnard* 'remain[s] the fount of the modern jurisdiction to award exemplary damages': *Axa Insurance UK Plc v Financial Claims Solutions Ltd* [2017] EWHC 3803 (QB) [15] (Judge Andrew Keyser QC).

Rookes that 'the permissibility of awards of exemplary damages in tort cases is much restrained by formal rules in English law'.[18]

Lord Devlin sought to justify the 'categories test' on the basis of both precedent (he contended that the categories '[we]re established as part of the common law') and principle (he argued that there were principled reasons calling for the retention of the power to award punitive damages in these categories of case).[19] As we will show, neither contention is convincing, and it is tolerably clear that Lord Devlin's real reason for establishing the 'categories test' was simply his desire to restrict to the greatest possible extent a remedy that he considered to be anomalous.[20] It is unsurprising that *Rookes* has not been followed in any other jurisdiction.[21]

i. *Bad Formal Reasoning*

According to Atiyah and Summers, 'a particular formal reason may be bad … It may rest on law that is not really valid law; or it may misconstrue that law or it may go beyond that law as properly interpreted and applied'.[22] Lord Devlin employed such 'bad formal reasoning' in *Rookes* in contending that the first and second categories were justified by previous decisions. After reviewing various authorities regarding punitive damages, Lord Devlin said:

> These authorities convince me … that there are certain categories of cases in which an award of exemplary damages can serve a useful purpose in vindicating the strength of the law … I propose to state what these two categories are … The first category is oppressive, arbitrary or unconstitutional action by the servants of the government … Cases in the second category are those in which the defendant's conduct has been calculated by him to make a profit for himself which may well exceed the compensation payable to the plaintiff … To these two categories which are established as part of the common law there must of course be added any category in which exemplary damages are expressly authorised by statute … I must now return to the authorities I have already reviewed and make quite plain what it is that I have not accepted from them.[23]

Lord Devlin considered that three decisions – *Wilkes*, *Huckle* and *Benson v Frederick* – demonstrated the existence of 'category 1' (ie, oppressive conduct

[18] Atiyah and Summers, above n 3, 86.

[19] *Rookes* [1964] AC 1129, 1226, 1228.

[20] Lord Devlin wrote that 'so far as I know, the idea of exemplary damages is peculiar to English law … your Lordships … have to consider whether it is open to the House to remove an anomaly from the law of England' (*Rookes* [1964] AC 1129, 1221). He also referred to '[t]he anomaly inherent in exemplary damages' (*Rookes* [1964] AC 1129, 1227).

[21] Ultimate appellate courts declined to follow *Rookes* in Australia (*Uren* (1966) 117 CLR 118), Canada (*Vorvis v Insurance Corp of British Columbia* [1989] 1 SCR 1085 ('*Vorvis*')), New Zealand (*Taylor v Beere* [1982] 1 NZLR 81) and Singapore (*ACB v Thomson Medical Pte Ltd* [2017] SGCA 20, [2017] 1 SLR 918 ('*ACB*')). cf *Allan v Ng & Co* [2012] HKCA 119, [2012] 2 HKLRD 160 ('*Allan*') in which *Rookes* was cited in passing.

[22] Atiyah and Summers, above n 3, 28.

[23] *Rookes* [1964] AC 1129, 1225–28.

by government servants).[24] However, *Huckle* was arguably concerned with aggravated rather than punitive damages,[25] and in none of the cases did the courts attach importance to the fact that the defendant was a public servant. Rather, it was the arbitrary and outrageous conduct of the defendant that justified the awards, and it was simply coincidental that the defendant was a government servant. Thus, judges and commentators writing during our first period considered the defendant's conduct (rather than the defendant's capacity) as triggering the punitive response in the above cases.[26] For example, according to Winfield:

> [I]n exemplary damages [the court] can punish the defendant for … an especially outrageous attack on the plaintiff's security … [This] is illustrated by the cases deciding against the legality of the search warrants which were issued against John Wilkes and others during the latter part of the eighteenth century.[27]

There is no reference to the defendant's capacity as a public servant in Winfield's discussion of *Wilkes*. Similarly, Jenks wrote that punitive damages may be awarded 'especially in the following cases: … where the plaintiff has been deprived of a constitutional right (*Huckle v Money*)'.[28] Again, there is nothing to suggest that the exercise of executive power by the defendant was important.

As to the second category, Lord Devlin again contended that three cases supported its existence: *Bell v Midland Railway Co*, *Williams v Currie* and *Crouch v Great Northern Railway Co*.[29] It is arguable that the latter two cases were not in fact concerned with punitive damages but with aggravated damages.[30] However, even if those decisions did involve punitive damages, by far the better view is that the courts did not regard the existence of a profit motive as a pre-condition to an

[24] *Wilkes* (1763) Lofft 1, 98 ER 489; *Huckle* (1763) 2 Wils KB 205, 95 ER 768; *Benson v Frederick* (1766) 3 Burr 1845, 97 ER 1130 ('*Benson*').

[25] There is no reference to punishment or a punishment-related goal in the Court's reasons. The fact that the term 'exemplary damages' is used in the Court's reasons is inconclusive because punitive and aggravated damages were not clearly distinguished at that time.

[26] However, at least one textbook of that period refers to 'abuses by officers of the law' as a case category in which punitive damages may be awarded: see WE Ball, *Principles of Torts and Contracts* (London, Stevens and Sons, 1880) 110 (citing *Duke of Brunswick v Slowman* (1849) 8 CB 317, 137 ER 532 in support).

[27] P Winfield, *A Textbook on the Law of Torts*, 5th edn (London, Sweet & Maxwell, 1950) 150.

[28] E Jenks, *A Digest of English Civil Law*, 3rd edn (London, Butterworth, 1938) 347. See also CG Addison, *Wrongs and Their Remedies: Being a Treatise on the Law of Torts* (London, Stevens and Sons, 1860) 788–89; F Pollock, *The Law of Torts*, 2nd edn (London, Stevens and Sons, 1890) 170; W Salmond, *The Law of Torts*, 5th edn (London, Sweet & Maxwell, 1920) 129–30. cf J Sayer, *The Law of Damages* (London, Strahan and Woodfall, 1770) 220 who argues that the punitive damages award in *Huckle v Money* was justified because the injury was 'done under the colour of authority'.

[29] *Bell v Midland Railway Co* (1861) 10 CBNS 287, 142 ER 462 ('*Bell*'); *Williams v Currie* (1845) 1 CB 841, 135 ER 774 ('*Williams*'); *Crouch v Great Northern Railway Co* (1856) 11 Exch 742, 156 ER 1031 ('*Crouch*').

[30] Lord Devlin himself interpreted *Williams* as an aggravated damages case (and, it seems, rightly so): *Rookes* [1964] AC 1129, 1229. As for *Crouch*, only one of the three judges who decided that case, Martin B, used terminology – 'vindictive' damages – that was potentially consistent with the concept of punitive damages. However, that language is hardly decisive considering that the terms 'vindictive', 'exemplary' and 'aggravated' damages were used apparently more or less interchangeably at the time.

award of punitive damages but as reinforcing the conclusion that an award was merited.

In relation to *Bell*, Lord Devlin relied on Erie CJ's remark that an award of £1,000 for private nuisance was not excessive because the 'company [had] set up a wharf of their own, and, careless whether they were doing right or wrong, prevented all access to the plaintiff's wharf, *for the purpose of extinguishing his trade and advancing their own profit*'.[31] However, Erie CJ did not suggest that the aim of making a profit was a pre-condition to awarding punitive damages. It is far more plausible to think that the defendant's profit motive was not regarded as a *condition* that had to be satisfied in order to enliven the jurisdiction to award punitive damages but merely as an *indication* that punitive damages were warranted on the facts.

Similarly, in *Williams* Maule J, who was the only judge to mention the issue of profit, said merely:

> When … we consider that the acts of which the plaintiff complains were not only detrimental to the plaintiff, but profitable to the defendant, and that the verdict does not very much exceed the amount of actual damage proved, I think we should be usurping the legitimate province of the jury if we were to interfere.[32]

The better view is that Maule J simply considered that the fact that the wrong yielded a profit called for a large award, and did not regard the existence of profit motive as a pre-condition to the award.

As to *Crouch*, Lord Devlin relied on the following passage from Martin B's reasons:

> [I]f … the plaintiff was a carrier, and … his business was to collect goods for the purpose of sending them down by railway, and … the defendants designedly refused to carry parcels … *for the purpose of getting a monopoly in their hands* and destroying the plaintiff's trade – … *upon being satisfied that the railway company willfully transgressed the law with a view to get a monopoly of a certain class of business* and destroy the business of another, I am not prepared to say that a jury might not properly give vindictive damages to a person so oppressed. But that is not this case. Whenever the question arises, I shall be perfectly free to give an opinion upon it.[33]

Even if Martin B contemplated an award of punitive damages as opposed to aggravated damages, he only did so in relation to a hypothetical scenario and reserved his opinion as to whether the scenario called for an award.

Before leaving the present point, it is worth adding that although *Rookes* is an excellent illustration of formalism in English law, it is also in some ways a striking counter-example to Atiyah and Summers' more general claim that one incident of the highly formal English legal system is that 'the courts … are often unwilling to make the changes which seem desirable' and that the judiciary is generally

[31] *Bell* (1861) 10 CBNS 287, 304, 142 ER 462, 469 (emphasis added).
[32] *Williams* (1845) 1 CB 841, 848, 135 ER 774, 776–77.
[33] *Crouch* (1856) 11 Exch 742, 759, 156 ER 1031, 1038 (emphasis added).

'cautious in exercising [its] law-making function'.[34] It is difficult in some respects for Atiyah and Summers to accommodate *Rookes* given that Lord Devlin assumed an unusually active role in changing the law, especially for the time. His Lordship's attitude in *Rookes* was also unusual because, unlike most 'English appellate judges', he did not 'rely more heavily on the arguments of counsel and much less heavily on [his] own research'.[35] The summary of counsel's argument in the report of *Rookes* in the Appeal Cases does not contain any reference to the categories. It appears that they are entirely based on Lord Devlin's own research.

ii. Content Formality: Lord Devlin's 'Categories' are Not Principled

Lord Devlin considered that principle as well as precedent justified awarding punitive damages in specified categories of case. He contended that principle supported the first category because the 'power [of government servants] must always be subordinate to their duty of service'.[36] The second category, Lord Devlin said, was 'necessary to teach a wrongdoer that tort does not pay'.[37] However, the 'categories test' comprises what Atiyah and Summers characterised as 'content formality' because the rule established by that test is 'under-inclusive … in relation to its objectives'.[38] It is under-inclusive because it excludes from its scope cases that should be embraced given the purposes of awarding punitive damages, which purposes Lord Devlin identified as being punishment and deterrence.[39] The problem is that the interest in punishment and deterrence is not confined to cases of oppressive conduct by public servants (category 1) or to instances of profit-seeking conduct (category 2). Those are manifestly not the only situations in which conduct that is deserving of punishment and in respect of which there is a need for deterrence can occur. Consider, for example, *Loudon v Ryder*.[40] In this case, the defendant entered the claimant's flat through a window and attacked the claimant. Although the defendant's conduct falls outside the *Rookes* categories (because the defendant was not a public servant and did not act with a profit motive), the behaviour plainly merited the award of punitive damages according to the rationales for the remedy.

iii. A Counter-example to the English Norm

Atiyah and Summers observed that one of the formal characteristics of English law was that 'lower courts are expected to – and do – conform without question

[34] Atiyah and Summers, above n 3, 141, 269.
[35] ibid 279.
[36] *Rookes* [1964] AC 1129, 1226.
[37] ibid 1227.
[38] Atiyah and Summers, above n 3, 13.
[39] 'The object of exemplary damages is to punish and deter': *Rookes* [1964] AC 1129, 1220.
[40] *Loudon v Ryder* [1953] 2 QB 202 (overruled in *Rookes* [1964] AC 1129, 1229).

to the rulings of higher courts'.[41] By contrast, in a more substantive system, 'precedents … are expected to be disregarded or overruled if they seem wrong or unjust or bad or obsolete'.[42] *Broome*, which concerned a claim in respect of a defamatory publication, is an arresting counter-example to that thesis. In *Broome*, the Court of Appeal (Lord Denning MR, Salmond and Phillimore LJJ) unanimously concluded that *Rookes* should not be followed to the extent that it endorsed the categories because those categories were 'hopelessly illogical and inconsistent' as well as contrary to previous authority.[43] This refusal, although it was technically obiter since the Court of Appeal would have decided the appeal in the same way even if they had followed *Rookes*, provides an excellent English example of divergence from the norm of loyalty to superior courts by employing substantive reasoning. Atiyah and Summers themselves identified the Court of Appeal's decision in *Broome* as exceptional in English law generally.[44] Unsurprisingly, however, given English formalism, the House of Lords on a further appeal in *Broome* sharply rebuked the Court of Appeal and emphasised the obligation of all courts to adhere strictly to the House's judgments.[45]

C. Formalism's Grip Tightens: The 'Pre-1964 Test' (1993–2000)

Perhaps the most extreme illustration of commitment to formalism in the English law of punitive damages, and perhaps in the English law of obligations more generally, is the decision of the Court of Appeal in *AB v South West Water Services*.[46] In that case, the Court relied on obiter dicta in the House of Lords' decision in *Broome* to establish what is known as the 'pre-1964 test' (or 'cause of action test'). According to that test, punitive damages can be awarded only in respect of causes of action for which they had been awarded before 1964 (that being the year in which *Rookes* was decided). It had the effect of precluding punitive damages from being awarded in proceedings in, for example, deceit,[47] negligence,[48] public nuisance[49] and patent infringement.[50] The 'pre-1964 test' also prevented punitive damages from being awarded for statutory torts created after 1964.[51] In short, it comprised

[41] Atiyah and Summers, above n 3, 289–90.

[42] ibid 414.

[43] *Broome v Cassell & Co Ltd* [1971] 2 QB 354, 381 (Lord Denning MR).

[44] Atiyah and Summers observed, with reference to the Court of Appeal's decision in *Broome v Cassell & Co Ltd*, in which Lord Denning was part of the constitution, that 'Lord Denning was an exception to th[e] generalization [that] English judges accept the traditions of loyalty to higher court rulings': Atiyah and Summers, above n 3, 290 (footnotes omitted).

[45] *Broome v Cassell & Co Ltd* [1972] AC 1027, 1054, 1084, 1098–99, 1107, 1113, 1131–32 ('*Broome*').

[46] *AB* [1993] QB 507.

[47] *Broome* [1972] AC 1027, 1076, 1130.

[48] *AB* [1993] QB 507.

[49] ibid.

[50] *Catnic Components Ltd v Hill & Smith Ltd* [1983] FSR 512.

[51] See, eg, unlawful discrimination based on the Race Relations Act 1976 (UK) (see *Deane v Ealing London Borough Council* [1993] ICR 329). cf *Bradford City Metropolitan Council v Arora* [1991] 2 QB 507.

a high hurdle (additional to the 'categories test') that had to be surmounted before the jurisdiction to award punitive damages was available.

According to Atiyah and Summers:

> [f]ormality degenerates into formalistic reasoning when, for example, judges refuse to recognise the excessive arbitrariness of a common law rule and adhere to that rule where this would not be justifiable … A formalistic reasoning involves a failure to take substantive considerations into account *when they ought to be taken into account*.[52]

AB exemplifies Atiyah and Summers' description of formalistic reasoning. The Court fixated on the precise language used in *Broome*, and it elected to permit awards of punitive damages only if it had been held in a pre-1964 case that they were available in the cause of action concerned. The fact that an award of punitive damages may otherwise have been warranted given the facts of the individual case was irrelevant. As the author of the fifteenth edition of *Winfield & Jolowicz on Tort* pointedly observed, the 'pre-1964 test' meant that the availability of punitive damages 'depend[ed] not on principle but upon the accidents of litigation (or even of law reporting) before 1964'.[53]

D. A More Substantive Approach Strikes Back (2001–)

Since 2001, the English law of punitive damages has followed a more substantive approach. In *Kuddus v Chief Constable of Leicestershire Constabulary*,[54] the House of Lords unanimously abolished the 'pre-1964 test'. Lord Nicholls' speech is arguably the best example of substantive reasoning regarding punitive damages by a British judge since the Court of Appeal's decision in *Broome* or, conceivably, the era prior to *Rookes*. Not only did he recognise that the 'pre-1964 test' 'represent[ed] in practice an arbitrary and irrational restriction on the availability of exemplary damages'[55] but he also said that 'the availability of exemplary damages should be co-extensive with its rationale … [T]he underlying rationale lies in the sense of outrage which a defendant's conduct sometimes evokes, a sense which is not always assuaged fully by a compensatory award of damages'.[56]

Despite the removal of the 'pre-1964 test' in 2001, several cause of action restrictions on the award of punitive damages that are also based on formal reasoning nonetheless survive in English law. For example, the dominant view is that punitive damages are not available for equitable wrongs. According to the authors of a leading textbook on equity, 'in England, received legal opinion has long been that exemplary damages awards for breach of purely equitable obligations are

[52] Atiyah and Summers, above n 3, 28–29.
[53] WVH Rogers, *Winfield and Jolowicz on Tort*, 15th edn (London, Sweet & Maxwell, 1998) 746.
[54] *Kuddus* [2001] UKHL 29, [2002] 2 AC 122.
[55] ibid [55].
[56] ibid [65].

not permitted – and English law therefore precludes them'.[57] Similarly, in *Mosley v News Group Newspapers Ltd*, Eady J held that punitive damages were not available for breach of confidence 'since there [wa]s no existing authority (whether statutory or at common law) to justify such an extension'.[58] The reliance on (the absence of) precedent in this regard is significant for present purposes since it suggests that this cause of action bar is based not on substantive reasons (such as, for example, a reason rooted in the nature of equity) but on formal grounds.

Another residual cause of action restriction concerns claims for breach of contract. It is widely thought that such claims do not engage the jurisdiction to award punitive damages. For example, according to Ewan McKendrick, 'punitive damages … cannot be awarded in a purely contractual action, even where the defendant has calculated that he will make a profit from his breach of contract'.[59] This bar ultimately owes its existence to the decision of the House of Lords in *Addis v Gramophone Co Ltd*,[60] which courts and commentators have blindly assumed establishes that punitive damages are unavailable for claims in contract.[61] It has also been contended that the longevity of the bar on punitive damages in the contractual context might render their introduction inappropriate.[62] This position exemplifies a formal approach.

In addition to *Kuddus*, several other developments since 2001 reflect a more substantive approach including the Court of Appeal's decision in *Rowlands v Chief Constable of Merseyside Police*[63] and the enactment of section 34 of the Crime and Courts Act 2013 (UK). The claimant in *Rowlands* had been physically restrained by a policeman who also procured her detention and gave false evidence in an attempt to secure her conviction. The claimant sued the Chief Constable of Merseyside Police for assault, false imprisonment and malicious prosecution. The Court of Appeal was concerned with whether punitive damages could and should be awarded against a defendant whose liability was vicarious rather than personal. Moore-Bick LJ considered that although 'it is contrary to principle to punish a person whose behaviour is not in any way blameworthy' there were still substantive reasons justifying the availability of punitive damages in such cases.[64] First, he said, awarding punitive damages would express the Court's disapproval

[57] JD Heydon, MJ Leeming and PG Turner, *Meagher, Gummow and Lehane's Equity: Doctrines and Remedies*, 5th edn (Sydney, LexisNexis Butterworths, 2015) para 23.600.

[58] *Mosley v News Group Newspapers Ltd* [2008] EWHC 1777 (QB) [197] ('*Mosley*').

[59] E McKendrick, *Contract Law*, 12th edn (Basingstoke, Palgrave MacMillan, 2017) 370.

[60] *Addis v Gramophone Co Ltd* [1909] AC 488 ('*Addis*').

[61] One of us has argued that this understanding is incorrect, and that *Addis*, contrary to prevailing wisdom, says nothing about the availability of punitive damages in contract: see J Goudkamp, 'Exemplary Damages' in G Virgo and S Worthington (eds), *Commercial Remedies: Resolving Controversies* (Cambridge, Cambridge University Press, 2017) 321–22.

[62] Law Commission, *Aggravated, Exemplary and Restitutionary Damages* (Law Com No 247, 1997) 118; S Rowan, 'Reflections on the Introduction of Punitive Damages for Breach of Contract' (2010) 30 *OJLS* 495, 504, 516.

[63] *Rowlands v Chief Constable of Merseyside Police* [2006] EWCA Civ 1773, [2007] 1 WLR 1065 ('*Rowlands*').

[64] *Rowlands* [2006] EWCA Civ 1773, [2007] 1 WLR 1065 [46].

of the conduct of both the individual police officer and the police force as an institution.[65] Secondly, Moore-Bick LJ considered that awarding punitive damages was 'desirable as a matter of policy [because] … [o]nly by this means can awards of an adequate amount be made against those who bear public responsibility for the conduct of the officers concerned'.[66]

The Crime and Courts Act 2013 affects the availability of punitive damages against certain media defendants. In outline, the salient provisions authorise the award of punitive damages in respect of 'relevant claims'[67] arising from the publication of 'news-related material'[68] against a 'relevant publisher'[69] who was not a member of an 'approved press regulator'[70] at the material time. Before an award can be made, it is necessary that '(a) the defendant's conduct has shown a deliberate or reckless disregard of an outrageous nature for the claimant's rights, (b) the conduct is such that the court should punish the defendant for it, and (c) other remedies would not be adequate to punish that conduct'.[71] The new regime departs from previous formal restrictions on punitive damages in two ways. First, it explicitly authorises the award of punitive damages for misuse of private information and breach of confidence and thus overcomes residual judicial cause of action restrictions in this area.[72] Secondly, although the Act brings cases to which it applies within category 3 of the 'categories test' (ie, statutory authorisation to award punitive damages), in a sense it loosens the strictures of that test by enabling the award of punitive damages against press defendants whenever there was 'a deliberate or reckless disregard of an outrageous nature for the claimant's rights' without any requirement for a "profit motive"'.[73]

E. Assessment

Although the jurisdiction to award punitive damages has been liberalised in various ways since 2001, overall, the English law of punitive damages remains highly formal, largely due to the 'categories test' but also because of certain residual cause of action restrictions. It is important, however, that the position

[65] ibid [42].
[66] ibid [47].
[67] Crime and Courts Act 2013 (UK), s 42(4). Relevant claims are 'civil claims in respect of (a) libel; (b) slander; (c) breach of confidence; (d) misuse of private information; (e) malicious falsehood; and (f) harassment'.
[68] ibid s 42(7). News-related material means '(a) news or information about current affairs, (b) opinion about matters relating to the news or current affairs, or (c) gossip about celebrities, other public figures or other persons in the news'.
[69] ibid s 41.
[70] ibid s 42(2). An approved regulator means 'a body recognised as a regulator of relevant publishers'.
[71] ibid s 34(6). Note that punitive damages can also be awarded against a member of the press who has signed up to be regulated, under certain circumstances (see ibid s 34(3)).
[72] See *Mosley* [2008] EWHC 1777 (QB) [197].
[73] Crime and Courts Act 2013 (UK), s 34(6)(a).

not be overstated. Despite embracing a highly formalistic approach, the English law of punitive damages has always contained traces of substantive reasoning. Four examples merit mention. First, the rule that the defendant's wealth is relevant to the assessment of punitive damages[74] is based on the idea that in order to punish and deter effectively, awards of punitive damages need to be tailored to the defendant's individual circumstances.[75] Secondly, the imposition of other sanctions for the same conduct is relevant to both the decision to award punitive damages and to the quantification of the award.[76] This also reflects a concern not to punish the defendant excessively and to avoid over-deterrence. Third, provocation by the claimant is considered in determining whether punitive damages should be awarded and, if so, in what amount.[77] This rule is similarly intelligible from a substantive perspective since provocation by the claimant may diminish the defendant's blameworthiness.[78] Fourth, when several claimants are entitled to punitive damages in respect of the same wrongful conduct, those damages are shared equally between them.[79] A rule that required the full punitive damages award to be paid to each claimant would be incompatible with the goals of achieving proportionate punishment and efficient deterrence.

III. Australia

The Australian law of punitive damages is much more substantive than the corresponding English law in significant respects. The High Court of Australia was the first ultimate appellate court in the Commonwealth to reject the *Rookes* categories, which step it dramatically took in *Uren v John Fairfax & Sons Pty Ltd*.[80] In refusing to follow *Rookes*, the High Court engaged extensively with the justifications for punitive damages. It hence preferred substance over form. However, traces

[74] *Benson* (1766) 3 Burr 1845, 97 ER 1130, 1846; *Rookes* [1964] AC 1129, 1227–28; *Hassan v Cooper* [2015] EWHC 540 (QB), [2015] RTR 26 [80]–[92] ('*Hassan*').

[75] '[T]he means of the person to pay the [punitive] damages are relevant … [I]f you have an award made in the case of a person who will be completely destroyed and broken by it, that is to go too far … Equally if you have a rich defendant, it is relevant to bear in mind that a very modest award is no deterrent': *Hassan* [2015] EWHC 540 (QB), [2015] RTR 26 [80] (Butler J).

[76] *Wilkes* (1763) Lofft 1, 98 ER 489, 490; *Archer v Brown* [1985] QB 401, 423; *Axa Insurance UK Plc v Thwaites* (Norwich County Court, 8 February 2008) [12]; Crime and Courts Act 2013 (UK), s 35(2). cf *Borders (UK) Ltd v Commissioner of Police of the Metropolis* [2005] EWCA Civ 197; *AT v Dulghieru* [2009] EWHC 225 (QB).

[77] *Russell v Home Office* [2001] Po LR 29 (QB) [204]–[206].

[78] It is for this reason that the criminal law takes cognisance of provocation in relation to sentencing. As Ashworth notes 'courts are expected to take [provocation] into account when assessing culpability for the purpose of sentencing': A Ashworth, *Sentencing and Criminal Justice*, 6th edn (Cambridge, Cambridge University Press, 2015) 149.

[79] *Riches v News Group Newspapers Ltd* [1986] QB 256.

[80] *Uren* (1966) 117 CLR 118. For discussion, see M Lunney, 'The Unexpected Cold War Contribution to Exemplary Damages in Defamation: *Uren v John Fairfax & Co*' in D Rolph (ed), *Landmark Cases in Defamation Law* (Oxford, Hart Publishing, 2019) (forthcoming).

of formal reasoning can nonetheless be found in the Australian law of punitive damages.

Uren concerned two defamatory publications in the *Sun Herald* that connected Tom Uren, a Member of Parliament, with a Russian spy. The imputation was that Mr Uren had been duped by the spy into asking questions in Parliament with a view to extracting from the Prime Minister and the Minister for Defence information about secret defence establishments in Australia. The High Court robustly rejected the 'categories test'. Substantive reasoning features very prominently in, in particular, Taylor J's reasons. Taylor J wrote:

> I do not feel as Lord Devlin did, that such a far-reaching reform as he proposed … was justified by asserting that punishment was a matter for the criminal law … Indeed, the statement of the categories in which exemplary damages may be awarded concedes that, in some cases, at least, it is the function of the civil law to permit an award of damages by way of punishment … I am unable to see any grounds, either in principle or upon authority, justifying the formulation of th[ese] … categor[ies]. This observation has … special force when it is seen that in many cases much the same functions are performed in precisely the same manner and in the exercise of much the same authority by both "servants of the government" and other persons. There is … even more force in the observation when it is observed that the second category … relates to acts done by any person but it is confined to acts done by a defendant who "with a cynical disregard for a plaintiff's rights has calculated that the money to be made out of his wrongdoing will probably exceed the damages at risk". … I am quite unable to see why the law should look with less favour on wrongs committed with a profit-making motive than upon wrongs committed with the utmost degree of malice or vindictively, arrogantly or high-handedly with a contumelious disregard for the plaintiff's rights.[81]

The effect of rejecting the 'categories test' was that the availability of punitive damages turned simply on whether the defendant's conduct exhibited a contumelious disregard for the claimant's rights.[82] An appeal to the Privy Council was dismissed with Lord Morris remarking on behalf of the Board that '[t]heir Lordships are not prepared to say that the High Court were wrong in being unconvinced that a changed approach in Australia was desirable'.[83]

A substantive approach was reaffirmed in *Gray v Motor Accident Commission* in which the High Court held that punitive damages are available in claims in the tort of negligence because conduct that is actionable in that tort may merit punishment.[84] And in *Lamb v Cotogno* the High Court upheld an award of punitive

[81] *Uren* (1966) 117 CLR 118, 131, 137–38.

[82] See, eg, Taylor J in *Uren* (1966) 117 CLR 118, 138 quoting with approval Knox CJ's remark in *Whitfeld v De Laurent & Co Ltd* (1920) 29 CLR 71, 77 that punitive damages 'are given only in cases of conscious wrongdoing in contumelious disregard of another's rights'.

[83] *Australian Consolidated Press Ltd v Uren* [1969] 1 AC 590, 644.

[84] *Gray v Motor Accident Commission* [1998] HCA 70, (1998) 196 CLR 1, 1 ('*Gray*') (giving the example of an employer systematically and deliberately disregarding risks or cases of outrageous departure from the standard of care that would have been achieved by the reasonable person). See further K Barker et al, *The Law of Torts in Australia*, 5th edn (Melbourne, Oxford University Press, 2012) 698.

damages against a defendant motorist who had purchased compulsory third-party liability insurance pursuant to a statutory scheme. Consistently with a substantive approach the Court reasoned that deterrence 'extends beyond the actual wrongdoer and the exact nature of his wrongdoing' and that the award appeases the victim and assuages any urge for revenge.[85]

Despite the overall substantive approach to the law of punitive damages that prevails in Australia, several illustrations of formal reasoning can nevertheless be found. A good example with far reaching consequences in practice is the arbitrary prohibition by statute in New South Wales, Queensland and the Northern Territory of the award of punitive damages in cases involving negligently inflicted personal injury or death.[86] Cause of action restrictions supply another illustration of formal reasoning. Although a 'cause of action test' equivalent to that which existed in England has never been adopted in Australia, Australian law nonetheless bars the recovery of punitive damages in certain causes of action on formal grounds. For example, the High Court has confirmed that punitive damages cannot be awarded in claims for breach of and contract and apparently did so on the footing that, according to established principle, the assessment of damages in contract is unaffected by the reprehensibility of the breach.[87] This reflects a formal approach since it appeals to the rule that damages for breach of contract are compensatory rather than linking the punitive damages jurisdiction to its rationales, namely punishment and deterrence. In *Hospitality Group Pty Ltd v Australian Rugby Union Ltd*, the Federal Court engaged in formal reasoning when it said that punitive damages are unavailable in claims for breach of contract because 'this was authoritatively decided by the House of Lords in *Addis*'.[88] Finally, in *Harris v Digital Pulse Pty Ltd*,[89] a majority of the New South Wales Court of Appeal held that punitive damages cannot be awarded in a claim for breach of fiduciary duty.[90] It did so mainly on formal grounds. Thus, the majority said that punitive damages should not be awarded for equitable wrongs because never in its history did equity award punitive damages.[91] However, the

[85] *Lamb v Cotogno* (1987) 164 CLR 1, 5.

[86] Civil Liability Act 2002 (NSW), s 21; Civil Liability Act 2003 (Qld), s 52; Personal Injuries (Liabilities and Damages) Act 2003 (NT), s 19. With the exception of the Northern Territory, these jurisdictions still allow punitive damages for dust diseases and smoking or other tobacco-related injuries. See also the Competition and Consumer Act 2010 (Cth), s 87ZB(1) which prohibits punitive damages for death or personal injury in proceedings under the Australian Consumer Law.

[87] Consider the remarks in *Butler v Fairclough* (1917) 23 CLR 78, 89 (Griffith CJ) (emphasis added): 'The motive or state of mind of a person who is guilty of a breach of contract is not relevant to the question of damages for the breach … A breach of contract may be innocent, even accidental or unconscious … Or it may be wilful, and even malicious and committed with the express intention of injuring the other party. *But the measure of damages is not affected by any such considerations*.' This passage was quoted in *Gray* [1998] HCA 70, (1998) 196 CLR 1 [13].

[88] *Hospitality Group Pty Ltd v Australian Rugby Union Ltd* [2001] FCA 1040 [142].

[89] *Harris v Digital Pulse Pty Ltd* [2003] NSWCA 10, (2003) 56 NSWLR 298 ('*Harris*').

[90] cf *Jane Doe v Australian Broadcasting Corporation* [2007] VCC 281 [187]–[193] regarding the action for breach of confidence.

[91] *Harris* [2003] NSWCA 10, (2003) 56 NSWLR 298 [23] (Spigelman CJ): 'The fact that the relevant behaviour has occurred in the same kind of context over the course of centuries, without equity having

majority also offered substantive reasons, such as the idea that punishment is alien to equity,[92] which reason reveals attentiveness to the rationale for awarding punitive damages.

IV. The United States

Although the law regarding punitive damages in the US is subject to certain constitutional limitations that apply uniformly across the country,[93] by and large the law of punitive damages in America varies considerably from state to state. In these circumstances, and in order to keep the discussion within manageable bounds, this chapter will take the rules that are propounded in the *Restatements of the Law* published by the American Law Institute as representing the law in the US.

Section 908 of the *Restatement (Second) of Torts* reads:

> (1) Punitive damages are damages, other than compensatory or nominal damages, awarded against a person to punish him for his outrageous conduct and to deter him and others like him from similar conduct in the future.
>
> (2) Punitive damages may be awarded for conduct that is outrageous, because of the defendant's evil motive or his reckless indifference to the rights of others. In assessing punitive damages, the trier of fact can properly consider the character of the defendant's act, the nature and extent of the harm to the plaintiff that the defendant caused or intended to cause and the wealth of the defendant.

Section 908 clearly endorses a highly substantive approach. The rationales for awarding punitive damages are also the criteria that determine when the punitive damages jurisdiction is available and how it should be exercised. Consistently with the stated goals of awarding punitive damages, punitive damages are not available in claims against the personal representatives of a deceased tortfeasor.[94] This makes sense from a substantive approach since the award cannot serve any punitive purpose in such circumstances. Also in line with substantive considerations is the fact that punitive damages can be granted even though the claimant suffered no harm.[95] Since wrongdoers who fail to cause harm may nonetheless deserve to be sanctioned and need to be deterred, this rule is explicable from a substantive viewpoint.

developed a remedy of the character now urged on the Court, of itself indicates that the development of the law in a case of this kind is inappropriate.'

[92] *Harris* [2003] NSWCA 10, (2003) 56 NSWLR 298 especially [57]–[61], [306], [337]–[339], [401].

[93] The leading cases are *BMW of North American Inc v Gore* 517 US 559 (1996); *State Farm Mutual Auto Insurance Co v Campbell* 538 US 408 (2003) ('*State Farm*'). We return to these constitutional limitations below in the text accompanying nn 97–99.

[94] *Restatement (Second) of Torts*, § 908, cmt *a*, § 925, cmt *b*(4).

[95] 'Although a defendant has inflicted no harm, punitive damages may be awarded because of, and measured by, his wrongful purpose or intent, as when he unsuccessfully makes a murderous assault upon the plaintiff, who suffers only a momentary apprehension': § 908, cmt *b*.

Also of interest is cmt *d* to § 100 of the *Restatement (Third) of Trusts*. Section 100 lays down the normal measure of damages in a claim for breach of trust.[96] Comment *d* reads:

> Ordinarily, a recovery under this Section would not be supplemented by an additional award of exemplary damages. The rule stated in Clause (a) of this Section is restorative … not punitive … In the egregious case, however, punitive damages are permissible under the laws of many jurisdictions. This is especially so if the trustee has acted maliciously, in bad faith, or in a fraudulent, particularly reckless, or self-serving manner. Among the facts and circumstances that are relevant when punitive damages are being considered in such jurisdictions are the nature and extent of the trustee's wrongdoing, the trustee's conduct in presenting an accounting or defending a surcharge action, and the extent to which punitive damages are important in order to punish the trustee, to recognize the harm to the beneficiaries, and to deter similar misconduct.

This suggests that punitive damages can exceptionally be awarded in claims for breach of trust where the goals of punishment and deterrence justify that remedial response. Again, this is generally consistent with a substantive approach.

According to § 355 of the *Restatement (Second) of Contracts*, '[p]unitive damages are not recoverable for a breach of contract unless the conduct constituting the breach is also a tort for which punitive damages are recoverable'. According to cmt *a* to § 355, the basis of this general prohibition is that 'the purpose of awarding contract damages is to compensate the injured party'. This reflects formal reasoning because there is no consideration of the justification for this cause of action restriction. Instead, § 355 is based on the norm that damages in contract are compensatory.

Before leaving the relevant law in the US, it is convenient briefly to discuss the constitutional limitations that we mentioned at the outset of this section. In *State Farm Mutual Auto Insurance Co v Campbell*, Kennedy J, delivering reasons with which Rehnquist CJ, Stevens, O'Connor, Souter and Breyer JJ joined, confirming guideposts that the Supreme Court had identified previously, said that in order to guard against the risk of grossly excessive or arbitrary punishment, courts reviewing punitive damages awards should consider three matters. Those matters are:

> (1) the degree of reprehensibility of the defendant's misconduct; (2) the disparity between the actual or potential harm suffered by the plaintiff and the punitive damages award; and (3) the difference between the punitive damages awarded by the jury and the civil penalties authorized or imposed in comparable cases.[97]

[96] 'A trustee who commits a breach of trust is chargeable with (a) the amount required to restore the values of the trust estate and trust distributions to what they would have been if the portion of the trust affected by the breach had been properly administered; or (b) the amount of any benefit to the trustee personally as a result of the breach.'

[97] *State Farm* 538 US 408 [6] (2003).

All three of those considerations are, speaking very broadly, animated by the stated goals of awarding punitive damages and hence reflect substantive concerns.[98] Certainly, none of them constitutes a restriction resembling a rule such as the English 'categories test', which test is fundamentally disconnected from the rationales for the punitive damages jurisdiction.[99]

Finally, it is worth noting that Atiyah and Summers identified the use of civil juries in the US as being consistent with a substantive approach. They wrote:

> the permissibility of awards of punitive damages in tort cases is much restrained by formal rules in English law, while in America the tendency of recent years has increasingly been to leave such questions to the jury with only the vaguest directions as to when such an award is appropriate.[100]

They further noted that although:

> the substantive vision in America may well be largely responsible for the extensive role of the jury in civil litigation … the price paid for the use of civil jury in America is heavy indeed, in terms of sacrifices of predictability and uniformity in law.[101]

However, empirical research in the US suggests that judges and juries do not differ substantially from each other in determining whether to award punitive damages or in assessing the quantum of such awards.[102]

V. Canada

Canadian courts have generally taken a highly substantive approach to punitive damages. The decision in *Paragon* provides an early and excellent example of

[98] However, it is arguable that restrictions based on the ratio between the amount of compensatory damages and the amount of punitive damages are arbitrary and therefore not substantive. In *State Farm* 538 US 408 [16] (2003), the Supreme Court said that 'an award of more than four times the amount of compensatory damages might be close to the line of constitutional impropriety' although it recognised that ratios are instructive rather than binding.

[99] Different and more formal limitations were propounded by the Supreme Court in *Exxon Shipping Co v Baker* 554 US 471 (2008), in which the Court held that in the general maritime law punitive damages cannot exceed a 1:1 ratio with compensatory damages.

[100] Atiyah and Summers, above n 3, 86 (footnotes omitted).

[101] ibid 425.

[102] 'Juries and judges award about the same amount of punitive damages per dollar of compensatory damages. The simplest explanation of this similarity is that judges and juries behave similarly … Prior results indicate that judges and juries award punitive damages at similar rates': T Eisenberg et al, 'Judges, Juries, and Punitive Damages: Empirical Analyses Using the Civil Justice Survey of State Courts 1992, 1996, and 2001 Data' (2006) 3 *Journal of Empirical Legal Studies* 263, 278, 288. cf T Eisenberg and M Heise, 'Judge–Jury Differences in Punitive Damages Awards: Who Listens to The Supreme Court?' (2011) 8 *Journal of Empirical Legal Studies* 325, 332. In England, it appears that civil juries, which are now virtually extinct, did not differ significantly from judges in how they decided punitive damages issues: J Goudkamp and E Katsampouka, 'An Empirical Study of Punitive Damages' (2018) 38 *OJLS* 90, 116.

substantive reasoning.[103] In that case, the Alberta Supreme Court refused to follow *Rookes* and decided that punitive damages may be awarded when the defendant's conduct is 'sufficiently censurable to invoke the principle upon which the award rests'.[104] Clement JA said:

> [*Rookes*] recognises the principle of exemplary damages, but in restricting its application it … does injustice to the principle. The basis of such an award is actionable injury to the plaintiff done in such a manner that it offends the ordinary standards of morality or decent conduct in the community in such marked degree that censure by way of damages is, in the opinion of the Court, warranted. The object is variously described to include deterrence to other possible wrongdoers, or punishment for maliciousness, or supra-compensatory recognition of unnecessary humiliation or other harm to which the claimant has been subjected by the censurable act. It is the reprehensible conduct of the wrongdoer which attracts the principle, not the legal category of the wrong out of which compensatory damages arise and in relation to which the conduct occurred. To place arbitrary limitations upon its application is to evade the underlying principle and replace it with an uncertain and debatable jurisdiction.[105]

In *Vorvis v Insurance Corp of British Columbia*,[106] the Supreme Court of Canada confirmed the rejection of the 'categories test'. McIntyre J said that punitive damages are merited 'in respect of conduct which is of such nature as to be deserving of punishment' and cited with approval the above passage from *Paragon*.[107] In *Whiten*, Binnie J who delivered the reasons of the majority of the Supreme Court, noted that:

> the attempt to limit punitive damages by "categories" does not work and was rightly rejected in Canada in *Vorvis* … The control mechanism lies not in restricting the category of case but in rationally determining circumstances that warrant the addition of punishment to compensation in a civil action.[108]

The substantive approach of the Canadian jurisprudence on punitive damages is also reflected by the fact that it has long been the law in that country that a punitive damages award can be made in any type of tort action (including negligence[109]), in breach of contract[110] and in respect of equitable wrongs.[111] Punitive damages

[103] *Paragon* (1972) 24 DLR (3d) 156.
[104] ibid.
[105] ibid 167.
[106] *Vorvis* [1989] 1 SCR 1085.
[107] ibid 1108.
[108] *Whiten* 2002 SCC 18, [2002] 1 SCR 595 [67].
[109] 'The contention that exemplary damages cannot be awarded in actions based on negligence must fail … [I]t would seem that exemplary damages may be granted in all cases where the conduct of the defendant has been such as to merit condemnation by the court': *Robitaille v Vancouver Hockey Club Ltd* (1979) 124 DLR (3d) 228, 250 (the Court). See also L Klar and C Jefferies, *Tort Law*, 6th edn (Toronto, Thomson Reuters, 2017) 144 (pointing out that, although punitive damages are available in proceedings in the tort of negligence, they are very rarely awarded).
[110] *Vorvis* [1989] 1 SCR 1085; *Whiten* 2002 SCC 18, [2002] 1 SCR 595; *Sun Life Assurance Co of Canada v Fidler* 2006 SCC 30, [2006] 2 SCR 3.
[111] See, eg, *Weisenger v Mellor* [1989] BCWLD 2129; *Norberg v Wynrib* [1992] 2 SCR 226 (especially McLachlin J and L'Heureux-Dubé J).

are simply made available based on whether their justifications merit the award thereof. It is noteworthy that the more generous rules regarding the availability of punitive damages in Canada do not seem to have triggered large punitive damages awards in that country. According to Klar and Jefferies, punitive damages even for the most outrageous behaviour have been very moderate and most awards are well under CAD100,000 and frequently less than CAD50,000.[112] These findings cast significant doubt on suggestions in Australia[113] and England[114] that the jurisdiction to award punitive damages needs to be restricted in order to prevent excessive awards from being made.[115]

Although no 'cause of action test' exists in Canada, Canadian courts have accepted a bizarre restriction on the jurisdiction to award punitive damages for breaches of contract, namely, that the defendant's conduct constitute an 'independent actionable wrong'.[116] For example, in *RCR Catering Ltd v Scimp* the Nova Scotia Court of Appeal said that there was a 'threshold principle that punitive damages in a breach of contract case … arise when there has been an *independent wrong committed by the defendant over and above the breach of contract*'.[117] Similarly, in *Whiten*, Binnie J said that:

> a breach of the contractual duty of good faith is independent of and in addition to the breach of contractual duty to pay the loss. It constitutes an 'actionable wrong' within the *Vorvis* rule … *An independent actionable wrong is required*, but it can be found in *breach of a distinct and separate contractual provision or other duty* such as a fiduciary obligation.[118]

This restriction is a striking illustration of bad formal reasoning as it rests on a misreading of *Vorvis*. *Vorvis* involved a wrongful dismissal claim. The defendant failed to give the claimant reasonable notice when terminating the claimant's employment. Prior to the wrongful dismissal, the claimant had been harassed by his supervisor. Punitive damages were not awarded because none of the conduct in issue was sufficiently outrageous. However, McIntyre J observed that no award would be made in relation to the harassment for the additional reason that it 'was not considered sufficiently offensive, standing alone, to constitute actionable wrong … and … was not of such nature as to justify the imposition of an award of punitive damages'.[119] It is clear from McIntyre J's reasons that he did not hold that an independent breach of duty was required before punitive damages can

[112] Klar and Jefferies, above n 109, 144–45.
[113] Barker et al, above n 84, 377.
[114] Law Commission, *Aggravated, Exemplary and Restitutionary Damages: A Consultation Paper* (Law Com CP No 132, 1993) 82, 113.
[115] Punitive damages awards are apparently modest in England: see Goudkamp and Katsampouka, above n 102, 103.
[116] *Whiten* 2002 SCC 18, [2002] 1 SCR 595, 640.
[117] *Schimp v RCR Catering Ltd* 2004 NSCA 29, 236 DLR (4th) 461 [75] (emphasis added).
[118] *Whiten* 2002 SCC 18, [2002] 1 SCR 595, 639–40 (emphasis added).
[119] *Vorvis* [1989] 1 SCR 1085, 1110.

be awarded in respect of a breach of contract. Unfortunately, that is not how his reasons have been understood.[120]

VI. Conclusion

In 1991, Atiyah and Summers wrote that '[m]ore work remains to be done with respect to our thesis that the English system is more formal' than that in the US.[121] We hope to have shown in this chapter that Atiyah and Summers' thesis still holds in so far as the law of punitive damages is concerned. We also contended that the relevant Australian law falls in a similar spot on the spectrum between form and substance as American law whereas the material rules in Canada represent the most substantive approach of the jurisdictions under consideration.[122]

[120] See further J McCamus, 'Prometheus Bound or Loose Cannon? Punitive Damages for Pure Breach of Contract in Canada' (2004) 41 *San Diego Law Review* 1491, 1504; *PH Hydraulics & Engineering Pty Ltd v Airtrust (Hong Kong) Ltd* [2017] SGCA 26, [2017] 2 SLR 129 [114]–[115] ('*PH Hydraulics*').

[121] Atiyah and Summers, above n 3, 428.

[122] Due to space constraints we confined our analysis to these four jurisdictions and did not consider the relevant law in, eg, Hong Kong, Singapore and New Zealand. We briefly note that the relevant law in Hong Kong and New Zealand can probably be regarded as occupying an intermediate position in the spectrum between form and substance, along with Australia and the US, although Hong Kong may adopt the *Rookes* categories (see *Allan* [2012] HKCA 119, [2012] 2 HKLRD 160, 170). By contrast, Singapore, like Canada, adopts a highly substantive approach with the Court of Appeal tending to examine thoroughly the normative justifications for rules in this area (see, eg, *ACB* [2017] SGCA 20, [2017] 1 SLR 918 [170]–[177], [199]–[206] (rejecting the *Rookes* categories and ruling in favour of the availability of punitive damages for inadvertent negligence) and *PH Hydraulics* [2017] SGCA 26, [2017] 2 SLR 129 [67]–[136] (ruling against the introduction of punitive damages for breach of contract)).

15

Statute Law in the Law of Obligations: Dimensions of Form and Substance

MARK LEEMING*

> We too need education in the obvious – to learn to transcend our own convictions and to leave room for much that we hold dear to be done away with short of revolution by the orderly change of law.[1]

Holmes' words introduced Summers' article published four decades ago: 'General Equitable Principles under Section 1–103 of the Uniform Commercial Code'.[2] The article was directed to a statute that made 'the principles of law and equity, including the law merchant' applicable to the Uniform Commercial Code unless displaced by the particular provisions of the Act – thereby softening the impact of a new legislative regime.[3] In turn, Atiyah and Summers drew upon the effect of that provision and others like it as part of the explanation for the greater emphasis on substance in the US legal system, contrasting it with the relative formality of the English legal system.[4] It is no surprise that the pair – one steeped in the English common law, the other with a deep expertise in the Uniform Commercial Code (which in part is a reaction against common law[5] and reflects the heritage of Field[6]) –

* I acknowledge the research assistance of Mr Marcel Delany. All errors are mine.

[1] OW Holmes, 'Law and the Court' in *Speeches by Oliver Wendell Holmes* (Boston, MA, Little, Brown & Co, 1934) 102.

[2] RS Summers, 'General Equitable Principles under Section 1-103 of the Uniform Commercial Code' (1978) 72 *Northwestern University Law Review* 906.

[3] See generally D Litowitz, *Perspectives on the Uniform Commercial Code*, 2nd edn (Durham, NC, Carolina Academic Press, 2007) especially 8–11. The provision is associated with Karl Llewellyn, who was its principal drafter and leading exponent. See A Kamp, 'Between-the-Wars Social Thought: Karl Llewellyn, Legal Realism and the Uniform Commercial Code in Context' (1995) 59 *Albany Law Review* 325 and G Gilmore, 'In Memoriam: Karl Llewellyn' (1962) 71 *Yale Law Journal* 813, 814–15, coincidentally noting that: 'Revolutionary as his early writings were thought to be, Karl abhorred abrupt departures, sudden breaks and the revealed certainty of novel illumination. He was a man of tradition, of continuity, of ordered growth and gradual change' (at 814).

[4] PS Atiyah and RS Summers, *Form and Substance in Anglo-American Law: A Comparative Study of Legal Reasoning, Legal Theory, and Legal Institutions* (Oxford, Clarendon Press, 1987) ch 4.

[5] See F Snyder, 'Clouds of Mystery: Dispelling the Realist Rhetoric of the Uniform Commercial Code' (2007) 68 *Ohio State Law Journal* 11.

[6] See F Lechner, *The American Exception* (New York, Palgrave Macmillan, vol 1, 2017) 155–56. For Field's influence in England in relation to the Judicature legislation, see M Lobban, 'Preparing for Fusion: Reforming the Nineteenth-Century Court of Chancery' (2004) 22 *Law & History Review* 389, 565.

contrasted the different roles of statute in those legal systems. They maintained that many US statutes (notably, constitutional statutes) were drafted with 'broad and vague language',[7] while in the UK, legislation was relied upon 'so much more readily to resolve questions that in America are left to the courts'.[8] They also maintained that American courts displayed a greater willingness to engage in purposive rather than textual construction.[9] They contended that 'the English political-legal system relies more heavily than the American on statute law and less on case-law, and that, because statute law is more formal than case-law, this is one factor which makes English law more formal'.[10]

It might be of interest to consider whether, some 30 years later, those distinctions are now as pronounced as they once seemed. Both legal systems have changed. The work of Atiyah and Summers preceded landmarks such as *Pepper v Hart*,[11] the enactment of the Human Rights Act 1998 (UK) and the appointment of Antonin Scalia to the US Supreme Court. The mode of reasoning seen in the UK Supreme Court in much public law litigation (for example, the recent civil partnerships case[12] and, more remarkably, in *Unison*),[13] and the growth of textualism in US courts[14] may have been unanticipated in 1986. But analysis of such matters would make for a different chapter.

This chapter employs Holmes' aphorism as to the need for 'education in the obvious', in an area explored by Atiyah and Summers, namely, the role of statutes in common law legal systems. It focusses upon the diversity of statutes and their dynamic interaction with judge-made law. Most lawyers, practising or academic, instinctively know something of the range of statutes and the ways in which private law is shaped by them. Yet curiously little has been written about this issue, and the learning that exists is often a little simplistic and fails to capture the richness of the interaction.

Statutes are an essential element of any account of a legal system. Of course, it is vital to distinguish between different classes of statutes. For example, many

[7] Atiyah and Summers, above n 4, 101.

[8] ibid 299.

[9] ibid 101–4, concluding: 'It is common for American lawyers to poke fun at seemingly formalistic and wooden decisions by English judges, and at their apparently simplistic faith in the belief that statutes have a simple or plain meaning which can be arrived at by methods of literal interpretation. Conversely, English layers are easily shocked by what they see as the free-wheeling and sometimes "substantivistic" methods of American judges which seem on occasion to pay scant regard to the wording of the legislative text at all' (footnotes omitted). Atiyah and Summers regarded both criticisms as unfruitful.

[10] ibid 298.

[11] *Pepper v Hart* [1993] AC 593.

[12] *R (on the application of Steinfeld and Keidan) v Secretary of State for International Development* [2018] UKSC 32, [2018] 3 WLR 415 ('strict scrutiny' of justification; four-stage test of proportionality).

[13] *R (on the application of Unison) v Lord Chancellor* [2017] UKSC 51, [2017] 3 WLR 409 (rule of law and access to the courts driving determinations of invalidity of executive action in imposing fees on access to employment tribunals). cf *Commissioner of Corrective Services v Liristis* [2018] NSWCA 143 [75], J Basten, '*UNISON*, The Parole Board and Principle of Legality' (2018) 29 *Public Law Review* 187 and R Rawlings, 'The *UNISON* case: A New High-water Mark' (2018) 29 *Public Law Review* 190.

[14] Indeed, the familiarity of the meme 'we are all textualists now' in US academic literature is itself remarkable: see, eg, J Schacter, 'Text or Consequences?' (2011) 76 *Brooklyn Law Review* 1007, 1008.

statutes are constitutive in the sense of conferring power: rather than imposing norms of conduct and sanctions for their breach, they authorise the creation of companies, or wills, or contracts, or bills of sale, or they create agencies and instrumentalities and corporations with important powers. Those statutes are not of present concern. Large swathes of legislation regulate particular areas of conduct, and within those areas impose norms of conduct and specify sanctions for their breach in ways that resemble judge-made law. And some statutes (probably, only a small minority of the total in this 'age of statutes') achieve their effect through engaging directly with judge-made law. In Australia, notable examples are the Civil Liability Act 2002 (NSW) and its counterparts and some of the consumer protection provisions of the Competition and Consumer Act 2011 (Cth). Those two examples illustrate the distinction drawn by Atiyah and Summers between open- and close-ended statutes: the former closely engaged with the existing law of negligence, while the latter created new norms including those broadly based on unconscionable conduct but left it to the courts to flesh out the details. If one is to analyse the role of statute in common law legal systems, it is important to appreciate this variety. As I have elsewhere said:[15]

> Justice Frankfurter said that 'enactments such as the Sherman Law that embody a felt rather than defined purpose and necessarily look to the future for the unfolding of their content, making of their judicial application an evolutionary process nourished by relevant changing circumstances'.[16] Judge Friendly described such statutes as open- rather than close-ended.[17] Open-ended statutes, which turn on broadly expressed concepts, like 'misleading or deceptive' or 'manner of manufacture',[18] naturally and indeed necessarily attract a more purposive and less minutely textual mode of construction. What is more, different parts of the same statute may be construed differently;[19] consider the general prohibition in the copyright legislation in some jurisdictions against authorising infringing conduct and the narrowly articulated 'safe harbour' provisions which guarantee a defence. Judge Robert Katzmann has said, in his elegant account of judging in the Second Circuit, that 'Statutes vary in design and substance, and so the interpretive task may change and the tools used may vary depending on the particular statutory issue at hand'.[20]

It simply does not do justice to the richness of the legal system to conflate all these categories of legislation as the premise of an argument. There is a real descriptive loss if they are treated as a homogeneous category.

[15] M Leeming, 'Equity: Ageless in the Age of Statutes' (2015) 9 *Journal of Equity* 108, 116–17.

[16] *United States v Union Pacific Railroad Co* 353 US 112, 122 (1957). More recently, see *State Oil Co v Khan* 522 US 3 (1997).

[17] H Friendly, *Benchmarks* (Chicago, The University of Chicago Press, 1967) 204.

[18] See, eg, what Crennan and Kiefel JJ termed the 'celebrated NRDC case' of *National Research Development Corp v Commissioner of Patents* (1959) 102 CLR 252, 262 on the 'concept of patent law ultimately traceable to the use in the Statute of Monopolies of the words "manner of manufacture"': *Apotex Pty Ltd v Sanofi-Aventis Australia Pty Ltd* [2013] HCA 50, (2013) 304 ALR 1 [216]. See for a recent example *Research Affiliates LLC v Commissioner of Patents* [2014] FCAFC 150, (2014) FCR 378 [6]–[8] (Kenny, Bennett and Nicholas JJ).

[19] See H Xanthaki, *Drafting Legislation: Art and Technology of Rules for Regulation*, (Oxford, Hart Publishing, 2014) chs 7–16.

[20] R Katzmann, *Judging Statutes* (New York, Oxford University Press, 2014) 55.

There is also a temporal, or dynamic, dimension to the relationship between statute law and judge-made law and the substance/form distinction to which both contribute. Atiyah said 30 years ago, in an article published shortly before his work with Summers, that 'the relationship between common law and statute law must be seen as the relationship between two developing and moving bodies of law; and the way in which they interact on each other becomes a matter of no little importance'.[21] Some accounts that treat judge-made law and statute as separate systems fail to recognise this important interaction;[22] a well-known article by Burrows is a notable exception.[23] Paradoxically, while it is important to pause before treating the class of statutes (or even the sub-class of norm-creating statutes) as a single homogeneous category, it is also important to bear in mind that the distinction between judge-made law and statute law can itself be illusory when the temporal dimension is considered. Most of the time, as Windeyer J said, 'it is misleading to speak glibly of the common law in order to compare and contrast it with a statute'.[24] As Burrows has put it, 'common law and statute are more fully integrated than has traditionally been thought'.[25]

This chapter presents three examples drawn from the law of obligations, in the areas of contract, tort and equity, illustrating these distinctions. None is unfamiliar, although it is hoped that there are insights in each. Hence the invocation of Holmes. The first example is the divergent approaches in Australia, New Zealand and the UK to whether statutory apportionment is available to reduce a judgment for breach of a contractual duty of care. The second is the divergence between the Australian and English law of exemplary damages for defamation following *Rookes v Barnard*,[26] which was the occasion for pointed observations on how judge-made law was to be read. The third relates to the way in which the already expansive notion of unconscionable conduct in Australia has been altered by a series of statutes in the quarter century between 1986 and 2011.

I. Statute Treated as Judge-made Law

White and Summers stated provocatively at the outset of their work on the Uniform Commercial Code that 'In our system of law statutory law tends to be transformed into case law'.[27] This is by no means confined to ancient statutes like the Statute of

[21] P Atiyah, 'Common Law and Statute Law' (1985) 48 *MLR* 1, 1.

[22] See, eg, R Posner, *The Problems of Jurisprudence* (Cambridge, MA, Harvard University Press, 1990) 247.

[23] A Burrows, 'The Relationship between Common Law and Statute in the Law of Obligations' (2012) 128 *LQR* 232.

[24] *Gammage v The Queen* (1969) 122 CLR 444, 462.

[25] Burrows, above n 23, 233. See further M Leeming, 'Theories and Principles Underlying the Development of the Common Law: The Statutory Elephant in the Room' (2013) 36 *University of New South Wales Law Journal* 1002.

[26] *Rookes v Barnard* [1964] AC 1129 ('*Rookes*').

[27] J White and R Summers, *Handbook of the Law under the Uniform Commercial Code* (St Paul, Minn, West Publishing Co, 1972) third sentence of preface.

Elizabeth, which remains a mainstay of the modern law of charity.[28] In modern statutes that tendency is regularly seen when an open-ended statute invites or requires elucidation by courts. But it may also be seen in narrowly drafted statutes. Last week, I heard this exchange:[29]

> SACKVILLE AJA: I'm just wondering whether your construction of s 5D is supported by the authorities. It's not self-evident from the language.
>
> COUNSEL: Well, in fact, the language doesn't use the 'but for' in its terms, but it's accepted that that's what it means; *Adeels Palace v Moubarak* lays it down.

It may seem a little strange that both the statutory defined term 'factual causation' and the perfectly precise statutory language of 'necessary condition' were glossed by a reference to what has been said by a court. The High Court had no difficulty in *Adeels Palace* stating that factual causation required by section 5D(1)[30] was determined by the 'but for' test.[31] What else could the precise language of 'necessary condition' possibly mean in this context? But in a system where a primary mode of advocacy involves persuading a judicial officer that she or he is bound by the decision of a higher court, it is unsurprising that advocates prefer to cite High Court decisions construing a statute rather than relying on the statute itself. That is one 'obvious' way in which statute becomes treated as common law, and this despite the oft-repeated command that one must start with the statute.[32]

Different modes of reasoning apply in a statutory context as opposed to a judge-made law context. A good example is contributory negligence. This neglected area has greatly benefited from recent analyses, extending to legal history[33] and empirical studies.[34] In Australian law, as I have sought to explain more fully elsewhere,[35] it continues to develop – in large measure because of the number of, and latent

[28] In Australia, notably by the modes of analogical and inferential reasoning endorsed in *Incorporated Council of Law Reporting of the State of Queensland v Federal Commissioner of Taxation* (1971) 125 CLR 659 and *Royal National Agricultural and Industrial Association v Chester* (1974) 48 ALJR 304.

[29] The reference is to the hearing in *Lim v Cho* [2018] NSWCA 145.

[30] s 5D(1) of the Civil Liability Act 2002 (NSW) provides:

> (1) A determination that negligence caused particular harm comprises the following elements:
>
> (a) that the negligence was a necessary condition of the occurrence of the harm ('factual causation'), and
>
> (b) that it is appropriate for the scope of the negligent person's liability to extend to the harm so caused ('scope of liability').

[31] *Adeels Palace Pty Ltd v Moubarak* [2009] HCA 48, (2009) 239 CLR 420 [45].

[32] See, eg, *Ogden Industries Pty Ltd v Lucas* [1970] AC 113, 127: 'It is quite clear that judicial statements as to the construction and intention of an Act must never be allowed to supplant or supersede its proper construction and courts must beware of falling into the error of treating the law to be that laid down by the judge in construing the Act rather than found in the words of the Act itself'.

[33] See, eg, P Mitchell, *A History of Tort Law 1900–1950* (Cambridge, Cambridge University Press, 2015) ch 13.

[34] See, eg, J Goudkamp and D Nolan, *Contributory Negligence: Principles and Practice* (Oxford, Oxford University Press, 2018) 3–4, 77–122; J Goudkamp and D Nolan, *Contributory Negligence in the Twenty-First Century* (Oxford, Oxford University Press, 2019).

[35] M Leeming, 'Statutory Interpretation *as* Private Law' in P Vines and S Donald (eds), *Statutory Interpretation in Private Law* (Alexandria, Federation Press, 2019).

complexity in, statutory amendments. This section of this chapter focusses on just one point: statutory apportionment for contractual claims. The point is reasonably familiar but illustrates as clearly as anything else the distinction I wish to emphasise.

Like many common law jurisdictions, the Australian states enacted legislation in the form of the Law Reform (Contributory Negligence) Act 1945 (UK), which turned on 'fault':

> Where any person suffers damage as the result partly of his own fault and partly of the fault of any other person or persons, a claim in respect of that damage shall not be defeated by reason of the fault of the person suffering the damage, but the damages recoverable in respect thereof shall be reduced to such extent as the court thinks just and equitable having regard to the claimant's share in the responsibility for the damage.[36]

'Fault' was defined to mean 'negligence, breach of statutory duty or other act or omission which gives rise to a liability in tort or would, apart from this Act, give rise to the defence of contributory negligence'. Note the narrowly prescriptive first clause of the provision, in contrast with the open-ended concluding clause, referring to what a court thinks 'just and equitable'.

The reform was driven by the harshness of the defence of contributory negligence at common law, and the obscurities attending to exceptions to it. But law does not stand still. The expansion of negligence associated with *Henderson v Merrett Syndicates Ltd* has led to a growing overlap in claims which could be framed either in contract or for breach of duty of care.[37] In such cases, could the recovery in a plaintiff's claim in contract be reduced by the statute? How did the statutory text apply in changed circumstances half a century later?

After some decisions pointing in the opposite direction,[38] the English and New Zealand Courts of Appeal sanctioned the availability of the section in some but not all contractual cases.[39] The section was not available where the contractual obligation did not depend on negligence,[40] but was available where the liability in contract was the same as that in tort, or else arose from a contractual obligation to take care even if it did not correspond to an independently existing common law duty.[41] That approach fastened upon the breadth of the term 'fault' in the opening clause and the perceived awkwardness of a plaintiff obtaining different judgments for the same breach of identical duties in contract and in tort. At the same time that construction downplayed the original purpose of the provision, and the limiting

[36] Section 1(1).

[37] *Henderson v Merrett Syndicates Ltd* [1995] 2 AC 145.

[38] Notably, the *volte-face* by Neill LJ between *AB Marintrans v Comet Shipping Co Ltd* [1985] 1 WLR 1270 and *Forsikringsaktieselskapet Vesta v Butcher* [1989] AC 852, 875 ('*Butcher*').

[39] *Butcher* [1989] AC 852; *Mouat v Clark Boyce* [1992] 2 NZLR 559, 564–65; *Vining Realty Group Ltd v Moorhouse* [2010] NZCA 104, (2011) 11 NZCPR 879.

[40] See *Barclays Bank plc v Fairclough Building Ltd* [1995] QB 214.

[41] These three categories were identified by Hobhouse J in *Forsikringsaktieselskapet Vesta v Butcher* [1986] 2 All ER 488 at first instance.

effect of the words 'shall not be defeated by reason of the fault of the person suffering the damage'.

In 1999 the point came before the High Court of Australia, in *Astley v Austrust Ltd*,[42] where the defendant firm of solicitors was subject to concurrent contractual and tortious duties to take reasonable care. The client sued for breach of retainer, and the firm relied on statutory apportionment. The local legislation followed the English text verbatim.[43] Yet the High Court departed from English and New Zealand authority and held that the word 'negligence' in the definition of 'fault' was limited by the words 'which gives rise to a liability in tort',[44] with the result that contributory negligence was not a defence to breach of an implied term to perform services with reasonable care and skill. The majority judgment noted that the 'theoretical foundations for actions in tort and contract are quite separate', with contractual obligations implied at law long preceding the 'imperial march of modern negligence law'.[45] This construction was said best to accord with the purpose of the legislation, which sought to remedy a harshness in the law of tort, and had nothing to say about contract law. The majority judgment was conscious of the inconsistent remedies which would be available in cases of concurrent liability in tort and contract:

> Perhaps the apportionment statute should be imposed on parties to a contract where damages are payable for breach of a contractual duty of care. If it should, and we express no view about it, it will have to be done by amendment to that legislation. If courts are to give effect to the will of the legislature, it is not possible to do so having regard to the terms of apportionment legislation, based on the United Kingdom legislation of 1945, and the evil that it was designed to remedy.[46]

The decision was criticised,[47] and promptly overturned legislatively.[48]

It may be that some of the criticism of *Astley v Austrust Ltd* was misplaced, owing to a misapprehension of the nature of the issue presented on appeal. The position would have been quite different if there had been two parallel developments in *judge-made* law. Suppose the common law had seized upon the considerable deficiencies of the traditional doctrine of contributory

[42] *Astley v Austrust Ltd* [1999] HCA 6, (1999) 197 CLR 1 ('*Astley*').

[43] Wrongs Act 1936 (SA), s 27A.

[44] *Astley* [1999] HCA 6, (1999) 197 CLR 1 [71]–[83].

[45] ibid [48].

[46] ibid [88].

[47] See, eg, J Swanton, 'Contributory Negligence is not a Defence to Actions for Breach of Contract in Australian Law: *Astley v Austrust Ltd*' (1999) 14 *Journal of Contract Law* 251 and J Davis, 'Contributory Negligence and Breach of Contract: *Astley v Austrust Ltd*' (1999) 7 *Torts Law Journal* 117.

[48] See Law Reform (Miscellaneous Provisions) Amendment Act 2000 (NSW); Law Reform (Contributory Negligence) Amendment Act 2001 (Qld); Law Reform (Contributory Negligence and Apportionment of Liability) Act 2001 (SA); Tortfeasors and Contributory Negligence Amendment Act 2000 (Tas); Wrongs (Amendment) Act 2000 (Vic); Law Reform (Contributory Negligence and Tortfeasors' Contribution) Amendment Act 2003 (WA); Civil Law (Wrongs) Act 2002 (ACT); Proportionate Liability Act 2005 (NT).

negligence, and, perhaps influenced by the position in admiralty and a handful of nineteenth-century jury decisions,[49] developed a doctrine of apportionment for contributing fault.[50] If so, one could advance a powerful argument based on coherence for that *judge-made* doctrine to accommodate itself with the parallel growth of concurrent duties in contract and tort. One basic attribute of the body of judge-made law is to strive against such inconsistencies.[51]

Perhaps because of the thousands of decisions on the discretionary power created by statutory apportionment, focussing on concepts such as 'causal potency' and 'relative culpability' in elucidating the open-ended part of the provision ('as the court thinks just and equitable'), sight was lost of the more narrowly drafted language in which the balance of the section is framed. But the issue in *Astley* remained one of statutory construction, rather than the development of judge-made law. The *relevant portion* of the statutory text was precise, and quite narrowly directed to cases of liability in tort,[52] enacted in a context which pre-dated the expansion of negligence. It is one thing to change the law so as to extend a judge-made rule to circumstances outside its original scope, but which nonetheless fall within its purpose – especially if the need to do so is due to an expansion of that other area of the law. It is an entirely different thing to expand the legal meaning of a fixed statutory text written in prescriptive terms, which ordinarily is to be read literally. Hence the High Court's reference to 'give effect to the will of the Legislature', which continued to speak half a century later in different circumstances. There are occasions when the changed legal landscape causes the legal meaning of a statute to change, but they are rare.[53]

Sir Victor Windeyer memorably captured the distinction in an address delivered in Canada in the year after his retirement after 14 years on the High Court of Australia, which is less well known than it should be:

> The words and phrases in Acts of Parliament have an intractable stubbornness under our traditional system of statutory interpretation. The dictates of Parliament must

[49] A form of apportionment existed in Admiralty for collision cases, which was preserved by the Judicature Act 1873 (36 and 37 Vict c 66) and continued in a modern form under the Brussels Convention on Collisions at Sea (1910), reflecting the influence of civil law: see F Lawson, 'Notes on the History of Tort in the Civil Law' (1940) 22 *Journal of Comparative Legislation and International Law* (3rd series) 136, 142–44. There are also instances of apportionment for contributory negligence in jury verdicts, which were sustained on appeal: see M Leeming, *The Statutory Foundations of Negligence* (Sydney, Federation Press, 2019) ch 5.

[50] This is no idle fancy; it is precisely what occurred in Florida and California in the absence of statutory reform: see *Hoffman v Jones*, 280 So 2d 431 (Fla 1973) and *Li v Yellow Cab Company of California*, 13 Cal 3d 804, 532 P 2d 1226 (1975). The various approaches taken in the US are beyond the scope of this chapter, but see V Schwartz, *Comparative Negligence*, 5th edn (New Providence, NJ, LexisNexis, 2010).

[51] An early contribution to the now burgeoning literature on coherence, directed to this area, is B Hepple, 'Negligence: The Search for Coherence' (1997) 50 *Current Legal Problems* 69.

[52] Contrast the breadth of 'just and equitable', which has led to consideration of the 'relative culpability' and the 'causal potency' of each party's conduct.

[53] An example may be seen in *Daniels v Australian Competition and Consumer Commission* [2002] HCA 49, (2002) 213 CLR 543 [35] (recognition that legal professional privilege is a substantive right, rather than a rule of evidence, altering the construction of 'reasonable excuse' in legislation authorising compulsive examinations).

> be obeyed and applied according to the letter. The words may sometimes take their meaning by an appreciation of the policy and purpose of the statute read against a background knowledge of the mischief it was enacted to remedy. They are not to be glossed, expanded, modified, or explained by a court, in the way that judicial statements of common law may be slowly broadened down from precedent to precedent.[54]

Judgments are not to be read as statutes. Less familiar, but equally true, is the converse aphorism that statutes are not to be read as judgments: 'the judicial task in statutory construction differs from that in distilling the common law from past decisions'.[55] Inevitably, statutes are more formal, more textual, to be read more *literally* (as Windeyer observed, 'to the letter'), and accordingly have an anchoring effect against incremental change. The metaphor employed by Baroness Hale and Lord Reed captures the temporal anchoring of statutes: they deprecated treating judicial statements like statutes which were 'set in stone'.[56]

II. Judge-made Law Treated as Statutes

Sometimes *principles* from judge-made law are incorporated in terms in statutes. Consistently with one theme of this chapter, that occurs in several different ways. For example, the modern incarnations of the Statute of Frauds recognise the exceptions developed by the courts in cases of resulting and constructive trusts and the doctrine of part performance.[57] The equitable doctrines of applying the statute of limitations by analogy and declining to apply it in cases of concealed fraud are themselves incorporated in some modern statutes of limitation.[58] Sometimes the *text* of a court's reasons is incorporated. An example may be seen in section 5B of the Civil Liability Act 2002 (NSW), which very largely – but not entirely – picks up the language of the so-called 'calculus' in Mason J's judgment in *Wyong Shire Council v Shirt*, save for substituting 'not insignificant' risks for risks which are real in the sense of being neither far-fetched or fanciful.[59] A third form of legislative incorporation occurs when statute overturns a particular decision. Sometimes, as in the reversal of *Astley*, where the issue is binary, the construction of the statute is clear; but sometimes such provisions give rise to large questions of construction. For example, in *Wynbergen v Hoyts Corporation Pty Ltd* the High Court unanimously held that when a defendant had tortiously injured a plaintiff, the damages could not be reduced to zero, a result which was then overturned by

[54] V Windeyer, 'History in Law and Law in History' (1973) 11 *Alberta Law Review* 123, 130–31.

[55] See, eg, *McNamara v Consumer Trader and Tenancy Tribunal* [2005] HCA 55, (2005) 221 CLR 646 [40].

[56] *Woodland v Swimming Teachers Association* [2013] UKSC 66, [2014] AC 537 [38]. See also *NA v Nottinghamshire County Council* [2017] UKSC 60, [2018] AC 355 [35]–[36].

[57] See, eg, Conveyancing Act 1919 (NSW), ss 23C(2), 54A(2).

[58] See, eg, Limitation Act 1969 (NSW), s 23 and Limitation Act 2005 (WA), s 27. See also P Handford, 'A New Limitation Act for the 21st Century' (2007) 33 *University of Western Australia Law Review* 387, 400–02 and M Leeming, '"Not Slavishly Nor Always" – Equity and Limitation Statutes' in P Davies, S Douglas and J Goudkamp (eds), *Defences in Equity* (Oxford, Hart Publishing, 2018) 293, 299, 302–03.

[59] See *Bunnings v Giudice* [2018] NSWCA 144 [52]–[53].

legislation enacted by three Australian states and one territory.[60] But it is unclear what principles apply to the new legislation. Statute has overturned the authoritative construction determined by the High Court, but has failed to explain how the newly amended provision is to be applied.[61]

An entirely different phenomenon occurs when judgments are treated as if they were statutes. No legislative activity is present, and it seems necessary to recall that the reasons for judgment are not legislation. As a unanimous High Court recently said,[62] it is necessary to bear in mind that 'the words of a principle stated in a judge's reasons for decision require consideration of what those reasons convey about the principle and are not to be applied literally', citing what had been said by Gummow J in *Brennan v Comcare*:

> The frequently repeated caution is against construing the terms of those judgments as if they were the words of a statute. The concern is not with the ascertainment of the meaning and the application of particular words used by previous judges, so much as with gaining an understanding of the concepts to which expression was sought to be given.[63]

The caution is 'frequently repeated' because it is so easily forgotten. One striking example arose in *Rookes*,[64] which was argued in the House of Lords over 15 days in July and November 1963, with the main issue being the tort of intimidation and its relationship with the Trade Disputes Act 1906 (6 Edw 7 c 47). All law lords addressed the main issue, which was promptly overturned by statute.[65] Presently relevant is the cross-appeal on exemplary damages, which was addressed only by Lord Devlin, with whom in this respect Lords Reid, Evershed, Hodson and Pearce simply agreed.[66] Lord Devlin identified two categories of case where the common law authorised the award of exemplary damages, and did so in terms which were expressed to be exhaustive.[67] The categories were introduced as 'oppressive, arbitrary or unconstitutional action by servants of the government', and cases where 'the defendant's conduct has been calculated by him to make a profit for himself which may well exceed the compensation payable to the plaintiff'.[68]

[60] *Wynbergen v Hoyts Corporation Pty Ltd* (1997) 72 ALJR 65. In New South Wales, Queensland, Victoria and the Australian Capital Territory, s 5S of the Civil Liability Act 2002 (NSW) and its equivalents, enacted in response to the decision, expressly authorise determinations of 100% contributory negligence.

[61] These and other examples are discussed in more detail in Leeming, above n 49.

[62] *Stewart v Atco Controls Pty Ltd (in liq)* [2014] HCA 15, (2014) 252 CLR 307 [32].

[63] *Brennan v Comcare* (1994) 50 FCR 555, 572.

[64] *Rookes* [1964] AC 1129.

[65] Trade Disputes Act 1965 (UK).

[66] *Rookes* [1964] AC 1129, 1179, 1197, 1203, 1238.

[67] Notably, his statement that 'I am well aware that what I am about to say will, if accepted, impose limits not hitherto expressed on such awards and that there is powerful, though not compelling, authority for allowing them a wider range' (*Rookes* [1964] AC 1129, 1226); and 'the judge should not allow [a case for exemplary damages] to be left to the jury unless he is satisfied that it can be brought within the categories I have specified' (*Rookes* [1964] AC 1129, 1228).

[68] *Rookes* [1964] AC 1129, 1226. Goudkamp and Katsampouka in the present volume identify this as one of the best examples of the role of formal reasoning in the law of obligations: J Goudkamp and E Katsampouka, 'Statute Law in the Law of Obligations: Dimensions of Form and Substance', this volume, ch 14.

Lord Devlin seemed to recognise a larger role for aggravated damages for cases which might formerly have been awarded exemplary damages. As a judicial swansong (Lord Devlin had retired 11 days before judgment was delivered),[69] *Rookes* contrasts starkly with his statement in 1962 'I doubt if judges will now of their own motion contribute much more to the development of the law'.[70]

Almost a year before *Rookes* was delivered, a Sydney newspaper published a story which imputed that Tom Uren, a sitting Member of Parliament, had been duped by a Russian spy. At the commencement of the trial, the publisher abandoned its pleas,[71] made an apology and left damages as the only issue for the jury. As is well known, the Australian High Court declined to follow *Rookes*,[72] while the further appeal to the Privy Council (argued over eight days) was dismissed, Lord Morris concluding with the statement that 'Their Lordships are not prepared to say that the High Court were wrong in being unconvinced that a changed approach in Australia was desirable'.[73]

Most members of the Australian High Court took Lord Devlin's speech at face value. Not so Windeyer J. Perhaps it was unduly charitable, perhaps with an eye to the inevitability of a further appeal, Windeyer J gave a devastatingly persuasive account of the way in which defamation was historically grounded in crime while at the same time suggesting that the result was merely 'to produce a more distinct terminology'.[74] He emphasised the narrowness of the verbal distinctions: contrast the traditional formulation ('conscious wrongdoing in contumelious disregard') and the essence of Lord Devlin's approach ('cynical disregard of a plaintiff's rights by a calculating defendant').[75] Windeyer J rejected the publisher's submission:

> We were asked to read Lord Devlin's statement of the second category of cases fit for exemplary damages as if it were not descriptive, but exhaustively definitive. We were asked to construe it literally and rigidly as if it were a statute. We were asked to subordinate the statement of principle to an illustration of that principle.[76]

A few years later, the same issue arose in the English Court of Appeal. Lord Denning, unlike the High Court of Australia, was directly bound by *Rookes* yet was unrestrained in his criticism. He said of Lord Devlin's speech that:

> I must say a word, however, for the guidance of judges who will be trying cases in the meantime. I think the difficulties presented by *Rookes v Barnard* are so great that the judges should direct the juries in accordance with the law as it was understood

[69] See *Rookes* [1964] AC 1129 p ix 'Memoranda'.

[70] P Devlin, *Samples of Lawmaking* (London, Oxford University Press, 1962). Indeed, *Rookes* was truly of the Court's own motion – it seems that the reformulation was not the subject of argument.

[71] Litigation at common law proceeded under the unreformed pre-Judicature system associated with the 3rd edition of Bullen & Leake.

[72] *Uren v John Fairfax & Sons Pty Ltd* (1966) 117 CLR 118 ('*Uren*').

[73] *Australian Consolidated Press Ltd v Uren* (1967) 117 CLR 221, 241.

[74] *Uren* (1966) 117 CLR 118, 152.

[75] ibid 164.

[76] ibid 153.

> before *Rookes v Barnard*. Any attempt to follow *Rookes v Barnard* is bound to lead to confusion.[77]

A majority of the House of Lords disagreed. The decision is complex, and for present purposes just one aspect will be mentioned. Lord Reid said that 'It seems to me obvious that the Court of Appeal failed to understand Lord Devlin's speech'.[78] The passage which followed is worth reproducing in full, despite its length:

> The very full argument which we have had in this case has not caused me to change the views which I held when *Rookes v Barnard* was decided or to disagree with any of Lord Devlin's main conclusions. But it has convinced me that I and my colleagues made a mistake in simply concurring with Lord Devlin's speech. With the passage of time I have come more and more firmly to the conclusion that it is never wise to have only one speech in this House dealing with an important question of law. *My main reason is that experience has shewn that those who have to apply the decision to other cases and still more those who wish to criticise it seem to find it difficult to avoid treating sentences and phrases in a single speech as if they were provisions in an Act of Parliament.* They do not seem to realise that it is not the function of noble and learned Lords or indeed of any judges to frame definitions or to lay down hard and fast rules. It is their function to enunciate principles and much that they say is intended to be illustrative or explanatory and not to be definitive. *When there are two or more speeches they must be read together and then it is generally much easier to see what are the principles involved and what are merely illustrations of it.* I am bound to say that, in reading the various criticisms of Lord Devlin's speech to which we have been referred, I have been very surprised at the failure of its critics to realise that it was intended to state principles and not to lay down rules.[79]

I do not wish to enter into the debate as to the merits of joint judgments of appellate courts, save to say that it is one thing for there to be a joint judgment with its inevitable compromises of style and substance in an appeal in a settled area of the law which turns on its own facts, while it is another where a question of law is unsettled or developing or, to use Lord Reid's language, there is an 'important question of law'. To return once again to a theme of this chapter, why ever should it be thought that there should be a simple one-size-fits-all answer to a question as basal as whether there should be joint judgments in something as richly complex as the legal system?

One should be cautious to avoid the 'textualisation' of precedent.[80] It is revealing that a judge as sophisticated and experienced as Lord Reid was sufficiently concerned by the misreading of judgments on important questions of law as to recommend separate reasons.

[77] *Broome v Cassell & Co Ltd* [1971] 2 QB 354, 384.

[78] *Broome v Cassell & Co Ltd* [1972] AC 1027, 1084 ('*Broome*').

[79] *Broome* [1972] AC 1027, 1084–85 (emphasis added).

[80] See, eg, *Comcare v PVYW* [2013] HCA 41, (2013) 250 CLR 246 [15]–[16]; P Tiersma, 'The Textualization of Precedent' (2007) 82 *Notre Dame Law Review* 1187.

III. Statutes Co-existing with Judge-made Law

One focus of Atiyah and Summers' work was §1-103 of the Uniform Commercial Code and its counterparts, which they described as 'extensive provisions enabling whole statutes or programmes to be overridden or modified by substantive considerations at the point of application', and to which there was said to be nothing comparable in England.[81] The section was said to be 'probably the most important single provision in the Code'.[82]

Section 1-103, in the form it then took, provided:

> Unless displaced by the particular provisions of the Uniform Commercial Code, the principles of law and equity, including the law merchant and the law relative to capacity to contract, principal and agent, estoppel, fraud, misrepresentation, duress, coercion, mistake, bankruptcy, and other validating or invalidating cause supplement its provisions.

It bears a close resemblance to section 61(2) of the Sale of Goods Act 1893 (56 and 57 Vict c 71).[83] What does §1-103 add? It is axiomatic that statute always displaces inconsistent judge-made law, so that can scarcely have been its main function. Certainly, the section repels any inference that the statute – which is, after all, described as a 'Code' – is exhaustive in the sense of covering the field to the exclusion of all judge-made law. It then treats the law merchant as included within 'the principles' of law and equity, and then, lest there be any doubt about it, identifies a series of particular doctrines which are expressly preserved, subject to their being displaced by particular provisions of the Code. No express guidance is given as to when a particular provision 'displaces' a principle of judge-made law. This is left to the courts.

Perhaps §1-103 says something about how courts are to interpret the entirety of the Uniform Commercial Code. It is in a sense exhortatory – it encourages a certain curial attitude to the statute. I am speculating, but it may be that the codification movement in the US, which was much more extensive than in England and Australia, would have led to a different approach to construction in the US in the

[81] Atiyah and Summers, above n 4, 113.

[82] White and Summers, above n 27, 6.

[83] 'The rules of the common law, including the law merchant, save in so far as they are inconsistent with the express provisions of this Act, and in particular the rules relating to the law of principal and agent and the effect of fraud, misrepresentation, duress or coercion, mistake, or other invalidating cause, shall continue to apply to contracts for the sale of goods'. The local counterpart is s 4(2) of the Sale of Goods Act 1923 (NSW). The wider form in the Code, which includes the words 'and equity' means that a large question of construction in the British and Australian legislation does not arise in the US. The issue is mentioned by G Williams, 'Language and the Law – III' (1945) 61 *LQR* 293, 302, reviewed in the New South Wales Law Reform Commission's report *Sale of Goods* (New South Wales Law Reform Commission, *Sale of Goods* (Report 51, 1987) 10–12) and in M Bridge (ed), *Benjamin's Sale of Goods*, 9th edn (London, Sweet & Maxwell, 2014) 11 ('an issue which has never been authoritatively determined in this country').

absence of the express command in §1-103, and for that reason was regarded by White and Summers as being of heightened importance.

An Australian counterpart, which also picks up and encourages the development of judge-made law, whilst at the same time declining to provide how that is to occur, may be seen in the proscription of unconscionable conduct. The legislative history is complex.[84] Complexity is an important part of the theme of this chapter, but it can also distract. Accordingly, what follows is simplified in two respects. I have omitted reference to the parallel state developments under the Fair Trading Acts,[85] and also the parallel federal regulation, insofar as unconscionable conduct relates to the supply of financial services, under the Australian Securities and Investments Acts 1989 and 2001 (Cth),[86] although I cannot avoid the confusion caused by sections being renumbered and statutes being renamed. The account commences in the mid 1980s, when the High Court had given prominence to the equitable principle in *Commercial Bank of Australia Ltd v Amadio*,[87] and similar legislation in some specialist areas was being developed.[88]

A. 1986 – Unconscionable Conduct Directed to Consumers (s 52A)

A statutory prohibition against unconscionable conduct was first introduced into the Trade Practices Act 1974 (Cth) in 1986.[89] The new section 52A(1) provided that: 'A corporation shall not, in trade or commerce, in connection with the supply or possible supply of goods or services to a person, engage in conduct that is, in all the circumstances, unconscionable'.

[84] Contrast its counterpart in the Uniform Commercial Code, §2-302 and s 140A of the Consumer Credit Act 1974 (UK), considered in *Plevin v Paragon Personal Finance* [2014] UKSC 61, [2014] 1 WLR 4222.

[85] Broadly speaking, these tended to follow the amendments to the Trade Practices Act (for example, s 43 of the Fair Trading Act 1987 (NSW) mirrored ss 52A and 51AC), but did not extend to forms analogous to s 51AA. They ceased to have a separate existence after the commencement of the Australian Consumer Law.

[86] The Financial Sector Reform (Consequential Amendments) Act 1998 (Cth) introduced equivalents to ss 51AA and 51AB insofar as those norms of conduct applied to financial services: ss 12CA and 12CB of the Australian Securities and Investments Act 1989 (Cth). This seems primarily to have reflected a policy decision confirming ASIC, as opposed to the ACCC, was the regulator for financial services. An equivalent to s 51AC was belatedly added in 2001, at the same time the 1989 Act was replaced by the Australian Securities and Investments Commission Act 2001 (Cth). When s 12CC was introduced into the ASIC Act, a right to damages for breach of each of the prohibitions under ss 12CA–12CC was introduced (under s 12GF).

[87] *Commercial Bank of Australia Ltd v Amadio* (1983) 151 CLR 447 ('*Amadio*').

[88] Notably in employment law, such as the proscription of 'harsh and unconscionable' contracts of work under s 88F of the Industrial Arbitration Act 1940 (NSW) and its successors, which influenced the drafting of the Contracts Review Act 1980 (NSW). See J Peden, *The Law of Unjust Contracts: Including the Contracts Review Act 1980* (Sydney, Butterworths, 1981) 73–74.

[89] By the Trade Practices Revision Act 1986 (Cth), s 22.

Contravention did *not* give rise to a right to damages.[90] Contravention did entitle an application for a range of 'other orders' under section 87, within a two-year time period.[91] Section 52A(2) set out a list of five non-exhaustive factors which could (but need not) be taken into account by the court in considering whether conduct had been unconscionable.[92] The scope of the provision was limited to goods and services ordinarily acquired for personal, domestic or household use or consumption and not for re-supply or being used in some manufacturing process.[93]

Note the complexity on the face of the statute. There were evaluative judgments to be made in relation to the five factors regard to which is authorised by section 52A(2) (which include the 'legitimate interests' of the corporation and whether it employs 'unfair tactics'). The court was then required to make a further evaluative judgment, namely, whether, in those and all other circumstances, the corporation had engaged in conduct that is 'unconscionable'. No express guidance was given as to what amounted to unconscionable conduct, save for the enumeration of the factors to which regard may be had. Thus the statute confirmed a core area of the ambit of the concept, but said nothing expressly as to its outer limits. However, statute chose to label the new norm of conduct by 'unconscionable', which had been given prominence in *Amadio*, and one available construction was that it meant no more and no less than the equitable doctrine.

B. 1992 – Unwritten Law Unconscionable Conduct (s 51AA)

At first, section 52A was the only provision regarding unconscionable conduct, and it was directed toward consumers. This changed in 1992. Section 52A was renumbered section 51AB. An additional prohibition, section 51AA was added: 'A corporation must not, in trade or commerce, engage in conduct that is unconscionable within the meaning of the unwritten law, from time to time, of the States and Territories'.[94] Unlike section 51AB (formerly section 52A), section 51AA was not expressly limited by reference to the class of plaintiffs. However, no differently from that section, contravention of the new section 51AA did not entitle a plaintiff to damages.

[90] See s 82(3), amended by the Trade Practices Revision Act 1986 (Cth), s 52.

[91] See the new s 87(1C) inserted by the Trade Practices Revision Act 1986 (Cth), s 55.

[92] The parties' bargaining positions (Trade Practices Act 1974 (Cth), s 52A(2)(a)); whether the consumer was required to comply with conditions not reasonably necessary for the protection of the legitimate interests of the corporation (s 52A(2)(b)); whether the consumer was able to understand the documents relating to the transaction (s 52A(2)(c)); whether there was any undue influence or pressure or unfair tactics (s 52A(2)(d)); and a comparison of the value of the goods and services in the transaction at hand and in the market generally (s 52A(2)(e)).

[93] By the Trade Practices Act 1974 (Cth), sub-ss 52A(5), (6).

[94] By the Trade Practices Legislation Amendment Act 1992 (Cth).

Four points may be made about section 51AA.

1. First, the reference to 'the unwritten law, from time to time, of the States and Territories' does not bear its literal meaning. The implicit contrast with 'written law' reflected the distinction between the *conceptual* system of judge-made law with the *textual* system of statute law. The High Court subsequently held that there was but one common law of Australia, which is reflected in the form now taken by the successor provision (section 20 of the Australian Consumer Law).[95]
2. Secondly, the statute was a legislative imprimatur to equitable doctrine developed at that time, and expressly acknowledged that those equitable principles would develop over time. If there were any doubts as to the relative breadth of the equitable doctrine as formulated by Australian courts, there was nothing in section 51AA to discourage that development.[96]
3. Thirdly, unlike section 51AB, section 51AA was not limited in its terms by statute to consumer transactions (although on one view the application of equitable principle may have supplied similar limits).
4. Fourthly, section 51AA(2) provided that 'this section does not apply to conduct that is prohibited by section 51AB'. Accordingly, section 51AB must be taken to have some meaning separate from the meaning of unconscionability in equitable doctrine, lest it be entirely otiose.

C. 1998 – Business Unconscionable Conduct (s 51AC)

Section 51AC was added in 1998.[97] It provided:

> A corporation must not, in trade or commerce, in connection with
>
> (a) the supply or possible supply of goods or services to a person (other than a listed public company); or
>
> (b) the acquisition or possible acquisition of goods or services from a person (other than a listed public company);
>
> engage in conduct that is, in all the circumstances, unconscionable.[98]

The provision did not apply to transactions valued at more than A$1 million. The difference between section 51AB (formerly section 52A) and section 51AC turned upon the monetary cap and the exclusion of listed public companies from the class of applicants who could avail themselves of it. The extrinsic materials stated that

[95] See *Lange v Australian Broadcasting Corporation* (1997) 189 CLR 520 and *John Pfeiffer Pty Ltd v Rogerson* [2000] HCA 36, (2000) 203 CLR 503.

[96] Coincidentally, judgment in *Louth v Diprose* (1992) 175 CLR 621 was delivered shortly after the bill passed through the Senate, and before assent was given to it.

[97] By the Trade Practices Amendment (Fair Trading) Act 1998 (Cth).

[98] Section 51AC(2) was identical save that it dealt with the supply and acquisition of goods and services to and from a corporation (other than a listed public company) by a person.

'the government has accepted the principle that small business people are entitled to a legal protection against unconscionable conduct which is comparable to that accorded to consumers'.[99] The provision authorised the court to have regard to the same five factors already found in section 51AB, and to six further factors.[100] It probably followed that the form of statutory unconscionability in section 51AC was broader than that in section 51AB.

A much more important difference was in remedy. Section 82 was also amended so that a breach of section 51AC would give rise to a right to damages under that section. That was doubly innovative. Not only does it represent a signal change from the position in equity, where rescission is the standard relief, and monetary relief is problematic,[101] but it also reflected a large departure from the discretionary relief equity would ordinarily order. Particularly in a traditional case involving rescission for unconscientious conduct, discretionary factors (such as delay) might be a powerful factor telling against granting relief. But notwithstanding the value-laden determination of the 11 matters to which courts were authorised to have regard, and the evaluative determination of 'unconscionable', if that determination be made, then a party who could show loss was entitled *as of right* to obtain damages if proceedings were commenced within three years.

There was no equivalent delineation between sections 51AA and 51AC at that stage.[102] It would appear to follow that the same conduct might contravene both sections, although the latter but not the former would give rise to an entitlement to damages. This was addressed in 2001, effectively albeit a little cryptically, by an amendment which inserted three letters and one semicolon into section 82.[103]

D. 2001, 2007 and 2008 – Monetary Limits Increased

In 2001, the monetary limit for transactions to which section 51AC applied was raised to A$3 million.[104] In 2007, the monetary limit was expanded again to A$10 million.[105] A further factor to which courts were authorised to consider

[99] Commonwealth of Australia, *Parliamentary Hansard*, House of Representatives, 30 September 1997, 8800 (The Hon Mr Reith MP).

[100] Whether the defendant acted consistently in its conduct to the plaintiff and other like counterparties (Trade Practices Act 1974 (Cth), s 51AC(3)(f)); the requirements of codes of conduct applying to particular industries (sub-ss 51AC(g), (h)); whether the defendant had 'unreasonably failed to disclose' to the plaintiff certain risks to the plaintiffs (s 51AC(3)(i)); whether the defendant was willing to negotiate (s 51AC(3)(j)); and whether the parties had acted in good faith (s 51AC(3)(k)).

[101] See *Munchies Management Pty Ltd v Belperio* (1988) 58 FCR 274 284–286 and *Nadinic v Drinkwater* [2017] NSWCA 334, (2017) 94 NSWLR 518 [34]–[36].

[102] Contrast s 51AA(2), mentioned above.

[103] See Trade Practices Amendment Act (No 1) 2001 (Cth), sch 1, item 18, which inserted '; IVA' after 'Part IV'.

[104] See Trade Practices Amendment Act (No 1) 2001 (Cth), sch 1, item 2.

[105] Trade Practices Amendment Act (No 1) 2007 (Cth), sch 3, items 7 and 8.

was added to unconscionable conduct directed at consumers, namely, whether the defendant had a contractual right to vary a term of the contract unilaterally. Finally, in 2008, the monetary limits were repealed.[106]

E. 2010 – Re-labelling as the Australian Consumer Law

In 2010 the Trade Practices Act was renamed the Australian Competition and Consumer Act 2010 (Cth).[107] The three statutory norms remained, but were now found in sections 20, 21 and 22 of what was termed the Australian Consumer Law, which was in Schedule 3 to the Act. The reference to the 'unwritten law, from time to time, of the States and Territories' was replaced by 'unwritten law from time to time', catching up with what the High Court had held a decade earlier. The right to damages for breaches of each of sections 20–22 continued.[108] Despite the statute's new name of the legislation, the unconscionable conduct provisions directed to businesses remained. Indeed, a new factor was added to the new section 22 (formerly section 51AC), namely, whether the defendant was willing to negotiate, the terms of the contract and whether those terms had been complied with, and any conduct of the defendant after the entry into the contract.

F. 2011 – Coalescence of Consumer and Business Unconscionable Conduct

In 2011, sections 21 and 22 were repealed and replaced by a single provision, section 21.[109] The distinction between the former sections 51AB and 51AC was removed, although section 20, the successor to section 51AA, was not amended. There was now a single statutory prohibition on unconscionable conduct in section 21, and a list of factors which could be taken into account in section 22. Those factors were the same as those which could previously be taken into account in assessing section 51AC. Finally, section 21(4)(a) provided that 'It is the intention of the Parliament that this section is not limited by the unwritten law relating to unconscionable conduct'.

[106] Trade Practices Amendment Act 2008 (Cth), sch 3, item 12.
[107] By the Trade Practices Amendment (Australian Consumer Law) Act (No 2) 2010 (Cth). For how this works in light of the limitations on federal legislative power, see J Dietrich, 'Service Guarantees and Consequential Loss Under the Australian Consumer Law: The Illusion of Uniformity' (2012) 20 *Competition and Consumer Law Journal* 43.
[108] Australian Competition and Consumer Act 2010 (Cth), s 236.
[109] By the Competition and Consumer Legislation Amendment Act 2011 (Cth).

G. Effects

What is the effect of this legislative history upon judge-made law? First of all, and unsurprisingly in light of the extent and recency of legislative change, there have been relatively few decisions and fewer appellate decisions. That may also be a consequence of the residual nature of the norm; a plaintiff who has a cause of action in contract, or tort, or breach of fiduciary duty, or for misleading and deceptive conduct is apt to litigate a well-established claim in preference to something more contestable. And it is also probably a consequence of the inherent uncertainty of the language in which it is expressed.[110] The legislation has incorporated the language of 'unconscionable conduct', and it will be recalled that Mason J emphasised at the outset of his judgment in *Amadio* that: 'It goes almost without saying that it is impossible to describe definitively all the situations in which relief will be granted on the ground of unconscionable conduct'.[111]

Secondly, what does emerge from the legislative history over a quarter of a century is a steady expansion of the statutory norm, which may be contrasted with the equitable principle. That seems to be clear from (a) the increasing list of factors consideration of which is expressly sanctioned, (b) the extension to 'business' or 'commercial' transactions, (c) the ever-increasing monetary limits upon the conduct to which the provision applied and (d) the fact that the statutory concept has (since 1992) sat alongside a federal law which picked up the 'unwritten law' and (since 2011) has been expressly not limited by the unwritten law. In short, there would seem to be an overwhelming case based on legislative history for an expansionist reading of the provisions. Section 21(4)(a) appears to be even more exhortatory than §1-103.

Thirdly, the legislative text and history make it all the more important to identify some limits to the doctrine. Most famously, attempts have been made to limit its scope to conduct involving a 'high level of moral obloquy'.[112] Whether this is so remains unresolved. There is now some authority to the effect that such a submission is unhelpful,[113] as well as authority that it may be useful, largely to emphasise

[110] See P Strickland, 'Rethinking Unconscionable Conduct Under the Trade Practices Act' (2009) 37 *Australian Business Law Review* 19 and R Baxt, 'What Place Does "Moral Obloquy" Have in the Evaluation of Statutory Unconscionable Conduct?' (2014) 88 *Australia Law Journal* 396.

[111] *Amadio* (1983) 151 CLR 447, 461. See also *Blomley v Ryan* (1956) 99 CLR 362, 405.

[112] These are associated with *Attorney General of New South Wales v World Best Holdings Ltd* [2005] NSWCA 261, (2005) 63 NSWLR 557, although it is far from clear that Spigelman CJ's reasons are so to be read.

[113] See, eg, (and without purporting to be exhaustive) *PT Ltd v Spuds Surf Chatswood Ltd* [2013] NSWCA 446 [101]–[102], *Colin R Price & Associates Pty Ltd v Four Oaks Pty Ltd* [2017] FCAFC 75, (2017) 251 FCR 404 [52] and *Commonwealth Bank of Australia v Kojic* [2016] FCAFC 186, (2016) 249 FCR 421 [54]–[60], [69]–[72], [88]. See also S McLeod, 'Statutory Unconscionable Conduct Under the ACL: The Case Against a Requirement for "Moral Obloquy"' (2015) 23 *Competition and Consumer Law Journal* 123.

the extent of the departure from accepted community standards.[114] But given the text, the legislative history and the nature of the equitable principle from which the statute derives, it seems unlikely that it can readily be circumscribed by curial gloss.

Fourthly, it is to be recalled that language is slippery, and as one distinguished commentator has very recently observed of Hohfeld's campaign for precision in legal language: 'even lawyers are deceived by the two-faced nature of much of legal language, looking in one way at legal usage and in another at the pre-legal ideas that the law intends to regulate'.[115] The distinctiveness of the statutory norm, which is broader than equitable principle and whose contravention now gives rise to a right to damages, provides a further reason to bear in mind whether one is drawing upon equitable principle or is instead engaged in an exercise of statutory construction. That is in one sense helpful. It reminds me of a single lane bridge just around a blind corner near my grandmother's home, which to this day has fended off all attempts to widen it, on the basis that 'It's so dangerous that it's safe'.[116] Sections 20 and, especially, 21 of the Australian Consumer Law bear a similar character. The interrelationship between statute and equity is complex and intertwined and requires careful attention.

IV. Conclusion

How does this relate to the theme of this book? As has been observed,[117] precise definitions of 'form' and 'substance' are elusive. I have sought to explain that the role of statutes in a legal system answers at least one definition of its 'formality', and so the ways in which statute law is treated as judge-made law, and vice versa, may be said to reflect *dimensions* of the form/substance distinction. Most if not all of the examples in this chapter may be familiar, but that is really the point. Legal reasoning and legal decision-making deals with judgments and statutes all the time, and the roles of judge-made law and statute law and their interrelationship have profound implications on the nature of the legal system. Sometimes it is useful to step back and look again, with fresh eyes, on matters that may seem obvious.

[114] For recent examples see *Ipstar Australia Pty Ltd v APS Satellite Pty Ltd* [2018] NSWCA 15, (2018) 329 FLR 149 [193]–[195] and *Mastronardo v Commonwealth Bank of Australia Ltd* [2018] NSWCA 136 [18]–[22].

[115] F Schauer, 'Hohfeld on Legal Language' in S Balganesh, T Sichelman and H Smith (eds), *The Legacy of Wesley Hohfeld: Edited Major Works, Select Personal Papers, and Original Commentaries* (Cambridge, Cambridge University Press, 2019) (forthcoming).

[116] It may be seen on Google Maps (Oatley, south of the Sydney CBD, where Boundary Rd crosses the railway line).

[117] A thoughtful and wide-ranging exploration of the role of form is found in R Summers, *Form and Function in a Legal System: A General Study* (New York, Cambridge University Press, 2006) especially 61–63.

16

Interpretive Formalism in the Law of Obligations: Thirty Years after *Form and Substance*

BEN CHEN AND JEFF GORDON

I. Introduction

A central plank of Atiyah and Summers' thesis is that the degree of 'interpretive formality' – that a written text is interpreted literally rather than by reference to its underlying rationale – is higher in England than in the US.[1] When interpreting a statute, written contract or some other legal document, English courts pay close attention to the text but US courts allow the judicially-divined purpose of the text to control. Due to sufficient affinity between the English and Australian interpretive approaches around the time of the publication of *Form and Substance*,[2] Atiyah and Summers' thesis also applied to the Australian legal system. Up until the 1980s, Australian statutory interpretation methodology was highly deferential to English authority.[3] And contractual interpretation methodology similarly deferred to English precedent.[4]

In this chapter, we argue that things have changed in the last 30 years. When it comes to statutory interpretation, Australia and the US have significantly converged: the US has become more formal, and Australia more substantive. Neo-formalism in the US is driven by the rise of textualism. *Form and Substance* was published scarcely a year after Antonin Scalia's appointment to the US Supreme Court.

[1] PS Atiyah and RS Summers, *Form and Substance in Anglo-American Law: A Comparative Study of Legal Reasoning, Legal Theory, and Legal Institutions* (Oxford, Clarendon Press, 1987) 14–16, 100–12 ('*Form and Substance*').

[2] See below Section II.C.2.

[3] M Sanson, *Statutory Interpretation*, 2nd edn (Oxford, Oxford University Press, 2017) 5.

[4] See below Section II.C.2. As late as 2002, in a contractual interpretation case, it was necessary for the High Court of Australia to clarify for lower courts that, if they discern any inconsistency between a High Court case and a House of Lords case, then they should follow the views of the High Court. *Royal Botanic Gardens and Domain Trust v South Sydney City Council* [2002] HCA 5, (2002) 240 CLR 45 [39].

Over the next 30 years, Scalia influentially advocated for more interpretive formalism, championing strict textualism in statutory interpretation and originalism in constitutional interpretation. In Australia, the trend has been in the opposite direction. Aided and abetted by amendments to the Acts Interpretation Act 1901 (Cth) and by *Pepper (Inspector of Taxes) v Hart*[5] in the UK, Australian courts have adopted a 'text in context' approach.[6]

The form/substance distinction is useful for classifying the different approaches to statutory interpretation. But, we argue, the form/substance distinction intersects with another issue, immanent in the case law, that is inadequately addressed: to what extent does a statute displace anterior law? Judges typically address this question by asking whether the statute is a 'code'. But the code/non-code distinction is not binary; it is continuous. The binary view of statutory interaction with the background *corpus juris* is not tailored to today's legislative reality. We introduce the *displacement continuum*, which supplies a useful conceptual resource for situating a statute in the anterior law. The displacement continuum supplements rather than replaces the traditional debates over statutory interpretation methodology.

We use private law statutes to illustrate our claims. Several decades ago, the judicial mind in the Anglo-Australian world saw private law as 'governed by the common law, tempered but slightly with equity, and disfigured but little by statute'.[7] The same might be said of the then-prevailing American attitude.[8] In modern times, rarely is any private law obligation untouched by legislation.[9] Scalia's influence in the US, therefore, not only shows significantly more interpretive formalism but also significantly more formalism. Similarly, a more substantive approach to statutory interpretation in Australia affects a vast range of private law statutes. Since statutes are everywhere,[10] movement in interpretive formalism

[5] *Pepper (Inspector of Taxes) v Hart* [1993] AC 593 ('*Pepper*').

[6] Our claim is limited to formality in statutory interpretation. It could be argued, for example, that the Australian High Court's approach to developing the common law, which requires taking into account any relevant statute, is formal because statutes are inherently formal. 'In considering the development of the common law of Australia', said the High Court, 'it is necessary to consider whether there is a "consistent pattern of legislative policy to which the common law in Australia can adapt itself"'. *Imbree v McNeilly* [2008] HCA 40, (2008) 236 CLR 510 [64] (quoting *Esso Australia Resources Ltd v Federal Commissioner of Taxation* [1999] HCA 67, (1999) 201 CLR 49 [23] ('*Esso*')). We express no view on this argument, except to say that it is about formality in developing the common law, not about formality in statutory interpretation. *Esso* [1999] HCA 67, (1999) 201 CLR 49 [20] (quoting PS Atiyah, 'Common Law and Statute Law' (1985) 48 *MLR* 1, 6).

[7] O Dixon, 'Science and Judicial Proceedings' in SHZ Woinarski (ed), *Jesting Pilate: and other papers and addresses* (Melbourne, Lawbook, 1965) 11, 13.

[8] HF Stone, 'The Common Law in the United States' (1936) 50 *Harvard Law Review* 4, 22–23.

[9] Tort law, eg, is '"drenched" in statute, and to exclude statutes from accounts of tort is to present a grossly incomplete picture'. TT Arvind and J Steele, 'Introduction: Legislation and the Shape of Tort Law' in TT Arvind and J Steele (eds), *Tort Law and the Legislature: Common Law, Statute and the Dynamics of Legal Change* (Oxford, Hart Publishing, 2013) 1, 13.

[10] Consider, eg, the civil liability legislation introduced across Australia in 2002 and 2003, which enacted 'easily the most significant modifications to tort law ever made in that country (legislative or judicial)'. J Goudkamp, 'Statutes and Tort Defences' in TT Arvind and J Steele (eds), *Tort Law and*

bespeaks broader change, including, of course, in the law of obligations. Indeed, increasing formalism in the US and increasing substantivism in Australia is not limited to statutory interpretation. These trends are reflected in contractual interpretation too.[11]

Mindful of the great diversity of private law statutes today, we do not advocate for any particular interpretive methodology. In fact, we conclude that, in the ever-expanding area of statutory private law, there are good reasons for believing that Australian courts have become more substantive than their American counterparts. We illustrate this claim by reference to the constructive trust in bankruptcy and the legislative authorisation of equitable relief. Both of these are examples of an equitable doctrine operating within a statutory regime.[12] These examples highlight the continuous nature of statutory displacement of anterior law. They also reveal that the extent of displacement can depend on the chosen statutory drafting style and interpretive methodology.

Section II below explores the driving forces behind the apparent reversal of trend in American and Australian interpretive methodologies. That section also elaborates upon the displacement continuum. Illustrating our broader claims, Section III compares the American and Australian approaches to the constructive trust in bankruptcy, while Section IV does the same for the legislative authorisation of equitable relief. Section V concludes.

II. Trends in Interpretive Methodology

A. Textualism and Purposivism in the US and Australia

Scalia championed textualism and reinvented statutory interpretation in the US. For the past three decades – since Scalia was elevated to the Supreme Court in 1986 – the debate between textualism and purposivism has dominated statutory interpretation.[13] Some argue that it is time to leave that debate behind. But Scalia, said Justice Elena Kagan, 'taught everybody how to do statutory interpretation differently'.[14] Brett Kavanaugh, the newest addition to the US Supreme Court,

the Legislature: Common Law, Statute and the Dynamics of Legal Change (Oxford, Hart Publishing, 2013) 41. After those reforms, 'tort law in Australia can no longer be regarded as largely a common law field'. B McDonald, 'Legislative Intervention in the Law of Negligence: The Common Law, Statutory Interpretation and Tort Reform in Australia' (2005) 27 *Sydney Law Review* 443, 443.

[11] See below Section II.C.

[12] See below Sections III, IV.

[13] JJ Brudney and L Baum, 'Protean Statutory Interpretation in the Courts of Appeals' (2017) 58 *William & Mary Law Review* 681, 685.

[14] E Kagan, 'The Scalia Lecture: A Dialogue with Justice Kagan on the Reading of Statutes' (*Harvard Law Today*, 17 November 2015) 8:12 https://today.law.harvard.edu/in-scalia-lecture-kagan-discusses-statutory-interpretation/.

thought that '[s]tatutory interpretation has improved dramatically over the last generation, thanks to the extraordinary influence of Justice Scalia'.[15] Kagan said that after Scalia, 'we're all textualists now'.[16]

In many ways, Scalia's outsize influence was anticipated by the publication of *Form and Substance* in 1987. Atiyah and Summers rightly observed that '[f]ew matters affect the style of a legal system in a modern state more than the methods used to interpret statutes'.[17] Regarding *interpretive* formality, they stipulated that an interpretation of a legal text is highly formal if it focuses on the literal meaning of words. Statutes, of course, are susceptible to high degrees of interpretive formality.[18] Yet Atiyah and Summers argued that statutory interpretation in the US tended to be substantive. American courts, they said, treated statutory text as relatively unimportant; statutes were vessels for purposes, rationales or policies that trump the particular words adopted by the legislature.[19] English judges, by contrast, focused on ordinary meaning, considered statutory purpose only if the words had no determinate ordinary meaning, and divined statutory purpose from limited sources (text or antecedent statute or common law). American judges paid less attention to ordinary meaning, considered statutory purpose to determine whether the ordinary meaning was determinate in the first place, and freely drew from all available legislative history.[20]

It's worth pausing to note that Atiyah and Summers' normative project overlapped with Scalia's. They said that 'contrary to frequent American practice, we do not use the term "formal" pejoratively', and that 'one of our principal purposes is to rehabilitate formal legal reasoning'.[21] Similarly, Scalia thought it 'mindless' to criticise textualism as formalistic.[22] He said: '*of course it's formalistic*! The rule of law is *about* form'.[23] Atiyah and Summers agreed, marvelling that English lawyers 'would be amazed' to hear Judge Richard Posner say that 'a judge "rarely starts his inquiry with the words of the statute, and often if the truth be told, he does not look at the words at all"'.[24] 'Most American judges', said Atiyah and Summers, 'are willing to consider evidence of purpose in deciding whether the words are unclear in the first place'.[25] Nearly ten years later, Scalia would make the same criticism in his own distinctive way:

> Resort to legislative history has become so common that lawyerly wags have popularized a humorous quip inverting the oft-recited (and oft-ignored) rule as to when its use

[15] BM Kavanaugh, 'Fixing Statutory Interpretation' (2016) 129 *Harvard Law Review* 2118, 2118.
[16] Kagan, above n 14, 8:28.
[17] Atiyah and Summers, above n 1, 100.
[18] ibid 15, 97.
[19] ibid 100.
[20] ibid 100–02.
[21] ibid 7.
[22] A Scalia, *A Matter of Interpretation*, 2nd edn (Princeton, Princeton University Press, 2018) 25.
[23] ibid.
[24] Atiyah and Summers, above n 1, 101–02 (quoting R Posner, 'Statutory Interpretation – In the Classroom and in the Courtroom' (1983) 50 *University of Chicago Law Review* 800, 807–08).
[25] ibid.

> is appropriate: 'One should consult the text of the statute,' the joke goes, 'only when the legislative history is ambiguous.' Alas, that is no longer funny. Reality has overtaken parody.[26]

Things have changed as a result of the Scalian revolution in American statutory interpretation. Atiyah and Summers' general claims need updating to reflect the formal turn. The gathering consensus is that statutory interpretation in the US is more formal today than it was in the late 1980s. The current US Supreme Court is 'dominantly textualist'.[27] Both liberal and conservative justices now refuse to 'allow … ambiguous legislative history to muddy clear statutory language'.[28] 'Thanks to the great intellectual efforts of textualists, purposivists, and pragmatists over the past three decades', said a legislation scholar, '[a]ll sides … largely have converged on a middle-ground, text-focused position that, for most practitioners and judges (even if not for Justice Scalia himself), includes recourse to broader context, including, in disciplined fashion (again largely thanks to Justice Scalia), legislative materials'.[29] American statutory interpretation today is significantly more formal than it was in 1987.

For most of the twentieth century, Australian courts held fast to the traditional common law rule that excluded reliance on extrinsic material.[30] The High Court reaffirmed that rule as late as 1977.[31] Justice Gibbs thought it 'neither irrational nor outmoded', but 'based upon sound practical reasons'.[32] Justice Mason said it was 'so firmly entrenched that the courts should not depart from it, notwithstanding that it may in isolated cases produce unintended results'.[33] He thought it 'peculiarly a matter for Parliament' to determine whether courts should rely on legislative history.[34]

Parliament accepted the invitation. By the early 1980s, formal statutory interpretation was out of favour. In his 1980 Fullagar Lecture, Lord Scarman assailed the High Court as 'more English than the English' on statutory interpretation.[35]

[26] Scalia, above n 22, 31.

[27] FH Easterbrook, 'The Absence of Method in Statutory Interpretation' (2017) 84 *University of Chicago Law Review* 81, 81.

[28] *Milner v Department of Navy* 562 US 562, 572 (2011) (Kagan J) ('*Milner*'); *NLRB v SW Gen Inc* 137 S Ct 929, 943 (2017) (Roberts CJ).

[29] AR Gluck, 'Justice Scalia's Unfinished Business in Statutory Interpretation: Where Textualism's Formalism Gave Up' (2017) 92 *Notre Dame Law Review* 2053, 2058–59.

[30] JA Scutt, 'Statutory Interpretation and Recourse to Extrinsic Aids' (1984) 58 *Australian Law Journal* 483; JW Barnes, 'Statutory Interpretation, Law Reform and Samford's Theory of the Disorder of Law – Part One' (1994) 22 *Federal Law Review* 116; JW Barnes, 'Statutory Interpretation, Law Reform and Samford's Theory of the Disorder of Law – Part Two' (1995) 23 *Federal Law Review* 77; RS Geddes, 'Purpose and Context in Statutory Interpretation' (2005) 2 *University of New England Law Journal* 1.

[31] *Commissioner for Prices & Consumer Affairs (SA) v Charles Moore (Aust) Ltd* (1977) 139 CLR 449 ('*Charles Moore*').

[32] *Charles Moore* (1977) 139 CLR 449, 461.

[33] ibid 478.

[34] ibid.

[35] L Scarman, 'Ninth Wilfred Fullagar Memorial Lecture: The Common Law Judge and the Twentieth Century – Happy Marriage or Irretrievable Breakdown?' (1980) 7 *Monash Law Review* 1, 6. Pat Brazil quoted Lord Scarman's comment in his opening remarks to a 1981 symposium on statutory interpretation: Geddes, above n 30, 8.

In 1984, the *Sydney Morning Herald* editorialised on 'the extreme literalism of courts in recent years'.[36] The legislative reform effort in Australia was spearheaded by the Commonwealth Attorney-General, Peter Durack, and Pat Brazil (later head of the Attorney-General's Department). Ten days after Lord Scarman's Fullagar Lecture, Durack suggested that 'particular legislation, regulatory in nature', could require courts 'to have regard to an explanatory memorandum which would be submitted to the Parliament and attached to the legislation'.[37] Within a year the Commonwealth Attorney-General introduced, and Federal Parliament enacted, the legislation inserting section 15AA into the Acts Interpretation Act 1901 (Cth). Section 15AA required courts to adopt 'a construction that would promote the purpose or object underlying the Act (whether that purpose or object is expressly stated in the Act or not)'.[38]

Durack and Brazil also organised a 1983 symposium in Canberra on 'Extrinsic Aids to Statutory Interpretation' – one of Durack's 'initiatives in the field of statutory interpretation … of unusual éclat'[39] – attended by Lord Wilberforce and five members of the High Court.[40] The *Australian Law Journal* noted that Lord Wilberforce's 'brilliant paper' advocated 'enlarging the matrix' of legitimate sources for legislative interpretation.[41] 'There appears', reported the *Australian Law Journal*, 'general approval for an amendment of the *Acts Interpretation Act*' permitting courts to consider 'the contents of any document which is declared by the Act to be a relevant document'.[42] Justice Macrossan of the Supreme Court of Queensland recalled a more general consensus: a vote taken at the 1983 symposium 'favoured, by a vast majority, the view that judges should be free to have regard to any material which they might think relevant', and that a 'majority also thought that some statutory provision was desirable to ensure that use was made of this opportunity'.[43] This more liberal approach to extrinsic materials prevailed. From 1984, courts were permitted to refer to extrinsic material

[36] 'The Language of the Law', *Sydney Morning Herald* (Sydney, 2 April 1984) 8.

[37] 'Current Topics: The "Purposive" versus the "Literal" Construction of Statutes' (1981) 55 *Australian Law Journal* 175, 176.

[38] Statute Law Revision Act 1981 (Cth), sch 1; 'Current Topics: Statutory Guidelines for Interpreting Commonwealth Statutes' (1981) 55 *Australian Law Journal* 711, 711; 'Guidelines for Interpretation in Australia' (1981) 2 *Statute Law Review* 181.

[39] 'Current Topics: Contribution to Law Reform of Senator Durack QC as Attorney-General, 1977–1983' (1983) 57 *Australian Law Journal* 320, 321.

[40] 'Current Topics: Canberra Symposium on Extrinsic Aids to Statutory Interpretation, February 1983' (1983) 57 *Australian Law Journal* 191, 192. The symposium was attended by at least two future High Court justices and was 'chaired by the leading force behind the moves for reform and the procedure of a public discussion, Mr Pat Brazil': 'What Does It Mean?' [1983] *Reform (Australian Law Reform Commission)* 62. Pat Brazil convened an earlier 1981 symposium: 'An Australian Symposium on Statutory Interpretation' (1982) 3 *Statute Law Review* 172. We thank Professor Neil Foster for drawing our attention to Pat Brazil.

[41] 'Current Topics: Canberra Symposium on Extrinsic Aids to Statutory Interpretation, February 1983' (1983) 57 *Australian Law Journal* 191, 192.

[42] ibid 193.

[43] JM Macrossan, 'Judicial Interpretation' (1984) 58 *Australian Law Journal* 547, 549.

to confirm the text's ordinary meaning, to resolve textual ambiguity, or to avoid absurd results.[44]

Australia's legislative reform was a prelude to a 'modern' or 'contextual' approach to statutory interpretation.[45] In the aftermath of the legislative reform, Australian courts were initially cautious, refusing to rely on legislative history unless the text was ambiguous or its ordinary meaning produced absurdity.[46] Then, assisted by a relaxation at common law of the traditional exclusionary rule,[47] a less formal approach developed. Australian courts today consider legislative history (and other extrinsic materials) as part of the entire range of surrounding circumstances relevant to a question of statutory interpretation. Legislative history is primarily used 'to identify the purpose or policy of the statutory provision or the statute as a whole', and secondarily as evidence of the meaning of the statutory text.[48]

It should be noted that circa 2010, there were whispers in the High Court that text was to be categorically privileged over context.[49] Even then, however, the Chief Justice of New South Wales cautioned against placing too much weight on the High Court's methodological asides.[50] Subsequent commentary from Justice Kenny supported this view.[51] In September 2017, the High Court in *SZTAL* confirmed that text and context are considered simultaneously.[52] The 'text in context' approach of *SZTAL* has been enthusiastically embraced by the intermediate appellate courts, including a five-judge bench of the New South Wales Court of Criminal Appeal.[53]

At a broad methodological level, then, the Australian High Court's approach to statutes is less interpretively formal than the US Supreme Court's. The US Supreme Court views the statutory text as the privileged source: it is legitimate

[44] Acts Interpretation Amendment Act 1984 (Cth), s 7 (inserting s 15AB of the Acts Interpretation Act 1901 (Cth)).

[45] See especially *CIC Insurance Ltd v Bankstown Football Club Ltd* (1997) 187 CLR 384, 408 ('*CIC Insurance*'); J Dharmananda, 'Outside the Text: Inside the Use of Extrinsic Materials in Statutory Interpretation' (2014) 42 *Federal Law Review* 333; J Barnes, 'Contextualism: "The Modern Approach to Statutory Interpretation"' (2018) 41 *University of New South Wales Law Journal* 1083.

[46] *Re Australian Federation of Construction Contractors; Ex parte Billing* (1986) 68 ALR 416, 420.

[47] The House of Lords relaxed the exclusionary rule in *Pepper* [1993] AC 593.

[48] Dharmananda, above n 45, 356.

[49] *Alcan (NT) Alumina Pty Ltd v Commissioner of Territory Revenue* [2009] HCA 41, (2009) 239 CLR 27 [47] (Hayne, Heydon, Crennan and Kiefel JJ); *Saeed v Minister for Immigration and Citizenship* [2010] HCA 23, (2010) 241 CLR 252 [33]–[34] (French CJ, Gummow, Hayne, Crennan and Kiefel JJ).

[50] JJ Spigelman, 'The Intolerable Wrestle: Developments in Statutory Interpretation' (2010) 84 *Australian Law Journal* 822.

[51] S Kenny, 'Constitutional Role of the Judge: Statutory Interpretation' (2014) 1 *Judicial College of Victoria Online Journal* 4, 11.

[52] *SZTAL v Minister for Immigration and Border Protection* [2017] HCA 34, (2017) 347 ALR 405 [14] (Kiefel CJ, Nettle and Gordon JJ), [37] (Gageler J) ('*SZTAL*').

[53] *Xiao v The Queen* [2018] NSWCCA 4, (2018) 96 NSWLR 1 [223]–[224]. See also *AD v Commissioner of the Australian Federal Police* [2018] NSWCA 89, (2018) 332 FLR 285 [45]–[46]; *Public Service Association and Professional Officers' Association Amalgamated Union of New South Wales v Industrial Relations Secretary* [2018] NSWCA 39, (2018) 96 NSWLR 762 [113]; *Australian Competition and Consumer Commission v Cement Australia Pty Ltd* [2017] FCAFC 159 [377]–[388].

to rely on extrinsic material *only if* the text is unclear.[54] Textual ambiguity is the gateway to extrinsic material; legislative history 'is meant to clear up ambiguity, not create it'.[55] The Australian High Court is not so formal. Its approach 'allows a court to consider the purposes of an Act in determining whether there is more than one possible construction'.[56] The much-quoted joint judgment in *CIC Insurance* said that extrinsic material can be considered 'in the first instance, not merely at some later stage when ambiguity might be thought to arise'.[57] The US Supreme Court, by granting statutory text lexical priority to other sources, has adopted an approach that is more literal, and therefore more interpretively formal, than the Australian High Court's.

Or so they say. Whether lower courts actually do what the respective supreme courts say is an open question. It is notoriously difficult, for example, to avert the judicial gaze from legislative history, even under specific instructions. Recent studies of the US Courts of Appeals support a 'protean' or 'eclectic' approach to statutory interpretation, reflecting widespread use of legislative history despite the grave warnings issued by the US Supreme Court.[58] This tendency has been around for a long time. In 1981, when UK courts were under a strict injunction to refrain from relying on legislative history altogether, Quintin Hogg, the Lord Chancellor, colourfully explained to the House of Lords that anyone who 'think[s] that courts and practitioners do not read Blue Books[59] in order to find out what statutes mean [is] living in a complete fool's paradise'.[60] As one US federal judge put it recently, '[t]he suggestion that you follow some kind of methodological rule in terms of looking at legislative history tends to be overly formalist and not in the real world'.[61]

B. Statutes, Common Law and the Displacement Continuum

We all know the story: for most of its history, the common law was hostile to statute. Legislation, in Harlan Fiske Stone's indelible turn of phrase, was seen as 'an alien intruder in the house of the common law'.[62] The common law's abiding hostility to statute led to a separation between unwritten and written law akin

[54] AM Samaha, 'If the Text is Clear – Lexical Ordering in Statutory Interpretation' (2018) 94 *Notre Dame Law Review* 155.

[55] *Milner* 562 US 562, 572 (2011) (Kagan J).

[56] *Mills v Meeking* (1990) 169 CLR 214, 235 (Dawson J).

[57] *CIC Insurance* (1997) 187 CLR 384, 408.

[58] Brudney and Baum, above n 13; AR Gluck and R Posner, 'Statutory Interpretation on the Bench: A Survey of Forty-Two Judges of the Federal Court of Appeals' (2018) 131 *Harvard Law Review* 1298.

[59] 'Blue Books' are the books bound in blue that typically contain official British Government publications like parliamentary reports.

[60] HL Deb 26 March 1981, vol 418, cols 1345–46.

[61] Gluck and Posner, above n 58, 1325.

[62] Stone, above n 8, 15.

to 'oil and water'.[63] But now, aided by a star-studded cast of twentieth-century academic lawyers – Pound,[64] Atiyah,[65] Finn,[66] Beatson[67] – we are finally working through statute and common law's 'symbiotic relationship'.[68] Assisted by recent interventions from other luminaries – Burrows,[69] Leeming[70] – we realise that no statute is born in a vacuum. No statute, we might say, is an island.

Understanding how a statute interacts with the background *corpus juris* is necessary for deciding what a statutory provision requires. For example, one of the 'strong-arm' provisions of the US *Bankruptcy Code* empowers the trustee in bankruptcy to assume the position of a hypothetical bona fide purchaser at the commencement of the case.[71] This provision is drafted to enable avoidance of any unperfected interest in real property forming part of the bankrupt estate. However, whether the strong-arm provision permits avoidance of a constructive trust – an equitable remedy with proprietary consequences – is highly controversial. In determining the requirements of the strong-arm provision, the court must form a view on whether the Code displaces the unwritten law governing constructive trusts in bankruptcy.[72]

The question usually asked is whether the statute enacts a 'code'.[73] If so, then the statute 'neither requires nor permits resort to any other law in the determination of the rights, duties and liabilities which it creates'.[74] But the code/non-code distinction is not binary; it is continuous. Even if a statute enacts a code that replaces the common law, 'an appeal to earlier decisions can be justified if the language of the statute is itself doubtful or if some other special ground is made out'.[75] Characterising the statute as a code does not create an absolute rule that pre-code decisions cannot be relied on.

A statute's interaction with the background *corpus juris* occurs on a *displacement continuum*. At one end of the continuum are 'codes', which replace anterior common law wholesale. Ordinarily, antecedent unwritten law cannot be relied on when interpreting, for example, a criminal code.[76] Located in the middle of

[63] J Beatson, 'Has the Common Law a Future?' (1997) 56 *CLJ* 291, 300.
[64] R Pound, 'Common Law and Legislation' (1908) 21 *Harvard Law Review* 383.
[65] PS Atiyah, 'Common Law and Statute Law' (1985) 48 *MLR* 1.
[66] P Finn, 'Statutes and the Common Law' (1992) 22 *University of Western Australia Law Review* 7; P Finn, 'Statutes and the Common Law: The Continuing Story' in S Corcoran and S Bottomley (eds), *Interpreting Statutes* (Annandale, Federation Press, 2005) 52.
[67] J Beatson, 'The Role of Statute in the Development of Common Law Doctrine' (2001) 117 *LQR* 247.
[68] *Brodie v Singleton Shire Council* [2001] HCA 29, (2001) 206 CLR 512 [31] (Gleeson CJ).
[69] A Burrows, 'The Relationship between Common Law and Statute in the Law of Obligations' (2012) 128 *LQR* 232.
[70] M Leeming, 'Equity: Ageless in the "Age of Statutes"' (2015) 9 *Journal of Equity* 108.
[71] 11 USC § 544(a)(3).
[72] See below Section III.
[73] See, eg, *Carlton and United Breweries Ltd v Tooth & Co Ltd* (1986) 5 NSWLR 1, 12–16 (Hodgson J).
[74] *Philip Morris Inc v Adam P Brown Male Fashions Pty Ltd* (1981) 148 CLR 457, 543 (Wilson J).
[75] *Gamer's Motor Centre (Newcastle) Pty Ltd v Natwest Wholesale Australia Pty Ltd* (1987) 163 CLR 236, 243–44 (Mason CJ).
[76] *Brennan v The Queen* (1936) 55 CLR 253, 263 (Dixon and Evatt JJ).

the continuum are statutes that modify or supplement the unwritten law. The *Australian Consumer Law* overlaps and adopts unwritten law.[77] At the other end of the continuum are statutes that minimally displace the unwritten law. Typically such statutes establish sui generis legislative schemes. Statutory 'interim control orders', for example, have no common law analogue.[78]

To begin with, the displacement continuum is helpful because it illustrates that statutes cannot completely escape antecedent law, but they can be more or less pre-emptive. Even a code is not 'written on a *tabula rasa*, with all that used to be there removed and forgotten'; it is, rather, 'written on a palimpsest, with the old writing still discernible behind'.[79] For example, the High Court has held that the Native Title Act 1993 (Cth) constitutes an exclusive code governing the recognition, protection, extinguishment and impairment of native title.[80] But, as Brennan J recognised in *Mabo v Queensland (No 2)* and Gummow J recognised in *Wik Peoples v Queensland*, native title 'takes [its] place in the general legal order' and 'may be protected by such legal or equitable interests established by the evidence, whether proprietary or personal and usufructuary in nature and whether possessed by a community, a group or an individual'.[81]

Further, the displacement continuum is helpful because it clarifies whether common law analogies are legitimate in statutory interpretation. The more pre-emptive the legislation, the less legitimate a common law analogy. Of course, a common law analogy may not be very helpful in interpreting a minimally-displacing statute, especially if the statute enacts a sui generis legislative scheme. But that is a different question from whether it is legitimate to use an analogy.

Some factors indicate where a statute falls on the displacement continuum. A statute expressly abolishing anterior law is maximally-displacing.[82] But not all statutes are clear. Textually detailed statutes are more likely to displace antecedent law. Comprehensive and reticulated statutes, such as codes, are maximally-displacing and highly detailed. To be sure, a maximally-displacing statute is not always textually detailed; in those instances, a court may not rely on anterior unwritten law but may rely on substantive reasons like policy considerations. Moreover, a statutory refusal to adopt the language and concepts of the unwritten law – the conscious creation of a sui generis legislative scheme – is an indicator that the statute does not displace but is intended to exist alongside the unwritten law. However, when a statute *does* adopt the language and concepts of the unwritten law, it can be a difficult question whether the statute either picks up the unwritten law or creates a new complex of statutory rights and duties under an old label. Section III below will provide an example to illustrate this point.

[77] Competition and Consumer Act 2010 (Cth), sch 2, ss 18, 20.

[78] *Thomas v Mowbray* [2007] HCA 33, (2007) 233 CLR 307 [17] (Gleeson CJ), [120] (Gummow and Crennan JJ), [338] (Kirby J).

[79] *Vallance v The Queen* (1961) 108 CLR 56, 76 (Windeyer J).

[80] *Western Australia v Commonwealth (Native Title Act Case)* (1995) 183 CLR 373, 453.

[81] *Mabo v Queensland (No 2)* (1992) 175 CLR 1, 61; *Wik Peoples v Queensland* (1996) 187 CLR 1, 197.

[82] See, eg, Maintenance, Champerty and Barratry Abolition Act 1993 (NSW).

The displacement continuum also intersects with the important distinction between open-ended and close-ended statutory language.[83] Open-ended statutory words 'embody a felt rather than defined purpose and necessarily look to the future for the unfolding of their content, making of their judicial application an evolutionary process nourished by relevant changing circumstances'.[84] Examples include the *Australian Consumer Law*'s prohibition on 'misleading or deceptive' conduct. Close-ended statutory language – such as a 'specific grant [of an easement] contained in a specific statute designed to achieve a specific contemporaneous goal' – 'does not gain meaning from time' and 'the judicial task is to ascertain what content was conveyed' at the time of enactment.[85]

The distinction between open- and close-ended statutory language is 'important and underappreciated',[86] but the displacement continuum shows that it is also insufficient. Ordinarily, perhaps, an open-ended section adopts or builds on unwritten law rather than displaces it; and close-ended language may usually displace anterior unwritten law. But this is not always the case, and moderately-displacing statutes create particular difficulties. In 2017, the High Court held that the word 'inflicts' in section 35 of the Crimes Act 1900 (NSW) is open-ended, 'adaptable to new circumstances' and 'contemporary ideas and understanding'.[87] Relying on Lord Steyn's speech in *R v Ireland*, which interpreted similar language in an 1861 UK Act, the Court reasoned that the 'generality' of the language 'attracts the operation of the always speaking approach, and so includes the reckless infliction of sexual disease'.[88] But the real question is not whether 'inflicts' is open-ended; it is whether section 35 swept away *Ireland*. The Court did not grapple with that question.[89]

C. Correlated Trends in Contract Interpretation

While Atiyah and Summers did not dwell on contracts, recent comparative studies lend support to their thesis: contract doctrine and theory tend to be more substantive in US jurisdictions than in many other common law jurisdictions.[90] This section argues for a more complex picture; it reveals a strong trend in favour of textualism in the US, and an oscillation between textualism and contextualism in Australia.

[83] HJ Friendly, 'Mr Justice Frankfurter and the Reading of Statutes' in W Mendelson (ed), *Felix Frankfurter: The Judge* (New York City, Reynal & Hitchcock, 1964) 38.

[84] *United States v Union Pacific Railroad Co* 353 US 112, 122 (1957) (Frankfurter J, dissenting).

[85] *United States v Union Pacific Railroad Co* 353 US 112, 122 (1957) (Frankfurter J, dissenting).

[86] Leeming, above n 70, 22.

[87] *Aubrey v The Queen* [2017] HCA 18, (2017) 260 CLR 305 [30], [40] ('*Aubrey*').

[88] *Aubrey* [2017] HCA 18, (2017) 260 CLR 305 [40].

[89] ibid [26].

[90] See, eg, L Nottage, 'Changing Contract Lenses: Unexpected Supervening Events in English, New Zealand, US, Japanese, and International Sales Law and Practice' (2007) 14 *Indiana Journal of Global Legal Studies* 385; L Nottage, 'Tracing Trajectories in Contract Law Theory: Form in Anglo-New Zealand Law, Substance in Japan and the United States' (2013) 4 *Yonsei Law Journal* 175.

i. US Trends in Favour of Textualism

Illustrating the crux of our arguments is a favourite classroom case about a mockumentary entitled *Borat: Cultural Learnings of America for Make Benefit Glorious Nation of Kazakhstan*. A Maryland-based driving instructor tells the story. In May 2005, someone working for a California-based film producer made oral representations to solicit the driving instructor's participation in a 'documentary about the integration of foreign people into the American way of life'.[91] The driving instructor agreed to participate for $500, and the filming was scheduled to take place in Washington DC in June 2005. On the day of filming, the production crew arrived 90 minutes late with $500 for the driving instructor and a standard-form document for him to sign. In a hurry and relying on previous conversations, the driving instructor signed the document without reading it. The scene that was filmed that day involved the driving instructor giving lessons to comedian Sacha Baron Cohen, in character as Borat, who was 'driving irresponsibly and erratically engaging in conversation with strangers and making derogatory and offensive remarks'.[92]

The driving instructor brought claims in fraud and misrepresentation against the film producer, Cohen and others in a New York federal court, seeking compensation for emotional harm and disgorgement. The plaintiff's claims critically depended on the oral representations that induced his participation. However, the standard-form document that he signed contained a merger clause acknowledging that he was 'not relying upon any promises or statements made by anyone about the nature of the film'.[93] That merger clause was reinforced by an exclusive forum-selection clause and a choice-of-law clause nominating New York courts and New York law, respectively.

Why would the drafter of the standard-form document, who worked for a California-based film producer, include clauses that prefer New York courts and New York law? To secure the enforcement of the merger clause to the letter. This was indeed the outcome in the driving instructor's case. He had to sue in New York after these clauses successfully barred his claims brought elsewhere.[94] The trial judge in New York found no ambiguity in the merger clause, and therefore enforced the clause according to its literal meaning. The result was a summary dismissal of the fraud and misrepresentation claims.[95] This was affirmed on appeal.[96]

[91] *Psenicska v Twentieth Century Fox Film Corp* Nos 07 Civ 10972(LAP), 08 Civ 1571(LAP), 08 Civ 1828(LAP), 2008 WL 4185752, 1 (SDNY Sept 3, 2008) (quoting the complaint) ('*Psenicska*').

[92] *Psenicska v Twentieth Century Fox Film Corp* Nos 07 Civ 10972(LAP), 08 Civ 1571(LAP), 08 Civ 1828(LAP), 2008 WL 4185752, 1 (SDNY Sept 3, 2008) 2.

[93] *Psenicska v Twentieth Century Fox Film Corp* Nos 07 Civ 10972(LAP), 08 Civ 1571(LAP), 08 Civ 1828(LAP), 2008 WL 4185752, 1 (SDNY Sept 3, 2008) 3 (quoting the complaint). This document is on file with the authors.

[94] K Raygor and B Bahktari, 'Great Success! "Borat's" Release Agreement', *The New York Law Journal* (New York, 18 July 2008).

[95] *Psenicska v Twentieth Century Fox Film Corp* Nos 07 Civ 10972(LAP), 08 Civ 1571(LAP), 08 Civ 1828(LAP), 2008 WL 4185752, 1 (SDNY Sept 3, 2008) (quoting the complaint) 5–7.

[96] *Psenicska v Twentieth Century Fox Film Corp* 409 Fed Appx 368 (2nd Cir 2009).

While the contract-interpretation methodology favoured in many other US jurisdictions is more contextual than the common law approach in New York,[97] the Borat cases illustrate a broader pattern in contract drafting that leads to the practical domination of the textualist methodology. A widely-cited empirical study suggests that almost half of US commercial contracts nominate New York law.[98] The same study reveals that 15 per cent choose the law of Delaware – another textualist jurisdiction.[99] In stark contrast, only about eight per cent choose the law of California – a contextualist jurisdiction.[100] Emboldened by these statistics, influential lawyer-economists have endorsed New York's textualist approach as the majority default rule in commercial cases, primarily to reduce expected adjudication costs and to maximise party control.[101]

Textualism in US contract law and practice is not limited to commercial cases; it clearly has infiltrated consumer and employment cases. This is the result of the formalist turn in the arbitration jurisprudence of the US Supreme Court. Section 2 of the Federal Arbitration Act, a century-old provision, provides that arbitration agreements 'shall be valid, irrevocable, and enforceable, save upon such grounds as exist at law or in equity for the revocation of any contract'.[102] In the late 1980s, the Court began to promote arbitration. The Court was initially substantive, endorsing arbitration on economic grounds.[103] Then, in a series of classic Scalia opinions, the Court's textualism continued arbitration's steady march.[104] Recent opinions of the Court carry on Scalia's legacy, upholding agreements that mandate individual rather than aggregate arbitration and stultifying consumer and employee protection laws.[105] Empirical studies consistently reveal widespread inclusion of arbitration clauses in consumer and employment contracts.[106]

[97] A Schwartz and RE Scott, 'Contract Interpretation Redux' (2010) 119 *Yale Law Journal* 926, 928, 932 (footnotes omitted).

[98] T Eisenberg and GP Miller, 'The Flight to New York: An Empirical Study of Choice of Law and Choice of Forum Clauses in Publicly-Held Companies' Contracts' (2009) 30 *Cardozo Law Review* 1475, 1478.

[99] *Alta Berkeley VI CV v Omneon, Inc* 41 A 3d 381, 385–86 (Del 2012).

[100] Eisenberg and Miller, above n 98, 1490.

[101] See, eg, Schwartz and Scott, above n 97, 961–63; L Bernstein, 'Custom in the Courts' (2015) 110 *Northwestern University Law Review* 63, 105.

[102] 9 USC § 2.

[103] JM Glover, 'Disappearing Claims and the Erosion of Substantive Law' (2015) 124 *Yale Law Journal* 3052, 3061–63.

[104] ibid 3066–68 (discussing Scalia's majority opinions in *AT&T Mobility LLC v Concepcion* 563 US 333 (2011), *American Exp Co v Italian Colors Restaurant* 570 US 228 (2013)).

[105] See, eg, *Kindred Nursing Centers Limited Partnership v Clark* 137 S Ct 1421 (2017); *Epic Systems Corp v Lewis* 138 S Ct 1612 (2018).

[106] See, eg, T Eisenberg, GP Miller and E Sherwin, 'Arbitration's Summer Soldiers: An Empirical Study of Arbitration Clauses in Consumer and Nonconsumer Contracts' (2008) 41 *University of Michigan Journal of Law Reform* 871, 883; US Government Consumer Financial Protection Bureau, *Arbitration Study: Report to Congress, pursuant to Dodd–Frank Wall Street Reform and Consumer Protection Act § 1028(a)* 2–9 (March 2015) (footnotes omitted); AJS Colvin, 'The Growing Use of Mandatory Arbitration: Access to the Courts Is Now Barred for More Than 60 Million American Workers' (Report, Economic Policy Institute 6 April 2018) 4–13 (footnotes omitted).

Well-drafted arbitration clauses can remove from courts claims of unconscionability[107] as well as fraud, duress or mistake.[108] Some scholars argue that arbitration even leads to changes in the substantive content of the law.[109]

However, contract-drafting practices and forum shopping in the US seem unable to eliminate contextualism completely. Textualism cannot infiltrate goods contracts falling within the scope of Article 2 of the *Uniform Commercial Code*.[110] Drafted by eminent legal realists well before the publication of *Form and Substance*, this nationally-uniformed Article mandates a contextualist approach to contract interpretation.[111] Because the UCC is enacted state-by-state, reaching nationwide consensus to amend it is extremely difficult.[112] Hence we do *not* argue that prior comparative studies are wrong to suggest that US contract doctrine and theory seem highly substantive.[113] We only qualify those studies by drawing attention to a strong trend in favour of textualism in the US.

ii. Australian Developments

Constitutional, statutory and contractual interpretation are correlated. Scalia promoted formalism in constitutional and statutory interpretation,[114] and there are similarities in statutory and contractual interpretation.[115] In the period leading to the publication of *Form and Substance*, the Privy Council could hear direct appeals from Australian state supreme courts on state matters. This entrenched the formalism that prevailed in Australian courts in contractual and statutory interpretation.

While the Privy Council was looming large, Australian courts could not develop an interpretive methodology that departed significantly from the formalism that Atiyah and Summers observed in the UK. As William Gummow observed, even Sir Owen Dixon 'suffered constraint in the scope of his judicial work'.[116] Dixon preferred contextualism.[117] His Honour wrote in *Commissioner for Railways (NSW) v Agalianos* that '*the context, the general purpose and policy* of a [statutory]

[107] *AT&T Mobility LLC v Concepcion* 563 US 333 (2011).

[108] GA Bermann, 'The "Gateway" Problem in International Commercial Arbitration' (2012) 37 *Yale Journal of International Law* 1, 33–34 (surveying and discussing the US cases in point).

[109] Glover, above n 103.

[110] UCC §§ 2-102, 2-201.

[111] UCC § 2-202.

[112] See generally WH Henning, 'Amended Article 2: What Went Wrong?' (2009) 11 *Duquesne Business Law Journal* 131.

[113] See above n 90.

[114] See above Section II.A.

[115] See, eg, M Kirby, 'Towards a Grand Theory of Interpretation: The Case of Statutes and Contracts' (2003) 24 *Statute Law Review* 95; A Robertson, 'Purposive Contract Interpretation' (2019) *Legal Studies* (forthcoming).

[116] W Gummow, 'The 2017 Winterton Lecture: Sir Owen Dixon Today' (2018) 43 *University of Western Australia Law Review* 30, 35.

[117] ibid.

provision and its consistency and fairness are surer guides to its meaning than the logic with which it is constructed'.[118] In the shadow of the Privy Council, and under the extraordinary influence of the House of Lords,[119] the High Court of Australia did not accept Dixon's purposive approach to statutory interpretation.[120] Yet, about a decade after the complete abolition of appeals to the Privy Council,[121] the High Court quoted Dixon's statement in *Agalianos* to embrace purposivism in statutory interpretation.[122]

In the era of Privy Council appeals, the then-prevailing British formalism also imposed constraints on Australian courts' approach to contract interpretation. In *Port Jackson Stevedoring Pty Ltd v Salmond & Spraggon (Australia) Pty Ltd*, the Privy Council intervened to smother disagreement with its contract-interpretation precedents expressed by two High Court Justices.[123] In *BP Refinery (Westernport) Pty Ltd v Shire of Hastings*,[124] the Privy Council reversed the Victorian Supreme Court to establish a stringent test for the implication of contractual terms in fact. Factual implication is commonly understood to involve an interpretive task.[125]

Contextualism claimed adherents among the British judiciary even before the abolition of Privy Council appeals from Australian courts. By the time *Form and Substance* was published, Lord Wilberforce had already delivered several speeches to endorse a contextual approach to contract interpretation.[126] However, his Lordship's approach was not accepted as orthodoxy until its emphasis by Lord Hoffmann in 1998.[127] Similarly, as noted above, at least by 1981 Lord Wilberforce was advocating for a purposive approach to statutory interpretation that permitted recourse to extrinsic materials, and his views were influential in Australia.[128]

[118] *Commissioner for Railways (NSW) v Agalianos* (1955) 92 CLR 390, 397 ('*Agalianos*') (emphasis added).

[119] B Kercher, *An Unruly Child: A History of Law in Australia* (St Leonards, Allen & Unwin, 1995) 166–69.

[120] Above, text accompanying nn 30–34.

[121] Australia Act 1986 (Cth, UK).

[122] *Project Blue Sky v Australian Broadcasting Authority* [1998] HCA 28, (1998) 194 CLR 355, 381.

[123] *Port Jackson Stevedoring Pty Ltd v Salmond & Spraggon (Australia) Pty Ltd* (1980) 144 CLR 300, 304–05.

[124] *BP Refinery (Westernport) Pty Ltd v Shire of Hastings* (1977) 180 CLR 266.

[125] See, eg, A Robertson, 'The Limits of Interpretation in the Law of Contract' (2016) 47 *Victoria University of Wellington Law Review* 191; *Codelfa Construction Pty Ltd v State Rail Authority of NSW* (1982) 149 CLR 337, 345 (Mason J) ('*Codelfa*'); *Attorney General of Belize v Belize Telecom Ltd* [2009] UKPC 10, [2009] 1 WLR 1988 [21]–[22]. cf *Marks and Spencer plc v BNP Paribas Securities Services* [2015] UKSC 72, [2016] AC 742 [22]–[31] (Lord Neuberger, with whom Lord Sumption and Lord Hodge agreed); JW Carter and W Courtney, '*Belize Telecom*: A Reply to Professor McLauchlan' [2015] *Lloyd's Maritime and Commercial Law Quarterly* 245.

[126] *Prenn v Simmonds* [1971] 1 WLR 1381; *Reardon Smith Line Ltd v Yngvar Hansen-Tangen* [1976] 1 WLR 989.

[127] *Investors Compensation Scheme Ltd v West Bromwich Building Society* [1998] 1 WLR 896, 912–13 (Lord Hoffmann); T Bingham, 'A New Thing under the Sun? The Interpretation of Contract and the *ICS* Decision' (2008) 12 *Edinburgh Law Review* 374 (approved in *Wood v Capita Insurance Services Ltd* [2017] UKSC 24, [2017] AC 1173 [10] ('*Wood*')).

[128] Above, text accompanying nn 39–44.

Since Privy Council appeals were abolished, Australian contractual interpretation oscillates between textualism and contextualism. Professor John Carter recently observed that contract interpretation in Anglo-Australian jurisdictions has gradually moved away from strict textualism.[129] As Carter writes, 'The expressions "commercial construction" and "commercial interpretation" describe both the characteristics of the [Anglo-Australian] construction process and the desired result of that process'.[130] Very recently, Professor Andrew Robertson argued that purposive interpretation rationalises both the interpretation of express contractual terms and the factual implication of contractual terms. This purposive approach is a form of contextual interpretation that gives effect to 'commercial common sense'.[131] However, the Anglo-Australian approach to contract interpretation is not 'unfaithful or disloyal to the text'.[132] It is a sliding-scale approach that pays greater attention to the text as the text becomes clearer, and/or greater care seems to have been taken to draft it.[133]

There is today controversy in Australia as to whether recourse to extrinsic materials is permitted when there is no ambiguity in the contractual text. Such an 'ambiguity gateway' is supported by High Court authority decided before the abolition of Privy Council appeals.[134] Various remarks in recent High Court cases have thrown the 'ambiguity gateway' into doubt.[135] The majority view among Australian intermediate appellate courts is against retaining the 'ambiguity gateway'.[136] Moreover, the 'ambiguity gateway' controversy in Australia concerns the extent to which extrinsic materials may be used for the *purpose of interpretation*. Carter points out the importance of considering the purpose for

[129] See generally JW Carter, *The Construction of Commercial Contracts* (Oxford, Hart Publishing, 2013) paras 1.24–1.26 (footnotes omitted). cf J Sumption, 'A Question of Taste: The Supreme Court and the Interpretation of Contracts' (2017) 17 *Oxford University Commonwealth Law Journal* 301 (arguing that the UK approach to contractual interpretation may be retreating from contextualism).

[130] Carter, above n 129, para 1.22.

[131] Robertson, above n 115.

[132] ibid.

[133] ibid (discussing *Arnold v Britton* [2015] UKSC 36, [2015] AC 1619 [18]; *Wood* [2017] UKSC 24, [2017] AC 1173 [10], [13]).

[134] *Codelfa* (1982) 149 CLR 337, 352 (Mason J) (still a binding authority according to *Royal Botanic Gardens and Domain Trust v South Sydney City Council* [2002] HCA 5, (2002) 240 CLR 45 [49] (Gleeson CJ, Gaudron, McHugh, Gummow and Hayne JJ); *Western Export Services Inc v Jireh International Pty Ltd* [2011] HCA 45, (2011) 86 ALJR 1 [3]–[4]).

[135] See, eg, *Electricity Generation Corp v Woodside Energy Ltd* [2014] HCA 4, (2014) 251 CLR 640 [35]; *Ecosse Property Holdings Pty Ltd v Gee Dee Nominees Pty Ltd* [2017] HCA 12, (2017) 261 CLR 544 [16]; *Victoria v Tatts Group Ltd* [2016] HCA 5, (2016) 90 ALJR 392 [51]–[75] (considering the context and purpose of a contractual provision after finding no ambiguity in its text). See generally J Eldridge, 'Contracts: Construction – "True Rule" in Codelfa Construction v State Rail Authority (NSW) – No Requirement of Ambiguity before Regard is Had to Surrounding Circumstances' (2018) 92 *Australian Law Journal* 249; J Eldridge, '"Surrounding Circumstances" in Contractual Interpretation: Where are we Now?' (2018) 32 *Commercial Law Quarterly* 3. We thank Patricia Lane and John Eldridge for drawing our attention to these recent developments.

[136] *Mainteck Services Pty Ltd v Stein Heurtey SA* [2014] NSWCA 184, (2014) 89 NSWLR 633 [71]–[86]; *Cherry v Steele-Park* [2017] NSWCA 295, (2017) 96 NSWLR 548 [76]–[83] (Leeming JA, with whom Gleeson JA agreed), [123]–[124] (White JA) and the cases discussed therein.

which extrinsic materials are excluded.[137] Australian law does not prevent recourse to extrinsic materials for the non-interpretive purposes of ascertaining fraud or misrepresentation.[138] This is true regardless of where one stands on the 'ambiguity gateway' debate. In stark contrast, the New York courts took a textualist approach in the Borat cases to enforce the unambiguous merger clause without regard to extrinsic evidence of fraud and misrepresentation.

III. Constructive Trusts in Bankruptcy

Focusing on American and Australian cases concerning constructive trusts in bankruptcy,[139] this section illustrates how the textual and substantive interpretive methods interact with the background *corpus juris*. In both countries, the constructive trust is an equitable remedy, and bankruptcy is a creature of statute. Section A will show great similarities between the equitable principles governing the constructive trust in Australian law and in prevailing US law. However, while the US bankruptcy statute has highly-detailed provisions that may displace the anterior equitable principles, the relevant statutory provisions in Australia are open-ended. The American and Australian cases thus present a natural experiment for understanding the interaction of a potentially-displacing statute and its background *corpus juris*. In this light, Sections B and C will compare the different interpretive methods that American and Australian courts have taken to resolve constructive trust claims in bankruptcy. Section D will highlight the main lessons from this comparative exercise.

A. Constructive Trusts in Anterior Law

Australian law and prevailing US law employ similar equitable principles to govern constructive trusts. Stating the prevailing view in US jurisdictions, the *Restatement (Third) of Restitution and Unjust Enrichment* ('*R3RUE*') understands the constructive trust as a flexible equitable remedy.[140] An order awarding a constructive trust construes the holder of the legal title of some contested property as a trustee who owes specified obligations to the constructive trust claimant. In particular, the respondent – the constructive trustee – can be directed to transfer the contested property to the claimant.[141]

[137] Carter, above n 129, para 8.04.

[138] JW Carter, *Contract Law in Australia*, 7th edn (Chatswood, LexisNexis Butterworths, 2018) paras 12.07, 12.12, 12.16 (footnotes omitted).

[139] Because this section primarily concerns US law, we use the word 'bankruptcy' to describe both individual bankruptcy and corporate insolvency. We expressly emphasise the individual/corporate distinction when it is relevant.

[140] *Restatement (Third) of Restitution and Unjust Enrichment* (2011), § 55 cmt *a*.

[141] ibid.

In the same vein, Australian courts of equity exercise their remedial discretion to frame a constructive trust to do 'full justice'[142] or 'practical justice'.[143] A constructive trust so granted is 'predominantly remedial'[144] rather than 'institutional'; it is the result of an exercise of the equitable discretion to grant the appropriate relief at the time of litigation, although such discretion extends to choosing a specified date from which the relief becomes operative.[145] Thus, like in prevailing US law, the equitable principles governing constructive trusts in Australian law exhibit great flexibility as well as sensitivity to the particular facts and circumstances of the case.

In both Australia and the US, the constructive trust is particularly valuable to its claimant when the respondent is bankrupt, because the claimant is traditionally ranked above the general creditors in the distribution of the bankruptcy estate. This traditional position reflects the general law orthodoxy that the 'property' of a bankrupt does not include what he or she holds on trust for another person.[146] However, as Sections B and C will reveal, the American and Australian bankruptcy statutes may displace the general law orthodoxy to different degrees.

B. Highly-detailed Provisions in the US Bankruptcy Statute

i. The 'Strong-Arm' Provision

Writing at the turn of the twenty-first century, Professor Andrew Kull – the chief reporter of the *R3RUE* – laments:

> [T]he Uniform Commercial Code and the Bankruptcy Code were drafted as common-law statutes. In theory, at least, they displace the preexisting common law only to the extent they alter it, and they presume the continued existence of this background law to govern every question not otherwise resolved. In practice it does not work quite like that. Lawyers and judges who deal regularly with commercial materials come to expect that any problem worth arguing about has been made the subject of an express statutory provision, their usual task being to locate and explicate the relevant statutory language. In consequence, the neglected background law recedes still further – until we reach a point at which the most orthodox legal proposition, if not tied to a specific code section, may actually be challenged as spurious.[147]

[142] *John Alexander's Clubs Pty Ltd v White City Tennis Club Ltd* [2010] HCA 19, (2010) 241 CLR 1 [128].

[143] *Grimaldi v Chameleon Mining NL (No 2)* [2012] FCAFC 6, (2012) 200 FCR 296 [583] ('*Grimaldi*').

[144] *Muschinski v Dodds* (1985) 160 CLR 583, 615.

[145] ibid.

[146] *Restatement (Third) of Restitution and Unjust Enrichment* (2011), § 60 cmt *f*, reporter's note f (footnotes omitted); M Murray and J Harris, *Keay's Insolvency: Personal & Corporate Law and Practice*, 10th edn (Pyrmont, Lawbook, 2018) paras 4.90, 14.15 (footnotes omitted).

[147] A Kull, 'Restitution in Bankruptcy: Reclamation and Constructive Trust' (1998) 72 *American Bankruptcy Law Journal* 265, 266–67.

As Section III.B.3 will elaborate, Professor Kull's criticism is directed at a line of textualist opinions that erode the traditional priority of constructive trusts in bankruptcy, despite the express preservation of equitable interests in the Bankruptcy Code.[148] These textualist opinions primarily rely upon § 544(a)(3) of the Code, a seemingly pre-emptive provision. It relevantly states:

> (a) The [trustee in bankruptcy,] … without regard to any knowledge of the trustee or of any creditor … may avoid any transfer of property of the debtor or any obligation incurred by the debtor that is voidable by—
>
> …
>
> (3) a bona fide purchaser of real property … from the debtor, against whom applicable law permits such transfer to be perfected, that obtains the status of a bona fide purchaser and has perfected such transfer at the time of [the filing of the bankruptcy application], whether or not such a purchaser exists.

Known as the 'strong-arm' provision, § 544 functions to allow the trustee in bankruptcy to avoid unperfected security interests in the bankruptcy estate. A consequence of avoidance is the holder of the unperfected security interest becomes a general creditor. Section 544(a)(3) in particular has the potential to defeat the traditional forensic advantage of a constructive trust, because it is junior to the legal title of a (hypothetical) bona fide purchaser for value without notice. Thus, drafted by reference to a general law concept (the bona fide purchaser for value without notice), § 544(a)(3) creates a difficult question as to whether it preserves the background *corpus juris*.

State law is the core of the background *corpus juris* for the Bankruptcy Code. As a rule of thumb, a US federal court applies the decisional law of the state (including state choice-of-law rules) in which it sits, unless a valid federal law requires otherwise. In federal bankruptcy proceedings, the deference to state law can be outcome-determinative because private law is often diverse across states. The well-known *Butner* principle preserves applicable state property law unless some 'federal interest' requires otherwise.[149]

When applied to constructive trusts, the *Butner* principle neatly illustrates the dilemma that courts often face in determining the extent of statutory displacement of anterior law; more precisely, the two questions are:

1. whether the constructive trust amounts to a 'property interest' under applicable state law; and
2. whether some 'federal interest' contradicts the state law result.

[148] 11 USC § 541(d) ('Property in which the debtor holds, as of the commencement of the case, only legal title and not an equitable interest … becomes property of the [bankruptcy estate] only to the extent of the debtor's legal title to such property, but not to the extent of any equitable interest in such property that the debtor does not hold.').
[149] *Butner v United States* 440 US 48, 54–55 (1979).

Neither the text of the Bankruptcy Code nor its legislative history unambiguously addresses these questions.[150] There thus arises an opportunity for substantive reasons to inform the resolution of these questions.

Duly restating the orthodoxy in the *R3RUE*, Kull characterises constructive trusts as 'property interests', even though their availability and precise form depend on judicial discretion.[151] The leading opponent of the *R3RUE* position is Professor Emily Sherwin, who argues that the law governing constructive trusts does not provide sufficiently determinate rules to govern what is owned and who owns it. As a result of this indeterminacy, constructive trusts are not 'property interests' capable of operating in rem and supporting transactions.[152] These substantive arguments continue to influence many courts.

Substantive arguments also invoke the 'federal interests' manifested by the Bankruptcy Code. One such argument is there is a federal policy against ostensible property interests,[153] and constructive trusts are at best ostensible property interests. Another argument is denying priority to constructive trust claimants better preserves the bankruptcy estate for collective and orderly reorganisation or liquidation.[154]

ii. Substantive Interpretation

While Kull's traditional view continues to attract judicial support in some US jurisdictions,[155] the majority view there is now Sherwin's.[156] Some courts of strategic importance have taken substantive approaches to construing § 544(a)(3), resulting in the constructive trust largely losing its traditional priority in bankruptcy.

Ringing the bells of rebellion against the orthodoxy, the Court of Appeals for the Sixth Circuit in *In re Omegas Group, Inc* took a substantive approach to construing § 544(a)(3).[157] While it quoted Sherwin's property-interest analysis at length,[158] the Sixth Circuit was more concerned with the extent to which the policy of rateable distribution – one of the underlying policies of the Bankruptcy Code – pre-empts state general law.[159]

[150] *Restatement (Third) of Restitution and Unjust Enrichment* (2011), § 60 reporter's n f.

[151] ibid § 55 reporter's n d, § 61 cmt *a*.

[152] E Sherwin, 'Why *In re Omegas Group* Was Right: An Essay on the Legal Status of Equitable Rights' (2012) 92 *Boston University Law Review* 885, 889–90.

[153] See, eg, *DuBay v Williams* 417 F 2d 1277, 1288 (9th Cir 1969).

[154] Kull, above n 147, 294–95 (footnotes omitted).

[155] See, eg, *In re Mississippi Valley Livestock, Inc* 745 F 3d 299 (7th Cir 2014).

[156] R Levin and HJ Sommer (eds), *Collier on Bankruptcy*, 16th edn (Newark, Matthew Bender Elite Products, vol 5, 2010) 544.02[3] (footnotes omitted).

[157] *In re Omegas Group, Inc* 16 F 3d 1443 (6th Cir 1994) ('*Omegas Group*').

[158] *Omegas Group* 16 F 3d 1443, 1449 (6th Cir 1994) (quoting EL Sherwin, 'Constructive Trusts in Bankruptcy' (1989) *University of Illinois Law Review* 297, 301).

[159] *Omegas Group* 16 F 3d 1443, 1451–52 (6th Cir 1994). See also *In re Morris* 260 F 3d 654 (6th Cir 2001) (clarifying 11 USC § 544(a)(3) does not destroy constructive trusts impressed by applicable state law upon the bankruptcy estate prior to the filing of the bankruptcy application).

The Court of Appeals for the Second Circuit in *In re First Central Financial Corp* took a different line of substantive reasoning, but arrived at the same outcome.[160] In that case, the Second Circuit rejected the constructive trust claim on multiple state law grounds, one of which was the inappropriateness of granting a constructive trust in bankruptcy. The Second Circuit agreed with the Sixth Circuit in respect of the policy of rateable distribution, but *disagreed* with the understanding that that policy pre-empts state general law governing constructive trusts. However, in addition to the underlying policies of bankruptcy, the Second Circuit was also concerned with the need to minimise conflict between state general law and a nationally-uniform statute.[161] Aiming to reconcile these substantive considerations with an unwillingness to find pre-emption, the Second Circuit found solutions in *state general law* instead. New York general law – the state general law that applied in this case – granted an equitable discretion. The applicable standard was whether 'under such circumstances that in equity and good conscience [the constructive trust respondent] ought not to retain [the contested property]'. Exercising that equitable discretion against the constructive trust claimant, the Second Circuit found that while the bankruptcy estate may have been enriched by the value of the constructive trust claims, 'it was not unjustly enriched'.[162] As reiterated in a subsequent opinion, the Second Circuit's view is *not* that the Bankruptcy Code pre-empts New York law, but that New York law *itself* is understood as not treating 'retention by the bankruptcy estate of assets that, absent bankruptcy, would go to a particular creditor [as] inherently unjust'.[163]

Thus both the Sixth Circuit and the Second Circuit take a decidedly substantive approach to construing the Bankruptcy Code. Paying no attention to the nuances of the text, both Courts have implemented bankruptcy policies in a sweeping way to destroy the traditional priority of constructive trusts.

iii. Textual Interpretation

Since the ascendancy of Justice Scalia, textualism has been the dominant methodology for resolving bankruptcy disputes. A widely-held belief is the US Supreme Court tends to favour arguments that explicate the plain meaning of the Bankruptcy Code to the exclusion of policy arguments.[164] A notable exception is *BFP v Resolution Trust Corporation*, in which Justice Scalia led the majority to affirm a lower court decision that prefers upholding state property law over the

[160] *In re First Central Financial Corp* 377 F 3d 209 (2^{d} Cir 2004) ('*First Central*').
[161] *First Central* 377 F 3d 209, 217–18 (2^{d} Cir 2004) (footnotes omitted).
[162] *First Central* 377 F 3d 209, 218 (2^{d} Cir 2004).
[163] *In re Ades and Berg Group Investors* 550 F3d 240, 245 (2^{d} Cir 2008) (footnotes omitted).
[164] RJ Mann, *Bankruptcy and the US Supreme Court* (Cambridge, Cambridge University Press, 2017) 11–13 (surveying the academic literature).

plain meaning of the relevant Code provision.[165] Nonetheless, textualism remains the norm.[166]

Rather than invoking substantive considerations, US federal courts with jurisdiction over Delaware typically adopt a textual interpretation of § 544(a)(3) to deny the traditional bankruptcy priority of constructive trusts.[167] For example, in *In re Paul J Paradise & Associates*, a lender transferred some real property to a corporate home-builder, in order to allow the home-builder to use the property as collateral to obtain a construction loan.[168] The lender did not obtain a mortgage or make a public filing, and only obtained a promissory note from the home-builder. After the failure of its construction plan and without having made any payment on the note, the home-builder filed for bankruptcy while the real property was still under its name. The lender sought to recover the property by making a constructive trust claim (and other claims), which was summarily dismissed by the Bankruptcy Court. Dismissing the appeal that followed, the District Court took a decidedly textual approach: reconciling the language of § 544(a)(3) with another provision of the Bankruptcy Code that purports to exclude equitable interests from the bankruptcy estate.[169] Notably, the District Court refused to endorse the substantive reasons stated in *Omegas Group*,[170] even as it endorsed the Sixth Circuit's *conclusion* – that the Code destroys the traditional priority of constructive trusts.

The view of the Delaware federal courts – that the constructive trust loses its traditional priority – is of primary strategic importance in bankruptcy cases. New York federal courts largely reach the same conclusion (albeit for different methodological reasons). The forum-selection provision of the Bankruptcy Code only requires the bankrupt to have some minimal connection with the forum in which the bankruptcy application is filed.[171] That flexible provision facilitates forum shopping; empirical studies consistently reveal that more than 40 per cent of corporate bankruptcy applications are filed in Delaware.[172] Moreover, almost

[165] *BFP v Resolution Trust Corporation* 511 US 531, 534, 544–55 (1994).

[166] L Dembart and BA Markell, 'Alive at 25? A Short Review of the Supreme Court's Bankruptcy Jurisprudence, 1979–2004' (2004) 78 *American Bankruptcy Law Journal* 373; M McDermott, 'Justice Scalia's Bankruptcy Jurisprudence: The Right Judicial Philosophy for the Modern Bankruptcy Code?' (2017) *Utah Law Review* 939.

[167] *In re Paul J Paradise & Associates, Inc* 249 BR 360, 367 (D Del 2000) ('*Paradise*') (footnotes omitted); *Singh v Attorney General of US* 677 F 3d 503, 516, n 16 (3d Cir 2012). Delaware opinions that preserve the traditional priority of constructive trusts in bankruptcy also typically take a textualist approach; the disagreement pertained to the reconciliation of 11 USC §§ 541(d), 544(a)(3): see generally Levin and Sommer, above n 156, para 544.02[3].

[168] *Paradise* 249 BR 360, 362 (D Del 2000).

[169] *Paradise* 249 BR 360, 366–67 (D Del 2000) (reconciling 11 USC §§ 541(d), 544(a)(3)). 11 USC § 541(d) is set out in above n 148.

[170] *Paradise* 249 BR 360, 368–70 (D Del 2000).

[171] 28 USC § 1408.

[172] See, eg, JA Ellias, 'What Drives Bankruptcy Forum Shopping? Evidence from Market Data' (2018) 47 *Legal Studies* 119.

30 per cent of corporate bankruptcy applications are filed in New York,[173] which is within the jurisdiction of the Second Circuit. Thus, due to forum shopping, US constructive trust claimants have largely lost their traditional priority in bankruptcy.

Compared with the textual approach, the substantive approaches do not necessarily lead to greater or lesser displacement of the background *corpus juris*. Notice the text of § 544(a)(3) only covers real property. Such drafting has led textualist courts to hold that in personal property cases, the constructive trust *retains* its traditional priority in bankruptcy,[174] even though such priority is lost in real property cases. By comparison, the substantive approaches taken by the Second and Sixth Circuits deny priority to constructive trusts in both real property and personal property cases. Hence these substantive approaches have displaced the anterior law governing constructive trusts to a greater extent than the textual approach. However, under the *alternative* substantive approach favoured by the *R3RUE* and some other courts, constructive trusts retain their traditional bankruptcy priority in both real property and personal property cases.

C. Open-endedness in the Australian Corporations Statute

This section will show that, in contrast to the textualist approach that the US Supreme Court and the Delaware courts tend to favour, the Australian approach to granting constructive trusts in bankruptcy is decidedly substantive. Recall that Australian law and prevailing US law employ similar equitable principles to govern constructive trusts.[175] However, unlike US courts, Australian courts are not restricted by highly-detailed statutory provisions in the bankruptcy statute; the Australian Corporations Act 2001 (Cth) – governing corporate bankruptcy – is *silent* on whether a bankruptcy estate includes properties that the bankrupt holds on trust for someone else.[176] This is a form of open-endedness. Thus, in corporate bankruptcy cases, Australian courts are free to preserve the anterior law on the constitution of a bankruptcy estate.[177]

Unrestricted by pre-emptive statutory provisions, Australian courts of equity exercise their discretion to grant constructive trusts in a manner that is practically consistent with the *R3RUE* position (which is the minority position in the US).[178] More precisely, Australian courts of equity can grant a proprietary right to the

[173] ibid.

[174] See, eg, *In re DVI, Inc* 306 BR 496, 503 (Bankr D Del 2004); *In re Bake-Line Group, LLC* 359 BR 566 (Bankr D Del 2007); *Restatement (Third) of Restitution and Unjust Enrichment* (2011), § 55 reporter's n d, § 60 comment f.

[175] Above Section III.A.

[176] Murray and Harris, above n 146, para 14.15.

[177] See, eg, *Re Stansfield DIY Wealth Pty Limited (in liq)* [2014] NSWSC 1484, (2014) 291 FLR 17; Murray and Harris, above n 146, para 14.15. The Australian individual bankruptcy statute expressly excludes trust properties from bankruptcy estates: Bankruptcy Act 1966 (Cth), s 116(2)(a).

[178] Above, text accompanying n 156.

constructive trust claimant, which right removes some or all of the bankruptcy estate from the unsecured creditors. This would prefer the interests of the constructive trust claimant above some innocent third parties', and is therefore not done routinely. Consideration of third-party interests has manifested a judicial preference for granting an equitable lien to the constructive trust claimant.[179] Rather than a bright-line rule, the Australian approach has produced cases that 'exhibit diversity in the relief granted'.[180] Thus the Australian approach openly prizes individualised justice over predictability and generality. This is a clear example of substantive judicial reasoning, and a stark contrast to the textualist approach that modern US bankruptcy opinions tend to exhibit.

D. Similar Anterior Law, Different Degrees of Displacement

American and Australian cases on constructive trusts in bankruptcy provide an instructive example of the interaction of a statute and its background *corpus juris*. Although Australian law and prevailing US law employ similar equitable principles to govern constructive trusts, the bankruptcy statutes in both countries are very different. While the Australian corporate bankruptcy statute is open-ended with respect to constructive trusts, the US bankruptcy statute has highly-detailed provisions that may be pre-emptive. Thus, while Australian courts can simply apply the anterior law to resolve constructive trust claims in bankruptcy proceedings, US courts must confront the difficult question as to the extent of displacement. The example of constructive trusts in bankruptcy thus confirms the general observation, made in Section II.B, that statutory provisions that seemingly adopt general law concepts in a textually-detailed way present a difficult question as to the degree of displacement. That question seems to be simplified greatly if the statutory language is open-ended, as the Australian experience reveals. Moreover, the US experience shows that different interpretive methods can lead to different degrees of displacement.

IV. Legislative Authorisation of Equitable Relief

A. Statutes Referring to Anterior Law

It's inevitable that statutes use words and concepts from the unwritten law. In *Wilson v Anderson*,[181] the High Court of Australia held that a 'lease' in perpetuity

[179] *Grimaldi* [2012] FCAFC 6, (2012) 200 FCR 296 [583].
[180] JD Heydon and MJ Leeming, *Jacob's Law of Trusts in Australia*, 8th edn (Chatswood, LexisNexis Butterworths, 2016) para 13.11 (footnotes omitted).
[181] *Wilson v Anderson* [2002] HCA 29, (2002) 213 CLR 401 ('*Wilson*').

granted under the Western Lands Act 1901 (NSW) conferred a right of exclusive possession within the meaning of the Native Title Act 1993 (Cth). Gaudron, Gummow and Hayne JJ cautioned against 'reasoning that as an interest was described as a "lease" it is to be presumed that a right of exclusive possession was conferred'.[182] Indeed, the Native Title Act 'postulates the existence of an interest which, although described as a "lease", is not a lease at common law'.[183] Gleeson CJ thought it unsurprising 'that the incidents of a statutory lease are not exhaustively defined by statute, and may include incidents of a lease as provided by the common law'.[184]

By contrast, recently in *Marvin M Brandt Revocable Trust v US*,[185] the US Supreme Court interpreted a statutory 'right of way' as nothing more than a simple easement whose incidents were found in the four corners of the statute. The textualist opinion held that, on abandonment, the statutory right of way goes to the private party who acquired the underlying land. The Court remarked that '[a]pter words to indicate the intent to convey an easement would be difficult to find'.[186] True, the Court relied on 'basic common law principles' and the dissent objected that statutory rights of way were '*sui generis* property rights not governed by the ordinary common-law regime'.[187] But 'basic common law principles' were invoked only as a matter of plain meaning. The Court did not rely on anterior law because that would have involved the application of state property law. The incidents of the statutory right of way were exhaustively defined by the text of the statute.

Although courts do not usually frame the issue in this way, their task is to locate the statute on the displacement continuum. Cases like *Wilson* show that Australian courts are reluctant to conclude that a statutory lease displaces anterior law wholesale: ordinarily, the unwritten law 'incidents' of a statutory lease continue to exist. But American courts tend to conclude that statutory interests are defined by text alone. When deciding that a statutory right of way conveyed an easement and not a limited fee, the US Supreme Court focused on the text. Anterior law (state property law) was irrelevant to that holding.

B. Statutory Injunctions in Australian Legislation

Australian regulatory statutes often empower courts to enjoin contraventions. When a person violates the Corporations Act 2001 (Cth), for example, section 1324 provides that a court may 'grant an injunction, on such terms as the Court thinks appropriate, restraining' the person and, 'if in the opinion of the

[182] *Wilson* [2002] HCA 29, (2002) 213 CLR 401 [59].
[183] ibid.
[184] ibid [19].
[185] *Marvin M Brandt Revocable Trust v US* 134 S Ct 1257 (2014) ('*Marvin*').
[186] *Marvin* 134 S Ct 1257, 1264 (2014) (quoting *Great Northern Railway Co v United States* 315 US 262, 271 (1942)).
[187] *Marvin* 134 S Ct 1257, 1269 (2014).

Court it is desirable to do so, requiring that person to do any act or thing'. The word 'desirable' confers a broad discretion.[188] Similarly, section 80 of the Competition and Consumer Act 2010 (Cth) empowers a court to 'grant an injunction in such terms as the Court determines to be appropriate', if the court is satisfied that a statutory violation has occurred.

Absent statutory authorisation of injunctive relief, a court of equity may enforce a statutory obligation by injunction.[189] Yet the court exercises a statutory jurisdiction under sections 1324 and 80 rather than an equitable one. Although sections 1324 and 80 both use the word 'injunction', today Australian courts hold that these statutory remedies differ from injunctions traditionally understood. The threshold question is where the statute is situated on the displacement continuum. Does the statute adopt, supplement or displace the traditional conditions for the award of injunctive relief?

Section 80 of the Competition and Consumer Act (Cth) expanded the availability of injunctive relief. For one thing, the statute confers standing on 'the regulator or any other person' to seek an injunction, 'a significant broadening of locus standi'.[190] Also, the conduct which can be enjoined includes not only contraventions and attempted contraventions, but also aiding, abetting, counselling, procuring, inducing, attempting to induce, or 'being in any way, directly or indirectly, knowingly concerned in, or party to' contraventions, and conspiring to contravene. The statute removes other significant equitable limits on injunctive relief, including requirements that the defendant previously engaged, or intends in the future to engage, in the prohibited conduct. Lockhart J, in an influential judgment, thought that section 80 gave the court 'the widest possible injunctive powers, devoid of traditional constraints, though the power must be exercised judicially and sensibly'.[191]

Section 80, however, did not wholly displace anterior equitable limitations. The statute's expansion of injunctive relief 'does not mean that the traditional equitable doctrines are irrelevant'.[192] Lockhart J emphasised, for example, that even though previous engagement in prohibited conduct is not necessary for granting a statutory injunction, it is nevertheless important. The legislative scheme for injunctive relief, said Lockhart J, 'is not … a new statutory house, rather an old house with some modern extensions'.[193] Other statutory injunction provisions modelled on section 80, such as division 14 of Part 17 of the Environment Protection and

[188] *World Series Cricket Pty Ltd v Parish* (1977) 16 ALR 181, 185 (Bowen CJ) ('*World Series Cricket*').

[189] JD Heydon, MJ Leeming and PG Turner, *Meagher, Gummow & Lehane's Equity: Doctrines & Remedies*, 5th edn (Chatswood, LexisNexis Butterworths, 2015) 728–38.

[190] *Re ICI Australia Operations Pty Ltd v Trade Practices Commission* [1992] FCA 474, (1992) 38 FCR 248, 266 (Gummow J) ('*ICI*').

[191] *ICI* [1992] FCA 474, (1992) 38 FCR 248, 256.

[192] ibid 256–57.

[193] ibid 257.

Biodiversity Conservation Act 1999 (Cth), are similarly regarded as old remedial houses with modern extensions.[194]

The same conclusions obtain regarding section 1324 of the Corporations Act (Cth), which is similar in terms to section 80 of the Competition and Consumer Act (Cth). Courts exercise statutory jurisdiction under section 1324, not traditional equity jurisdiction.[195] They are not confined by conventional equitable doctrine when issuing section 1324 injunctions. 'That said', as Ward JA put it, 's 1324 does not displace the court's equitable jurisdiction and it has been said that equitable principles represent a sound basis for undertaking a preliminary assessment' for a statutory injunction.[196] Even though 'the analogy between the statutory injunction and the injunction in the court's traditional equitable jurisdiction has become more and more remote', section 1324 has not wholly displaced traditional equitable considerations.[197] Just like section 80, section 1324 is an old equitable house with some modern statutory extensions.

C. 'Appropriate Equitable Relief' in ERISA

In the US, the Employee Retirement Income Security Act of 1974 (ERISA) prescribes national minimum standards for disclosure and investment safeguards concerning employee benefit (retirement and health) plans. A remedial provision, § 502(a)(3), authorises a plan beneficiary, participant or fiduciary to bring a civil action to enjoin a violation of ERISA or the plan, or 'to obtain other appropriate equitable relief' to redress the violation or enforce ERISA or the plan.[198]

From 2002 to 2016, the US Supreme Court decided five cases interpreting the phrase 'appropriate equitable relief'.[199] Four presented the same basic facts: a plan fiduciary sought reimbursement for medical expenses after a beneficiary recovered money from a third party. In his characteristically textual mode, Justice Scalia for the Court held in 2002 that '"[e]quitable" relief must mean *something* less than *all* relief' and that the interpretation of § 502(a)(3) must not 'render the modifier ["equitable"] superfluous'.[200] Accordingly, 'the term "equitable relief"

[194] *Humane Society International Inc v Kyodo Senpaku Kaisha Ltd* [2006] FCAFC 116, (2006) 154 FCR 425 [18].

[195] *Australian Securities and Investments Commission v Mauer-Swisse Securities Ltd* [2002] NSWSC 741, (2002) 42 ACSR 605 [19], [36] ('*Mauer-Swisse Securities*').

[196] *Re Idyllic Solutions Pty Ltd; Australian Securities and Investments Commission v Hobbs* [2013] NSWSC 106, (2013) 93 ACSR 421 [66].

[197] *Mauer-Swisse Securities* [2002] NSWSC 741, (2002) 42 ACSR 605 [31].

[198] Section 502(a)(3) of ERISA is codified at 29 USC § 1132(a)(3).

[199] *Great-West Life & Annuity Insurance Co v Knudson* 534 US 204 (2002) ('*Great-West Life*'); *Sereboff v Mid Atlantic Medical Services Inc* 547 US 356 (2006); *CIGNA Corp v Amara* 563 US 421 (2011); *US Airways Inc v McCutchen* 569 US 88 (2013); *Montanile v Board of Trustees of the National Elevator Industry Health Benefit Plan* 136 S Ct 651 (2016) ('*Montanile*').

[200] *Great-West Life* 534 US 204, 209–10 (2002).

in § 502(a)(3) must refer to those categories of relief that were *typically* available in equity'.[201] To operationalise its narrow interpretation, the Court consults 'standard treatises on equity, which establish "the basic contours" of what equitable relief was typically available in *premerger* equity courts'.[202] (The federal courts were merged in 1938.)

The 'historical analysis' prescribed by the US Supreme Court means that § 502(a)(3) is a minimally-displacing and open-ended provision. It is minimally-displacing because the Court interpreted it to adopt not replace equitable relief. And it is open-ended because it relies on judicial articulation to unfold its content. As Samuel Bray argued, the Court's invocation of the tradition of equity under § 502(a)(3) is a judicially constructed ideal.[203] So, while the statutory language is open-ended, the Court has interpreted it narrowly.

The formal approach of American courts to the legislative authorisation of equitable relief is not limited to ERISA. For example, the Racketeer Influenced and Corrupt Organizations Act of 1970 (RICO) authorises a court 'to prevent and restrain violations of [RICO] by issuing appropriate orders'.[204] The Court of Appeals for the District of Columbia Circuit fixated on the phrase 'prevent and restrain' to hold that 'the jurisdiction is limited to forward-looking remedies that are aimed at future violations'.[205] Disgorgement, therefore, was not available because it 'is a quintessentially backward-looking remedy focused on remedying the effects of past conduct'.[206] To hold that RICO conferred a plenary equitable jurisdiction would 'effectively ignor[e] the words "prevent and restrain" altogether', and would 'nullif[y] the plain meaning of the terms and violate[] our canon of statutory construction that we should strive to give meaning to every word'.[207]

D. Old American Houses, New Australian Extensions

The difference between the American approach to § 502(a)(3) and the Australian approach to statutory injunctions is evident. To strain Lockhart J's metaphor, the US Supreme Court has refused to build statutory extensions onto the old equitable house. The textual formalism that is now so influential in the US limits the efficacy of comprehensive legislative schemes. Australian courts have taken a different tack. They have liberalised the statutory injunction, holding that statutory injunctions displace some, but not all, of the anterior law.

[201] ibid 210.
[202] *Montanile* 136 S Ct 651 (2016).
[203] SL Bray, 'The Supreme Court and the New Equity' (2015) 68 *Vanderbilt Law Review* 997, 1014–16, 1022.
[204] 18 USC § 1964(a).
[205] *United States v Philip Morris USA Inc* 396 F 3d 1190, 1198 (DC Cir 2005) ('*Philip Morris*').
[206] *Philip Morris* 396 F 3d 1190, 1198 (DC Cir 2005).
[207] *Philip Morris* 396 F 3d 1190, 1198 (DC Cir 2005).

It is interesting to compare the Australian and American approaches when different statutory interpretation methodologies held sway. So, for example, before Justice Scalia's ascendancy, the US Supreme Court was sympathetic to an approach that amplified statutory grants of equity jurisdiction. In 1946, the Court held that a statutory grant of general equitable jurisdiction includes 'all inherent equitable powers … for the proper and complete exercise of that jurisdiction'.[208] The grant was presumed plenary – 'the full scope of that [equitable] jurisdiction is to be recognized and applied' – unless 'in so many words, or by necessary and inescapable inference', Congress required otherwise.[209] Indeed, the Court encouraged an inferior tribunal to 'go beyond the matters immediately underlying its equitable jurisdiction … and give whatever other relief may be necessary under the circumstances'.[210]

Prior to the emergence of the modern approach to statutory interpretation in the mid-1990s, the Australian attitude to the legislative authorisation of equitable relief resembled current American practice. In 1977, the Full Court of the Federal Court of Australia approached section 80 of the Competition and Consumer Act (Cth) (then called the Trade Practices Act 1974 (Cth)) as though it adopted generally applicable equitable rules for injunctive relief.[211] And in 1984, when a plaintiff sought a statutory order restraining the defendant from exercising voting rights attaching to illegally acquired shares, McPherson J of the Queensland Supreme Court thought that 'the general approach' was supplied by traditional equitable considerations.[212] Now, it is true that the legislation (especially corporations legislation) has changed since these cases were decided. But it is equally true that Australian courts today are less reluctant to build statutory extensions on old equitable houses.

V. Conclusion

Our primary thesis is that much has changed since *Form and Substance* was published 30 years ago. There is now strong support for interpretive formalism and textualism in the US. These American trends stand in contrast to Australia's enthusiasm for purposivism and contextualism.

We have described the immediate causes of the shift in interpretive formalism in Australia and the US. In Australia, the shift away from interpretive formalism was prompted by the Barwick Court's literal approach to taxation

[208] *Porter v Warner Holding Co* 328 US 395, 398 (1946) ('*Porter*').

[209] *Porter* 328 US 395, 398 (1946).

[210] ibid.

[211] *World Series Cricket* (1977) 16 ALR 181, 185 (Bowen CJ).

[212] *Adsteam Building Industries Pty Ltd v Queensland Cement and Lime Company Ltd* [1984] 2 Qd R 1, 5–6.

statutes – Lionel Murphy memorably called the Court a 'tax avoider's temple'.[213] In the US, the extraordinary influence of Antonin Scalia, as well as the selection of textualist jurisdictions by contract drafters and litigators, pushed interpretive methodology in a more formal direction. But there are deeper dynamics at play. The shift towards interpretive formalism in the US is typically seen as part of a broader conservative reaction to the constitutional revolution launched by the US Supreme Court under Earl Warren.[214] Scalia was an important conservative lieutenant.[215] In Australia, the movement away from interpretive formalism is part and parcel of a fundamental development: legal independence from the UK and, consequently, the need 'to part, in some respects at least, from the philosophy of … legal formalism'.[216]

[213] Kercher, above n 119, 181.

[214] MJ Graetz and L Greenhouse, *The Burger Court and the Rise of the Judicial Right* (New York City, Simon & Schuster, 2016) 341–45.

[215] SM Teles, *The Rise of the Conservative Legal Movement: The Battle for Control of the Law* (Princeton, Princeton University Press, 2008) 1, 141–42, 158.

[216] P Finn, 'Unity, Then Divergence: The Privy Council, the Common Law of England and the Common Laws of Canada, Australia and New Zealand' in A Robertson and M Tilbury (eds), *The Common Law of Obligations: Divergence and Unity* (Oxford, Hart Publishing, 2016) 37, 44–48 (quoting A Mason, 'Future Directions in Australian Law' (1987) 13 *Monash University Law Review* 149, 154–55).

17

Misrepresentation, Misleading Conduct and Statute through the Lens of Form and Substance*

JEANNIE MARIE PATERSON AND ELISE BANT

I. Introduction

Doctrines that provide various rights of redress for misrepresentation and misleading conduct hold a central place across the spectrum of commercial and consumer law, including in tort, contract, and equity, as well as pursuant to statutory schemes of regulation and redress.[1] Strong reasons for the law's interest in such behaviour are not difficult to find: parties who have been induced to enter into contracts on the basis of misleading conduct have not exercised genuine choice and a trader who attracts customers through misleading conduct distorts the market and harms other more truthful competitors.[2] In England, a key statutory intervention in this field is the Misrepresentation Act 1967 (Misrepresentation Act). The Act provides some practical remedial benefits to contracting parties. But it has not perhaps had the impact that might have been expected at its inception. Introduced to 'make improvements to the law as to the effect of misrepresentation

* This chapter forms part of a broader project funded by an Australian Research Council Discovery Grant entitled 'Remedies under the Australian Consumer Law and the Common Law: Evolution and Revolution'. Our thanks go to Joseph Huntley and Gavin Rees for their helpful research assistance throughout the writing of this chapter.

[1] 'Misleading conduct' is a broader category than misrepresentation, encompassing the latter but also capturing a range of acts and omissions that go beyond 'representations' or statements. The range of doctrines at common law and in equity focused on the regulation of misleading conduct in all its forms include the torts of deceit, negligent misstatement, defamation, passing off, injurious falsehood, as well as rescission for misrepresentation and estoppel. Other doctrines commonly address misleading conduct as part of the factual grounds of the complaint, albeit with a different doctrinal focus, such as restitution for mistake and breach of fiduciary duty. The statutory treatments of misleading conduct in Australia using the original prohibition – now found in s 18 of the Australian Consumer Law (ACL), in Sch 2 of the Competition and Consumer Act 2010 (Cth) – number in the dozens.

[2] See also *First Tower Trustees Ltd v CDS (Superstores International) Ltd* [2018] EWCA Civ 1396 [104] (Leggatt LJ) ('*First Tower Trustees*').

on a contract',[3] it was almost immediately overtaken by developments in the tort of negligent misrepresentation, and its intended protective force reduced by contractual drafting techniques.

Section 2(1), dealing with damages, has not been subject to the rigorous judicial scrutiny that one might expect from a statutory incursion into common law remedies. A similar observation may be made of the treatment by English courts of section 3, dealing with contract terms that exclude or restrict liability for misrepresentation. Judicial and scholarly attention has tended to focus on the characterisation of the binding effect of non-reliance clauses – variously through contractual interpretation or contractual estoppel – rather than the circumstances in which the Act will apply to regulate such provisions and the requirements of reasonableness if it does. At least until recently, the Act has generally made a desultory appearance at the end of the decision or commentary to confirm that it has little or no bearing on the key issues.

On its face, this is surprising: one might expect that legislation specifically directed towards the consequences of misrepresentation inducing entry into a contract would be central to analysis in this context. We suggest that one way of understanding this treatment of the statutory regulation of contracts induced by misrepresentation is in terms of Atiyah and Summers' distinction between form and substance in law and legal reasoning, and their observation that English law is, in general, highly formal.[4] Both the drafting of the statutory regime and the interpretative response that it prompts in courts are consistent with Atiyah and Summers' thesis. As we explain below, the predominantly narrow and prescriptive form of the Misrepresentation Act has led to it failing to keep pace with legal developments and inviting evasive contract drafting. The English courts' traditional preference for formal reasoning has compounded these consequences through the literal interpretation largely given to the statute.

The formal nature of both the English statute and the judicial response that it has provoked is highlighted through a contrast with the Australian statutory treatment of misleading conduct. Two Australian jurisdictions also adopted the Misrepresentation Act, following the UK example.[5] However, for all practical purposes, these Acts have been rendered redundant through the introduction of a broad-based statutory prohibition on misleading conduct 'in trade or commerce',[6] which operates throughout the Australian states and territories, and is accompanied by a suite of flexible and wide-ranging remedies. The Australian prohibition on misleading conduct does not cover quite the same ground as the Misrepresentation Act,

[3] PS Atiyah and GH Treitel, 'Misrepresentation Act 1967' (1967) *MLR* 369, 369.

[4] PS Atiyah and RS Summers, *Form and Substance in Anglo-American Law: A Comparative Study of Legal Reasoning, Legal Theory, and Legal Institutions* (Oxford, Clarendon Press, 1987) 1. See also RS Summers, 'Form and Substance in Anglo-American Law' (1987) 14 *Cornell Law Forum* 2, 2.

[5] Misrepresentation Act 1972 (SA); Law Reform (Misrepresentation) Act 1977 (ACT), later replaced by the Civil Law (Wrongs Act) 2002 (ACT), s 175.

[6] Originally in s 52 of the Trade Practices Act 1974 (Cth) (TPA), but now replaced by s 18 of the ACL.

containing a primary prohibition as well as a remedial regime. Nonetheless, the response of Australian courts to the scheme is instructive. The very design of the legislative regime has prompted in Australian courts a stable and effective regulatory response to misleading conduct that is integrated with the common law and equitable responses that cover similar ground.

Atiyah and Summers also highlighted the correlation between prevailing legal theories about the role of courts and styles of legal reasoning.[7] Here we suggest that the relationship between statutes and the judicial response to those statutes becomes more complex. The way in which legislation is drafted may, through the courts' commitment to the formal rules of statutory interpretation, determine the kind of response produced to the task of interpreting and applying the statutory provisions in question.

The contrast between rules and standards in statutory drafting is significant here. As we will see below, judges may find reason to engage with the legislative purpose even in an apparently categorical rule-based regime; likewise, principle-based drafting does not necessarily push judges towards a substantive engagement with the purposes of the legislation.[8] Nonetheless, legislative reliance on detailed rules will tend to prompt a more formal interpretative response than broadly-framed legislative provisions. By contrast, the use of standards will tend to allow courts greater scope for drawing on the relevant general law context, and give courts little choice other than to engage directly with the purposes of the legislation. This divergence does not arise as the product of some political commitment to formal or substantive approaches to statutory interpretation. Rather it is, at least partly, the product of a shared judicial commitment to principles of statutory interpretation. Whatever their proclivity for form or substance, judges must respond to the text before them.

In England, the narrowly drafted right to damages in section 2(1) of the Misrepresentation Act has been met with a formal response that defers to the constrained language and hence operation of its provisions. One result is that the statutory remedial scheme became quickly disengaged from its evolving general law context. The section 3 review of clauses that exclude or restrict liability for misrepresentation inducing entry into a contract has commonly been sidelined by technical questions of contractual characterisation that will determine the operation of the legislation, deferring the questions of the 'reasonableness' of the clause to an afterthought. As we shall see, English courts have only recently moved

[7] See Atiyah and Summers, above n 4, 241–45, noting a correlation between positivist methodology and formal methods of statutory interpretation.

[8] We discuss examples of substantive engagement with the purpose of the Misrepresentation Act below, text accompanying nn 97–105. Conversely, in the early days of interpreting the Australian prohibition on misleading conduct, some Australian courts initially struggled to give full effect to the protective purpose of the legislation, using general law concepts to read down the novel statutory prohibition. This, however, was quickly corrected in light of the peremptory language and explicitly instrumental purpose of the statute: E Bant and JM Paterson, 'Misleading Conduct before the Federal Court: Achievements and Challenges' in P Ridge and J Stellios (eds), *The Federal Court's Contribution to Australian Law: Past, Present and Future* (Leichhardt, Federation Press, 2018) 165.

towards a more substantive engagement with the effect of contractual non-reliance clauses and the extent to which they are caught by the Act. This approach is made necessary by the courts' commitment to ensuring that the legislative provision has effect and is not rendered nugatory by drafting techniques.[9]

A striking contrast is again provided by the Australian experience of a more substantive judicial engagement with the purposes and context of the statutory prohibition on misleading conduct and its associated remedies. Significantly, however, this response is consistent with a formal response to the statutory text, which directs courts to a substantive inquiry through the open-textured drafting in which it is expressed. In other words, the way in which the statute is drafted in Australia leads courts to a substantive engagement with its purpose and context by very reason of the courts' formal commitment to prioritising the text in the process of statutory interpretation.

In this chapter, we explore these trends by reference, first, to the legislative direction as to damages under both pieces of legislation and, secondly, the comparative success of non-reliance and no-representation clauses negotiated by parties seeking to reduce the risk of liability for misleading conduct. We commence the inquiry by considering some key characteristics of formal and substantive reasoning identified by Atiyah and Summers, as found in statute and under general (common and equitable) law. We then consider the Misrepresentation Act provisions dealing with damages and contracting out, before turning to the prohibition on misleading conduct in trade and commerce in Australia.

II. Form and Substance in Legislation and General Law

A. Form and Substance in Anglo-American Law

In their seminal work, *Form and Substance in Anglo-American Law*, Atiyah and Summers argued that there are comprehensive differences between English and American law and modes of legal reasoning.[10] They proposed that 'the English approach to law is relatively formal, whereas the American approach is relatively substantive'.[11] As Atiyah subsequently observed, Australia probably falls between the two.[12]

[9] See, eg, *Parmar v Barclays Bank plc* [2018] EWHC 1027 (Ch); *First Tower Trustees* [2018] EWCA Civ 1396.

[10] Atiyah and Summers, above n 4. See also PS Atiyah, 'Form and Substance in Contract Law' in *Essays on Contract* (Oxford, Oxford University Press, 1986) 93.

[11] Summers, above n 4, 2.

[12] PS Atiyah, 'Justice and Predictability in the Common Law' (1992) 15 *University of New South Wales Law Journal* 448, 454.

Atiyah and Summers' primary focus was on modes of judicial reasoning. Formal reasoning seeks a legally authoritative basis for a decision.[13] This should not be confused with 'formalistic' reasoning, a degenerate species of formal reasoning that occurs when judges adhere to formal reasoning in the face of a pressing need to take substantive considerations into account.[14] By contrast, substantive reasoning looks to 'moral, economic, political, institutional, or other social considerations' in reaching a decision.[15] Atiyah and Summers argued that English courts favoured formal over substantive reasoning styles. The relative formality of English law meant that English courts were more likely to:

> insist that a statutory text or a common law rule should be applied without regard to consequences or even to possible equitable or other considerations which might appear to require the literal rule to be modified when it comes to be applied.[16]

Atiyah and Summers also argued that the form and substance dichotomy was reflected in the relative prevalence of statute in English law. They argued that statute plays a significant role in English law, more so than in American law, and that English statutory law is a more formal kind of law.[17] For example, they argued that statute is the 'paradigmatic type of formal law'.[18] This is because 'statute law is embodied in a fixed form of words – in canonical form – and it is those very words which constitute law'.[19]

This preference for formality in English legal reasoning and legislation is repeated in the English courts' approach to statutory interpretation. The formal reasoning Atiyah and Summers saw as preferred by English courts favours a literal interpretation of statutory provisions. Consistently, Atiyah and Summers argued that the English system is:

> more formal in its methods of statutory interpretation, still adhering to a 'plain meaning' or literal approach in which the interpretation less often goes directly to policies and rationales.[20]

They observed that English judges typically 'emphasise the overall primacy of the ordinary meaning of the words used in the statute far more than do American judges'.[21] It follows that English courts[22] are less likely to refer to the purposes of the statute than American judges.[23] American judges are more sceptical of the idea

[13] Atiyah and Summers, above n 4, 1.
[14] ibid 28–29.
[15] ibid 1. Atiyah and Summers also identified a degenerate form of substantive reasoning, unhappily labelled 'substantivist', in which appropriate formal reasons are ignored: ibid 30–31.
[16] Atiyah, above n 12, 456.
[17] Atiyah and Summers, above n 4, 96.
[18] ibid 97.
[19] ibid.
[20] ibid 96.
[21] ibid 101.
[22] ibid.
[23] ibid 102.

of a plain meaning and are more willing to go behind a legislative text to give effect to the intention of the legislature.[24]

Atiyah and Summers observed that the different styles of judicial reasoning correlated with historical, cultural, and institutional factors,[25] and reflected different underlying visons of law in the two jurisdictions.[26] In particular, the interpretive method of English courts was notable for its deference to the will of Parliament,[27] and the value it placed on stability and certainty in the legal system.[28] Indeed, Atiyah argued that one of the strengths of the English preference for legal formality was the high degree of predictability and certainty that it yielded for English law.[29]

B. Form and Substance in Understanding Judicial Responses to Misleading Conduct

These insights from Atiyah and Summers on form and substance are a useful lens for understanding the judicial response to legislation in England and Australia that regulates misrepresentation. The field is of interest because, as noted at the outset of this chapter, doctrines providing relief from contracts induced by misrepresentation or, more broadly, from misleading conduct, occupy a central place in commercial and consumer law. Regardless of the degree to which a legal system adopts the rhetoric of freedom of contract, its responses to misrepresentation will be central to the integrity of the regime. This is because such conduct distorts and undermines the principle of autonomous choice on which contract law is premised. Misrepresentation inducing entry into a contract is singled out for special treatment throughout the general law, and most common law jurisdictions have also legislated to regulate such conduct. In some cases this statutory intervention provides a substantive right of action to affected persons, either generally or when acting as consumers, and/or providing remedies and limiting the extent to which liability for conduct that misleads can be excluded or limited.[30]

[24] ibid 110–11.
[25] ibid 3.
[26] ibid 4.
[27] ibid 105.
[28] ibid 104.
[29] Atiyah, above n 12, 456.
[30] Beyond those discussed in this chapter, see, eg, Cap 284 Misrepresentation Ordinance (Hong Kong) (a local equivalent of the Misrepresentation Act); Fair Trading Act 1986 (NZ), s 9 (modelled on the Australian regime). In protecting consumers, see the Consumer Rights Act 2015 (UK) and the Consumer Protection (Fair Trading) Act (Singapore) (Cap 52A, 2009 Rev Ed), s 4, discussed in JM Paterson and V Wong, 'Consumer Protection, Statute and the Ongoing Influence of the General Law in Singapore' (2016) 28 *Singapore Academy of Law Journal* 1079–1110. The US has a plethora of state statutory prohibitions, complementing the federal prohibition found in Federal Trade Commission Act 1914, 15 USC § 45, which address 'unfair and deceptive practices': see the critical survey in CL Carter, *Consumer Protection in the States: A 50-State Report on Unfair and Deceptive Acts and Practices Statutes* (National Consumer Law Center, 2009).

In Australia, the breadth of the prohibition on conduct that is 'misleading or deceptive or likely to mislead or deceive' reduces the need for plaintiffs to appeal to general law doctrines such as estoppel, negligent misrepresentation, or deceit in pursuing their claim.[31] Yet, as we will see below, these general law doctrines have also provided important insights for the operation of the novel statutory scheme, enabling courts to refine their understanding of its distinctive regulation of misrepresentation and misleading conduct, and to place it in its wider legal context. Similarly, even the more restrictive approach of the Misrepresentation Act – which addresses remedial issues against the assumed background of the general law on misrepresentation – demands direct engagement with the substance of the law's prohibition. The assessment of misrepresentation is necessarily dependent on the factual context in which it occurs, assessed against community standards and the substantive reasons for prohibiting such conduct. As we shall see, the pattern of response arising from this web of interactions is not straightforward. Rather, the form of the legislation may affect the judicial response to both the legislation and the broader legal context.

Legislation, like legal reasoning, reflects a choice between form and substance, which may often manifest in the choice between rules and standards[32] or, in alternate terminology, between 'fussy' and 'fuzzy' styles of legislative drafting.[33] Duncan Kennedy explains that:

> The first dimension of rules is that of formal realizability … The extreme of formal realizability is a directive to an official that requires him to respond to the presence together of each of a list of easily distinguishable factual aspects of a situation by intervening in a determinate way.[34]

By contrast:

> A standard refers directly to one of the substantive objectives of the legal order … The application of the standard requires the judge to both discover the facts of a particular situation and to assess them in terms of the purposes or social values embodied in the standard.[35]

The form of a statutory provision will reflect the values and proclivities of the legislature.[36] A rule-based regime may be preferred for its direct and

[31] Although, on this issue of the relationship between tort and the prohibition on misleading conduct, see *ABN AMRO Bank NV v Bathurst Regional Council* [2014] FCAFC 65, (2014) 224 FCR 1. See also JM Paterson and E Bant, 'In the Age of Statutes, Why Do We Still Turn to the Common Law Torts?: Lessons from the Statutory Prohibitions on Misleading Conduct in Australia' (2016) 23 *Torts Law Journal* 139.

[32] See D Kennedy, 'Form and Substance in Private Law Adjudication' (1976) 89 *Harvard Law Review* 1685.

[33] K Mason, 'The Intent of Legislators: How Judges Discern It and What They Do if They Find It' (2006) 27 *Australian Bar Review* 253, 259.

[34] Kennedy, above n 32, 1687–88.

[35] ibid 1688.

[36] Hence the approach adopted by legislatures over time is by no means static: a recent trend in Australian drafting towards redundancy and rules-based prolixity has been the subject of stringent

focused operation. Open-textured standards allow greater scope for courts to respond to the circumstances of the cases before them in promoting the purposes of the legislation.[37]

Importantly, for our purposes, the form in which legislation is drafted will, to a considerable degree, dictate the kind of inquiry undertaken by courts in interpreting and applying the legislation. It will tend to do this regardless of the proclivities and values of the courts, provided that the overriding judicial value being applied is fidelity to the statute through the principles of statutory interpretation. These principles of interpretation, informed by the courts' commitment to giving effect to the will of the legislature in the English and, we suggest, Australian traditions, mean that the style of response, formal or substantive, can be influenced by the particular form of statutory regime. The courts' commitment to the core principles of statutory interpretation requires them to respond to the legislation in a manner that is consistent with the way in which it is drafted, and may therefore prompt formal or substantive reasoning styles regardless of the historical or ideological preference of the courts for one or other style.

III. The English Statutory Response to Misleading Conduct

In England, the primary legislation of general application directed at misleading conduct is the Misrepresentation Act (we leave for the moment the consumer protection regime in the Consumer Rights Act).[38] This regime does not disturb the general law that identifies when conduct is misleading, but regulates the consequences of misrepresentations that induce entry into a contract. Our focus is on two aspects of the regime: the provision for damages in section 2(1), and the control exercised over attempts by the parties to exclude or restrict liability through their contract in section 3.

A. Damages under the Misrepresentation Act

Section 2(1) of the Misrepresentation Act provides:

> Where a person has entered into a contract after a misrepresentation has been made to him by another party thereto and as a result thereof he has suffered loss, then, if the

criticism: see, eg, *Wingecarribee Shire Council v Lehman Brothers Australia Ltd (in liq)* [2012] FCA 1028, (2012) 301 ALR 1 [948] (Rares J); S Rares, 'Striking the Modern Balance between Freedom of Contract and Consumer Rights' (2014) 28(3) *Commercial Law Quarterly* 7, 13.

[37] See Kennedy, above n 32, 1688.

[38] See further E Bant and JM Paterson, 'Consumer Redress Legislation: Simplifying or Subverting the Law of Contract' (2017) 80 *MLR* 895–926.

> person making the misrepresentation would be liable to damages in respect thereof had the misrepresentation been made fraudulently, that person shall be *so liable* notwithstanding that the misrepresentation was not made fraudulently, unless he proves that he had reasonable ground to believe and did believe up to the time the contract was made the facts represented were true.[39]

Section 2(1) provides a right to damages for misrepresentation inducing entry into a contract, without a representee needing to establish fault or a duty of care, placing the onus on the representor to provide that it acted honestly and reasonably. It was enacted in response to concerns expressed in the Tenth Report of the Law Reform Committee in 1962 that the law did not currently provide an adequate remedy to plaintiffs who had been misled in a context where fraud was difficult to prove.[40] Subsequently, the decision in *Hedley Byrne & Co Ltd v Heller & Partners Ltd*[41] established a pathway to damages for negligent misrepresentation. Uncertainties about this basis for damages meant that the provision was enacted as recommended.[42] Nonetheless, it has been commented that:

> Had the imminence of the *Hedley Byrne* decision been realised at the time the Committee reported in 1962, the need for the statutory intervention – or at least for this aspect of it – might have been considered to have been met by the advent of the new tortious liability.[43]

Almost from the outset, the form of section 2(1) has been subject to criticism. Writing in 1967, Atiyah and Trietel commented that:

> Some of the reforms introduced [by the *Misrepresentation* Act] are enacted in a manner which is quite extraordinarily tortuous and obscure.[44]

It is well established that the measure of damages under section 2(1) is based in tort not contract.[45] The prevailing authorities suggest that, in light of the words italicised above, the relevant measure of tort damages is that for deceit.[46] It follows that the remoteness rules in deceit will apply, and the defendant will be liable for all loss that is a direct and natural consequence of the misrepresentation, regardless

[39] Misrepresentation Act 1967 (UK), sub-s 2(1) (emphasis added).

[40] Law Reform Committee, *Innocent Misrepresentation* (Tenth Report, Cmnd 1782, 1962) para 17.

[41] *Hedley Byrne & Co Ltd v Heller & Partners Ltd* [1964] AC 465.

[42] WR Anson and J Beatson, *Anson's Law of Contract*, 28th edn (Oxford, Oxford University Press, 2002) 248.

[43] J Edelman (ed), *McGregor on Damages*, 20th edn (London, Thomson Reuters, 2018) para 49.049.

[44] Atiyah and Treitel, above n 3, 369, 378.

[45] *Royscot Trust Ltd v Rogerson* [1991] 2 QB 297, 304–05 (Balcombe LJ) ('*Royscot*'). See also *South Australia Asset Management Corp v York Montague Ltd* [1997] AC 191, 216 ('*South Australia Asset Management*'); *Smith New Court Securities Ltd v Citibank NA* [1997] AC 254, 267, 283 ('*Smith New Court Securities*').

[46] *Royscot* [1991] 2 QB 297, 304–05 (Balcombe LJ). See also *William Sindall plc v Cambridgeshire County Council* [1994] 1 WLR 1016, 1037 ('*William Sindall*'); *Bridgegrove Ltd v Smith* [1997] 2 EGLR 40, 42; *Spice Girls Ltd v Aprilia World Service BV* [2002] EWCA Civ 15, [2002] EMLR 27 [12]; *Ng Buay Hock v Tan Keng Huat* [1997] SGHC 58, [1997] 1 SLR(R) 507; *South Australia Asset Management* [1997] AC 191, 216. The question was, however, left open in *Smith New Court Securities* [1997] AC 254, 267 (Lord Browne Wilkinson), 283 (Lord Steyn).

of whether such loss was reasonably foreseeable.[47] This very literal interpretation of liability under the Act follows from the 'fiction of the fraud' device employed in the language of the provision, which treats a non-fraudulent defendant as if they had been fraudulent ('so liable') for the purposes of allowing the plaintiff access to damages.[48]

The approach is consistent with a formal response to the legislative rule. However, concerns over coherence between statutory and common law outcomes have led leading legal minds to argue in favour of a different, more purposive interpretation of the provision.[49] This line of criticism of the current approach is largely focused on the English courts' failure to recognise the possibility of the 'ambulatory' operation of the provision.[50] Scholars have argued that it is incongruous to hold a defendant who has, at most, made a negligent misrepresentation, to the more demanding remedial responsibilities arising from liability in deceit when the sole purpose of the statute was to allow the plaintiff a damages remedy in the absence of fraud on the part of the defendant.[51] If it is accepted that the purpose of the provision was to produce a more accessible remedial regime in response to misrepresentation inducing entry into a contract, the literal approach to its interpretation preferred by courts appears overreaching and even incongruous.

In *RBC Properties Pte Ltd v Defu Furniture Pte Ltd*,[52] Andrew Phang Boon Leong JA (delivering the judgment of the court) propounded a different interpretation of the scope of section 2(1), although a conclusive view was not necessary to resolve the dispute. Andrew Phang Boon Leong JA considered that the difficulty of applying this measure of damages to liability under section 2(1) was that the section 'does *not* concern a situation that pertains to *actual fraud* as such, but one that, on the contrary, falls *short* of it'.[53] These situations lack the

[47] *Doyle v Olby (Ironmongers) Ltd* [1969] 2 QB 158, 167 (Lord Denning MR); *Smith New Court Securities* [1997] AC 254, 264–67 (Lord Browne Wilkinson), 283 (Lord Steyn).

[48] J Cartwright, *Misrepresentation, Mistake and Non-Disclosure*, 3rd edn (London, Sweet & Maxwell, 2012) para 7.33.

[49] See, eg, ibid; R Hooley, 'Damages and the Misrepresentation Act 1967' (1991) 107 *LQR* 547; I Brown and A Chandler, 'Deceit, Damages and the Misrepresentation Act 1967, s 2(1)' [1992] (February) *Lloyds Maritime and Commercial Law Quarterly* 40; HG Beale (ed), *Chitty on Contracts*, 31st edn (London, Sweet & Maxwell, 2012) para 6.075; E Peel, *Treitel on the Law of Contract*, 13th edn (London, Sweet & Maxwell, 2011) para 9.066.

[50] Ambulatory construction has been contentious in England: compare, eg, *Fitzpatrick v Sterling Housing Association Ltd* [2001] 1 AC 27; *R v Ireland* [1998] AC 147, 158–59 (Lord Steyn); *Birmingham City Council v Oakley* [2000] UKHL 59, [2001] 1 AC 617. In Australia, see *Paciocco v Australia and New Zealand Banking Group Ltd* [2015] FCAFC 50, (2015) 236 FCR 199, 291–95 [382]–[396] (Besanko J). As Besanko J explained at [391], an 'ambulatory' construction contrasts with what Bennion calls a 'fixed-time' provision (O Jones, *Bennion on Statutory Interpretation*, 6th edn (London, LexisNexis, 2013) section 288) to which the maxim, *contemporanea expositio est optima et fortissima in lege* (the best and surest mode of construing an instrument is to read it in the sense which would have been applied when it was drawn up), is to be applied (RH Kersley and H Broom, *Broom's Legal Maxims*, 10th edn (London, Sweet & Maxwell, 1939) 463).

[51] Cartwright, above n 48, para 7.33.

[52] *RBC Properties Pte Ltd v Defu Furniture Pte Ltd* [2014] SGCA 62, [2015] 1 SLR 997 ('*RBC Properties*'). See also *Xia Zhengyan v Geng Changqing* [2015] SGCA 22, [2015] 3 SLR 732 [97].

[53] *RBC Properties* [2014] SGCA 62, [2015] 1 SLR 997 [83].

'moral turpitude' attributable to a situation of fraudulent misrepresentation.[54] His Honour expressed the view that use of the language of 'fraud' in section 2(1) was 'intended to signal the fact that s 2(1) offered a *statutory* remedy for damages which was hitherto available only in the context of the (more serious) situation of fraudulent misrepresentation or deceit'.[55] Instead, section 2(1) operated as the 'analogue of the common law action for negligent misrepresentation'.[56] Andrew Phang Boon Leong JA considered that this moral scale suggested that the measure of damages under section 2(1) should be that of negligent misstatement, rather than fraud.[57]

Justice James Edelman writing in *McGregor on Damages* describes the construction of section 2(1) in *Royscot*[58] as 'unfortunate'.[59] Edelman argues that it is difficult to justify making a negligent defendant liable to pay the same damages, however remote, as a defendant who has defrauded the plaintiff.[60] Edelman submits that:

> there is a clear alternative interpretation possible and that all that s 2(1) is purporting to say is this: before the Act the person induced by misrepresentation not forming part of the contract had only an action for fraudulent misrepresentation, now he has one also for negligent misrepresentation.[61]

This is an overtly more purposive interpretation than that taken by English courts to date in interpreting section 2(1). It suggests that the common law developments in distinguishing between the scope of liability for damages for negligence and fraudulent misstatement should equally be reflected in the interpretation of the legislation. This interpretation accordingly favours coherence in the substantive relationship between the regime and the surrounding general law over a formalistic adherence to the letter of the provision.

B. Excluding or Restricting Liability under the Misrepresentation Act

Section 3 of the Misrepresentation Act provides that:

> If a contract contains a term which would exclude or restrict—
>
> (a) any liability to which a party to a contract may be subject by reason of any misrepresentation made by him before the contract was made; or
>
> (b) any remedy available to another party to the contract by reason of such a misrepresentation,

[54] ibid [84].
[55] ibid.
[56] ibid.
[57] ibid.
[58] *Royscot* [1991] 2 QB 297.
[59] Edelman, above n 43, para 49.056.
[60] ibid.
[61] ibid.

> that term shall be of no effect except in so far as it satisfies the requirement of reasonableness as stated in section 11(1) of the Unfair Contract Terms Act 1977; and it is for those claiming that the term satisfies that requirement to show that it does.

The section subjects contract terms purporting to exclude or restrict liability to a test of reasonableness.[62] Reasonableness of its nature requires courts to consider the substantive effect of a term in the context in which it appears. However, the judicial approach to the section has relied on a formal characterisation of contractual terms, reducing the opportunities for application of the substantive test. This has occurred because parties have attempted to reduce the likelihood of liability for misleading conduct and avoid the application of this section through drafting strategies, including the use of 'non-reliance' clauses.

Non-reliance clauses are contractual statements that one or both parties has not relied on any or specified statements of the other party in making the decision to enter into the contract. These clauses do not directly exclude or reduce liability. Rather they seek to prevent liability arising in the first place by seeking to displace any link between the misrepresentation and entry into the contract.[63] The victim of a misleading statement must generally show that they have relied on the statement in order to obtain rescission or damages. The inclusion of a contractual statement that there has been no reliance on any pre-contractual representation is an attempt either categorically to preclude an actionable claim, or at least to provide an evidential basis for finding that the preconditions for a remedy do not exist in the circumstances of the case.[64]

English courts have accepted that a clearly drafted clause acknowledging that the plaintiff has not relied on any representation by the other party to the contract may be effective to preclude the plaintiff from later raising reliance on that representation as a reason for avoiding the contract or claiming damages for misrepresentation.[65] The primary authority is *Springwell Navigation Corp v JP Morgan Chase Bank*. In this case, Aikens LJ observed that parties are free to contract for whatever state of affairs they may choose. Aitkens LJ said:

> If A and B enter into a contract then, unless there is some principle of law or statute to the contrary, they are entitled to agree what they like … [T]here is no legal principle that states that parties cannot agree to assume that a certain state of affairs is the case at the

[62] For the various iterations of this provision, see Atiyah and Treitel, above n 3, 379.

[63] ibid 381.

[64] See G McMeel, *McMeel on the Construction of Contracts: Interpretation, Implication, and Rectification*, 3rd edn (Oxford, Oxford University Press, 2017) para 26.93.

[65] See, *Peekay Intermark Ltd v Australia and New Zealand Banking Group Ltd* [2006] EWCA Civ 386, [2006] 2 Lloyd's Rep 511 [56]–[57] (Moore-Bick LJ) ('*Peekay*'); *Springwell Navigation Corp v JP Morgan Chase Bank* [2010] EWCA Civ 1221 [143] (Aikens LJ) ('*Springwell*'). See also *Rock Advertising Ltd v MWB Business Exchange Centres Ltd* [2018] UKSC 24, [2018] 2 WLR 1603 [10] (Lord Sumption, with whom Lady Hale, Lord Wilson and Lord Lloyd-Jones agreed, affirming the effectiveness of a no oral modification clause on similar grounds). See also G McMeel, 'Documentary Fundamentalism in the Senior Courts: The Myth of Contractual Estoppel' [2011] *Lloyd's Maritime and Commercial Law Quarterly* 185.

> time the contract is concluded or has been so in the past, even if that is not the case, so that the contract is made upon the basis that the present or past facts are as stated and agreed by the parties.[66]

The importance of courts recognising the effect of such contractual strategies has been affirmed on the grounds of the value of commercial certainty and predictability. Thus, in *Springwell*, Aikens LJ saw 'commercial utility in such clauses being enforceable, so that parties know precisely the basis on which they are entering into their contractual relationship'.[67] Provided the parties' intention 'is clear', the clauses will be upheld.[68]

It has also been recognised by courts that the 'in principle' binding effect of such clauses is subject to the factors recognised as vitiating contractual consent.[69] Thus, in *Peekay*, Moore-Bick LJ stated that the effectiveness of non-reliance clauses 'may be challenged on the grounds that the contract as a whole, including the clause in question, can be avoided if in fact one or other party was induced to enter into it by misrepresentation'.[70] But this seems to invert the proper progress of the inquiry. Rather than assuming that the no reliance clause is effective to show the parties did not rely on any pre-contractual misrepresentations, unless there has been established a misrepresentation of the whole of the contract, the substantive effect of any misrepresentation should be considered against the whole of the circumstances of the case, including the non-reliance clause. Another way of saying this is that the question of whether the contract is voidable for misrepresentation is logically separate from the characterisation of the terms of the contract that purport to reduce the opportunity for reliance on misrepresentation as a reason for seeking relief from the contract.

From this perspective, the English approach to the issue is highly formal; it treats the character of the non-reliance clause as separate from the analysis of whether the impugned conduct was misleading. Rather than adopting a holistic approach, the analysis is broken down into a series of steps: (1) the basis on which the non-reliance clause is binding; (2) whether the non-reliance clause is an exclusion or limitation clause for the purposes of section 3 of the Misrepresentation Act and section 11(1) of the Unfair Contract Terms Act 1977; and (3) assuming the application of those statutes, whether the non-reliance clause is reasonable. While much academic commentary has focused on the first question, our focus is somewhat different. We note that the effect of the first two, more formal stages of the inquiry has been to reduce the opportunities for courts to engage with the substantive question prompted by the statute, which is whether a clause reducing or limiting liability for misrepresentation is reasonable.

[66] *Springwell* [2010] EWCA Civ 1221 [143] (Aikens LJ).
[67] ibid.
[68] *Peekay* [2006] EWCA Civ 386, [2006] 2 Lloyd's Rep 511 [57] (Moore-Bick LJ).
[69] McMeel, above n 64, para 26.70; McMeel, above n 65, 201–02. See also *Prime Sight Ltd v Lavarello* [2013] UKPC 22, [2014] AC 436 [47].
[70] *Peekay* [2006] EWCA Civ 386, [2006] 2 Lloyd's Rep 511 [57] (Moore-Bick LJ).

As we will see below, recent decisions suggest less tolerance with the traditional approach and a shift towards a more substantive engagement with the protective policy of the statute.

i. The Basis for Binding Effect

As to the first issue, non-reliance clauses might simply be treated as statements of past fact and given evidential weight depending on the circumstances in determining whether a party has been misled in entering into the contract, an approach as we will see below preferred by Australian courts.[71] Where it is felt necessary to give greater weight to the parties' contractual statements, it may be possible to imply a promise accompanying a non-reliance clause not to bring an action alleging that one party was misled in entering into the contract.[72] Under this contractual approach, non-reliance clauses would be enforceable because:

> Since the parties have agreed X to be the case, then the party which denies that X is in fact the case is in breach of contract. The Courts will not permit a party to benefit from its own wrong – including its own breach of contract.[73]

Since the decisions in *Springwell and Peekay*, English courts have, however, preferred to analyse the effect of non-reliance clauses through estoppel;[74] initially evidential estoppel,[75] and now contractual estoppel.[76] The contractual estoppel arising from a non-reliance clause prevents a party who has, through the contract, acknowledged a state of affairs to be the case from subsequently claiming the facts were different.[77] Significantly, unlike estoppel by representation, contractual estoppel does not require the parties to prove detrimental reliance.[78]

[71] See also D McLauchlan 'The Entire Agreement Clause: Conclusive or a Question of Weight' (2012) 128 *LQR* 521.

[72] McMeel, above n 64, para 26.26; K Loi 'Contractual Estoppel and Non-Reliance Clauses' [2015] *Lloyd's Maritime and Commercial Law Quarterly* 346.

[73] *Credit Suisse International v Stichting Vestia Groep* [2014] EWHC 3103 (Comm) [310] (Andrew Smith J).

[74] See McMeel, above n 64, paras 26.49–26.52; J Braithwaite, 'The Origins and Implications of Contractual Estoppel' (2016) 132 *LQR* 120.

[75] *Lowe v Lombank* [1960] 1 WLR 196; *EA Grimstead & Son Ltd v McGarrigan* [1999] EWCA Civ 3029 ('*EA Grimstead*'); *Watford Electronics Ltd v Sanderson CFL Ltd* [2001] EWCA Civ 317, [2001] 1 All ER (Comm) 696 ('*Watford*').

[76] *Peekay* [2006] EWCA Civ 386, [2006] 2 Lloyd's Rep 511 [56]–[57] (Moore-Bick LJ, Mr Lawrence Collins concurring), [70] (Chadwick LJ); *Springwell* [2010] EWCA Civ 1221 [143]–[144] (Aikens LJ). Also *Cassa di Risparmio della Repubblica di San Marino SpA v Barclays Bank Ltd* [2011] EWHC 484 (Comm), [2011] 1 CLC 701 [505] (Hamblen J) and, in relation to non-advisory clauses, *IFE Fund SA v Goldman Sachs International* [2007] EWCA Civ 811, [2007] 2 Lloyd's Rep 449 [28] (Waller LJ) ('*IFE Fund SA*'); *Titan Steel Wheels Ltd v Royal Bank of Scotland plc* [2010] EWHC 211 (Comm), [2010] 2 Lloyd's Rep 92 [89] (David Steel J) ('*Titan Steel*'); *Barclays Bank plc v Svizera Holdings BV* [2014] EWHC 1020 (Comm), [2015] 1 All ER (Comm) 788 [61] (Flaux J) ('*Barclays Bank*'); *Thornbridge Ltd v Barclays Bank plc* [2015] EWHC 3430 (QB) [109] (Moulder J) ('*Thornbridge*'); *Marz Ltd v Bank of Scotland plc* [2017] EWHC 3618 (Ch) [160] (Rosen QC) ('*Marz*'); *Carney v NM Rothschild and Sons Ltd* [2018] EWHC 958 (Comm) [76] (Waksman QC, sitting as a judge of the High Court) ('*Carney*').

[77] See *Peekay* [2006] EWCA Civ 386, [2006] 2 Lloyd's Rep 511 [70] (Chadwick LJ).

[78] *Springwell* [2010] EWCA Civ 1221 [177] (Aitkens LJ).

The use of contractual estoppel to explain the binding effect of non-reliance clauses has been criticised by scholars and commentators on the ground that it is inconsistent with the core concept of the estoppel doctrine.[79] Once the requirements of detrimental reliance are stripped away, the estoppel appears to add little to the core elements of the usual contractual inquiry. As Justice Leeming (writing extrajudicially) has observed:

> If there is to be a doctrine which gives rise to enforceable rights by reason of a clause in a written contract, for which detrimental reliance is not required, why call it 'contractual estoppel'? Why not refer to it simply as part of the law of contract?[80]

It may yet be that reliance in this context of the novel doctrine of contractual estoppel will be reconsidered. In *Chen v Ng*, the Privy Council observed that:

> the description contractual or conventional estoppel may in reality be a confusing misnomer, in circumstances where the parties can (even if there is also reliance on the truth of the agreed proposition) simply be regarded as having committed themselves by contractual term to a particular proposition.[81]

For present purposes, we may observe that the debate over the contractual estoppel characterisation of non-reliance clauses, diverts attention from what we would consider the core substantive inquiry into whether in the circumstances a party has been misled. It also delays, and in some instances avoids, engagement with the protective purposes of the statute.

ii. Application of s 3 of the Misrepresentation Act

It is only once it has been determined that a non-reliance clause is, on its face, binding that courts turn to consider section 3 of the Misrepresentation Act. The section is concerned with clauses that exclude or restrict liability. Non-reliance clauses do not, on their face, purport to exclude or restrict liability for misrepresentation inducing entry into a contract. Their operation occurs earlier in the contracting process to prevent liability from arising at all. If a court was to take a highly formal approach to the interpretation of the statute and the contract – because non-reliance clauses do not explicitly seek to limit liability, but rather seek to define the basis on which the parties contracted – they would not fall within the scope of section 3 of the Misrepresentation Act.[82] The question as to whether section 3 of the Misrepresentation Act applies would start and end with the form of the clause.[83]

[79] See, eg, McMeel, above n 64; Loi, above n 72. But see also Braithwaite, above n 74.

[80] M Leeming, 'Receipts Clauses and "Contractual Estoppel" Revisited' (2018) 134 *LQR* 171, 175.

[81] *Chen v Ng* [2017] UKPC 27, [2017] 5 LRC 462 (British Virgin Islands) [30] (Lord Neuberger, Lord Mance, Lord Clarke, Lord Sumption and Lord Hodge) ('*Chen*').

[82] The approach may be consistent with the insight of Professor Coote that exclusion clauses differ only in form from other terms defining the scope of the parties' obligations: BG Coote, *Exception Clauses: Some Aspects of the Law Relating to Exception Clauses in Contracts for the Carriage, Bailment and Sale of Goods* (London, Sweet & Maxwell, 1964).

[83] See, eg, *William Sindall* [1994] 1 WLR 1016; *Barclays Bank* [2014] EWHC 1020 (Comm), [2015] 1 All ER (Comm) 788 [61] (Flaux J); *Thornbridge* [2015] EWHC 3430 (QB) [109] (Moulder J).

In order to prevent the legislative regime being rendered redundant by ingenious drafting,[84] courts have been increasingly prepared to look beyond the form of the clause to its effect.[85] This change in approach arises out of a concern to preserve the integrity of the statutory prohibition. Thus, as Toulson J commented in *IFE Fund SA*, a 'party cannot by a carefully chosen form of wording circumvent the statutory controls on exclusion of liability for a representation which has on proper analysis been made'.[86] This approach is consistent with that taken by the Law Commission in introducing legislation to regulate the use of exclusion clauses under the Unfair Contract Terms Act, which focused on the 'mischief' of the clause.[87] English courts have, increasingly, been alive to the point that the sole practical purpose of non-reliance clauses is to reduce the risk of liability for misrepresentation.

In determining whether a non-reliance clause is subject to review for reasonableness under the Misrepresentation Act, courts typically refer to the 'key question' identified by Christopher Clarke J in *Raiffeisen*,[88] and affirmed by Aitken LJ in *Springwell*.[89] This question asks 'whether the clause attempts to rewrite history or parts company with reality'.[90] A clause that attempts to 'rewrite history' by denying reliance on a misrepresentation that has already occurred, and been relied upon, is in substance excluding or restricting liability and should be subject to review under section 3.[91] The point is illustrated in the oft quoted example from *Raiffeisen*, in which Christopher Clarke J explained that:

> [T]o tell the man in the street that the car you are selling him is perfect and then agree that the basis of your contract is that no representations have been made or relied on, may be nothing more than an attempt retrospectively to alter the character and effect of what has gone before and in substance be an attempt to exclude or restrict liability.[92]

[84] See, eg, where non-reliance clauses have been found to be in substance exclusion clauses: *Government of Zanzibar v British Aerospace (Lancaster House) Ltd* [2000] 1 WLR 2333 [53] (Raymond Jack QC) ('*Government of Zanzibar*'); *Raiffeisen Zentralbank Osterreich AG v Royal Bank of Scotland plc* [2010] EWHC 1392 (Comm), [2011] 1 Lloyd's Rep 123 [313] (Chrisopher Clarke J) ('*Raiffeisen*'); *First Tower Trustees* [2018] EWCA Civ 1396 [51] (Lewison LJ with whom Sir Colin Rimer agreed), [99] (Leggatt J).

[85] See, eg, *Government of Zanzibar* [2000] 1 WLR 2333 [53] (Raymond Jack QC); *Avrora Fine Arts Investment Ltd v Christie, Manson & Woods Ltd* [2012] EWHC 2198 (Ch) [145] (Newey J) ('*Avrora*'); *First Tower Trustees* [2018] EWCA Civ 1396.

[86] *IFE Fund SA* [2007] EWCA Civ 811, [2007] 2 Lloyd's Rep 449 [68]–[69] (Toulson J).

[87] Law Commission, *Exemption Clauses* (Law Com No 69, 1975) para 146.

[88] *Raiffeisen* [2010] EWHC 1392 (Comm), [2011] 1 Lloyd's Rep 123 [202].

[89] *Springwell* [2010] EWCA Civ 1221 [181].

[90] *Raiffeisen* [2010] EWHC 1392 (Comm), [2011] 1 Lloyd's Rep 123 [314] (Christopher Clarke J). See also *IFE Fund SA v Goldman Sachs International* [2006] EWHC 2887 (Comm), [2007] 1 Lloyd's Rep 264 [68]–[69] (affirmed by the Court of Appeal: *IFE Fund SA* [2007] EWCA Civ 811, [2007] 2 Lloyd's Rep 449 [28]) (Toulson J) ('*Goldman Sachs*').

[91] *Raiffeisen* [2010] EWHC 1392 (Comm), [2011] 1 Lloyd's Rep 123 [287] (Christopher Clarke J): There is 'an important distinction between a provision which makes clear that no (or only a qualified) representation is being made and one which purports to exclude a representation that has been made'.

[92] *Raiffeisen* [2010] EWHC 1392 (Comm), [2011] 1 Lloyd's Rep 123 [315].

In practice, and outside the realm of simple consumer cases, the distinction between a non-reliance clause that defines the basis of the parties' transaction and one that rewrites history is not an easy one.[93] This is largely because the functional outcome of the two categories of clause is the same. In *Carney*, Waksman QC, sitting as a judge of the High Court, considered that relevant factors, none of which was solely determinative, included the language and factual context of the clause and its location within the contract, noting that a clause located with a 'myriad of standard terms may point to it being exclusionary, especially if alongside express exclusions of liability'.[94] As we will see below, these are factors that Australian courts also consider. However, Australian courts address them from the outset, as an intrinsic aspect of assessing whether the defendant has engaged in conduct that is misleading; a substantive inquiry prompted by the standard-based drafting in the Australian statutory regime. As well as being more conceptually compelling, this more direct approach also provides clearer guidance to contracting parties as to the effectiveness of such clauses than the comparatively convoluted process of analysis followed in England.

English courts have generally approached the distinction between a clause that defines the basis on which the parties contract, and one that attempts to rewrite history – thus being an exclusion clause – on the basis of impression, which provides little real guidance to the relevant considerations. For example, in *Springwell*, Aikens LJ held that terms under which the plaintiff agreed that it was a sophisticated investor who had placed no reliance on advice from the bank, defined the basis on which the bank was willing to contract and therefore fell outside section 3 of the Misrepresentation Act.[95] By contrast, terms to the effect that 'no representation or warranty, express or implied, is or will be made by [the bank] in or in relation to such documents or information', and 'the Holder has not relied on and acknowledges that [the bank] has not made any representations or warranty with respect to the advisability of purchasing this Note', were held by the court to be attempts to exclude or restrict liability and were therefore subject to review under section 3 of the Misrepresentation Act. This was because, if there had been misrepresentations made to the plaintiff, they were 'an attempt retrospectively to alter the character and effect of what has gone on before'.[96] The dividing line between these two categories of clause is unclear, and therefore difficult to replicate with any degree of certainty.

A more straightforward approach, and one more consistent with the protective purposes of section 3 of the Misrepresentation Act, would be to accept that

[93] *Carney* [2018] EWHC 958 (Comm) [83] (Waksman QC). See also E MacDonald, 'Exclusion Clauses: The Ambit of s 13(1) of the Unfair Contract Terms Act 1977' (1992) 12 *Legal Studies* 277, 278.

[94] *Carney* [2018] EWHC 958 (Comm) [94]. Also *Marz* [2017] EWHC 3618 (Ch) [273]–[275] (Rosen QC); MacDonald, above n 93, 288.

[95] *Springwell* [2010] EWCA Civ 1221 [181].

[96] *Springwell* [2010] EWCA Civ 1221 [182] (Aikens LJ). See also *Colin Ali, Melanie Davis, Owain Golding, Ian Mcgreavy v Abbeyfield VE Limited* [2018] EWHC 669 (Ch) [154] (Kelyn Bacon QC) ('*Abbeyfield*').

non-reliance clauses are drafted with an aim of reducing the risk of liability for misrepresentation, and so fall within the scope of review under section 3. The Court of Appeal in *First Tower Trustees* suggested little ongoing tolerance for such clauses, or indeed attempts to distinguish between exclusion clauses caught by the Act and other types of clauses that produced a functionally similar outcome. Lord Justice Lewison stated that:

> Where a duty is imposed by law and not because it is a term of a contract agreed between the parties, the distinction between a contract term which excludes liability and one which prevents liability from arising by giving rise to a contractual estoppel is a distinction without a difference. In such circumstances it cannot be said that the contract term is merely creating and defining the extent of the parties' obligations. The term is seeking to exclude a liability which would otherwise be there.[97]

This approach would free courts to engage directly with the substantive inquiry into the context of the parties' contracting behaviour when assessing the reasonableness of a clause excluding, or restricting, liability for misrepresentation inducing entry into a contract.

iii. The Reasonableness of the Clause

As an evaluative standard, the requirement of reasonableness necessarily prompts a substantive inquiry into the circumstances of the case in light of the purposes of the provision. Consistently, the Unfair Contract Terms Act 1977, section 11(1) provides:

> In relation to a contract term, the requirement of reasonableness for the purposes of … section 3 of the Misrepresentation Act 1967 … is that the term shall have been a fair and reasonable one to have been included having regard to the circumstances which were, or ought reasonably to have been, known to or in the contemplation of the parties when the contract was made.

Despite courts' concern to uphold the binding effect of non-reliance clauses in order to support clarity and stability on commercial contracting,[98] there does not seem to have been any detrimental loss of certainty in subjecting non-reliance/exclusion clauses to this standard. In cases where there is relative equality of bargaining power between the parties, non-reliance clauses are typically treated as a reasonable expression of the principle of freedom of contract.[99]

[97] *First Tower Trustees* [2018] EWCA Civ 1396 [99] (Lewison LJ with whom Sir Colin Rimer agreed). See also [98] (Leggatt LJ).

[98] *Springwell* [2010] EWCA Civ 1221 [143] (Aikens LJ).

[99] See, eg, *Raiffeisen* [2010] EWHC 1392 (Comm) [314]–[315]; *Goldman Sachs* [2006] EWHC 2887 (Comm), [2007] 1 Lloyd's Rep 264 [68]–[69]; *Springwell* [2010] EWCA Civ 1221 [183]–[184] (Aitken LJ); *FoodCo UK LLP (t/a Muffin Break) v Henry Boot Developments Ltd* [2010] EWHC 358 (Ch) [175]–[177] (Lewison J); *Avrora* [2012] EWHC 2198 (Ch) [145] (Newey J). See also (basis and non-advisory clauses): *Titan Steel* [2010] EWHC 211 (Comm), [2010] 2 Lloyd's Rep 92 [105] (David Steel J); *Marz* [2017] EWHC 3618 (Ch) [273]–[275] (Rosen QC); *Carney* [2018] EWHC 958 (Comm) [356] (Waksman QC, sitting as a judge of the High Court).

For example, in *E A Grimstead*, Chadwick LJ assumed, without deciding, that the non-reliance clause fell within the scope of section 3 of the Misrepresentation Act.[100] Chadwick LJ also considered that the clause satisfied the requirement of being reasonable. Echoing a common theme, Chadwick LJ emphasised the value to the parties of 'commercial certainty'. Chadwick LJ also posited that 'the price to be paid reflects the commercial risk which each party – or, more usually, the purchaser – is willing to accept'.[101] Similarly, in *Springwell*, although non-reliance and no-representation clauses were found to be subject to the Misrepresentation Act as attempts to limit liability, they were considered to be reasonable. This was largely because of the 'fact that [the plaintiff] was a sophisticated investor in emerging market investments who was conscious of the risks of this type of investment', and who was aware of the relevant clauses and their effect.[102]

By contrast, in *First Tower Trustees*, a non-reliance clause was held to be ineffective to exclude liability for pre-contractual statements.[103] In that case, a landlord misrepresented to the tenant in its replies to pre-contract inquiries that it had no knowledge of any environmental problems affecting the property, when in fact it knew that the property contained asbestos which needed to be removed. The non-reliance clause in the lease purported to exclude liability for reliance on any statement made by the landlord. The Court of Appeal held that the clause was subject to section 3 of the Misrepresentation Act. The clause would have the effect of excluding liability for misrepresentation.[104] The clause was not reasonable because it rendered the opportunity to make pre-contractual inquiries worthless and, indeed, misleading.[105]

iv. Substantive Reasoning Prompted by Fidelity to the Integrity of the Legislative Scheme?

We can observe from this analysis that the response of English courts to non-reliance clauses consists of a series of staged inquiries into the binding effect of the clause, its characterisation as a matter of contractual interpretation, the effect of the legislation, and its measure as against the standard of reasonableness. This process is exceedingly formal, although it arrives eventually at a more substantive analysis. This substantive analysis is required to avoid the danger of the legislative purpose – of regulating the use of contractual terms to exclude liability for misrepresentation inducing entry into a contract – being undermined by clever drafting.

[100] *EA Grimstead* [1999] EWCA Civ 3029.

[101] ibid p 35A-C, cited at *Watford* [2001] EWCA Civ 317, [2001] 1 All ER (Comm) 696 [39] (Chadwick LJ). See also *Carney* [2018] EWHC 958 (Comm) [349] (Waksman QC).

[102] *Springwell* [2010] EWCA Civ 1221 [183] (Aitken LJ).

[103] *First Tower Trustees* [2018] EWCA Civ 1396. See also *Abbeyfield* [2018] EWHC 669 (Ch) [158].

[104] *First Tower Trustees* [2018] EWCA Civ 1396 [67] (Lewison LJ with whom Sir Colin Rimer agreed), [98] (Leggatt LJ).

[105] *First Tower Trustees* [2018] EWCA Civ 1396 [75] (Lewison LJ with whom Sir Colin Rimer agreed), [112] (Leggatt LJ).

It therefore reflects the courts' own commitment to the integrity of the legislative regime. If it is not to be more than an empty and easily avoided prohibition, the Misrepresentation Act requires courts to inquire into the substance of any non-reliance clause, and not merely to assume that its form takes it outside the purview of the regime.

While English courts may have avoided the charge of formalistic reasoning, the staged method of inquiry risks distracting from the impact of the legislative regime, and does little to ensure the overall coherence of this area of law. A more direct engagement with the substantive reasons underpinning the statutes would reduce complexity, promote certainty, and give better effect to the protective purposes of the statute. It would also accord with the formal primacy of legislation over common law. In that regard, the statutory controls over contracting out of liability should not be a mere add-on qualification to an otherwise effective contractual device. There can, after all, be no contractual estoppel if the non-reliance clause is in any event invalid.

More fundamentally, as noted above, we would also suggest that the substantive impact of the alleged misrepresentation on the contracting process should be addressed as a central question relevant to the validity of the contract. The contractual term in that context becomes merely one piece of evidence going to the heart of the substantive inquiry. This kind of inquiry should also be necessitated by the courts' commitment to the integrity of the contracting process. English courts should not countenance a complete fiction in contracting, whereby parties claim that there has not been any misrepresentation inducing entry into a contract when, in fact, this has been the case. To take any other approach would be, in Atiyah and Summers' terms, not formal in the sense of rigorous and rule following, but formalistic – leading the law into disrepute. This theme is well illustrated through the contrast with the approach of Australian courts to non-reliance clauses, to which we return below.

IV. Australia

Australia has long contained a statutory prohibition on misleading conduct, now found in section 18 of the ACL which provides, in simple and categorical terms:

> A person must not, in trade or commerce, engage in conduct that is misleading or deceptive or is likely to mislead or deceive.

The ACL regulation of misleading conduct clearly has a wider reach than the Misrepresentation Act. The ACL promotes explicitly instrumental ends, namely fair business practices and consumer protection. While the ACL does not define what is misleading or deceptive conduct, courts have found, consistently with the language and purpose of the statute, that the range of conduct caught by the prohibition is broader than that often the subject of general law doctrines. Most strikingly, no element of intent or fault is required in order for the prohibition to be contravened.[106] Both business-to-consumer and business-to-business conduct is covered. A breach of the prohibition on misleading conduct in the ACL moreover provides a plaintiff with access to a range of far-reaching and flexible remedies.[107] There is also the possibility of enforcement by the regulator leading to the imposition of civil pecuniary penalties.[108]

By removing the need to prove intention to mislead and making a generous suite of remedies available to plaintiffs,[109] the regime built upon, but also consciously departed from, its surrounding general law context. In these ways, the statutory scheme has invited courts to engage with considerations and interests that go well beyond the immediate parties to the dispute. This is consistent with the Australian embrace of equitable doctrines such as unconscionable dealing, which also show a considerable concern with generalised moral standards as a basis for adjudication.[110] It is this interplay between the form of the legislation and judicial interpretive techniques, including the consideration given to the words of the provision, its legislative purpose and the surrounding common law context, that provide an interesting contrast to English courts' treatment of the Misrepresentation Act, and one which we suggest is useful despite the different roles played by the two legislative regimes.

A. Statutory Damages and Other Remedies

As already noted, the ACL provides a veritable 'remedial smorgasbord',[111] both for misleading conduct and unconscionable conduct, with a right to damages for 'loss or damage' caused by the conduct pursuant to ACL s 236, and wide-ranging discretionary and compensatory orders available under ACL ss 237, 243.[112] When exercising their discretion to mould relief, section 237 requires that the orders must operate to 'compensate' or 'prevent or reduce' 'loss or

[106] *Parkdale Custom Built Furniture Pty Ltd v Puxu Pty Ltd* (1982) 149 CLR 191, 197 (Gibbs CJ).

[107] ACL, ss 236, 237, 243; previously TPA ss 82, 87.

[108] Australian Securities and Investment Commission Act 2001 (Cth), s 12GBA (ASIC Act). See also JM Paterson and E Bant, 'Intuitive Synthesis and Fidelity to Purpose? Judicial Interpretation of the Discretionary Power to Award Civil Penalties under the Australian Consumer Law' in P Vines and S Donald (eds), *Statutory Interpretation in Private Law* (Leichhardt, Federation Press, 2019).

[109] *Akron Securities Ltd v Iliffe* (1997) 41 NSWLR 353, 364 (Mason P) ('*Akron*').

[110] See generally P Finn, 'Statutes and the Common Law' (1992) 22 *University of Western Australia Law Review* 7, especially 12, 25, noting through the 1980s, parallel themes of enhanced remedial regimes under the TPA and a reformation of common law and equitable doctrine.

[111] *Akron* (1997) 41 NSWLR 353, 364 (Mason P).

[112] The illustrative range of orders given under s 243 includes orders declaring that the impugned contract is void *ab initio* or from a certain date; orders varying the impugned contract; orders refusing to enforce part or all of a contract; orders to refund money or return property to the injured person; and orders directing the respondent to pay the injured person the amount of the loss or damages. Similar provisions exist under the ASIC Act, ss 12GF, 12GM, 12GNB. See also E Bant and JM Paterson, 'Limitations on Defendant Liability for Misleading or Deceptive Conduct Under Statute: Some Insights from Negligent Misstatement' in K Barker, R Grantham and W Swain (eds), *The Law of Misstatements: 50 Years On from Hedley Byrne v Heller* (Oxford, Hart Publishing, 2015).

damage' suffered because of misleading conduct. Again, none of these terms are defined by the statute. Courts have embraced the task of giving content to these terms, and the accompanying range of potential orders by reference to the language and purpose of the statute, viewed in light of their general law context. Some of the statutory remedies, such as the power to vary a contract under section 243(b)(1), are not typically available under the general law.[113] However, other statutory orders available under the Act find ready (if not uncontentious) parallels in common law and equitable remedies; for example, in the form of tort damages and equitable rescission.

The Australian courts' response to these provisions models a willingness to embrace the potential for development of new law. In approaching the interpretation and application of the statute, the High Court has emphasised on numerous occasions that '[a]nalogy … is a servant not a master'.[114] Primacy must be given to the words and purpose of the statute. Yet at the same time, the body of surrounding law provides analogies that, while not controlling, 'represent an accumulation of valuable insight and experience which may be useful in applying the Act'.[115] The approach stands in contrast to the isolated operation of section 2(1) of the Misrepresentation Act, which we have seen has been separated from its evolving general law context, and is therefore less able either to influence the law around it or, in turn, to draw from relevant contextual aims and principles to develop a more integrated law of misrepresentation.

One illustration of the Australian approach in searching for interpretative clues in the text, and purpose, of the legislation to shape the evolving jurisprudence is in the treatment of fault at the remedial stage. While the general statutory prohibition on misleading conduct is expressed in absolute terms, the remedial consequences of liability in claims for private redress are strongly separated within the structure of the statute,[116] emphasising the discrete nature of the inquiry. This structure, the very breadth of the remedial scheme, the role allocated within the scheme for judicial discretion, and the explicit attention paid under the scheme to the mechanics of deterrence suggest that the legislation is, in a number of respects, scaled to the degree of fault attributable to the defendant in the form of intentional, reckless, or careless conduct.

In the evolving Australian jurisprudence, the courts' interpretation of the statutory right to damages for 'loss or damage' suffered because of misleading conduct has come to be strongly influenced by ideas of fault informed by appropriate general law analogues. Thus courts have looked to guidance from deceit,[117]

[113] cf *Vadasz v Pioneer Concrete (SA) Pty Ltd* (1995) 184 CLR 102, 115–16 ('*Vadasz*'), notably a decision expressly influenced by the statutory scheme in a potential example of the 'gravitational influence' of the statute discussed further below.

[114] *Marks v GIO Australia Holdings Ltd* (1998) 196 CLR 494 [103] (Gummow J) ('*Marks*').

[115] *Henville v Walker* [2001] HCA 52, (2001) 206 CLR 459 [18] (Gleeson CJ) ('*Henville*').

[116] The prohibition is contained in s 18 (ch 2), while the private law rights of redress are found in ss 232–43 (ch 5) of the ACL.

[117] *Gould v Vaggelas* (1985) 157 CLR 215, 236 (Wilson J), 250 (Brennan J).

in determining that courts may make an inference that the plaintiff relied on the misleading conduct of the defendant in circumstances where the conduct in question was calculated to induce that reliance.[118] Principles from the tort of deceit have likewise been influential in determining the scope of the losses for which the defendant will be held responsible for conduct that is misleading under the statute.[119] Here, both plaintiff and defendant fault have operated to delimit the defendant's scope of liability. This advertence has been reinforced by recent amendment to the statutory scheme which requires courts to consider the parties' respective and relative fault in apportioning damages awards for contravention of the section 18 prohibition.[120]

Deceit has not been the only source drawn upon by courts in determining the defendant's scope of liability.[121] Negligent misstatement has also been influential, and the very language and structure of the statute leaves open the possibility of limiting defendant liability by reference to ideas of mitigation, relative culpability, and responsibility.[122]

Ideas of fault and culpability have similarly been adapted to the statutory scheme of remedies beyond damages; for example, the combination of statutory orders akin to rescission. Here, courts have drawn upon general law ideas of fault (and, conversely, what is reasonable conduct) in the context of plaintiff mitigation, the effect of delay,[123] counter-restitution and change of position[124] – not only to guide the development of the jurisprudence concerning the operation of the statutory scheme – but to enable insights from the statutory context to inform parallel general law principles. As examples of this reverse 'gravitational'[125] effect of the statute, the scheme has arguably influenced the development in Australian law of

[118] See, eg, *Ricochet Pty Ltd v Equity Trustees Executors and Agency Company Ltd* (1993) 41 FCR 229, 233; *Lord Buddha Pty Ltd (in liq) v Harpur* [2013] VSCA 101, (2013) 41 VR 159 [132] (Vickery AJA, Weinberg and Tate JJA agreeing). Courts have also emphasised that inferences of reliance drawn in this manner may be rebutted by the circumstances of the transaction: *Campbell v Backoffice Investments Pty Ltd* [2009] HCA 25, (2009) 238 CLR 304 [143] (Gummow, Hayne, Heydon and Kiefel JJ) ('*Campbell*'); *De Bortoli Wines Pty Ltd v HIH Insurance Ltd (in liq)* [2012] FCAFC 28 [67], [91]–[94] (Jacobson, Siopis and Nicholas JJ); *Razdan v Westpac Banking Corporation* [2014] NSWCA 126 [15]–[18] (McColl JA).

[119] *Henville* [2001] HCA 52, (2001) 206 CLR 459 [19] (Gleeson CJ), [130]–[134] (McHugh J); *Marks* (1998) 196 CLR 494 [41] (McHugh, Hayne and Callinan JJ), [102]–[103] (Gummow J), [137]–[138] (Kirby J); *HTW Valuers (Central Qld) Pty Ltd v Astonland Pty Ltd* [2004] HCA 54, (2004) 217 CLR 640 [65] (Gleeson CJ, McHugh, Gummow, Kirby and Heydon JJ).

[120] Competition and Consumer Act 2010 (Cth), s 137B.

[121] Courts have also drawn on the tort of passing off for guidance, particularly on issues of causation and the role of damages calculated on a user principle: see E Bant and JM Paterson 'Exploring the Boundaries of Compensation for Misleading Conduct: The Role of Restitution Under the ACL' (2019) *Sydney Law Review* (forthcoming).

[122] Bant and Paterson, above n 112.

[123] On mitigation and delay, see *Henjo Investments Pty Ltd v Collins Marrickville Pty Ltd* (1988) 39 FCR 546, 565–66 ('*Henjo Investments*').

[124] See, eg, *Munchies Management Pty Ltd v Belperio* (1988) 58 FCR 274.

[125] J Beatson, 'The Role of Statute in the Development of Common Law Doctrine' (2001) 117 *LQR* 247, 259.

more flexible approaches to equitable rescission,[126] the standard of 'reasonableness' in reliance in estoppel,[127] and provides significant guidance for the developing change of position defence.[128]

B. Non-Reliance Clauses

The breadth of the Australian prohibition on misleading conduct makes it relatively straightforward for courts to hold that parties cannot contract out of or exclude liability for misleading conduct under the regime, on the grounds that this would be contrary to public policy.[129] In *Henjo Investments*, Lockhart J explained:

> Section 52 [TPA/ACL s 18] is a section in the consumer protection provisions of an Act concerned to protect the public from misleading or deceptive conduct and unfair trade practices which may result in contravention of the Act. It has been held that exclusion clauses, of which special conditions 6 and 7 are examples, cannot operate to defeat claims under s 52 … such exclusion clauses will generally be ineffective because they cannot break the nexus between the conduct in contravention of s 52 and the making of the agreement.[130]

The approach of Australian courts to non-reliance clauses provides a relevant and illuminating contrast with the approach of the English courts to the restrictions in section 3 of the Misrepresentation Act. Australian courts have accepted that an appropriately worded disclaimer, such as a non-reliance or no representation clause, if sufficiently prominent and contemporaneous with the allegedly misleading conduct, may prevent that conduct from being misleading, or make it difficult for a person to show actual reliance on the misleading conduct so as to give rise to a right to a remedy.[131] However, whether such provisions will be effective is a factual inquiry, depending on the circumstances of the case, with factors such

[126] *Vadasz* (1995) 184 CLR 102, 115–16.

[127] *Waltons Stores (Interstate) Ltd v Maher* (1988) 164 CLR 387; *EK Nominees Pty Ltd v Woolworths Ltd* [2006] NSWSC 1172 [137]–[139], [147], [261], [268], discussed in E Bant, 'Statute and Common Law: Interaction and Influence in Light of the Principle of Coherence' (2015) 38 *University of New South Wales Law Journal* 367, 387–91.

[128] Eg, on the question of the application of the defence to non-reliance-based changes of position, as discussed in E Bant, 'Rescission, Restitution and Compensation' in S Degeling and J NE Varuhas (eds), *Equitable Compensation and Disgorgement of Profit* (Oxford, Hart Publishing, 2017).

[129] *Henjo Investments* (1988) 39 FCR 546, 561.

[130] ibid. See also *Bowler v Hilda Pty Ltd* (1998) 80 FCR 191, 207.

[131] *Butcher v Lachlan Elder Realty Pty Ltd* [2004] HCA 60, (2004) 218 CLR 592, 608 (Gleeson, Hayne and Heydon JJ) ('*Butcher*'). See also *Campbell* [2009] HCA 25, (2009) 238 CLR 304 [130], cited in *Forty Two International Pty Ltd v Barnes* [2014] FCA 85, (2014) 97 AC-SR 450 [486]; *Re Colorado Products Pty Ltd (in prov liq)* [2014] NSWCA 789, (2014) 101 AC-SR 233 [124] ('That clause would not exclude a claim that the relevant statements were nonetheless misleading and the Defendants in fact relied upon them'). See also *Guirguis Pty Ltd v Michel's Patisserie System Pty Ltd* [2017] QCA 83 [28]–[29], [63], [64] (Fraser JA, McMurdo JA and Boddice J agreeing).

as the sophistication of the plaintiff and the significance of the information in question central to the determination.[132]

In *Campbell*, Gummow, Hayne, Heydon and Kiefel JJ observed that:

> [N]either the inclusion of an entire agreement clause in an agreement nor the inclusion of a provision expressly denying reliance upon pre-contractual representations will necessarily prevent the provision of misleading information before a contract was made constituting a contravention of the prohibition against misleading or deceptive conduct by which loss or damage was sustained … whether conduct is misleading or deceptive is a question of fact to be decided by reference to all of the relevant circumstances, of which the terms of the contract are but one.[133]

In other words, and in contrast with the approach taken by the English courts, the effect of a non-reliance clause is considered at the outset as part of a matrix of considerations relevant to determining whether the plaintiff has been misled.[134] As French CJ commented in the same case: 'The question is not one of law, but of fact'.[135] In England, this inquiry is only prompted where the Misrepresentation Act is raised, and then only at the end of a courts' analysis of the alleged misrepresentation and the effect of a non-reliance clause in light of the doctrine of contractual estoppel.

For example, in *Jewelsnloo Pty Ltd v Sengos*, the NSW Court of Appeal found that a 'No Reliance' provision in the contract for purchase of business precluded a claim of misleading conduct, in circumstances where the bargain was made on the basis that the purchaser would pay a 'severely discounted price to reflect the fact that it was not able to rely upon the accuracy of [sales figures provided by the seller and covered by the non-reliance clause]'.[136] By contrast, in *Shah v Hagemrad*, the Court was satisfied that the plaintiff placed reliance on the defendants' representations despite the inclusion in the contract of a non-reliance clause, and notwithstanding the fact that the plaintiff had the benefit of legal advice and was aware of the risk of some inflation of the sales figures in question.[137] In *Westpac Banking Corporation v Lee*,[138] written non-reliance declarations in the contract did not have the effect of qualifying misleading oral advice in circumstances where the plaintiff advised the bank's officer that he had not read the disclosure documents for the investment product in question,[139] and there was no evidence that

[132] See generally *Butcher* [2004] HCA 60, (2004) 218 CLR 592.

[133] *Campbell* [2009] HCA 25, (2009) 238 CLR 304 [130].

[134] See *Butcher* [2004] HCA 60, (2004) 218 CLR 592 [152] (McHugh J); *Havyn Pty Ltd v Webster* [2005] NSWCA 182, (2005) 12 BPR 22,837 [86]–[96] (Santow, Tobias JJA and Brownie AJA); *Campbell* [2009] HCA 25, (2009) 238 CLR 304 [130].

[135] *Campbell* [2009] HCA 25, (2009) 238 CLR 304 [31]. See also *Butcher* [2004] HCA 60, (2004) 218 CLR 592 [39] (Gleeson CJ, Hayne and Heydon JJ).

[136] *Jewelsnloo Pty Ltd v Sengos* [2016] NSWCA 309 (Beazley ACJ, Macfarlan JA, Payne JA).

[137] *Shah v Hagemrad* [2018] FCA 91 [106]–[107].

[138] *Westpac Banking Corporation v Lee* [2013] NSWCA 375 ('*Westpac*').

[139] *Westpac* [2013] NSWCA 375 [175] (Barratt, Emmett and Gleeson JA).

the bank's officer specifically brought the non-reliance clauses to the attention of the plaintiff when being asked specific questions about the product.[140]

Given the courts' focus on the whole of the circumstances, including the interaction between the alleged misleading conduct and the non-reliance clause, there is little scope for the operation of estoppel by convention or contractual estoppel operating to preclude reliance on pre-contractual representations where the contract contains a no reliance clause.[141]

V. The Approaches Compared

Four interrelated observations follow from this comparison of the English and Australian approaches to legislation dealing with misrepresentation and misleading conduct. The first concerns the relationship between statute and the general law. The work of Burrows and other scholars has alerted us to the fallacy of an oil and water approach, and the importance of an integrated analysis.[142] In the context of misrepresentation, this should mean that we should not think about the effectiveness of contractual attempts to reduce liability without also considering the statutory overlay of the Misrepresentation Act. This regime affects the substantive outcome for contracting parties as much as the nuances of the doctrinal characterisation of non-reliance clauses. We have seen that the latter attempts to define the scope of the contract, or may give rise to a contractual estoppel. The statutory overlay, however, requires consideration of the substantive object and effect of those clauses, and therefore cuts across any doctrinal characterisation.

The second observation relates to the way in which the form of the legislation influences the style of judicial reasoning. The prescriptive expression of the Misrepresentation Act has encouraged the English judicial proclivity for formal reasoning identified by Atiyah and Summers. The result is a convoluted, and often unclear, response to attempts to limit liability for misrepresentation inducing entry into a contract. Only after a process of doctrinal analysis and characterisation of the non-reliance and similar clauses do courts engage with the substantive inquiry

[140] *Westpac* [2013] NSWCA 375 [177].

[141] See further *Franklins Pty Ltd v Metcash Trading Ltd* [2009] NSWCA 407, (2009) 76 NSWLR 603; *Saleh v Romanous* [2010] NSWCA 274, (2010) 79 NSWLR 453. See also N Seddon, 'Can Contract Trump Estoppel?' (2003) 77 *Australian Law Journal* 126.

[142] A Burrows, 'The Relationship between Common Law and Statute in the Law of Obligations' (2012) 128 *LQR* 232. See further PS Atiyah, 'Common Law and Statute Law' (1985) 48 *MLR* 1; J Beatson, 'Has the Common Law a Future?' (1997) 56 *CLJ* 291; Beatson, above n 126; M Leeming, 'Theories and Principles Underlying the Development of the Common Law: The Statutory Elephant in the Room' (2013) 36 *University of New South Wales Law Journal* 1002; Finn, above n 110; P Finn, 'Statutes and the Common Law: The Continuing Story' in S Corcoran and S Bottomley (eds), *Interpreting Statutes* (Annandale, Federation Press, 2005) 52; WMC Gummow, 'The Common Law and Statute' in *Change and Continuity: Statute, Equity, and Federalism* (Oxford, Oxford University Press, 1999) 1.

into reasonableness of that clause required by the legislation. By contrast, a similar judicial commitment to the principles of statutory interpretation in Australia has produced a relatively straightforward approach to the statutory regime overlaying the common law in the field of misleading conduct, which is consistent with the principles-based drafting employed by the ACL.

The third observation relates to the correlation between styles of reasoning and drafting, and the predictability of outcomes. The perceived advantages of formality in legal reasoning and in statutory design are its certainty and propensity to promote predictable and consistent case outcomes, albeit at the expense of 'precision in the achievement of the objectives lying behind the rule'.[143] There are certainly circumstances in which a rule-based regime is entirely desirable and appropriate to promote a desired result, and where a loss of nuance may well be countered by the benefits of certainty.[144] However, bright-line rules may provide less of a benefit where the underlying circumstances with which they are dealing are necessarily complex, such as with cases of alleged misrepresentation or misleading conduct.

Any consideration of misrepresentation inducing entry into a contract must necessarily address the circumstances in which the contract was made, the terms of the relevant contract, as well as the body of applicable general law doctrines. Equally, the factual impact of a non-reliance clause on the claim to be misled is dependent on the circumstances of the case. The tendency of English courts to focus on the binding effect and characterisation of such clauses in answering this question, and the application of the statutory regime, only makes for murkier analysis. It certainly does not make the relevant inquiry more stable, as recent judicial expressions of intolerance with such devices indicate.[145]

The fourth observation relates to the relationship between statute and the surrounding general law. As we have seen in the remedial context of the Misrepresentation Act, and the comparison with the statutory prohibition on misleading conduct in Australia, highly prescriptive and specific legislative interventions tend to be isolated from their surrounding context and contained within their original historical, and legal reason for being. This can be contrasted with the use of broadly-framed standards that have the benefit of allowing courts to locate them within their broader legal (common law, equitable, and statutory) context as an integral part of the interpretative process. In turn, this promotes ongoing interaction between statutory provisions and general law doctrines to promote a more integrated overall law that can evolve over time.

[143] Kennedy, above n 32, 1689.

[144] Atiyah, above n 12. A common example given in the literature of a circumstance where bright line rules are desirable road rules: see, eg, HB Schaefer, 'Legal Rules and Standards' in CK Rowley and F Schneider (eds), *The Encyclopedia of Public Choice* (Dordrecht, Kluwer Academic Publishers, 2004) 347.

[145] See above, nn 81 and 97.

VI. Conclusion

The distinction between form and substance provides a useful lens for analysing judicial reasoning and styles of legislative drafting. This article has explored the influence of the form of legislation as a way of understanding the judicial response to the Misrepresentation Act, and its contrast with judicial responses to the Australian statutory prohibition on misleading conduct. The English response to misrepresentation inducing entry into a commercial contract is, as Atiyah and Summers suggest, relatively formal. English courts accept that non-reliance clauses may, through the device of contractual estoppel, preclude claims of this kind. In England, a substantive engagement with the relationship between alleged misrepresentations, and non-reliance clauses, in precluding remedial responses to that conduct, is only prompted at the later stages of the courts' inquiry by the need to apply section 3 of the Misrepresentation Act. By contrast, this is precisely the threshold response of Australian courts in approaching such claims.

As Atiyah and Summers themselves recognised, the distinction between form and substance enables identification of general trends in law and legal reasoning. It does not demand that legal reasoning be one or the other: rather, it allows judicial and legislative approaches to be understood along a spectrum of reasoning from more formal to more substantive, accepting that both methods will usually be present in any one case. We have suggested that the comparison of judicial responses to legislation regulating misrepresentation and misleading conduct illustrates the way in which the form of legislation can nudge courts towards more formal or more substantive styles of reasoning. Judicial commitment to the principles of statutory interpretation means that they must take the form of legislation seriously. Precise legislative rules accordingly prompt a strongly formal response. By contrast, legislation drawing on open-textured standards will prompt early engagement with the substantive content of the material regulated by the provision. The contrast explored in this article between English and Australian approaches to legislation regulating the consequences of misleading conduct makes apparent the limitations and difficulties associated with a strongly formal approach to legislative design and application. Indeed, we suggest that the contrast between the English and Australian approaches, on both fronts, is eloquent on the benefits of re-engaging with substance over form.

There is unlikely to be any perceived urgency to redraft the troublesome provisions of the Misrepresentation Act 1967 to reflect a more standard-based response to misrepresentation. Nonetheless, indications of an approach more focused on the substance of the misconduct and the legislative regime are evident, particularly in the stated preference of the Privy Council in *Chen*[146] for treating the binding effect of non-reliance clauses as a matter of interpretation not estoppel, and

[146] *Chen* [2017] UKPC 27, [2017] 5 LRC 462 [30].

in the Court of Appeal's approach in *First Tower Trustees*[147] in assessing whether such a clause operates to exclude liability. The approach in these decisions indicates a more substantive engagement with the purpose, and effect, of contract terms and, in the case of *First Tower Trustees*, the statutory enactment. This is, we suggest, ultimately more analytically robust and, moreover, may promote greater certainty for those dealing in the market.

[147] *First Tower Trustees* [2018] EWCA Civ 1396 [66], [111].

18

Form and Substance: Three Observations on the State of Debate

KIT BARKER

Anyone reading the excellent range of chapters in this volume, or who attended the Obligations IX conference that gave rise to it, will gain the impression that the distinction between formal and substantive approaches to law is very deep-seated. In my experience, however, 'formalists' and 'substantivists' often differ on rather less than they seem to. In his excellent and thought-provoking book, *Beyond the Formalist-Realist Divide*,[1] Brian Tamanaha recently concluded that, in one context at least, too much has been made of the division. Both 'formal' and 'substantive' approaches have been present in some proportion in the law at different times. Those who excoriate 'formalism' have too often been engaged in the burning of straw men – the destruction of impossible views about the law that no-one ever really held, or holds.[2] Similarly, very few, if any, modern critics of legal 'realism' really believe that the law is reducible to a purely mechanical enterprise in which answers are derived through the application of deductive logic and adherence to text, without reference to its core, underlying values. The disagreements between adherents to legal 'form' and 'substance' are therefore much more subtle – and more varied – than bare reference to the distinction itself reveals. This does not make the distinction redundant, but it does mean that, if it is to be at all useful, we must articulate very precisely what we mean by it and be alert to the great variety of different views that potentially underpin it.

The aim of this chapter is limited to making three, brief, observations about current debates regarding form and substance, which are prompted in the main by the papers offered at the conference that gave rise to this volume. The first, which follows the theme of my opening paragraph, is analytical in nature and relates to

[1] B Tamanaha, *Beyond the Formalist-Realist Divide: The Role of Politics in Judging* (Princeton, Princeton University Press, 2010).

[2] ibid, especially 59–63, chs 9, 10.

the nature of the distinction itself. 'The' distinction between form and substance is actually, I suggest, a set of associated, binary distinctions, not any single one, and this in turn explains both its difficulty and its fertility. The second observation relates to the appreciable rise (or resurrection – depending on your point of view)[3] of 'formalist' approaches to private law in recent years. I suggest some possible explanations for this. Finally, I wish to say a few words about Hohfeld, whose work now appears once more to be much in vogue amongst legal academics and to be increasingly cited by courts. Hohfeld is interesting because, although his schema for understanding legal relations is the archetype of 'formality' in one sense, it has, over the years, appealed to conservatives and realists alike. There are some forms of formalism, in other words, that do not stand in opposition to realist or 'substantivist' approaches to the law at all, but which are useful to everyone, whatever their political or philosophical persuasion.

I. The Distinction(s)

The distinction between 'formalism' and 'substantivism' is more than one distinction and is used to understand more than one aspect of the legal enterprise. During the Obligations IX conference alone, it was used to characterise different approaches to legal taxonomy,[4] to the law's creation, its development, its interpretation and the way it is applied by judges to facts. Commentators also cast the distinction itself in a wide variety of ways that are loosely connected, but identifiably different. I stopped counting at 13. In using the nouns 'form' and 'substance', authors hence referred to distinctions between: (i) legal rules or text (form) and their reasons, merits or justifications (substance);[5] (ii) the law's institutional structure (for example, the bi-partite nature of private litigation) and its rules or purposes;[6] (iii) the 'name' or 'label' attached to a legal concept and its content; (iv) the law's 'appearance' and its 'reality' or 'truth';[7] (v) the law's procedures (for example, the old forms of action) and its primary or secondary norms; and (vi) the law's 'method' and its 'results' (or, analogously, its 'rules' and its 'effects in practice'[8]). When using the same words adjectivally to describe approaches to legal reasoning, they distinguished between (vii) 'open' (formal) and 'closed'

[3] According to Tamanaha, ibid, 'formalism' as it is sometimes demonised in the modern day never really existed historically. Compare and contrast W Fisher III, M Horwitz and T Reed (eds), *American Legal Realism* (Oxford, Oxford University Press, 1993) xi–xv, according to whom formalism (here interpreted as 'classical legal thought') materialised in the US after the Civil War, only then to be subsumed again by legal realism in the twentieth century.

[4] See, eg, Robertson's injunction against 'lumping' together taxonomically (or doctrinally) things that are substantively different; and against 'splitting' things that are substantively the 'same' (A Robertson, 'The Form and Substance of Equitable Estoppel', this volume, ch 11).

[5] This is perhaps the most common way the distinction is cast.

[6] See, eg, R Stevens, 'Private Law and the Form of Reasons', this volume, ch 6.

[7] See, eg, A Burrows, 'Form and Substance: Fictions and Judicial Power', this volume, ch 2.

[8] See, eg, B McFarlane, 'Form and Substance in Equity, this volume, ch 9.

(hidden, substantive) reasoning;[9] (viii) reasoning that is highly constrained (automatic, dictated by authority, text, lexical priority, or categorisation) and that which is less constrained (flexible, discretionary, multifactorial, responsive to context, able to span different organisational frameworks); (ix) reasoning that is 'internal' or 'intrinsic' to legal rules (formal) and that which is 'external' or 'extrinsic' to them (substantive, instrumental, social, moral); (x) reasoning that is logical, mechanical or syllogistic and reasoning based on values, interests, or purposes; (xi) reasoning that is abstract and general (as found in a civilian code) and that which is fact-specific and particular; (xii) reasoning that places priority upon certainty and that which favours 'justice on the case'; and (xiii) reasoning that is technical, subsidiary or trivial and reasoning that is of great, or even conclusive normative importance.

It is therefore clearly possible to be formalist in one way and substantivist in another, which I personally consider a source of relief, even if it is complicating. Categorising oneself (always a tricky task and increasingly so as one becomes older, I have found) involves characterising one's commitments in respect of a wide variety of complex, but connected, binary questions. Determining whether one is a formalist or a 'substantivist' proves no exception to the rule. Do I believe in commitment to a rule's text, or purpose? Do I support the use of legal fictions?[10] Is authority conclusive in determining legal outcomes? Is certainty prior to justice? Should legal categories be organised around common reasons for claims, or according to history, procedure, or context? Should the bipartite nature of private litigation limit our understanding of its purposes? Is law an autonomous discipline, or socially embedded? Should judges make 'policy'? It is only when one has answered all of these questions (and more) – not just any single one – that one will know quite where one stands on the full range of debates concerning form and substance in the modern day. In respect of many of these questions, one may be tempted to answer neither 'yes', nor 'no', but 'something in between' or 'sometimes', or one may feel the need to insist on further specification as to the question's precise meaning before feeling fully comfortable in answering it.

One conclusion that one might draw from this is that, because deciding whether one is committed to form or substance involves so many different questions, the distinction itself is fragmentary and useless. My own view is that the reverse is in fact true, provided care is taken. Practices are generally better understood when deconstructed from the point of view of multiple, binary questions, rather than singular ones. Indeed, if the distinction between form and substance were a solitary distinction, then understanding the law in terms of it would be a rather unsophisticated, black-and-white business. The distinction is all the more fertile for its diversity, although it certainly requires clear and disciplined handling.

[9] See, eg, L Murphy, 'The Formality of Contractual Obligation', this volume, ch 7 (contract law is 'formal' because it does not wear its instrumental justifications openly on its face).

[10] For further assistance in making your mind up on this question, see L Fuller, *Legal Fictions* (Stanford, Stanford University Press, 1967); M Del Mar and W Twining (eds), *Legal Fictions in Theory and Practice* (Cham, Springer, 2015).

This also leaves open the question whether all of the distinctions set out above as 'binary' are genuinely so. The line that Atiyah and Summers famously drew between 'formalism' and 'formalistic' reasoning prompts this query, because that distinction is, on their own account, one of degree and it appears to turn on questions of substance (here meaning reason): 'formalistic' reasoning is a 'degenerate' type of 'formal' reasoning and is different to it in the extent to which it is *unjustified* by reference to (substantive) *reasons* that 'ought to be taken into account'.[11] The very definition of (acceptable) formalism in this account therefore rests in part upon substantive questions of justification. This feature may not be true of some of the distinctions drawn between form and substance, but may well be of others.

II. The Rise of a 'New' Formalism

The second observation relates to what I perceive to be a resurgence in formalism (some types of it, at least)[12] in private law in recent years. This is most obviously manifest in the important philosophical work of Ernest Weinrib[13] and those who have helped to develop and apply his ideas about private law across a broad range of legal doctrine. It is also reflected to some extent in the US in the revived interest in private law doctrine symbolised by the 'New Private Law' movement[14] and in extensive recent Restatement projects on the law of torts[15] and unjust enrichment law.[16] In this volume, it can be found in Rob Stevens' view (similar to Weinrib's) that private law must be understood in terms of – and limited in its ambitions by – the bipartite form of litigation;[17] as well as in the warning at the end of Birke Häcker's chapter against the abandonment of general rules in favour of discretionary, evaluative judgments.[18] Even realists now place more store by rules than once they did.[19]

[11] PS Atiyah and RS Summers, *Form and Substance in Anglo-American Law: A Comparative Study of Legal Reasoning, Legal Theory, and Legal Institutions* (Oxford, Clarendon Press, 1987) 29. Note also that whether or not such substantive reasons ought to be taken into account is also itself dictated by (jurisdiction-specific) reasons for resolving an issue formally: ibid.

[12] Very few, if any, scholars or practitioners advocate a return to the historical 'forms of action' and this forms no part of the modern formalist agenda, as far as I know.

[13] Most definitively stated in E Weinrib, *The Idea of Private Law* (Cambridge, MA, Harvard University Press, 1995).

[14] See New Private Law: Project on the Foundations of Private Law, http://blogs.harvard.edu/nplblog/.

[15] *Restatement of the Law (Third) Torts, Products Liability* (1997); *Apportionment of Liability* (2000); *Liability for Physical and Emotional Harm* (2010); *Liability for Economic Harm* (2018). Additional projects on *Intentional Torts to Persons* and *Property Torts* are currently underway.

[16] *Restatement of the Law Third, Restitution and Unjust Enrichment* (2018).

[17] See Stevens, above n 6.

[18] See B Häcker, '"Substance Over Form": Has the Pendulum Swung Too Far?', this volume, ch 3.

[19] Hanoch Dagan is a notable example, seating himself very much in the former tradition of Karl Llewellyn, rather than that of intervening rule-sceptics. See H Dagan, *Reconstructing American Legal*

This is no place to conduct a full debate and I wish to confine my attention to identifying some possible reasons for the resurgence of formal instincts at this particular point in time. It is, in my view, partly symptomatic of a broader sense of loss of control – a common intellectual anxiety that the legal world is disintegrating, too complicated, incoherent and lacking in some important way in legitimacy. The formal instinct is in part, I suggest, a psychological desire to impose order upon chaos.

Before we come to this – and before I am mistaken for someone who places no store by form – it is worth re-iterating the very good reasons why the law concentrates on it.[20] Form (understood for this purpose as the shape and public 'text' or 'statement' of rules) is key to the law's certainty, predictability, transparency and accessibility and therefore to values associated with the rule of law. It is also facilitative – providing objective evidence of our commitments and intentions, cautioning actors and assisting to channel their behaviour.[21] Beyond this, a focus on form helps to co-ordinate different systems of rules. In Federal or international legal systems this is especially important, but even in singular ones, 'formal' texts, such as a statutes, codes, restatements and bills of rights help to moderate the degree of legal variation across different geographical and social domains. At common law, the ability to co-ordinate legal and equitable doctrines triggered by the same facts also clearly depends on the norms of those doctrines being ascertainable and clean-edged. The co-ordinating function of form is important both from a 'system management' point of view and from the important perspective of ensuring equal treatment and respect for citizens. Equality and rationality require comparison and only that which is ascertainable is comparable.

There is therefore an undeniable sense in which ascertainable, public form is essential to law. This proposition is different to the assertion that the 'form' (this time I mean the structure and rules) of the law is inherently prior to its substance (content, values or purposes). Of course, it is true to say that the legal aims we can achieve depend on the tools we have. Practicing lawyers simply have to get on with the job of litigation, given the available structures and rules at any given point in time. At the same time, however, there is no intrinsic reason why we cannot change the form of the tools we have, to achieve the aims we want. That is simply a matter of public will. Philosophically, form is no more prior to substance (reason) than the chicken is to the egg.[22] Given that law is a deliberative human construct, the more credible historical view in fact seems to be that aims came before legal forms (we intended before we constructed), but the key point is that the relationship between forms and ends is reflexive and susceptible to constant adjustment.

Realism and Rethinking Private Law Theory (Oxford, Oxford University Press, 2013); E Sherwin, 'Rule-Oriented Realism' (2005) 103 *Michigan Law Review* 1578.

[20] See further Atiyah and Summers, above n 11, 23–28.

[21] L Fuller, 'Consideration and Form' (1941) 41 *Columbia Law Review* 799, 800–01.

[22] Interestingly, the view that neither chicken nor egg is prior to the other is now also proposed by quantum physicists: University of Queensland, 'Quantum weirdness in "chicken or egg" paradox' (*ScienceDaily*, 4 September 2018), www.sciencedaily.com/releases/2018/09/180904114733.htm.

None of the important virtues of form explains, however, why formalism is ascendant again in private law at this point in time. My suggestion is that this is in part a reaction (whether reasoned or visceral) to the growing uncertainties and insecurities of the age – that it represents a grasp for security, coherence and legitimacy at a time when each of these values has come to be thought of as threatened. What, then are the contemporary threats to which the new formalism might seek to respond?

One is undoubtedly the politicisation of private law, which is particularly marked in the US. Ernest Weinrib's formalist project[23] must, I think, be understood as a reaction to the worst excesses of (at least some types of) realism in that jurisdiction and the sense that it goes too far in instrumentalising the legal relationship between wrongdoers and their victims for social purposes, without evincing due respect for the private rights of the parties to a given dispute, or the proper limits on the role of adjudicators. Similar concerns about judges' involvement in policy pervade Robert Stevens' work on the law of torts.[24] Modern reversions to formalism also coincide with the rise of neo-liberalism and the retraction of the state from traditional social welfare objectives. At a time when welfarism is generally politically derided, it is probably thought particularly inapposite for judges and private law to be engaging in it.[25]

A second concern is the increased complexity of private law. The vast increase in statutory regulation through the course of the twentieth century, the burgeoning of reported cases, and the complex interaction of multiple sources of law can easily give rise to the sense that the legal world is becoming less 'manageable' and rapidly more incoherent. Proper co-ordination between various legal actors and norms (common law, equitable, statutory and constitutional) is difficult to achieve and there are frequent overlaps, clashes and contradictions.[26] Some statutes are now so vast and labyrinthine in construction that no general shape or aim is discernible in them;[27] and some are rushed through parliaments so quickly as to later prove a serious source of concern and interpretive puzzlement.[28]

[23] Weinrib, above n 13.

[24] R Stevens, *Torts and Rights* (Oxford, Oxford University Press, 2007). See also B Tamanaha, *Law as a Means to an End: Threat to the Rule of Law* (Cambridge, Cambridge University Press, 2006) (warning that unrestrained instrumentalism can threaten the rule of law).

[25] For the avoidance of doubt, I am not suggesting that 'formalists' are necessarily neo-liberals, or that either Professor Weinrib or Professor Stevens is anti-welfare. Their stance (as far as I know) is simply that if welfare is our aim, private law is the wrong way to go about it. The point in the text is simply that if welfarism is derided in Parliaments, this relieves judges of any pressure to engage in it and is indeed likely to steer them away from it, in case they contradict the expressed intentions of the people. That results in less 'politics' (of this sort at least) in private law.

[26] On the problems of co-ordination in complex systems, see K Barker, 'Private Law as a Complex System: Agendas for the Twenty-First Century' in K Barker, K Fairweather and R Grantham (eds), *Private Law in the 21st Century* (Oxford, Hart Publishing, 2017).

[27] The Corporations Act 2001 (Cth) is an excellent example. It runs to 1,643 sections.

[28] The classic recent example in Australia is the Civil Liability Acts, brought in very swiftly at the behest of insurance companies and other lobbyists as a response to the economic turbulence of the early part of the current century.

In this environment, it is scarcely surprising that the legal community advocates certainty, transparency, clear demarcation, lower-level reasoning and smaller numbers of set rules over ad-hoc, purposive judgements and multiple, overlapping systems. This is a time for doctrinal trimming, the application of Occam's razor, rationalisation, codification, merger, harmonisation and unification. The aim is partly to combat overkill, redundancy and inefficiency, but partly also to increase the law's moral integrity, transparency and intelligibility for its citizens. A clear symptom of the current difficulties caused for courts by multiple, conflicting sets of rules and standards is the common judicial designation of 'coherence' as an important priority in the common law's development.[29] Second-order rules for the co-ordination and management of multiple first-order ones are of increased visibility and importance.

A third factor is the emergence of a battery of new and undoubtedly difficult doctrinal challenges. A good example is the relatively recent development of unjust enrichment law, which has proven particularly unsettling to some. The category has sometimes (unfairly, I personally think) been perceived as a rapacious devourer of traditional private law frameworks, fictions and principles – a destroyer of the old order and a threat to general security. Even now, there is disagreement about its basic shape and scope. The response of those supporting its elaboration has been to seek to legitimise and stabilise it using a formal, ordered, symmetrical, quasi-scientific method, so that the subject is given both its own clear, internal logic and a stable place on the private law 'map', which minimises its overlap and conflict with other subjects such as contract, tort and property law.[30] As we shall see further below, some commentators have used formal Hohfeldian analytical tools to try to work though some of its difficulties. One writer, Professor Burrows, has tried to calm the choppy waters in England and Wales by drafting a concise restatement of its main principles.[31] In these instances, 'formalism' has been deployed as both a diplomatic mediator of change ('don't panic everyone – we are proceeding in a disciplined way and according to both authority and science') and a mechanism via which our intelligence can extend its hand to grasp and explain the unfamiliar.

Other sources of real instability in the current age include: the shift from the (apparent) certainties of 'all-or-nothing' systems of responsibility in private law to ones in which compromises are struck and responsibility for events and their consequences is shared between multiple parties in fractions according to

[29] For a critical review of this phenomenon in Australian law, see A Fell, 'The Concept of Coherence in Australian Private Law' (2018) 41 *Melbourne University Law Review* 1160.

[30] The leading figure in this enterprise in England and Wales and a staunch supporter of the disciplined analytical and taxonomic method was Peter Birks: P Birks, *An Introduction to the Law of Restitution* (Oxford, Clarendon Press, rev edn, 1985); P Birks, *Unjust Enrichment*, 2nd edn (Oxford, Oxford University Press, 2005).

[31] A Burrows, *A Restatement of the English Law of Unjust Enrichment* (Oxford, Oxford University Press, 2012).

criteria that are vague and in practice hard to apply;[32] the increasingly difficult relationship between 'public' and 'private' law that has come about with the rise of the modern administrative state and the development of human rights jurisprudence; the expansion of the types of human interest that private law is expected to protect;[33] and the observable preference in some quarters for tests of legal duty that are based upon the weighing of a wide range of normative factors, rather than hard-and-fast rules.[34] These multifactorial tests are in large measure a reflection of judges' recognition of the difficulty of many modern legal questions and their attempt to grapple with the key normative issues in new cases, but they infuriate and confuse anyone trying to make an accurate prediction of the outcome of a case, or wanting a simple 'yes' or 'no' answer to questions of basic obligation. They dull 'bright lines'. Individual tort victims who encounter the law only rarely and who care little for planning may not be overly worried by this, but repeat commercial actors and markets are edgy about uncertainty and, it is sometimes thought, prone to responding to it through distortive practices, with undesirable social consequences. In these times of economic fragility, certainties and stability in form tend to be regarded as especially important.

It is therefore understandable why there might be a deep sense of unease about the state of private law at this time. To the extent that it is possible to do so, we should clearly address each of the above sources of concern. In some instances, 'formalism' of one sort or another may indeed provide a partial answer. At the same time, however, it is important to accept that some level of insecurity and uncertainty is inevitable in a complex and changing world. Whilst a focus on the form of law is a good place to start, we should not allow our anxieties regarding uncertainty to frustrate our attempts to achieve worthwhile purposes either. We must learn to differentiate between that which we can control and that which we cannot – to change what we can, accept what we cannot and have the wisdom to know the difference.

III. Hohfeld Resurrected – A Limited Reconciliation

My final observation relates to the increased recent use in legal scholarship of the work of Wesley Newcomb Hohfeld.[35] I see this as being in part a symptom of

[32] This is evidenced in doctrines such as the partial defences of contributory negligence and change of position, contribution, and 'proportionate liability', all of which are relatively recent additions to our law – see generally, T Weir, 'All or Nothing?' (2004) 78 *Tulane Law Review* 511; K Barker and R Grantham (eds), *Apportionment in Private Law* (Oxford, Hart Publishing, 2018).

[33] Eg, psychiatric, emotional, economic and privacy interests.

[34] This has been particularly notable in Australian appellate courts dealing with the duty of care question in complex modern negligence cases. See, eg, *Caltex Refineries (Qld) Pty Ltd v Stavar* [2009] NSWCA 258, (2009) NSWLR 649 [102]–[105] (Allsop P); *Makawe Pty Ltd v Randwick City Council* [2009] NSWCA 412, (2009) 171 LGERA 165.

[35] WN Hohfeld, *Fundamental Legal Conceptions as Applied in Judicial Reasoning* (W Cook ed, New Haven, Yale University Press, 1919). For a full appraisal of Hohfeld's influence and modern uses,

the new 'formalism' and a reaction to the modern insecurities about burgeoning rights-speak, but the interesting thing about Hohfeld's approach is that, although it is formal in the sense that it provides an elegant analytical scheme for thinking and talking about rights, it has actually been used by writers of all political persuasions – by conservatives and radicals, doctrinalists and realists alike. It has hence been deployed in recent years (more or less successfully) to deconstruct traditional property conceptions;[36] to explain the nature of 'rights', 'liabilities' and remedies in unjust enrichment law,[37] tort and contract;[38] the relationship between legal and equitable rights; the impact of public discretions on private law duties, liabilities and immunities;[39] the relationship between private law, courts and the state;[40] and to illuminate our understanding of parts of public law, including human rights law,[41] administrative law,[42] comparative law[43] and international law.[44] Hohfeld was related to the eminent German zoologist and philosopher Ernst Heinrich Haeckel (1834–1919), who designed his own (rather eclectic) genealogical tree charting relationships between different types of animals and there is an intriguing parallel between the analytical techniques both men brought to bear upon their work in their different fields.

It is not just academic commentators who are showing renewed interest in Hohfeld's scheme of rights. Figure 1 below provides a graphical representation of patterns of citation across US, UK and Australian courts since

see K Barker, 'Private Law, Analytical Philosophy and the Modern Value of Wesley Newcomb Hohfeld: A Centennial Appraisal' (2018) 38 *OJLS* 585.

[36] It has, eg, played an important part in the story of the 'bundle of rights' theory of property that is dominant in the US. See also, for examples of use in rethinking modern property: H Dagan, 'The Craft of Property' (2003) 91 *California Law Review* 1517; B McFarlane, *The Structure of Property Law* (Oxford, Hart Publishing, 2008).

[37] P Jaffey, 'Hohfeld's Power-Liability/Right-Duty Distinction in the Law of Restitution' (2004) 17 *Canadian Journal of Law and Jurisprudence* 295; K Barker, 'Damages Without Loss: Can Hohfeld Help?' (2014) 34 *OJLS* 631.

[38] On tort and rights, see Stevens, above n 24, ch 2. On remedies more generally, see S Smith, 'Duties, Liabilities and Damages' (2012) 125 *Harvard Law Review* 1727.

[39] K Barker, 'Public Power, Discretion and the Duty of Care' in K Barker, S Degeling, K Fairweather and R Grantham (eds), *Private Law and Power* (Oxford, Hart Publishing, 2017) 207.

[40] Most notably in what is known in the US as 'Civil Recourse' theory, pioneered by Ben Zipursky and John Goldberg. For an early piece, see B Zipursky, 'Civil Recourse, Not Corrective Justice' (2003) 91 *Georgetown Law Journal* 695. For fuller treatment and references, see Barker, above n 35.

[41] There are some reservations about the use of Hohfeld in this field, on the basis that his conception of rights is too cramping: R Cruft, 'Human Rights as Rights' in G Ernst and J Heilinger (eds), *The Philosophy of Human Rights: Contemporary Controversies* (Berlin, de Gruyter, 2011) 129.

[42] J Varuhas, 'The Reformation of English Administrative Law? "Rights", Rhetoric and Reality' (2013) 72 *CLJ* 369, 396–412; N Bamforth, 'Hohfeldian Rights and Public Law' in M Kramer (ed), *Rights, Wrongs and Responsibilities* (Basingstoke, Palgrave Macmillan, 2001) 1 (guarded support for the scheme in public law generally).

[43] See, eg, M Van Hoecke, 'Hohfeld and Comparative Law' (1996) 9 *International Journal for the Semiotics of Law* 185.

[44] G Hughes, 'Hohfeld in Occupied Territory' (1963) 4 *Sydney Law Review* 249; J Morss, 'The Legal Relations of Collectives: Belated Insights from Hohfeld' (2009) 22 *Leiden Journal of International Law* 289; J Morss, 'Power and International Law: Hohfeld to the Rescue' [2011] *The Western Australian Jurist* 93.

the 1920s, including citations by both judges and counsel. This has been compiled through the use of on-line electronic databases,[45] so that its accuracy cannot be 100 per cent guaranteed, but it serves nonetheless to illustrate the general trend.[46] What is perhaps most striking is not so much the total number of citations, as the dramatic increase in the rate of citation toward the end of the twentieth century and in the first two decades of the twenty-first century. In the US, 35 per cent of citations have occurred since the year 2000; in Australia 70 per cent, and in the UK (including Scotland) some 90 per cent (although the overall figures in this part of the world are the lowest by far and there appears to be no single instance that I could find in which either the House of Lords or the UK Supreme Court has referred to Hohfeld directly, approvingly or otherwise). He has been cited five times in the United States Supreme Court[47] and twelve times in the High Court of Australia.[48]

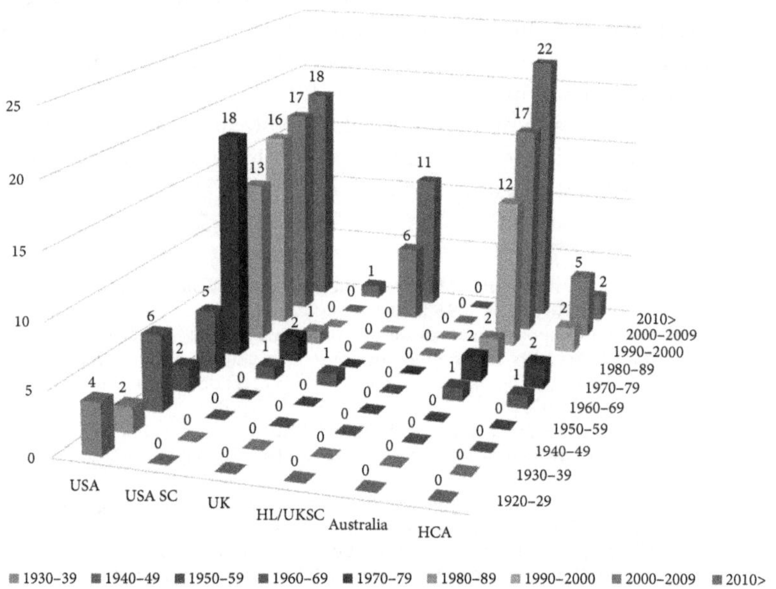

Figure 1 Number of Citations of Hohfeld in Courts (by decade and jurisdiction)

[45] For Australian, English and Scottish cases, LexisAdvance was used. For US case law, Westlaw. Data presented is based on a search conducted on 11 December 2017.

[46] For a much more detailed analysis of case citations, see Barker, above n 35.

[47] *Heffernan v City of Paterson* 136 S Ct 1412 (2016); *Golden State Transit Corp v Los Angeles* 493 US 103 (1989); *Zablocki v Redhail* 434 US 374 (1978); *United States v Richardson* 418 US 166 (1974); *Flast v Cohen* 392 US 83 (1968).

[48] *Maloney v R* [2013] HCA 28, (2013) 252 CLR 168; *JT International SA v Commonwealth of Australia; British American Tobacco Australasia Ltd v The Commonwealth* [2012] HCA 43, (2012) 250 CLR 1; *Chang v Laidley Shire Council* [2007] HCA 37, (2007) 234 CLR 1; *New South Wales v Commonwealth of Australia* [2006] HCA 52, (2006) 229 CLR 1; *Western Australian Planning Commission v Temwood Holdings Pty Ltd* [2004] HCA 63, (2004) 221 CLR 30; *Minister for Immigration and Multicultural and Indigenous Affairs v Al Khafaji* [2004] HCA 38, (2004) 219 CLR 664;

This is not to say that Hohfeld's analytical system is always cited with approval, or that courts and commentators always refer to legal relations in the way that he did. He has nonetheless become an important reference point in modern discussions about the meaning of rights. I have speculated elsewhere as to some of the reasons why his approach is particularly well adapted to the challenges of the current age.[49] The precise reasons for the recent explosion of interest in him are difficult, however, to prove definitively. My suggestion here is that they might be connected in some way to recent reactions against openness and vagueness in law and the sense that, in difficult and uncertain times when legal relationships are becoming increasingly complex and ever more rights are being demanded, we all need a stable vocabulary for understanding what is going on and talking out our differences, before final decisions are made.[50]

In any event, Hohfeld has, I believe, an important message for modern debates about form and substance. It is that whatever our substantive (normative) commitments, there is always value in terminological clarity and in deconstructing very carefully what we mean in any given instance by legal 'rights'. His view was not that the formal analytical method should be the end of law, but that it could and should be used to serve it – that a disciplined and consistent method for thinking about what rights mean is an essential precondition to determining whether or not we should have them and, if so, how they should be configured. 'Formal' thinking is hence not – contrary to the opposition which the traditional 'distinction' implies – necessarily opposed to the law's 'substantive' aims and purposes, but, in one manifestation at least, an important tool for ensuring that those purposes are properly identified, considered and delivered, whatever they may be. This limited reconciliation of formalism (of at least one type) with 'substantivism', is, I suggest, credible and useful. It offers some common ground and an important set of critical tools to those who otherwise find themselves on opposite sides of the various 'form and substance' debates, or who find themselves talking at cross-purposes. This conclusion provides an appropriately optimistic way of ending this volume even if it does not pretend to represent the final word on many of the questions it raises.

Attorney-General (Qld) v Australian Industrial Relations Commission [2002] HCA 42, (2002) 213 CLR 485; *Crimmins v Stevedoring Industry Finance Committee* [1999] HCA 59, (1999) 200 CLR 1; *Yanner v Eaton* [1999] HCA 53, (1999) 201 CLR 351; *Downs v Williams* (1971) 126 CLR 61; *Mathieson v Burton* (1971) 124 CLR 1; *Ogden Industries Pty Ltd v Lucas* (1967) 116 CLR 537.

[49] Barker, above n 35.

[50] Another possible explanation is that increased citation rates are attributable to other, random factors, such as the extent to which judges have increased their engagement with, and referencing of, academic work.

INDEX

NB: locators in *italics* refer to information in figures